Botswana
Safari Guide

Okavango Delta • Chobe

Northern Kalahari

the Bradt Travel Guide

Chris McIntyre

edition
5

www.bradtguides.com

Bradt Travel Guides Ltd, UK
The Globe Pequot Press Inc, USA

BOTSWANA: OKAVANGO DELTA, CHOBE, NORTHERN KALAHARI

ANGOLA

Okavango

Caprivi Strip

NAMIBIA

Rundu

The Tsodilo Hills, a
UNESCO-listed gallery of
ancient Bushman art
page 427

Shakawe

Moremi Game Reserve, the oldest
protected section of the Okavango
Delta and magnet for self-drivers
page 309

NAMIBIA

Okavango

Sepupa

Tsodilo
Hills

Seronga

KEY

Main town or city	●
Other town	○
Airport	✈
Tarred road	———
Gravel road (may require 4x4)	———
4x4 track	======
International boundary	- - - -

Etsha 6

Etsha

Jao

Moremi
Game Reserve

Gumare

Okavango Delta

Nokaneng

Boro

Aha Hills

The extraordinary wildlife-rich
islands and waters of the
Okavango Delta
page 407

Maun

Tsau

Toteng

*Motshabeng
Flats*

Sehithwa

Lake
Ngami

Khwebe Hills

Tautsa Flats

Ngwanalekau Hills

BOTSWANA
map coverage

N

Central
Kalahari
Game
Reserve

Bradt

0	50km
0	30 miles

Windhoek

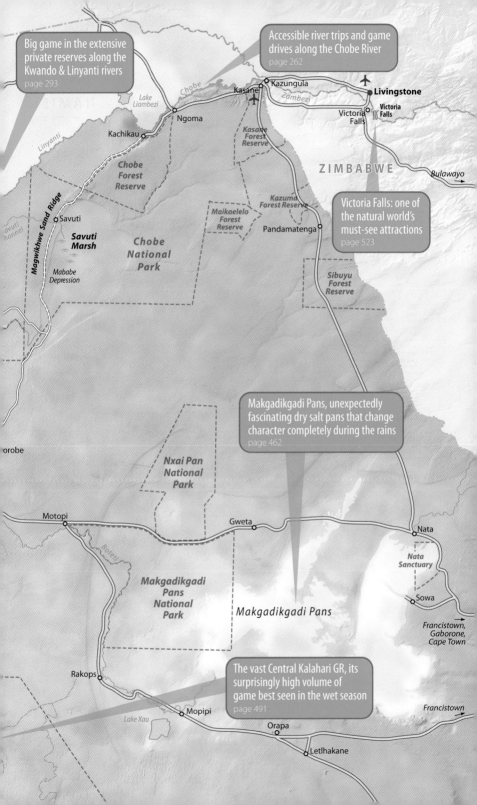

Big game in the extensive private reserves along the Kwando & Linyanti rivers
page 293

Accessible river trips and game drives along the Chobe River
page 262

Victoria Falls: one of the natural world's must-see attractions
page 523

Makgadikgadi Pans, unexpectedly fascinating dry salt pans that change character completely during the rains
page 462

The vast Central Kalahari GR, its surprisingly high volume of game best seen in the wet season
page 491

Lake Liambezi

Chobe

Zambezi

Kazungula

Kasane

Livingstone

Victoria Falls

Victoria Falls

Ngoma

Kachikau

ZIMBABWE

Bulawayo

Kasane Forest Reserve

Chobe Forest Reserve

Linyanti

Magwikhwe Sand Ridge

Savuti

Savuti Marsh

Mababe Depression

avuti hannel

Chobe National Park

Maikaelelo Forest Reserve

Kazuma Forest Reserve

Pandamatenga

Sibuyu Forest Reserve

Nxai Pan National Park

orobe

Motopi

Boteti

Gweta

Nata

Nata Sanctuary

Sowa

Francistown, Gaborone, Cape Town

Makgadikgadi Pans National Park

Makgadikgadi Pans

Rakops

Mopipi

Lake Xau

Francistown

Orapa

Letlhakane

Botswana
Don't miss...

The Okavango Delta
Once a vast inland lake, the Okavango Delta swells to three times its size during the dry winter months, creating Africa's biggest oasis, a refuge for everything from waterbirds to elephants
(TD/AWL) pages 309–445

The Kwando and Linyanti rivers
In wetter years this is a delta, providing a refuge for a wide range of wildlife such as lion
(TH) page 293–307

Makgadikgadi Pans

Fascinating dry salt pans that can be explored on foot, by 4x4 or on quadbikes

(JG) pages 462–76

Chobe riverfront

A magnet for wildlife, including thirsty giraffe

(AVZ) pages 262–70

Moremi Game Reserve

With some of the richest ecosystems in Africa, Moremi is populated by a diverse range of animals, including large numbers of elephant

(TH) pages 309–43

EL 32
UP CLOSE ON
YOUR *ADVENTURE*

A vast expanse stretches before you. You are enthralled by the beauty of the savannah,
which is revealed in every single conceivable shade of brown and green. A silhouette
of thousands of gnus, antelope and zebras migrating can be seen in the blazing sun.
But your attention is drawn in an instant to a young cheetah that is carefully
stalking a gazelle. It suddenly sets off in pursuit of its prey at an incredible speed.
You've never been as close as this to the action, thanks to the EL 32 binoculars.
SWAROVISION technology allows you to enjoy this unforgettable encounter with
wildlife displayed in razor-sharp, vivid and lifelike images. With SWAROVSKI OPTIK
the world belongs to those who can see beauty.

SEE THE UNSEEN
WWW.SWAROVSKIOPTIK.COM

SWAROVSKI
OPTIK

AUTHOR

Chris McIntyre went to Africa in 1987, after reading physics at Queen's College, Oxford. He taught with VSO in Zimbabwe for almost three years and travelled around extensively, mostly with a backpack. In 1990, he co-authored the UK's first guidebook to Namibia and Botswana, published by Bradt, before spending three years as a shipbroker in London.

Since then, Chris has concentrated on what he enjoys most: Africa. He wrote the first guidebook to Zambia for Bradt in 1996, the first edition of their Namibia guide in 1998 and this Botswana guide in 2003; he also co-authors guides to Tanzania and Zanzibar. While keeping these guidebooks up to date, his day job is managing director of Expert Africa – a specialist tour operator which organises high-quality trips throughout Africa for individual travellers from around the world, including a very wide range of trips to Botswana. This also includes the Wild about Africa programme of small group trips lead by top professional guides.

Chris maintains a keen interest in development and conservation issues, acting as advisor to various NGOs and projects associated with Africa. He is a Fellow of the Royal Geographical Society, and contributes photographs and articles to various publications. Now based in Surrey, Chris and his wife, Susan, still regularly travel and research in Africa.

Chris can usually be contacted by email on e chris.mcintyre@expert.africa.

MAJOR CONTRIBUTORS

Writing this book has been a team effort; I'm indebted to many that have made researching a pleasure and this book possible. For this fifth edition, these include:

Tricia and Bob Hayne updated much of the text for this edition, having worked extensively on three previous editions, as well as on Chris's other guides to Namibia, Zambia and Zanzibar. Formerly editorial director of Bradt Travel Guides, Tricia is now a freelance travel writer. When not researching in the wilds of Botswana, she and Bob are likely to be found toting backpacks on long-distance hiking trails.

Richard Ball studied zoology at university before becoming a guide in Botswana. His passion for wildlife and for Botswana sees him travelling there frequently, expanding his knowledge of the region, its people and its ecosystems – which led him to join Expert Africa in 2016. Richard contributed to several chapters, including the Kalahari Salt Pans, the CKGR, the Panhandle and the Okavango Delta.

Amanda Bond has always loved to travel, and Africa has been one of her favourite parts of the world since her first visit in 2004. After graduating with a degree in geography, Amanda returned to Africa to manage lodges in Zanzibar and South Africa. She now works as part of the Zambia team at Expert Africa, and updated the Livingstone chapter for this edition.

Josh Flatman first visited South Africa while studying for a degree in conservation biology and ecology. Following a masters in biosciences, and work on wildlife conservation and research projects in the UK, Norway and Cyprus, he volunteered and travelled in Namibia for three months. He now works for Expert Africa and helped to update the sections on Maun and the Okavango Delta.

Tom Morris first visited southern Africa in 2009, and since then has travelled the region extensively. He joined Expert Africa in 2015, where his original focus on Namibia and Zimbabwe has been extended to include Botswana. For this edition, Tom helped to update the sections covering Kalahari Salt Pans, the Panhandle and Northwest Kalahari, the Central Kalahari, Maun and the private reserves of the Okavango Delta.

Mike Unwin is an award-winning freelance natural-history writer and illustrator, and author of Bradt's *Southern African Wildlife: A Visitor's Guide*. Mike contributed much expert natural-history information, and wrote most of the chapter on the Kalahari's great salt pans. He now lives in England, having spent seven years in southern Africa pursuing wildlife around all corners of the region.

However, this guide has been built very much on the solid foundations laid by contributors to previous editions. Foremost among these are African expert and fellow author, Philip Briggs, who allowed me to build on his original text to create the *Botswana Wildlife Guide*; Octavia Kenny, who wrote most of the history in the first chapter; and my colleagues at Expert Africa, Megan Green and Tracy Lederer, who are authorities on Botswana in their own right, and who have both contributed much significant information and detail over the last two editions.

Contents

LIST OF MAPS

Botswana meant little to me at first; it was never in the news. Then, finding myself in Zimbabwe, I remembered an old friend's enthusiasm for the Okavango Delta. So, in April 1988, three of us set off from Victoria Falls and hitched a lift in an open pick-up into Chobe. We were badly prepared, but even our lack of food and close encounters with hyenas added to the magic. No fences here; everything was so wild.

From Maun we splashed out on a few days' camping trip on a mokoro. While the boatman spoke little English, the Delta was magical, almost surreal – like floating on a tropical fish tank with animals everywhere around. The Okavango's lush greenery contrasted with the harsh dryness of the rest of the subcontinent. Iridescent birds flashed past, while terrapins sunbathed and otters played. All added to the feeling of paradise; we left entranced.

Thus started my love affair with the country. Since then I've been lucky enough to return many times. I've been guided by some of the best, learning more about the bush and its animals and plants. I've flown over the dry Kalahari and the verdant Delta, mesmerised by the ancient patterns of watercourses, islands and game trails. And I've walked and driven around, exploring for myself on the ground, exhilarated by the sense of freedom. Yet still I feel as if I've only scratched the surface of Botswana, and I always leave wanting to return.

HOW TO USE THIS GUIDE

AUTHOR'S FAVOURITES Finding genuinely characterful accommodation or that unmissable off -the-beaten-track café can be difficult, so the author has chosen a few of his favourite places throughout the country to point you in the right direction. These 'author's favourites' are marked with a *.

PRICE CODES For accommodation price codes, see page 153. For restaurant price codes, see page 154.

MAPS
Keys and symbols Some maps include alphabetical keys covering the locations of those places to stay, eat or drink that are featured in the book.

Grids and grid references Some maps use grid lines to allow easy location of sites. Map grid references are listed in square brackets after listings in the text, with page number followed by grid number, eg: [94 C3]. Please note that, in order to keep the maps legible, not all sites have been pinpointed on the maps, but grid references have been supplied to highlight their general location.

NOTE ON DATUM FOR GPS CO-ORDINATES For all the GPS co-ordinates in this book, note that the datum used is WSG 84 – and you must set your receiver accordingly before copying in any of these co-ordinates.

All GPS co-ordinates in this book have been expressed as degrees, minutes and decimal fractions of a minute. Note that this now differs slightly from the format used by the Shell map, which uses degrees, minutes and seconds.

Note that Google Earth satellite images for some lodges, camps and key GPS locations in this book can be accessed directly at www.expert.africa.

Introduction

It's tempting here, by way of introduction, to list Botswana's main highlights as areas, one by one, describing each to entice the reader. I'd probably start by waxing lyrical about the Okavango Delta being a world-class attraction for exclusive wildlife viewing; I'd then marvel at the scale of the reserves around the Chobe, Kwando and Linyanti rivers, and perhaps eulogise about the almost spiritual experience of visiting the vast salt pans. But to do this would be misleading. For me, Botswana has just three overriding attractions – which transcend its geography.

First comes the wildlife. Whether this is your first safari or your 50th, Botswana won't disappoint. The sheer variation of the country, from the arid Kalahari to lush, well-watered forest glades, ensures tremendous variety. Botswana is serious about its big game. It has spectacular herds of elephants and buffalo, and prolific populations of predators. Experienced safari enthusiasts can bounce across the bush following a pack of wild dogs: Botswana has probably the continent's best population of these highly endangered predators. Yet often it's the country's smaller residents that will keep you entertained, from tiny painted reed frogs and barking geckos to troops of entertaining meerkats.

Second – and the underlying reason why many come here – is the feeling in Botswana that you're within an endless pristine wilderness, almost devoid of human imprint. For city-dwellers, such space is the ultimate luxury. In Botswana, animals wander freely across vast reserves which are measured in thousands of square kilometres, not merely hectares. Exploring these wilder corners is invariably deeply liberating.

Third, and missed by some, is Botswana's rich history. It's often barely hinted at but, veiled and mysterious, it's all the more enticing. It reveals itself in the paintings at Tsodilo, and the magic that seems to surround those hills. You'll catch a glimpse of it as you search for Stone Age arrowheads on the Makgadikgadi Pans. And standing on an ancient riverbed, or the wave-washed hills around Savuti, it's hard not to look into the geology and wonder what forces shaped this country, long before you, or indeed any people, first set eyes on it.

Back in the present, the world is changing fast. On a very positive note, 2009 and the following two years saw record water levels in the Okavango Delta and Kwando–Linyanti river systems, filling many channels that had been dry for decades. Initially the Boteti flowed for much of its course, the long-dry Magwegqana Spillway filled with water and the Savuti Channel reached the Savuti Marsh. Although the waters have receded somewhat, there is still water for about 2–4km of the spillway, and the Boteti continues to flow.

Despite this good news, most of the earth's great wilderness areas are under threat – and not just from climate change. The 21st century is an age when even the earth's wildest corners must earn their keep, adapt or change irrevocably. Botswana's government has, to date, been a beacon of prosperity and stability within a troubled continent. Financed largely by income from some of the world's largest diamond mines, it has set many examples of how to run a country. However, Botswana's diamonds aren't forever. Current deposits are running out, and while new ones are discovered, many expect the industry's output is likely to plateau and decline within a few decades at most. When this happens, it will leave a gaping hole in the economy. Tourism is the obvious way to fill this, but exactly how is not obvious.

As it stands, Botswana's thriving tourist industry is the envy of the continent: minimising impact by admitting only small numbers who pay handsomely to rejuvenate themselves in its pristine environments. Some of the revenue has been channelled back into the poorer communities in the areas concerned. This first-rate approach has been a very responsible one; it hasn't been a quick way for the country to get rich through tourism, but it has been sustainable.

In the last decade we've seen the government flirt with the idea of higher-volume tourism in one or two areas. Although the original policy of high-cost, low-density tourism across most of northern Botswana seems to have won the day, there is a move towards increasing the number of camps in each of the private concessions. While many of these areas are large enough to sustain the move, some of these new camps will be occupying more marginal areas in terms of wildlife, and in others, there is at least the possibility of activities being slightly less exclusive. Elsewhere, there's a move to encourage new lower-cost properties along the Panhandle area, enabled in part by the construction of a bridge over the Okavango at Mohembo, and thus giving easier and cheaper access to an experience of the Okavango Delta from its western fringe.

Both steps to increase tourism revenue are moderate, and far from some of the more drastic, damaging proposals that have been mooted. However, as both progress, it remains to be seen if this pace of change will be enough to satisfy the economic imperative for tourism to generate a larger slice of the national income.

So my plea to the reader is twofold. First, go now and support Botswana's small-scale camps and responsible tourism; the country needs you. Second, having committed many of Botswana's secret corners to paper here, I ask you to use this guide with respect. Botswana's wild areas need great care to preserve them. Local people are easily offended, and their cultures eroded, by a visitor's lack of sensitivity. Enjoy – but be a thoughtful visitor, for the country's sake.

🏠	Hotel/lodge/guesthouse etc
Λ	Campsite
–·–· International boundary	
═══ Tarred road	🏠Λ Accommodation covered in a different chapter
═══ Gravel road (may require 4x4)	e Internet
═════ 4x4 track	† Church/cathedral
═══ Railway	⅏ Waterfall
✈ Airport	⌂ Cave/rock shelter
✛ Airstrip	➤ Bird sanctuary
⛴ Car ferry	♧ Isolated woodland feature
🚌 Bus station	○ Waterhole/borehole
⛽ Fuel station/garage	▲ Summit (height in metres)
P Car park	⊕ GPS location
i Tourist information	⟼ Border post
🏺 Museum	x–x Gate
⚲ Statue/monument	• Other place of interest
$ Bank	═══ Marsh
✉ Post office	Salt pan
✚ Hospital/clinic	National park/reserve
✚ Pharmacy	Shopping centre/market
	Urban park

FEEDBACK REQUEST

Every guidebook is a snapshot in time. Restaurants open, lodges change hands, tour operators come and go – and prices change. The author and publisher would appreciate any feedback you may have from your travels, whether to tell us about somewhere new that you have discovered or to share your experience of places mentioned in the guide. Such feedback will make a huge difference when it comes to the next edition, and will ensure that this guide continues to evolve and broaden its scope for future readers.

So why not write and tell us about your experiences? Contact us on ☎ 01753 893444 or e info@bradtguides.com. We will forward emails to the author who may post updates on the Bradt website at www.bradtupdates.com/botswana. Alternatively, you can add a review of the book to www.bradtguides.com or Amazon.

ATTENTION WILDLIFE ENTHUSIASTS

For more on wildlife in Botswana, why not check out Bradt's *Southern African Wildlife*? Visit www.bradtguides.com/shop for a 10% discount on all our titles.

Part One

GENERAL INFORMATION

BOTSWANA AT A GLANCE

Location Southern Africa, between 20° and 30°E, and between 18° and 27°S
Size 581,730km^2
Climate Subtropical. Summer (November–March): 19–35°C; winter (June–August): 5–23°C. Rainy season November–March.
Status Republic
Population 2,230,905 (Statistics Botswana, 2016 estimate)
Population growth per year 1.8% (World Bank, 2016 estimate)
Life expectancy at birth 64.5 years (UNDP, 2016)
Infant mortality 34.8/1,000 live births (UNDP, 2016)
Capital Gaborone, population 257,993 (Statistics Botswana, 2016 estimate)
Other main towns Francistown, Lobatse, Selebi-Phikwe, Orapa
Economy Major earners: diamonds, tourism, nickel, beef
GNI US$6,610 per capita (World Bank, 2016)
GDP growth rate 2.9% (Bank of Botswana, 2016)
Currency Pula (BWP, abbreviated to P)
Rate of exchange US$1 = P9.64, £1 = P13.57, €1 = P11.83 (April 2018)
Language English (official), Setswana (national), Shona, other local languages
Religion Christianity, traditional beliefs
International telephone code +267
Time GMT +2
Electricity 220 volts
Weights and measures Metric
Flag Broad, light-blue horizontal stripes, divided by black central stripe bordered by narrow white stripes
National anthem *Fatshe leno la rona*: 'Blessed be this noble land'
Public holidays 1–2 January, Good Friday, Easter Monday, 1 May (Labour Day), Ascension Day, 1 July (Sir Seretse Khama Day), third Monday and Tuesday in July (President's Day), 30 September (Botswana Day), first Monday in October, 25–26 December
Tourist board www.botswanatourism.co.bw

SEND US YOUR SNAPS!

We'd love to follow your adventures using our *Botswana* guide – why not send us your photos and stories via Twitter (*@BradtGuides*) and Instagram (*@bradtguides*) using the hashtag #botswana? Alternatively, you can upload your photos directly to the gallery on the Botswana destination page via our website (*www.bradtguides.com/botswana*).

1

The Natural Environment

PHYSICAL ENVIRONMENT

TOPOGRAPHY Botswana lies landlocked in the heart of southern Africa, straddling the Tropic of Capricorn and covering about 581,730km², of which about two-thirds is in the tropics. Most of the country is a gently undulating sandsheet with an altitude of between 900m and 1,300m. This is punctuated by occasional isolated rock outcrops, which are rarely more than 100m tall. Two major features stand out from this: the enormous salt pans and the huge inland delta of the Okavango River.

A relatively narrow corridor of land on the southeast side of Botswana is rockier and less flat than the rest, with sandstone and granite hills leading down to the Shashe, Limpopo and Marico rivers. This land is much more suitable for agriculture, and is where most of the country's population is concentrated.

Geological history Looking back into Botswana's geological history gives us insights to explain how the great salt pans and the Okavango Delta were formed. It's a long story though, of which I can give only a brief outline here. For a deeper and much more scholarly approach, seek out John Reader's *Africa: A Biography of a Continent* and especially Mike Main's *Kalahari: Life's Variety in Dune and Delta* (see *Appendix 3*, page 543). Both are excellent, giving much more comprehensive discussions of the latest scientific thinking than I'm able to give here – the first in terms of Africa generally, and the second with immense detail specifically about Botswana.

Setting the scene To put discussions in perspective, and give our history a sense of scale, let me start at the beginning. Around 4,600 million years ago the earth's crust began to form and cool. A thousand million years later, fossils from South Africa's Barberton Mountain Land give us evidence of the first recorded, simple, single-celled bacteria.

By 3,300 million years ago more complex blue-green algae had appeared, though it took a further 2,300 million years for multi-cellular organisms to evolve. Palaeontologists say that around 600 million years ago there was an 'evolutionary explosion', when many different species evolved, including ancestors of most of the world's existing invertebrates.

About 230 million years ago the earth saw the emergence of both dinosaurs and the first mammals. For the next 165 million years the dinosaurs dominated the earth and the largest mammals that evolved were probably no bigger than present-day rabbits. Only around 65 million years ago, when some great calamity killed off most of the dinosaurs, did the mammals begin to rise to dominance and inherit the earth.

The supercontinent Meanwhile, somewhere between 135 and ten million years ago the supercontinent, Gondwanaland, broke up and the continents started to move

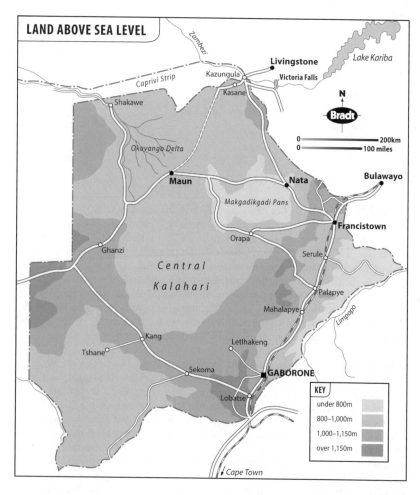

away from each other. By the time that the continents split from Gondwanaland, the basic rocks upon which southern Africa is built, the Karoo lavas, had been laid down. By about 65 million years ago – the end of the Cretaceous Period – most of the subcontinent's diamonds, gems and other mineral wealth had also been formed, and erosion was gradually wearing away at the land.

The world's earliest primate fossils are from Europe and North America, dating from around 65 million years ago, but it wasn't until about four million years ago that *Australopithecus* appeared in Africa – a prime candidate for being one of our earliest ancestors. This period, as our first ancestors were evolving, is about the time when we start looking at how Botswana's landforms were created.

The Kalahari's superlake During the Tertiary Period, which dates from about 65 million years ago, Botswana's climate was probably very arid, and as the region's rocks were gradually eroded, so the wind-blown sands accumulated and began to form what we now call the Kalahari.

Around four or five million years ago it's thought that the Okavango, Kwando and Zambezi rivers had completely different courses than they do today – probably

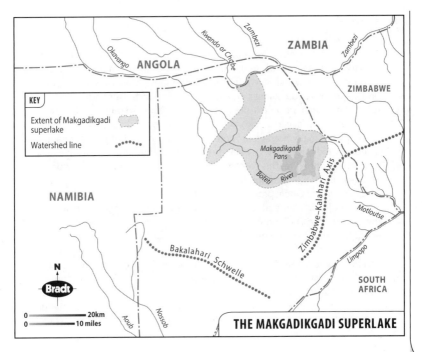

THE MAKGADIKGADI SUPERLAKE

all flowing into one channel which headed south through the Kalahari and into the Orange River and/or the Limpopo. (Different theories suggest different courses.)

Then, around two to four million years ago, it's thought that seismic shifts forced parts of southern and central Botswana upwards. Geologists identify the areas raised as the 'Zimbabwe–Kalahari Axis' and the 'Bakalahari Schwelle' – both of which are now watersheds in the region.

The net effect of these upward movements was to block the flow southwards of the rivers, and to form a superlake that had its deepest parts where the Makgadikgadi Pans are today. This greater Lake Makgadikgadi existed until very recently, though its extent varied greatly over the millennia, depending on the climate and inflows. It is thought that at its greatest, it covered an area of up to 80,000km², and that it probably only dried up in the last 10,000 years. At its largest it probably stretched as far as Lake Ngami in the west, what is now Chobe in the north, and beyond Nata to the edge of present-day Zimbabwe in the east.

Evidence suggesting the existence of this lake is dotted around its ancient shorelines. The great Magwikhwe Sand Ridge that you cross as you drive between Savuti and North Gate, probably defined one of its northwestern shorelines. Similarly, another is thought to have been the less obvious Gidikwe Sand Ridge, which lies just to the west of the Boteti River where it borders the present Makgadikgadi Pans National Park.

Look at the base of several of the Kalahari's isolated hills and you'll find rounded, water-washed pebbles and rocks worn smooth over the centuries by waves. The eastern side of the Ghoha Hills, north of Savuti, is a particularly clear example of this – though all of Savuti's hills show some of this history if you look carefully.

In some areas of the Makgadikgadi you can stroll around and pick up the flint arrowheads and other tools of Stone Age encampments, which must have sat beside the shores of this lake within the last few thousand years.

Diamond is a crystalline form of ordinary carbon formed under conditions of extreme pressure and temperature. In nature, such conditions are only found deep below the earth's surface, in the lower crust or upper mantle. Under specific circumstances, the rock matrix in which diamonds occur was subjected to such great pressure that it became fluid and punched its way up to the earth's surface in a volcanic pipe of liquid rock. This situation is similar to a conventional volcanic eruption, except that instead of basaltic magma being erupted through fissures in the crust, the volcanic material is a peculiar rock called kimberlite. This contains a wide assortment of minerals (including diamonds), often in addition to large chunks of other rocks that have been caught up in the whole process.

Although such kimberlite pipes occur throughout southern Africa, from the Cape to the DRC, only a small proportion of those discovered contain enough diamonds to be profitably worked. Among them are the Botswana mines at Orapa, Damtshaa, Letlhakane and Jwaneng. It's interesting to note that Botswana's western neighbour, Namibia, has diamond deposits along its Atlantic coast. These are 'secondary diamond deposits', because they do not come directly from kimberlite pipes. Instead, Namibia's diamonds are found in areas where ancient rivers have eroded kimberlite pipes in the interior, washing diamonds down to the sea, and depositing them in sediments there.

From rifts to deltas At some time in the last million years (none of my sources seems to be sure exactly when), this flow into the great Lake Makgadikgadi was gradually, probably quite slowly, cut off.

Northern Botswana has a series of deep, underlying faultlines running beneath its sands. These faults are thought to be the southernmost extensions of the same system of parallel faultlines that are pulling away from each other and have formed East Africa's Great Rift Valley. These extend south, forming the rift valleys of the Luangwa and Lower Zambezi, before cutting across the Zambezi at Victoria Falls. Here, amid the sands of the northern Kalahari, they are probably at their youngest and shallowest. In Botswana and Zimbabwe these two main faultlines run parallel to each other, from northeast to southwest.

Look at a map and you'll see the Zambezi flowing roughly south through western Zambia, until it reaches a point around Victoria Falls and what's known as the Middle Zambezi Valley (around where Lake Kariba is today). Effectively the Zambezi has been diverted, flowing into the Rift Valley and then northeast along it. This would have starved the great lake of its largest water supply, but clearer evidence of the faultlines can be seen in the present paths of two other rivers.

Look again at the map and you'll realise that the Kwando forms the Botswana–Namibia border, flowing southeast (roughly parallel to both the Zambezi and the Okavango). Then it clearly passes through an area where there's very little gradient, and forms a mini-delta, before abruptly changing direction to become the Linyanti River, and starting to flow northeast. (Note, in passing, the very clear parallels between the delta formations of the Okavango and Kwando/Linyanti rivers.)

This new course of the Linyanti River marks one faultline – known as the Linyanti–Gumare Fault. At Lake Liambezi, this river then seems to 'escape' from the confines of its fault to meander roughly southeast, until meeting another faultline parallel to the first. Here it is again renamed as the Chobe River, with

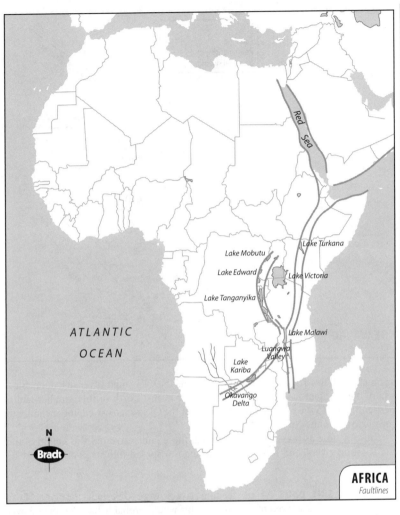

AFRICA
Faultlines

a clearly defined course, flowing northeast and parallel to the Linyanti, along another faultline.

The Selinda (or Magwegqana) Spillway also flows roughly along the Linyanti–Gumare Fault, and further west the line cuts across the flow of the Okavango, just south of the base of the Panhandle. It effectively marks the start of the Delta proper. Parallel to this, but at the south end of the Delta, are the Kunyere and Thamalakane faults. The latter is clearly marked by the position of the Thamalakane River, which marks the most southerly extent of the Delta. Here the Thamalakane River collects the meagre outflow from the Okavango's Delta and diverts it southwest along the faultline, and ultimately into Lake Ngami and the Boteti. Maun sits in the narrow space between the Kunyere and Thamalakane faults.

Just like the parallel faults of the rift valleys further northeast, the Linyanti–Gumare Fault in the north, and the Kunyere and Thamalakane faultlines in the south are gradually pulling away from each other. Between them, the underlying base rock has dropped relative to the land outside the faults – some geologists say by

KEY

Faultline	————
Permanent swamp	-·-·-·-
Seasonal swamp	··········

Mohembo

Shakawe

Panhandle

Faults

Seronga

Nqoga

Jao

N

Bradt

Gumare

Linyanti–
Gumare Fault

Thaoge

Kunyere

Kwando

Linyanti

Selinda Spillway

Linyanti–Gumare Fault

0 ———— 50km
0 ———— 30 miles

Moanachira

Khwai

Chief's
Island

Mogogelo

Boro

Thamalakane Fault

Kunyere Fault

Maun

Nhabe

Boteti

OKAVANGO
Faults

Lake
Ngami

as much as 300m. These have acted to 'capture' the Okavango River in a depression where the gradient is very shallow. (As an aside, just north of this, smaller faults, perpendicular to the main ones, act to restrict the Okavango's sweeping meander to the narrow confines of the Panhandle.)

Thus, in time as they gradually formed, these faults diverted the Zambezi and the Kwando rivers, and forced the Okavango to spread into its present-day delta formation.

The great salt pans As its feeding rivers were diverted, the great Lake Makgadikgadi was starved of its sources. This would probably have happened over a very long period of time. We know that the climate in Botswana varied greatly, and during periods of heavier rainfalls the lake might have persisted. Geologists have identified at least five clearly different levels of the lake, each of which has its own identifying features that are still visible. And for each the size of the lake must have been totally different.

But eventually, starved of inflow in a drier climate, the lake shrank. With no known outflows, it would probably have already been very brackish. Now its remaining salts were concentrated more and more, and eventually crystallised out where the last of its waters evaporated – at its lowest point, where the pans are now. Too saline for plants to grow, this residue formed the amazingly flat surface of the great salt pans that are now such a distinctive feature of the northern Kalahari.

The formation of the Okavango Delta The geological history outlined so far in this chapter explains how the Okavango has been constrained by faults, but it doesn't really help to explain how the Delta's strange and wonderful landscapes

NW–SE SIMPLIFIED GEOLOGICAL CROSS-SECTION FROM MOHEMBO TO MAUN

KEY
Okavango sediments
Kalahari sands
Base rocks

Mohembo   Seronga   Linyanti–Gumare Fault   Maun
Thamalakane Fault
Kunyere Fault

Bradt

came about. That's really due to much more recent processes, of which I'll try to give a brief summary here.

From the air Firstly, if you're flying over the Delta, note what you see. There are manmade tracks, like the straight lines of the buffalo fence, which surrounds part of the Delta. Or the close, parallel lines of bush tracks made by vehicles, sometimes curving, sometimes perfectly straight.

You'll also see more erratic, single tracks, often radiating from pans or waterholes; these are clear animal tracks. (Yes, animals have favourite paths that they like to use too.) Deeper in the Delta you'll find more and more winding drainage lines, of water channels which glint in the sun. Catch the light right and you'll realise that areas which you thought were thick, green vegetation are floodplains, which reflect the sky.

Look carefully at the 'browner' areas between these and you'll start to distinguish the dry land and the islands from the floodplains and the water. Look out for the small, round islands that often have a ring of palms around the outside of them. Note that some, at their centre, have barren patches of what looks like white salt.

Many islands will be longer. A few of these may look like a number of the small islands joined together. But many are long and narrow – we'll call them ribbon islands. Note how parallel their sides are, and how the vegetation on the edges looks that much more lush than the vegetation in the middle.

Building islands The Okavango's an amazing sight from the air – and all the more incredible if you understand a little of how its features were formed. Here are the basics of the main two methods.

Biological mechanism: round islands The Okavango's floods are erratic and its water levels variable, sometimes giving the chance for small mounds to develop which, when flooding returns, are above the level of the flood. Often, but not always, these are termite mounds, made by the *Macroternes michaelseni* termite.

Obtruding above the water level of the subsequent flood, the mound allows the termites to survive, and makes a handy perch for birds. Eventually seeds take hold, and grow into shrubs and trees, fertilised by the guano from the birds that rest there. In some areas of the Delta (the Jao flats stand out in my mind) you'll see these small islands at the early stages of their formation everywhere. Often the dominant plants are wild date palms (*Phoenix reclinata*), though *Ficus* species and the usual broad-leafed trees of the Delta will follow.

Once started, the trees will transpire, sucking water up with their roots to fuel photosynthesis. This lowers the water table directly under the island, which then attracts inflows from the surrounding floodplains seeping under the island. However, the tree roots don't take up many salts, and gradually the ground water under the island becomes saturated with salts – especially silica and calcite. Eventually these crystallise out underneath the roots. As this precipitate increases, the level of the ground around the edge of the island is raised.

This gradually acts to enlarge the island, raising it above the surrounding floodplains. However, as the island enlarges the groundwater that moves towards the centre of the island becomes increasingly saline – and eventually toxic to plants. The wild date palms die off first in the centre, as they are the least salt-tolerant, then the broadleaved trees, until finally the relatively salt-tolerant real fan palms (*Hyphaene petersiana*) will be the only trees in the centre. When the salt concentrations rise further they, too, die, leaving only salt-tolerant grasses like the spiky sporobolus (*Sporobolus spikatus*).

Capillary action and evaporation force the supersaturated water to the surface of the centre of the island, where salt deposits are now left and no plants can survive. This whole process is estimated to take at least a hundred years. The remaining crystalline salt deposits are known as 'trona' deposits, and are clearly visible as a white crystalline powder from the air or the ground.

Channel mechanism: linear islands The Okavango's water is at its richest in nutrients as it enters the Panhandle and the top of the Delta – as flowing over the nutrient-poor Kalahari sands of the Delta itself won't enrich it. In this Panhandle and upper Delta area, the deep waters are surrounded by the vigorous growth of papyrus (see box, page 335, for details).

These live and die fast, forming a mat of thick vegetal matter by the side of the channel. This builds up the sides of the channel, and gradually its deeper stems are compressed and start forming peat. Meanwhile, suspended sediments are deposited on the floor of the channel. Thus the whole channel, floor and papyrus surrounds, start to rise slightly above the surrounding floodplains.

Once this happens it only takes a hippo track, or some other leakage, for the water in the channel to cut through the peat sides of the channel and the papyrus beds find a completely alternative, lower path through the floodplains. This leaves behind a dry, slightly raised line of sandy deposits, lined on either side by high beds of peat. This higher land will encourage plants to grow, forming a long, narrow island, which can be enlarged by the biological mechanisms mentioned above.

Once dry, the peat eventually burns down to a thin layer of nutrient-rich ash, which now lines this island, encouraging what biologists call 'sweet' floodplains. These support nutrient-rich grasses and other high-quality vegetation, and a rich growth of trees and bushes at the edge of these long islands.

Meandering mechanism: alluvial islands Some islands in the Delta were probably built up first as sandy alluvial deposits during wetter periods in the Delta's history – as the banks beside meandering rivers. Then, when times became drier they were colonised by vegetation, and enlarged by the biological mechanisms mentioned above.

Geological mechanism: Chief's Island Chief's Island, the largest island in the Delta, is thought to have geological origins. Note that its western edge traces out a line which, if continued northwest, would coincide perfectly with the eastern faultline that constrains the Panhandle (see page 8 for a diagram showing this faultline).

Chief's Island was probably pushed up as higher land during the formative rifting/warping of the area, which fits with the observation that it is largely made up of uniform deposits of sand and clay.

CLIMATE Botswana is landlocked far from the coast and mostly in the tropics. It receives a lot of strong sunlight and most of the country is classed as either semi-arid or arid (the line being crossed when evaporation exceeds rainfall). In many respects, most of central and northern Botswana has a subtropical 'desert' climate, characterised by a wide range in temperature (from day to night and from summer to winter), and by low rainfall and humidity.

Botswana's climate follows a similar pattern to that found in most of southern Africa, with rainfall when the sun is near its zenith from November to April, and most areas receiving their heaviest rainfall in January and February. The rainfall is heavier in the north and east, and lighter in the south and, especially, the southwest. The precise timing and duration of the rains is determined by the interplay of three airstreams: the moist 'Congo' air mass, the northeastern monsoon winds, and the southeastern trade winds. The water-bearing air is the Congo air mass, which normally brings rain when it moves south into Botswana from central Africa. Effectively a belt of rain works its way south across the continent, reaching its southernmost point around January or February. If you listen to any local weather forecasts, they'll probably refer to this as the intertropical convergence zone, or the ITCZ. As the sun's intensity reduces, the Congo air mass moves back north, leaving Botswana dry by around April.

Thus **January** and **February** are the wettest months, when many areas will have regular and often torrential downpours in the late afternoon. When there are no clouds, temperatures can peak as high as 40°C. However, it's much more usual for them to be moderated by afternoon cloud cover and to stay between about 20°C and 30°C. Humidity fluctuates during the day, typically from about 50% to 80%.

By **March** the rainfall is decreasing, though still the afternoon clouds are around. Mornings and early afternoons will often be cloudless, and a few of the nights will go below 10°C even though the average of the nightly minimums is nearer 18°C.

April and **May** are lovely months. You may catch the odd afternoon shower in April, but these are gone by May – as are most of the clouds. The maximum day temperatures are around 33°C, and while the nightly minimum average is between 10°C and 15°C, this hides the occasional chilly nights when areas of the Kalahari will record temperatures just below freezing.

June and **July** are the coolest months, with daytime average highs around 25°C concealing the occasional day when the mercury just reaches 30°C. You'll still need

CLIMATE STATISTICS: MAUN

The average maximum and minimum temperatures for Maun are typical of the pleasant climate in northern Botswana – although as elsewhere in the world, things are changing; temperatures of 40°C or more are no longer particularly unusual in October. Nevertheless, Maun's temperatures are slightly less extreme than you might expect in one of the Kalahari's drier environments. Similarly, expect the highs and lows in the heart of the Delta to be more moderate than this (lower highs, and higher lows!):

	Temp °C		Temp °F		Rainfall
	max	min	max	min	mm
January	33	19	91	68	101
February	32	19	90	68	101
March	32	18	90	65	51
April	30	15	87	60	26
May	28	10	82	50	0
June	25	6	78	42	0
July	26	6	80	42	0
August	27	9	81	48	0
September	34	14	93	58	0
October	38	19	100	68	0
November	37	20	98	69	25
December	35	20	95	69	76

your shorts, T-shirt, sunhat and suncream for the middle of the day, but as dusk approaches you'll quickly need warmer clothes. The average night goes down to about 6°C, but cold snaps of well below freezing (typically –5°C) are common – especially in the drier areas of the Kalahari. **August** is very similar, though not quite as cold. You'd be very unlucky for it to go below freezing, even at night, and the days will often creep over 30°C.

September and **October** are really the heart of the dry season, and the daytime heat gradually builds as these months wear on. Typical early afternoon temperatures are in the low 30s (°C), and nights will seldom fall below 10°C, though most will be nearer to 20°C. The humidity is usually very low, typically 20–40%.

November is always interesting and can be unpredictable. Often much of it will simply be a continuation of October's heat and dryness. But eventually the humidity will build and clouds start to appear in the afternoons. These will block the sun, cool the temperatures, and eventually produce some showers in the late afternoon. November mornings will generally remain fine and hot, with blue skies.

During **December** temperatures usually stay around 20–30°C, day and night, and rain will be an increasingly regular occurrence in the afternoon. Humidity is normally 50–60%. The hottest days may just reach 40°C, but even so the coolest nights won't go below about 10°C.

HABITAT AND VEGETATION

In many ways a brief description of some of the main habitats for plants is really a step through the various types of environment that you'll encounter in Botswana.

As with animals, each species of plant has its favourite conditions. External factors determine where each species thrives, and where it will perish. These include temperature, light, water, soil type, nutrients, and what other species of plants and animals live in the same area. Species with similar needs are often found together, in communities which are characteristic of that particular environment. Botswana has a number of different such communities, or typical 'vegetation types', within its borders – each of which is distinct from the others. The more common include:

MOPANE WOODLAND The dominant tree here is the remarkably adaptable mopane (*Colophospermum mopane*), which is sometimes known as the butterfly tree because of the shape of its leaves. Although it doesn't thrive on the Kalahari's sands, it is very tolerant of poorly drained or alkaline soils, and those with a high clay content. This tolerance results in the mopane having a wide range of distribution throughout southern Africa; in Botswana it occurs mainly in the Okavango–Linyanti region, and throughout the eastern side of the country.

Mopane trees can attain a maximum height of 25m when growing on rich, alluvial soils. These are then called cathedral mopane, for their height and the graceful arch of their branches. However, shorter trees are more common in areas that are poor in nutrients, or have suffered extensive fire damage. Stunted mopane will form a low scrub, perhaps only 5m tall. All mopane trees are deciduous, and the leaves turn beautiful shades of yellow and red before falling during the late dry season. Then, with the first rains, the trees become tinged with light-green young leaves. They flower around December and January, with clusters of small, yellow-green flowers.

Ground cover in mopane woodland is usually sparse; just thin grasses, herbs and the occasional bush. The trees themselves are an important source of food for game, as the leaves have a high nutritional value – rich in protein and phosphorus

VEGETATION

KEY

Miombo woodland	Mopane dominated	
Wetland	Lake deposits	
Recent alluvium	Kalahari sandveld	

– which is favoured by browsers and is retained even after they have fallen from the trees. Mopane forests support large populations of rodents, including tree squirrels (*Peraxerus cepapi*), which are so typical of these areas that they are known as mopane squirrels.

PAN Though not an environment for rich vegetation, a pan is a shallow, usually seasonal, pool of water without any permanent streams leading to or from it. Mopane woodlands are full of these small pans during and shortly after the rainy season, the water being held on the surface by the clay soils. They are very important to the game that feeds here during the summer, but dry up soon after the rains cease.

SALT PAN A salt pan is, as its name implies, a pan that's salty. The huge Makgadikgadi Pans are the residues from ancient lakes. Because of the high concentrations of mineral salts found there – there are no plants there when they are dry. When they fill with water it's a slightly different story as algal blooms appear, sometimes attracting the attention of specialist filter-feeders like flamingos.

MIOMBO WOODLAND Although this would be the natural vegetation across most of neighbouring Zambia, in Botswana miombo woodland, and its associated *dambos* (see below), is uncommon. There are patches in central Chobe and the northeast of the country. It is found in areas where the soils are acid and not particularly fertile. Often they have been leached of minerals by the water run-off.

Miombo woodland consists of a mosaic of large wooded areas and smaller, more open spaces dotted with clumps of trees and shrubs. The woodland is broadleaved and deciduous (though just how deciduous depends on the available water), and the tree canopies generally don't interlock. The dominant trees are *Brachystegia*, *Julbernardia* and *Isoberlinia* species – most of which are at least partially fire-resistant. There is more variation of species in miombo than in mopane woodland, but despite this it is often known simply as 'brachystegia woodland'. The ground cover is also generally less sparse here than in mopane areas.

DAMBO A *dambo* is a shallow grass depression, or small valley, that is either permanently or seasonally waterlogged. It corresponds closely to what is known as a *vlei* in other parts of the subcontinent. These open, verdant dips in the landscape often appear in the midst of miombo woodlands and support no bushes or trees. In higher valleys among hills, they will sometimes form the sources of streams and rivers. Because of their permanent dampness, they are rich in species of grasses, herbs and flowering plants, like orchids – and are excellent grazing (if a little exposed) for antelope. Their margins are usually thickly vegetated by grasses, herbs and smaller shrubs.

TEAK FOREST In a few areas of the far north of Botswana, including the northern side of Chobe National Park, the Zambezi teak (*Baikaea plurijuga*), also known as Rhodesian teak, forms dry semi-evergreen forests on Kalahari sand. Often these woodlands occur on fossil dune-crests. As this species is not fire-resistant, these stands are only found where fire is rare, and slash-and-burn-type cultivation methods have never been used. Below the tall teak is normally a dense, deciduous thicket of vegetation, interspersed with sparse grasses and herbs in the shadier spots of the forest floor.

The teak is a lovely strong wood, with an even texture and deep red-brown colour. It is expensive, often exported, and widely used – from furniture to classy wooden floors.

KALAHARI SANDVELD A number of trees and bushes thrive on Chobe's extensive areas of Kalahari sand, including various *Vachellia*, *Senegalia*, *Terminalia* and *Combretum* species. 'Kalahari sandveld' is a general term that I'll use to describe any of these plant communities based on sand.

In appearance they range from a very open savannah with a few tall trees separated only by low undergrowth, to quite dense tickets of (often thorny) shrubs which are difficult to even walk through. If you want to be a little more technical about this, then biologists will often divide this into distinctive subgroups, including:

Terminalia sericea **sandveld** occurs where you find deep, loose sand – these are unfertile areas which cover large areas of the Kalahari. The main species found here are the silver terminalia (*Terminalia sericea*), or silver cluster-leaf as it's sometimes called, and the Kalahari appleleaf (*Philenoptera nelsii*). These generally occur with wild seringa bushes (*Burkea africana*) and the bushwillow (*Combretum collinum*). Underneath these you'll often find the rather beautiful silky bushman grass (*Stipagrostis uniplumis*).

Vachellia erioloba woodlands also occur on sand, but often where there are fossil river valleys that have an underground supply of water throughout the year. Camelthorn trees (*Vachellia erioloba*) have exceedingly long taproots that reach this, sustaining large stands of these mature trees reaching an impressive 16–17m in height. They grow slowly but give good shade, so the bush cover beneath them is fairly sparse.

Vachellia tortilis woodlands are not found on such deep sand; instead they prefer the fine alluvium soils, which water has deposited over time. Although it forms homogenous stands less often than the camelthorns, a number of the very distinctive, flat-topped umbrella thorns (*Vachellia tortilis*) can often be seen together. Between these you'll find low grasses rather than much undergrowth. This results in a beautiful, quintessentially African scene which fits many first-time visitors' picture of the continent as gleaned from the blockbuster film *Out of Africa*.

MOIST EVERGREEN FOREST In the areas of higher rainfall and (as is more likely in Botswana) near rivers, streams, lakes and swamps, where a tree's roots will have permanent access to water, dense evergreen forests are found. Many species occur, and this lush vegetation is characterised by having three levels: a canopy of tall trees, a sub-level of smaller trees and bushes, and a variety of ground-level vegetation. In

KARIBA WEED

At several checkpoints in Botswana, particularly near rivers, notices are posted warning of the problems posed by the invasive waterweed, *Salvinia molesta*. Known locally as *mosthimbambo*, and more widely by its common names, giant salvinia or Kariba weed, it was first identified in the Zambezi River over 50 years ago. Since then it has become widespread throughout the southern part of the continent, migrating to the Chobe River in the 1980s.

A native of Brazil, Kariba weed is a water fern that was at one time sold for ornamental use in aquariums and garden ponds. With an exceptionally fast rate of reproduction, the plant spread rapidly from these relatively narrow confines into larger bodies of warm, relatively sluggish water. As the plant multiplies, its originally flat green leaves die back and fold together, forming an impenetrable mat that can be as much as a metre deep. The implications for waterways such as the rivers of Botswana are considerable. Not only do the matted plants create an obstruction, impacting on boat traffic and blocking irrigation pipes and water supplies, they also create an ideal breeding ground for mosquitoes and other insects. The impact on the environment is no less devastating, with indigenous plants affected by loss of light and oxygen, an effect that is compounded as decaying plants sink to the riverbed and adversely affect the development of fish and other river wildlife.

Control of such a virulent plant has proved extremely difficult. While it can be sprayed, this is rarely fully effective, and the chemicals used are in themselves harmful to the environment. Rather more successful has been the introduction of a weevil imported from Australia, *Cyrtobagus salviniae*, whose adults and larvae feed on and damage the plants under the right circumstances.

The problem is by no means confined to Africa. Kariba weed is on the environmental hit-list of countries across the globe, from New Zealand to the US, where both sales and ownership of the plant are now banned. In Botswana, however, the challenge is to prevent serious damage to the country's aquatic ecosystem. With this in mind, the authorities have introduced strict measures, which include controlling the boats allowed on the country's waterways, and decontamination of those that are licensed.

effect, the environment is so good for plants that they have adapted to exploit the light from every sunbeam.

This type of forest is prevalent in the Okavango and Linyanti areas, and beside the country's larger rivers. It's perhaps worth distinguishing here between two very different types of this forest:

Riverine forests (occasionally called riparian forests) are very common. They line many of Botswana's major rivers and are found throughout the Okavango–Linyanti area. Typical trees and shrubs here include the jackalberry (*Diospyros mespiliformis*), African mangosteen (*Garcinia livingstonei*), sausage tree (*Kigelia africana*), large feverberry (*Croton megalobotrys*), knobthorn (*Senegalia nigrescens*), marula (*Sclerocarya birrea caffra*), raintree (*Philenoptera violacea*) and various species of fig. Move away from the river and you'll find riparian species thinning out rapidly.

Swamp forest – or something very akin to it – occurs in tiny patches on small islands in permanently flooded areas of the Okavango. These islands, which will themselves occasionally be flooded, might include a mixture of fig and waterberry species, plus lots of wild date palms (*Phoenix reclinata*) and a few tall real fan palms (*Hyphaenea petersiana*).

In the centre of slightly larger small islands, where the ground is salty from trona deposits (page 10), you will find only spiky sporobolus grassland (*Sporobolus spicatus*) – no trees at all!

FLOODPLAIN Floodplains are the low-lying grasslands on the edges of rivers, streams, lakes and swamps that are seasonally inundated by floods. The Okavango and, to a lesser extent, the Linyanti–Chobe region has some huge areas of floodplain. These often contain no trees or bushes, just a low carpet of grass species that can tolerate being submerged for part of the year. In the midst of most of the floodplains in the Okavango you'll find isolated small 'islands' slightly raised above the surrounding grasslands. These will often be fringed by swamp forest (pages 17–18).

Sometimes the communities of vegetation will be 'zoned' to reflect the extent and frequency of the flooding. In areas that become submerged for long periods you'll find species like wild rice (*Oryza longistaminata*) and the sedge *Cyperus articulatus*. Grasses such as *Imperata cylindrica* often dominate places that generally spend less time underwater.

CHANNELS Vegetation found in permanent channels includes the giant sedge or papyrus (*Cyperus papyrus*), which dominates large areas of the Okavango, plus species like the distinctive cylindrical hippo grass (*Vossia cuspidata*), the tall maize-like phragmites reed (*Phragmites australis*), used for thatching, and the unmistakable bulrush (*Typha capensis*).

LAGOONS Where the water is more still, in deep lagoons and side-channels where the surface is open but the water doesn't flow much, the bottom will often be covered with fairly stable peat deposits. This gives a stable base for many species of aquatic plants. Some are strictly submerged while others have floating leaves. An obvious indicator of this type of environment is the presence of waterlilies.

CONSERVATION

A great deal has been written about the conservation of animals in Africa; much of it is over-simplistic and intentionally emotive. As an informed visitor you are in the unique position of being able to see some of the issues at first hand, and to appreciate the perspectives of some of the local people. So abandon your preconceptions, and start by realising how complex the issues are.

Here I shall try to outline a few ideas common to current thinking on conservation, and to many areas in the region. Only then will I frame them in the context of Botswana.

BEING PRAGMATIC: CONSERVATION AND DEVELOPMENT Firstly, conservation must be taken within its widest sense if it is to have meaning. Saving animals is of minimal use if the whole environment is degraded, so we must consider conserving whole areas and ecosystems, not just the odd isolated species.

Observe that land is regarded as an asset by most societies, in Africa as it is elsewhere. (The San are a notable exception in this regard.) To 'save' the land for the animals, and use it merely for the recreation of a few privileged foreign tourists, is a recipe for huge social problems – especially if the local people remain excluded from benefit and in poverty. Local people have hunted animals for food for centuries. They have always killed game that threatened them or ruined their crops. If we now try to protect animals in populated areas without addressing the concerns of the people, then our efforts will fail.

The only pragmatic way to conserve Africa's wild areas is to see the *development* of the local people, and the *conservation* of the ecosystems, as interlinked goals. In the long term, one will not work without the other. Conservation without development leads to resentful local people who will happily, and frequently, shoot, trap and kill animals. Development without conservation will simply repeat the mistakes that most developed countries have already made: it will lay waste a beautiful land and kill off its natural heritage. Look at the tiny areas of undisturbed natural vegetation that survive in the UK, the USA or Japan. See how unsuccessful we in the northern hemisphere have been at long-term conservation over the past 500 years.

As an aside, the local people in Africa are sometimes wrongly accused of being the only agents of degradation. Many would like to see 'poachers' shot on sight, and slash-and-burn agriculture banned. But observe the importation of tropical hardwoods by the West to see the problems that our demands place on the natural environment in the developing world.

In conserving some of Africa's natural areas and assisting the development of its people, the international community has a vital role to play. It could effectively encourage African governments to practise sustainable long-term strategies, rather than grasping for the short-term fixes which politicians seem universally to prefer. But such solutions must have the backing of the people themselves, or they will fall apart when the foreign aid budgets eventually wane.

In practice, to get this backing from the local communities it is not enough for a conservation strategy to be compatible with development. Most rural Africans are more concerned about where they live, what they can eat, and how they will survive, than they are about the lives of small, obscure species of antelope that taste good when roasted.

To succeed in Africa, conservation must not only be *compatible* with development, it must actually *promote* it. Conservation efforts must also actively help the local people to improve their own standard of living. If that situation can be reached, then local communities can be mobilised behind long-term conservation initiatives.

Governments are the same. As the famous Zambian conservationist, Norman Carr, once commented, 'Governments won't conserve an impala just because it is pretty.' But they will work to save it *if* they can see that it is worth more to them alive than dead.

The continent's best current strategies involve trying to find lucrative and sustainable ways to use the land. They then plough much of the revenue back into the surrounding local communities. Once the local communities see revenue from conservation being used to help them improve their lives – to build houses, clinics and schools, and to offer paid employment – then such schemes rapidly get their backing and support.

Carefully planned, sustainable tourism is one solution that is working effectively. For success, local communities must see that visitors pay because they want the wildlife. Thus, they reason, the existence of wildlife directly improves their income, and they will strive to conserve it. It isn't enough for people to see that the wildlife helps the government to get richer; that won't dissuade a local hunter from shooting a duiker for dinner. However, if he is directly benefiting from visitors, who come to see the animals, then he has a vested interest in saving that duiker.

HIGH REVENUE, LOW VOLUME In the late 1980s Botswana's parks, and especially the Chobe riverfront area and Moremi, were being badly over-used. Many visitors were self-contained South Africans who would arrive with all their food and kit. They bought little in Botswana except their cheap park-entry tickets, and contributed little to the nation's economy.

In an effort to reduce numbers, and stave off serious environmental (and aesthetic) problems due to too many visitors, it was decided to increase the park fees by a factor of ten. This worked miraculously – reducing the number of visitors and their impact, but retaining the same level of revenue for the parks' authorities.

At the time this was revolutionary, even though now it seems obvious. Thus Botswana's policy of 'high-revenue, low-volume' tourism was born. Access to most of Botswana's wild areas is expensive in order to maximise revenues and keep environments pristine. The country is the envy of Africa for having a good, working system that is delivering increasing revenues as well as many local development initiatives.

This basic policy has been in place for almost 25 years, and there is every indication that it will continue. Indeed, the principle has extended way beyond the national parks and game reserves to embrace virtually the whole of northern Botswana.

NATIONAL PARKS AND RESERVES The national parks, like Chobe, and the game reserves, like Moremi, work on a simple system. Nobody lives in these (a handful of San in the CKGR being the exception). Anyone can visit, provided they pay the fees. These are scaled to be cheapest for citizens of Botswana, reasonable for residents and more costly for visitors. (See page 131 for these charges.)

Private concessions or reserves Outside of the national parks and game reserves, northern Botswana has been divided up into a series of wildlife management areas (WMAs). See the map on pages 346–7 for some of these. Those in northwestern Botswana, in Ngamiland, are numbered NG1, NG2, etc, up to NG51. These areas are normally referred to in Botswana as 'concessions' although in this guide I have used this term virtually interchangeably with the phrase 'private reserve' or simply just 'reserve'.

Within each of these the government, via the local 'land board', has defined who owns the wildlife, and what can be done with it. Until January 2014, limited (controlled and sustainable) hunting was allowed in many of the concessions, but this is now outlawed throughout Botswana.

Community concessions In most of these concessions, the approach taken centres around Community Based Natural Resource Management (CBNRM), a modern phrase for a strategy which tries to reconcile conflicts over resources between the people and the wildlife in its broadest sense.

CBNRM is based on the premise that the people living next to a resource are the ones best suited to protecting that resource, as they would lose most if that resource were lost, and gain most if it's managed well. There is also an ethical consideration: for example, the people who pay the costs of living near wildlife (destruction of crops and livestock, and loss of human life) should benefit from its conservation. Local people need to be involved in the decision-making process and to benefit from the areas around them, and CBNRM tries to make this possible.

Thus in most of Botswana's concessions, local communities now make decisions about how they are run, and they reap the rewards if they are run well and successfully. (See box, page 359, about NG22 and NG23, for an example of one such arrangement.)

TOURISM Botswana lies in the heart of sub-Saharan Africa – and its tourism is the envy of the continent in many ways. The country is regarded, quite rightly, as having some of the continent's best wildlife areas, which are still in generally pristine condition.

What's more, the expansion of tourism from the nucleus of the national parks to the areas around them has gradually increased the area effectively protected for wildlife since the 1980s. This is enlarging the contiguous area in northern Botswana available for wildlife, helping to ensure that game populations increase in size, and become more viable. In the words of the late Peter Sandenbergh, who ran safari camps and tourism operations in this area for longer than most, 'one of the greatest changes since coming to this area in 1983 has been the remarkable increase in animal numbers and species diversity.'

Tourism isn't yet as important to Botswana as diamonds or beef production, but it is increasing every year. By providing substantial employment and bringing foreign exchange into the country, it gives the politicians a reason to support conservation. When the diamonds run out – within the next few decades – Botswana needs to have an alternative, and renewable, source of income … and tourism is one of the most obvious contenders.

For the impact of tourism on the economy, see pages 86–7. And for ways in which you can support both conservation initiatives and small local charities that directly help the people of Botswana, see pages 158–60.

Hunting issues Big-game hunting, where visiting hunters pay large amounts to kill trophy animals, was for years practised on a number of private reserves and concessions. Just like photographic tourism, it was a valuable source of revenue in the long term for people living in the country's concessions.

In practical terms, there was room for both types of visitors in Botswana: the photographer and the hunter. The national parks, and some of the private reserves nearest the parks (eg: NG23, NG27A and NG27B), were designated for photographic visitors; here no hunting was allowed.

In many of the private reserves, controlled sustainable hunting was permitted, although a few (such as the concessions run by Wilderness Safaris, like NG15 and NG26) maintained a policy of no hunting. These concessions provide a buffer between the pristine national parks and the land around, a system designed to protect the national parks' animals from incursions by poachers, while the parks act as a large gene pool and species reservoir for the private concessions.

Despite this long-held policy, the government imposed a moratorium on commercial hunting, which includes trophy hunting, in January 2014. Effectively, this extended an earlier ban on lion hunting. The decision came as no surprise to many in Botswana, since it fulfilled a commitment to ban commercial hunting made by President Ian Khama prior to taking office in 2008.

Poaching It's perhaps worth adding that Botswana has very, very little poaching. There is always a little small-scale poaching of game 'for the pot' by local people … but large-scale commercial poaching operations are virtually unknown.

Occasionally there's a complaint about poachers coming across the river from Namibia – putting the blame on poachers from neighbouring countries is a very usual tactic in this part of the world. However, the Kwando, Linyanti and Chobe rivers, and the rest of the country's borders, are so well patrolled by the Botswana Defence Force (BDF) that this seems unlikely.

2

Botswana Wildlife Guide

For more on wildlife in Botswana, check out Bradt's Southern African Wildlife. *Get 10% off at www.bradtguides.com/shop.*

This wildlife guide is designed to help you name most of the mammals that you are likely to see in Botswana. Less common species are featured under the heading '*Similar species*' beneath the animal to which they are most closely allied or bear the strongest resemblance.

There are times, of course, when safari goers are presented with a series of animal tracks rather than the animal itself. A good guide can make these come alive, helping you to make sense of what you see in the bush. They show you, for example, that cats' tracks have three lobes at the bottom, whereas dog and hyena tracks feature only two; point out the cheetah's claws, usually absent from other cat tracks; or the direction in which an elephant is walking from small scuff marks around its track. To help your interpretation, we have included some of the more widely seen tracks in *Appendix 1* (pages 530–4); the more you learn, the more you'll enjoy about the bush.

For much more detailed information, see *Southern African Wildlife: A Visitor's Guide* by Mike Unwin, also published by Bradt Travel Guides. There are also very comprehensive field guides to the flora and fauna of southern Africa, which usually cover Botswana, and several guides dedicated just to Botswana. See *Appendix 3*, pages 542–3 for my suggestions.

MAMMALS

Because the Okavango area is so well-watered, its natural vegetation is very lush and capable of supporting a high density of game in the dry season. This spreads out to the

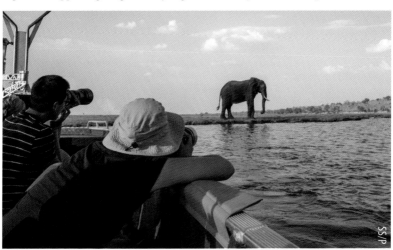

SSP

surrounding areas during the earlier months of the year – accounting for the sheer volume of big game to be found in northern Botswana's parks and private reserves.

Overall, Botswana's large mammals are typical of the savannah areas of southern Africa. The large predators are here: lion, leopard, cheetah, wild dog and spotted hyena. Cheetah are found in higher densities here than in most other areas of the subcontinent, and northern Botswana has one of Africa's three strong populations of wild dogs.

Elephant and buffalo occur in large herds that roam throughout the areas where they can find water. Black and white rhino, which had been wiped out throughout the wilds of northern Botswana, have now been reintroduced into the private areas of Moremi and the Delta, and are gradually spreading across the region.

Antelope are well represented, with impala, springbok, tsessebe and red lechwe each numerically dominant in different areas – depending on the environment. The sheer range of Botswana's ecosystems means that if you move about there is a really wide variety of species to be seen.

GAME MIGRATIONS: HISTORICAL FACTORS Like most of Africa's big game, some of Botswana's larger mammals undertake major seasonal migrations – or at least they did, until relatively recently. The 'big picture' was that large numbers of big herbivores put a great strain on the vegetation in any given locale, and so moving around gave the plants time to recover. Thus the basic pattern was for the game to move out into the Kalahari's drier areas during the rains, when it would have no difficulty finding small pools to drink from, and then gradually migrate back to sources of permanent water as the dry season progressed.

The main species involved were elephant, buffalo, zebra, wildebeest and hartebeest. These migrations still occur, and do affect the game densities in many areas, although they're much reduced due to two main factors.

First, competition for land from humans and their domestic stock, which has reduced the area over which the wildlife can range, and caused particular problems by monopolising some of the few areas of permanent water in the Kalahari.

Second, the erection of long, game-proof, disease-control fences which have appeared across historical migration routes in the Kalahari. The first of these was in 1954, in response to insistence by European trading partners that, to import Botswana's beef, the country must have an effective strategy for containing and dealing with outbreaks of foot-and-mouth disease.

The relative damage done by these two factors is still a hotly debated issue in Botswana, but the results were serious. In some years tens and possibly hundreds of thousands of animals, mostly wildebeest, died of thirst or starvation, many in very close proximity to the fences. (See page 494 for further comments.) Some blame the fences directly; others regarded them as a scapegoat for the real cause – the scale of human encroachment on the Kalahari. Whatever the cause, Botswana no longer has migrations of this scale.

See Mike Main's *Kalahari: Life's Variety in Dune and Delta* for a rational overview of this debate; various issues of *Botswana Notes and Records* (especially 1984) for more detailed partisan arguments; and Mark and Delia Owens' book *Cry of the Kalahari* for an impassioned but one-sided view of the people who observed it at first hand.

GAME MIGRATIONS: THE CURRENT STORY Mention the word 'migration' and there's a tendency to picture millions of wildebeest in the Serengeti, fording rivers of waiting crocodiles and filling endless flat plains. That's not what you get in Botswana, so forget those images.

What you do find is a modest but noticeable drift of game away from the main water points of the Chobe, Linyanti and Okavango around the start of the rains – usually some time during November – and a gradual return as the dry season progresses. However, the precise details vary with the species of game.

Elephant and **buffalo** make broadly similar movements. As the rains come, their large herds split into much smaller family groups, of which some move away from the Linyanti and Okavango systems. They spread out into the drier areas, especially the vast swathes of land dominated by mopane which lie between these areas (Wildlife Management Areas NG14/15/16/18/20; see page 20 for an explanation of WMAs). Those from the Chobe riverfront areas similarly split, heading into the Chobe Forest Reserve and the rest of Chobe National Park, while some move east of Chobe National Park into Zimbabwe's Hwange National Park, and the Matetsi area between that and the Zambezi.

From around May the animals start to head back, and gradually join up into larger herds, until by September and October the riverfronts of the Chobe and Kwando–Linyanti have some of the most amazing densities of buffalo and (especially) elephants that you'll find anywhere in Africa.

The migrations of **zebra** are somewhat more complex, and still the topic of research, but it seems that during the rains large herds of zebra congregate on both Makgadikgadi and Nxai pans, forming an amazing spectacle (if you can find them). During the dry season these animals gather in numbers beside the Boteti River, the western boundary of Makgadikgadi National Park. Separate populations from the Okavango, Chobe and Linyanti areas move to more open areas of the Kalahari. Some of these groups always seem to pass through the sweet grass plains of the Savuti area around April–May, and often this coincides with their foaling season.

Wildebeest in the north of the country follow a similar pattern to the zebra, but those in the centre and south of the Kalahari are effectively now a separate population. It seems that numbers in the central area of the Kalahari have fluctuated wildly since records began; before the fences there was probably a big annual migration northeast in the dry season to Lake Xau – the nearest water point to the CKGR. Like **hartebeest** in the Central Kalahari, they certainly move around with the season, but the complexities of their current migration patterns are unclear.

CATS AND DOGS

Lion (*Panthera leo*) Shoulder height 100–120cm; weight 150–220kg. Africa's largest predator, the lion, is the animal that everybody hopes to see on safari. It is a sociable creature, living in prides of five to over 20 animals and defending a territory of 20–200km². Lions often hunt at night, and their favoured prey is large or medium-sized antelope such as wildebeest and impala – although they may take prey as large as buffalo or giraffe. Most hunting is done by females, but dominant males normally feed first after a kill. Rivalry between males is intense and takeover battles are frequently fought to the death, so two or more males often form a coalition. Young males are forced out of their home pride at three years of age, and cubs are usually killed after a successful takeover.

When not feeding or fighting, lions are remarkably indolent – they spend up to 23 hours of any given day at rest – so the anticipation of a lion sighting is often more exciting than the real thing. Lions naturally occur in any habitat, except desert or rainforest. They once ranged across much of the Old World, but these days they are all but restricted to the larger conservation areas in sub-Saharan Africa (with one residual population existing in India).

Lions occur throughout Botswana, and are very common in the main northern areas of Chobe, Linyanti–Kwando and the Okavango. They also range across the

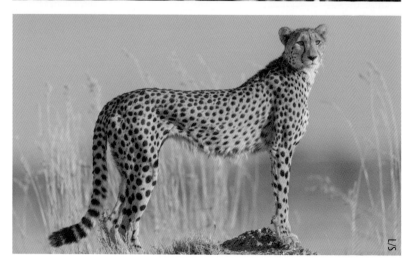

Kalahari, in the Nxai/Makgadikgadi areas and the Central Kalahari Game Reserve, though the relative scarcity of prey leads to small, dissociated pride structures which have vast territories.

In the northern reserves, where food is plentiful, the converse is the case. Large prides are the norm and some, like those around North Gate and Savuti, have become so big that they make a speciality of killing young and juvenile elephants in order to have enough meat to go around. Even if visiting these prolific reserves for just a few days, you'd be unlikely not to see at least some lions.

Leopard (*Panthera pardus*) Shoulder height 70cm; weight 60–80kg. The leopard is the most solitary and secretive of Africa's big cats. It hunts at night, using stealth and power, often getting to within 5m of its intended prey before pouncing. If there are hyenas and lions around then leopards habitually move their kills up into trees to safeguard them. This species can be distinguished from the cheetah by its rosette-like spots, lack of black 'tearmarks' and more compact, low-slung, powerful build.

The leopard is the most common of Africa's large felines. Some of Botswana's bush offers perfect habitat, with plenty of thickets, cover and big trees. The riverine woodlands found throughout the Chobe, Linyanti–Kwando and Okavango areas are firm favourites with them. Here they're quite often seen by sharp-eyed observers who scan low-hanging branches for these lounging felines. Meanwhile drives around dusk and early evening in the private concessions will sometimes yield good sightings of leopard going out on hunting forays as the light fades. Remarkably, leopard often seem unperturbed by the presence of a vehicle and spotlight, and will often continue whatever they are doing regardless of an audience; watching a leopard stalk is captivating viewing.

Leopard are very adaptable. There are many records of individuals living for years undetected in close proximity to humans, for example in the suburbs of major African cities like Nairobi, where they prey on domestic dogs. Given this, it's no surprise that they're also found throughout the Kalahari, though in lower densities commensurate with the relative lack of prey.

Cheetah (*Acynonix jubatus*) Shoulder height 70–80cm; weight 50–60kg. This remarkable spotted cat has a greyhound-like build, and is capable of running at 70km/h in bursts, making it the world's fastest land animal. Despite superficial similarities, you can easily tell a cheetah from a leopard by the former's simple spots, disproportionately small head, streamlined build, diagnostic black tearmarks, and preference for relatively open habitats. It is typically seen pacing the plains restlessly, either on its own or in a small family group consisting of a mother and her offspring. Diurnal hunters, cheetah favour the cooler hours of the day to hunt smaller antelope like springbok, steenbok and duiker; plus young wildebeest, tsessebe and zebra, and also warthog, large birds and small mammals such as scrub hares.

Given that cheetah never occur in high densities, Botswana is a better place than most to see them. In areas of plentiful game, they often lose their prey to lion or spotted hyena, so the relative scarcity of competition in areas like Nxai, Makgadikgadi and the Central Kalahari make these locations ideal. These locations also harbour large populations of springbok – a cheetah's ideal prey – and their ability to go for long periods without water gives them flexibility to move far from waterholes. Although cheetah are often thought of as animals of the open savannah, they do need some cover from which to sprint – so the Kalahari's thin scrub is perfect for them.

Having said that, all of my sightings of cheetah in Botswana have been in some of the central Okavango's areas of densest game – on Mboma Island and in the Mombo Concession! Looking through the sightings records at the camps, it's

A trio of lions prepares for an evening's hunting in Chobe National Park certainly notable that many of these cats move further into the Delta as the waters recede, and then move back out into the surrounding Kalahari to avoid the floods.

Estimates suggest that there are about 4,500 cheetah left in southern Africa, plus 2,500 or so in east Africa, and a barely sustainable number in Iran. (They did occur throughout India and Pakistan, but are now considered extinct there.) Scientists, noting a marked lack of genetic diversity among all living cheetah, have suggested that the species must have gone through a 'genetic bottleneck' in the past – thus perhaps all living cheetah are descended from one female. This goes some way to explaining why they are very susceptible to disease.

Serval (*Leptailurus serval*) Shoulder height 60cm; weight 9–18kg. This long-legged cat is the tallest of Africa's 'small cats'. It has a slim build with a short tail and black-on-gold spots giving way to streaking near the head. Seldom seen, it is widespread and quite common in moist grassland, reedbeds and riverine habitats throughout Africa, including northern Botswana. It's largely absent from the drier areas of the Kalahari.

Serval do particularly well in wetter areas where there is lots of long grass – and are common throughout the Okavango and Linyanti–Kwando area, although they're relatively rarely seen. Until recently, there have been consistent reports of good sightings from night drives alongside the Savuti Channel, but now that it is flowing again, this is no longer the case. Serval prey on mice, rats, small mammals, birds, snakes and lizards and will sometimes even take fish or the young of small antelope. They use their big ears to locate their prey precisely by sound, and their long legs to see over tall grass, and to spring high as they pounce.

Caracal (*Caracal caracal*) Shoulder height 40cm; weight 15–20kg. Smaller but heavier than the serval, caracal resemble lynx, with their uniform tan coat, short tail and tufted ears. They are solitary, mainly nocturnal hunters which feed on birds, small antelope and young livestock. Caracal are remarkable hunters for their size, and will often take prey as large as, or even larger than, they are. Their style is very much like that of a leopard; they normally stalk their prey as closely as possible, before springing an ambush. They may also take many of the same species at once, even caching their prey in trees to return and feed later, and can be quite acrobatic hunters, known to bat birds out of the air.

Caracal

Caracal occur throughout sub-Saharan Africa, easily adapting to a variety of environments. They're found throughout Botswana and while night drives in the early evening provide your best chance of a glimpse of them, they're still very rarely seen.

Similar species The smaller **African wildcat** (*Felis sylvestris lybira*) ranges from the Mediterranean to the Cape of Good Hope, and is similar in appearance to the domestic tabby cat. It has a ringed tail, a reddish-brown tinge to the back of its ears and an unspotted torso – which should preclude confusion with the even smaller **small spotted**

cat (*Felis nigripes*), a relatively rare resident of the central and southern Kalahari which has a more distinctively marked coat. Both species are generally solitary and nocturnal, often utilising burrows or termite mounds as daytime shelters. They prey upon reptiles, amphibians and birds as well as small mammals.

Wild dog (*Lycaon pictus*) Shoulder height 70cm; weight 25kg.

Also known as the painted hunting dog, the wild dog is distinguished from other African dogs by its large size and mottled black, brown and cream coat. Highly sociable, living in packs of up to 20 animals, wild dogs are ferocious hunters that literally tear apart their prey on the run. The most endangered of Africa's great predators, they are now threatened with extinction. This is the result both of relentless persecution by farmers, who often view the dogs as dangerous vermin, and of their susceptibility to diseases spread by domestic dogs; wild dogs are now extinct in many areas where they were formerly abundant, such as the Serengeti, and they are common nowhere. The global population of fewer than 3,000 is concentrated in southern Tanzania, Zambia, Zimbabwe, Botswana, South Africa and Namibia.

Wild dogs prefer open savannah with only sparse tree cover, if any, and packs have enormous territories, typically covering 400km² or more. They travel huge distances in search of prey, so few parks are large enough to contain them. Northern Botswana has one of the healthiest and most prolific populations in Africa, and is probably the best place on the continent to see them. These range right across Chobe, the Kwando–Linyanti and Okavango areas, and spread out beyond these into Namibia and the northwest areas of the Kalahari.

Packs generally den around July to early October, and this is the only time when you can be fairly sure of seeing them in any given area. Sometimes they'll den in the same area for several years running, while at other times they'll change from year to year. For the best chances of a sighting – and a possibility of following a pack as they hunt (an amazing, exhilarating experience) – choose a mainly dry reserve with plenty of open ground. Make sure that off-road driving is permitted, or you'll never be able to follow them, and ideally night drives should be allowed. Selinda, southern Kwando, Kwara and Vumbura would all currently be high on my list – and I've seen dogs in all of these. Better still, ask someone who knows the Delta and the reserves well where specific packs have denned the previous season, and go where they suggest.

Given that dogs will take most antelope and always run down their prey, the only strategy that their prey can adopt to avoid death is to run as far, and as fast, as they can. They will do this as soon as they realise that dogs are in the area. Thus if you ever see game seriously sprinting with a purpose, and just not stopping, then look hard: maybe there's a pack of dogs behind them!

AVZ

Black-backed jackal (*Canis mesomelas*)
Shoulder height 35–45cm; weight 8–12kg. The black-backed jackal is an opportunistic feeder capable of adapting to most habitats. Most often seen singly or in pairs at dusk or dawn, it is ochre in colour with a prominent black saddle flecked by a varying amount of white or gold. It is probably the most frequently observed small predator in Africa south of the Zambezi, and its eerie call is a characteristic sound of the bush at night. It is found throughout Botswana, with the exception of the far north of the country around the Chobe and Linyanti–Kwando areas, and is fairly common in the drier areas of the Kalahari.

Side-striped jackal (*Canis adustus*)
Shoulder height 35–40cm; weight 8–12kg. Despite its prevalence in other areas of Africa, the side-striped jackal is common nowhere in Botswana. It occurs in the far north of the country, including Chobe, the Linyanti–Kwando area and the Okavango. It is about the same size as the previous species, but greyish in colour, with an indistinct pale horizontal stripe on each flank and often a white-tipped tail. These jackals are also usually seen singly or in pairs, at dusk or dawn. Both the side-striped and the black-backed jackal are opportunistic feeders, taking rats, mice, birds, insects, carrion, wild fruits and even termites.

Bat-eared fox (*Otocyon megalotis*) Shoulder height 30–35cm; weight 3–5kg. This endearing small, silver-grey insectivore is unmistakable, with its huge ears and black eye-mask. It can be found throughout Botswana, anywhere that the harvester termite (*Hodotermes mossambicus*) occurs. The best areas are usually short grass plains that receive relatively low rainfall – Savuti Marsh was a favourite habitat when the marsh was dry.

This canine is mostly nocturnal, but can sometimes be seen in pairs or small family groups during the cooler hours of the day, usually in dry open country. It digs well, and will often 'listen' to the ground (its ears operating like a radio-dish) while wandering around, before stopping to dig with its forepaws. As well as termites, bat-eared foxes will eat lizards, gerbils, small birds, scorpions, beetle larvae and other insects.

Insect populations vary with the seasons and bat-eared foxes will move with them. When conditions allow, some areas will have very high densities.

Similar species The **Cape fox** (*Vulpes chama*) is an infrequently seen dry-country predator which occurs throughout central and western Botswana, but is absent from Chobe and the north side of the Okavango. It lacks the prominent ears and mask of the bat-eared fox, and its coat is a uniform sandy-grey colour.

Spotted hyena (*Crocuta crocuta*) Shoulder height 85cm; weight 70kg. Hyenas are characterised by their bulky build, sloping back (lower hindquarters), coarse brownish coat, powerful jaws and dog-like expression. Contrary to popular myth, spotted hyenas are not exclusively scavengers; they are also adept hunters, which hunt in groups and kill animals as large as wildebeests. Nor are they hermaphroditic, an ancient belief that stems from the false scrotum and penis covering the female hyena's vagina. Sociable animals, hyenas live in loosely structured clans of about ten animals, led by females, who are stronger and larger than males, and based in a communal den.

Hyenas get more out of their kills than most predators, digesting the bones, skin and even teeth of antelope. This results in the distinctive white colour attained by their faeces when dry – an easily identified sign of their presence in an area.

The spotted hyena is the largest hyena, identified by its light-brown, blotchily spotted coat. It is found throughout most of Botswana, only absent from the eastern areas around Ghanzi, and perhaps the country's furthest southern edge. These predators are common throughout the north, and will frequently scavenge around camps and campsites at night. Savuti's campsite was, for years, completely plagued by them, while few camps in the Delta are without a story of hyena breaking into kitchens or eating their way through larders.

Although mainly nocturnal, spotted hyenas can often be seen around dusk and dawn, and their distinctive, whooping calls are one of the most wonderful, yet spine-chilling, sounds of the African night.

Brown hyena (*Hyaena brunnea*) Shoulder height 75–85cm; weight 40–47kg. Although rare (with only about 8,000 animals left in the wild), this secretive, apparently solitary hyena occurs in the most arid parts of Namibia, and throughout Botswana, being absent only from the far north. It is unmistakable, with a shaggy, dark-brown coat – not unlike a large, long-haired German shepherd dog – with faint black stripes and sloping back.

In contrast to the spotted hyena, brown hyenas do tend to scavenge rather than hunt, and are generally solitary while doing so. They are the dominant carnivore in the drier areas of the Namib and Kalahari, where clans (typically two to ten animals) will defend enormous territories against neighbouring clans. Individuals normally forage on their own and eat whatever they can, from small birds and mammals to the remains of kill, as well as fruit and vegetables. They can go without water for long periods, gaining moisture from tsama melons as well as other food.

Brown hyena are very rarely seen on game drives, although in the last few years researchers based at Jack's Camp have habituated a small clan of hyena to their presence – making this probably the best place in Africa to see them. (See box, page 480 for more information on brown hyena.)

Aardwolf (*Proteles cristata*) Shoulder height 45–50cm; weight 7–11g; with a tawny brown coat and dark, vertical stripes, this insectivorous hyena is not much bigger than a jackal and occurs in low numbers in most parts of Botswana. It is active mainly at night, gathering harvester termites (specifically those of the genus *Trinervitermes*), its principal food, with its wide, sticky tongue. These termites live underground (not in castle-like termite mounds) and come out at night to cut grass and drag it back down with them. Occasionally the aardwolf will also take other insects, mice, birds and carrion.

Open grassland or lightly wooded areas form the typical habitat for aardwolves, which can sometimes be spotted around dusk, dawn or on very overcast days, especially during the colder months. The *Trinervitermes* termites often thrive on overgrazed land, which means that aardwolf are often more common on farmland than in national parks. I don't know of anywhere in central or northern Botswana where they're seen frequently.

PRIMATES
Chacma baboon (*Papio ursinus*) Shoulder height 50–75cm; weight 25–45kg. This powerful terrestrial primate, distinguished from any other monkey by its much larger size, inverted-U-shaped tail and distinctive dog-like head, is fascinating to watch from a behavioural perspective. It lives in large troops that boast a complex, rigid social structure characterised by a matriarchal lineage and plenty of inter-troop movement by males seeking social dominance. Omnivorous and at home in almost any habitat, the baboon is the most widespread primate in Africa, frequently seen in most of Botswana. The centre of the Kalahari (including the CKGR) is the only area from which it is absent.

There are three African races, regarded by some authorities as full species. The chacma baboon (*P. c. ursinus*) is grey, and confined largely to areas south of the Zambezi. The yellow baboon (*P. c. cynocephalus*) is the yellow-brown race occurring in Zambia, northern Mozambique, Malawi, southern and eastern Tanzania and eastern Kenya. The olive or anubis baboon (*P. c. anubis*) is a hairy green-to-brown baboon found in Ethiopia, Uganda, northern Tanzania and Kenya.

With a highly organised defence system, the only predator that seriously affects baboons is the leopard, which will try to pick them off at night while they are roosting

Vervet monkey

in trees or cliffs. Campers in Chobe and Moremi should treat these animals with respect; long exposure to humans has taught them to steal, and not to be afraid.

Vervet monkey (*Cercopithecus aethiops*) Length (excluding tail) 40–55cm; weight 4–6kg. Also known as the green or grivet monkey, the vervet is probably the world's most numerous monkey and certainly the most common and widespread representative of the *Cercopithecus* guenons, a taxonomically controversial genus associated with African forests. An atypical guenon in that it inhabits savannah and woodland rather than true forest, the vervet spends a high proportion of its time on the ground. It occurs throughout the northern and eastern parts of the country, but is absent from the drier areas of central, western and southern Botswana. Vervets like belts of tall trees with thick vegetation within easy reach of water, and much of northern Chobe, the Kwando–Linyanti area and the Okavango is ideal for them.

The vervet's light-grey coat, black face and white forehead band are distinctive – as are the male's garish blue genitals. Vervet monkeys live in troops averaging about 25 animals; they are active during the day and roost in trees at night. They eat mainly fruit and vegetables, though are opportunistic and will take insects and young birds, and even raid tents at campsites (usually where ill-informed visitors have previously tempted them into human contact by offering food).

Lesser bushbaby (*Galago senegalensis*) Length (without tail) 17cm; weight 150g. The lesser bushbaby is the most widespread and common member of a group of small and generally indistinguishable nocturnal primates, distantly related to the lemurs of Madagascar. In Botswana it occurs throughout the northern half of the country, including in Nxai and Makgadikgadi.

More often heard than seen, the lesser bushbaby can sometimes be picked out by tracing a cry to a tree and shining a torch into the branches; its eyes reflect as two red dots. These eyes are designed to function in what we would describe as total darkness. Lesser bushbabies feed on insects – some of which are caught in the air by jumping – and also on sap from trees, especially acacia gum.

Lesser bushbabies inhabit wooded areas, and prefer acacia trees or riverine forests. I remember being startled by a small family once; they raced through the trees above us, bouncing from branch to branch while chattering and screaming out of all proportion to their size.

LARGE ANTELOPE

Sable antelope (*Hippotragus niger*) Shoulder height 135cm; weight 230kg. The striking male sable is jet black with a distinct white face, underbelly and rump, and long decurved horns – a strong contender for the title of Africa's most beautiful antelope. The female is chestnut brown and has shorter horns, while the young are a lighter red-brown colour. Sable are found throughout the wetter areas of southern and eastern Africa, but are common nowhere.

In Botswana they occur in the north, as far west as the central Okavango. The Chobe riverfront is a good place to look for them in the dry season, usually between Kasane and Chobe Game Lodge, where several herds frequent the valleys and come down to drink.

Similarly, sable are occasionally seen near the Kwando and Linyanti rivers. They're not common in the Delta region, but are seen periodically. Good sightings have been recorded around the Gomoti River, and in NG20 and NG21. The Vumbura Concession (NG22) probably offers the highest density of sable in the Delta, while they're generally absent from NG26, NG27, NG30 and further west.

Sable are normally seen in small herds: either bachelor herds of males, or breeding herds of females and young, which are often accompanied by the dominant bull in that territory. The breeding females give birth around February or March; the calves remain hidden, away from the herd, for their first few weeks. Sable are mostly grazers, though will browse, especially when food is scarce. They need to drink at least every other day, and seem especially fond of low-lying dewy vleis in wetter areas.

Roan antelope (*Hippotragus equinus*) Shoulder height 120–150cm; weight 250–300kg. This handsome horse-like antelope is uniform fawn-grey with a pale belly, short decurved horns and a light mane. It could be mistaken for the female sable antelope, but this has a well-defined white belly, and lacks the roan's distinctive black-and-white facial markings. The roan is relatively rare; common almost nowhere in Africa (Malawi's Nyika Plateau being the obvious exception to this rule). In Botswana, small groups are found in the Chobe and Kwando–Linyanti areas, and occasionally some will wander as far as the drier parts of the Okavango Delta – but they're always something of a rarity. Ngwezumba Pans is probably the best location to search for them, but they're not seen regularly even there.

Roan need lots of space if they are to thrive and breed; they don't generally do well where game densities are high. This alone precludes them from success in most of the Delta. Game farms prize them as one of the most valuable antelope. They need access to drinking water, but are well adapted to subsist on relatively high plateaux with poor soils.

Oryx or gemsbok (*Oryx gazella*) Shoulder height 120cm; weight 230kg. This is the quintessential desert antelope, unmistakable with its ash-grey coat, bold black facial marks and flank strip, and unique long, straight horns. Of the three races of oryx in Africa, the gemsbok is the largest and most striking. It occurs throughout the Kalahari and Namib and is widespread all over central and western Botswana. The dominant large antelope in the CKGR, it can be seen there in large numbers during the early months of the year.

As you might expect, gemsbok are very adaptable. They range widely and are found in areas of dunes, alkaline pans, open savannah and even woodlands. Along with the much smaller springbok, they can sometimes be seen tracking across open plains with only dust-devils and mirages for company. Gemsbok can endure extremes of temperature, helped by specially adapted blood capillaries in their nasal passages that can cool their blood before it reaches their brains. Thus although their body temperature can rise by up to 6°C, their brains remain cool and they survive. They do not need drinking water and will eat wild melons and dig for roots, bulbs and tubers when grazing or browsing becomes difficult.

Waterbuck (*Kobus ellipsiprymnus*) Shoulder height 130cm; weight 250–270kg. The waterbuck is easily recognised by its shaggy brown coat and the male's large, lyre-shaped horns. The common race of southern Africa (*K. e. ellipsiprymnus*) and areas east of the Rift Valley has a distinctive white ring around its rump. The defassa race (known as *K. e. defassa* or *K. e. crawshayi*) of the Rift Valley and areas further west has a full white rump.

Only the common waterbuck occurs in Botswana, and it is restricted to the Chobe, Kwando–Linyanti and eastern sides of the Delta. Favourite areas include the northern side of the Linyanti Concession (NG15), and also Vumbura (NG22), but it is relatively uncommon elsewhere. Waterbuck certainly used to occur at Savuti when the channel flowed, but they deserted the area when the marsh dried up.

Waterbuck need to drink very regularly, so usually stay within a few kilometres of water, where they like to graze on short, nutritious grasses. At night they may take cover in adjacent woodlands. It is often asserted that waterbuck flesh is oily and smelly, which may discourage predators.

Blue wildebeest (*Connochaetes taurinus*) Shoulder height 130–150cm; weight 180–250kg. This ungainly antelope, also called the brindled gnu, is easily identified by its dark coat and bovine appearance. The superficially similar buffalo is far more heavily built; when they have enough space and conditions are right, blue wildebeest can multiply rapidly and form immense herds – as perhaps a million do for their annual migration from Tanzania's Serengeti Plains into Kenya's Maasai Mara.

In Botswana during the middle of the 20th century wildebeest were probably the most numerous large herbivore, forming herds estimated at a quarter of a million individuals. Although they are still found throughout Botswana, these numbers have fallen drastically. (See *Fauna* in *Chapter 16, The Central Kalahari*, pages 493–6, for further discussion of this.)

Wildebeest are best adapted to take large mouthfuls of short, nutritious grasses, and they need access to drinking water every two or three days. This limits them to remaining relatively close to a source of water, and if that dries up they will journey as far as necessary to find another.

Red hartebeest (*Alcelaphus buselaphus*) Shoulder height 125cm; weight 120–150kg. Hartebeests are ungainly antelope, readily identified by the combination of

Gemsbok

AVZ

Waterbuck

PO/MP/FLPA

Blue wildebeest

TH

large shoulders, sloping back, glossy, red-brown coat and smallish horns in both sexes. Numerous subspecies are recognised, all of which are generally seen in small family groups in reasonably open country. Though once hartebeest were found from the Mediterranean to the Cape, only isolated populations still survive.

The only subspecies native to Botswana is the red hartebeest, which is found throughout the arid central, southern and western areas of the country. It can be seen in Nxai and Makgadikgadi, and is one of the more numerous large mammals in the CKGR. Hartebeest may occur in the drier, southwestern corners of the Delta, or in the drier parts of southern Chobe, but I've no records of them being seen in either location.

Hartebeests are more or less exclusively grazers, and although they like access to water they will eat melons, tubers and rhizomes when necessary. In the Central Kalahari they'll range widely, often with wildebeest, following thunderstorms in search of fresh, green shoots.

Tsessebe (*Damaliscus lunatus*) Shoulder height 120cm; weight 125–140kg. Tsessebe are basically a slightly smaller, darker version of hartebeest, coloured red-brown with an almost purple sheen, though their lower legs are distinctly paler. (A closely related subspecies is known as topi in east Africa.) The two look similar in profile or at a distance, although often in the field you can make a good guess from the environment which antelope you're looking at long before you're close enough to examine its colouring.

The tsessebe is found in northern Botswana, and is one of the most common antelope in some parts of the Okavango Delta. Its favourite habitat is open grassland, where it is a selective grazer, eating the younger, more nutritious grasses. This makes it efficient in pastures where some grasses are old and some fresh, or in more broken country, but less efficient than, say, wildebeest where the pasture is uniformly short, good grass. The tsessebe is one of the fastest antelope species, and jumps very well.

Kudu (*Tragelaphus strepsiceros*) Shoulder height 140–155cm; weight 180–250kg. The kudu (or, more properly, the greater kudu) is the largest member of the genus *Tragelaphus*. These medium-sized to large antelopes are characterised by their grey-brown coats with up to ten stripes on each flank. The male has magnificent double-spiralled corkscrew horns. Occurring throughout Mozambique, Zimbabwe, Zambia and Namibia, kudu are found all over Botswana.

These handsome antelope are particularly common in the well-wooded areas of Chobe, the Kwando–Linyanti area and the Okavango, though they also occur throughout the drier areas of the Kalahari. They are browsers that thrive in areas with mixed tree savannah and thickets, and the males will sometimes use their horns to pull down the lower branches of trees to eat.

Wherever they occur, kudu are normally seen in small herds, consisting of a couple of females and their offspring, usually accompanied by a male. Otherwise the males occur either singly or in small bachelor groups.

Eland (*Taurotragus oryx*) Shoulder height 150–175cm; weight 450–900kg. Africa's largest antelope, the eland is light brown in colour, sometimes with a few faint white vertical stripes. Relatively short horns and a large dewlap accentuate its somewhat bovine appearance. It was once widely distributed in eastern and southern Africa, though the population has now been severely depleted. Small herds of eland frequent grasslands and light woodlands, often fleeing at the slightest provocation. (They have long been hunted for their excellent meat, so perhaps this is not surprising.)

Eland are very rare in the Okavango area and although they probably occur throughout Chobe, they are seldom seen. Better areas to see them are in the Kalahari's salt pans or, better still, the Central Kalahari. They are opportunist browsers and grazers, eating fruit, berries, seed pods and leaves as well as green grass after the rains, and roots and tubers when times are lean.

These large antelope run slowly, though can trot for great distances and jump exceedingly well. Eland have a very special significance for the San people –

Bushbuck

illustrated by the highlight of the famous 'van der Post panel' at the Tsodilo Hills (see page 435), which is a painting of a particularly magnificent eland bull.

MEDIUM AND SMALL ANTELOPE

Bushbuck (*Tragelaphus scriptus*) Shoulder height 70–80cm; weight 30–45kg. This attractive antelope, a member of the same genus as the kudu, is widespread throughout Africa and shows great regional variation in its colouring. (The animals found in sub-Saharan Africa are often claimed to be a subspecies, the 'Chobe bushbuck', though it seems likely that they're simply a colour variation of the main species.)

Bushbuck occur in forest and riverine woodland, where they are normally seen singly or in pairs. The male is dark brown or chestnut, while the much smaller female is generally a pale reddish brown. The male has relatively small, straight horns and both sexes are marked with white spots and sometimes stripes, though the stripes are often indistinct.

Bushbuck tend to be secretive and very skittish, except when used to people, when they relax and can become almost tame. They depend on cover and camouflage to avoid predators, and are often found in the thick, herby vegetation around rivers – and are the only solitary antelope in Africa that does not defend a territory. They will freeze if disturbed, before dashing off into the undergrowth. Bushbuck are both browsers and grazers, choosing the more succulent grass shoots, fruit and flowers. In Botswana they have a limited distribution around the Okavango, beside the Kwando–Linyanti and the Chobe. Look for them slowly picking their way through the thick bush near the water. (Serondela used to be a favourite spot, and the island on which Kwetsani stands had several fairly relaxed resident individuals when I last visited.)

Impala (*Aepeceros melampus* Shoulder height 90cm; weight 45kg. This slender, handsome antelope is superficially similar to the springbok, but in fact belongs to its own separate family. Tawny in colour, and lighter underneath than above, the impala has diagnostic black and white stripes running down its rump and tail, and the male has large lyre-shaped horns. The impala is one of the most widespread and successful antelope species in eastern and southern Africa. It is often the most common antelope in wooded savannah habitats, including most of Chobe and the drier, more forested parts of the Okavango Delta – though is rarely seen west of the Okavango, or south of Nxai Pan. Although they can survive without drinking, impala prefer to live near water and are largely absent from the Kalahari.

As you might expect of such a successful species, impala both graze and browse, depending on what fodder is available. Despite some people's tendency to overlook them as common, take a close look and you'll realise that they're exceptionally beautiful animals. Socially you'll normally see large herds of females and young, lorded over by a dominant male, and small bachelor groups of males.

Female impala

TW/S

Springbok (*Antidorcas marsupialis*) Shoulder height 60cm; weight 20–25kg. Springbok are graceful herbivores, similar in size to impala. Visitors from east Africa, noticing their passing resemblance to Thomson's gazelle (*Gazella thomsonii*), will not be surprised that they're southern Africa's only member of the gazelle family.

Even from a distance, springbok are unlikely to be confused with anything else; their finely marked short coats have fawn-brown upper parts and a white belly, separated by a dark brown band. Springbok generally occur in herds and favour dry, open country, preferring plains or savannah, and avoiding thick woodlands and mountains. They can subsist without water for long periods, provided that there is moisture (minimum of 10%) in the vegetation that they graze or browse.

Since springbok are more dependent on food than water, they congregate in huge numbers during the rains on areas where they can find fresh, green shoots – such as the pans of the CKGR. In contrast, during the dry season they spread out across the vast arid parks of the Kalahari. This is exactly the opposite pattern to that followed by most water-dependent antelope, which typically congregate during the dry season (around rivers to remaining pans), while spreading out during the rains. This explains why the Kalahari's game is at its densest during the rains, whereas the game in Chobe and the Okavango is at its most prolific during the dry season.

Springbok occur throughout central and southern Botswana, where they are usually the most common small antelope by far; in Nxai, Makgadikgadi and the CKGR they number in the thousands.

Springbok

SE/S

Reedbuck (*Redunca arundinum*) Shoulder height 80–90cm; weight 45–65kg. Sometimes referred to as the southern reedbuck (as distinct from mountain and Bohor reedbucks, found further east), these slender antelope are uniformly fawn in colour, and lighter below than above. Only males have horns, but both sexes show a distinctive black glandular patch below each ear. They are generally found in reedbeds and tall grasslands, often beside rivers, and are easily identified by their loud, whistling alarm call and distinctive bounding running style.

In Botswana; reedbuck are found only where there is close access to water in the north: in northern Chobe, the Kwando–Linyanti region and throughout the Delta. They live in monogamous pairs that defend a territory.

Puku (*Kobus vardonii*) Shoulder height 80cm; weight 60–75kg. Easily confused with the lechwe at a glance, the puku has an orange-tawny colour overall, which is lighter underneath than above. Its legs have no black markings, and its tail is a lighter yellow. Puku are smaller and slightly shaggier than lechwe, and the males have smaller, stouter horns than those of lechwe.

Puku are found all over eastern and central Africa, and are one of the most common antelopes in Zambia. Typically they inhabit open areas near rivers and marshes, though in Zambia are found in a wider variety of habitats. In Botswana their distribution is restricted to the floodplain areas of the Chobe riverfront, and often virtually the only place that you'll see them is around the aptly named Puku Flats, just west of Chobe Game Lodge.

Red lechwe (*Kobus leche*) Shoulder height 90–100cm; weight 80–100kg. Red lechwe are sturdy antelope with a chestnut-red coat, paler underneath than on top, and beautiful lyre-shaped horns. They need dry land on which to rest, but otherwise are adapted for life in the seasonal floodplains that border lakes and rivers. They will spend much of their time grazing on grasses and sedges, standing in water if necessary. Their hooves are splayed, adapted to bounding through their muddy environment when fleeing from the lion, hyena and wild dog that hunt them, making them the most aquatic of antelope after sitatunga.

Lechwe reach the southern limit of their distribution in the Okavango and Linyanti areas. They are also found in the DRC, Angola, Namibia's Caprivi Strip, and in Zambia, their stronghold; wherever they occur, the males are generally larger and darker than the females; when conditions are right, they can be found in huge numbers, and they are the most numerous antelope in the shallow-water environments of the Delta.

Sitatunga (*Tragelaphus spekei*) Shoulder height 85–90cm; weight 105–115kg. This semi-aquatic antelope is a widespread but infrequently observed inhabitant of west and central African papyrus swamps, from the Okavango in Botswana to the Sudd in Sudan. In Botswana sitatunga are concentrated in the Okavango – which has a strong population – though they're also seen periodically in the Kwando–Linyanti and Chobe systems. The best places to spot them are deep-water areas with plenty of papyrus, including Moremi and in NG21, 22, 23, 24 and 25 concessions.

Because of their preferred habitat, sitatunga are elusive and seldom seen, even in areas where they are relatively common. They are also less easy to hunt/poach than many other species, although they are exceedingly vulnerable to habitat destruction. Sitatunga are noted for an ability to submerse themselves completely, with just their nostrils showing, when pursued by a predator.

Klipspringer

Klipspringer (*Oreotragus oreotragus*) Shoulder height 60cm; weight 13kg. The klipspringer is a strongly built little antelope, normally seen in pairs, and easily identified by its dark, bristly grey-yellow coat, slightly speckled appearance and unique habitat preference. Klipspringer means 'rockjumper' in Afrikaans and it is an apt name for an antelope which occurs exclusively in mountainous areas and rocky outcrops, from Cape Town to the Red Sea. Klipspringers are mainly browsers, though they do eat a little new grass; when spotted they will freeze, or bound at great speed across the steepest of slopes.

Though often thought to be absent from all but the extreme southeast corner of Botswana, there were several reliable reports of sightings on Qumxhwaa Hill, near Savuti Marsh, at the end of the 1970s. Given that they only live in rocky hills and kopjes, and that most of Botswana is amazingly flat (or gently rolling at best), it's no surprise that only the odd isolated population exists. It's the same in other parts of their range. I've no reports of them at the Tsodilo Hills, but it would be a perfect habitat for them.

Steenbok

Steenbok (*Raphicerus cempestris*) Shoulder height 50cm; weight 11kg. This rather nondescript small antelope has red-brown upper parts and clear white underparts, and the male has short straight horns. It is one of the most commonly observed small antelope, especially on farmland; if you see a small antelope fleeing from you across grassland, then it is likely to be a steenbok. Like most other small antelopes, the steenbok is normally encountered singly or in pairs and tends to 'freeze' when disturbed, before taking flight.

Similar species The **Oribi** (*Ourebia ourebi*) is a relatively widespread but generally uncommon antelope, which occurs in very localised areas

Common duiker

ROT/NP/FLPA

throughout sub-Saharan Africa. It is usually found only in large, open stretches of dry grassland, where there are also patches of taller grass for cover. It looks much like a steenbok but stands about 10cm higher at the shoulder and has an altogether more upright bearing. In Botswana it is thought to occur in Chobe, and specifically in the Ngwezumba Pans area – although sightings of it even there are not common. **Sharpe's grysbok** (*Raphicerus sharpei*) is similar in size and appearance, though it has a distinctive white-flecked coat. It occurs alongside the steenbok in the far northeastern corner of Botswana, around northern Chobe and the Kasane area, but is almost entirely nocturnal in its habits and so very seldom seen.

Common duiker (*Sylvicapra grimmia*) Shoulder height 50cm; weight 20kg. This anomalous duiker holds itself more like a steenbok or grysbok and is the only member of its (large) family to occur outside of forests. Generally grey in colour, the common duiker can most easily be separated from other small antelopes by the black tuft of hair that sticks up between its horns. It occurs throughout Botswana, and across virtually the whole of southern Africa, with the exception of the Namib Desert. Common duikers tolerate most habitats except for true forest and very open country, and are tolerant of nearby human settlements. They are opportunist feeders, taking fruit, seeds and leaves, as well as crops, small reptiles and amphibians. Despite their widespread occurrence, duiker are relatively rarely seen.

OTHER LARGE HERBIVORES
African elephant (*Loxodonta africana*) Shoulder height 2.3–3.4m; weight up to 6,000kg. The world's largest land animal, the African elephant is intelligent, social and often very entertaining to watch. Females live in closely knit clans in which the eldest female plays matriarch over her sisters, daughters and granddaughters. Elephants' life spans are comparable with those of humans, and mother–daughter bonds are strong and may last for up to 50 years. Males generally leave the family group at around 12 years to roam singly or form bachelor herds. Under normal circumstances, elephants range widely in search of food and water, but when concentrated populations are forced to live in conservation areas their habit of uprooting trees can cause serious environmental damage.

A matriarchal herd of elephants drink thirstily from
the permanent waters of the Chobe River

Elephants are widespread and common in habitats ranging from deserts to rainforest; but they require trees and access to drinking water. They are very common in the north of Botswana.

The Chobe, Kwando–Linyanti and Okavango areas have one of Africa's greatest populations of elephants. During the rains, from December onwards, these disperse in the interior of the country, into the vast expanses of mopane forest and into the drier areas of the northern Kalahari. They split up into smaller family groups and spread out all over the place in order to find water (the clay pans of the mopane woodlands are especially valuable as sources).

Despite their range having become more restricted by human expansion over the years, individuals will often wander widely, turning up in locations from which they have been absent for years. However, as the dry season progresses and the waterholes dry up, small groups gradually coalesce into larger herds, and head for the permanent sources: the rivers and the Delta. Thus by September and October you can normally see huge herds of elephants along the Chobe, Kwando and Linyanti rivers. The number and size of herds in the Okavango increases also.

In many areas elephants have no natural predators (the huge prides of lion in the Savuti and North Gate areas are an exception to this rule); they are generally constrained by lack of suitable habitat (ie: trees and water), by man and by diseases such as anthrax. Thus in many confined national parks in southern Africa, there are programmes to cull elephants to restrict their numbers. This is controversial, even among ardent conservationists. Botswana has no such policy. The result, some argue, is an over-population of elephants here, and the severe environmental degradation to be seen around the riverfront in Chobe, where the riverine forests have been severely depleted; while not denying the observation, it's well worth remembering that there was a sawmill in this area, and extensive logging during the 1930s and early 1940s – so humans should take part of the blame for this.

Black rhinoceros (*Diceros bicornis*) Shoulder height 160cm; weight 1,000kg. This is the more widespread of Africa's two rhino species, an imposing and rather temperamental creature. Black rhino were once found all over northern Botswana,

Black rhino

White rhino

but were thought to have been poached to extinction here during the 1990s, while becoming highly endangered in many other countries within their range. Now, following the successful reintroduction of white rhino, black rhino have also been reintroduced, with their populations continuously monitored. If you want to help with this work, then see *Travelling positively* on pages 158–60.

Black rhino exploit a wide range of habitats from dense woodlands and bush to arid semi-desert, and are generally solitary animals. They can survive without drinking for four to five days. However, their territorial behaviour and regular patterns of movement make them an easy target for poachers. Black rhino can be very aggressive when disturbed and will charge with minimal provocation. Their hearing and sense of smell are acute, while their eyesight is poor (so they often miss their target).

White rhinoceros (*Ceratotherium simum*) Shoulder height 180cm; weight 1,500–2,000kg. The white rhino is in fact no paler in colour than the black rhino: 'white' and 'black' are *not* literal descriptions. The description 'white' derives from the Afrikaans *weit* (wide) and refers to the animal's flattened mouth, an ideal shape for cropping grass. This is a good way to tell the two rhino species apart, since the mouth of the black rhino, a browser in most parts of its range, is more rounded with a hooked upper lip.

Unlike their smaller cousins, white rhino are generally placid grazing animals and are very rarely aggressive. They prefer open grassy plains and are often seen in small groups. In the accounts of the first trips across Africa by the early white explorers, white rhino were found (and shot) in huge numbers.

This species was almost extinct by the end of the 19th century, reduced to a tiny population in South Africa's Umfolozi and Hluhluwe reserves. Intensive conservation subsequently nurtured a recovery and gradually animals were reintroduced into selected locations across southern Africa. By the 1980s, it had become much more numerous than the black rhino, whose numbers were by then falling fast. Sadly, the early 21st century saw poaching resume, with South Africa's once safe populations targeted ruthlessly. Today, Botswana's wild areas are viewed as safer havens from poaching than South Africa's game ranches. Thus transfers of animals from South Africa, and natural

51

Hippopotamus

population growth, have resulted in a surge in Botswana's population (see box, page 340 for background information). Visitors are increasingly seeing evidence of this, as sightings of white rhino are becoming less of a rarity across northern Botswana.

Hippopotamus (*Hippopotamus amphibius*) Shoulder height 150cm; weight 2,000kg. Characteristic of Africa's large rivers and lakes, this large, lumbering animal spends most of the day submerged but emerges at night to graze. Strongly territorial, herds of ten or more are presided over by a dominant male who will readily defend his patriarchy to the death. Hippos are abundant in most protected rivers and water bodies and are still quite common outside reserves.

Hippos are widely credited with killing more people than any other African mammal. They are clearly very, very dangerous – but I know of no statistics to support this claim, and many reliable sources suggest that elephant and lion kill just as many people. Crocodiles certainly kill more.

In Botswana you'll find hippo in good numbers in all of the major river systems: Chobe, Kwando–Linyanti and the Okavango. It would be difficult to go on safari in any of the wetter areas of northern Botswana without seeing large numbers.

Buffalo (*Syncerus caffer*) Shoulder height 140cm; weight 700kg. Frequently and erroneously referred to as water buffalo (which is actually an Asian species), the Cape, or African, buffalo is a distinctive, highly social, ox-like animal that lives as part of a herd. It prefers well-watered savannah, though also occurs in forested areas. Buffalo are primarily grazers and need regular access to water, where they swim readily. Lion often follow herds of buffalo, their favourite prey in some areas.

Huge herds are generally fairly peaceful, and experienced guides will often walk straight through them on walking safaris. However, small bachelor herds, and especially single old bulls, can be very nervous and aggressive. They have a reputation for charging at the slightest provocation, often in the midst of thick bush, and are exceedingly dangerous when wounded.

Buffalo smell and hear well, but it's often claimed that they have poor eyesight. This isn't true, though when encountered during a walking safari, if you keep still and the wind is right they won't be able to discern your presence.

Common and widespread in sub-Saharan Africa, in Botswana the buffalo is limited to the north of the country, largely by the absence of sufficient water

Buffalo

elsewhere. Their annual movements mirror those of elephants in general terms. During the rains, from December onwards, they disperse into the mopane forests and into the drier areas of the northern Kalahari, splitting up into smaller groups and spreading out. However, as the dry season progresses, they gather together into larger herds, and congregate near permanent sources of water: along the Chobe, Kwando and Linyanti rivers, and throughout the Okavango Delta. Then you'll see them in most reserves with water, though the open plains of NG23 (Duba Plains) seem to have particularly high concentrations of buffalo.

Giraffe (*Giraffa camelopardis*) Shoulder height 250–350cm; weight 1,000–1,400kg. The world's tallest and longest-necked land animal, a fully grown giraffe can measure up to 5.5m high. Quite unmistakable, giraffe live in loosely structured herds of up to 15 head, though herd members often disperse, when they are seen singly or in smaller groups. Formerly distributed throughout eastern and southern Africa, in Botswana these great browsers are now found only in the centre and north of the country. The CKGR has a very healthy population, as do Makgadikgadi and Nxai, and they are also found through the Chobe, Kwando–Linyanti and Okavango areas.

Giraffe

Giraffe are adapted to browse vegetation that is beyond the reach of all the other large herbivores, with the exception of elephant. They prefer *Acacia* and *Combretum* species, and a 45cm tongue ensures that they can pluck the leaves from the most thorny of branches.

Plains zebra (*Equus quagga*) Shoulder height 130cm; weight 300–340kg. Also known as common zebra, this attractive striped horse is common and widespread throughout most of eastern and southern Africa, where it is often seen in large herds alongside wildebeest. There are many subspecies of zebra in Africa, and most

Zebra

southern races, including those in Botswana, have paler brownish 'shadow stripes' between the bold black stripes (which are present in all races).

Zebra are common in most conservation areas, from northern South Africa and Namibia all the way up to the southeast of Ethiopia. In Botswana they occur in Makgadikgadi, Nxai and to the north – but I don't believe that they still occur within the CKGR. If the rains have been good in the Makgadikgadi Pans area, then during the first few months of the year you can witness huge herds of zebra roaming across the open plains in search of the freshest new grass.

Warthog (*Phacochoerus africanus*) Shoulder height 60–70cm; weight up to 100kg. This widespread and often conspicuously abundant resident of the African savannah is grey in colour with a thin covering of hairs, wart-like bumps on its face, and rather large, upward-curving tusks. Africa's only diurnal swine, the warthog is often seen in family groups, trotting around with its tail raised stiffly (a diagnostic trait) and a determinedly nonchalant air.

Warthog occur throughout Botswana, with the exception of the far south, although they don't usually fare well near settlements, as they are very susceptible to subsistence hunting/poaching. Wherever they occur, you'll often see them grazing beside the road, on bended knee.

Similar species Bulkier, hairier and browner, the **bushpig** (*Potomochoerus larvatus*) only occurs in the wetter areas of northern Botswana – northern Chobe, the Kwando–Linyanti and the Okavango. Like warthog, bushpig don't survive well near settlements: they damage crops and so are persistently hunted. That said, even where they do occur, they are rarely seen due to their nocturnal habits and preference for living in dense vegetation.

SMALL MAMMALS

African civet (*Civettictis civetta*) Shoulder height 40cm; weight 10–15kg. This bulky, long-haired, rather feline creature of the African night is primarily carnivorous, feeding on small animals and carrion, but will also eat fruit. It has a pale fawn coat, densely blotched with large black spots that merge into stripes towards the head. Civets are widespread and common throughout a band across northern Botswana, including Chobe, the Kwando–Linyanti and Okavango areas. They occur in many habitats, and make frequent cameo appearances on night drives.

Note that although they are occasionally referred to as 'civet cats', this is misleading. They are more closely related to the mongooses than the felines and belong in the same genus as genets.

Similar species Both the **small-spotted genet** (*Genetta genetta*) and the **large-spotted genet** (*Genetta tigrina*) are members of a large group of similar small predators found in Botswana. All the genets are slender and rather feline in appearance (though they are *not* cats), with a grey to gold-brown coat marked with black spots and bars, and a long ringed tail. However, as even experts often can't tell the various species apart without examining their skins by hand, precise identification of genets is difficult.

You're most likely to see genets on nocturnal game drives or occasionally scavenging around game-reserve lodges. The small-spotted genet is found all over Botswana, whereas its larger cousin is thought to be restricted to the northern areas of Chobe, Kwando–Linyanti and Okavango. Genets are excellent climbers and opportunists, eating birds, small mammals and large insects.

Banded mongoose (*Mungos mungo*) Shoulder height 20cm; weight around 1kg. The banded mongoose is probably the most commonly observed member of a group of small, slender, terrestrial carnivores. Uniform dark grey-brown except for a dozen black stripes across its back, it is a diurnal mongoose occurring in playful family groups, or troops, in most habitats throughout northern and northwestern Botswana. It feeds on insects, scorpions, amphibians, reptiles and even carrion and bird's eggs, and troops can move through the bush at quite a pace.

Similar species Several other mongoose species occur in Botswana. Some are social and gather in troops; others are solitary. Several are too scarce and nocturnal to be seen by most visitors.

The water or **marsh mongoose** (*Atilax paludinosus*) is large, normally solitary and has a very scruffy brown coat; it is widespread in the Chobe, Kwando–Linyanti and Okavango regions, generally found near water.

The **white-tailed mongoose** (*Ichneumia albicauda*), or white-tailed ichneumon, is a solitary, large brown mongoose with long, coarse hair. It is nocturnal and easily identified by its bushy white tail if seen crossing roads at night. It occurs across northern Botswana and it can also be found in a few cattle-ranching areas, where it eats the beetle-grubs found in manure.

The **slender mongoose** (*Galerella sanguinea*) is also widespread throughout Botswana wherever it can find cover. It, too, is solitary, but it is very much smaller (shoulder height 10cm) and has a uniform brown or reddish coat and blackish tail tip. Its tail is held up when it runs.

The **large grey mongoose** (*Herpestes ichneumon*), also called the Egyptian mongoose, is a large mongoose with coarse, grey-speckled body hair, black lower legs and feet, and a black tip to its tail. It is found in the same northern areas of Botswana, but is common nowhere. It is generally diurnal, and is either solitary or lives in pairs. Large grey mongooses eat small rodents, reptiles, birds and also snakes, generally killing rather than scavenging.

Selous' mongoose (*Paracynictis selousi*) is smaller, with fine, speckled grey fur, and a white tip at the end of its tail. It likes open country and woodlands, occurring in many northern and further eastern areas of Botswana. It is nocturnal and solitary, eating mainly insects, grubs, small reptiles and amphibians. It seems especially fond of the larvae of dung beetles, and so is sometimes found in cattle country.

The **yellow mongoose** (*Cynitis penicillata*) is a small, sociable mongoose with a tawny or yellow coat, and is commonly found across most of Botswana – even in the drier areas of the Central Kalahari. It normally forages alone and is easily identified by the white tip on the end of its tail. This species often shares burrow systems with ground squirrels.

Finally, the **dwarf mongoose** (*Helogale parvula*) is a diminutive (shoulder height 7cm), highly sociable light-brown mongoose often seen in the vicinity of the termite mounds where it nests. This is Africa's smallest carnivore, and occurs in higher densities than any other. It is widespread throughout the Chobe, Kwando–Linyanti and Okavango areas, and often seen. Groups of 20–30 are not unknown, consisting of a breeding pair and subordinate others. These inquisitive little animals can be very entertaining to watch.

Meerkat or suricate (*Suricata suricatta*) Shoulder height 25–35cm; weight 650–950g. Found throughout central and southwest Botswana, and much of neighbouring Namibia, meerkats are absent from the Chobe, Kwando–Linyanti and Okavango regions. The best places to see them are Makgadikgadi, the CKGR and further towards the southwest corner of Botswana (eg: the KD1 concession, south of Ghanzi, and the Kgalagadi Transfrontier Park).

Meerkats also belong to the mongoose family. These small animals are sandy to silvery-grey in colour, with dark bands running across their backs. They are exclusively diurnal and have a distinctive habit of sitting upright on their hind legs. They do this when they first emerge in the morning, to sun themselves, and throughout the day.

Living in complex social groups, meerkats are usually seen scratching around for insects, beetles and small reptiles in dry, open, grassy areas; while the rest forage, one or two of the group will use the highest mound around as a sentry-post – looking out for predators using their remarkable eyesight. Meerkats' social behaviour is very complex: they squeak constantly to communicate and even use different alarm calls for different types of predators. Because of their photogenic poses and fascinating social behaviour, they have been the subject of several successful television documentaries filmed in the southern Kalahari.

Honey badger (*Mellivora capensis*) Shoulder height 30cm; weight 12kg. Also known as the ratel, the honey badger is black with a puppyish face and grey-white back. It is an opportunistic feeder best known for its allegedly symbiotic relationship with a bird called the honeyguide which leads it to beehives, waits for it to tear them open, then feeds on the scraps. The honey badger is among the most widespread of African carnivores, and also among the most powerful and aggressive for its size. It occurs all over Botswana, but is thinly distributed and infrequently seen, except where it has lost its fear of people and started to scavenge from safari camps.

Similar species Other mustelids occurring in the region include the **striped polecat** (*Ictonyx striatus*), a common but rarely seen nocturnal creature with black underparts and a bushy white back.

Cape clawless otter (*Aonyx capensis*) Shoulder height 20–30cm; weight 3–5kg. This is the larger of the two species of otter that occur in southern Africa. It has a chocolate-brown coat with a pale cream-to-white chin and throat. In Botswana, it is restricted to the northern river systems of Chobe, Kwando–Linyanti and the Okavango (it's not found in broad, tropical rivers like the Zambezi), though will occasionally move away from there, across dry land, in search of other pools and waterways.

Cape clawless otters are active mostly around dusk and dawn, although they will sometimes be seen in broad daylight or at night. Rough skin on their paws gives excellent grip, and with this they prey mostly on frogs and fish. They'll also take freshwater mussels, and will use rocks to help them crack these open.

Although very shy (they'll usually flee when approached by a boat or people), these animals are delightful to watch, seeming very playful, with a variety of aquatic acrobatics, and cleaning their face and paws scrupulously after every meal. Visiting Botswana, you're most likely to see otters in the shallow floodplain areas of the Okavango when on a quiet mokoro trip.

Similar species The smaller **spotted-necked otter** (*Lutra maculicollis*) is darker with light white spots on its throat – though difficult to distinguish from its larger cousin unless you're familiar with them both. Its distribution and habits are similar to the Cape clawless, though it is more diurnal, and more tied to bodies of water.

Aardvark (*Orycteropus afer*) Shoulder height 60cm; weight up to 70kg. This singularly bizarre nocturnal insectivore is unmistakable with its long snout, huge ears and powerful legs, adapted to dig up the nests of termites, on which it feeds. Aardvarks occur throughout southern Africa, except in the driest western areas of the Namib. Though their distinctive three-toed tracks are often seen, and they are not uncommon animals, sightings of them are rare.

Aardvarks prefer areas of grassland and sparse scrub, rather than dense woodlands, so much of Botswana's bush suits them well. You're most likely to see them on a late-night game drive, and many guides say that they are seen more often during the rainy season, from December to March.

Pangolin (*Manis temmincki*) Total length 70–100cm; weight 8–15kg. Sharing the aardvaak's diet of termites and ants, the pangolin is another very unusual nocturnal insectivore, with distinctive armour plating and a tendency to roll up in a ball when disturbed. (Then it can swipe its tail from side to side, inflicting serious damage on its aggressor.) Sometimes known as Temminck's pangolins, or scaly anteaters, these strange animals walk on their hindlegs, using their tail and front legs for balance. They are both nocturnal and rare, and their distribution is little known, although they are thought to occur throughout Botswana. Sightings are exceedingly rare; thus an average of three sightings of pangolin per year in NG31 Reserve counts as a remarkably prolific record by the standards of most areas in Africa!

In some areas further south, particularly Zimbabwe, local custom is to make a present of any pangolin found to the paramount chief (often taken to mean the president). This has caused great damage to their population.

Cape clawless otter

ZSSD/MP/FLPA

Aardvark

STA

Pangolin

SC/MP/FLPA

Porcupine (*Hystrix africaeaustralis*) Total length 80–100cm; weight 15–25kg. This is the largest rodent found in the region, and occurs all over southern Africa, except for the western reaches of the Namib Desert. It is easily identified by its black-and-white-striped quills, generally black hair and shambolic gait. If heard in the dark, then the rustle of its foraging is augmented by the slight rattle of its quills. These fall out fairly regularly, and are often found in the bush.

Porcupines have a varied diet, and they are fairly opportunistic when it comes to food. Roots and tubers are favourites, as is the bark of certain trees; they will also eat meat and small reptiles, or birds if they have the chance. You're most likely to see porcupines on night drives, as individuals, pairs or small family groups.

Similar species Also spiny, the **Southern African hedgehog** (*Erinaceus frontalis*) has been recorded in eastern and southeastern areas of Botswana, though it is small and nocturnal, so rarely seen even where it does occur. Hedgehogs are about 20cm long (much smaller than porcupines), omnivorous and uncommon.

Rock hyrax (*Procavia capensis*) Shoulder height 20–30cm; weight 4kg. Rodent-like in appearance, hyraxes (also known as dassies) share an ancient evolutionary lineage with elephants. This species and the similar **yellow-spotted rock hyrax** (*Heterohyrax brucei*) are often seen sunning themselves in rocky habitats, and become tame when used to people.

Hyraxes are social animals, living in large groups, and are largely herbivores, eating leaves, grasses and fruits; where you see large numbers, watch out for black eagles and other raptors, which prey extensively on them. In Botswana they're restricted to the southeast of the country, although places like the Tsodilo Hills would seem an ideal habitat for them.

Scrub hare (*Lepus saxatilis*) Shoulder height 45–60cm; weight 1–4.5kg. This is the largest and most common African hare or rabbit, occurring everywhere in Botswana. In some areas a short walk at dusk or after nightfall might reveal three or four scrub hares. They tend to freeze when disturbed.

Similar species Very similar, the **Cape hare** (*Lepus capensis*) has been recorded in Botswana, both in the southwest and in an area to the north of the great salt pans. However, distinguishing between these two similar species at night, when they are most likely to be seen, would be very difficult.

Ground squirrel (*Xerus inauris*) Shoulder height 20–30cm; weight 400–700g. This terrestrial rodent is common in the more arid parts of Botswana, including the Central Kalahari, and southeastern areas. It is grey to grey-brown with a prominent white eye ring and silver-black tail; within its range, it might be confused with the meerkat, which also spends much time on its hind legs. Unlike the meerkat, the ground squirrel has a characteristic squirrel mannerism of holding food in its forepaws.

The ground squirrel is a social animal; large groups share one communal burrow. It can often be spotted searching for vegetation, seeds, roots and small insects, while holding its tail aloft as a sunshade.

Bush squirrel (*Paraxerus cepapi*) Total length 35cm; weight 100–250g. This common rodent is a uniform buff colour, with a long tail that is furry but not bushy. It is widely distributed all over southern and east Africa, and occurs throughout northern Botswana in most woodland habitats. Bush squirrels are so numerous in mopane woodlands that it can be difficult to avoid them, hence the species' other common names, the mopane or tree squirrel.

Bush squirrels live alone, in pairs or in small groups, usually nesting in a drey of dry leaves, in a hole in a tree. They are diurnal and venture to the ground to feed on seeds, fruit, nuts, vegetable matter and small insects; when alarmed they often bolt up the nearest tree, keeping on the side of the trunk away from the threat, out of sight as much as possible. If they can find a safe vantage point with a view of the threat, then they'll sometimes make a loud scolding alarm call.

Flap-necked chameleon

62

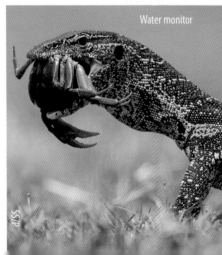

Water monitor

Botswana's numerous ecosystems are home to more than 140 species of reptile – including the Nile crocodile.

NILE CROCODILE (*Crocodylus niloticus*) Length up to 5m; weight up to 1,000kg. Few visitors to Botswana will want to miss the opportunity to see this antediluvian creature. With its powerful serrated tail, horny plated skin and up to 100 peg-like teeth crammed into a long, sinister smile, the Nile crocodile is the stuff of nightmares and action movies. Contrary to the more lurid myths, crocodiles generally avoid people (understandably, given the slaughter they have suffered). Yet while they will not usually launch themselves into boats or come galloping after you on land, humans are still potential prey for a big one, and tragedies do occasionally occur; when in crocodile country, it is sensible to keep your distance from the water's edge.

Crocodiles inhabit lakes, rivers and swamps. They can live up to 100, but reach sexual maturity at 12–15 years. Whereas youngsters are boldly marked in black and green, adults are generally a muddy grey-brown colour – usually lighter in rivers than in lagoons. Theirs is an amphibious life: basking on land, jaws agape to lose heat, or cruising the waters, raised eyes and nostrils allowing them to see and breathe undetected. As well as eating fish such as bream and barbel, adult crocs will ambush mammals up to the size of buffalo, grabbing them with an explosive sideways lunge from the water, before dragging them under to drown. Large numbers of crocodiles gather to scavenge big carcasses, churning up the water as they thrash and spin to dislodge chunks of flesh. They will even leave the water to steal a nearby lion kill.

LIZARDS The largest of the lizard species in Botswana are the monitor lizards, which can grow to over 2m in length, but there are also a large number of skinks, sand lizards, geckos, chameleons and agamas. With the arguable exception of the monitor lizards, which could in theory inflict a nasty bite if cornered, all are harmless to humans.

The **water monitor** (*Varanus niloticus*) is regularly observed by tourists, particularly on the banks of the Okavango's water ways, where you will often hear one splash into the water before seeing it. Size alone might make it possible to fleetingly mistake a monitor for a small crocodile, but the lizard's more colourful yellow-dappled skin and smaller head precludes sustained confusion. This species, and the less frequently seen **rock or white-throated monitor** (*Varanus exanthematicus*), are predatory omnivores, feeding on anything from birds' eggs to smaller reptiles and mammals, and occasional carrion.

Also very common are various **agama** species, distinguished from other common lizards by their relatively large size of around 20–25cm, their large heads and their almost plastic-looking scaling. Depending on the species, this can be a combination of blue, purple, orange or red, with the flattened head generally a different colour from the torso. Another common family are the **skinks**: small, long-tailed lizards, most of which are quite dark and have a few thin black stripes running from head to tail. Botswana's only chameleon is the **flap-necked chameleon** (*Chamaeleo dilepis*), found throughout the Okavango Delta. During the day its excellent camouflage can make this lizard almost impossible to spot, as the light coming off the surrounding vegetation is picked up by cells in the chameleon's skin (chromatophors and melanophors) which then replicate that colour. At night, however, chameleons are much more visible as they find it impossible to replicate the surrounding colours due to the lack of light.

Puff adder

SNAKES Of the 72 species of snake found in Botswana, roughly 80% are non venomous, and most are unlikely to be seen unless actively sought. The most frequently spotted non-venomous snake on safari is Africa's largest, the **rock python** (*Python sebae*), which has gold-on-black mottled skin and can grow to 5m or more. Pythons kill their prey – small antelopes, large rodents and similar animals – by strangulation, wrapping their muscular bodies around it until it cannot breathe, then swallowing it whole and dozing off for a couple of months while it is digested. Few are large or bold enough to tackle an adult human, but many could kill a small child. Much smaller but also frequently seen is the slender **stripe-bellied sand snake** (*Psammophis subtaeniatus*), which grows up to 1m long and feeds on smaller reptiles, birds and rodents. It has large eyes, and a yellow underside with stripes down either side, and is strictly diurnal.

One of the most commonly encountered venomous snakes is the **puff adder** (*Bitis arietans*), a large, thick-set resident that is rightly considered the most dangerous of African snakes – not because it is the most venomous or aggressive but because its notoriously sluggish disposition means it is more often disturbed than other snakes. Although it feeds mainly on rodents, it will strike when threatened, bending itself into a defensive S-shape.

Other venomous species, such as the **black mamba** (*Dendroaspis polylepis*), **boomslang** (*Dispholidus typus*) and **Mozambique spitting cobra** (*Naja mossambica*), are seldom seen and usually flee or go into cover way before you have a chance to observe them.

Rock python

Stripe-bellied sand snake

Leopard tortoise

VG/MP/FLPA

TORTOISES AND TERRAPINS Tortoises and terrapins are unique in being protected by a prototypal suit of armour formed by their heavy exoskeleton.

The most common of the terrestrial tortoises is the **leopard tortoise** (*Stigmochelys pardalis*), which is named for its gold-and-black mottled shell, and can weigh up to 30kg. There's also the much smaller **Kalahari (serrated) tent tortoise** (*Psammobates oculifer*), found throughout Botswana, but much less common in the Delta.

Terrapins are essentially the freshwater equivalent of turtles. Somewhat flatter in shape than tortoises, they generally have a plainer brown shell. They might be seen sunning on rocks close to water or peering out from roadside puddles. Botswana's five species of terrapin are found largely around the Okavango swamps, along the Panhandle and in the Linyanti/Chobe region. These include the hinged terrapins and the **Okavango mud turtle** (*Pelusios bechuanicus*), which is one of the biggest of the species with quite a long, elongated, pronounced shell. The **marsh (or helmeted) terrapin** (*Pelomedusa subrufa*), however, is present throughout the country, even in the semi arid desert areas that include the Makgadikgadi and the Kalahari. During the drier months, it will dig deep underground to keep moist and cool, emerging as soon as the rains come.

FROGS The members of the frog family that are most frequently seen in Botswana are the **painted reed frogs**. Keep a close eye out when in a mokoro, and you'll spot these colourful little frogs folded up and stuck to the reeds with their sucker-pad toes. Up to about 40mm long, adults have extremely variable colours and patterns, from clear stripes through to dots, patches and vermiculations – and from bright green and yellow through to red and dark brown. Given the huge colour variability in these frogs, a precise identification will challenge many herpetologists, but the Angolan painted reed frogs (*Hyperolius parallelus*) and the painted reed frog (*Hyperolius marmoratus*) are two key candidates. Listen at night beside water: the chorus of gentle individual notes, as if from tiny bells, is very distinctive: that's the frogs calling.

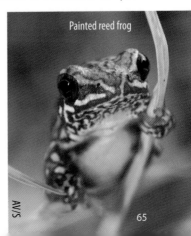

Painted reed frog

AV/S

65

Large areas of Botswana are still covered by relatively undisturbed natural vegetation, and hunting is not a significant factor for most of Botswana's 597 recorded species of birds. Thus, with a range of natural habitats, Botswana is a superb birding destination.

There are fairly clear distinctions between the birds that you're likely to find in areas of swamp or open water, those that frequent riverine forest, and those found in the drier areas. None are endemic, though several have very restricted distributions. These include the slaty egret and the wattled crane, which are restricted to the Okavango, Linyanti and Chobe river systems, the brown firefinch, and the Natal nightjar. The Okavango Delta is a particularly good place for birdwatching as the habitats change from dry, to flooded, to deep-water over very short distances.

MIGRANTS In addition to its resident bird species, Botswana receives many migrants. In September and October the Palaearctic migrants (ie: those that come from the northern hemisphere – normally Europe) appear, and they remain until around April or May. This is also the peak time to see the intra-African migrants, which come from further north in Africa. The rains from December to around April see an explosion in the availability of most birds' food: seeds, fruits and insects. Hence this is the prime time for birds to nest, and the best season in which to observe them in their breeding plumage, even if it is also the most difficult time to visit the more remote areas of the country.

BIRDING HIGHLIGHTS Many of Botswana's birds are safari highlights in their own right, so even if you're intent on seeing the big five, be prepared to be entranced by some of the country's avifauna.

In wetland areas, look out for the delicate African jacana, also known as the Jesus bird for its apparent ability to walk on water. In the reeds above, the tiny malachite kingfisher is given away by its jewel-like colouring and bright orange beak, while

1. The striking **saddle-billed stork** (*Ephippiorhynchus senegalensis*) stands tall above the wetlands at a height of around 145cm, its wingspan stretching up to 2.7m. Females are smaller than males, and are distinguished by their yellow eyes. (JG)
2. Also known as the lily-trotter or the Jesus bird, the **African jacana** (*Actophilornis africanus*) is unmistakable with its rich chestnut torso and wings. Exceptionally widely spread toes allow it to walk on lily pads and other light floating vegetation. (SS/P)
3. The rare **slaty egret** (*Egretta vinaceigula*) is largely confined to the shallow waters of the Okavango Delta, Linyanti and Chobe River areas. With its habit of creating umbrella-like shade with its wings when fishing, it's fascinating to watch – as well as relatively easy to identify. (SS/P)
4. Named after the French for a juggler or tightrope walker, the **bateleur** (*Terathopius ecaudatus*) exhibits a tilting flight pattern, reminiscent of a circus performer wobbling along a suspended line. A large and widespread eagle, it has predominantly black plumage offset by a bright-red face mask, beak and legs. In unusual circumstances, when threatened, both male and female will successively divebomb the threat, folding their wings into a V shape and making a number of fast, low passes that engender an attendant loud rush of air. (SB/S)
5. Conspicuous along the shores of most rivers and lakes, the **African fish eagle** (*Haliaeetus vocifer*) is a magnificent raptor with a chestnut belly and a yellow base to its large hooked bill. Its far-carrying banshee wail of a call – often heard as a duet – is one of the most evocative sounds of the African bush. (SS/P)
6. Africa's heaviest flying bird, the **kori bustard** (*Ardeotis kori*) is a widespread resident of grassland habitats, and is especially common in areas like the dry Savuti Marsh. (DD/FLPA)

the larger pied kingfisher is regularly seen hovering as it prepares to dive for its prey. Look higher, perhaps on a rock or a dead branch, to spot the sinuous African darter, then higher still for the distinct dark brown and white of the African fish eagle, which often perches on the tops of trees overlooking the river. Back in the treeline, a uniform tawny plumage may give away Pels' fishing owl, one of the Delta's most sought-after species that is notoriously difficult to spot.

Of the larger wetland inhabitants, top of the list is the extraordinary saddle-billed stork, a monogamous bird that is often seen in pairs. Around the edge of small pools and pans, spoonbills may jostle for position with storks – yellow-billed, marabou, open-billed and more – along with herons, egrets, pelicans, lapwings and ibis. But for a real spectacle, pay a visit to one of Botswana's heronries at Gcodikwe and Kanana, where thousands of birds congregate to breed towards the end of the dry season. This is also the time of year when a flash of crimson and turquoise signals the return of the carmine bee-eaters to nest in sandy riverbanks – though you may also see them on the wing after a fire, swooping on insects drawn out by the flames.

In drier areas, the lilac-breasted roller is no less dazzling for being relatively common. Equally spectacular, if far less common, is the African paradise whydah, which is in full breeding plumage between February and April. You'll find most of the hornbills here, too, along with Meyer's parrots and swallow-tailed bee-eaters.

The open plains are home to some of the larger birds, from ostriches to the kori bustard – Africa's largest flying bird, and claimed by Botswana as the national bird. High above, birds of prey range from the almost ubiquitous yellow-billed kite to the strongly marked bateleur, or short-tailed eagle, its chiselled head sometimes clear in silhouette against the sky. And then there are the vultures – many of them now endangered as a result of feeding on animals that have been given drugs such as diclofenac, which can prove fatal to the birds.

For more detail on the birdlife of Botswana's individual habitats, see the entries in the individual chapters.

1. Of the nine species of kingfisher that occur in Botswana, the gem-like **malachite kingfisher** (*Alcedo cristata*) most strongly resembles its European namesake. It is often observed perched motionless on reeds or shrubs alongside rivers and lakes, but is given away by its bright coloration. (CS/P)

2. A firm safari favourite, the insectivorous **lilac-breasted roller** (*Coracias caudate*) prefers a woodland habitat, and will often perch conspicuously on a single branch, almost as if posing for photographs. (SS/P)

3. With stunning colouring, the **carmine bee-eater** (*Merops nubicoides*) is a welcome arrival in the summer months. The largest of the bee-eater family in southern Africa, it often congregates in colonies near rivers and marshes, where it nests in holes in steep sandy banks. (CS/P)

4. Unlike the carmine, the **swallow-tailed bee-eater** (*Merops hirundineus*) is resident all year. Slightly larger than the equally common little bee-eater, and with bluish rather than brown underparts, it is distinctive for its forked tail. (FT/S)

5. Large and very distinctive, **Pel's fishing owl** (*Scotopelia peli*) is top of the wish list for many birders. Although it's by no means as rare as its fame would suggest, it is notoriously difficult to spot, spending most of the day perched high in the canopy of a large tree. (WD/FLPA)

6. Most often seen in flight, when it exhibits a blue-green back, the colourful and gregarious **Meyer's parrot** (*Poicephalus meyeri*) also enlivens broad-leaved trees in its woodland habitat. (AP/A)

Botswana

Okavango Delta, Chobe,
Linyanti, Central Kalahari,
Makgadikgadi Pans and beyond

Individually tailored safaris to East and Southern Africa, with expert advice and personal service

History, Politics and Economy

We can learn a lot about Botswana today by looking back into its history. Its far distant past, explaining some of the main features of its landscapes, is covered as part of *The physical environment*, at the start of *Chapter 1*. A potted overview of Botswana's more recent human history is given here, casting some light on its current politics and economics.

HISTORY

EARLY PEOPLES Read about the country's geological history and it's framed in terms of hundreds, or at least tens, of millions of years. Thus it's sobering to realise how relatively recent any human history is, and how much more compressed its timescales are.

Our knowledge about early human life in Botswana is derived from archaeology and from oral histories, which go back about 700 years. Written records date only from the arrival of Europeans in the 18th and 19th centuries. Most of these are personal accounts, which are interesting, but subjective. In many places the story is confused and incomplete, or even deliberately misleading (pages 89–106).

However, archaeological evidence suggests that hunter-gatherer peoples have lived for about 60,000 years at sites like the Tsodilo Hills in the Kalahari. We know, too, that the ancestors of the Khoisan (comprising both the San and the Khoi people; pages 72–3) were once widely dispersed throughout the continent, and probably had exclusive occupation of southern, central and eastern Africa from about 60,000 years ago up to the last 3,000 years.

Skeletons of a Khoisan-type people, dating back 15,000 years and more, are found throughout southern and eastern Africa. It is believed to be these people who made the rock paintings of people and animals that are found all over eastern and southern Africa and even in the Sahara Desert. The earliest paintings have been found in Namibia (the 'Apollo 11' cave) and are thought to date back 26,000 years.

Rock paintings found at the Tsodilo Hills are evidence that the living was good enough to allow the people to develop a vibrant artistic culture. Most experts believe that many of the paintings have deeper significance, probably connected with spiritual, religious or mythological beliefs. It is impossible to interpret them accurately without an in-depth knowledge of the culture and beliefs of those who created them. Unfortunately no group today claims historical responsibility. The local Zhu Bushmen claim that their god, Gaoxa, made the paintings.

The animals of Africa, such as antelope, eland, rhinos and giraffe, are the subject of many paintings. The images beautifully capture the form and the spirit of each animal. Humans also appear; one painting at the Tsodilo Hills shows a group of 15 men exhibiting the permanent erection, or semi-erection, which is a distinctive feature of San men from birth to death. Later paintings, featuring black men and sometimes war, are thought to depict the arrival of the Bantu farmers.

The San The San were perfectly adapted to their desert environment and had learned to survive its harsh extremes of climate – drought, unrelenting heat and sun in the winter, and heavy rains and floods in the summer.

Predominantly hunter-gatherers, it is thought that at various times, when the climate was more favourable, the San may also have owned and grazed stock. Several times in past millennia the climate of Botswana has been much wetter, and at others much drier than it is at the moment. Periodically the huge pans that are a distinctive feature of the landscape, such as at Makgadikgadi and Nxai, became great lakes, full of water and supplied by several rivers. Probably some San groups took advantage of plentiful supplies of water to acquire stock. Now the rivers have dried up and the Okavango Delta has receded, the pans are full of water only during the rainy season and the San are herders no longer. There are also more recent records of them owning and trading copper from secret mines in the Kalahari, and bartering it for iron.

The Khoi Around 3000BC, Late Stone Age hunter-gatherer groups in Ethiopia, and elsewhere in North and West Africa, started to keep domestic animals, sow seeds, and harvest the produce: they became the world's first farmers.

By around 1000BC these new pastoral practices had spread south into the equatorial forests of what is now the Democratic Republic of Congo, to around Lake Victoria, and into the northern area of the Great Rift Valley, in northern Tanzania. However, agriculture did not spread south into the rest of central/southern Africa immediately. Only when the technology, and the tools, of ironworking became known did these practices start their relentless expansion southwards.

It's thought that during the last centuries BC many Khoi-speaking peoples in northern Botswana converted their lifestyle to pastoralism – herding cattle and sheep on the rich pastures exposed by the retreating wetlands of the Okavango Delta and Lake Makgadikgadi.

It used to be thought that the Khoi acquired their stock during the (black) Iron Age, from Bantu-speaking farmers who are thought to have migrated into their area around 1,500 years ago. However, finds of sheep bone dating back 3,000 years now suggest that the Khoi had obtained stock long before the arrival of the Bantu, probably from East Africa where they had been herded for thousands of years. The Khoi spread, migrating with their livestock through central Namibia, as far south as the Cape of Good Hope, by about 70BC.

When the first Dutch settlers saw the Khoi in about AD1600 they lived in groups with a leader, but were split into smaller clans under their own headman. The clans came together only in times of stress or war. Because water was vital for the stock animals, the Khoi dug wells that were owned exclusively by the clan and group. In times of drought, when water was scarce, fights might erupt over these waterholes. Then each clan sent men to fight to protect the group's interests.

Each clan lived in a village, which was built inside a circular thorn hedge. In the centre were thorn enclosures to pen and protect the stock, surrounded by a circle of houses. Khoi houses are of a 'bender' or dome-tent construction type; that is, long flexible poles are bent to form arches and the ends stuck into the ground. They are then covered with mats. When the clan needed to move to find more water or grazing these huts were simply taken down and strapped on to the back of their animals.

Tlou and Campbell (see *Appendix 3*, page 540) describe one such village, which is known to have existed at Toromoja on the Boteti River (about 11 miles east of Rakops) around AD1200. A group of Khoi known as the Bateti lived there and kept long-horned cattle, sheep and goats, but they lived mainly on fish, zebra and other animals which they caught in the pits they dug by the river. They also ate plants, particularly waterlily roots. They had San servants who hunted and collected wild food for them. Sometimes they traded skins and ivory for iron tools, copper and tobacco, with the people living at Maun in the northwest, or the Toutswe people to the southeast.

Archaeologically speaking the Khoisan peoples were examples of Late Stone Age cultures; that is, their tools and weapons were made of wood, bone and stone. The Late Stone Age refers not to a period of time, but to a method and style of tool construction. Human beings had made stone tools for millennia and the name Late Stone Age refers to stylistic refinements and to the manufacture of tools developed for specific uses.

Specifically, experts define the transition from Early to Middle Stone Age technology as indicated by a larger range of stone tools often adapted for particular uses, and signs that these people had a greater mastery of their environment. This was probably in progress around 125,000 years ago in Botswana. They normally characterise the Late Stone Age by the use of composite tools, those made of wood and/or bone and/or stone used together, and by the presence of a revolutionary invention: the bow and arrow. This first appeared in southern Africa, and throughout the world, about 15,000 years ago. Skeletons of some of these Late Stone Age hunters had a close physical resemblance to the modern Khoisan people.

The Bantu-speaking farmers The next people to arrive in Botswana were the Bantu-speakers. This collective term refers to a number of different tribes, from a related linguistic group, who over the course of thousands of years gradually migrated down into southern Africa from north of the Equator. The date of their arrival in Botswana is hard to pinpoint.

The Bantu were grain farmers (agriculturalists) as opposed to pastoralists or hunter-gatherers and they brought Iron Age technology with them; that is, their tools and weapons were made of iron. Physically these Iron Age farmers were much taller and heavier than the Khoisan, and they became the ancestors of the modern black Africans in southern Africa.

Crucial to the production of iron is a smelting furnace capable of reaching very high temperatures. Associated with the Iron Age is a new kind of pottery, which also had to be fired at high temperatures. Archaeologists use the finds of pottery and iron to date the arrival of the new people on the landscape of Botswana.

It is thought that the Bantu-speakers arrived in two main waves, bringing western and eastern Bantu languages. From West Africa, Late Stone Age farmers on the upper Zambezi were converted to the use of iron tools by about 300BC. From East Africa, Early Iron Age farming spread south along the east coast as far as the Zambezi by around 20BC.

By 200BC, in the Okavango–Makgadikgadi region, people were making a kind of pottery which archaeologists think was Khoi pottery influenced by western Iron Age (Bantu) styles, suggesting an initial contact between the two groups. The major Bantu influx probably occurred around the first few centuries AD, and the ancestors of the Khoisan people, with their simple Stone Age technology and hunter-gatherer existence, just could not compete. Since then the Khoisan have gradually been either assimilated into the migrant groups, or effectively pushed into the areas which could not be farmed. Thus the older Stone Age cultures persisted for much longer in the Kalahari (which is more difficult to cultivate) than in the rest of the country.

In theory, the stronger iron weapons of the Bantu should easily have made them the dominant culture. However, it took a very long time for Bantu language and culture to replace that of the Khoi; as late as the 19th century people were still speaking Khoi on the Boteti River. This supports a theory of communities living peacefully there, side by side, for a thousand years or more. In fact, there is some evidence of inter-marriage or inter-breeding between the two groups. The Batswana today have a mixture of Bantu and Khoisan features and they are noticeably lighter in skin colour than Bantu-speakers further north. They also tend to have the almond-shaped eyes, high cheekbones and thin lips of the Khoisan.

MORE IMMIGRANTS There are numerous problems with compiling a record of Bantu history in Botswana. We are dependent on oral history and archaeological records, and the two sometimes conflict with each other. The situation is very complex because of the number and mobility of the tribes involved.

The earliest dated Iron Age site in Botswana is an iron-smelting furnace in the Tswapong Hills, which is dated to around AD190. There is evidence of an early farming settlement of beehive huts made of grass matting, dating to around AD420 by the Molepolole River and a similar one has been found co-existing with Khoisan sites in the Tsodilo Hills, dating to around AD550.

By the 4th or 5th century AD, Iron Age farmers had certainly settled throughout much of southern Africa. As well as iron-working technology, they brought with them pottery, the remains of which are used by archaeologists to work out the migrations of various different groups of these Bantu settlers. These migrations continued, and the distribution of pottery styles suggests that the groups moved around within the subcontinent: this was much more complex than a simple north–south influx. Many of the tribes roamed over the whole of southern Africa, before various colonial authorities imposed artificial country borders in order to carve out territories for themselves.

This situation was complicated more recently by the prolonged and horrifically bloody tribal wars of the 19th century, known to historians as the Difaquane Wars.

BATSWANA HISTORY The Batswana rose to domination from among a number of powerful dynasties that spread out from the western Transvaal around AD1200–1400. During the period 1500–1600 the Phofu dynasty in western Transvaal disintegrated, with junior brothers forming breakaway, independent chiefdoms. Oral history traditions explain this as a response to drought. The archaeological record shows populations expanding into open country in small villages with cattle corrals, but by around 1700 the settlements were often larger towns built of stone and situated on hills, reflecting the growth of hostile states, and the need for a strong defence.

The Difaquane Wars The whole of southern Africa was subject to increasing disruption, migration and war from about 1750 onwards, as trading and raiding for ivory, cattle and slaves spread inland from the coasts of Mozambique, the Cape Colony and Angola. The tribes often captured opponents during battle and sold them to slave raiders. Some of the battles themselves may have been slave raids against an enemy tribe.

Paramount among the aggressors in these wars was an ambitious Zulu leader named Shaka, who controlled a large slice of Natal by around 1810. The Ngoni people, which includes the Zulu nation, refer to the wars which Shaka initiated as the Mfecane, or 'the crushing'. However, the Batswana people, who were among the victims of Shaka's wars of expansion, refer to them as the Difaquane, which means 'the scattering'. Because they scattered, so they dispersed others.

A good explanation of this period is covered in John Reader's excellent *Africa: A Biography of the Continent* (see *Appendix 3*, page 540). He summarises the root causes:

> Thus they [the Zulus] were trapped in 'the trans-continental cross-fire of interrelated European plunder systems'. It was the unrelenting advance of settlers from the west, and the predacious demands of slavers in the east – exacerbated by intermittent drought – that set southern Africa in turmoil during the early eighteenth century. Not Shaka, not the Zulus, not the Mfecane.

Eventually, after the wars passed in the 1840s, the Batswana states of Ngwaketse, Kwena and the Ngwato rose to prosperity. They organised their people into wards with their own chiefs, but all paying tribute to the king. The states were in competition over trade benefits for ivory and ostrich feathers, down new roads, south to the Cape Colony. These roads also brought Boer trekkers and Christian missionaries to Botswana.

One of the Batswana kings, Sechele of the Kwena (1829–92), was baptised by David Livingstone, who passed through Botswana on his missionary travels. However, it was the Ngwato, who superseded the Kwena in trading supremacy, who produced the most remarkable and famous dynasty – and upon whom the following pages will concentrate.

Ngwato dynasty In *Serowe: Village of the Rain Wind* (see *Appendix 3*, page 539), Bessie Head describes this remarkable dynasty, beginning with the reign of Khama the Great. He was king when the capital of the Bamangwato (Ngwato) moved to Serowe in 1902. Previously the capital had been a hundred miles away at Shoshong, and then at Palapye, but each time the tribe was forced to move on when water sources dried up. In 1902, two rivers, the Sepane and the Manonnye, flowed through Serowe, although both have subsequently dried up.

Khama the Great Khama was the eldest son of Segkoma I, who was the chief when David Livingstone, the missionary explorer, first moved northwards through Botswana in the 1840s. While the capital had still been at Shoshong, Livingstone had converted Khama and his brothers to Christianity. Although their father had allowed the missionaries to stay with them, and was interested to talk to them, he had refused to give up the traditional ways.

Eventually this led to a war between father and son, which Khama won, becoming king of the Bamangwato. Khama was a poetic visionary who changed the customs of his people in line with his Christian beliefs, and who foresaw the need for strong protection in the colonial carve-up of Africa, and campaigned strongly for the British Protectorate of Bechuanaland. (See also the box on pages 110–11.)

Segkoma II In 1916, Khama was kicked on the knee by a horse. At this time he invited his son Segkoma II, who had been in exile for ten years governing his own branch of the Bamangwato, to come home and rule at Serowe. This he did, and subsequently ruled at Serowe for nine years, although for most of that time he remained in the shadow of King Khama. Most importantly Khama insisted that

Segkoma marry a woman given to him by the Bamangwato, and the heir from this marriage was Seretse, who would later become the first president of Botswana.

Tshekedi Khama Following the death of Khama, and shortly afterwards of Segkoma II, Tshekedi Khama (Khama's son from a late second marriage) stepped in as regent until the four-year-old Seretse should come of age.

Where Khama was a visionary and politician, Tshekedi was full of pragmatic common sense and his rule, from 1926 to 1959, is marked by educational advances and self-help projects. When he first became leader there was only a primary school in Serowe. Then Tshekedi used his own money to send the young people of the village to South Africa for further education. From there they came home to teach in the village school. Later a secondary school and subsequently a college were built, using the voluntary labour of what were known as the age regiments (see box, pages 110–11). Also known as the *mephato*, these were groups of young men of about the same age, usually formed from those who had graduated from the tribal initiation ceremony (known as *bogwera*) at the same time. They could be called upon to carry out services for the good of the community, ranging from routine community tasks to helping out with emergencies.

Moeng College of Higher Education is exciting for the principles on which it was founded, which gave equal weight to traditional knowledge and craft skills alongside academic instruction. As an experiment in social relations the houses built for the teaching staff were the equivalent of houses for white government officials. It was the only college in southern Africa at the time where houses for white and black teachers were equal and where they lived together in the same hostel.

Seretse Khama During the reign of Tshekedi, a problem arose over the future of Seretse Khama. Seretse was educated abroad, in London, Fort Hare University in South Africa, and Oxford. In 1948, Seretse wrote to inform his uncle that he wanted to marry an Englishwoman, Ruth Williams. Tshekedi opposed the marriage on the grounds that a king or chief could not do as he pleased because he was the servant of the people, and an heir to the chieftaincy was at stake. Traditionally the chief's wife was chosen by the *morafe* or tribal group. Seretse insisted on his right to choose his own wife and married the Englishwoman.

They were still arguing when the British took matters into their own hands. In a case that created an international scandal, the British government barred Seretse from the chieftaincy of the Bamangwato, and exiled him for six years. They invited him to Britain, where they forced him to stay. They also banned Tshekedi Khama from entering the Bamangwato reserve.

Secret documents have since confirmed that this British intervention was in order to satisfy the South African government, which objected to Seretse Khama's marriage to a white woman at a time when the policy of racial segregation, apartheid, was being enforced in South Africa.

Seretse, Tshekedi and their people fought against this banishment. The Bamangwato refused to pay taxes, sent delegations to the British and led protests. They refused to accept a British-nominated chief, and many people, including women, were flogged for this refusal.

Finally Tshekedi visited Seretse in London and the two resolved their differences. Seretse returned to Botswana with Ruth. Although a condition of his return was that he remained barred from the chieftancy, both he and Tshekedi continued to play an active role in the politics of Botswana, and were instrumental in the lead-up to independence.

DAVID LIVINGSTONE

David Livingstone's *Missionary Travels and Researches in South Africa* excited great interest in England. This account of his journeys across southern Africa in the 1840s and 50s had all the appeal that undersea or space exploration has for us now. Further, it captured the imagination of the British public, allowing them to take pride in their country's exploration of Africa, based on the exploits of an explorer who seemed to be the epitome of bravery and righteous religious zeal.

Livingstone had set out with the conviction that if Africans could see their material and physical well-being improved – probably by learning European ways, and earning a living from export crops – then they would be ripe for conversion to Christianity. He was strongly opposed to slavery, but sure that this would disappear when Africans became more self-sufficient through trade.

In fact Livingstone was almost totally unsuccessful in his own aims, failing to set up any successful trading missions, or even to convert many Africans permanently to Christianity. However, his travels opened up areas north of the Limpopo for later British missionaries, and by 1887 British mission stations were established in Zambia and southern Malawi.

Traders The earliest Europeans to come to Botswana were adventurers, explorers, hunters and missionaries. Travel in Botswana was very expensive, even then. A year's travel could cost up to US$600 – equivalent to what a soldier of the period might earn during 30 years in the army. So early travellers came to trade for ivory, which made them huge profits with which to finance their expeditions. They travelled in wooden wagons, drawn by oxen or horses, and brought guns, beads, clothing and other, less-valuable items, which they bartered for significant amounts of ivory.

One of the biggest problems on the journey was the lack of water. There were often stretches of 50km or more without any. Water would be carried on the wagons, but not enough for both men and beasts. Sometimes the oxen died of thirst. There are stories of the wagons being unhitched and the oxen led to the nearest water – which could be some kilometres distant – and then returning to pull the wagons further. Oxen often died from drinking bad water or from tsetse-fly bite, while horses died of tickbite. A distance of 20km per day was thought to be a good rate of travel.

However, a wagon that did make it could return with about 200 elephant tusks – worth around £1,200 when sold in Cape Town. As they heard tales of huge profits, more traders began to venture into the region and gradually introduced money, which had been unknown until then. Previously barter and exchange systems functioned in the village – one goat equals one woven grass basket, and so on. Subsequently money became important in trade and people were forced to either sell something, or sell their labour, to get money. Little paid work could be found in Botswana, so large numbers of people were forced to emigrate to find work, often in the mines in South Africa.

Meanwhile the traders began to settle in Botswana at Shoshong, though the Bamangwato chiefs, Segkoma and Khama, were keen to prevent them from going further into the interior, so that they could maintain their trading supremacy.

The missions Following the traders came the missionaries, and missionary societies, who were already active in South Africa. Robert Moffat of the London Missionary Society (LMS) established a station at Kudumane, which succeeded in bringing Christianity to the Batswana and in training African evangelists to spread the word. It was to Kudumane that David Livingstone came in 1841. In 1845, he married Moffat's daughter, Mary, and they settled among the Bakwena.

Although ostensibly a missionary, Livingstone was primarily interested in exploration and in 1849 he and his party became the first whites to see Lake Ngami. He died in 1873 in Zambia, while looking for the source of the Nile.

Khama and his Bamangwato family at Shoshong were converted by the missionaries of a German Lutheran society, although he later joined the London Missionary Society Church. Most missionaries tried to change local Setswana customs, which they considered heathen and inferior to European Christian customs. Most of all they fought against the medicine men, who defended the old traditional customs. However, despite leaders like Khama who abolished male and female initiations, rain-making and beer drinking, some customs still flourish because people like them.

The early missionaries affected disinterest in politics, although they inevitably supported Christians against non-Christians. Their position was always precarious because they needed to retain the goodwill of the chiefs to remain in their mission posts. However, during the Protectorate, missionaries who knew they had the backing of the British government became quite cavalier, demanding the removal of chiefs who resisted Christianity.

Although the missionaries tried to destroy local cultures, they also provided education and established the first schools. They introduced useful tools such as the plough and the wagon, and taught gardening and crop irrigation. The missionaries' wives taught sewing and baking and helped to nurse the sick and deliver babies.

Botswana and the British British foreign policy in southern Africa had always revolved around the Cape Colony, which was seen as vital to British interests in India and the Indian Ocean. Africa to the north of the Cape Colony had largely been ignored. The Boers were on the whole left to their farming in the Transvaal area, since they posed no threat to the Cape Colony.

However, from the 1850s to the 1870s the Batswana leaders appealed to the British for protection against the Boers, who had formed their own free state ruling the Transvaal, but were continually threatening to take over Batswana lands in Botswana.

When Germany annexed South West Africa (now Namibia) in 1884, the British finally began to take those threats seriously. They became afraid that the Boers might link up with the Germans and prevent British access to the 'north road', leading to the interior of Africa – now Zambia and Zimbabwe. It was really to safeguard this road that the British finally granted Botswana protection in 1885. Significantly, the German government was told about the British Protectorate of Bechuanaland before the chiefs in Botswana.

Cecil John Rhodes Initially the British government had fully intended to hand the supervision of the Protectorate over to the government of the Cape Colony, but the Cape was unwilling to take on the responsibility and the potential expense.

In 1886, the Boers discovered large gold deposits in the Witwatersrand (around Johannesburg). The influx of money from this boosted the Boer farmers, who expanded their interests to the north, making a treaty with Khama's enemy to the east, the powerful Lobengula. This in turn prompted the British to look beyond the Limpopo, and to back the territorial aspirations of a millionaire British businessman and prominent Cape Colony politician, Cecil Rhodes. By 1888 Rhodes, a partner in the De Beers consortium, had control of the lucrative diamond-mining industry in

Kimberley, South Africa. He was hungry for power, and dreamt of linking the Cape to Cairo with land under British control.

Rhodes was fuelled by the belief that other areas of Africa had great mineral wealth and he wanted to colonise them and reap that wealth. In order to do so he formed the British South Africa Company (BSAC) in 1889. At that time, if companies or individuals could obtain concessions to African land from the owners, they were able to colonise it for the Crown. The British government expected that these concessions would be obtained honestly. However, they were often gained fraudulently, by persuading illiterate African chiefs to sign (or put their mark on) documents which were presented to them as treaties, but which actually appropriated their lands.

The immediate reason for forming the BSAC was in order to colonise the land of the Amandabele and the Mashona (now Zimbabwe). In 1888, Rhodes's men had obtained, by trickery, a treaty known as the Rudd Concession from the King of the Amandabele, Lobengula. This granted Rhodes all mineral rights on the king's land. Although the king rejected the treaty when he discovered its real intention, Rhodes was nevertheless granted a royal charter by the British government.

The British also promised to transfer the Bechuanaland Protectorate to the BSAC, on condition that Rhodes first obtained the agreement of the Batswana rulers. Rhodes wanted the Protectorate, because he needed the right to build a railway across Bechuanaland. He further wanted to annex the Protectorate to Rhodesia (now Zimbabwe), and from there attack the Boer state of Transvaal from the north.

Rhodes and other British businessmen had stakes in the highly profitable gold mines at Witwatersrand (Johannesburg), but the state was controlled politically by the Boers. Rhodes wanted British rule in the Transvaal, to protect his profits from the gold mines.

The three chiefs In 1895, three Batswana chiefs, Khama, Bathoen and Sebele, travelled to London to plead a case against the British government handing over the Protectorate to Rhodes, whom they did not trust. Some Batswana chiefs had already signed concessions with the BSAC, but in nearly all cases they did not realise that they had given away their land. It was, in any case, against Setswana law to sell or give away land. Rhodes attempted to stop the kings in Cape Town and prevent them from going to Britain but he was unsuccessful.

In a meeting with Joseph Chamberlain, then the British Colonial Secretary, the three chiefs criticised the BSAC and asked that:

- Bechuanaland should remain a Protectorate directly under the Queen.
- Their independence should be preserved.
- Their lands should not be sold.
- Liquor drinking should be prohibited in their areas.

Chamberlain told them that the British government could not go back on its promise to transfer the Protectorate to the BSAC. However, he also said that the company would obey the Queen, so it was the same as being governed by her. Hence the chiefs must reach an agreement with the BSAC. Then he went on holiday.

Instead the chiefs toured England, seeking the support of the British people against the company. Their campaign was organised by the London Missionary Society, and supported by temperance groups, anti-slavery and humanitarian groups and businesses that feared the effect of a costly war if the transfer went ahead. Chamberlain returned from holiday to find letters to this effect. Worried that the affair might become an election issue and lose the government votes, he agreed to the chiefs' demands, with the provisos that they must all cede the land which Rhodes required for the railway, and that taxation would be introduced to pay for the administration of the Protectorate.

The Jameson Raid A month later, in October 1895, Rhodes found a pretext for attacking the Transvaal. The raid was led by Dr S Jameson on behalf of the non-Boer whites or 'Uitlanders' in the Transvaal, who had complained of unequal treatment by the Boers. This famous raid, which came to be known as the Jameson Raid, was carried out from within the Bechuanaland Protectorate. However, it failed. The anticipated uprising of the Uitlanders never happened, so the raiders soon surrendered to the Boers.

The fact that Britain had allowed the Protectorate to be used to attack another country caused an international scandal. The British government, angered at being brought into disrepute by Rhodes, refused to transfer the Protectorate to the BSAC, and removed control of the Batswana lands that had been obtained for the raid.

It was the failure of the Jameson Raid, and Rhodes's subsequent if temporary disgrace, which protected the independent future of Botswana. Rhodes did later receive land for a railway strip and some blocks of 'Crown Land' – the Gaborone, Lobatse and Tuli blocks. These, together with the Tati Block and Ghanzi, which had been settled earlier, became the only European areas in Bechuanaland.

The Protectorate Britain continued to administer the Protectorate for 70 years, through the Anglo-Boer War (1899–1902) and two world wars. However, Britain disliked spending money on its colonies, and from the time the Union of South Africa was formed in 1910 it was always intended to transfer the Protectorate to the Union. The Batswana continued to fight against it, especially as they witnessed the poor treatment of black Africans in that country.

By 1955, the policy of the British government had changed. This was due in part to the problems with Seretse and Tshekedi Khama and the Bamangwato (page 76), and partly because of South Africa's gradual move towards apartheid and away from the more egalitarian values of the post-war society that was emerging in the UK and the rest of the West.

In 1956, Seretse, who was supported by many groups in Britain, including Members of Parliament, spoke strongly against the British government's intervention. Tshekedi also turned against the British, accepting Ruth as the rightful wife and demanding Seretse's return to Bechuanaland. He believed that the British wanted to use the problem to break his tribe, and as an excuse to transfer the Protectorate to South Africa.

However, by then the issue of transferring the Protectorate to South Africa's control was dead in the minds of the British government. Clearly Botswana would have to be diplomatically protected from South Africa's ambitions, but the British didn't seem to have a plan for it beyond that.

MODERN HISTORY
The dangerous decade The years between 1956 and 1966 were a dangerous, formative decade in Botswana's history. For a detailed, insider's view of it read *Botswana: The Road to Independence*, by Peter Fawcus and Alan Tilbury. The authors were two of Britain's most senior administrators who were at the sharp end of steering relations between Britain and the Protectorate during this period.

While the British government couldn't see into the future, supporters of Seretse Khama had organised political movements as early as 1952. Eventually a legislative council was set up in 1961, based on an interim constitution and limited national elections. Then Seretse Khama joined the legislative council, and the Protectorate's new executive council.

Meanwhile local politics was developing rapidly. The Bechuanaland People's Party (BPP) was founded in 1960, and later split into two factions, which were eventually to become the Botswana Independence Party (BIP) and the Botswana People's Party (BPP).

Both factions espoused a fairly radical agenda calling for immediate independence, the abolition of the chiefs, nationalisation of some lands and the removal of most whites from the civil service. With the material support of other nationalist movements in Ghana and Tanzania, 1960–61 saw support for the BPP grow rapidly in the townships of eastern Botswana.

From his position on the inside of government, Seretse Khama could see the danger that these parties posed to the constitution that was developing, and to the smooth running of the civil service after independence. Hence early in 1962, under a marula tree in Gaborone, he and five others (Ketumile Masire, A M Tsoebebe, Moutlakgola Nwako, Tsheko Tsheko and Goareng Mosinyi) formed the Botswana Democratic Party (BDP) to campaign for a more ordered transition to independence. All were experienced, educated men and between them had strong links throughout the country, in both the educated elites and the poorer rural communities.

In particular, Seretse Khama and Ketumile Masire, as president and general secretary of the party, formed a strong partnership, without any signs of the feuds and splits that had beset the opposition. One was from the north, the other from the south; one a chief, the other a commoner. Gradually their conservative message began to win over the electorate. This was helped by the fear that any radical new government could provoke problems with South Africa – which still apparently had an appetite for control of Bechuanaland.

Independence Fawcus and Tilbury observe that between 1956 and 1966, 'constitutional and political development far outstripped economic and social advance. The thought that independence might be at the end of the road only emerged in the early 1960s and was discounted by Lord Hailey as late as 1963.'

Fortunately since about 1956 there had been a slow build-up in Britain's financial grants to the Protectorate. By 1963, a £10 million plan was in place for development that covered the transition period around independence. This included the immediate start to constructing a new administrative capital, at Gaborone – as previously Bechuanaland had been administered from Mafikeng, over the border in South Africa.

During this time, Sir Ketumile Masire, Bechuanaland's first deputy prime minister and second president, commented that there was a high 'degree of consultation and co-operation between the local representatives of the British government and the people of Botswana' and that there was 'immense goodwill on both sides'. Perhaps this, more than anything else, explains how the transition was completed so peacefully.

On 1 March 1965, a remarkably peaceful election was held, with voters placing coloured symbols in envelopes to allow for the largely illiterate electorate. This worked without problems. The Bechuanaland Democratic Party (BDP) won 28 out of the 31 seats, and on 3 March 1965 Seretse Khama became the country's first prime minister. Within this new administration, a number of senior British public servants were kept on – including the minister of finance and the attorney general, and a senior civil servant in each of the ministries.

This clear victory for the BDP, and stable administration, gave the new government the platform from which to amend the constitution. The new Setswana name of the Republic of Botswana was chosen for the country, and on 30 September 1966, Sir Seretse Khama became the first president.

Politics since independence

1966–80: President Sir Seretse Khama Seretse Khama inherited a poor country. In 1965, the population stood at about 550,000 with a low level of literacy, and the country was gripped by a bad drought. Fortunately Britain was sympathetic to continuing to cover substantial costs of the new nation's administration, although with the discovery of diamonds at Orapa in 1967 by geologists from De Beers, and the subsequent mining operations which began in 1971, this assistance was only needed for six years after independence.

Botswana had long been in the Southern African Customs Union – and in 1969 it succeeded in renegotiating the terms of this, to become more financially independent. (Previously it had received a fixed percentage of total customs union income, rather than the income that was due directly from its own territory.)

During the 1970s Botswana's economy grew steadily, typically by around 12–13%, as Botswana extended its basic infrastructure for both mining development and basic social services for its population. Despite threats from, among others, the Marxist-leaning Botswana National Front (BNF), Sir Seretse Khama steered the country on a fairly moderate line – and the BDP was consistently re-elected in generally fair elections.

With civil war in Rhodesia throughout the 1970s, and apartheid regimes in South Africa and South West Africa (Namibia), Botswana's position was tricky. It accepted refugees from neighbouring countries, but refused to be used as a base for resistance organisations. Such neutrality was often severely tried, not least when, in February 1978, the Rhodesian army crossed the border and massacred 15 Botswana soldiers at Lesoma (see box, page 253).

Zimbabwe gained independence in 1980, and the same year saw the foundation of the Southern African Development Coordination Conference (SADCC), with the aim of co-ordinating the region's disparate economies in the face of the huge economic muscle wielded by South Africa's apartheid regime.

Sir Seretse Khama died in July 1980 and, as envisaged by the constitution, was succeeded by his deputy, Sir Ketumile Masire. He left behind him an impressive legacy of a stable, prosperous country amid a changing subcontinent. He had skilfully steered Botswana, with foresight and prudence, during perhaps its most vulnerable period – leaving it with the firm foundations of a democratic tradition, and well-trained executive and administrative branches of government.

The 1980s: President Sir Ketumile Masire Masire's succession was mandated by another victory for the BDP in a general election to the National Assembly in 1984 – although at the same time they lost control of all the town councils except Selebi-Phikwe. This sign of discontent was widely ascribed to high levels of unemployment.

Just as the 1970s had witnessed upheavals in Rhodesia, so the 1980s saw the intensification of pressure on the white regime in South Africa to give way to majority rule.

Botswana continued to welcome refugees, but refused to harbour bases for the ANC's war on apartheid in South Africa. During this period Botswana had a delicate balancing act to play. Like most countries it was calling for an end to apartheid, and geographically it was one of the 'front-line' states in the battle against apartheid. However, Botswana's economy was so dependent on its southern neighbour that it couldn't afford to apply the sanctions that most countries were calling for.

In 1981, tensions arose with South Africa over the supply of military equipment from the USSR for the Botswana Defence Force (BDF), though by 1986 Britain and the USA were offering hardware to the BDF to deter South African incursions into Botswana.

Meanwhile on its eastern border, relations with Robert Mugabe's ZANU government were businesslike rather than terribly friendly. The early 1980s saw Mugabe's notoriously ruthless Fifth Brigade terrorising Matabeleland – the province adjacent to Botswana. Zimbabwean refugees flooded into Botswana including, in March 1983, the leader of ZAPU, Mugabe's opposition in the elections, Joshua Nkomo.

Nkomo left for London rapidly, but later allegations that the refugee camps were harbouring armed dissidents caused problems, culminating in a border skirmish in 1983 between the BDF and 'armed men wearing Zimbabwean military uniforms'. It wasn't until April 1989 that Botswana felt able to revoke the 'refugee' status for Zimbabwean nationals and, soon after, the refugees left – although Botswana continued to have many illegal migrants from Zimbabwe.

Internally, political tensions between the BDP and the BNF peaked in early 1987 with a referendum on constitutional amendments to the electoral system, which was boycotted by the BNF. However, by October 1989, the BDP demonstrated its substantial support by winning 65% of the votes in an election (a result which was again challenged by the BNF in several constituencies). In October the new National Assembly returned Masire to the president's office for a third term.

During this time there were several incursions into Botswana by South African troops – including two raids on alleged ANC offices in Gaborone in 1985 and 1986. But a few years later, tensions began to ease as South Africa's President De Klerk started to set his country on a course for majority rule. One of his first steps was independence for Namibia in 1990.

1990–98: President Sir Ketumile Masire The early 1990s saw several corruption scandals in which a number of ministers resigned – including, in March 1992, the vice president, Peter Mmusi. (Contrast these with the paucity of resignations that occur during corruption scandals in most governments and you'll realise this is a good sign, not a bad one, for the integrity of Botswana's government!)

The general election of October 1994 saw the BNF triumphing in the urban areas, winning 13 seats (37.7% of the vote), while the BDP, with 40 seats (53.1% of the vote), continued to command the support of the rural constituencies. The elections were peaceful, with around a 70% turnout, and at last Botswana had an opposition party capable of a serious challenge to the BDP.

During this time relations with Botswana's neighbours were generally good. However, in 1992, a border squabble arose between Botswana and Namibia over a tiny island (called Sedudu by Botswana, and Kasikili by Namibia) in the Chobe River. (For details of this argument, see page 250.) A potentially much more serious issue arose in 1996 when Namibia announced plans to construct a pipeline to take water from the Okavango River at Rundu. Given that this would impact directly on the Okavango Delta, the possibility of such a pipeline remains a source of great concern for Botswana.

Then, in 1998, an influx of refugees from Namibia's Caprivi Strip arrived, including Mishake Muyongo, who had been suspended as president of Namibia's opposition party, the Democratic Turnhalle Alliance. He and other leading Caprivians had campaigned for independence for the province. By 1999, over 2,000 refugees were living near Gaborone. Namibia's extradition demands were refused, although eventually a settlement was brokered by the UNHCR whereby the most prominent refugees were granted asylum in Denmark, and the rest returned to Namibia under an amnesty.

Internal electoral reform had long been on the agenda in Botswana, with some consensus about the need for it from all the political parties. In 1997, various amendments to the constitution were passed, including a reduction in the voting age from 21 to 18 years old, the establishment of an electoral commission that is independent of the government, and a measure to restrict the president to a maximum of two terms in office.

When Masire retired in March 1998, it was at a time of infighting in the opposition, the BNF. This led to a split in the party, with dissident members forming the Botswana Congress Party (BCP). After 11 of the BNF's 13 deputies had defected, the BCP was declared the official opposition in July 1998.

1998–2008: President Festus Mogae
The day after Masire's retirement, his vice president, Festus G Mogae, head of the BDP, was inaugurated. Mogae was born in 1939 and trained at Oxford as an economist. He served as executive director at the IMF for anglophone Africa, and later in various senior government posts, including Governor of the Bank of Botswana. His new cabinet was virtually identical to the old one; the only new minister was Lt General Seretse Khama Ian Khama, son of Botswana's first president (the late Sir Seretse Khama), who in 1998 became vice president. Both men remained in office following elections in 1999 and 2004.

In 2003, Ian Khama became chairman of the BDP and five years later, when President Mogae stepped down at the end of his second term in office, he took on the presidency.

2008–present: Lt General Seretse Khama Ian Khama
The new president took office in April 2008. Elections the following year returned the BDP with 53% of the votes, securing 45 seats in parliament, while their BNF and BCP rivals came away with just ten seats. Five years later, Khama remained in office after the BDP was once again returned to government, despite garnering less than 50% of the votes. By contrast, the four opposition parties – the BNF and BCP, along with the Botswana Movement for Democracy and the Botswana People's Party – took 53% of the vote between them.

The president was born in the UK in 1953, and trained at Britain's military academy, Sandhurst, before joining the newly formed Botswana Defence Force, rising to take charge in the late 1980s. Known as an ardent conservationist, he is actively involved in environmental organisations, and in 2014 he introduced a hunting ban throughout Botswana. He has promoted the importance of diversification within Botswana's economy, with a view to lessening the country's dependence on diamond mining. More controversial, though, has been the introduction of the Directorate of Internal Security, with its own powers separate from the police force; Khama is considered something of an authoritarian, which has rendered him unpopular in many quarters.

On the international stage, Khama has often taken a hard line, sometimes finding himself a lone voice within the African Union. In 2011, he was one of the first to break off relations with Libya's Colonel Gaddafi, and in 2016 he called for Zimbabwe's president Robert Mugabe to step down (which he finally did in late

2017). He risked a backlash from the influential Chinese leadership, too, over a planned visit to Botswana by the Dalai Lama in 2017, although the Tibetan leader is said to have cancelled his trip at the last minute.

Under the constitution, the president will step down from office in 2018 in favour of his deputy, Mokgweetsi Masisi, who was appointed in 2014. Masisi, a trained teacher and minister of education, will then have 18 months to prepare for elections in November 2019. This time, however, the elections will have a new edge as in February 2017 Botswana's four opposition parties announced that they had joined forces under the Umbrella for Democratic Change (UDC). It remains to be seen how strong the coalition will prove to be, but for the first time the opposition could present a serious challenge to the BDP's 50-year hold on power.

GOVERNMENT AND ADMINISTRATION

Botswana's parliament consists of two houses: the National Assembly and the House of Chiefs. Elections to the National Assembly are held every five years, with results based on a first-past-the-post system, similar to that in the UK. As a result, the electoral system affords little chance for minority parties to gain ground, and attempts by opposition parties to pool their resources against the might of the BDP have so far come to nothing.

The president is appointed by parliament rather than directly elected. This is a controversial issue, but in 2008 parliament rejected calls for the system to be changed in favour of a popular vote. Each president may serve for a maximum of two terms, after which the vice president takes over. He or she is then given 18 months to prepare for a general election.

For administrative purposes, the country is divided into a mix of rural and urban districts.

ECONOMY

In economic terms, Botswana has long been one of Africa's success stories, reflecting both the country's natural mineral wealth and a political and social stability which far outweighs that of its neighbours. Underpinning this success has been the exploitation of Botswana's diamond mines, although other growth sectors have been in tourism, cattle farming and financial services.

In the 30-year period following independence in 1966, the economic growth rate averaged just over 9% a year, marking the economy out as the fastest growing in the world, according to the World Bank. By the turn of the century, this had stabilised at around 7% a year. Despite plummeting to –7% in 2009, when Botswana's mining sector was reeling from the effects of a worldwide recession, the annual growth rate bounced back to 8% the following year. By 2016, however, the economy was experiencing something of a downturn, with high youth unemployment and growth slowed to just 2.9% a year.

ECONOMIC DEVELOPMENT Prior to independence, Botswana's economy was primarily based on farming, particularly cattle. Even in 1993, some 46% of the country's land was permanent pasture. Since the 1970s, however, the extraction of mineral resources, particularly diamonds, has been big business, and today the sector accounts for a significant proportion of the country's wealth.

In the face of finite diamond resources, however, the need to diversify is clear. In particular, the tourism, technology and financial services sectors have been earmarked for potential development, while the processing of diamonds and semi-precious stones is also targeted. Cattle-raising also remains significant.

INTERNATIONAL TRADE Total exports in 2016 were estimated at over US$7.32 billion, up by almost a quarter since 2012. Of these, diamonds and other minerals accounted for almost 85%, with other revenue sources including tourism (5.8%) and meat (1.45%). Major export markets are Belgium and India, with South Africa, Namibia and the UAE also significant.

In the same year, Botswana's imports were valued at around US$6.1 billion, with some 65% of these coming from South Africa, which supplies most of the country's electricity, as well as non-industrial diamonds. This last reflects in part the move to Gaborone in 2013 of De Beers' international centre for diamond sales and sorting. Other imports range from foodstuffs and textiles to machinery and petroleum products.

Botswana is a member of the Southern African Customs Union (SACU), an economic bloc comprising South Africa, Botswana, Namibia, Lesotho and Swaziland. Goods produced in Botswana enter the markets of the other four member states free of duty or any other restrictions. Botswana is also an active member of the Southern African Development Community (SADC), a body which groups together 15 countries within the region and has its headquarters in Gaborone.

Diamond mining Botswana's economic success is founded on its natural resources, particularly diamonds. Today, alongside Russia, it remains one of the leading producers of gem-quality diamonds in the world. Diamonds account for around a third of the country's GDP, and the employment – directly and indirectly – of some 25% of the workforce. In an attempt to broaden the value of its diamond industry, the government has also encouraged the establishment in Botswana of diamond-processing factories, luring them away from their stronghold in India.

For over three decades after mining began in 1971, the industry catapulted the economy on to a course of sustained growth. Despite the global recession in 2008–09, and a slump in sales in 2015, the market has since recovered to record a total value of US$6.02 billion in 2016.

Until 2011, most diamond mining was carried out by Debswana, a 50/50 partnership between De Beers and the Botswana government that was formed in 1969. Of the company's four large, open-cast operations, the first to be in production was at Orapa, west of Francistown. Opened in 1971, it was for many years the world's largest open-cast diamond mine. It was joined in 1975 by the nearby Letlhakane mine, and in 1982, by Jwaneng in the south of the country, which is classed as the world's richest diamond mine, and is anticipated to remain in production until 2024 and beyond. Debswana's fourth mine is the much smaller Damtshaa, near Orapa.

In 2011, the controversial Ghaghoo diamond mine was opened within the Central Kalahari Game Reserve. Operated by Gem Diamonds Botswana, the mine has a potential yield of up to 20.5 million carats, but was mothballed in early 2017 when faced with a downturn in the market for commercial diamonds. A similar situation has arisen at the Lerala mine, operated by Australian company Kimberley Diamonds.

Tourism Botswana's natural environment is a major attraction for tourists, as highlighted in this guide. The government's policy of encouraging small numbers of upmarket visitors to its pristine wilderness areas is proving successful within the overall aim of protecting the environment.

The number of overseas tourists visiting the country is expected to reach 1,797,000 in 2017, with almost two-thirds coming from the USA, Germany and the UK. Although this is down from a peak of more than two million in 2008, the trend is now back on the upward trajectory that started in 1994, with visitor numbers projected to hit 2.73 million in 2027. In 2016, tourism accounted directly for 3.9% of GDP, a figure that is forecast to rise to 4.3% in 2027. Translated into jobs, this equates to 2.6% of the workforce in 2016, or 25,000 jobs, and is expected to rise to 4.8% within the next decade. A further 43,500 jobs were indirectly supported by the industry.

When the diamonds run out – within the next few decades – Botswana needs to have an alternative, and renewable, source of income, and tourism is one of the most obvious contenders. The difficulty for the government will be trying to increase substantially tourism's revenues while still keeping tourism a premium product, and hence at a low density. It is noticeable that when leases in the wildlife concessions come up for review, the operators are being allowed to construct additional camps, thus giving them the capacity for more visitors. While there is certainly space in some of the concessions for this, in others there is likely to be a knock-on effect in terms of exclusivity.

In the meantime, in order to increase the benefits from tourism without adverse impact on the environment, attempts are being made to diversify into smaller 'ecotourism' projects that will benefit local communities at ground level, and to offset the negative effects of a clash between tourism projects and the needs of local people. Among these are new community-based projects in both Kasane and the Tsodilo Hills, aimed at boosting cultural tourism.

WORKFORCE With a highly literate workforce, and largely good industrial relations, Botswana has reaped the rewards of the success of the mining industry to the country's economy. At US$6,788, GDP per capita was among the highest in Africa in in 2016. This, though, masks a broad social divide. Unemployment continues to average almost 18% a year, and around a third of the population is considered to be close to the poverty line, living on less than US$1.25 per day.

FOREIGN INVESTMENT The combination of political stability, low rates of taxation and the lack of exchange controls, which were abolished in 1999, makes Botswana attractive to investors. Key to any prospective investment is the Botswana Investment and Trade Centre (*www.bitc.co.bw*), which is instrumental in pursuing government policies of privatisation and diversification.

4

People and Culture

POPULATION OVERVIEW

Botswana's population was estimated at 2,230,905 in 2016, reflecting a population growth per year of some 1.8%.

This growth rate is low by African standards, and results from two conflicting issues. On the plus side, just over half of fertile women use contraceptives, which is exceptional for sub-Saharan Africa and reflects an educated people with a prosperous and generally developed economy. Conversely, while average life expectancy is currently estimated at 64.5 years, almost back to that of the mid 1990s, the intervening period saw it fall as low as 36 years, as the country battled with high levels of HIV/AIDS. Although some 17.6% of citizens are still living with HIV – the second-highest rate in the world – this is significantly lower than the peak of around 40%. Nevertheless, about a third of the population is still under the age of 15.

UNICEF's statistics indicate that more than 96% of the population has access to safe water, 64% to adequate sanitation, and almost every child under one has been immunised against polio, diphtheria and BCG. These are very good levels by the continent's standards, and are no doubt helped by the government's policy of paying the full cost of all these vaccines.

However, these statistics say nothing of what Botswana's people are like. If you venture into the more rural areas, take a local bus, or try to hitchhike with the locals, you will often find that people are curious about you. Chat to them openly, as fellow travellers, and you will find most to be delightful. They will be pleased to assist you where they can, and as keen to help you learn about them and their country as they are interested in your lifestyle and what brings you to Botswana. That said, it's not uncommon, especially in the towns, to find people surly and largely uninterested sometimes … just as they are in London, or New York, or many other modern cities.

SOCIAL GROUPS OR 'TRIBES'

The people of Africa are often viewed, from abroad, as belonging to a multitude of culturally and linguistically distinct tribes – which are often portrayed as being at odds with each other. While there is certainly an enormous variety of different ethnic groups in Africa, most are closely related to their neighbours in terms of language, beliefs and way of life. Modern historians eschew the simplistic tag of 'tribes', noting that such groupings change with time.

Sometimes the word 'tribe' is used to describe a group of people who all speak the same language; it may be used to mean those who follow a particular leader or to refer to all the inhabitants of a certain area at a given time. In any case, 'tribe' is

Historians, anthropologists and social scientists are divided, and often perplexed, about what name to use for the people known as 'Bushmen'. The confusion is compounded by the mix of different tribal tags used in historical texts, often for reasons of political correctness.

San, Bushmen, San/Bushmen, Khoisan and Khoi are all used, often apparently randomly. In Botswana you'll also hear RAD (Remote Area Dweller) or Masarwa/Basarwa used, but the former is exceedingly vague and the latter (meaning 'people without cattle') often considered insulting. Equally insulting is the colonial term 'Hottentot'. Some avoid the term 'Bushmen', regarding it as debasing and sexist, often using 'San' in preference – which others claim to be a derogatory Nama word. Meanwhile 'Khoisan' is a language grouping, not a specific race or tribe, and also encompasses the Khoi (or Khoe or Khoi-Khoi or Khoi-khoin), and hence also Namibia's Damara and Nama people. All have similar 'click' languages, but they live very differently from many of the people who we think of as the Bushmen.

Ideally, we would use the term which these people use themselves, but there lies the rub. Ask villagers in the Kalahari and they will describe themselves as members of the Ju-/wasi, the !Kung, the Hai-//omn – or any one of a dozen other language groups. (See box, page 99 for an explanation of the !, / and // in these names.) If we used these much more precise linguistic terms (see box, pages 104–5, for a few of the main ones), they would overly complicate our discussions and require an accuracy that is beyond me.

These people have no label for the broad racial category that we regard as 'the Bushmen'. They simply don't think of themselves as belonging to one race of people. Therefore, the concept of an overall grouping of people that we call 'Bushmen' must have originated from someone other than the people themselves. In truth, it is an invention of those who came to this corner of Africa later – a legacy of colonialism in its broadest sense.

Given the questionable validity of any term, I have used San throughout this book: not because I believe it to be more accurate than the alternatives, but simply because this is a term that is widely used in southern Africa, and widely understood elsewhere. It's also the term adopted by the Kalahari People's Fund (*www.kalaharipeoples.org*), and agreed by various San communities in Namibia. That said, it's a vague term; just try to make it precise and you'll realise how inadequate it is. I apologise if it is, in any language, derogatory; it isn't meant to be.

a vague word that is used differently for different purposes. The term 'clan' (blood relations) is a smaller, more precisely defined, unit – though rather too precise for our broad discussions here.

Certainly, at any given time, groups of people or clans who share similar language and cultural beliefs do band together and often, in time, develop 'tribal' identities. However, it is wrong to then extrapolate and assume that their ancestors will have had the same groupings and allegiances centuries ago.

In Africa, as elsewhere in the world, history is recorded by the winners. Here the winners, the ruling class, may be the descendants of a small group of immigrants who achieved dominance over a larger, long-established community. Over the years, the history of that ruling class (the winners) usually becomes regarded as the history of the whole community, or tribe. Two 'tribes' have thus become one, with one history – which will reflect the origins of that small group of immigrants, and not the ancestors of the majority of the current tribe.

Botswana is typical of many African countries. As you will see, there are cultural differences between the people in different parts of the country. However, in many ways these are no more pronounced than those between the states of the USA, or the different regions of the (relatively tiny) UK. There continues to be lots of inter-marriage and mixing of these peoples and cultures – perhaps more so than there has ever been, due to the efficiency of modern transport systems. Generally, though, there is very little friction between these communities (whose boundaries, as we have said, are indistinct), and Botswana's various peoples live peacefully together.

THE KHOISAN: THE SAN AND THE KHOI The Khoisan is a language grouping rather than a specific race or tribe, and includes the various peoples of both the San, discussed at length here, and the Khoi, covered in the following section. All have relatively light golden-brown skin, almond-shaped eyes and high cheekbones. Their stature is generally small and slight, and they are now found across southern Africa.

There is not another social/language group on this planet which has been studied, written about, filmed and researched more than the San, or Bushmen, of the Kalahari. Despite this, or indeed because of it, popular conceptions about them, fed by their image in the media, are often strikingly out of step with the realities. Thus they warrant a separate section devoted to them.

The aim of these next few pages is to try and explain some of the roots of the misconceptions, to look at some of the realities, and to make you think. Despite having spent a lot of time with San in the Kalahari, I find it difficult to separate fact from oft-repeated, glossy fiction. If parts of this discussion seem disparate, it's a reflection of this difficulty.

Recent scientific observations on the Khoisan Our view of the San is partly informed by some basic anthropological and linguistic research, mostly applying to the Khoisan, which is worth outlining to set the scene.

Anthropology The first fossil records that we have of our human ancestors date back to at least 60,000 years ago in East Africa. These are likely to have been the ancestors of everyone living today.

Archaeological finds from parts of the Kalahari show that human beings have lived here for at least 40,000 years. These are generally agreed to have been the ancestors of the modern Khoisan peoples living in Botswana today.

Language research Of the world's 20 linguistic 'families', four are very different from the rest. All these four are African families – and they include the Khoisan and the Niger-Congo (Bantu) languages. This is among the evidence that has led linguists to believe that human language evolved in Africa, and further analysis has suggested that this was probably among the ancestors of the Khoisan.

The Khoisan languages are distinguished by their wide repertoire of clicking sounds. Don't mistake these for simple: they are very sophisticated. It was observed by Dunbar in 'Why gossip is good for you' (see *Appendix 3*, page 541) that, 'From the phonetic point of view these [the Khoisan languages] are the world's most complex languages. To speak one of them fluently is to exploit human phonetic ability to the full.'

4

At some point the Khoisan languages diverged from a common ancestor, and today three distinct groups exist: the northern, central and southern groups. Languages gradually evolve and change as different groups of people split up and move to new areas, isolated from their old contacts. Thus the evolution of each language is specific to each group, and reflected in the classifications described later in this chapter.

According to Mike Main in *The Visitor's Guide to Botswana* (now *The African Adventurer's Guide to Botswana*; see *Appendix 3*, page 543), the northern group are San and today they live west of the Okavango and north of Ghanzi, with representatives found as far afield as Angola. The southern group are also San, who live in the area between Kang and Bokspits in Botswana. The central group is Khoi, living in central Botswana, and extending north to the eastern Okavango and Kasane, and west into Namibia, where they are known as the Nama.

Each of these three Khoisan language groups has many dialects. These have some similarities, but they are not closely related, and some are different to the point where there is no mutual understanding. Certain dialects are so restricted that only a small family group speaks them; it was reported recently that one San language died out completely with the death of the last speaker.

This huge number of dialects, and variation in languages, reflects the relative isolation of the various speakers, most of whom now live in small family groups as the Kalahari's arid environment cannot sustain large groups of people living together in one place as hunter-gatherers.

Genetic discoveries Most genetically normal men have an X- and a Y-chromosome, while women have two X-chromosomes. Unlike the other 22 pairs of (non-sex) chromosomes that each human has, there is no opportunity for the Y-chromosome to 'swap' or 'share' its DNA with any other chromosome. Thus all the information in a man's Y-chromosome will usually be passed on, without change, to all of his sons.

However, very rarely a single 'letter' in the Y-chromosome will be altered as it is being passed on, thus causing a permanent change in the chromosome's genetic sequence. This will then be the start of a new lineage of slightly different Y-chromosomes, which will be inherited by all future male descendants.

In November 2000, Professor Ronald Davis and a team of Stanford researchers (see *Appendix 3*, page 541) claimed to have traced back this lineage to a single individual man, contesting that a small group of East Africans (Sudanese and Ethiopians) and Khoisan are the closest present-day relatives of this original man. That is, their genetic make-up is closest to his. (It's a scientific 'proof' of the biblical Adam, if you like.)

This is still a very contentious finding, with subsequent researchers suggesting at least ten original male sources ('Adams') – and so, although interesting, the jury remains out on the precise details of all these findings. If you're interested in the latest on this, then you'll find a lot about it on the web; start searching with the keywords: 'Khoisan Y chromosome'.

Historical and current views of the San Despite much evidence and research, our views of the San seem to have changed relatively little since both the Bantu groups and the first Europeans arrived in southern Africa.

The settlers' view Since the first Bantu farmer migrated south through East Africa, the range of territory occupied by the foragers, whose Stone Age technology had dominated the continent, began to condense. By the time the first white settlers appeared in the Cape, the Khoisan people were already restricted to Africa's southwestern corners and the Kalahari.

All over the world, farmers occupy clearly demarcated areas of land, whereas foragers will move more and often leave less trace of their presence. In Africa, this made it easier for farmers, first black then white, to ignore any traditional land rights that belonged to foraging people.

Faced with the loss of territory for hunting and gathering, the foragers – who, by this time were already being called 'Bushmen' – made enemies of the farmers by killing cattle. They waged a guerrilla war, shooting poison arrows at parties of men who set out to massacre them. They were feared and loathed by the settlers, who, however, captured and valued their children as servants.

Some of the Khoisan retreated north from the Cape – like the ancestors of Namibia's Nama people. Others were forced to labour on the settlers' farms, or were thrown into prison for hunting animals or birds which had been their traditional prey, but which were now designated property of the Crown. This story is told by Robert J Gordon in *The Bushman Myth: The Makings of a Namibian Underclass* (see *Appendix 3*, page 539). He shows that throughout history the hunter-gathering San have been at odds with populations of settlers who divided up and 'owned' the land in the form of farms. The European settlers proved to be their most determined enemy, embarking on a programme of legislation and massacre. Many San died in prison, with many more shot as 'vermin'.

Thus the onslaught of farmers on the hunter-gatherers accelerated between the 1800s and the mid 1900s. This helped to ensure that hunter-gathering as a lifestyle continued to be practical only in marginal areas that couldn't be economically farmed – like the Kalahari.

Western views of the San in the 1800s Though settlers in the Cape interacted with Khoisan people, so did Europe and the US, in a very limited way. Throughout the 1800s and early 1900s a succession of Khoisan people were effectively enslaved and brought to Europe and the US for exhibition. Sometimes this was under the guise of anthropology, but usually it didn't claim to be anything more than entertainment.

One of the first was the 'Hottentot Venus' – a woman who was probably of Khoisan extraction who was exhibited around London and Paris from 1810 to 1815, as an erotic curiosity for aristocrats. A string of others followed – for example, the six Khoisan people exhibited at the Coney Island Pleasure Resort, beside New York, and later in London in the 1880s, and billed as the 'missing link between apes and men'; or the 'wild dancing bushman' known as Franz, brought to England around 1913 by Paddy Hepston (see Q N Parsons' piece in *Botswana Notes and Records*, detailed in *Appendix 3*, page 540).

Impressions of the San from the 1950s In the 1950s, a researcher from Harvard, John Marshall, came to the Kalahari to study the Kung! San. He described a peaceful people living in harmony with nature, amid a land that provided all their needs. The groups had a deep spirituality and no real hierarchy: it seemed like the picture of a modern Eden (especially when viewed through post-war eyes). Marshall was a natural cameraman and made a film that follows the hunt of a giraffe by four men over a five-day period. It swiftly became a classic, both in and outside of anthropological circles.

TRADITIONAL LIFE FOR THE SAN

Looking at the lifestyle of the San who until recently remained in the more remote areas of the Kalahari, it's difficult not to lapse into a romantic view of ignoring present realities. There are too many cultural aspects to cover here, so instead I've just picked out a few that you may encounter.

NOMADS OF THE KALAHARI Perhaps the first idea to dispel is that the San are nomads. They're not. San family groups have clearly defined territories within which they forage, called a n!ore (in the Ju/'hoansi language). This is usually centred on a place where there is water, and contains food resources sufficient for the basic subsistence of the group.

Groups recognise rights to the n!ore, which is passed on from father to first-born son. Any visiting people would ask permission to remain in these. Researchers have mapped these areas, even in places like the Central Kalahari.

HUNTER-GATHERERS Any hunter-gatherer lifestyle entails a dependence on, and extensive knowledge of, the environment and the resident fauna and flora found there. In the Kalahari, water is the greatest need and the San know which roots and tubers provide liquid to quench thirst. They create sip wells in the desert, digging a hole, filling it with soft grass, then using a reed to suck water into the hole, and send it bubbling up the reed to fill an ostrich egg. Water-filled ostrich eggs are also buried at specific locations within the group's 'area'. When necessary the San will strain the liquid from the rumen of a herbivore and drink that.

Researchers have observed that any hunting is done by the men. When living a basic hunting and gathering lifestyle, with little external input, hunting provides only about 20% of their food. The remaining 80% is provided largely by the women, helped by the children, who forage and gather wild food from the bush. By the age of 12 a child might know about 200 plant species, and an adult more than 300.

SOCIAL SYSTEM The survival of the San in the harsh environment of the Kalahari is evidence of the supreme adaptability of humans. It reflects their detailed knowledge of their environment, which provides them not only with food, but with materials for shelter and medicine in the form of plants.

Another very important factor in their survival is the social system by which the San live. Social interaction is governed by unwritten rules that bind the people in friendship and harmony. One such mechanism is the obligation to lend such few things as are individually possessed, thereby incurring a debt of obligation from the borrower. The San also practise exogamy, which means they have an obligation to marry outside the group. Such ties bind the society inextricably together, as does the system of gift exchange between separate groups.

Further research agreed, with researchers noting a great surfeit of protein in the diet of the Kung! San and low birth rates akin to modern industrial societies.

Again the San were seen as photogenic and sources of good copy and good images. Their lives were portrayed in romantic, spiritual terms in the book and film *The Lost World of the Kalahari* by Laurens van der Post (see *Appendix 3*, page 542). This documentary really ignited the worldwide interest in the San and led to subsequent films such as *The Gods Must be Crazy*. All the images conveyed an idyllic view of the San as untainted by contact with the modern world.

Owing to environmental constraints a group will consist of between 80 and 120 people, living and moving together. In times of shortage the groups will be much smaller, sometimes consisting of only immediate family – parents, grandparents and children. They must be able to carry everything they possess. Their huts are light constructions of grass, and they have few possessions.

Because no-one owns property, no-one is richer or has more status than another. A group of San has a nominal leader, who might be a senior member of the group, an expert hunter, or the person who owns the water rights. The whole group takes decisions affecting them, often after vociferous discussions.

HUNTING The San in the Kalahari are practised hunters, using many different techniques to capture the game. Their main weapons are a very light bow, and an arrow made of reed, in three sections. The arrowhead is usually poisoned, using one of a number of poisons obtained from specific plants, snakes and beetles. (Though most San know how to hunt with bows and arrows, the actual practice is increasingly uncommon when it's not done to earn money from observing visitors.)

All the hunters may be involved in the capture of large game, which carries with it certain obligations. The whole group shares in the kill and each member is entitled to a certain portion of the meat.

There are different methods for hunting small game, which only the hunter's family would usually share. One method for catching spring hares involves flexible poles, sometimes 4m long, made of thin sticks, with a duiker's horn (or more usually now a metal hook) fastened to the end. These are rammed into the hare's hole, impaling the animal, which is then pulled or dug out.

TRANCE DANCING Entertainment for the San, when things are good, usually involves dancing. During some dances, which may often have overtones of ritual or religion, the dancers may fall into a trance and collapse.

These trances are induced by a deliberate breathing technique, with a clear physiological explanation. Dances normally take place in the evening, around a fire. Then the women, children and old people will sit around and clap, while some of the younger men will dance around the circle in an energetic, rhythmic dance. Often this is all that happens, and after a while the excitement dies down and everyone goes to sleep.

However, on fairly rare occasions, the dancers will go into a trance. After several hours of constant exertion, they will shorten their breathing. This creates an oxygen deficiency, which leads to the heart pumping more strongly to compensate. Blood pressure to the brain increases; the dancer loses consciousness and collapses.

4

The reality was much less rosy than the first researchers thought. Some of their major misconceptions have been outlined particularly clearly in chapter 13 of John Reader's *Africa: A Biography of the Continent* (see *Appendix 3*, page 540). He points out that, far from being an ideal diet, the nutrition of the San was often critically limited, lacking vitamins and fatty acids that would usually be associated with a lack of animal fat in their diet. Far from a stable population with a low birth rate, it seems likely that there had been a decline in the birth rate in the last few generations. The likely cause for this was periods of inadequate nourishment during the year when the San lost weight from lack of food, stress and the great exertions of their lifestyle.

In fact, it seems likely that the San, whom we now see as foragers, are people who, over the last two millennia, have become relegated to an underclass by the relentless advance of both black and white farmers who did not recognise their original rights to their traditional land.

The San and the modern media Though scientific thought has moved on since the 1950s, much of the media has not. The San are still perceived to be hot news.

The outpost of Tsumkwe is the centre for many of the San communities in Namibia. It's a tiny crossroads with a school and a handful of buildings, in a remote corner of northeastern Namibia. Despite its isolation, in 2001 this desert outpost hosted no fewer than 22 film crews. Yes, really. That's an average of almost two each month – and I'm not counting a whole host of other print journalists and photographers.

Talk to virtually any of the directors and you'll realise that they arrive with very clear ideas about the images that they want to capture. They all think they're one of the first, they think they're original, and they want to return home with images which match their pre-conceived ideas about the San as 'the last primitive hunter-gatherers'.

As an example, you'll often see pictures in the media of San hunters in traditional dress walking across a hot, barren salt pan. When asked to do these shoots the San's usual comment is, 'Why? There's no point. We'd never go looking for anything there.' But the shots look spectacular and win prizes … so the photographers keep asking for them. From the San's perspective, they get paid for the shots, so why not pose for the camera? I'd do the same!

Thus our current image of the San is really one that *we* are constantly recreating. It's the one that we expect. But it doesn't necessarily conform to any reality. So on reflection, popular thinking hasn't moved on much from Marshall's first film in the 1950s.

Current issues for the San

There are several issues affecting the rights of the San and their place in modern society. It's a fundamental tenet of the Botswana government that it doesn't allow any of its policies to favour one ethnic group or another. This is generally held to be a very sensible approach, framed to avoid creating ethnic divisions and strife. However, the San are not recognised within the power structure accorded to the various chiefs of Botswana's other tribal groups; there's no San representation in the House of Chiefs (Botswana's second legislative chamber), and no traditional land rights accorded to them. This puts them at a major political disadvantage. In addition, under Botswana law, hunting and gathering isn't recognised as a formal category of land use – so in local disputes the needs of the San are frequently subjugated to those of Botswana's farmers. All this serves to underpin their continuing fight for the right to live in the Central Kalahari Game Reserve.

Central Kalahari Game Reserve

We know this land belonged to our great grandparents. But now, just because we are Bushmen, our land is being taken from us.

Bushman woman, Central Kalahari Game Reserve

One of the more contentious issues facing Botswana in recent years – with much rhetoric from all quarters – is whether or not the San have an ongoing right to live within the Central Kalahari Game Reserve (CKGR), continuing a presence that is estimated to date back some 20,000 years.

The CKGR was proclaimed in 1961 in the last days of the British Protectorate with the intention of placating international concern over the well-being of the San, by safeguarding it for the San hunter-gatherers who were living there. Although for ease of administration it was designated as a game reserve, the needs of its people were a prime motivating factor in its declaration. Following independence, the rights of the San within the reserve were confirmed by Botswana's first president, Sir Seretse Khama. At that time, the population of the San within the CKGR was estimated at around 5,000 people.

It was an underlying assumption that the San would continue with their traditional lifestyle. So while hunting has always been banned within the game reserve, as it is in other Botswana reserves, hunting with bows and arrows was tacitly accepted. Similarly, the San's traditional means of sourcing and storing other food and water were in keeping with the sustainable approach to managing a game reserve.

Gradually, however, things started to change, as people from the San communities came into greater contact with modern society. Over several years, small homesteads were built within the reserve, crops were grown, and domestic animals introduced. When miners prospecting for minerals in the reserve drilled a borehole for water, in the south of the reserve, the water was made available to the San community. Later, it is alleged that rifles were substituted for bows and arrows, and donkeys or horses introduced for transport. Government estimates suggested that if hunting within the reserve continued to grow, the wildlife would be decimated within decades. (That said, the dramatic loss of wildlife within the reserve over the last 30 years can also be laid at the foot of the cattle fences, which have served to prevent game from following their natural migration routes in search of water during the dry season.)

As early as 1986 a government white paper spelled out that the new policy was for the residents of the CKGR to be relocated outside the reserve, ostensibly so that they could access health, education and other facilities in common with other citizens. From then until 2002, the story was one of the government using carrots and sticks to attain this aim.

By 1996, the San population within the CKGR had been reduced to an estimated 1,482. At this stage, the largest settlement, a small village called Xade in the south of the reserve, had a borehole which supplied water, and a few basic buildings. Just six years later, in 2002, only one extended family of 22 people remained – the only San people never to leave the reserve.

The San v the government Supporters of the San's right to remain alleged that from the mid 1990s until 2002, the government and its servants, including the park's game scouts, applied more and more pressure on the local people, forcing them to resettle to new locations outside the reserve. (The best-known of these is named, with Orwellian flair, New Xade.) They alleged that San individuals were beaten and otherwise coerced into moving, and that even the water supply was stopped for those who elected to stay.

For its part, the government denied that they ever used force and insisted that any relocations were voluntary. Their view was that the water borehole – drilled by prospectors – was only ever intended to be temporary and that other services – such as mobile clinics – were withdrawn from Xade for reasons of practicality and cost.

Either way, it seemed likely that the government had, at best, been a little 'over-zealous' in its resettlement policy, and at worst may have committed serious injustices to the people in the reserve.

For me, the most pertinent question was 'Why bother?' The official line that the resettlement policy was to protect the game seemed implausible, given the bad press that this generated throughout the world. There were two obvious theories. One recognised that the government is putting an increasing emphasis on tourism, and was concerned that the presence of the San would detract from the tourist's experience. This really doesn't add up, as tourism could integrate well with the communities if given a chance, and provide a real income for them – and the whole process was started many years before tourism to the CKGR on any scale was viewed as a viable prospect. A second suggested that the government wanted to clear the way for the possibility of exploiting mineral claims in the area: diamond prospectors have long been looking for another find like Orapa beneath the Kalahari. This made little sense either; if an economic diamond pipe were found here – which has since proved to be the case – then no regulations would stand in the way of its exploitation! Implausible though it may seem, I believe that the government started by thinking, rather naively, that removal of the San from the CKGR was the 'best thing for all concerned' and were taken aback by the international campaign against it. Then they found themselves unable to backtrack without both losing face and making an exception for one ethnic group, which they didn't want to do.

In 2002, with the backing of the UK human rights organisation Survival International (www.survival-international.org), 243 San people brought a case against the government, asserting their rights under the constitution to return to their ancestral lands. It was a long-running case, but finally, in December 2006, the three judges in the High Court ruled, by a majority of two to one, that the government's action was 'unlawful and unconstitutional', and 'failed to take account of the knowledge and culture' of the San. One judge added, 'In my view the simultaneous stoppage of the supply of food rations and the stoppage of hunting licences is tantamount to condemning the remaining residents of the Central Kalahari Game Reserve to death by starvation.'

Far from being the end of the dispute, however, the judgement served in part to prolong it. Despite the verdict, there was no requirement for the government to provide services such as water for those electing to return to the reserve. On his inauguration in 2008, President Khama sought to find a way forward by calling a meeting between the San and the government (although he is quoted by Survival International as saying that the San's way of life was an 'archaic fantasy'). A draft management plan was circulated among cabinet ministers prior to discussion with local residents' groups and relevant non-governmental organisations (NGOs). Yet despite this initiative, little has changed. The government has provided a new borehole for the small San community. And diamond mining within the reserve has commenced.

Most of those who have 'returned' in fact come and go, spending weeks in the reserve, then leaving in order to collect benefits (known as 'destitute rations' – coupons that can be exchanged for eligible provisions such as oil or flour), or water, or food. They are not allowed to drill further boreholes, to build any permanent structure, to use any form of transport, or to take in any new domestic animals such as goats. Hunting continues to be banned inside the CKGR and, although the San people can apply for special game licences for hunting in the wildlife management areas that abut the reserve, their lawyers argue that they should not have to apply for what is theirs by right.

In a further blow to the San, in August 2013, their British lawyer was barred from the country, and a month later the High Court ruled that, for procedural reasons, they would not permit the San's latest legal attempt to gain free access to their ancestral land to proceed.

What next? For Survival International, the campaign goes on, and they have called for tourists to boycott Botswana in an attempt to force the government's hand. Meanwhile, the San living in the settlements outside the reserve face different challenges. In New Xade, where there is housing, water and government welfare agencies, the children benefit from both primary and secondary schools, and health needs are met by a modern hospital. Nevertheless, many complain that, with no opportunity to practise their traditional skills, the legacy of countless generations is being wiped out. And with no recent farming tradition, self-sufficiency is difficult. Some have found work on cattle farms or game farms and reserves, others in the tourist industry, but unemployment among the San is considerably higher than the national level of 18%. For many, the resulting disenfranchisement has led to situations of extreme poverty, with alcoholism a problem among some San populations.

Hope for the future? Perhaps one of the few rays of hope is that as a consequence of the prevailing image of the San, visitors really are willing to pay to see something of their 'traditional culture'. Hence the springing up of various traditional villages and tourism projects in both Botswana and neighbouring Namibia.

These vary from really interesting, genuine insights into the people and their skills, to little more than curiosity shows put on for the benefit of visitors.

I'd probably argue that virtually all are worthwhile for the San – provided that they bring a substantial income into the community involved, and do so without actively harming the people's self-esteem. Meanwhile, from experience of the best, I know they can be absolutely fascinating personal interactions for the visitor, as well as acting to reinforce the community's own self-esteem and value in their own skills, while bringing much-needed money into the community.

CULTURAL SENSITIVITY AND LANGUAGE

Cultural sensitivity isn't something that a guidebook can teach you, though reading the section on cultural guidelines at the end of this chapter may help. Being sensitive to the results of your actions and attitudes on others is especially important in this area.

The San are often a humble people, who regard arrogance as a vice. It is normal for them to be self-deprecating among themselves, to make sure that everyone is valued and nobody becomes too proud. So the less you are perceived as a loud, arrogant foreigner, the better.

Very few foreigners can pick up much of the local language without living here for a long time. (Readers may already realise that spellings of the same word can vary greatly.) However, if you want to try to pronounce the words then there are four main clicks to master. In the well-documented Ju/'hoansi language, these are:

/ a dental click, a sucking sound, made by putting the tongue just behind the front teeth.
// a clucking sound, like that used in English to urge on a horse.
! a sharp popping sound, like a cork coming out of a bottle, made by pulling the tongue down quickly from the roof of the mouth.
(a soft popping sound, made by putting your tongue just behind the ridge at the back of the front teeth (this is usually the hardest).

4

What's become very, very clear is that making such a tourist–community interaction really successful for both parties needs the permanent commitment of someone on the ground who has been working with the community for a long period – and understands both the community and the tourists. Without this, such projects invariably fail.

The Khoi The San are often described as hunter-gatherers and the Khoi as pastoralists. The distinction between the two Khoisan peoples is not quite so clear-cut, but it is generally useful. The Khoi, who live in central Botswana and Namibia, have herds of cattle, but continue to source some of their food from hunting and gathering, supplemented by milk products. Because of the intrinsic value of the animals, the Khoi milk their herds but do not kill them for food; stock animals are only killed to mark special occasions.

The ownership of property (stock) by the Khoi has created a more rigid and complex social structure than among the San. Property creates wealth, which can be inherited after the death of the owner, and so laws of inheritance have been developed, as well as laws to protect property. Wealth brings with it the power to control others, thus creating leaders. It also leads to a wealth-based economy that depends on the exchange of goods and work that have an economic value. What must be freely given among the San must be bought and paid for among the Khoi.

Little is known about the religious beliefs of the Khoi, though they believe in a Supreme Being and it is thought that some beliefs are similar to the San and can be traced back to a common source.

OTHER SOCIAL GROUPS
Bantu-speaking peoples After a complex history of conflict, a number of tribes of Bantu origin can now be found in Botswana. As discussed on pages 89–91, today the word 'tribe' has colonial connotations, but unfortunately we do not have a suitable alternative. Likewise, definition by ethnic group is not considered politically correct in Botswana; all people are primarily Batswana (the people of Botswana), and only secondarily Bayei, Bakwena, European, etc. (Tribal names are frequently preceded by 'Ba', which means 'the people of …'.) Sometimes you'll also see the singular 'Motswana' or 'Matswana', used to mean a person from Botswana.

Batswana Although the same name applies to all the people of Botswana, the Batswana (or Tswana) are also the largest ethnic group in the country. (As an aside, colonial partitioning led to three-quarters of the Batswana actually living in South Africa.) The name embraces a number of different offshoots. The Batswana speak Setswana, which is the second language of Botswana, English being the official language.

The Bakalanga The Bakalanga are the country's second-largest population group after the Batswana, despite having been divided by colonial boundaries. Today over 80% of them live in Zimbabwe. Those in Botswana live mainly in the area around Francistown, although they are scattered as far afield as Maun, Palapye, Serowe, Mahalapye and Mochudi. Their origins are unclear, though some of them have probably lived in the region of the upper Shashe River for at least a thousand years. For the last 600 years they have been ruled by other peoples, but interestingly their conquerors have always ended by inter-marrying with the Bakalanga and adopting their customs and language.

The Bakalanga are primarily agriculturalists and this is reflected in their religion and culture, but cattle and goats are also kept, usually by the chief on behalf of his tribe. The chief would give cattle to people who had performed services to the tribe, or those who needed them in order to get married or to sacrifice to the ancestors. The primary importance of agriculture is shown by the traditional marital gifts of specially forged iron hoes that were given to the bride's parents to symbolise the continuity of her livelihood.

The Basubiya, the Bayei and the Hambukushu Around AD1600, these three groups of river-dwelling people all lived close together in the region to the south of the Chobe River. Their closeness is reflected in the similarity of their customs. Significantly, their system of inheritance meant that wealth and status were not passed to the first son, but through to the children of the father's eldest sister. So a man inherited the chieftancy if his mother was the eldest sister of the chief.

The Basubiya According to tradition, after a fight over a lion skin the Bayei were defeated by the Basubiya. They moved away to the Linyanti River, but they still came under the rule of the Basubiya.

Meanwhile, the Hambukushu were driven from their homeland by the expansionist and tribute-seeking chief of the Balozi, whose capital used to be at Katima Mulilo (but is now in western Zambia). To avoid paying the tribute and escape his attentions, the Hambukushu left the Zambezi River and moved nearer to the Chobe and Linyanti rivers, into a region which was already occupied by the Bayei.

In time, the Basubiya grew very powerful and had a large state which stretched westwards from Luchindo on the Chobe River towards the Okavango. Eventually they were defeated by the Balozi and were incorporated into the Lozi empire until its collapse in 1865. According to Campbell, the Basubiya were mainly agriculturalists who also kept some cattle, sheep and goats. They cultivated the floodplains, which they prepared by hoeing in the autumn before the winter floods and planting crops such as millet, sweet reeds and melon when the floods had receded. Today they still live in the Northwest and Chobe districts of the country.

The Bayei (and Banoka) In response to the Basubiya invasion, the Bayei moved away from the Chobe River, into the Okavango, and between 1750 and 1800 they firmly established themselves in the area of the Okavango Delta around Lake Ngami. This shallower, southern section of the Delta perfectly suited the Bayei, who lived mainly from fishing. They also kept cattle, but used them only as pack animals. In the Delta they encountered a group of Khoi called the Banoka (otherwise known as the River Bushmen), who had adapted their hunter-gatherer skills to the environment of the Delta.

The two peoples seem to have co-existed peacefully and even swapped skills. For example the Bayei taught the Banoka to fish with nets where before they had only used baskets. The Bayei made nets from the twisted fibres of succulent plants, which they then trawled behind their boats, called *mekoro*. A *mokoro* ('mekoro' is the plural form) is a dugout canoe that is poled from the rear. In return the Banoka taught the Bayei how to dig pits, filled with sharp pointed sticks, in the middle of a game trail, to trap unsuspecting animals on their way to the river.

A prize catch for the Bayei was the hippo, which is notoriously bad-tempered and dangerous and is liable to attack if surprised in the water. Sometimes it was hunted from the mekoro, when the Bayei's method, like that of the old whale hunters, was to harpoon the hippo from the boat. Instantly the animal would take flight, towing the mokoro in its wake. The hunters had to kill the hippo with their spears, before it either broke loose or killed them. This they did by attempting to reach the bank in their boats, tying the rope attached to the harpoon to a tree and waiting for the hippo to tire before approaching it with spears. Another favourite method of hippo hunting was to place a spear weighted with rocks suspended from a tree over a hippo trail. This capitalised on the fact that hippos live in the water during the day, but come out at night to graze, when they tend to keep to the same tracks.

While mekoro today are more likely to be transporting tourists for a spot of hippo watching, and may well be made of fibreglass instead of wood, they are still often poled by a Bayei man.

The Hambukushu Meanwhile the Hambukushu found that settling on the Chobe did not take them far enough from the Balozi tribute seekers, so they moved again and settled in the more northerly, upper reaches of the Okavango Delta. Being agriculturalists as well as hunters and fishermen, they preferred the deeper water there. Unlike the lower regions, this area did not flood when the rains came and so was more suitable for agriculture. They cleared the bush and planted crops along the river, such as millet, sugarcane, pumpkins and root crops.

Like the Bayei, the Hambukushu used mekoro, but instead of poling them standing up, they sat down and used paddles to propel them through the deeper water.

Alec Campbell's *The Guide to Botswana* (see *Appendix 3*, page 543) describes how the Hambukushu hunted for elephants:

> They took the blade of a spear which had a barb in it and fixed this into a heavy piece of wood. They dug shallow holes on paths used by elephants and then set these spear blades facing upwards. The elephant stood on this, driving the blade deep into the bottom of its foot, after which it couldn't walk. When it was weak, men came with axes and slashed the tendons in its back legs so that it fell down and could be speared.

Today the Hambukushu are most famous for their beautiful hand-woven baskets, which are internationally recognised for their craftsmanship and design. The wide variety of basket types reflects the numerous purposes for which they were traditionally used, ranging from enormous grain-storage baskets, to tightly woven beer baskets for holding the local brew. Unfortunately, the baskets are now being produced commercially, which enables the makers to earn a reasonable living, but has led to over-exploitation of the natural resources from which the baskets are made. The Hambukushu are also renowned as rain-makers, another skill which they have exploited commercially by selling their services to neighbouring tribes.

The Ovaherero and the Ovambanderu The Ovaherero (or Herero) and their relatives the Ovambanderu are pastoralists, who keep large herds of sheep, goats, and especially cattle, which have a religious significance for them. According to their oral history tradition they seem to have moved southwest from central Africa, probably to escape the tsetse fly which spreads sleeping sickness and kills cattle and people.

The religious life of the tribe was of great importance. The tribe was divided into religious clans under a priest/chief. He owned the most cattle and he maintained a sacred herd on behalf of the tribe. On his death the priesthood and the care of the sacred herd passed to his son. The Ovaherero practised ancestor worship, and one of the priest's main religious duties was appeasing the dead relatives of the tribe.

As pastoralists, the clans led their herds in search of grazing but each clan had a designated area. Within this area the women built round huts from a framework of branches covered with mud. The huts were built in a circle around corrals for the animals. As well as tending the herds, the men hunted with wooden spears (their only iron came from trading with the Batswana). The women also collected wild food and made *omaere*, a kind of sour milk which was their staple food.

The presence of the Ovaherero people in Botswana dates back to the beginning of the 20th century, when they were living in what is now northern Namibia, but were becoming increasingly unhappy about their loss of land to the German colonists. In January 1904, their leader, Samuel Maherero, ordered a Herero uprising against the colonial forces. Initially the Hereros had success in taking many German farms and smaller outposts, and in severing the railway line between Swakopmund and Windhoek. However, later that year the German General von Trotha led a large German force including heavy artillery against the Hereros. By August the Hereros had been pushed back to their stronghold of Waterberg, with its permanent waterholes. On 11 August, the Germans attacked, and the battle raged all day. Though it was not decisive, the Hereros' spirit was beaten by the superior firepower and they fled east, into the Kalahari and towards Maun. Many perished; the rest settled in what is now northern Botswana. They had lost their cattle and were forced to work as servants to another tribe, the Batawana. However, they soon rebuilt their herds and also learned agriculture from the Batawana, which they used to supplement their traditional diet of soured milk.

Today, although most of the Ovaherero live in Namibia, some are still to be found in Botswana. The women are recognisable because they continue to dress in the clothes they were taught to wear by Victorian Christian missionaries, including long bulky dresses and elaborate headdresses.

The Kagalagadi This name (not to be confused with the name of the transfrontier park in Botswana and South Africa) is applied to different people of varied descent who currently live in the Kalahari Desert. There are five major groups who have settled in different areas of the Kalahari. They all have their own tribal names and customs and they speak a variety of languages – the combined form of which is a Sotho language, not a dialect of Setswana.

Of these groups, the Bakgwatheng remain in the east of the Kalahari on the fringes of the desert, which receives sufficient rainfall for their crops of sorghum, melons and beans. They also keep small herds of cattle, sheep and goats, and mine and work iron. As iron ore was not available in the heart of the Kalahari, these factors all restricted them to the desert's fringe.

The Bangologa and the Babolaongwe, on the other hand, are pastoralists with large herds of sheep and goats, and a few cattle. They obtain most of their food from hunting and gathering, so they are not reliant upon agriculture and they trade for iron, so they were able to live a nomadic existence within the desert. The other two groups are the Baphaleng and the Bashaga.

Others

White Batswana The current white population of Botswana is much lower than that of its surrounding neighbours, and many of these are not permanent residents. This reflects the unusual history of Botswana: the fact that the country was a 'protectorate' rather than a colony.

Note that these small numbers of white Batswana are very different from the expatriate community (page 106), who are often white but simply working in the country on a temporary basis. Many white Batswana will trace their families back to colonial immigrants who came over during British rule, but most are citizens of

BOTSWANA'S MAIN LANGUAGE GROUPS

For more scientifically minded readers, here's a list of most of Botswana's main language groups, with their linguistic family roots and a few brief notes on where they're spoken. This tells you the history of that language, starting with the main group to which it belongs, and defining it more specifically. Thus English and Afrikaans are both Indo-European languages, and more specifically Germanic and West. That means they both originally derive from one ancient language: West Germanic. The classification of the Khoisan and Bantu languages gives a similar view of their history and relationships. Obviously the information below is best read in conjunction with the whole section on social groups.

BANTU LANGUAGES

Setswana *Classification: Niger-Congo, Atlantic-Congo, Volta-Congo, Benue-Congo, Bantoid, Southern, Narrow Bantu, Central, S, Sotho-Tswana (S30), Tswana.* Around 70% of the population speak Setswana (also known as Tswana). Some official business is conducted in Setswana, the media often use English and Setswana interchangeably, and it's the lingua franca between different citizens who don't speak English.

Tswapong *Classification: Niger-Congo, Atlantic-Congo, Volta-Congo, Benue-Congo, Bantoid, Southern, Narrow Bantu, Central, S, Sotho-Tswana (S30), Tswapong.* Several thousand speakers, in the Central District and Mahalapye Sub-district.

Kagalagadi *Classification: Niger-Congo, Atlantic-Congo, Volta-Congo, Benue-Congo, Bantoid, Southern, Narrow Bantu, Central, S, Sotho-Tswana (S30), Kgalagadi.* Estimated total of about 35,000 speakers in Botswana.

Birwa *Classification: Niger-Congo, Atlantic-Congo, Volta-Congo, Benue-Congo, Bantoid, Southern, Narrow Bantu, Central, S, Sotho-Tswana (S30), Sotho.* Estimated total of about 10,000 speakers in Botswana.

Kalanga *Classification: Niger-Congo, Atlantic-Congo, Volta-Congo, Benue-Congo, Bantoid, Southern, Narrow Bantu, Central, S, Shona (S10).* Estimated total of about 160,000 speakers in Botswana.

Ndbele *Classification: Niger-Congo, Atlantic-Congo, Volta-Congo, Benue-Congo, Bantoid, Southern, Narrow Bantu, Central, S, Ngui.* Estimated total of about 10,000 speakers in the Northeast District, though this is the main language over the border in Zimbabwe's Matabele Province.

Herero *Classification: Niger-Congo, Atlantic-Congo, Volta-Congo, Benue-Congo, Bantoid, Southern, Narrow Bantu, Central, R, Herero.* Estimated total of about 31,000 speakers scattered among other ethnic groups in Botswana, often having their own area in towns and villages. This is one of Namibia's major ethnic groups.

Yeyi *Classification: Niger-Congo, Atlantic-Congo, Volta-Congo, Benue-Congo, Bantoid, Southern, Narrow Bantu, Central, R, Yeye.* Estimated total of about 27,000 speakers in Botswana, with probably another 20,000 ethnic Bayeyi who do not actually speak Yeyi.

Mbukushu *Classification: Niger-Congo, Atlantic-Congo, Volta-Congo, Benue-Congo, Bantoid, Southern, Narrow Bantu, Central, K, Kwangwa.* Estimated total of about 12,000 speakers in Botswana, located in the Northwest District, especially in Gomare and the villages to the north of there, and in the Okavango Delta.

Subiya *Classification: Niger-Congo, Atlantic-Congo, Volta-Congo, Benue-Congo, Bantoid, Southern, Narrow Bantu, Central, K, Subia (L50).* Estimated total of about 12,000 speakers in Botswana, mostly living in the Northwest and Chobe districts.

KHOISAN LANGUAGES

!Xoo *Classification: Khoisan, southern Africa, Southern, Hua.* There are between 3,000 and 4,000 speakers of this Khoisan language, and its related dialects, living in Botswana.

=/Hua *Classification: Khoisan, southern Africa, Southern, Hua.* Around 1,000–1,500 speakers, living mainly in the southern Kalahari Desert and the Kweneng District.

//Gana *Classification: Khoisan, southern Africa, Central Tshu-Khwe, Northwest.* Around 1,000 speakers living around the Ghanzi District, in villages and farms, and in the Central Kalahari Game Reserve. Speakers are also found in the Central District (Boteti Sub-district) and the cattle-posts south and west of Rakops.

/Anda *Classification: Khoisan, southern Africa, Central Tshu-Khwe, Northwest.* About 1,000 speakers live in the Northwest District, mostly around the Khwai River and Mababe Village areas.

Ksoe *Classification: Khoisan, southern Africa, Central Tshu-Khwe, Northwest.* Speakers of this language, often known as the 'River Bushmen', number around 1,700–2,000, and live in and around the Northwest District, mainly in the villages of Gan, Cadikarauwe, Mohembo, Shakawe, Kaputura, /Ao-Kyao, Sikonkomboro, Ngarange, Sekanduko, Xongoa, Cauwe, Moxatce, Dungu, Seronga, Beyetca, Gudigoa, Sikokora, Geixa, /Qom-ca, Tobere, 0/Umbexa, Djaxo and Kangwara.

Deti *Classification: Khoisan, southern Africa, Central Tshu-Khwe, Central.* Spoken in the Central District, the Boteti Sub-district, and in the villages which are strung out along the Boteti River.

Nama *Classification: Khoisan, southern Africa, Central Tshu-Khwe, Central.* There are about 200–1,000 Nama speakers in Botswana, mostly in the Kgalagadi District around Tsabong, Makopong, Omaweneno and Tshane villages, and in the Ghanzi District, in the villages along the Ghanzi–Mamuno road. It's also spoken by a much larger population in Namibia.

Ganadi *Classification: Khoisan, southern Africa, Central Tshu-Khwe, North Central.* Spoken in the Northeastern area.

Shua *Classification: Khoisan, southern Africa, Central Tshu-Khwe, North Central.* Counted together with the Tshwa group, there are around 19,000 Shua speakers in Botswana, located in the Central District and Tutumi Sub-district.

//Gwi *Classification: Khoisan, southern Africa, Central, Tshu-Khwe, Southwest.* There are around 800 speakers in villages in the Kweneng and Ghanzi districts.

Naro *Classification: Khoisan, southern Africa, Central Tshu-Khwe, Southwest.* Botswana has an estimated 8,000 speakers of Naro.

Ju/'hoansi *Classification: Khoisan, southern Africa, Northern.* This is one of the larger Khoisan languages, with 4,000–8,000 speakers in Botswana, and many more in Namibia, around the Tsumkwe area.

=/Kx'au//'ein *Classification: Khoisan, southern Africa, Northern.* There are about 3,000 speakers in Botswana, mostly in the Ghanzi District, both in the villages and working on commercial farms.

EUROPEAN LANGUAGES

English *Classification: Indo-European, Germanic, West, English.* English is the official language in Botswana, the language of government and schools, although official work is increasingly being carried out in Setswana (Tswana).

Afrikaans *Classification: Indo-European, Germanic, West; Low Saxon-Low Franconian, Low Franconian.* There are some 20,000 people in Botswana whose native tongue is Afrikaans, mainly on the commercial farms in the Ghanzi District. In addition, many of the white community who have close links with South Africa can communicate in Afrikaans.

Botswana rather than, say, British. This is generally an affluent group of people, a number of whom own and run their own businesses.

Expatriates Totally distinct from the permanent population of citizens of Botswana who are white, there is also a significant 'expat' community in Botswana. These foreigners usually come to Botswana for two or three years to work on short-term contracts, often for multi-national companies or aid agencies. Most are highly skilled individuals who come to share their knowledge with local colleagues – often teaching skills that are in short supply in Botswana.

There is also a significant number of foreigners working in the safari industry. These are often residents of other southern African nations who come to guide or manage camps for a few years, although as work permits become increasingly difficult to obtain, the number of expats in the safari business is slowly starting to fall.

LANGUAGE

Botswana's official languages are English and Setswana: 70% of the population speaks Setswana. Many people are at least bilingual, speaking English and their mother tongue, and possibly Setswana or Afrikaans, depending on what is locally required to get work.

According to data from 'Ethnologue: Languages of the World' (*www.ethnologue. com*), there are at least 26 languages spoken in Botswana. For a scientific overview of these, see box, pages 104–5.

It's worth reiterating here that all the world's languages have been grouped into around 20 linguistic families, of which four are from Africa. These include the Khoisan and Bantu languages, the former being among the world's most complex languages. For some hints on mastering its series of clicks, see box, page 99.

RELIGION

Officially Botswana is a Christian country, with almost two-thirds of the population claiming membership of a Christian group. These mostly belong to the Anglican, Methodist and United Congregational churches, but among several other denominations there are also Catholics, Lutherans and Zion Christians. (Members of this last are noted for the khaki dress worn when attending services.) Services are usually in Setswana, though the larger churches in the main towns also have English services, and the smaller, rural ones will sometimes use the local languages. Faith healing is often incorporated into services. Other religions, such as Islam, are represented only in the larger towns; their following is small, mainly among expat workers.

As usual in the subcontinent, many of Botswana's religions blend Christian beliefs with aspects of traditional beliefs. In times of crisis or ill health, most people are as likely to seek out a traditional healer as they are to visit a priest or a hospital. More often still, they will pursue both a traditional and a more Western approach at the same time. (From a medical standpoint, the best practices of traditional healers are increasingly lauded throughout southern Africa as holistic approaches, which can complement Western medicine.)

People's traditional beliefs depend largely on ancestry, differing widely from tribe to tribe, but generally incorporating a great respect for ancestors, a belief in their continued existence in the spirit world, and a certainty that the spirits affect everyone's day-to-day lives.

EDUCATION

Botswana's education system follows a ten-year course focusing on both academic and practical skills. Children start in primary school at the age of six, moving on after standard seven to a further three years at junior secondary school. Examinations held at the end of form 3 – roughly aged 15 – determine whether or not a child may continue into senior secondary education, to study for the Botswana General Certificate of Education. Success in this opens up the option of attending technical college or the University of Botswana.

Primary education is compulsory for all children and is free up to the age of 13, after which 95% of the cost is funded by the government. Primary school attendance is around 90/92% for boys/girls, falling considerably at secondary level to around 52/59%. Adult literacy comes out at 80/82%. This pattern of the girls generally receiving more education is unusual in Africa, where sons are often favoured by their parents over daughters – but given women's pivotal role in bringing up children and running households in this traditional society, it bodes well for the future.

CULTURE

Botswana's diverse ethnic mix results in an equally diverse cultural heritage, although the importance of music and dance runs like a common thread throughout. Visitors to the country will often be treated to displays of traditional dancing and singing that will reflect in part the area in which they're based, and in part the traditions of those taking part. (For notes on San culture, see box, pages 94–5.)

Bessie Head's book, *Serowe: Village of the Rain Wind* (see *Appendix 3*, page 539), offers an invaluable and very readable introduction to Batswana culture, Bamangwato style. (The Bamangwato tribe rose to ascendancy over the other tribes, following the Difaquane Wars. This was due partly to their prime location for trading contacts and partly to visionary leadership.)

The book gives a wonderful insight into an African village and the lives, knowledge and skills of the inhabitants. Writing in 1981, Head describes Serowe as a typical traditional village. Most people had three homes: one in the village, one at the lands where they ploughed, and one at the cattle post where they kept their cattle. The homes were all round, thatched mud huts and people moved from home to home all the time.

We learn how the homes are constructed – that the walls of the mud huts were built and externally decorated by the women, but were thatched by the men. The weaving of grass baskets was a woman's occupation, but tanning hide to make leather Batswana mats and blankets was a man's profession.

MUSIC Botswana's musical traditions are as varied as its culture. In traditional Batswana culture, the teaching of music and dance was incorporated into the initiation rites at puberty, and dancing, accompanied by the beat of drums, was once used to mark special occasions such as hunting or the annual harvest. Today, choral singing is particularly popular, with village choirs often coming together to celebrate national holidays – and guests at the safari lodges may well be regaled by staff with spontaneous and exceptionally harmonious singing.

Comments here are intended to be a general guide, just a few examples of how to travel more sensitively. They should not be viewed as blueprints for perfect Botswana etiquette. Cultural sensitivity is really a state of mind, not a checklist of behaviour – so here we can only hope to give the sensitive traveller a few pointers in the right direction.

When we travel, we are all in danger of leaving negative impressions with local people that we meet. It is easily done – by snapping that picture quickly, while the subject is not looking; by dressing scantily, offending local sensitivities; by just brushing aside the feelings of local people, with the high-handed superiority of a rich Westerner. These things are easy to do, in the click of a shutter, or flash of a dollar bill.

However, you will get the most representative view of Botswana if you cause as little disturbance to the local people as possible. You will never blend in perfectly when you travel – your mere presence there, as an observer, will always change the local events slightly. However, if you try to fit in and show respect for local culture and attitudes, then you may manage to leave positive feelings behind you.

One of the easiest, and most important, ways to do this is with **greetings**. African societies are rarely as rushed as Western ones. When you first talk to someone, you should greet them leisurely. So, for example, if you enter a bus station and want some help, do not just ask outright, 'Where is the bus to … ?' That would be rude. Instead you will have a better reception (and a better chance of good advice) by saying:

Traveller:	'Good afternoon.'
Local:	'Good afternoon.'
Traveller:	'How are you?'
Local:	'I am fine, how are you?'
Traveller:	'I am fine, thank you. (pause) Do you know where the bus to …'

This goes for approaching anyone – always greet them first. For a better reception still, learn the greetings in Setswana (see *Appendix 2*, pages 537–8), or even the local language. While most people in Botswana understand English, a greeting in an appropriate local language will be received with delight.

Very rarely in one of the towns you may be approached by someone who doesn't greet you. Instead s/he tries immediately to sell you something, or even hassle you in some way. These people have learned that foreigners aren't used to greetings, and so have adapted their approach accordingly. A surprisingly effective way to dodge their attentions is to reply to their questions with a formal greeting, and then politely – but firmly – refuse their offer.

Another part of the normal greeting ritual is **handshaking**. As elsewhere, you would not normally shake a shop-owner's hand, but you would shake hands with someone to whom you are introduced. Get some practice when you arrive, as there is a gentle, three-part handshake used in southern Africa which is easily

With the policy of integration implemented at independence in the mid 1960s came a decline in individual cultural traditions. Since then, however, there has been a resurgence of interest. Traditional songs and dancing are widely taught in schools, and during the 1980s there was a revival of instruments such as the *segaba*, a simple violin used to accompany folk singing. Simpler still are the thumb pianos learned. It consists of taking each other's right hand, as for a normal handshake, but just shaking once, up and down. Then while leaving the thumbs linked, the grip is changed by both people raising their hands, until their arms make a right-angle. Each then grasps the other person's thumb and the top of their hand firmly. Then this is swiftly relaxed, with thumbs still interlinked, and the hands are dropped back into one last normal 'shake'.

Your **clothing** is an area that can easily give offence. Most people in Botswana frown upon skimpy or revealing clothing, especially when worn by women. Shorts are fine for walking safaris, but otherwise dress conservatively and avoid short shorts, especially in the more rural areas. Respectable locals will wear long trousers (men) or long skirts (women).

Homosexuality remains illegal in Botswana, although no-one – as far as I know – has ever been prosecuted, and same-sex relationships have never been a problem for guests in safari camps. While it's not at all unusual in traditional societies to see two men – or two women – casually holding hands, public **displays of affection** between two people (gay or straight) may create tension and are best avoided.

Photography is a tricky business. Most people in Botswana will be only too happy to be photographed – provided you ask their permission first. Sign language is fine for this question: just point at your camera, shrug your shoulders, and look quizzical. The likelihood is that then everyone will smile for you, producing the type of 'posed' photograph that you may not want. However, stay around and chat for 5 or 10 minutes, and people will get used to your presence and stop posing; then you will get more natural shots (a camera with a quiet shutter is a help).

Note that special care is needed with photography near government buildings, bridges, mines, and similar sites of strategic importance. You must ask permission before photographing anything here, or you risk people thinking that you are a spy. (To be fair to the country, I've never come across such problems in Botswana, though I'd still exercise the same caution as in any other country.)

If you're seeking directions to somewhere, don't be afraid of **asking questions**. Most people will be polite and keen to help – so keen that some will answer 'yes' to questions if they think that this is what you want to hear. So try to avoid asking leading questions. For example, 'Yes' would often be the typical answer to the question, 'Does this road lead to … ?' And in a sense the respondent is probably correct – it will get you there. It's just that it may not be the quickest or shortest way. To avoid misunderstandings, it is often better to ask open-ended questions like, 'Where does this road go to?' or 'How do I drive to … ?'

The examples above are general by their very nature. But wherever you find yourself, if you are polite and considerate to the people of Botswana that you meet, then you will rarely encounter any cultural problems. Watch how they behave and, if you have any doubts about how you should act, then ask someone quietly. They will seldom tell you outright that you are being rude, but they will usually give you good advice on how to make your behaviour more acceptable.

or *setinkane*, like miniature xylophones made with sheets of scrap metal on a small wooden base, and once widely played.

Recently, there has been an explosion of musical influence from overseas, resulting in a more modern culture of hip-hop artists and performers of *kwasa-kwasa* – a suggestive dance form akin to the rumba.

Because he was a deeply committed Christian convert, Khama, the leader of the Bamangwato, began to make changes to the traditional way of life. He reformed the *bogadi* tradition, under which a woman's children belonged to her husband, even if they were born after his death. Khama also laid down laws and regulations for his people to live by, including banning the consumption of alcohol.

One of his most significant changes was the abolition of the initiation ceremonies for men and women. One elderly man described the men's initiation ceremony or *bogwera*:

> Not only was the foreskin cut and the youths put through endurance tests, but one of us had to remain behind. He was killed in a painful way, in the secrecy of the bush. When we came home, it was made out that the youth had died because he could not stand up to the tests. Everyone knew the truth but it was treated as a deep secret. That was why Khama abolished *bogwera*.

However, the ritual was still important to mark the passing of boyhood into manhood, so Khama preserved the tradition of 'age regiments'. All young men had their coming of age marked by a gathering with prayers and lectures. Those who came of age at the same time formed an age regiment. From Khama's time on, the age regiments began to volunteer to work on community projects such as building schools or churches and many things were accomplished.

It was also largely due to the efforts of Khama that Botswana became a British Protectorate, known as the British Bechuanaland Protectorate. This probably saved the country from becoming another South Africa or Rhodesia (Zimbabwe) and resulted in Botswana's peaceful independence in 1966.

ARTS AND CRAFTS While the ancient rock art of the Tsodilo Hills has gained international recognition, modern visual arts are much harder to find, at least outside of Gaborone, which is home to the National Museum and Art Gallery.

Visitors, however, should have no problem in finding examples of local crafts, especially basketwork. The tradition stems from items woven for practical purposes such as storing or winnowing grain. Most of these are produced by women from the Bayei and Hambukushu groups in northwest Botswana, where the *mokolwane* palm – source of the fibres for basket weaving – is widely grown. Now increasingly popular as souvenirs, these baskets can be deceptively complex in construction, something that is reflected in their costs. Many are plain, but others have intricate patterns woven into their design.

Clay pots also have their place in traditional culture, being used both for storing water and for brewing beer, as well as for cooking. In rural villages, such pots were moulded from natural clays, then baked in the sun to dry, but today most potteries use kilns to fire their work.

When the Protectorate was finally granted, Khama expressed his gratitude and laid down the following principles of government, in a document which related primarily to the Bamangwato, but was later applied to the whole country:

I am not baffled in the government of my town, or in deciding cases among my own people according to custom. I have to say that there are certain laws of my country which the Queen of England finds in operation, and which are advantageous to my people, and I wish these laws should be established and not taken away by the Government of England. I refer to our law concerning intoxicating drinks, that they should not enter the country of the Bamangwato, whether among black people or white people. I refer further to our law which declares that the lands of the Bamangwato are not saleable. I say this law is also good; let it be upheld and continue to be law among black people and white people.

The system of traditional law to which Khama referred in this document was well established. It centred upon the chief, whose position of prestige and power carried with it the obligation that the good of the tribe must be placed above personal desire. The chief held property and land on behalf of the tribe and had always to be available to his people to settle disputes and business affairs.

There was also a tribal court, known as a *kgotla*, to help him make decisions. This consisted of the headmen of the wards into which the village was divided, and of senior tribesmen. Disputes which could not be settled within the ward were brought to the kgotla. There was an obligation for people to be open in all their dealings with each other and to act in the best interests of the community.

SEND US YOUR SNAPS!

We'd love to follow your adventures using our *Botswana* guide – why not send us your photos and stories via Twitter (🐦 *@BradtGuides*) and Instagram (📷 *@bradtguides*) using the hashtag #botswana? Alternatively, you can upload your photos directly to the gallery on the Botswana destination page via our website (*www.bradtguides.com/botswana*).

5

Planning and Preparation

WHEN TO GO AND HIGHLIGHTS

There simply isn't one 'best time' to visit Botswana, or any of its wild areas. Most tourists visit during the dry season, from around May to the end of October. Within that season, the period from mid-July to mid-October is definitely the busiest – although Botswana's small camps/lodges and private reserves ensure that it never feels busy, even when everywhere is full. (In fact, the country's capacity for tourism remains tiny compared with that of South Africa, Kenya or Tanzania.)

Most of those visiting outside of this season are cognoscenti, who visit early or late in the season – May to July or late October to November – when the camps are quieter and often costs are lower.

A much smaller number of visitors come during the rains, from December to April, when camps will frequently be quiet for days. This often means that they will give visitors a much more personal experience, with private drives; their rates are often lower too, and they're usually far more flexible about bringing children on safari.

Much of the blame for this 'glut or famine' of visitors lies with overseas tour operators. Many who advertise trips here just don't know Botswana well enough to plan trips which work during the rainy season. It's much easier for them to make blanket generalisations, telling enquirers who don't know any better that it's 'not interesting' or that 'you won't see any game' if you visit in the wet season. None of this is true, as long as you choose your destinations carefully, but of course most people don't know this in advance.

While the rains are not the ideal time for everybody's trip, they are a fascinating time to visit and should not be dismissed without serious thought.

Here is some guidance on various issues to help you decide what the best time for your visit would be. However, one of the biggest reasons for coming to the Okavango – and you may only realise this once you've visited – is not the game or the birds. It's simply the whole general ambience of being able to float over lily-covered lagoons with the sun on your back and a gentle breeze in your hair. This is certainly best when the skies are fairly clear of clouds – from April to November.

WEATHER For a detailed description of the weather that can be expected, see the section on *Climate*, pages 11–13, and note that Botswana's rainy season normally occurs between December and April, with January and February usually being the wettest months.

Dry season (May to November) This is the easiest time to travel, as then you are unlikely to meet rain and can expect clear blue skies. This is ideal if this is your first trip to Africa, or if seeing lots of big game is top of your wish-list.

Within this, you'll find June–August the coolest, when night temperatures in the Kalahari can drop below freezing. Then from September onwards the heat gradually builds up. The interior areas of the Kalahari, including central Chobe and the great salt pans, get very hot towards the end of October. Occasions when it reaches over 40°C in the shade have earned this the tag of 'suicide month'.

That said, note that in the Okavango, where there are large areas of water and green vegetation, the extremes of temperature are much more pleasant and moderated: the nights in August never reaching freezing, and the days in October are never unbearable.

Everywhere November is a variable month. Some days will be hot. Some will be cooler, as gathering clouds shield the country from the sun. Sometimes these bring welcome showers; sometimes they simply build, and with them come tension and humidity.

Wet season From December to March, or even April, the scenario is totally different, although the days can still vary enormously from one to the next. Even within a day, skies can change from sunny to cloudy within minutes and then back again. Downpours are usually heavy and short – and usually late in the afternoon – although there are often a few days when the sky remains grey and overcast. You will need a good waterproof for the rainy season, but I've always felt that the rains are seldom long enough to stop you doing anything.

Having said this, on one February visit, the rain didn't ever seem to end, and the skies remained grey for days – so I should perhaps recant this. In fact, I take the view that Africa's weather is just becoming harder to predict, and I was unlucky!

TRAVELLING CONDITIONS Travelling around Botswana in the dry season often has its challenges, but in some places in the wet season it's a totally different game. Then

OKAVANGO FLOOD LEVELS

KEY
2016
2011
2009
2007
2005
2004
2002
1994
1992
1984

The Okavango River's flow rate, measured at Mohembo, in thousands of m³ per second

THE OKAVANGO'S ANNUAL FLOOD

This very complex variable is really a minor point for most visitors – who will find the Okavango Delta enchanting whenever they visit. However, the flooding levels will have some influence on certain activities, and may even influence your choice of where you want to visit in the Delta.

The water levels at any point in the Okavango Delta depend mainly on three variables: first, the local rainfall in your location; second, the height of the seasonal flood of the Okavango; and third, your location within the Delta – the further north you are in the Okavango, the more water you're likely to have.

The local summer rains and the arrival of the seasonal floods are generally out of sync by around two to six months, depending on exactly where you are within the Delta. This represents the time taken for the peak of the rains in the Okavango River's main catchment area – the Angolan highlands – to make it down the Okavango River and into the various areas of the Delta.

These annual floods have for years been monitored very carefully at Mohembo, where the river enters Botswana – see the graph opposite. From this we know that the peak of the flood at Mohembo generally occurs between mid-March and mid-May – just after the local summer rains in the region of the Delta have come to an end. Given the tiny gradient and very slow flow rate, this surge of water from Angola can take up to six months to work its way from the Panhandle to the far extremities of the Delta's waterways.

Hence expect the highest water levels in most areas of the Delta to occur after the rains – from about May to August. After that, levels will generally fall until around February, when the local rains start to slowly raise water levels prior to the main flood.

the areas of pure sand are still fine to drive on, and even a bit firmer than they are when it's hot and dry.

Driving yourself In some areas where the soil has a high clay content, the bush tracks become quagmires – the track from Rakops to the Central Kalahari Game Reserve's Matswere Gate near Kuke Corner is a fine example, as are most of the Makgadikgadi Pans. Some tracks, especially those in the Delta–Linyanti region, like the old route between Xakanaxa and North Gate, become submerged completely. Thus travel in Botswana during the wet season requires careful research, and scrupulous attention to your emergency precautions. If you're heading for somewhere remote in the wet season, then travelling with two or more vehicles is wise.

Flying around In contrast, the weather is seldom a problem if you're flying into one of Botswana's safari camps. All are used to the vagaries of the weather and the water levels, although they may affect your activities. Similarly, if you're heading out on a budget mokoro trip or safari, it shouldn't affect your trip significantly – though your vehicle may need the occasional push!

Although there are fewer visitors around during this period, Botswana's flight schedules don't change much, and only a few of its camps will close. (Many will close during this period for a few weeks of planned maintenance or any building work that's needed. Those that remain open are often very quiet – so if you've often

Ten years ago, taking children on safari in Botswana might have been considered unusual, but things are changing, and the country's lodges and camps haven't been slow to pick up on the trend.

The idea of taking a child on safari might at first seem obvious. You'll be out in a wilderness environment, with plenty of animals to watch, and seemingly non-stop entertainment. But that, of course, is part of the problem. The 'entertainment' cannot be guaranteed, so during a typical 3-hour game drive, there's often time when things that might fascinate you – colourful birds, the construction of a termite mound, last night's hyena tracks, even a(nother) herd of impala – will be of little interest to a child. And when big game is spotted, instead of being able to leap up and down with excitement, your child is expected to be absolutely quiet and still. Then there's the often unspoken concern of a sensitive child witnessing a kill.

Add to this the rather exclusive make-up of many safari camps, the safety issues within camp (dangerous wildlife, high walkways and unguarded pools being just a few), and the lack of opportunity for letting off steam, and the considerations mount up.

So how can it work? Although many lodges still maintain a very adult atmosphere, designating a high minimum age for children, several offer some form of 'family' accommodation. Sometimes that's simply a room with an extra bed or two, rather than anything particularly child-friendly; at others, it's a suite of rooms, either sharing a bathroom or with each of them en suite, and occasionally with their own lounge area. One or two lodges, such as the Shinde Enclave and Linyanti Ebony, have a group of tents or chalets that are slightly separate from the main camp, so work particularly well for families. And more specifically, a handful of places – including Khwai Tented Camp – have built entirely separate houses that are exceptionally well suited to families, with space to run around, and your own chef so that you can eat at times that suit your family rather than other guests. Mealtimes in many lodges can be a trial for children, though some will prepare meals early, so that you can dine with other guests while a member of staff (albeit not a qualified childminder) babysits for you. Another option is private family dining, at a time to suit you.

Even when lodges do accept families, many insist that those with children under, say, eight years old reserve a private vehicle and guide. If this at first seems draconian, consider too that this is for the benefit of the children, as well as for other guests. With your own guide, you select where you stop and spend time, and if your children

been to Africa in the dry season, then this is a fascinating time to visit – like being introduced to a different side of an old friend.)

VEGETATION During the wet season, the foliage runs wild. The Kalahari springs into life as the bush turns many shades of green. Open clay pans become small pools in the bush and it's a time of renewal, when a gentler light dapples Botswana's bush.

When the rains end, the leaves in the Kalahari gradually dry and many eventually drop. More greys and browns appear, and good shade becomes harder to find. Eventually, by late September and October, most plants look dry and parched, coloured from straw yellow to shrivelled brown.

However, note that large areas of the Okavango have their own permanent water supply – regulated more by the annual floods than the rainfall – and so don't follow this pattern so clearly. See box, page 115.

want to ask questions, that's fine. At camps run by Kwando Safaris, you can organise a specialist guide who will travel with your family and will even keep children occupied during siesta time – which can otherwise be particularly challenging. You'll need to book a private vehicle (from US$220 per day for a family of four at Kwando, but rising to a steep US$600 plus at some camps), and a specialist guide will cost a further US$300 per day, but your safari experience will be considerably enhanced.

Several camps accept quite young children but insist on a minimum age, for safety reasons, before a child can go on a mokoro trip or bush walk. The smaller camps, such as Motswiri, can often be more flexible here, with guides who will assess the maturity of individual children rather than applying a one-size-fits-all age limit. Other camps, such as those owned by Wilderness Safaris, tend to apply the 'rules' more strictly.

Putting children at the heart of safaris, Ker & Downey have a three-day Young Explorers safari for children of seven or older. Based at Shinde Enclave or Footsteps Camp, a specially trained guide will be allocated to your family, focusing on the children both on safari and back in camp – though that doesn't include childminding. He/she can also accompany you to other Ker & Downey camps, including Okuti, thus broadening the experience for all. Depending on the ages of the children, activities might include making bows and arrows, fishing, bushcraft and quizzes – but the odd game of football or frisbee could also be thrown in. The key here is entertainment – bored children are the bane of everyone's life on safari, so be aware that if you opt for a conventional trip, you will need to take plenty to occupy your offspring when in camp.

A couple of other options can widen the choice. The first is to base yourself in a family-friendly hotel in Kasane, where you'll be rewarded with plenty of wildlife on game drives and boat trips into Chobe National Park without feeling cooped up the rest of the time. The other is to opt for a mobile safari, where children are less likely to feel restrained, and will probably relish the camping element. Four that spring to mind in Maun are Harkness Safaris and Barclay Stenner Safaris, both of whom are very child-friendly, Endeavour Safaris, which has no age restrictions; and Letaka Safaris, who have a special two-bedroom family tent with a lockable entrance, so you and your children will be secure under one roof – something that is particularly reassuring with younger age groups. Then, with your children both happy and safe, you can get on with enjoying a family safari.

GAME From the point of view of most herbivores, the wet season is much more pleasant than the dry season. During the wet season, most animals live in enormous salad bowls, with convenient pools of water nearby. It's a good time to have their young and eat themselves into good condition.

Visitors who have been to Africa before will often find something special about seeing all the animals when they aren't struggling with thirst and a lack of vegetation. It gives a sense of luxuriance and plenty, which isn't there in the dry season.

Migration patterns Before people started to have a big impact on Botswana's landscape (arguably, only in the last 150 years or so), many of the animals used to follow regular seasonal migration patterns, often over very large distances. It was the same throughout Africa originally; many species, especially the herding species of plains game, would move around to where the best food sources were to be found.

Despite the changes wreaked by man since then, the remnants of these migrations still happen. Understanding them will help you to work out what the best times are to visit the various parks – so first read the section on *Game migrations* on pages 24–5 for detailed comments.

The finer details of each area are covered under sections entitled *When to go*, which are spread throughout the book, but in very general terms:

Chobe Areas with riverfront are at their best during July–October. Traditionally, the Savuti Marsh area is totally different, with some good game all year, but probably at its best around March–May and (if the rains have arrived) November – when herds of zebra and plains game are passing through.

Kwando/Linyanti Follows the same basic pattern as Chobe's riverfronts – so it is best in the late dry season, when it's the only source of water for miles around.

Okavango/Moremi The central areas of the Delta have permanent water all year, and equally permanent populations of animals. Thus many game species stay here all year, and densities of animals (excluding elephant and buffalo) don't change that much. However, in the dry season the permanent populations of game found on the edges of the Delta are swelled by an influx of animals from the parched Kalahari. Thus, the game densities on the accessible edges of the Delta often rise significantly as the dry season progresses.

Nxai Pan Can be erratic, but always used to be at its best when wet, from December to March – though often still very good into May and June. However, the artificial pumping of a waterhole a couple of kilometres north of the gate has changed this pattern. During the rest of the year, you'll find plains game staying here in numbers, often accompanied by a few lion.

Makgadikgadi Pans The pans themselves can be superb when wet, December to April; large herds of zebra and other plains grazers appear. On their western border, the Boteti River (or its channel) follows the opposite pattern, attracting game at the end of the dry season, around August to early November.

Central Kalahari Game congregates in the huge grassy valleys here, most famously in Deception Valley, when the vegetation is lush during and shortly after the rains, from about December to May.

Seasonal highlights
The bottom line is probably that if game viewing is your overriding priority, or this is one of your first trips to Africa, then you'll be better visiting during the dry season. Then the animals are much easier to spot, as no thick vegetation obscures the view, and they are forced to congregate at well-known water points, like rivers, where they can be observed.

However, more experienced African travellers are missing out if they never travel during the rains – as it's completely different and can be superb. A few specific highlights of Botswana's animal calendar would include:

February–April Most of the herbivores are in their best condition, having fed well on the lush vegetation. It's a perfect time to catch huge concentrations of springbok and oryx on the short grass plains of the Central Kalahari's fossil river valleys.

May–June Probably my favourite time to be in Botswana (and most of southern Africa!). It's a great time to visit Savuti Marsh, and in the Okavango the floodwater moves down the Delta.

July–August Leopard are generally easier to see, as they come out more during the twilight hours. Further into the year, they often wait until it is cool, only appearing later in the evening.

September–October Elephant and buffalo tend to amalgamate into larger, more spectacular herds. (They splinter again just before the rains.) Lion sights become more frequent, as they spend more time near the limited remaining water sources.

November Can be a great month as often the rains haven't arrived, leaving amazing game densities in the riverfront areas (yet visitors are thin on the ground and prices are low). However, too many cloudless days can mean high midday temperatures.

December–January Crocodiles are nesting, and so found on or near exposed sandbanks. Various baby animals start to appear in November, followed by most of the mammals that calve sometime during the rainy season.

BIRDLIFE The birdlife in Botswana is certainly best when the foliage is most dense, and the insects are thriving, ie: in the wet season. Then many resident birds are nesting and in their bright, breeding plumage. This coincides to a large extent with the 'summer' period, from around October to March, when the Palaearctic migrants from the northern hemisphere are seen.

To give you an idea of the richness of the avifauna here, in the Okavango–Linyanti–Chobe areas during the rainy season it isn't difficult for competent ornithologists to record 100 different species between dawn and midday. Really energetic birdwatchers can notch up as many as 200 different species in a 24-hour period in somewhere as rich as the northern Chobe riverfront area. A real enthusiast might count about 320 species (out of the 550 or so which occur) during a two-week trip here.

Birding highlights The highlights of Botswana's birding calendar include:

March–July Wattled cranes and other opportunists follow the floods in the Okavango, snapping up drowning insects and reptiles.

August–October 'Fishing parties' of herons, egrets and storks will arrive at pools as they dry up, to feed on the stranded fish.

September–November Nesting carmine bee-eaters colonise soft vertical riverbanks, skimmers nest on exposed sandbanks, and large breeding colonies of storks and herons gather at places like the Kanana heronry and Gcodikwe Lagoon. Migrant waders appear beside the edge of most pans and lagoons.

November–April Most of the weavers are in breeding plumage.

February–April Red bishop birds, yellow-billed storks and the spectacular paradise whydahs have their breeding plumage on display. If the rains have been good then the flamingos may be nesting on Sua Pan; ostriches gather in numbers on the pans of the Central Kalahari.

April–June Juvenile birds of many species abound as this season's young are fledged and leave their nests.

PHOTOGRAPHY

I find the light clearest and most spectacular during the rainy season. Then the rains have washed the dust from the air, and the bright sunlight can contrast wonderfully with dark storm clouds. The vegetation's also greener and brighter, and the animals and birds often in better condition. However, it will rain occasionally when you're trying to take shots, and the long periods of flat, grey light through clouds can be very disappointing; you'll get few good shots then. Sometimes it can seem as if you're waiting for the gods to grant you just a few minutes of stunning light, between the clouds.

A much more practical time to visit is just after the rains, around April to June, when many of the advantages remain but you are less likely to be interrupted by a shower. (This is one of my reasons for being a fan of May as a great time to travel!)

The dry season's light is reliably good, if not quite as inspirational as that found during the rains. You are unlikely to encounter any clouds, and will get better sightings of game to photograph. Do try to shoot in the first and last few hours of the day, when the sun is low in the sky. During the rest of the day use a filter (perhaps a polariser) to guard against the sheer strength of the light leaving you with a memory card full of washed-out shots.

During the hotter months around October, you're also likely to encounter more bush fires than normal, which can leave a thin pall of smoke covering a large area. (This can especially be a problem near the border area with Namibia, when smoke from the many manmade fires there can drift across.)

WALKING SAFARIS

For safe and interesting walking, you need the foliage to be low so that you can see through the surrounding bush as easily as possible. This means that the dry season is certainly the best time for walking – and even then I'd counsel you to choose where you visit very, very carefully as standards of walking guides can be highly variable. (See my comments on the safety of walking safaris on pages 187–91.)

I wouldn't advise anyone looking for a serious walking trip to visit Botswana in the wet season. Walking through shoulder-high grass is nerve-racking with the best of walking guides, and only two or three operations in Botswana are really likely to have anything like that calibre of guide. The best months for walking are May to October, though away from the moderating influence of the Okavango's waters, October can be very hot for longer walks.

COSTS OF TRIPS

Aside from the airfares to get here, which vary in their own way (pages 137–8), some safari operators also lower their rates when business is quieter. Generally July to October is the peak season when prices are highest; January and February is the green season when prices are lowest, and the rest of the year falls somewhere in between.

PUBLIC HOLIDAYS

Botswana's public holidays are as follows:

1 January	New Year's Day
2 January	
March/April	Good Friday and Easter Monday
1 May	Labour Day
Thursday in May/early June	Ascension Day

1 July	Sir Seretse Khama Day
3rd Monday and Tuesday in July	President's Day
30 September	Botswana Day
1st Monday in October	
25 December	Christmas Day
26 December	Boxing Day

ORGANISING AND BOOKING YOUR TRIP

How you organise your holiday depends on what kind of a trip you're taking. Generally the more expensive the trip, the more organisation it needs.

ORGANISING A FLY-IN TRIP Most tourists who come to Botswana for a few weeks' safari fly between a series of remote safari camps; this is by far the easiest and most popular way to visit the country. Combinations of the Okavango Delta, and the Kwando–Linyanti and Chobe areas are most common, with relatively few people venturing further south or west into the Kalahari.

When to book? These trips are not difficult to arrange for a knowledgeable tour operator. If you have a favourite camp or operation, or will be running to a tight schedule, then book as far ahead as you can. Eight to ten months in advance is perfect. Bear in mind that most camps are small, and thus easily filled. They organise their logistics with military precision and so finding space at specific camps at short notice, especially in the busier months, can be tricky.

Unless you're lucky, or book very early, expect one or two of your chosen camps to be full. Usually there will be good alternatives available. That said, it's fairly rare for visitors to have a really bad time in any of the upmarket camps in Botswana, as standards are generally high – so don't be put off just because your first choice isn't immediately available.

The exception to this is usually the rainy season – when camps often close for maintenance for a few weeks; those that do stay open, however, are seldom full.

How much? Safaris in Botswana are not cheap. The standards for an average fly-in safari camp are high, but so are the prices. For the most part, expect to pay around US$630–1,780 per person sharing per night in the high season, between June and October, but note that the very top camps will cost substantially more: up to US$3,000 per person. This will include all meals, most drinks, laundry, activities and local drinks. Light aircraft transfers from Maun to the camps average around US$200 per person one-way.

Depending on the particular camps, April, May and November should cost less. At this time of year, expect something nearer US$465–2,265 per person sharing per night – which again includes everything except internal (and international) flights. Prices in the wet season are generally lower (the exception being the camps in the Kalahari); then a rough cost of US$350–1,930 per person sharing per night should be quite realistic.

If you stay for a longer spell with some camps (and 'longer' can mean anything from three to seven nights), or groups of camps, then these rates will drop slightly; if you fly between camps every day or two, only spending one or two nights at each camp (not recommended) then they'll rise.

These trips are expensive, so you should expect a good level of service and knowledge from the operator who is arranging it for you. If you don't get it, go elsewhere.

How to book? It's best to arrange everything at the same time, using a reliable, independent tour operator. Many operators sell trips to Botswana, but few know the country and the camps well. Insist on dealing directly with someone who does. Botswana's areas, camps and lodges do change, so up-to-date local knowledge is vital in putting together a trip that runs smoothly and suits you.

Booking directly with the Botswana companies is possible, but piecing together a jigsaw of complex transfers and flights can be tricky, and you will have little recourse if anything goes wrong. By contrast, UK and European operators are bonded, so your money is protected if they go broke. (If you're still nervous, pay with a credit card.) Remember, too, that the safari companies are primarily interested in selling space at their own camps and lodges – regardless of whether or not these are the best camps for you, so it's wise to seek out an independent operator. Indeed, most of the bigger groups of camps and lodges work largely with the overseas travel trade, which has special contracts with them. And as if to reinforce the point, many of these groups make it clear on their websites that they don't accept direct bookings, and that these should be made through a specialist travel agent or tour operator. So, paradoxically, the best way of booking a fly-in safari in Botswana is usually by arranging it many months prior to your trip through a specialist tour operator based outside Africa.

European, US and other overseas operators usually work on commission for the trips that they sell, which is deducted from the basic cost that the visitor pays. Perhaps because of the UK's historical links, or the high number of British safari-goers, there seems to be more competition among UK tour operators than elsewhere. Hence they've a reputation for being generally cheaper than US operators for the same trips – and the best usually work out much cheaper than similar trips booked directly.

Which tour operator? Botswana looks on the surface like an easy country to sell, and you'll find scores of brochures that feature a trip or two there. Many will include only camps from one local operator – perhaps using only Wilderness Safaris, or only &Beyond camps, or visiting nothing but Desert & Delta places. This is a really bad sign, as no one operator in Botswana has a monopoly of the best camps.

However, start asking detailed questions about the alternatives and you'll rapidly sort the best from the rest. Don't let anyone convince you that there are only half-a-dozen decent safari camps in Botswana; that's rubbish. If the person you're talking to hasn't been to the camps that you are interested in – or doesn't offer a genuinely wide choice to suit you – then find someone who does.

Here I must, as the author, admit a personal interest in the tour-operating business. I organise and personally run the UK operators Expert Africa (see opposite) and Wild about Africa (page 124). We are currently one of the leading tour operators to Botswana – based on my team's detailed personal knowledge of the country. We organise trips for travellers to Africa from all over the world, especially the UK and America. Our website has detailed original maps, extensive reviews from many of our travellers, and fully costed trips that include the widest choice of Botswana lodges and camps.

The best Botswana operators are specialists. Their brochures and websites will have unique pictures that you won't find elsewhere, cliché-free text that isn't copied from other websites, and staff who can talk to you from first-hand experience about the camps that interest you. You'll always get the best advice (and the best chance of problem-free trips) from people who know the places that you're thinking of going to personally.

International tour operators featuring Botswana include the following – and note that several of the UK operators have offices in the USA and elsewhere. Whoever you book through, make sure first that the company has in place a 'bond' to protect your money in case they go bust. The most usual form of this in the UK is the ATOL licence; if a company doesn't have one of these, then question them very carefully indeed. All the companies below have good track records, and currently have ATOL bonds for your protection.

UK tour operators

Aardvark Safaris Aspire Business Centre, Ordnance Rd, Tidworth, Hants SP9 7QD; 01980 849160; e mail@aardvarksafaris.com; www. aardvarksafaris.co.uk. Small upmarket operator with good knowledge of Botswana.

Abercrombie & Kent St George's Hse, Ambrose St, Cheltenham, Glos GL50 3LG; 01242 386500; e info@abercrombiekent.co.uk; www. abercrombiekent.co.uk. Large, long-established posh operator worldwide, with a wide choice of Africa trips. (Note that Botswana's Sanctuary Retreats is under the same ownership.)

Audley Travel New Mill, New Mill Lane, Witney, Oxon 0448 9SX; 01993 838000; e africa-botswana@audleytravel.com; www.audleytravel. com. Specialist tailor-made operator with worldwide coverage including Botswana.

Botswana Specialists The Old Dairy, Wood Farm, Ipswich Rd, Otley, Suffolk IP6 9JW; 01473 599083; e info@botswanaspecialists.co.uk; www. botswanaspecialists.co.uk. Tribes Travel offer a selection of trips worldwide based on strong fair-trade principles; this new brand is an alternative way to book their Botswana trips. See ad, page 112.

Cazenove & Loyd Argon Mews, Fulham Broadway, London SW6 1BJ; 020 7384 2332; e enquiries@cazloyd.com; www.cazloyd.com. Posh operator with tailor-made trips worldwide. Good local knowledge & service; high price tag.

Cox & Kings 30 Millbank, London SW1P 4EE; 020 3813 9287; e info@coxandkings.co.uk; www.coxandkings.co.uk. Long-established operator famed for its Indian trips. More recent programmes worldwide, include fly-in trips to Botswana.

Drive Botswana 34 Birch Valley Rd, Stoke-on-Trent ST7 4GN; 0161 408 4316/7, +267 492 1824 (Botswana); e info@drivebotswana.com; www. drivebotswana.com; this company also has an office in Botswana, specialising in fully inclusive tailor-made self-drive safaris, primarily in fully equipped Toyota Land Cruisers. See ad, inside-back cover.

Expert Africa 9 & 10 Upper Sq, Old Isleworth, Middx TW7 7BJ; 020 3405 6666; e info@expert.africa; www.expert.africa. A team of enthusiastic Africa experts run by Chris McIntyre – this book's author. I believe we have the best range of fly-in & mobile-safari trips to Botswana! See ads, pages 1 & 344.

The Explorations Company Fraser Hse, Southrop, Glos GL7 3NR; 01367 850566; e info@africanexplorations.com; www. explorationscompany.com. Old-school operator, formerly known as African Explorations, now working worldwide.

Gane & Marshall 01822 600600; e info@ ganeandmarshall.com; www.ganeandmarshall. com. Long-established travel company. See ad, page 112.

Hartley's Safaris The Old Chapel, Chapel Lane, Hackthorn, Lincs LN2 3PN; 01673 861600; e info@hartleysgroup.com; www.hartleys-safaris. co.uk. Established tailor-made specialists to East/ southern Africa & Indian Ocean islands, with close historical connections to Botswana.

Journeys Discovering Africa 0800 088 5470, +1 888 428 2772 (USA); e enquiries@ journeysdiscoveringafrica.com; www. journeysdiscoveringafrica.com. UK company with well-established operations in Uganda & Rwanda now offering trips to southern Africa, inc Botswana. See ad, 3rd colour section.

Original Travel 1st Flr, 111 Upper Richmond Rd, London SW15 2TL; 020 7978 7333; e ask@ originaltravel.co.uk; www.originaltravel.co.uk. Upmarket worldwide company incorporating the former Tim Best Travel – & including top-end fly-in lodges in Botswana.

Rainbow Tours 2 Waterhouse Sq, 138–140 Holborn, London EC1N 2ST; 0207 666 1276; e info@rainbowtours.co.uk; www.rainbowtours. co.uk. Established Africa specialists, now part of the Western & Oriental Group, with a varied Botswana programme. See ad, inside-front cover.

Safari Consultants Africa Hse, 2 Cornard Mills, Mill Tye, Gt Cornard, Suffolk CO10 0GW; 01787

888590; e info@safari-consultants.com; www.
safari-consultants.com. Very old-school tailor-
made specialists to East/southern Africa & Indian
Ocean with a competent Botswana programme.
See ad, page 70.

Safari Drive Trainer's Office, Windy Hollow,
Sheepdrove, Lambourn, Berks RG17 7XA; \01488
71140; e info@safaridrive.com; www.safaridrive.
com. Specialist African operator with 1st-class
knowledge of Botswana, concentrating on self-drive
trips using their own well-equipped Land Rovers &
Toyota Land Cruisers. See ad, 3rd colour section.

Steppes Africa 51 Castle St, Cirencester,
Glos GL7 1QD; \01285 601750; e enquiry@
steppestravel.co.uk; www.steppestravel.co.uk.
Posh tailor-made specialist covering destinations
including central, eastern & southern Africa.

Ultimate Travel Company 25–27 Vanston Pl,
London SW6 1AZ; \020 3131 5588; e enquiry@
theultimatetravelcompany.co.uk; www.
theultimatetravelcompany.co.uk. Wide-ranging
operator including central, eastern & southern
Africa among their destinations.

Wild about Africa Sunvil Hse, Upper Sq, Old
Isleworth, Middx TW7 7BJ; \020 3495 6655;
e safari@wildabout.africa; www.wildabout.
africa. A sister company of Expert Africa that
focuses on private trips led by top wildlife
guides & exclusive camps for the most
discerning travellers.

Wildlife Worldwide Sutton Manor Farm,
Bishop Sutton, Hants SO24 0AA; \01962 302086;
e reservations@wildlifeworldwide.com; www.
wildlifeworldwide.com. Worldwide operator
offering tailor-made & small-group wildlife
holidays to all corners of the globe.

Zambezi Safari & Travel 6 Delamore Pk,
Pitman's Lane, Cornwood, Devon PL21 9QP;
\01752 878858; e info@zambezi.com;
www.zambezi.com. Specialist safari planners
concentrating on East, central & southern Africa.

Other tour operators
USA/Canada

Adventure Travel Desk (ATD) 308
Commonwealth Av, Wayland, MA 01778; \0800
552 0300; e atd@african-safari.com; www.african-
safari.com

The Africa Adventure Company 2601
E Oakland Park Bd, Suite 600, Fort Lauderdale,
FL 33306; \0800 882 9453; e safari@
africanadventure.com; www.africanadventure.
com. See ad, 3rd colour section.

Ker & Downey 6703 Highway Bd, Katy, TX
77494; \0800 423 4236; e info@kerdowney.com;
www.kerdowney.com

Overseas Adventure Travel 1 Mifflin Pl, Suite
400, Cambridge, MA 02138; \0800 955 1925;
www.oattravel.com. Members-only organisation
who run group trips for 10–16 participants aged
over 50.

Australia

The Classic Safari Company 124A Queen
St, Woollahra, NSW 2025; \+61 2 9327 0666;
e info@classicsafaricompany.com.au; www.
classicsafaricompany.com.au

South Africa

Drifters \+27 11 888 1160; e drifters@drifters.
co.za; www.drifters.co.za. Specialists in overland trips.

Jenman African Safaris \+27 21 683 7826;
e info@jenmansafaris.com; www.jenmansafaris.
com. Family-run company with a wide range of
options. See ad, 3rd colour section.

Pulse Africa \+27 11 325 2290; e info@
pulseafrica.com; www.pulseafrica.com. Tailor-
made trips to Africa & the Indian Ocean.

France

Makila Voyages 4 place de Valois, 75001 Paris;
\+33 1 42 96 80 00; www.makila.fr

Suggested fly-in itineraries
Most fly-in trips to Botswana last between ten
days and three weeks, and are often limited more by travellers' available budgets
than anything else. The Okavango Delta, Kwando–Linyanti and Chobe areas
are the most common destinations, but the Central Kalahari, Nxai Pan and the
Makgadikgadi Pans also have their own landing strips and are sometimes added on
to the start or end of trips.

Less commonly, it's quite possible to plan a trip that's part mobile or self-
drive, followed by a few days of relative luxury at a fly-in camp or two (usually in
the Delta).

Concentrating on the fly-in element, the key to an interesting fly-in trip is variation: making sure that the different camps that you visit really are different. For me this means that they're in different environments and have different activities. So mix deep-water camps with shallow-water ones, and forested areas with open ones. That way you'll not only have the greatest variety of scenery, of which there's a lot in the Delta, but also see the widest variety of game.

I also prefer to mix camps run by different companies – one from Wilderness, one from &Beyond and one from Kwando, for example. I find that this makes a more interesting trip than staying at camps which are all run by the same company (sometimes in predictably similar styles).

When flying in, the costs of visiting the camps in the parks are very similar to the costs of those in the private concessions. Because of the ability to do night drives, to drive off-road, and (sometimes) to go walking, I generally prefer to use camps in private areas. Hence I've included relatively few of the camps which are inside the parks here.

For most trips, if you work on spending around three nights at each camp that you visit, that's ideal. Four would be lovely, though often visitors haven't got that much time (or money), whereas two nights is OK for some camps, but a fraction too short for most.

Here I'll give you a few ideas for combinations of areas that I think work well together, giving a real variation to trips. These are **not** lists of my all-time favourite camps; I have deliberately chosen not to pick out just my favourites (simply because the type of camps that I love – the simpler, smaller ones with their emphasis on guiding and wildlife – may not be so ideal for you). Instead, these are trips in which I think the various areas, camps and experiences go well together – and demonstrate what I mean about varying the areas that you stay in and the companies that you use.

Livingstone, Kwando–Linyanti and Okavango Delta: 11 nights/ 12 days
- 2 nights Livingstone, a hotel or lodge
- 3 nights Linyanti Bush Camp, CH1 – riverine areas with a balance of dry and wet areas
- 3 nights Kwara, NG20 – for deep-water motorboat trips plus some game viewing in areas of denser vegetation
- 3 nights Kwetsani, NG25 – for picturesque shallow-water mokoro trips, plus some game viewing in open floodplains

Livingstone, Kwando–Linyanti, Okavango and the Pans: 15 nights/ 16 days
- 2 nights Livingstone, a hotel or lodge
- 3 nights Lagoon, NG15 – dry-land game viewing in mostly riverine forest
- 4 nights Vumbura, NG20 – for some deep-water, some shallow-water mokoro trips, and some game viewing in an open floodplain environment
- 3 nights Sandibe, NG31 – for game viewing in a more forested environment
- 3 nights Jack's Camp – something totally different on the great salt pans

Just the Okavango Delta: 8 nights/9 days
- 3 nights Xakanaxa Camp, Moremi – for dry-land game viewing
- 2 nights Xugana, NG21 – transfer from Xakanaxa for deep-water trips
- 3 nights Nxabega, NG31 – for shallow-water trips and game viewing

Gordon Rattray (🐦@gordonrattray), updated by Endeavour Safaris

For wheelchair users and people who have difficulties walking, Botswana is a relatively accessible safari destination. It is possible to book through a specialised operator and be sure that your needs are met, or to do enough preparation in advance and travel independently. Either way, with some endeavour, everybody can experience the unique highlights this country has to offer.

TRANSPORT

Air travel Most international travellers arrive via Johannesburg, where the services and facilities for disabled people rival and sometimes better those in Europe. Air Botswana and Airlink connect Johannesburg with Maun, but limited cargo space on this route means that they do not always allow heavy chairs; it's important to notify them in advance of the dimensions and weight of your wheelchair to ensure that it will be loaded. In Maun, the current airport terminal has an aisle chair, the staff are extremely efficient and there is a spacious (albeit not officially wheelchair-accessible) toilet. Once the airport is rebuilt, it's hoped that facilities will improve.

The shorter flights from Maun into the Okavango Delta, Moremi Game Reserve, etc, are also quite possible; when I went, the pilot helped lift me first on to the plane floor and then on to my seat, and there was room to stow my wheelchair with the luggage. However, these planes are small so a folding wheelchair and soft baggage are essential. Also, do note that airfields in the Delta are usually just a landing strip with few other facilities, and if an aisle chair is needed in Kasane, this should be ordered from Gaborone in advance.

By road Safari vehicles in Botswana are often 4x4, and therefore higher than normal cars. This means that – unless you use a specialised operator with adapted cars and a hydraulic lift or manual ramps – wheelchair transfers may be more difficult. My advice is to thoroughly explain your needs and always stay in control of the situation.

It is possible to hire self-drive vehicles, but I know of no company providing cars that are adapted for disabled drivers.

Distances are large and roads are often bumpy, so if you are prone to skin damage you may need to take extra care. Place your own pressure-relieving cushion on top of (or instead of) the original car seat and, if necessary, pad around knees and elbows.

There is no effective legislation in Botswana to help facilitate disabled travellers' journeys by bus.

ACCOMMODATION In **Maun**, both Island Safari Lodge (page 208) and Thamalakane River Lodge (pages 206–7) have two chalets with roll-in showers; Maun Lodge (page 207) has two rooms with roll-in shower but both have a 15cm step to enter the rooms; Cresta Riley's (page 207) has one step-free room with a bath, and the new Cresta Maun (page 207) has one room with a roll-in shower.

In **Kasane,** Mowana Safari Resort & Spa (page 238) and Chobe Marina Lodge (page 237) have adapted rooms; Chobe Bush Lodge (pages 238–9) has two rooms with roll-in showers accessible by ramp, and Chobe Safari Lodge (page 239) has two rooms with roll-in showers; and Chobe Game Lodge (page 267) has two rooms with roll-in showers. Bakwena Lodge (page 237) also has two rooms with roll-in outside showers, but you'll need a plank to access the shower and the toilet space is very limited.

There are several lodges and camps in the **Okavango Delta** that have a degree of accessibility, depending on your needs. Motswiri (page 304) has a spacious tent designed for wheelchair users, with handles and a roll-in shower, but is accessible only by air in small Cessna planes. Other camps are accessible by road: Savute Safari Lodge (page 288), which has one tent with a ramp, roll-in shower and plenty of manoeuvring space; Okuti (pages 326–7), which is in general very accessible for wheelchair users, with very spacious rooms and level-entry showers, although the doors accessing the bathroom and shower room are quite tight; and Camp Xakanaxa (page 326), which has ramps to access the main area and roll-in showers in the rooms, but no space next to the toilet for a wheelchair. In the Khwai area, Machaba Camp (page 320) has a spacious tent designed for wheelchair users, with handrails and a roll-in shower. **Outside the Delta**, Leroo La Tau Lodge (page 483), has a tent with a ramp, roll-in shower and plenty of manoeuvring space; and Dinaka Safari Lodge (page 504) has a tent with ramp and roll-in shower, though details could change following refurbishments in 2017.

In Zambia's **Livingstone**, the Royal Livingstone and Avani Victoria Falls Resort hotels (page 517) each have two highly adapted rooms.

HEALTH AND SAFETY In general, doctors will know about 'everyday' illnesses, but you must understand and be able to explain your own particular medical requirements. Rural clinics are often basic so, if possible, take all necessary medication and equipment with you. It is advisable to pack this in your hand luggage during flights in case your main luggage is delayed.

It's well worth taking out membership of Okavango Air Rescue (*www. okavangorescue.com*), which has a medically staffed and equipped helicopter with an emergency doctor for the Okavango Delta and the Kalahari.

Botswana can be extremely hot. If this is a problem for you, be careful to book accommodation with fans or air conditioning. A useful cooling aid is a plant-spray bottle.

Security For anyone following the usual security precautions (page 175) the chances of robbery are greatly reduced. In fact, as a disabled person I often feel more 'noticed', and therefore a less attractive target for thieves. But the opposite may also apply, so do stay aware of where your bags are and who is around you, especially during car transfers and similar activities.

SPECIALIST TOUR OPERATORS
Endeavour Safaris (pages 225–6) The leader in disability travel in Botswana with custom-designed mobile-camping equipment, several adapted vehicles, & the option of boating safaris in the Delta.

FURTHER INFORMATION
www.gov.uk/guidance/foreign-travel-for-disabled-people General information about travelling for people with disabilities.
www.rollingrains.com A searchable website advocating disability travel.
www.youreable.com A UK-based general resource for disability information, with an active forum.

After reading this book you'll realise there are so many possibilities that you'd be wise to talk through your wishes with someone who knows the camps and can work out what's best for you.

ORGANISING A BUDGET OR BACKPACKING TRIP If you're backpacking then usually you're more restricted by money than by time. Many of the side-trips and safaris that you take will be organised at the time, on the ground – and trying to do too much in advance might be counter-productive.

So, read the book, and head off. Start by heading towards Maun or Kasane, keeping your eyes open and talking to people you meet to see what's going on. And enjoy! Much of the joy is the unpredictability of these trips; if you want everything fixed and arranged then backpacking isn't really for you!

ORGANISING A MOBILE SAFARI Mobile trips in Botswana range from cheap-and-cheerful budget safaris to absolutely top-class operations running privately guided trips for small family groups. Thus generalising among them is difficult, although levels of comfort vary. Typically, the cheapest are dubbed 'participation' safaris (where you pitch your own tent and muck in with all the chores). Then there's 'semi-participation', where you'll help – perhaps just pitching your own tent – but staff will be on hand; and 'non-participation' or 'fully serviced' – where the staff will do everything for you. As a general rule, the more they cost, the further in advance they should be booked. (For an indication of costs, see page 142.) The cheaper ones often survive on last-minute bookings from people who turn up; the more costly private ones can be booked up years in advance. Many safari companies are members of HATAB (Hospitality & Tourism Association of Botswana) and/or the Botswana Guides Association (BOGA), both of which have their own campsites that are reserved exclusively for tour operators.

Ideally, talk to someone who has been on safari with the mobile operator that you're considering before booking with them. If this isn't possible then don't hesitate to ask a lot of questions before you decide which trip is right for you. You'll be stuck with your guide and group for a week or more, so it's vital to make the right choice.

Most of these companies are based in Maun (pages 223–7), with only a few elsewhere – like Kasane. The best often have overseas tour operators who know them well, and will sell their trips at around the same price (or even cheaper) than they do directly.

ORGANISING A SELF-DRIVE TRIP Describing the roads in Botswana is like describing Dr Jekyll and Mr Hyde. The tarred main routes, and most of the roads in the towns, can be beautifully smooth roads with excellent signposts. They're often delightfully free of traffic: a dream to drive on. They're eminently suitable to potter around in a normal 2x4 such as a Toyota Corolla or VW Golf.

However, the tracks through the national parks and more remote areas can become nightmares. Inexperienced or badly prepared drivers will find themselves seriously challenged, with deep sand in the dry season, and glutinous mud when it's wet – often compounded by a complete lack of signposts or directions.

If you want to hire a self-drive vehicle for your trip, then you must treat Botswana's two personas very differently. Your biggest decision is your vehicle, as this will make or break the experience.

Hiring a 2x4 If you are sticking to the towns and tar roads then hire a 2x4 from one of the normal hire companies – Avis, Bidvest or Europcar would be the obvious three.

Contacting them directly, a medium-sized saloon (Group C) for about two weeks will cost you around US$50 per day, including 'super' CDW (collision damage waiver; page 130) insurance cover and unlimited mileage, but excluding 12% VAT. (See *Car hire* in the chapters on Maun and Kasane for the relevant contact details.)

Hiring a 4x4 If you want to explore Botswana in your own 4x4, then you have three options: to hire locally; to rent a vehicle from a South African-based company; or to go with a UK specialist.

Whoever you choose to hire from, think carefully. What you need to drive into the bush in Botswana is a serious, fully equipped vehicle – and what you'd be hiring off-the-peg isn't always, in my view, up to the job. You need a vehicle that you can rely on, with long-range tanks, a high-lift jack, a spade and decent tow-rope, extra fuel cans if necessary and all the other bits and pieces that make all the difference. Perhaps most vitally, you need to have confidence that if anything goes wrong, there's a system in place to help you swiftly.

Local hire Contacting the hire companies directly (page 205), you'll find a twin-cab 4x4 hired for about 2 weeks will cost you upwards of about US$160/day, including unlimited mileage, multiple drivers & standard insurance, but not CDW insurance cover, rising to at least US$190/day with camping kit – & more for a Toyota Land Cruiser. For full insurance cover, you can expect to pay around US$40/day. Some companies also charge a premium for the high-season months, usually Jul to Oct. Others may charge extra for VAT or for a 2nd driver, or indeed for mileage above a certain level – usually 150km/day.

South African 4x4s Several South African companies offer 4x4 hire, including:

🚙 **Avis** ✆+267 686 0039; e botswanares@ avis.co.bw; www.avis.com. For equipped rentals: e safarirental.reservations@avis.co.za
🚙 **Bidvest** ✆+267 686 3728; e reservations@ bidvestcarrental.co.za; www.bidvestcarrental.co.za
🚙 **Britz 4x4** ✆+27 11 230 5200; e bookings@ britz.co.za; www.britz.co.za
🚙 **Bushtrackers Africa** ✆+27 11 465 2559; e info@bushtrackers.com; www.bushtrackers.co.za
🚙 **Drive Africa** ✆+27 21 447 1144; e myrental@ driveafrica.co.za; www.driveafrica.co.za
🚙 **Kwenda Safari** ✆+27 44 533 5416; e rmath@global.co.za; www.kwendasafari.co.za

Backed-up 4x4s Most of the companies mentioned above simply deal with hiring out vehicles; they may make suggestions, but generally don't get involved with helping you plan your trip or give you any advice. A step up

from this, in both price & completeness, are companies that provide not only a vehicle, but also put their expertise at your disposal & provide additional back up. They cost more, but if you're not experienced in driving around southern Africa, then it's probably what you need. Neither of the operators listed below offers vehicle-only hire; to benefit from their knowledge & back up you must arrange a whole trip through them.

🚙 **Drive Botswana** (page 123) As the name suggests, Drive Botswana is a self-drive safari specialist offering trips in Botswana & across southern Africa. They have offices in both the UK & Botswana. Their camping-equipped fleet of vehicles is made up of a range of single- & double-cab vehicles, each set up for between 2 & 4 travellers. As well as camping equipment, Drive Botswana will also arrange satnavs & sat phones on request; for some areas they stipulate these as essential. See ad, inside-back cover.
🚙 **Safari Drive** (page 124) Specialist African operators based out of the UK who have vehicles & support based in Windhoek, Cape Town, Livingstone, Maun, Lilongwe & Arusha. Their fleet of Land Rovers and Land Cruisers are among the region's best camping-equipped vehicles & I have used them for many of my more adventurous research trips. As well as tents, cooking equipment, long-range fuel tanks, water tanks & camping equipment, each vehicle comes with a Garmin satnav loaded with Tracks4Africa & a sat phone. A 14-day trip combining camping & lodges starts from around £2,820 pp, excluding flights.

Checking the fine print The devil's in the detail, especially if you're looking at any of the cheaper options. You should check any rental agreement very carefully, so that you know your position. Preferably also discuss any questions or queries with someone within the company that is supplying you with the vehicle. A few specific pointers may help.

CDW insurance The insurance and the collision damage waiver (CDW) clauses are worth studying particularly closely. These spell out the 'excess' that you will pay in the event of an accident. These CDW excesses vary widely, and often explain the difference between cheap rental deals and better, but more costly, options.

Some hire companies have very high excesses (ie: the amounts that you pay if you have a major accident). An 80% CDW is normal – which means that you will always pay 20% of the cost of any damage. However, look around and you should be able to reduce this to zero – although most hiring companies will still want a deposit, in case you damage or lose any of their vehicle's equipment.

Other fine print Though accidents are fortunately uncommon, they do happen. Then it's very important to get the situation resolved swiftly and carry on with your trip. Some of the companies have quite onerous terms – so be aware of these before you agree to take the vehicle.

Booking accommodation If you're driving a 2x4 on the tar, then you can afford to find a campsite in Maun or Kasane when you get there. If you need a room, then you only need to book one in advance during the busy season. For the rest of the year you shouldn't have a problem finding one.

Generally, finding a campsite outside the national parks is not a problem, though if you're not at a designated private site, you should always seek permission first (see pages 183–4 for more on this). However, campsites within the national parks **must** be booked in advance (pages 131–3) and you should do this as far ahead as possible. Any lodges at which you plan to stay should also be reserved in advance.

Driving in the national parks Historically you could just arrive at any national park in Botswana and pay your park fees, but in 2009 the authorities decreed that, in line with campsite reservations (pages 131–3), entry fees for the national parks should be pre-booked. Then in 2011 things changed again. The official line now is that if you have your accommodation confirmation it is possible to pay fees at the park entrance gates. However, do not rely on this; finding out which gates accept payment is next to impossible. Further, only a few of the wardens seem to be authorised to accept payments; most are not allowed to issue permits or handle money, no matter how persuasive you try to be. So if you arrive at a gate when the appropriate wardens are not available, don't expect to be able to pass. The policy is strict: if you haven't got a paid permit, you won't be able to enter. That said, several experiences in recent years suggests that common sense applies where a genuine problem has arisen.

Bearing all this in mind, I recommend that you arrange park fees in advance at one of the Department of Wildlife and National Parks (DWNP) offices (page 132), as it may well save you long delays and significant stress.

Park rules and regulations Park opening hours are 06.00–18.30 from April to September, and 05.30–19.00 from October to March. No driving is permitted in the parks outside these hours, so it is imperative to allow plenty of time for your journey, and to be at the gates or your campsite well before closing. Campers may camp only at designated sites, with prior reservation, and should leave the park before 11.00, or they will be liable for an additional day's park fees (which are payable to staff at the gates). The speed limit in all the national parks is 40km/h – though you'd be hard pressed to exceed this almost anywhere.

Both walking and swimming are prohibited within all Botswana's parks.

Park fees and permits Most organised trips will include park entry fees in their costs, but if you are travelling on your own then you must pay these directly.

Park fees are usually made up of three components: for the people, for your vehicle and for a campsite. The amount payable will depend on your nationality/ immigration status, and where your vehicle is registered. Campsite fees, however, are no longer fixed; see below for rates at the various sites.

While fees for park permits can in theory be paid at the gates, it's advisable to pay these in advance at one of a designated number of offices (⊕ *usually 07.30– 16.30 Mon–Sat, 07.30–noon Sun*), but do double check these times before arrival to avoid disappointment. Offices are located in Gaborone, Tsabong, Ghanzi, Kang, Letlhakane, Maun, Kasane, Francistown and Two Rivers (Twee Rivieren Rest Camp, Kgalagadi National Park). For self-drive visitors in northern Botswana, the most accessible of these are likely to be in Maun (page 222) and Kasane (where the designated office is at the Sedudu Gate into Chobe National Park).

In theory, credit cards (Visa or Mastercard) can be used at the Sedudu and Ngoma gates, but it's as well to be prepared for the inevitable occasions when the card machines are not working. Cash payments should be made in pula; even where US dollars are accepted, the rate of exchange is not likely to be favourable; where possible it is best to have with you the correct change in pula.

Park and vehicle fees, and rates for campsites still in DWNP hands, have remained unchanged for many years, but are widely expected to increase within the life of this guidebook. In the meantime, fees for the privatised campsites have increased dramatically: see page 132.

Park entry fees (per person per day)

	Bots citizen	Bots resident	Non-resident
Adult (18+)	P10	P30	P120
Child (age 8–17)	P5	P15	P60
Infant (7 & under)	free	free	free

Vehicle fees (per day)

Foreign-registered vehicle	P50
Botswana-registered vehicle	P10

National parks' campsites Botswana's national parks have a scattering of campsites where, until the late 1980s, you could just turn up and pay the fees. Then, the introduction of the 'high-revenue, low-volume' policy (page 20) led to a restriction in the number of pitches at each location, and now, all campsites must be pre-booked; you cannot just turn up.

Sites are very, very limited and often booked out almost a year in advance, so if you're planning to camp inside the national parks, it remains *essential* to book as early as you can. Reservations cannot usually be made more than 11 months in advance, but booking this far ahead is usually the ideal.

Privatisation of most of the campsites in the last five years or so has fragmented an already challenging system, since – in theory at least – each of the operators handles bookings only for its own campsites. Thus if you want to stay at, say, Savuti, Third Bridge and South Gate, you'll need to pull together your itinerary working with three separate operators. That said, both SKL and the Xomae Group are prepared to help out with bookings through other operators, though given the difficulty of communications, this isn't always straightforward, so it's crucial to allow plenty of time. Most sites in the northern parks are in the hands of four separate operators, with only a few still handled by the DWNP:

Central Kalahari Game Reserve Lekhubu, Letiahau, Piper, Sunday, Passarge & Motopi (Bigfoot Tours); others (DWNP)
Chobe National Park Ihaha (Kwalate Safaris); Savuti & Linyanti (SKL)
Moremi Game Reserve Xakanaxa & Maqwee (South Gate) sites (Kwalate Safaris); Khwai (North Gate) Campsite (SKL); Third Bridge & Gcadikwe Island camps (Xomae Group)
Makgadikgadi Pans National Park Khumaga (SKL); Njuca Hills & Tree Island (DWNP)
Nxai Pan National Park South & Baines' Baobab (Xomae Group)

Once you have your campsites lined up, be sure to get written confirmation for each one stating not just the dates of your reservation, but also confirming the number of the pitch reserved. Only then will you be able to buy your park permits from the DWNP, either in advance or at the gate, as they will require written proof of your overnight accommodation booking before issuing a permit. The system is not just unwieldy, it's also pretty costly. While the remaining DWNP sites still charge P30 (US$3) per person, fees for international visitors at the privatised sites are US$38–50 per person per night – and that's exclusive of park fees and the P10 per-person bed levy. (These rates are for international visitors; locals and residents of the SADC countries are charged according to a different scale of fees.)

On the plus side, many of these campsites – and particularly their ablution blocks – do seem to be better maintained than in the past, though inevitably some are cleaner than others. This variation in standards runs through to the efficiency of the individual operators, too. While some seem to be very much on the ball, this is not always the case, so do double check that all your paperwork is in order.

All the campsite operators, except Bigfoot Tours, who are based in Gaborone, have offices in Maun (page 222), so are relatively easy for most overseas travellers to visit in person. That said, in reality you'll need to have confirmed everything months ahead of your arrival. Contact details of the operators and campsite fees for adult visitors are as follows:

Bigfoot Tours ℄ 395 3360, 391 0927; m 7355 5573; e reservations@bigfoottours.co.bw; www. bigfoottours.co.bw. Lekhubu, Letiahau, Piper, Sunday, Passarge & Motopi Central Kalahari campsites in the Central Kalahari. US$50 pp.
DWNP Central booking Gaborone ℄ 397 1405; e dwnp@gov.bw; Maun office ℄ 686 0368; Kasane office ℄ 625 0486. P30 pp.
Kwalate Safaris Maun ℄ 686 1448; Sedudu Gate ℄ 625 0235; e kwalatesafari@gmail.com; www. kwalatesafaris.com. Ihaha Campsite in Chobe National Park; Xakanaxa & Maqwee (South Gate)

sites in Moremi Game Reserve. US$40 pp.
SKL Maun ℄ 686 5365/6; Sedudu Gate ℄ 625 0113; e reservations@sklcamps.co.bw, sklcamps@ btcmail.co.bw; www.sklcamps.com. Savuti & Linyanti campsites in Chobe National Park; Khwai (North Gate) Campsite in Moremi Game Reserve; Khumaga Campsite in Makgadikgadi Pans National Park. Arguably the most efficient of the new campsite operators, with offices in Maun & the Sedudu Gate. US$50 pp.
Xomae Group ℄ 686 2221; m 7386 7221; e xomaesites@bctmail.co.bw; www.xomaesites.

com. Third Bridge & Gcadikwe 1 & 2 island camps in Moremi Game Reserve; South Camp & Baines Baobab sites in Nxai Pan National Park. *US$50 pp;* *island camps US$85 pp (but note that prices in pula are more competitive than those in US dollars).*

Camping costs To give you some idea of the total cost of camping within the national parks, the following figures are based on a foreign-registered vehicle with two adult visitors spending seven days' camping in one or more of the parks – ranging from the lowest possible campsite fees (DWNP sites) to the highest (currently SKL and the Xomae Group):

Park entry fees	P1,680 (2 x 7 x P120)
Vehicle entry fees	P350 (7 x P50)
Camping fees	from P420 (2 x 7 x P30) up to US$700 (2 x 7 x US$50)
Total costs	**P2,450 (US$245) up to P8,120 (US$810)**

That's an average cost per person per day from P175 (US$20/£13.50) up to (much more realistically) P580 (US$66/£44) at the privatised campsites.

Campsite facilities Each campsite has a designated number of pitches or individual 'campsites'. These are usually very large by European and American standards, and capable of taking several vehicles – perhaps a group of friends travelling together. However, if the campsite is busy, you can expect to share your site with one or even two other vehicles. Most of the campsites have relatively modern ablution facilities, but some – especially in the CKGR and Makgadikgadi – are more rudimentary, and hot water is decidedly hit or miss. And at the most basic sites you'll need to heat your water over a fire. Most individual pitches have a firepit, and perhaps a barbecue stand. Regulations prohibit the collection of firewood within all Botswana's national parks and game reserves, so do make sure that you take sufficient with you, along with all the food, fuel and drinking water you will need for your trip. Although the occasional site, such as Savuti and Third Bridge, now has a small 'tuck' shop, don't rely on it.

Suggested self-drive itineraries

If you're driving yourself outside the national parks, and have lots of time, then you can afford to have total flexibility in your route, and plan very little. However, if you're coming for a shorter time, and want to use any of the campsites in the national parks, then you would be wise to arrange your trip carefully in advance. Note that campsite bookings in the national parks can be quite difficult to get, and both payment and dates are fixed at the time of reservation. You cannot just turn up at the national park gates and expect to book a campsite. Further, independent drivers can no longer rely on paying park-entry fees at the park gates (see page 131 for further details). Effectively, this commits you to a specific route and schedule.

Perhaps the most obvious and instantly rewarding trip for your first self-drive trip across Botswana would be between Livingstone and Maun. This is best done in the dry season.

Livingstone, Chobe, Moremi and Maun: 11 nights/12 days
This really is the fastest trip that you should consider through this area if you want to have time to enjoy the parks. Allowing more time would be better, and another 3–4 nights camping in the parks (including both Third Bridge and Xakanaxa for a few nights each) would improve it enormously. Since you're unlikely to need a vehicle in Livingstone, I suggest arranging a road transfer across the border and picking up

your vehicle in Kasane. This will usually result in a better vehicle, better back-up and an easier trip.

- 2 nights Livingstone – hotel/lodge (or campsite)
- 2 nights Ihaha Campsite, Chobe
- 2 nights Savuti Campsite, Chobe
- 2 nights Khwai (North Gate) Campsite, Moremi
- 2 nights Xakanaxa or Third Bridge Campsite, Moremi
- 1 night Maun – hotel/lodge (or campsite)

Of course it can easily be reversed. Some prefer Livingstone at the start, to relax after the flight. Others prefer to leave it until the end, with the highlight of seeing Victoria Falls (and buying curios) at the end. If you do start in Livingstone, then consider picking up your vehicle on the day that you leave for Ihaha, as this could save you a few days of vehicle hire.

I recommend that you use a hotel or lodge, rather than camp, for your first and last few days – I find that this makes my trips much easier and gives me time to get organised more easily at the start and end.

The Panhandle plus Tsodilo, Aha and Gcwihaba hills: 14 nights/15 days To visit the hills of the northwest Kalahari, ideally consider a trip based out of Maun:

- 1 night Maun – hotel/lodge (or campsite)
- 1 night Guma Lagoon or Swamp Stop
- 2 nights Tsodilo Hills – camping
- 3 nights Nxamaseri Lodge or Shakawe River Lodge
- 1 night Aha Hills – basic camping
- 1 night Gcwihaba Caves – basic camping
- 1 night Maun – campsite or hotel/lodge
- 1 night Maun – campsite or hotel/lodge

In the dry season, August or after, you might tag on a few days after Maun to visit the Boteti River area, where the game concentrations should then be good.

Whenever you go, I'd visit Tsodilo before Aha; it's considerably more accessible. Whatever route you take, don't try to get to Aha and Gcwihaba without sufficient fuel, food, water and a back-up plan. The roads in this remote area are neither well travelled nor well maintained, and getting stuck in deep sand is a real possibility. Do remember, too, to fill up with fuel wherever possible: Sehithwa, Shakawe and Gumare are the safest bets.

Nxai Pan and the Central Kalahari Game Reserve: 16 nights/17 days If you're experienced in the African bush, feel a lot more adventurous, and don't mind the idea of spending hours digging yourself out of mud or sand, then consider a trip to Nxai and the northern part of the Central Kalahari Game Reserve. This would probably be at its best between April and July; if you're travelling earlier then getting around Makgadikgadi could be tricky so you might consider reducing your time there.

- 1 night Maun – hotel/lodge (or campsite)
- 3 nights South Camp, Nxai Pan – camping
- 2 nights Planet Baobab (campsite or lodge)

- 2 nights Khumaga Campsite Makgadikgadi Pans NP
- 2 nights Deception Valley, CKGR – campsite
- 2 nights Sunday Pan, CKGR – campsite
- 2 nights Passarge Pan or Phokoje Pan, CKGR – campsite
- 1 night Motopi Pan, CKGR – campsite
- 1 night Maun – hotel/lodge (or campsite)

As with any rainy-season trip or excursion into the Central Kalahari Game Reserve, you should be doing this with a minimum of two vehicles, and safety precautions like taking a satellite phone would be a good idea. You cannot rely on being able to restock on this trip, so you **must** ensure you take enough food, water and fuel with you from Maun.

RED TAPE

TOURISM LEVY In June 2017, it was announced that visitors to Botswana from outside the Southern African Development Community (SADC) would have to pay a tourism levy of US$30 per person at the point of entry, to be valid for 30 days. This was to be payable either at self-service machines in cash (US dollars only) or by debit or credit card. However, implementation of the scheme was on hold for several months, and in December 2017 it was cancelled to allow for further discussion. It's reasonable to assume, though, that something similar may well emerge during the life of this guidebook.

VISAS If you need a visa for Botswana, you must get one before you arrive. Currently, passport holders from numerous countries, including the following, **do not need a visa** and will be granted a 30-day entry permit on arrival (subject to payment of the tourism levy when it comes into operation):

- Most EU (European Union) countries (except Cyprus, Hungary, Lithuania, and Malta – whose citizens *do* need visas)
- USA, South Africa, Scandinavian countries
- UK and most Commonwealth countries (except Cameroon, Ghana, Nigeria, Bangladesh, India, Pakistan and Sri Lanka – whose citizens *do* need visas).

For more details, contact your local Botswana embassy or high commission (pages 136–7) – which is also the best place to verify that the information here is still current. Alternatively, and to download a visa application form, check on the Botswana government website (*www.gov.bw*).

The prevailing attitude among both Botswana's government and its people is that visitors are generally very good for the country as they spend valuable foreign currency – so if you look respectable then you should not find any difficulties in entering Botswana.

Given this logic, and the conservative nature of Botwana's local customs, the converse is also true. If you dress very untidily, looking as if you've no money when entering via an overland border, then you may be questioned as to how you will be funding your trip. Very rarely, you may even be asked for a return ticket as proof that you do intend to leave. Dressing respectably in Botswana is not only courteous, but will also make your life easier.

Visa extensions If you want to stay longer than 30 days, then you must renew your permit at the nearest immigration office; a fee of P100 is payable. For a visa lasting longer than 90 days, you should apply to the appropriate Regional Immigration Officer (*Gaborone department* \361 1300/27/44; *toll free* \0800 600777), preferably before entering Botswana; for details, see www.gov.bw. Note that it's a serious offence to stay longer than 90 days in a 12-month period without permission.

Botswana is quite strict about **work permits**. These are now granted only for jobs for which a suitably qualified Botswana citizen is not available; for information, see www.gov.bw. Work permits can be obtained from the Ministry of Labour and Home Affairs (*MLHA;* \361 1100; *toll free* \0800 600777).

EMBASSIES AND DIPLOMATIC MISSIONS

Botswana's diplomatic missions abroad
Embassies & high commissions include:

Ⓔ Australia (high commission) 130 Denison St, Deakin Act 2600, Canberra; \02 6234 7500; e botaus-info@gov.bw

Ⓔ Belgium/EU (embassy) Av de Tervuren 169, 1150 Brussels; \02 735 2070; e boteur@gov.bw; http://botswana-brussels.com

Ⓔ China (embassy) 1 Don San Jie, Sanlitun, Chaoyang District, Beijing 100600; \653 26898; e botchin@gov.bw

Ⓔ Germany (embassy) Lennestrasse 5, 10785 Berlin; \030 8871 95010; embassyofbotswana.de

Ⓔ India (high commission) F8/3, Vasant Vihar, New Delhi 110057; \9111 4653 7000; www.botswanahighcom.in

Ⓔ Japan (embassy) 6F Kearny Pl, 4-5-10 Shiba, Minato-ku, Tokyo 108-0014; \03 5440 5676; e info@botswanaembassy.or.jp; www.botswanaembassy.or.jp

Ⓔ Namibia (high commission) 101 Nelson Mandela Av, Klein Windhoek, PO Box 20359, Windhoek; \061 221941/2/7; e botnam@gov.bw

Ⓔ South Africa (high commission) 24 Amos St, Colbyn, Pretoria 0083, PO Box 57035, Arcadia 0007, Pretoria; \012 430 9640

Ⓔ Sweden (embassy) Tyrgatan 11, PO Box 26024, 10041 Stockholm; \08 545 25880; www.botswana.se

Ⓔ Switzerland (permanent mission to United Nations) 80 Rue de Lausanne, 1202 Geneva; \022 906 1060; e botgen@bluewin.ch

Ⓔ UK (high commission) 6 Stratford Pl, London W1C 1AY; \020 7647 1000

Ⓔ USA (embassy) 1531 New Hampshire Av NW, Washington, DC 20036; \202 244 4990; e info@botswanaembassy.org; www.botswanaembassy.org

Ⓔ Zambia (high commission) 5201 Pandit Nehru Rd, PO Box 31910, Lusaka; \0211 250019, 250555, 253903

Ⓔ Zimbabwe (embassy) 22 Phillips Av, Belgravia, PO Box 563, Harare; \04 794645/7/8; e botzim@gov.bw

Diplomatic representation in Botswana
The following will be of most help to readers:

Ⓔ Angola (embassy) 13232 Khama Crescent, Nelson Mandela Rd, P Bag BR 11, Gaborone; \390 0204

Ⓔ China (embassy) 3096 North Ring Rd, PO Box 1031, Gaborone; \395 2209; e chinaemb_bw@mfa.gov.cn; http://bw.china-embassy.org

Ⓔ France (embassy) 761 Robinson Rd, PO Box 1424, Gaborone; \368 0800; e frambots@orangemail.co.bw

Ⓔ Germany (embassy) 3rd Flr, Professional Hse, Segoditshane Way, Broadhurst, PO Box 315, Gaborone; \395 3143, 370 4900; m 7130 0139; e germanembassy@info.bw

Ⓔ India (high commission) 5375 President's Dr, P Bag 249, Gaborone; \397 2676; f 397 4636; e cons.gaborone@mea.gov.in; www.hcigaborone.in

Ⓔ Japan (embassy) Barclays Hse, 8842 Khama Crescent, P Bag 00222, Gaborone; \391 4456; e consular@gr.ofa.go.jp

Ⓔ Mozambique (high commission) Robinson Rd, Main Mall, P Bag 00215, Gaborone; \319 1251–2/61; e altocomgamb@info.bw

Ⓔ Namibia (high commission) 186 Morara Cl, PO Box 987, Gaborone; \390 2181; e namibhc@botsnet.bw

Ⓔ Russia (embassy) 4711 Tawana Cl, PO Box 81, Gaborone; \395 3389; e embrus@info.bw; www.botswana.mid.ru

Ⓔ South Africa (high commission) 29 Queen's Rd, P Bag 00402, Gaborone; \390 4800–3

📧 **UK** (high commission) 1079–1084 Main Mall, Queen's Rd, Gaborone; ☎395 2841; e ukinbotswana@gmail.com
📧 **USA** (embassy) Embassy Dr, Govt Enclave, PO Box 90, Gaborone; ☎395 3982, 7111 (after hrs)

📧 **Zambia** (high commission) 1120 Queen's Rd, PO Box 362, Gaborone; ☎395 1951; e zamhico@work.co.bw
📧 **Zimbabwe** (embassy) 8850 Orapa Cl, PO Box 1232, Gaborone; ☎391 4495; e zimgaborone@mega.bw

BOTSWANA TOURISM BOARD (*391 3111, 310 5601; e board@botswanatourism. co.bw; www.botswanatourism.co.bw*) In addition to a useful website, the tourist board is represented in most major towns in Botswana, including Maun and Kasane, and by two offices overseas:

ℹ️ **Germany** ☎030 4202 8464; e j.frenzel@interface-net.de, info@botswanatourism.de; www.botswanatourism.eu. Website in German, Italian & French.

ℹ️ **UK** ☎020 7647 1018; e dwilson@botswanatourism.org.uk

GETTING THERE AND AWAY

BY AIR The vast majority of visitors to northern Botswana fly via the gateways of Maun, which has an international airport, and Kasane, which is also effectively serviced by the nearby airports at Victoria Falls (in Zimbabwe) and Livingstone (in Zambia).

The national carrier, Air Botswana, does not fly outside southern Africa, and of the other airline links to Botswana, the most notable is Airlink, a subsidiary of South African Airways. A popular routing for visitors to the region is to fly to Livingstone (airline code LVI) or Kasane (BBK) via Johannesburg (JNB), then leave from Maun (MUB), again routing via Jo'burg. There are also regular flights between Maun and Cape Town. Botswana's capital, Gaborone (GBE), is relatively rarely visited if you're on your way to or from northern Botswana – although occasionally you might stop in Gaborone as you fly between Maun and Jo'burg.

However you arrange your flights, remember some basic tips. First, make sure your purchase is protected. Always book through a company that is bonded for your protection – which in the UK means holding an Air Travel Organiser's Licence (ATOL) – or use a credit card.

Second, note that airlines don't always give the best deals direct. Often you'll do better through a discounted flight centre or a tour operator.

Third, book the main internal flights at the same time – with the same company – that you book your flights to/from Johannesburg. Often the airline taking you to Africa will have cheap deals for add-on regional flights within Africa. You should be able to get Jo'burg–Livingstone flights, or Maun–Jo'burg flights, at discounted rates provided that you book them at the same time as your return flights to Jo'burg. Further, if you book all your flights together with the same company, then you'll be sure to get connecting flights, and so have the best schedule possible. Don't be talked into getting an apparently cheap return to Jo'burg on the basis that you'll be able to then get a separate ticket to Maun; it'll cost you a lot more in the end.

From Europe Johannesburg is invariably the best gateway as it's widely served by many carriers. From Europe, British Airways, South African Airways, Lufthansa and Air France (to name but a few) have regular flights to Jo'burg. Generally these are busy routes which fill up far in advance, so you're likely to get cheaper fares by booking well ahead rather than at the last minute; this is a virtual certainty during the busiest season from July to October, and in December–January around the Christmas period.

For a return from London to Jo'burg with a decent airline, expect to pay around US$975/£750 for most of the year, adding perhaps another US$117/£90 or so in October though for flights departing after 11 December, you'll be lucky to pay less than US$1,950/£1,500. Unless there's some major international upset, these flights become progressively more expensive as you get closer to the departure. So as with most long-haul destinations, book early for the cheapest flights.

One-way flights between Jo'burg and Maun, with Air Botswana (*www. airbotswana.co.bw*), should cost around US$260/£200. Between Jo'burg and Livingstone, one-way economy flights with British Airways (*www.britishairways. com*) or South African Airways (*www.flysaa.com*) should cost in the region of US$169–175/£130–150.

From North America If you are coming from the US, you will need to pass through Johannesburg, and it's often easiest to route via London or another European capital as well. There isn't much of a discounted long-haul flight market in the US, so booking all your flights in the US will not always save you money.

Investigate the flight prices between the US and Botswana bought in the US. Look especially closely at fares with Delta and South African Airways direct from the US to Jo'burg – and talk to 'consolidators' who are the nearest that the US gets to having discounted ticket agents.

Then compare these with buying a US–London return in the US, and London–Botswana tickets from a good source in London. London is Europe's capital for cheap flights, and visitors from the US often discover that flights bought from the UK, as well as trips from UK tour operators, offer better value than those in America.

From Australasia Qantas flies between Jo'burg and Sydney or Perth, while Singapore Airlines services routes to Asia, including Singapore.

From Namibia or Zambia It is possible, although rarely either easier or cheaper, to approach Botswana from one of the region's other capitals, Windhoek or Lusaka.

Air Namibia (*www.airnamibia.com.na*) no longer operates flights between Windhoek and Maun, but they do have connections between Windhoek and Victoria Falls in Zimbabwe, so it's possible to fly there and take a road transfer to Kasane.

Travel from Lusaka to Kasane is easier and more reliable, though think of it in two stages: Lusaka to Livingstone, then Livingstone to Kasane. Lusaka to Livingstone is a long 6-hour drive (though there are efficient and cheap coaches for the more adventurous), or a short 90-minute flight. There is a handful of good, small Zambian charter companies that will organise a charter flight on this route, or seats on a scheduled charter. Expect a cost of around US$250 per person with Proflight.

See opposite for options to get between Livingstone and Kasane, but note that it's very easy to arrange to be transferred by vehicle and boat for about US$60 per person one-way. The downside of travelling via Zambia is that most visitors, including those just in transit, will be liable for visa fees, although for those staying less than 24 hours the normal fee of US$50 per person is reduced to US$20.

OVERLAND Typically overland border posts open for about 8–12 hours a day, from between 06.00 and 08.00 in the morning. That said, some of the busier ones on main routes stay open considerably longer than this.

To/from Zambia Despite meeting Zambian territory only at a point, Botswana does have one border crossing with Zambia: a reliable ferry service across the Zambezi linking Kazungula with its namesake village in Zambia (⊕ *06.00–18.00; page 232*). All this is set to change in 2018, however, when the long-awaited bridge across the river is scheduled for completion.

To/from Zimbabwe Botswana has several border posts with Zimbabwe, of which the two most important are the one on the road between Kasane and Victoria Falls, at Kazungula (⊕ *06.00–20.00*), and the one on the main road from Francistown to Plumtree (and hence Bulawayo), at Ramokgwebana (⊕ *06.00–22.00*). A third, much smaller, post is at Pandamatenga (⊕ *08.00–17.00*). This is 100km south of Kasane, and sometimes used by visitors as a neat short cut into the back of Zimbabwe's Hwange National Park.

To/from Namibia Despite the long length of its border with Namibia, Botswana has very few border posts here. The most important of these by far is the post on the Trans-Kalahari Highway, the route between the towns of Ghanzi and Gobabis. Opening hours (⊕ *07.00–midnight*) are the same at Mamuno, on the Botswana side, as at Buitepos, on the Namibian side.

The other two major crossings are at Mohembo (north of Shakawe and at the south end of Namibia's Mahango National Park; ⊕ *06.00–18.00*) and across the Chobe River at Ngoma (⊕ *07.00–18.00*).

Rather less well known are three other possible crossings into Namibia. The first is at the Dobe border post (⊕ *07.30–16.30 Namibian time*), on the road between Tsumkwe, in Namibia, and Nokaneng, on the west of the Delta. The other two, geared to those spending time in lodges right on the Namibian border, are between Kasane and both Impalila Island and Kasika (⊕ *07.30–16.30*).

To/from South Africa South Africa has always been Botswana's most important neighbour politically and economically, and for many years (even before South Africa was welcome in the international fold) it was in a 'customs union' with South Africa and Namibia. Thus it's no surprise to find a range of border posts between Botswana and South Africa. In order from northeast to southwest, these are:

- Pontdrift (⊕ *08.00–16.00*)
- Platjan (⊕ *08.00–16.00*)
- Zanzibar (⊕ *08.00–16.00*)
- Martin's Drift (⊕ *06.00–22.00*) to Groblersburg
- Parr's Halt (⊕ *08.00–16.00*) to Stockpoort
- Sikwane (⊕ *07.00–19.00*) to Derdepoort
- Tlokweng, near Gaborone (⊕ *06.00–midnight*) to Kopfontein
- Ramotswa (⊕ *07.00–19.00*) to Swartkopfontein
- Pioneer Gate, near Lobatse (⊕ *06.00–midnight*) to Skilpadshek
- Ramatlabama (⊕ *06.00–22.00*)
- Phitshane Molopo (⊕ *07.30–16.30*) to Makgobistad
- Bray (⊕ *08.00–16.00*)
- Makopong (⊕ *08.00–16.00*)
- Tshabong (⊕ *06.00–18.00*) to McCarthy's Rest
- Middlepits (⊕ *08.00–18.00*)
- Bokspits (⊕ *08.00–16.00*)
- Twee Rivieren (⊕ *07.30–16.00*)

MONEY AND BUDGETING

Botswana has probably Africa's strongest and most stable currency, underpinned by the huge earnings of its diamond industry. The unit of currency is the pula – a word that also means 'rain' in Setswana, and hence tells you something about the importance of water in this country.

Theoretically each pula is divided into 100 thebe, although one thebe isn't worth that much, so most prices are rounded to the nearest ten thebe. Notes come in denominations of 200, 100, 50, 20 and 10 pula, with coins of 5, 2 and 1 pula, and 50, 25, 10 and 5 thebe. Notes in circulation prior to 2009 are no longer valid.

The pula's exchange rate is free-floating on the world market, so there is no black market for the currency. Thus don't expect to see any shady characters on the street hissing 'change money' as you pass; I never have. (If you do, then assume they're con men trying to dupe visitors who don't know any better!) As a result, US dollars, euros and UK pounds sterling are easily changed – and most of the more international businesses in the tourism sector set their prices in US dollars. Rates of exchange in April 2018 were as follows: US$1 = P9.64, £1 = P13.57, €1 = P11.83.

INFLATION Inflation has generally been relatively modest in Botswana. Between 1993 and 1998 the rate of inflation averaged 10.2%, but in the early 1990s it subsided to below 10% and by June 2002 the rate (based on a consumer price index) was 5.9%. Over the next decade or so it has risen and fallen, largely within these parameters, to average 2.8% in September 2016. For the latest figures, take a look at the website of Statistics Botswana (*www.statsbots.org.bw*).

Botswana's currency has generally gradually declined in value against the US dollar and the British pound over the last two decades. In 1998, the US dollar was worth P3.64, as against P10.51 in late 2017. Similarly, the rate of exchange against the British pound was P6.22 in 1998, compared with the latest figure of P13.57. Given the strength of Botswana's economy, this pattern seems likely to continue in the foreseeable future: with the pula gently declining relative to the world's major currencies.

BUDGETING Inevitably, the cost of visiting Botswana varies with the style in which you travel, and the places where you spend your time. However, Botswana's costs are relatively high. VAT (currently 12%) is charged on most transactions.

If you plan to get the most from what Botswana has to offer, you will probably need from US$675/£450 per night for a good mid-range camp in low season, rising dramatically to around US$3,000/£2,307 per night for the top camps in high season. Put into context, this means that an eight-night/nine-day fly-in trip from the UK to a good mid-range camp will start at about US$5,394/£4,149 per person. This is high by African standards, but what you get for it is high quality, and includes everything: your accommodation, activities, food, most drinks (usually excluding spirits and non-house wines), and even the odd charter flight between camps. You'll then be staying at a handful of small safari camps, each of which is situated in a different, but often stunning, corner of a pristine wilderness. This is one of the world's top wildlife experiences – the kind of magical trip at which Botswana excels.

At the other end of the spectrum, if you travel through Botswana on local buses, camping and staying near the towns, then the country isn't too expensive. A budget of US$80–110/£60–80 per day for food, accommodation and transport would suffice. However, most backpackers who undertake trips on this sort of budget won't be able to afford to visit any of the camps or more remote wildlife locations – which means that they'll be missing out on a lot of what makes Botswana unique.

Somewhere in the middle, at around US$160–220/£120–140 per day for a five-day trip, with six participants, you'll find some relatively basic budget-style safaris run out of Maun which will give you a real experience of the national parks and the Okavango Delta. They won't match what you'd find in the private concession areas, or further into the Delta, but they will make you glad you came to Botswana and probably harden your determination to return when you've a lot more money!

One of these mid-range options, though only one for those with substantial African experience, is to hire a fully equipped 4x4. Such a choice enables you to camp, buy food, and drive yourself around. This requires driving ability and planning, and isn't something to undertake lightly. But then four people in a decent vehicle (a slight squash, unless you're very well organised) would cost around US$160/£120 per person per day, including the vehicle, camping kit, equipment, park fees, fuel and food. Such trips are really much better for two people per vehicle, but in that case the daily costs would work out nearer US$260/£195 each.

Budgeting for safaris Botswana isn't a cheap country to visit. This is due to a combination of the high costs of the logistics needed to operate in remote areas, plus the deliberate policy of the government to maximise revenues from tourism, while preserving the pristine nature of the country by using high costs to limit the number of visitors. That said, different kinds of trips need very different budgeting.

For backpackers The cost of camping at organised sites may have risen in recent years, but camping is still the cheapest way to stay in most areas of Botswana, and a good bet if you're relatively self-sufficient. If you have your own equipment, you'll be looking at US$12–25/£9–19 per person per night, rising to US$50/£37 a night at some of the national parks' sites. Otherwise there are pre-erected tents at some sites, costing from around US$35–100/£26–74 for two people – or perhaps double that in the national parks.

Restaurant meals in the towns are cheap compared with Europe or America: expect to pay US$12–16/£9–12 for a good evening meal, including a local beer or two. Imported drinks are always more expensive than those from southern Africa – but as southern Africa has some first-class breweries and wineries, this really is seldom an issue. European wines and spirits, as you might expect, are ridiculously priced (and so make excellent gifts if you are visiting someone here). You will pay well over US$120/£90 for a bottle of decent French champagne!

For self-drivers If you have your own rugged 4x4 with equipment and the experience to use it and survive safely in the bush, then you will be able to camp and cook for yourself. This is then an affordable way to travel and see those remote areas of Botswana which are open to the public.

Your largest expense will be the hire of a decent and well-equipped vehicle. (Taking anything less into remote areas of wild bush is really very foolish.) See pages 128–9 for more comments on this, but expect it to cost from around US$190/£140 per day, including all your camping kit.

Your next largest expense will probably be park and camping fees in the national parks. These can be substantial, especially now that most of the campsites have been privatised. Rates vary, but with some of the more popular sites coming out at US$50 per person per night, you'll need to budget around US$66/£49 per day, based on two people. Note, however, that there are still many interesting areas outside of the national parks – including parts of Makgadikgadi, the Tsodilo Hills,

Aha Hills, Gcwihaba Caves and various offbeat areas of the Kalahari – where fees are considerably lower – or where no fees are payable.

The cost of food depends heavily on where you buy it, as well as what you buy – but most people will probably do one large shop in Maun or Kasane at the start of their trip, topping up on perishables as they progress. If you are sensible, US$12.50–18/£9–13 per day would provide the supplies for a good, varied diet without having to be at all stingy.

For mobile safaris The question 'how much are mobile safaris?' is as tricky to answer as 'how long is a piece of string?' It depends on where your trip is visiting, what the equipment, staff and guides are like, and how big the group is. In short, these trips vary greatly. To choose you must carefully prioritise what you want, what will suit you, and what you can afford to pay. Note also that prices for higher-end trips are heavily dependent upon the time of year that you travel.

On a bargain-basement trip for backpackers you will put up your tent, do the camp chores and even supply your own sleeping bag and drinks. On this you can expect to visit the parks, but not to have your time there maximised (parks are costly relative to staying outside them!). This would cost you from around US$160–220/£120–140 per day per person sharing, based on a five-day trip with six participants.

By contrast, a luxurious mobile safari, visiting pristine areas in the company of a small group with a top professional guide might cost up to US$600–645/£461–496 per person per day, including superb meals and all your drinks.

Between these two extremes, you ought to be able to get a trip of a decent quality for something around US$300–525/£230–404 per person per night sharing. Then expect to be camping in comfortable tents, with a small camp staff who will organise them, cook your meals and do all the chores.

As a final thought, if you value having a really comfortable bed at night, but still want the continuity of a good professional guide to stay with your group throughout the trip; if you like the idea of putting in a lot of time and energy game viewing in the parks, and don't mind a lot of time in a vehicle, then look at a mobile trip which moves between the lodges. These cost around US$890/£685 per person per day, again including superb meals and all your drinks.

For fly-in safaris to lodges and camps Again, the prices for fly-in trips vary considerably – though they're never cheap, and there's relatively little difference between the few bottom-end camps, and the vast majority of middle-market camps that provide good experiences in good areas.

Expect the most basic camp offering only mokoro and perhaps walking activities (which are cheaper to run than vehicles or boats) to cost up to US$295–445/220–330 per person per night sharing.

Otherwise a mid-range camp in a good area will usually be around US$580–905/£446–696 per person per night sharing, all-inclusive. By going off-season, or to slightly more offbeat, marginal areas, this can be reduced. However, note that quality of accommodation is only one factor in the price: some of the smallest, simplest bushcamps are among the most expensive places to stay.

If money really is no object, then there are a few really top-end places that cost a lot more than this. Abu and Mombo spring to mind. For these, you'll pay double this or more. But then, some would argue, you're getting the pinnacle of what Africa has to offer. Having said this, there are three obvious caveats. First, none of the prices here includes flight transfers. These probably average out at US$200/£154 per person per transfer, though working them out precisely is a complex business.

Second, you will almost always be quoted a rate for a 'package' of camps and flights; that's normal and often cannot be broken into its components.

And third, note that although the prices for camps given in this guide indicate what you can expect to pay (in 2018) if you book direct, this really should be a maximum figure. If you book through a good tour operator, you will usually be able to get them a little cheaper – and this is especially applicable to the more costly lodges. See the section on *Organising a fly-in trip*, earlier in this chapter, and note that, like airline tickets, the better rates for lodges are usually available indirectly.

TIPPING Tipping is a very difficult and contentious topic – worth thinking about carefully. Read the section on *Local payments*, page 194, and realise that thoughtlessly tipping too much is just as bad as tipping too little.

Ask locally what's appropriate; here I can only give rough guidance. Helpers with baggage might expect four or five pula for their help, while sorting out a problem with a reservation would be P20–30 (US$2–3/£1–2). Restaurants often add an automatic service charge to the bill, in which case an additional tip is not usually given. If they do not do this, then 10% would certainly be appreciated if the service was good.

At safari camps, tipping is not obligatory – despite the destructive assumption from some visitors that it is. If a guide has given you really good service then a tip of about US$5–15/£3–9 per day per person would be a generous reflection of this. A similar bonus for a tracker or mokoro poler might be around US$5/£3 per day per person. And if you'd like to leave something in the communal tip box for distribution to the camp staff, then consider around US$5/£3 per guest per day. Of course, if the service hasn't been that good, then don't tip.

Always tip at the end of your stay – not at the end of each day/activity. Do not tip after every game drive. This leads to the guides only trying hard when they know there's a tip at the end of the morning. Such camps aren't pleasant to visit and this isn't the way to encourage top-quality guiding. It's best to wait until the end of your stay, and then give what you feel is appropriate in one lump sum.

However, before you do this find out if tips go into one box for all of the camp staff, or if the guides are treated differently. Then ensure that your tip reflects this – with perhaps as much again divided between the rest of the staff.

HOW TO TAKE YOUR MONEY Taking your money in the form of both cash (ideally US dollars, but sterling is a reasonable back-up) and credit cards is probably the ideal. Always bring a mixture of US$1, US$5, US$10 and US$20 notes (US$1 notes make useful, if generous, tips for porters). Because of the risk of forgeries, people are suspicious of larger denomination notes, and US$100 and even US$50 bills are often rejected in shops and even banks. South African rand are sometimes accepted, though not as widely as dollars or pounds – and they're not very popular.

While US dollars (and/or credit cards) are most useful for those staying in hotels and lodges, and are usually accepted in restaurants and tourist shops, elsewhere you will really need to have pula, especially for smaller transactions and anything bought by the roadside. In more rural locations, nobody will accept anything else. Many fuel stations will accept only cash in pula; those that accept credit cards are still in the minority.

Travellers' cheques, although arguably preferable from a security point of view, as they are refundable if stolen, are no longer easy to exchange. If you do take them, be prepared for a hefty wait in the banks – we once queued in Kasane for almost 2 hours.

Credit cards Cashpoint (ATM) machines that work with foreign credit cards can be found in most large towns, including Maun and Kasane. That said, you may need to try more than one bank before you find one that accepts your card. Note, too, that Visa cards are more widely accepted than Mastercard, and generally cause fewer problems in shops too, so do bear this in mind when planning your trip. If necessary, you can obtain cash against a credit card inside the banks.

Most tourist lodges, hotels, restaurants and shops accept credit cards.

Banks If you need to change foreign currency, receive bank drafts, or do any other relatively complex financial transactions, then the banks here are perfectly capable and efficient. Their opening times vary, but expect them to start around 08.30 and finish by 15.30 during the week. The bigger banks open on Saturday, too, typically 08.30–noon.

WHAT TO TAKE This is an impossible question to answer fully, as it depends on how you intend to travel and exactly where you are going. If you are flying in for a short safari holiday then you need not pack too ruthlessly – provided that you stay within your weight allowance. However, note that smaller, privately chartered planes may specify a maximum weight of 10–12kg for hold luggage, which must be packed in a soft, squashable bag. Once you see the stowage spaces in a small charter plane, you'll understand the importance of not bringing along large or solid suitcases.

If you are backpacking then weight becomes much more important, and minimising it becomes an art form. Each extra item must be questioned: is its benefit worth its weight?

If you have your own vehicle then neither weight nor bulk will be so vital, and you will have a lot more freedom to bring what you like. Here are some general guidelines.

Clothing For most days all you will want is light, loose-fitting cotton clothing. Pure cotton, or at least a cotton-rich mix, is cooler and more absorbent than synthetic materials, making it more comfortable in the heat.

For men, shorts (not too short) are fine in the bush, and are increasingly acceptable in the towns and rural villages of northern Botswana. For women, a knee-length skirt, trousers or culottes are ideal. Botswana's dress code is generally conservative: a woman wearing revealing clothing in town could imply that she is a woman of ill repute, while untidy clothing suggests a poor person, of low social standing.

At the less serious camps you'll see a smattering of brighter coloured clothes among many dull bush colours, the former usually worn by first-time visitors who are less familiar with the bush. Note that washing is done daily at virtually all camps, so few changes of clothes are necessary. A squashable hat and a robust pair of sunglasses with a high UV-absorption are essential.

Finally, avoid anything which looks military. Leave all your camouflage patterns at home. Wearing camouflage is asking for trouble anywhere in Africa. You are very likely to be stopped and questioned by the genuine military, or at least the police, who will assume that you are a member of some militia – and question exactly what you are doing in Botswana. Few will believe that this is a fashion statement elsewhere in the world.

Footwear If you plan to do much walking, either on safari or with a backpack, then lightweight walking boots (with ankle support if possible) are sensible. This is mainly because the bush is not always smooth and even, and anything that minimises the chance of a twisted ankle is worthwhile. Secondly, for the nervous, it will reduce still further the minute chance of being bitten by a snake, scorpion or other creepy-crawly while walking.

Because of the heat, bring the lightest pair of boots you can find – preferably of canvas, or a breathable Goretex-type material. Leather boots are too hot for wearing in October, but thin single-skin leather is bearable for walking in July and August. Never bring a new pair, or boots that aren't completely worn in. Always bring several pairs of thin socks – two thin pairs of socks are more comfortable than one thick pair, and will help to prevent blisters.

For mokoro trips, or generally relaxing at camp during the day, rafting sandals or similar – with a strong sole and firmly fitting waterproof straps – are ideal. At night around camp, when you'll need to cover your feet/ankles against mosquitoes, lightweight boots of some sort are best.

Camping equipment If you are coming on an organised safari, then even the most simple bushcamp will mean tents with linen, mosquito nets and probably an en-suite shower and toilet. However, if you're planning on doing any camping, see pages 185–6 for ideas of what you should bring, and note that equipment is easier to buy in Europe or North America.

Other useful items Obviously no list is comprehensive, and only travelling can teach you what you need, and what you can do without. Here are a few of my own favourites and essentials, just to jog your memory. For visitors embarking on an organised safari, camps will have most things but useful items include:

- Sunblock and lipsalve – vital for protection from the sun
- Insect repellent
- Binoculars – essential for game viewing
- A small pocket torch (page 186)
- 'Leatherman' tool – never go into the bush without one
- A small water bottle, especially on flights (page 167)
- Electrical insulating tape – remarkably useful for general repairs
- Camera – a long lens is vital for good wildlife shots
- Basic sewing kit – with some really strong thread for repairs
- Cheap waterproof watch (leave expensive ones, and jewellery, at home)
- Couple of paperback novels
- Large plastic 'bin-liner' (garbage) bags, for protecting luggage from dust
- Simple medical kit

And for those driving or backpacking, useful extras are:

- Concentrated, biodegradable washing powder or liquid
- Long-life candles – African candles are often soft, and burn quickly
- Nylon 'paracord' – at least 20m for emergencies and washing lines
- Hand-held GPS navigation system, for expeditions to remote areas
- Good compass and a whistle
- More comprehensive medical kit (pages 186–7)

MAPS AND NAVIGATION

FINDING THE RIGHT MAP The best maps of northern Botswana for most visitors are those published in the Shell series, which stand head-and-shoulders above the

5

rest. The first of these was the ground-breaking *Shell Tourist Guide to Botswana*, originally published in 1998, which incorporated a short but very informative 60-page booklet on the country – effectively an impressive mini-guidebook – and a serious, well-researched, original map. These were produced by Veronica Roodt, an expert on the flora and fauna of the area (see *Appendix 3*, pages 542–3, for her excellent books on the flora). What really made the difference was that, on the reverse, were smaller, inset maps of all the main parks, complete with a number of GPS waypoints. It was this information which revolutionised independent trips around Botswana, and effectively opened the doors for more travellers into some of the country's less-known areas like the Central Kalahari.

Since then Shell have also published more detailed *Chobe* and *Moremi* maps, as well as those covering the *Okavango Delta and Linyanti*, and the *Kgalagadi*. These have much more specific coverage of game-viewing tracks – utilising satellite images, and including bird and animal checklists. All are worth having, in addition to the main Botswana map, if you're visiting these areas.

Relatively new on the market is a series of guides cum souvenirs from South African publisher Tinkers (*www.tinkers.co.za*), covering three oft-visited areas: the *Chobe River Tourist Map*, *Chobe National Park Tourist Map*, and *Moremi Game Reserve Tourist Map* – each with game-drive loops and GPS co-ordinates. These and some of the Shell maps may be on sale at the park gates into Chobe and Moremi, but it makes more sense to buy them before you set off.

If you want more detailed, Ordnance Survey-type maps, then by far the best plan is to go directly to the offices of the Department for Surveys and Mapping, in either Maun (page 204) or Gaborone (✆395 3251). Each of these two offices has roughly the same variety of excellent maps on offer, although some are always out of print. A particular favourite is the 1:350,000 map that covers the whole Okavango Delta area in detail. However, many of these maps were made several years ago; since then, tracks have changed, as has the location and number of safari camps. Therefore, unless you have plenty of time to interpret them, and can afford to carry around lots of maps, they're of limited use.

For something more up to date and altogether more useful you might consider visiting Ngami Data Services (page 204) in Maun, whose maps can be found hanging on the walls of many camps throughout Botswana. Their offerings range from historical souvenir prints to current maps with GPS co-ordinates. They even have a few helpful guides, of which the *Mobile Operators Campsite Guide* and the *Guide to the Tsodilo Hills World Heritage Site* are particularly good.

DIGITAL MAPPING Many overland travellers with a GPS (see opposite) would be lost – sometimes quite literally – without Tracks4Africa (*www.tracks4africa.co.za*), a digital mapping software package that covers the whole continent. That said, it is only compatible with Garmin devices, and while the Tracks4Africa mobile app is often useful, it isn't as good as the real thing, being decidedly hit and miss in certain areas. I have also experimented with using the free maps.me app and have been surprised and very impressed. I wouldn't recommend that travellers rely on Google maps; it's not (yet?) the right tool for driving in the bush.

For all of the above, you should certainly download any apps and maps that you need before you leave home, so you can use your device offline. Data roaming is prohibitively expensive, and even using a local SIM would leave you with a significant phone bill.

More general maps of Botswana, which you're most likely to find in bookshops and map stores outside Africa, are generally fine if you are visiting the towns and simply want to know roughly where the parks are. Among these is the expensive but tear-resistant Tracks4Africa map of *Botswana*, at 1:1m, with enlargements of eight key areas on the reverse, as well as an indication of driving times. Also tear-resistant is the double-sided offering from Reise Know-How at the same scale, with an indexed gazetteer – though the idea of using this to navigate anywhere off the tar is completely fanciful.

GPS systems
If you are heading into one of the more remote parks in your own vehicle, then you really should invest in a hand-held GPS (global positioning system). These can fix your latitude, longitude and elevation to within about 10m, using a network of American military satellites that constantly pass in the skies overhead. They will work anywhere on the globe.

What to buy
Commercial hand-held GPS units cost from around US$100/£80 in Europe or the USA. As is usual with high-tech equipment, their prices are falling and their features are expanding as time progresses.

I have been using a variety of Garmin GPS receivers for years now. The early ones ate batteries at a great rate and often took ages to 'fix' my position; more recent models not only have endless new functions and far better displays, but also use fewer batteries, fix positions much more quickly, and usually even work when sitting on the car's dashboard. Whatever make you buy, you don't need a top-of-the-range machine.

What a GPS can do
A GPS should enable you to store 'waypoints' and build a simple electronic picture of an area, as well as working out basic latitude, longitude and elevation. So, for example, you can store the position of your campsite and the nearest road, making it much easier to be reasonably sure of navigating back without simply retracing your steps.

It will also enable you to programme in points, using the co-ordinates given throughout this book and by the Shell maps, and use these for navigation. (See box, page vi for an important comment on datums.) Thus you should be able to get an idea of whether you're going in the right direction, and how far away your destination is.

When you return home, if you have a fast internet connection then knowing the GPS co-ordinates for a place will enable you to see satellite images of the place using programmes like Google Maps and Google Earth. See Expert Africa's website (*www.expert.africa*) for a demonstration of the satellite images of lodges that are possible.

What a GPS can't do
A GPS isn't a compass, and when you're standing still, it can't tell you which direction is which. It can only tell you a direction if you're moving. (That said, some of the most expensive GPS units do now incorporate electronic compasses that can do just this!)

Second, it can give you a distance and a bearing for where you might want to go but it can't tell you how to get there. You'll still need to find a track. You should NEVER just set out across the bush following a bearing; that's a recipe for disaster.

Finally, it can't replace a good navigator. You still need to be able to navigate and think to use a GPS effectively. If you're clueless on navigation then driving around the bush in Botswana will get you into a mess with or without a GPS.

Accessories
Most GPS units use quite a lot of battery power, so bring plenty of spare batteries with you. Also get hold of a cigarette lighter adapter for your GPS

when you buy it. This will enable you to power it from the car while you're driving, and thus save batteries.

Warning Although a GPS may help you to recognise your minor errors before they are amplified into major problems, note that such a gadget is no substitute for good map work and navigation. They're great fun to use, but shouldn't be relied upon as a sole means of navigation. You MUST always have a back-up plan – and an understanding of where you are – or you will be unable to cope if your GPS fails.

PHOTOGRAPHY AND OPTICS

Outside of Gaborone, optical equipment isn't widely available in Botswana – so bring everything that you will need with you. That's doubly important if you're shooting film. Note that it is illegal to fly a drone over any national park or game reserve without a licence.

Pictures taken around dawn and dusk will have the richest, deepest colours, while those taken in the middle of the day, when the sun is high, will seem pale and washed-out by comparison. Beware of the very deep shadows and high contrast that are typical of tropical countries – film just cannot capture the range of colours and shades that our eyes can. If you want to take pictures

WHICH BINOCULARS ARE BEST FOR ME?   *James Lowen*

Binoculars are a fabulous tool for getting close to nature – seeing animals well without disturbing them. But with hundreds of models available, and prices ranging from £20 to £2,000, selecting the right pair can feel daunting – whether it is an inaugural purchase or an upgrade. This guide aims to help.

BUYING BINOCULARS: THE BASICS To start, three guiding principles. First, what's right for me may not be for you. Binoculars are a personal thing, so never buy without testing. Second, prepare for trade-offs between weight, performance, practicality and price. Third, buy the best you can afford. You get what you pay for. My Swarovski 'bins', bought in 2004, remain as brilliant as on day one.

Binoculars are described in off-putting jargon. So let's explain the basics. Binocular names include two numbers, respectively the magnification factor and objective lens diameter (in mm). An 8x56 binocular magnifies objects by eight times through a 56mm-wide lens. Larger numbers usually mean heavier and more cumbersome binoculars, which are less convenient for travelling. I advise sticking to the ranges 7–10 (magnification) and 30–56 (lens). Avoid apparent marvels such as 20x50 'ex-army' binoculars, which are rubbish and heavy!

The ratio between the two numbers influences how much light the binocular lets in – and thus how bright the image is in dingy conditions. The larger the ratio, generally, the better such low-light performance. I favour a ratio of 1:4 (eg: 8477) or 1:5 (eg: 8x42); but up to 1:7 (eg: 8x56) may enhance use in shady forests or at twilight.

Numbers aside, binoculars are either 'roof-prisms' (H-shaped, slimline) or 'porro-prisms' (M-shaped, chunky). For tight budgets, porro-prisms arguably offer better value. Although pricier, roof-prisms tend to be better quality, easier to handle and more compact for travelling. All things being equal, they get my vote.

in full daylight, and capture details in the shadows, then you will need a good camera, and to spend some time learning how to use it fully. By restricting your photography to mornings, evenings and simple shots you will get better pictures and encounter fewer problems.

The bush is very dusty, so bring plenty of lens-cleaning cloths, and a blow-brush. Take great care not to get dust into the back of any camera, as a single grain on the back-plate can be enough to make a long scratch which ruins every frame taken.

For tips on photography from wildlife expert Jonathan Scott, see www.bradtguides.com/phototips.

BINOCULARS For a safari holiday, a good pair of binoculars is essential. They will bring you far more enjoyment than a camera, as they make the difference between merely seeing an animal or bird at a distance, and being able to observe its markings, movements and moods closely. Do bring one pair per person; one between two is just not enough.

There are two styles: the small 'compact' binoculars, perhaps 10–12cm long, which account for most popular modern sales, and the larger, heavier styles, double or triple that size, which have been manufactured for years.

Both vary widely in cost and quality. If you are buying a pair, then consider getting the larger style. The compact ones are fine for spotting animals; but are

TESTING BINOCULARS: WHAT TO LOOK FOR Pick them up. Is the weight evenly distributed? Can you hold them steady? Spectacle-wearers need eyecups that roll or slide so that the binocular offers 14–17mm of 'eye relief'. Now look through the optics. You want a wide field of view – but no need to go overboard. Ensure the image is sharp, ideally right to the edge of vision. How close can you focus? If you anticipate watching insects, choose a pair that focuses on your feet. Check that colours look natural – with no blue or yellow cast. Finally, examine a backlit object: if it is fringed yellow or purple, choose another pair.

WHAT MAKES BINOCULARS REALLY GOOD? Consider each candidate binocular's finer characteristics, which sort wheat from chaff across years of service. 'Fully multi-coated' lenses and prisms are recommended; they maximise light transmission, contrast and clarity. Look for an image so sharp it sears your eyes. Extra-low dispersion (ED) or high-density (HD) lenses correct colour fringing. Depth-of-field is important: you want to minimise time spent refocusing from a close animal to a distant one. Durability is key: seek high-strength but ideally lightweight housing. Weatherproofing is vital to keep out dust and water. Finally, if things go wrong, you want the manufacturer to stand by its product, offering a lifetime warranty. There's a reason why my Swarovskis go on… and on…

James Lowen (www.jameslowen.com) is a wildlife expert, award-winning writer and author of four Bradt wildlife titles.

difficult to hold steady, and very tiring to use for extensive periods. You will only realise this when you are out on safari, by which time it is too late.

Around 8 x 32 or 8 x 42 is an ideal size for field observations, as most people need some form of rest, or tripod, to hold the larger 10 x 50 models steady. Get the best-quality ones you can for your money. The cheapest cost from around US$60/£40, but to get a decent level of quality spend at least US$300/£200. In a different league entirely are top-of-the range binoculars manufactured by Leica and Swarovski (see ad, 1st colour section). You will be able to see the difference when you use them. For more on choosing binoculars, see the box, pages 148–9.

ELECTRICAL APPLIANCES

The local voltage is 220V, delivered at 50Hz. Sockets usually fit plugs with three square pins, like the current design in the UK, though plugs with three large round pins, like those in South Africa, are also widely in use. Ideally bring adapters for both.

When staying in bush lodges and even in the more upmarket camps, you are increasingly likely to have sockets in your room/tent. Even if you don't, it's usually easy to arrange to charge camera batteries, etc, as behind the scenes most camps run generators in order to power their kitchen and communications equipment. Don't, though, expect to be able to use a hairdryer out in the bush – few camps can cope with such a high-powered drain on their circuit.

GETTING AROUND

BY AIR There are two ways to fly within Botswana: on scheduled airlines or using small charter flights.

Scheduled flights The national carrier, Air Botswana, operates the scheduled network. This is limited in scope, but generally very efficient and reliable. Air Botswana links Maun directly with Kasane, Gaborone and Johannesburg, while Kasane is linked to both Gaborone and Johannesburg.

Charter flights Small charter flights operate out of the hub of Maun, with Kasane as a secondary focus, and ferry travellers around the camps of northern Botswana like a fleet of taxis. They use predominantly six- to 12-seater planes which criss-cross the region between a plethora of small bush runways. There's no other way to reach most camps, but flights are usually organised by the operator who arranges your camps as an integral part of your trip, and you'll never need to worry about arranging them for yourself.

Several people usually end up sharing these small flights, with timings scheduled by the companies a few days beforehand. Expect them to take under about an hour, during which you may stop at one or two other airstrips before reaching your destination. (See my comments under *From the air*, page 9, to help you understand a little about the patterns that you'll be able to see in the landscapes below.)

BY RAIL There is a railway that links South Africa with Lobatse, Gaborone, Palapye, Francistown and Bulawayo (in Zimbabwe), but that's the only railway in the country – so is rarely used by travellers to northern Botswana.

BY BUS Botswana has a variety of local buses which link the main towns together along the tarred roads. They're cheap, frequent and a good way to meet local people, although they can also be crowded, uncomfortable and noisy. In short, they are similar to any other local buses in Africa, and travel on them has both its joys and its frustrations.

There are two different kinds: the smaller minibuses, often VW combis, and the longer, larger, 'normal' buses. Both will serve the same destinations, but the larger ones tend to run to a timetable, go faster and stop less. Their smaller relatives usually wait to fill up before they leave the bus station, then go slower and stop at more places.

DRIVING Driving in Botswana is on the left, as in the UK, and seatbelts must be worn. If you're planning to drive, you should have either an international driving licence (available in the UK from the post office for £5.50) or a photo licence, though generally we've found that an old-style British paper licence is acceptable.

The standard of driving is relatively good, but traffic – and accidents – are increasing, so remain alert, and avoid driving at night in any circumstances. For comments on drink driving, see page 152.

Speed limits are generally 120km/h on major roads, decreasing to 80km/h outside towns and 60km/h in urban areas, with variations generally signposted. That said, travelling at 120km/h on even the best of Botswana's tarmac roads is foolhardy, given the potential for animals such as goats and even elephants wandering across the road; stick to 80km/h. In national parks, there is a blanket limit of 40km/h – though you'll rarely be in a position to come close to this.

The police have radar equipment, and actively set up radar traps, especially just outside towns. Speeding tickets may sometimes be paid on the spot, against a signed receipt from the officer, but often you'll have to report to the nearest police station within 48 hours. Botswana's police are efficient; it'd be foolhardy not to obey such a summons.

At the time of research, in autumn 2017, the price of fuel in Kasane was P7.56 (US$0.76) per litre for diesel, and P7.82 (US$0.78) for unleaded petrol. The further you travel away from the main centres, the more these prices are likely to increase.

Most roads in the towns, and the major arteries connecting these, are tarred and are usually in good condition, although traffic is increasing year on year. Away from these main arteries, though, and throughout virtually all of the wild areas covered by this guide, the roads are simply tracks through the bush made by whatever vehicles have passed that way. They are almost never maintained, and usually require at least a high-clearance vehicle – although often a high-clearance 4x4 is essential. During the wet season some of these tracks can be less forgiving, and become virtually impassable. Travelling on these bush tracks at any time of year is slow and time-consuming – but very much one of the joys of an adventurous trip to Botswana. For more details, see *Chapter 7*.

For details of vehicle hire and maps, see pages 128–9 and 145–8.

HITCHHIKING Hitchhiking is a practical way to get around the main towns – but very, very difficult as a means of getting around the national parks. Hitching on the tarred roads has the great advantage of allowing you to talk one-to-one with a whole variety of people, from local businesspeople and expats to truck drivers and farmers. Sometimes you will be crammed in the back of a windy pick-up with a dozen people and as many animals. Occasionally you will be comfortably seated in the back of a plush Mercedes, satisfying the driver's curiosity as to why you were standing beside a road in Botswana at all. It can be a great way to get to know the country, through the eyes of its people, though it is not for the lazy or those pressed for time.

Waiting times can be long, even on the main routes, and getting a good lift can take many hours. If you are in a hurry then combining hitchhiking with taking the odd bus can be a quicker and more pragmatic way to travel.

The essentials for successful hitching in Botswana include a relatively neat, conservative set of clothes, without which you will be ignored by some of the more comfortable lifts available. A good ear for listening and a relaxed line in conversation are also assets, which spring naturally from taking an interest in the lives of the people that you meet. Finally, always carry a few litres of water and some food with you, both for standing beside the road and for lifts where you can't stop to eat.

Dangers of drink driving Unfortunately, drinking and driving is relatively common in Botswana. It is more frequent in the afternoon/evening, and towards the end of the month when people are paid. Accepting a lift with someone who is drunk, or drinking and (simultaneously) driving, is foolish. Occasionally your driver will start drinking on the way, in which case you would be wise to start working out how to disembark politely.

An excuse for an exit, which I used on one occasion, was to claim that a close family member was killed while being driven by someone who had been drinking. Thus I had a real problem with the whole idea, and had even promised a surviving relative that I would never do the same ... hence my overriding need to leave at the next reasonable town/village/stop. This gave me an opportunity to encourage the driver not to drink any more, and when that failed (which it did), it provided an excuse for me to disembark swiftly. Putting the blame on my own psychological problems avoided blaming the driver too much, which might have caused a difficult scene.

Safety of hitchhiking Notwithstanding the occasional drunk driver, Botswana is generally a safe place to hitchhike for a robust male traveller, or a couple travelling together. However, although safer than in the UK, and considerably safer than in the USA, hitchhiking still cannot be recommended for single women, or even two women travelling together. This is not because of any known horror stories, but because women from outside of Botswana, and especially white women hitching, would evoke great curiosity among the local people, who might view their hitching as asking for trouble, while some would associate them with the 'promiscuous' behaviour of white women seen on imported films and TV programmes. The risk seems too high. Stick to buses.

ACCOMMODATION

Although northern Botswana's accommodation is dominated by hotels, lodges and campsites aimed at visiting tourists, there is still a considerable variety in terms of both style and prices. Most establishments are graded nowadays, with between one and five stars awarded on the basis of 'furnishings, service and guest care', but inevitably this gives only part of the picture.

Prices quoted in this guide are usually international rates – those payable by visitors from Europe, America and other Western countries. (Some establishments – and especially the national parks' campsites – have a two- or even three-tier pricing system, in favour of nationals of Botswana, and southern Africa.) All types of accommodation attract a tourism levy, or 'bed levy', of P10 per person per night. This is usually included in the rates, but in some of the cheaper establishments, or those where you pay per room rather than per person, it may be charged extra.

Note that while rates were correct at the time of research, in late 2017/early 2018, many will inevitably rise during the life of this guide.

As a final note: following the ban on commercial hunting in January 2014, at least some of Botswana's former hunting camps are reopening as photographic lodges, creating an upsurge of accommodation over the next few years.

ACCOMMODATION PRICES AND CODES Rates at most safari lodges in Botswana include full board and activities, whereas hotels and guesthouses are more usually priced for bed and breakfast. In both cases, we have coded prices in this guide to give an at-a-glance indication of relative costs. A few other establishments, however, fall outside this mould, and have not been allocated a code. These include campsites, and places where prices are based on dinner, bed and breakfast, or full board but without activities.

For urban establishments, and others offering **B&B accommodation**, rates are based on the cost of a double room with breakfast. Single supplements average around 20%, but may be significantly higher. VAT may be charged extra.

$$$$$	US$350+	£260+	P3,500+
$$$$	US$200–350	£150–260	P2,000–3,500
$$$	US$120–200	£90–150	P1,200–2,000
$$	US$60–120	£45–90	P500–1,200
$	up to US$60	up to £45	up to P500

For **all-inclusive** places, such as safari lodges and camps, rates are based on the cost of *one person sharing a room* per night, including full board and activities (FBA).

★★★★★	US$1,000+	£740+
★★★★	US$650–1,000	£480–740
★★★	US$300–650	£220–480
★★	US$125–300	£95–220
★	up to US$125	up to £95

HOTELS AND GUESTHOUSES Hotels in Botswana's towns tend to be aimed at visiting businesspeople, in which case they're functional but boring, regardless of price level. That said, they're also generally clean and rarely unpleasant. Expect costs in Maun to start from around US$65/£48 for a double room per night, but in Kasane – which is more geared to international tourists – you'll find very little under US$100/£75 a night.

In recent years a few guesthouses have sprung up in Botswana's larger towns, including Maun and Kasane, but these are still very limited, and often in such suburban locations that they're only practical if you've got your own vehicle. Some also tend to be on the pricey side, and don't seem to be good value for money.

LODGES AND CAMPS Botswana's lodges and camps vary from palatial residences crafted by top designers to simple spots with a few small tents, and a table in the shade. Given that range, the vast majority have rooms which are at least as comfortable as a good hotel room.

When the words 'tented camp' are mentioned, forget your memories of cramped scout tents and think instead of canvas designer chic. En-suite flushing toilets, running hot and cold water and battery-powered lights are standard, while many have electric fans, and an increasing number have air conditioning. Traditional bucket showers, where a bucket is filled with hot water and raised on a pulley for you by camp staff, are nowadays exceptionally rare.

Note that expensive does not always mean luxurious. Some of the top camps are very simply constructed. Equally, looking for basic, simple camps won't make your trip any cheaper. You're usually paying for virtually exclusive use of pristine wilderness areas, and will find little cost difference between a tiny bushcamp and the largest lodge. In fact, if anything there's increasingly a premium on space in the smaller camps. These need booking earlier as many find these friendlier than the larger ones.

FOOD AND DRINK

FOOD Talking of any one 'native cuisine' in Botswana is misleading, as what a person eats is dependent on where they live and the ethnic group they belong to. In the Kalahari and Okavango there was relatively little agriculture until recently; there, gathering and fishing, supplemented by hunting, provided subsistence for the various groups.

In the kinder climes east of the Kalahari, where there is enough rain for crops, sorghum is probably the main crop. This is first pounded into meal before being mixed with boiling water or sour milk. It's then made into a paste *bogobe* – which is thin, perhaps with sugar like porridge, for breakfast, then eaten thicker, the consistency of mashed potatoes, for lunch and dinner. For these main meals it will normally be accompanied by some tasty relish, perhaps made of meat (*seswa*) and tomatoes (*moro*), or dried fish. Maize meal, or *papa* (often imported as it doesn't tolerate Botswana's dry climate that well), is now often used in place of this. (In Zimbabwe this same staple is known as *sadza*, in Zambia it's *nshima* and in South Africa *mealie-pap*.) You should taste this at some stage when visiting. Safari camps will often prepare it if requested, and it is always available in small restaurants in the towns.

Camps, hotels and lodges that cater for overseas visitors serve a very international fare, and the quality of food prepared in the most remote camps is usually amazingly high. When coming to Botswana on safari your biggest problem with food is likely to be the very real danger of putting on weight.

Restaurant price codes Prices for restaurants listed in this guide have been coded as below, based on the average cost of a main course.

$$$$$	US$15+	£11+	P150+
$$$$	US$12.50–15	£9.25–11	P125–150
$$$	US$10–12.50	£7.50–9.25	P100–125
$$	US$6–10	£4.50–7.50	P60–100
$	up to US$6	up to £4.50	up to P60

Self-catering If you are driving yourself around and plan to cook, then get most of your supplies in Maun or Kasane. Both have several large, well-stocked supermarkets and a number of more specialist shops. However, it is important to be aware that northern Botswana is effectively ringed by a veterinary fence – widely known as the buffalo fence – with regular checkpoints along the roads to help prevent infection of the country's valuable cattle herds with foot-and-mouth disease. For this reason, taking red meat across the fence from a buffalo area into an area that is used for cattle farming is prohibited. Campers, take note!

It's usually best to stock up with food at these main centres, as away from them the range will become sparser. Expect villages to have just a bottle stall, selling the most popular cool drinks (often this excludes 'diet' drinks), and a small shop selling staples like rice and (occasionally) bread, and perhaps a few tinned and packet foods. Don't expect anything refrigerated.

DRINK

Alcohol Like most countries in the region, Botswana has two distinct beer types: clear and opaque. Most visitors and more affluent people in Botswana drink the **clear beers**, which are similar to European lagers and always served chilled. St Louis and Castle are the lagers brewed here by a subsidiary of South African Breweries. They are widely available and usually good. You'll also sometimes find Windhoek lager, from Namibia – which is similar and equally good.

The less affluent residents will usually opt for some form of the **opaque beer** (sometimes called Chibuku, after the market-leading brand). This is a commercial version of traditional beer, usually brewed from maize and/or sorghum. It's a sour, porridge-like brew: an acquired taste, and it changes flavour as it ferments; you can often ask for 'fresh beer' or 'strong beer'. As a visitor you'll have to make a real effort to seek out opaque beer; most bars that tourists visit don't sell it. Locals will sometimes buy a bucket of it, and then pass it around a circle of drinkers. It would be unusual for a visitor to drink this, so try some and amuse your companions. If you aren't sure about the bar's hygiene standards, stick to the pre-packaged brands of opaque beer like Chibuku.

Soft drinks Soft drinks are available everywhere, which is fortunate when the temperatures are high. Choices are often limited, though the ubiquitous Coca-Cola is usually there, along with the likes of Fanta in various flavours. Diet drinks are available in the towns, but rarely seen in the small bottle stores which pepper the rural areas – which is no surprise for a country where the rural population are poor and need all the energy their food can give them.

Water Water in the main towns is usually purified, provided there are no shortages of chlorine, breakdowns or other mishaps. It's generally fine to drink.

Out in the bush, most of the camps and lodges use water from boreholes. These underground sources vary in quality, but are normally free from bugs and so perfectly safe to drink. Sometimes it is sweet, at other times the water is a little alkaline or salty. Ask the locals if it is suitable for an unacclimatised visitor to drink, then take their advice.

The water in the Okavango Delta is generally fine to drink. You'll be expected to do so during most budget mokoro trips, which is fine for most backpackers who are in Africa for long trips. There are relatively few people living in the communities in the Delta; contamination levels are very low. However, if you've a sensitive stomach, or are visiting for a short trip, then you'd be best to avoid it and stick to borehole water, or travel with a filter bottle. (I'd recommend that you do not insist on bottled water as the costs/waste involved in transporting it to you are high, and borehole water is generally fine.)

CRAFTS AND CURIOS

Botswana's best bargains are handicrafts, and you'll find a variety. Look especially for hand-woven baskets made from the fronds of the real fan palm (*Hyphaene petersiana*), and the many different handicrafts of the San, like jewellery made from ostrich eggshells.

There's usually a divide between the simpler outlets, perhaps direct from the producers, and the more stylish, well-located shops which often have the best pieces, but invariably charge the highest prices.

If you're starting or ending your trip in Livingstone, then don't miss the curio stalls near the border post to Victoria Falls, or those in Livingstone's Mukuni Park. These are among the region's best places for carvings (though expect to bargain hard). Other places to seek out would be the various curio shops in Maun and Kasese, for excellent baskets, and the small basket shops in towns west of the Delta.

There are plenty of shops at the more stylish end of the spectrum, especially in Maun, and many lodges have small shops selling crafts and curios. Sometimes these are made by the staff or people in a local village; if that's the case, do buy some to support the initiative.

IMPORTS AND EXPORTS There is no problem in exporting normal curios, but you will need an export permit from the Department of Wildlife and National Parks to take out any game trophies. Visitors are urged to support both the letter and the spirit of the CITES bans on endangered species. In any case, without such permits you will probably have big problems when you try to import items back into your home country.

COMMUNICATIONS

POST BotswanaPost (*www.botspost.co.bw*), the government-owned postal service, is reliable, but often slow. They have post offices in all the larger towns, and a network of agencies in some of the larger villages. In northern Botswana, these include offices in Etsha 6, Ghanzi, Gumare, Gweta, Kasane, Kazungula, Maun, Nata, and Shakawe.

Letters are classified by size, with a 'standard' one being up to 120mm x 235mm x 20mm. For postcards and standard letters weighing less than 200g, postal rates are:

Botswana	Rest of Africa	Europe	Rest of world
P5	P10	P11	P12

Stamps are sometimes sold in curio shops, and most hotels and lodges will post letters on your behalf.

TELEPHONE Botswana's telephone system is generally very good, and you can dial some remarkably offbeat places from overseas. The presence of public phoneboxes on the streets is all but redundant nowadays. Mobile phones are ubiquitous – and few people have any need for the old-style cardphones.

To dial into Botswana from abroad, the international access code is 267. From inside the country, dial 00 to get an international line, then the country's access code (eg: 44 for the UK, 1 for the USA), then omit the first 0 of the number you are calling.

Essential telephone numbers
Ambulance ✆997
Police ✆999
Fire ✆998
Medical rescue ✆911
Medical air rescue ✆390 1601
BTC Call Centre ✆121; m 392 3141 (including international directory enquiries)
Directory enquiries ✆192; m 316 6651

Mobile phones Mobile-phone coverage has increased rapidly in recent years, with reception found even in relatively small villages. Outside of these, though, and in the national parks, a mobile phone will be of no use at all.

Local SIM cards in three sizes can be purchased in Kasane and Maun, significantly cutting the cost of calls from a mobile registered overseas. The major operators are Mascom (*www.mascom.bw*) and Orange (*www.orange.co.bw*), of which Mascom arguably has the better coverage. There's also BTC (*www.btc.bw*) and Be Mobile (*www.bemobile.co.bw*). Expect to pay about P10 for a SIM card, with top-up cards available in various denominations from P10.

EMAIL AND THE INTERNET Most businesses in Botswana nowadays have access to the internet, though it can be painfully slow and far from reliable. In general, it's best not to send large attachments until you're sure that the recipient can handle them, and if you don't get a reply from an email to Botswana within, say, 48 hours, it's a good idea to resend it.

THE MEDIA

With a small population, many in rural locations, the press here is equally small, and partly relies on the larger South African media companies. However, Botswana has several newspapers, radio and television stations.

INDEPENDENCE ISSUES Botswana's small media is generally fairly free and expresses its opinions, even when it disagrees with government policy. Even media which are owned by the government are obliged by law to give basic coverage of opposition views as well as the official versions. That said, disagreements do occur on a fairly regular basis, and clearly the independent press here fights a continuing battle to remain independent.

In May 2001, all government offices were instructed to stop using the two independent weekly papers, the *Botswana Guardian* and the *Midweek Sun*, following their criticism of Vice President Ian Khama. Given that the government is the largest advertiser in these papers, this had significant commercial impact. Shortly afterwards, following proceedings brought against the government by the papers' editors, a High Court judge ruled that the advertising ban was unconstitutional as the authorities were deemed to be applying unfair financial pressure on the papers in order to curtail their right to freedom of expression.

Occasionally the press also comes into the firing line for sensationalism, which is claimed to be fuelling ethnic tensions, and once recently a High Court judge started proceedings against *Mmegi* for defamation.

In April 2001, the head of news and current affairs at the official Botswana Television (BTV) station quit his job in protest about government interference in the station's editorial policy and programming. He alleged that officials had threatened him, and that the authorities had blocked the broadcast of a documentary on a South African woman who had been convicted of murder by a Botswana court and subsequently executed.

The subsequent, if controversial, establishment of a press council has resulted in a 'code of ethics' for the media, laying out standards of best practice that would seem to be free and fair.

THE PRESS Botswana's most widely read newspapers are the *Botswana Guardian* (*www.botswanaguardian.co.bw*) and *Mmegi* ('*The Reporter*': *www.mmegi.bw*), both published daily. *Mmegi* also has a sister publication, the *Monitor*, which comes out on a Monday. Other national papers include *The Botswana Gazette* (*www.thegazette. news*), the *Midweek Sun* (*www.themidweeksun.co.bw*), and the government's free weekday newspaper, the *Daily News* (*www.dailynews.gov.bw*), while the Maun area has the weekly *Ngami Times* (*www.ngamitimes.com*).

RADIO AND TELEVISION The government Department of Information and Broadcasting, based in Gaborone, runs both Botswana TV (*www.btv.gov.bw*) and Radio Botswana (*www.radiobotswana.gov.bw*). There is also the privately run Gaborone Television, which is owned by the Gaborone Broadcasting Company (GBC) and funded by advertising, and a trio of independent radio stations. That said, most people in Botswana with televisions are connected to one of the large South African networks, such as the MultiChoice digital satellite service (DStv).

The two state radio stations, Radio Botswana 1 (RB1) and Radio Botswana 2 (RB2), broadcast around the main towns, but away from these there's generally nothing but long-distance shortwave services. The non-commercial RB1 has no advertising and majors on news and current affairs, while the commercial station, RB2 – or FM 103 – features mainly popular music, from ballads, R&B, house, reggae, fusion and jazz to pop and disco. Within this you'll find the usual inane banter, as well as news bulletins at regular intervals, in a mix of Setswana and English. Independent stations include Yarona FM (106.6FM), Gabz FM (96.2FM) and Duma FM (93.0FM).

TRAVELLING POSITIVELY

Botswana is one of the richer of the developing nations, but despite this you may see scenes of poverty when you are visiting the country, especially in more rural areas. Beggars are fairly rare in the towns, but often the least able are dependent on charity. While giving a few coins to people is one way to put a sticking plaster over your feelings of guilt, this is not a long-term solution.

Similarly, although the visitor on an expensive safari is making a financial contribution to development and conservation in Botswana, he or she can do a lot more to help.

CONSERVATION The first thing to do if you want to help protect Botswana's wilder areas is to travel there, often; the income generated by tourism is the main hope to enable these areas to survive and thrive in the long term, and this in turn will make a positive contribution to conservation.

Many safari operators have programmes to help their local communities, having recognised that the mass of Botswana's people must benefit more (and more directly) from tourism if conservation is going to be successful in Botswana. Thus one very simple thing that you can do to help is to ask your operator:

- Besides employment, how do local people benefit from this camp?
- How much of this camp's revenue goes directly back to the local people?
- What are you doing to help the people living near this reserve?
- How much control do the local people have in what goes on in the area in which these safaris are operated?

If more visitors did this, it would make a huge difference in raising awareness of conservation and of the importance of local involvement in this sphere.

The second thing you can do is to support organisations such as those initiated by your tour operator, or one following, which work in promoting knowledge of

Botswana's wilder areas, in campaigning for environmental and social issues, and in research and conservation:

BirdLife Botswana 319 0540/1; e blb@ birdlifebotswana.org.bw; www.birdlifebotswana. org.bw. The local arm of BirdLife International has a bird population monitoring scheme that enables visitors as well as locals to contribute to data collection. Birders are asked to notify them about birds identified during Feb & Nov within a clearly defined area.

Kalahari Conservation Society 397 4557; e publicrelations@kcs.org.bw; www.kcs.org.bw
Wilderness Wildlife Trust e wildernesstrust@ wilderness.co.za; www.wildernesstrust.com. This Africa-wide charity has Botswana-based projects focused on several species, including wild dogs, zebra migration & the reintroduction of rhino.

In addition, helping the country's poorer communities (see below) will, ultimately, also help preserve the wildlife areas, as without sustainable economic development there's little long-term hope for the wildlife.

HELPING POORER AND DISADVANTAGED COMMUNITIES
There *are* ways in which you can make a positive contribution, but they require more effort than giving to someone on the street; perhaps this is the least you can do after an enjoyable trip to Botswana?

There is an established, trustworthy and reliable network of charities, churches and NGOs (non-governmental organisations). If you really want to help, then contact someone and make it happen!

Botswana has a whole range of good, small charities working at grassroots level to improve the lot of the poorest members of society here, and help them to develop economically. One good source of information is the website of the Ngamiland Council of Non-Governmental Organisations (*NCONGO; www. ncongo.info*), which provides a brief synopsis of many of the groups doing valuable work in northern Botswana. It doesn't include all charities, but would be a good start to your research. Another good port of call would be Travel for Impact, and detailed below are a few individual charities concentrated on the north of the country.

Travel for Impact Airport Rd, Maun; 686 4431; m 7230 7694; e tfibotswana@gmail. com; www.travelforimpact.com. Established in 2013, they work with a number of community initiatives, most notably Bana Ba Letsatsi (below), Women against Rape, AGLOW Polokong (focusing on the aged) & Maun Animal Welfare Society. Tfl is well placed to offer advice on where you can best help.
Bana Ba Letsatsi Maun; 686 4787; e info@ banabaletsatsi.org; www.banabaletsatsi.org. A local charity helping vulnerable children in Maun. See box, pages 200–2.
Ditshwanelo (The Botswana Centre for Human Rights) 390 6998; e admin.ditshwanelo@info. bw; www.ditshwanelo.org.bw. Ditshwanelo works with poorer communities all over Botswana on a range of human rights issues, from child advocacy

& the death penalty to the case of the San in the CKGR.
Gumare Counselling Centre 687 4235. Provides free counselling & HIV-testing services in Gumare & the wider Okavango area, & also works with orphans & other vulnerable children.
Love Botswana Outreach Mission Maun; 680 1114; e info@lovebotswana.org; http:// lovebotswana.org. Aims to provide leadership development through education, HIV/AIDS care & prevention, economic empowerment & spiritual development.
Thuso Rehabilitation Centre Maun; 686 0539. Rehabilitation centre for disabled people in the Chobe & Ngamiland community, providing therapy & vocational skills training such as dressmaking, weaving, leatherwork & agriculture.

5

VOLUNTEERING Botswana, like many African countries, hasn't been slow to take advantage of the upsurge in volunteering holidays. Despite this, there are many pitfalls for unwary volunteers, so be sure to do your homework – especially if you are trying to get involved with a local community.

Both Bana Ba Letsatsi and Love Botswana (page 159) have volunteer programmes, and it could well be worth contacting Travel for Impact (page 159) for other ideas. Before you start your search, some of the many issues to consider include:

- For every bona fide organisation, there will be others who are willing to take your cash without delivering on their side of the deal.
- Try to be realistic about your skills; they will probably define what you can usefully contribute. Communities in Botswana don't need unskilled hobbyists; they need professionals. To teach skills properly takes years of volunteering, not weeks. (How long did *you* take to learn those skills?) So, for example, if you're not a qualified teacher or builder in your home country, then don't expect to be let loose to do any teaching or building in Botswana.
- Most volunteers will learn much more than the members of the communities that they come to 'help'; be aware of this when you describe who is helping whom.
- Make sure that what you are doing isn't effectively taking away a job from a local person.

Time in Botswana will do you lots of good; make sure it's not to the detriment of your hosts.

6

Health and Safety

with Dr Felicity Nicholson

There is always great danger in writing about health and safety for the uninitiated visitor. It is all too easy to become paranoid about exotic diseases that you may catch, and all too easy to start distrusting everybody you meet as a potential thief – falling into an unfounded us-and-them attitude towards the people of the country you are visiting.

As a comparison, imagine an equivalent section in a guidebook to a Western country – there would be a list of possible diseases and advice on the risk of theft and mugging. Many Western cities are very dangerous, but with time we learn how to assess the risks, accepting almost subconsciously what we can and cannot do.

It is important to strike the right balance: to avoid being excessively cautious or too relaxed about your health and your safety. With experience, you will find the balance that best fits you and the country you are visiting.

HEALTH

BEFORE YOU GO

Travel insurance Visitors to Botswana should always take out a comprehensive **medical insurance policy** to cover them for emergencies, including the cost of evacuation to another country within the region. Such policies come with an emergency number (often on a reverse-charge/call-collect basis). You would be wise to memorise this, or indelibly tattoo it in as many places as possible on your baggage.

Personal-effects insurance is also a sensible precaution, but check the policy's fine print before you leave home. Often, in even the best policies, you will find a limit per item, or per claim – which can be well below the cost of replacement. If you need to list your valuables separately, then do so comprehensively. Check that receipts are not required for claims if you do not have them, and that the excess which you have to pay on a claim is reasonable.

Annual travel policies can be excellent value if you travel a lot, and some of the larger credit-card companies offer excellent policies. However, it can often be better to get your valuables named and insured for travel using your home contents insurance. These year-round policies will try harder to settle your claim fairly as they want your business in the long term.

Immunisations Having a full set of immunisations takes time, normally at least six weeks, although some protection can be had by visiting your doctor as late as a few days before you travel. Ideally, see your doctor or travel clinic (page 164) early on to establish an inoculation timetable.

Legal requirements There is no risk of yellow fever disease in Botswana, but a certificate for yellow fever vaccine is required for entry into Botswana if you are coming from a yellow fever endemic area, transiting through an airport of a yellow fever endemic area, or travelling on a passport issued in a country where yellow fever is endemic. Talk to a registered yellow fever centre to see if the vaccine is suitable for you.

Recommended precautions Preparations to ensure a healthy trip to Botswana require checks on your immunisation status: it is wise to be up to date on **tetanus**, **polio** and **diphtheria** (given as an all-in-one vaccine, Revaxis, that lasts for ten years), typhoid and hepatitis A. Immunisations against hepatitis B and rabies may also be recommended. Immunisation against cholera is not required for trips to Botswana, but there have been several reported cases recently, so may be worth considering if you are spending any length of time in highly populated areas.

Hepatitis A vaccine (eg: Havrix Monodos, Vaqta or Avaxim) comprises two injections given about a year apart. The course costs about £100, but may be available on the NHS; it protects for 25 years and can be administered even close to the time of departure. **Hepatitis B** vaccination should be considered for longer trips (one month or more), for those working with children, or in situations such as a hospital or contact sport where contact with blood is likely. Three injections are needed for the best protection and, for those aged over 16, can be given over a three-week period if time is short. Longer schedules give more sustained protection and are therefore preferred if time allows. Hepatitis A vaccine can also be given as a combination with hepatitis B as 'Twinrix', though two doses are needed at least seven days apart to be effective for the hepatitis A component, and three doses are needed for the hepatitis B. Again the former schedule applies only to those aged 16 or over.

Vaccination against **typhoid** is encouraged unless you are leaving within a few days for a trip of a week or less, when the vaccine would not be effective in time. Injectable vaccines (eg: Typhim Vi), last for three years and are about 70–80% effective, while three oral capsules (Vivotif) taken over five days will also last for about three years. However, the capsules may be less effective, although they are a useful alternative for those aged six and over.

Vaccination against **rabies** is advised for everyone (pages 172–3). Ideally you should have three pre-exposure injections over a minimum of 21 days, but this is especially important if you intend to have contact with animals and/or are likely to be more than 24 hours away from medical help. Contrary to popular belief these vaccinations are relatively painless.

Experts differ over whether a BCG vaccination against **tuberculosis** (TB) is useful in adults: discuss this with your travel clinic.

In addition to the various vaccinations recommended above, it is important that you should be properly protected against malaria. For detailed advice, see below.

Ideally you should visit your own doctor or a specialist travel clinic (page 164) to discuss your requirements if possible at least eight weeks before you plan to travel.

Malaria
Malaria is the most dangerous disease in Africa, and the greatest risk to the traveller. It occurs throughout northern Botswana, all the year round, so it is essential that you take all possible precautions against it. Key to these are prevention of mosquito bites, and taking a suitable prophylactic agent.

Malaria prevention Prophylaxis regimes aim to infuse your bloodstream with drugs that inhibit and kill the malaria parasites which are injected into you by a biting mosquito. This is why you must start to take the drugs *before* you arrive in a malarial area – so that they are established in your bloodstream from day one. Unfortunately, malaria parasites continually adapt to the drugs used to combat them, so the recommended regimes must adapt and change in order to remain effective. None is 100% effective, and all require time to kill the parasites – so unless there is a medical indication for stopping, it is important to complete the course after leaving the area as directed (usually one to four weeks depending on the regime). Falciparum (cerebral) malaria is the most common in Africa, and usually fatal if untreated, so it is worth your while trying to avoid it.

Seek current advice on the best anti-malarials to take: usually mefloquine, Malarone or doxycycline. If mefloquine (Lariam) is suggested, start this 2½ weeks (three doses) before departure to check that it suits you; stop it immediately if it seems to cause depression or anxiety, visual or hearing disturbances, severe headaches, fits or changes in heart rhythm. Side effects such as nightmares or dizziness are not medical reasons for stopping unless they are sufficiently debilitating or annoying. Anyone who has been treated for depression or psychiatric problems, has diabetes controlled by oral therapy or who is epileptic (or who has suffered fits in the past) or has a close blood relative who is epileptic, should probably avoid mefloquine.

In the past doctors were nervous about prescribing mefloquine to pregnant women, but experience has shown that it is relatively safe and certainly safer than the risk of malaria. That said, there are other issues, so if you are travelling to Botswana while pregnant, seek expert advice before departure.

Malarone (atovaquone/proguanil) is as effective as mefloquine. It has the advantage of few side effects and need only be continued for one week after returning. However, it is expensive and because of this tends to be reserved for shorter trips. Malarone may not be suitable for everybody, so take advice from a doctor. For most people, it can be taken safely for a year or more. It is suitable for children weighing 11–40kg, but can also be prescribed for those beneath this weight.

A third alternative is the antibiotic doxycycline (100mg daily). Like Malarone it can be started one to two days before arrival. Unlike mefloquine, it may also be used in travellers with epilepsy, although certain anti-epileptic medication may make it less effective. In perhaps 1–3% of people there is the possibility of allergic skin reactions developing in sunlight; the drug should be stopped if this happens. It is also unsuitable in pregnancy or for children under 12 years.

All tablets should be taken with or after the evening meal, washed down with plenty of fluid and, with the exception of Malarone (see above), continued for four weeks after leaving.

Despite all these precautions, it is important to be aware that no anti-malarial drug is 100% protective, although those on prophylactics who are unlucky enough to catch malaria are less likely to get rapidly into serious trouble. In addition to taking anti-malarials, it is therefore important to avoid mosquito bites between dusk and dawn (pages 168–9).

There is unfortunately the occasional traveller who prefers to 'acquire resistance' to malaria rather than take preventative tablets, or who takes homeopathic 'prophylactics' thinking these are effective against a killer disease. However, since homeopathy theory dictates treating like with like, it does not provide for prophylaxis or immunisation in a well person, so bona fide homeopaths do not advocate it. As for resistance, it takes at least 18 months residing in a malarial area for someone to get some immunity to malaria, so travellers to Africa will not acquire any effective resistance.

Travel clinics and health information A full list of current travel clinic websites worldwide is available on www.istm.org. For other journey preparation information, consult http://travelhealthpro.org.uk (UK) or http://wwwnc.cdc. gov/travel/ (US). Information about various medications may be found on www. netdoctor.co.uk/travel. All advice found online should be used in conjunction with expert advice received prior to or during travel.

Medical kit Pharmacies in Botswana's main towns, and in Livingstone, generally have good supplies of medicines, but away from these you will find very little. If you're venturing deep into the wilds on an independent trip, then you should take with you anything that you expect to need. If you are on an organised trip, an overlanding truck, or staying at hotels, lodges or safari camps, then you will not need much, as these establishments normally have comprehensive emergency kits. In that case, just a small personal medical kit might include:

- alcohol-based hand rub or bar of soap in plastic box
- antihistamine tablets
- antiseptic, eg: iodine or potassium permanganate (don't take antiseptic cream)
- blister plasters (if you plan any serious walking)
- condoms or femidoms and contraceptive pills
- impregnated bed-net or permethrin spray
- insect repellent
- lipsalve (ideally containing a sunscreen)
- malaria prophylaxis
- Micropore tape (for closing small cuts – and invaluable for blisters)
- moisturising cream
- paracetamol or aspirin (but note that aspirin should not be given in the event of snakebite, nor if you think you have dengue fever)
- sticking plaster (a roll is more versatile than pre-shaped plasters)
- sunscreen

However, if you are likely to end up in very remote situations, then you should also consider taking the following – and know how to use them:

- burns dressings (burns are a common problem for campers)
- antibiotics: ciprofloxacin or norfloxacin, for severe diarrhoea
- antibiotic eye drops, for sore, 'gritty', stuck-together eyes (conjunctivitis)
- injection swabs, sterile needles and syringes
- lint, sterile bandage and safety pins
- oral rehydration sachets
- steristrips or butterfly closures
- strong painkiller (eg: codeine phosphate – also use for bad diarrhoea)
- tweezers (perhaps those on a Swiss army knife)
- water purification equipment (page 167)
- a good medical manual (see *Appendix 3*, page 544)
- tinidazole for giardia or amoebic dysentery (see page 170 for regime)
- a digital thermometer

If you wear glasses, bring a spare pair. Similarly, those who wear contact lenses should bring spare ones, also a pair of glasses in case the dust proves too much for the lenses. If you take regular medication (including contraceptive pills) then

LONG-HAUL FLIGHTS, CLOTS AND DVT   *Dr Felicity Nicholson*

Any prolonged immobility, including travel by land or air, can result in deep-vein thrombosis (DVT) with the risk of embolus to the lungs. Certain factors can increase the risk and these include:

- History of DVT or pulmonary embolism
- Recent surgery to pelvic region or legs
- Cancer
- Stroke
- Heart disease
- Inherited tendency to clot (thrombophilia)
- Obesity
- Pregnancy
- Hormone therapy
- Older age
- Being over 6 foot or under 5 foot

A deep-vein thrombosis causes painful swelling and redness of the calf or sometimes the thigh. It is only dangerous if a clot travels to the lungs (pulmonary embolus). Symptoms of a pulmonary embolus (PE) – which commonly start three to ten days after a long flight – include chest pain, shortness of breath, and sometimes coughing up small amounts of blood. Anyone who thinks that they might have a DVT needs to see a doctor immediately.

PREVENTION OF DVT
- Wear loose comfortable clothing
- Do anti-DVT exercises and move around when possible
- Drink plenty of fluids during the flight
- Avoid taking sleeping pills unless you are able to lie flat
- Avoid excessive tea, coffee and alcohol
- Consider wearing flight socks or support stocking (*www.leghealthwarehouse.com*)

If you think you are at increased risk of a clot, ask your doctor if it is safe to travel.

bring a large supply with you – much easier than hunting for your usual brand in Botswana. Equally, it's worth having a dental check-up before you go, as you could be several painful days from the nearest dentist.

IN BOTSWANA Health care in Botswana is provided both by the government and on a private basis, with some facilities built and operated by mining companies.

Hospitals, dentists and pharmacies Botswana's main **hospitals**, in Maun (0800 600897), Francistown (0800 600891) and Gaborone (0800 600905), are capable of serious surgery and a good quality of care; they will also treat you first and ask for money later. However, the public health system is over-stretched and under-funded, so unless your illness is critical, it will take time for you to be attended to and treated at the public hospitals. Bear in mind, too, that a large number of patients in the public hospitals have serious infectious diseases, so there's a risk of coming away from these with something worse than you had when you arrived.

Assuming that you have comprehensive medical insurance as part of your travel cover – and you should check that you have – it is probably better go to one of the better-funded **private clinics** which are found in each of the main towns. These cater for both affluent citizens of Botswana and expats/diplomatic staff/travellers. They will accept payment from genuine travel-health insurance schemes. The best way to find details of the nearest private clinics is to look up 'medical – private clinics/practitioners' in the yellow pages at the back of the phone book.

In an emergency, contact:

Medical Rescue International Emergency 992; international emergency number +267 390 1601; helpdesk m 7132 2361; e enquiries@mri.co.bw; www.mri.co.bw. MRI organises 24hr medical evacuations from anywhere in Botswana. They insure individual travellers, & your own insurance company may pick up the bills if their services are needed, but many lodges are also members, covering you while you are staying there (though you will still need your own medical insurance).

Okavango Air Rescue Emergency 995, or +267 686 1506 from a satellite phone; office 686 1616; Maun m 7433 9743; e office@okavangorescue.com; www.okavangorescue.com. This not-for-profit organisation is on call 24/7. Their helicopter has a qualified doctor on board, & can airlift patients out if necessary. Many tour operators include their services, but individual membership costs just P175/year – around US$17.50/£13.

Ambulance 997 (public hospital emergency service)

Pharmacies in Botswana's main towns (and in Livingstone) generally have a good range of medicines, though specific brands are often unavailable. So bring with you all that you will need, as well as a repeat prescription for anything that you might run out of. Outside of the larger towns you probably won't be able to find anything other than very basic medical supplies. Thus you should carry a very comprehensive medical kit if you are planning to head off into the wilds (pages 164–5).

Staying healthy
Botswana is one of the healthiest countries in sub-Saharan Africa. It has a generally low population density, who are affluent by the region's standards, and a very dry climate, which means there are comparatively few problems likely to affect visitors. The risks are further minimised if you are staying in good hotels, lodges, camps and guest farms, where standards of hygiene are generally at least as good as you will find at home.

The major dangers in Botswana are car accidents (caused by driving too fast, or at night, on gravel roads) and sunburn. Both can be very serious, yet both are within the power of the visitor to avoid.

The following is general advice, applicable to travelling anywhere, including Botswana.

Food and storage
Throughout the world, most health problems encountered by travellers are contracted by eating contaminated food or drinking unclean water. If you are staying in safari camps or lodges, or eating in restaurants, then you are unlikely to have problems in Botswana.

However, if you are backpacking and cooking for yourself, or relying on local food, then you need to take more care. Tins, packets and fresh green vegetables (when you can find them) are least likely to cause problems – provided that clean water has been used in preparing the meal. In Botswana's hot climate, keeping meat or other animal products unrefrigerated for more than a few hours is asking for trouble.

Water and purification Tap water in Botswana's major towns, and borehole water – which is used in most of the more remote locations – is perfectly safe to drink for local residents. However, even the mildest of the local microbes may cause a slightly upset stomach for an overseas visitor so you would be wise to use bottled or treated water at all times – and this includes cleaning your teeth. Two-litre bottles of mineral water are available from most supermarkets; these are perfect if you're in a car. The majority of safari camps use borehole water that is extensively filtered, but increasingly they also have large containers of purified water, with which guests can fill their own water bottles (which are often supplied too). Bottled water is usually available as a back up, too.

If you're going it alone, you might want to consider using a bottle with a filter (eg: Aquapure). You can filter anything from river water to tap water without having to wait to drink it and the filter lasts for 350 litres. There is no need to boil the water either. If you don't have an Aquapure bottle, first filter out any suspended solids, perhaps by passing the water through a piece of closely woven cloth or something similar. Then bring it to the boil, or sterilise it chemically with chlorine dioxide. Boiling is much more effective, provided that you have the fuel available. Iodine tablets are no longer advised for water sterilisation. Another, albeit expensive, alternative is to use an electronic sterilisation device, such as a SteriPen.

Heat and sun Heatstroke, heat exhaustion and sunburn are often problems for travellers to Botswana, despite being easy to prevent. To avoid them, you need to remember that your body is under stress and make allowances for it. First, take things gently; you are on holiday, after all. Next, keep your fluid and salt levels high: lots of water and soft drinks, but go easy on the caffeine and alcohol. Third, dress to keep cool with loose-fitting, thin garments – preferably of cotton, linen or silk. Finally, beware of the sun. Hats and long-sleeved shirts are essential. If you must expose your skin to the sun, then use sun blocks and high-factor sunscreens (the sun is so strong that you will still get a tan). Be especially careful of exposure in the middle of the day and of sun reflected off water, and wear a T-shirt and lots of waterproof suncream (at least SPF25 and a UVA of four or more stars) when swimming. The glare and the dust can be hard on the eyes, too, so bring UV-protecting sunglasses and, perhaps, a soothing eyebath.

Prickly heat A fine pimply rash on the trunk is likely to be heat rash; cool showers, dabbing dry and talc will help. Treat the problem by slowing down to a relaxed schedule, wearing only loose, baggy, 100%-cotton clothes and sleeping naked under a fan; if it's bad you may need to check into an air-conditioned hotel room for a while.

Eye problems Bacterial conjunctivitis (pink eye) is a common infection in Africa; people who wear contact lenses are most open to this irritating problem. The eyes feel sore and gritty and they will often be stuck closed in the mornings. They will need treatment with antibiotic drops or ointment. Lesser eye irritation should settle with bathing in salt water and keeping the eyes shaded. If an insect flies into your eye, extract it with great care, ensuring you do not crush or damage it otherwise you may get a nastily inflamed eye from toxins secreted by the creature.

Small elongated red-and-black blister beetles carry warning colouration to tell you not to crush them anywhere against your skin.

Skin infections Any mosquito bite or small nick in the skin gives an opportunity for bacteria to foil the body's usually excellent defences; it will surprise many travellers how quickly skin infections start in warm humid climates and it is essential to clean and cover even the slightest wound. Creams are not as effective as a good drying antiseptic such as dilute iodine, potassium permanganate (a few crystals in half a cup of water) or crystal (or gentian) violet. One of these should be available in most towns. If the wound starts to throb, or becomes red and the redness starts to spread, or the wound oozes, and especially if you develop a fever, antibiotics will probably be needed: flucloxacillin (250mg four times a day) or cloxacillin (500mg four times a day). For those allergic to penicillin, erythromycin (500mg twice a day) for five days should help. See a doctor if the symptoms do not start to improve within 48 hours.

Fungal infections also get a hold easily in hot, moist climates so wear 100%-cotton socks and underwear and shower frequently. An itchy rash in the groin or flaking between the toes is likely to be a fungal infection. This needs treatment with an antifungal cream such as Canesten (clotrimazole); if this is not available try Whitfield's ointment (compound benzoic acid ointment) or crystal violet (although this will turn you purple!).

Avoiding insect bites The most dangerous biting insects in parts of Botswana are mosquitoes, because they can transmit malaria, dengue fever and a host of other diseases. Research has shown that using a mosquito net over your bed, and covering up exposed skin (by wearing long-sleeved shirts, and tucking trousers into socks) in the evening, are the most effective steps towards preventing bites. Bed-net treatment kits are available from travel clinics; these prevent mosquitoes biting through a net if you roll against it in your sleep, and also make old and holey nets protective. Mosquito coils and chemical insect repellents will help, and sleeping in a stream of moving air, such as under a fan, or in an air-conditioned room, will help to reduce your chances of being bitten.

DEET (diethyltoluamide) is the active ingredient in many repellents. The optimum concentration, of 50%, can safely be used in pregnancy and on babies from two months upwards. Note, however, that it will dissolve some plastics and synthetic materials, and may irritate sensitive skin, so care should be taken. Mosquito repellent must be applied to all exposed skin as mosquitoes will find any untreated skin.

Natural repellents are generally less effective than DEET-based ones and have to be used more frequently. Those who are genuinely allergic to DEET could use a repellent containing picaradin or a natural repellent containing p menthane diol (PND) derived from lemon eucalyptus. Both these repellents have to be applied more frequently than 50% DEET. Other remedies, such as eating garlic or taking vitamin B, are anecdotal and there is no evidence to suggest they work, so never substitute these for DEET.

Mosquitoes and many other insects are attracted to light. If you are camping, never put a lamp near the opening of your tent, or you will have a swarm of biters waiting to join you when you retire. In hotel rooms, be aware that the longer your light is on, the greater the number of insects which will be sharing your accommodation.

Aside from avoiding mosquito bites between dusk and dawn, which will protect you from elephantiasis and a range of nasty insect-borne viruses, as well as malaria (pages 162–3), it is important to take precautions against other insect bites. During the day it is wise to wear long, loose (preferably 100%-cotton) clothes if you are pushing through scrubby country; this will keep off ticks and also tsetse and day-biting *Aedes* mosquitoes which may spread viral fevers such as dengue fever and zika virus. You can also treat natural-fibre clothing with clothing sprays that contain permethrin, such as Lifesystems EX4. The insecticide will kill mosquitoes on contact with the fabric; the clothes will survive a few washes and will still be effective.

Tsetse flies are now rare in the Okavango Delta thanks to a government initiative to eradicate them. The flies hurt when they bite and it is said that they are attracted to the colour blue; locals will advise if they are a problem and whether they transmit sleeping sickness.

Minute pestilential biting blackflies spread river blindness in some parts of Africa between 19°N and 17°S; the disease is caught close to fast-flowing rivers since flies breed there and the larvae live in rapids. The flies bite during the day but long trousers tucked into socks will help keep them off. Citronella-based natural repellents (eg: Mosi-guard) do not work against them.

Tumbu flies or putsi, often called mango flies, are a problem where the climate is hot and humid. The adult fly lays her eggs on the soil or on drying laundry and when the eggs come into contact with human flesh (when you put on clothes or lie on a bed) they hatch and bury themselves under the skin. Here they form a crop of 'boils' each with a maggot inside. Smear a little Vaseline over the hole, and they will push their noses out to breathe. It may be possible to squeeze them out but it depends if they are ready to do so as the larvae have spines that help them to hold on.

In putsi areas either dry your clothes and sheets within a screened house, or dry them in direct sunshine until they are crisp, or iron them.

Jiggers, or sandfleas, are another flesh-feaster, which can be best avoided by wearing shoes. They latch on if you walk barefoot in contaminated places, and set up home under the skin of the foot, usually at the side of a toenail where they cause a painful, boil-like swelling. They need picking out by a local expert.

Snakes, spiders and scorpions Encounters with aggressive snakes, angry spiders or vindictive scorpions are more common in horror films than in Botswana. Most snakes will flee at the mere vibrations of a human footstep while spiders are far more interested in flies than people. You will have to seek out scorpions if you wish to see one. If you are careful about where you place your hands and feet, especially after dark, then there should be no problems. You are less likely to get bitten or stung if you wear stout shoes and long trousers. Simple precautions include not putting on boots without shaking them empty first, and always checking the back of your backpack before putting it on.

Snakes do bite occasionally, and you ought to know the standard first-aid treatment. First, and most importantly, *don't panic*. Most snakes are harmless and even venomous species will only dispense venom in about half of their bites. If bitten, you are unlikely to have received venom; keeping this fact in mind may help you to stay calm.

Even in the worst of these cases, the victim has hours or days to get to help, and not a matter of minutes. He/she should be kept calm, with no exertions to pump venom around the blood system, while being taken rapidly to the nearest medical help. The area of the bite should be washed to remove any venom from the skin, and the bitten limb should be immobilised. Paracetamol may be used as a painkiller, but never use aspirin because it may cause internal bleeding.

Most first-aid techniques do more harm than good: cutting into the wound is harmful and tourniquets are dangerous; suction and electrical inactivation devices do not work. The only effective treatment is antivenom. In case of a bite that you fear may be both serious and venomous:

- Try to keep calm. It is likely that no venom has been dispensed.
- Stop movement of the bitten limb by applying a splint.
- If you have a crêpe bandage, wrap it around the whole limb (eg: all the way from the toes to the thigh), as tight as you would for a sprained ankle or a muscle pull.
- Keep the bitten limb *below* heart height to slow the spread of any venom.
- Evacuate the victim to a hospital that has antivenom.
- *Never* give aspirin. You may offer paracetamol, which is safe.
- *Do not* apply ice packs.
- *Do not* apply potassium permanganate.

If the offending snake can be captured without any risk of someone else being bitten, take it to show the doctor. But beware, since even a decapitated head is able to dispense venom in a reflex bite.

When deep in the bush, heading for the nearest large farm or camp may be quicker than going to a town: it may have a supply of antivenom, or facilities to radio for help by plane.

DISEASES AND WHEN TO SEE A DOCTOR

Travellers' diarrhoea There are almost as many names for this as there are travellers' tales on the subject. Firstly, do resist the temptation to reach for the medical kit as soon as your stomach turns a little fluid. Most cases of travellers' diarrhoea will resolve themselves within 24–48 hours with no treatment at all. To speed up this process of acclimatisation, eat well but simply: avoid fats in favour of starches, and keep your fluid intake high. Bananas and papaya fruit are often claimed to be helpful. If you urgently need to stop the symptoms, for a long journey for example, then Lomotil, Imodium or another of the commercial anti-diarrhoea preparations will do the trick. They stop the symptoms, by paralysing the bowel, but will not cure the problem. They should be used only as a last resort and never if you have bad abdominal cramps with the diarrhoea.

If the diarrhoea persists for more than two days, or the stools contain blood, pus or slime, and/or you have a fever, you must seek medical advice. There are as many possible treatments as there are causes, and a proper diagnosis involves microscopic analysis of a stool sample, so go straight to your nearest hospital. The most important thing, especially in Botswana's climate, is to keep your fluid intake up. If it is not possible to reach medical help quickly then a dose of norfloxacin or ciprofloxacin repeated twice a day until reaching medical help may be appropriate. (If you are planning to take an antibiotic with you, note that both norfloxacin and ciprofloxacin are available only on prescription in the UK.) If the diarrhoea is greasy and bulky and is accompanied by sulphurous (eggy) burps, the likely cause is giardia. This is best treated with tinidazole (four x 500mg in one dose, repeated seven days later if symptoms persist).

The body's absorption of fluids is assisted by adding small amounts of dissolved sugars, salts and minerals to the water. Sachets of oral rehydration salts give the perfect biochemical mix you need to replace what is pouring out of your bottom but they do not taste so nice. Any dilute mixture of sugar and salt in water will do you good so, if you like Coke or orange squash, drink that with a three-finger pinch of salt added to each glass. The ideal ratio is eight level teaspoons of sugar and one level teaspoon of salt dissolved in one litre of water. Palm syrup or honey make good substitutes for sugar, and including fresh citrus juice will not only improve the taste of these solutions, but also add valuable potassium.

Drink two large glasses after every bowel action, and more if you are thirsty. If you are not eating you need to drink three litres a day *plus* whatever you are sweating *and* the equivalent of what's going into the toilet. If you feel like eating, take a bland diet; heavy greasy foods will give you cramps.

If you are likely to be more than a few days from qualified medical help, then come equipped with a good health manual and the selection of antibiotics which it recommends. *The Essential Guide to Travel Health* by Dr Jane Wilson-Howarth (see *Appendix 3*, page 544) is excellent for this purpose.

Malaria You can still catch malaria even if you are taking anti-malarial drugs so you should do everything possible to avoid mosquito bites. Untreated malaria is likely to be fatal, but even strains resistant to prophylaxis respond well to prompt treatment. Because of this, your immediate priority upon displaying possible malaria symptoms – including a rapid rise in temperature (over 38°C), and any combination of a headache, flu-like aches and pains, a general sense of disorientation, and possibly even nausea and diarrhoea – is to establish whether you have malaria, ideally by visiting a clinic.

A definite diagnosis of malaria is normally possible only by examining a blood sample under the microscope. It is best to get the problem properly diagnosed if possible, so don't treat yourself if you can easily reach a hospital first. You need three negative tests on consecutive days to be sure it isn't malaria, so stay within reach of a laboratory. It's worth noting that if you have a fever and the malaria test is negative, you may have typhoid or paratyphoid, which should also receive immediate treatment.

If (and only if) medical help is unavailable, then self-treatment is fairly safe, except for people who are pregnant or under 12 years of age. Should you be travelling to remote parts of Botswana, you would be wise to carry a course of treatment to cure malaria. Trying to use a rapid diagnostic kit if you are inexperienced and unwell often gives misleading results so is best avoided unless you are experienced in using them. With malaria, it is normal enough to go from feeling healthy to having a high fever in the space of a few hours (and it is possible to die from falciparum malaria within 24 hours of the first symptoms). In such circumstances, assume that you have malaria and act accordingly – whatever risks are attached to taking an unnecessary cure are outweighed by the dangers of untreated malaria.

There is some division about the best treatment for malaria, but either Malarone or Coarthemeter are the current treatments of choice. In Botswana you should always be able to get experienced local advice to tell you which will be the most effective.

Dengue fever This mosquito-borne disease – and other similar arboviruses – may mimic malaria but there is no prophylactic medication available to deal with it. The mosquitoes that carry this virus bite during the daytime, so it is worth applying repellent if you see any mosquitoes around. Symptoms include strong headaches, rashes, excruciating joint and muscle pains and high fever. Dengue fever only lasts for a week or so and is not usually fatal. Complete rest and paracetamol are the usual treatment. Plenty of fluids also help. Some patients are given an intravenous drip to keep them from dehydrating. It is especially important to protect yourself if you have had dengue fever before. A second infection with a different strain can result in the potentially fatal dengue haemorrhagic fever.

Sexually transmitted diseases AIDS is spread in exactly the same way in Africa as it is at home, through body secretions, blood and blood products. The same goes for the dangerous hepatitis B. Both can be spread through sex.

Remember that the risks of sexually transmitted disease are high, whether you sleep with fellow travellers or locals. About 40% of HIV infections in British heterosexuals are acquired abroad. If you must indulge, use condoms or femidoms, which help reduce the risk of transmission. If you do have unprotected sex, visit a clinic as soon as possible; this should be within 24 hours, or no later than 72 hours, for post-exposure prophylaxis. And if you notice any genital ulcers or discharge, get treatment promptly.

Hepatitis This is a group of viral diseases which generally start with Coca-Cola-coloured urine and light-coloured stools. It progresses to fevers, weakness, jaundice (yellow skin and eyeballs) and abdominal pains caused by a severe inflammation of the liver. There are several forms, of which the two most common are typical of the rest: hepatitis A (or infectious hepatitis) and hepatitis B (or serum hepatitis).

Hepatitis A and hepatitis E are spread by the faecal-oral route, that is by ingesting food or drink contaminated by excrement. They are avoided in the same ways you normally avoid stomach problems: by careful preparation of food and by drinking only clean water. But as there are now excellent vaccines against hepatitis A it is certainly worth getting inoculated before you travel (page 162).

In contrast, the more serious but rarer hepatitis B is spread in the same way as AIDS (by blood or body secretions), and is avoided the same way as one avoids AIDS. There is a vaccine which protects against hepatitis B, but three doses are needed over a minimum of 21 days. It is usually considered necessary only for medical workers, people working closely with children or if you intend to travel for six weeks or longer. There are no cures for hepatitis, but with lots of bed rest and a good low-fat, no-alcohol diet most people recover within six months. If you are unlucky enough to contract hepatitis of any form, use your travel insurance to fly straight home.

Rabies Rabies is carried by all warm-blooded mammals (beware the village dogs, and small monkeys that congregate around campsites in the parks) and is passed on to humans through a bite, a scratch, or simply saliva – on your skin, or into your eyes, nose or mouth. You must always assume any animal is rabid as they can often look well but still be infectious. Seek medical help as soon as possible after any potential exposure. Meanwhile scrub the wound with soap under a running tap or while pouring water from a jug for a good 10–15 minutes. The source of the water is not important, but if you have antiseptic to hand, then put this on afterwards. The soap helps stop the rabies virus entering the body and along with an antiseptic will guard against wound infections, including tetanus.

Post-exposure prophylaxis should be given as soon as possible, though it is never too late to seek help, as the incubation period for rabies can be very long.

Tell the doctor if you have had pre-exposure vaccine, as this will change the treatment you receive. If you have had three doses of pre-exposure vaccine, you will need only a couple of doses of rabies vaccine, ideally given three days apart.

Those who have not been immunised before (page 162) will need four or five doses of vaccine over 28–30 days and should also receive a product called rabies immunoglobulin (RIG – either human or horse). This is injected round the wound

NATIONAL PARKS AND ANTHRAX

Outbreaks of anthrax are relatively common among the animals in Botswana's national parks, but the Botswana authorities monitor the situation very closely, putting affected areas off-limits to visitors for a considerable period of time.

To allay any fears, it's worth noting a few facts about anthrax. It is a bacterial disease caused by the spore-forming *Bacillius anthracis*, and is primarily contracted by herbivores such as cattle, goats or sheep; outbreaks among carnivores are rare. Humans can contract the disease only if they come into direct contact with infected animals, their carcasses or material, including soil; it cannot be passed from one human to another. Fortunately the risk for travellers of getting anthrax is very low. Unless you're planning to eat the meat, or to get close enough to touch any animal or part of an animal, you're not at risk – though remember to avoid buying souvenirs made from animal skin, however tempting. For the most part, the disease occurs in the dry season when animals graze closer to the soil, where the spores can survive for a considerable period of time – hence the recurrence of outbreaks year on year. For this reason, proper disposal of carcasses, usually by incineration, is a crucial part of anthrax control measures.

Symptoms of anthrax vary, but usually occur within seven days. Most infections result from a cut or graze coming into contact with the bacteria. In this instance, what appears to be an insect bite grows within a couple of days into a painless ulcer about 1–3cm across, with a black centre, and surrounding lymph glands may swell. This type of infection usually responds well to antibiotics. Rarely, as a result of inhalation of spores, the apparent symptoms of a common cold progress to severe breathing problems, with a bleak outlook. A third form of the disease, which may follow the consumption of contaminated meat, leads to inflammation of the intestine, with potentially fatal consequences. While a vaccine is available, it is not normally recommended that visitors to Botswana should be inoculated.

to try and neutralise any rabies virus present and is a pivotal part of the treatment, but it is expensive and is not usually readily available in Botswana, so it is important to insist on getting to a place that has it. Another reason for having good insurance. And remember that, if you do contract rabies, mortality is 100% and death from rabies is probably one of the worst ways to go.

Tickbite fever African ticks are not the rampant disease transmitters they are in the Americas, but they may spread tickbite fever and a few dangerous rarities in Botswana. Tickbite fever is a flu-like illness that can easily be treated with doxycycline, but as there can be some serious complications it is important to visit a doctor. It is most prevalent in Botswana between November and January.

Ticks should ideally be removed as soon as possible as leaving them on the body increases the chance of infection. They should be removed with special tick tweezers that can be bought in good travel shops. Failing that you can use your fingernails: grasp the tick as close to your body as possible and pull steadily and firmly away at right angles to your skin. The tick will then come away complete, as long as you do not jerk or twist. If possible douse the wound with alcohol (any spirit will do) or iodine. Irritants (eg: Olbas oil) or lit cigarettes are to be discouraged since they can cause the ticks to regurgitate and therefore increase the risk of disease. It is best to get a travelling companion to check you for ticks; if you are travelling with small children, remember to check their heads, and particularly behind the ears.

Spreading redness around the bite and/or fever and/or aching joints after a tickbite imply that you have an infection that requires antibiotic treatment, so seek advice.

Bilharzia or schistosomiasis Though a low risk in Botswana, bilharzia is an insidious disease, contracted by coming into contact with contaminated water. It is caused by parasitic worms which live part of their lives in freshwater snails, and part of their lives in human bladders or intestines. A common indication of an infection is a localised itchy rash – where the parasites have burrowed through the skin – and later symptoms of a more advanced infection may include passing bloody urine. Bilharzia is readily treated by medication, and only serious if it remains untreated.

The only way to avoid infection completely is to stay away from any bodies of fresh water. Obviously this is restrictive, and could make your trip less enjoyable. More pragmatic advice is to avoid slow-moving or sluggish water, and ask local opinion on the bilharzia risk, as not all water is contaminated. It's generally thought that the Okavango Delta is not infected with bilharzia.

Generally bilharzia snails do not inhabit fast-flowing water, and hence rivers are free of it. However, dams and standing water, especially in populated areas, are usually heavily contaminated. If you think you have been infected, don't worry about it – just get a test done on your return at least six weeks after your last possible exposure.

Avoiding bilharzia If you are bathing, swimming, paddling or wading in fresh water which you think may carry a bilharzia risk, try to get out of the water within 10 minutes.

- Avoid bathing or paddling on shores within 200m of villages or places where people use the water a great deal, especially reedy shores or where there is lots of waterweed.
- Dry off thoroughly with a towel; rub vigorously.
- If your bathing water comes from a risky source try to ensure that the water is taken from the lake in the early morning and stored snail-free, otherwise it should be filtered or Dettol or Cresol added.
- Bathing early in the morning is safer than bathing in the last half of the day.
- Cover yourself with DEET insect repellent before swimming: it may offer some protection.

Returning home Many tropical diseases have a long incubation period, and it is possible to develop symptoms weeks after returning home (this is why it is important to keep taking anti-malaria prophylaxis for the prescribed duration after you leave a malarial zone). If you do get ill after you return home, be certain to tell your doctor where you have been. Alert him/her to any diseases that you may have been exposed to. Several people die from malaria in the UK every year because victims do not seek medical help promptly or their doctors are not familiar with the symptoms, and so are slow to make a correct diagnosis. Milder forms of malaria may take up to a year to reveal themselves, but serious (falciparum) malaria will usually become apparent within three to six months, and can start as early as one week into a malarial area.

If problems persist, get a check-up at one of the hospitals that specialise in tropical diseases: the Hospital for Tropical Diseases in the UK (*www.thehtd.org*), or in the USA the Centers for Disease Control (*www.cdc.gov*). Note that to visit such a hospital in the UK, you need a letter of referral from your doctor.

SAFETY

Botswana is not a dangerous country. If you are travelling on an all-inclusive trip and staying at lodges and hotels, then problems of personal safety are exceedingly rare. There will always be someone on hand to help you. Even if you are travelling on local transport, perhaps on a low budget, you will generally be perfectly safe if you are careful.

Outside of rougher parts of the main cities, crime against visitors, however minor, is rare. Even if you are travelling on local transport on a low budget, you are likely to experience numerous acts of random kindness, but not crime. It is certainly safer for visitors than the UK, USA or most of Europe.

To get into a difficult situation, you'll usually have to try hard. You need to make yourself an obvious target for thieves, perhaps by walking around at night, with showy valuables, in a less affluent area of a town or city. Provided you are sensible, you are most unlikely to ever see any crime here.

For women travellers, especially those travelling alone, it is doubly important to learn the local attitudes, and how to behave acceptably. This takes some practice, and a certain confidence. You will often be the centre of attention but, by developing conversational techniques to avert over-enthusiastic male attention, you should be perfectly safe. Making friends of the local women is one way to help avoid such problems.

> ### SAFETY FOR WOMEN TRAVELLERS *Janice Booth*
>
> When attention becomes intrusive, it can help if you are wearing a wedding ring and have photos of 'your' husband and children, even if they are someone else's. A good reason to give for not being with them is that you have to travel in connection with your job – biology, zoology, geography, or whatever. (But not journalism – that's risky.)
>
> Pay attention to local etiquette, and to speaking, dressing and moving reasonably decorously. Look at how the local women dress, and try not to expose parts of yourself that they keep covered. Think about body language. In much of southern Africa direct eye-contact with a man will be seen as a 'come-on'; sunglasses are helpful here.
>
> Don't be afraid to explain clearly – but pleasantly rather than as a put-down – that you aren't in the market for whatever distractions are on offer. Remember that you are probably as much of a novelty to the local people as they are to you, and the fact that you are travelling abroad alone gives them the message that you are free and adventurous. But don't imagine that a Lothario lurks under every bush: many approaches stem from genuine friendliness or curiosity, and a brush-off in such cases doesn't do much for the image of travellers in general.
>
> Take sensible precautions against theft and attack – try to cover all the risks before you encounter them – and then relax and enjoy your trip. You'll meet far more kindness than villainy.

THEFT Theft is not generally a problem in Botswana – which is surprising given the poverty levels among much of the population. The only real exception to this is theft from unattended vehicles, which is becoming more common in the larger towns. If you leave a vehicle with anything valuable on view, then you may return to find a window smashed and items stolen.

When staying at safari camps in the bush, you'll often find that there are no locks and keys on the doors and there is a tremendous amount of trust. Regardless of this, leaving cash or valuables lying around or easily accessible is both stupid and very unfair to the camp's staff. Your watch could easily be worth a year's salary to them; make sure you keep such items out of sight and out of the way of temptation. Most safari camps provide small safes in their rooms for such items.

Should you experience a theft in a camp, report it to the management immediately – but bear in mind that most such reports are solved with the realisation that the property's owner mislaid it themselves!

How to avoid it Like anywhere, thieves in the bigger cities here work in groups and choose their targets carefully. These targets will be people who look vulnerable and who have items worth stealing. To avoid being robbed, try not to look too vulnerable or too rich – and certainly not both. Observing a few basic rules, especially during your first few weeks in Botswana's cities, will drastically reduce your chances of becoming a target. After that you should have learned your own way of assessing the risks, and avoiding thefts. Until then:

- Try not to carry anything of value around with you.
- If you must carry cash, then use a concealed money-belt for your main supply – keeping smaller change separately and to hand.
- Try not to look too foreign. Blend into the local scene as well as you can. Act like a streetwise expat rather than a tourist, if possible. (Conspicuously carrying a local newspaper may help with this.)
- Rucksacks and large, new bags are bad. If you must carry a bag, choose an old battered one. Around town, a local plastic carrier bag is ideal.
- Move confidently and look as if you know exactly what you are doing, and where you are going. Lost foreigners make the easiest targets.
- Never walk around at night – that is asking for trouble.
- If you have a vehicle then don't leave anything in it, and avoid leaving it parked outside in a city.

Reporting thefts to the police If you are the victim of a theft then report it to the police – they ought to know. Also try to get a copy of the report, or at least a reference number on an official-looking piece of paper, as this will help you to claim on your insurance policy when you return home. Some insurance companies won't act without it. But remember that reporting anything in a police station can take a long time, and do not expect any speedy arrests for a small case of pickpocketing.

ARREST To get arrested in Botswana, a foreigner will normally have to try quite hard. There's no paranoia about foreigners, who are now generally seen as welcome tourists who bring money into the economy.

One simple precaution to avoid trouble is to ask for permission to photograph near bridges or military installations. This simple courtesy costs you nothing, and may avoid a problem later.

One excellent way to get arrested in Botswana is to try to smuggle drugs across its borders, or to try to buy them from 'pushers'. Drug offences carry penalties at least as stiff as those you will find at home – and the jails are a lot less pleasant. Botswana's police are not forbidden to use entrapment techniques or 'sting' operations to catch criminals. Buying, selling or using drugs in Botswana is just not worth the risk.

Failing this, arguing with any policeman or army official – and getting angry into the bargain – is a sure way to get arrested. It is essential to control your temper and stay relaxed when dealing with Botswana's officials. Not only will you gain respect, and hence help your cause, but you will also avoid being forced to cool off for a night in the cells.

If you are careless enough to be arrested, you will often be asked only a few questions. If the police are suspicious of you, then how you handle the situation will determine whether you are kept for a matter of hours or for days. Be patient, helpful, good-humoured, and as truthful as possible. Never lose your temper; it will only aggravate the situation. Avoid any hint of arrogance. If things are going badly after half a day or so, then start firmly, but politely, to insist on seeing someone in higher authority. As a last resort you do, at least in theory, have the right to contact your embassy or consulate, though the finer points of your civil liberties may be overlooked by an irate local police chief.

BRIBERY Bribery is not at all common in Botswana. Indeed, the country is widely rated as the least corrupt in Africa, and the government takes a very strict anti-corruption stance. Certainly no normal visitor should ever be asked for, or offer, a bribe. It would be just as illegal as offering someone a bribe back home. Forget it.

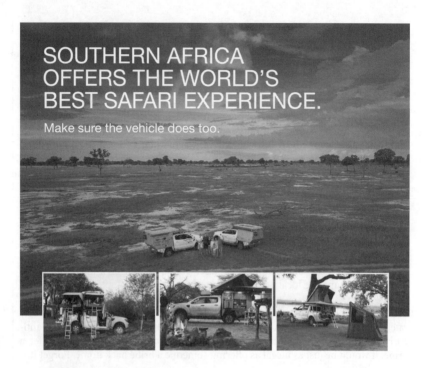

SOUTHERN AFRICA OFFERS THE WORLD'S BEST SAFARI EXPERIENCE.

Make sure the vehicle does too.

COMPARE BEFORE YOU COMMIT:

- Safety – Avis Safari Rental is the only safari rental company to offer a holistic safety package, including: vehicle stability programme – ESP, traction control, trailer sway control, all terrain tyres with an upgraded safari suspension system and with an extended 1,000km-range fuel tank.

- Green – All Avis Safari Rental vehicles are fitted with state-of-the-art solar-panelled charging systems.

- Comfort and convenience – Avis Safari Rental vehicles are the most comprehensively fitted safari hire vehicles available today.

- Latest vehicle models with extended-range fuel tank – The new Ford Ranger with full backing in Africa, is maintained to Avis' exacting standards.

- Safari experience and personal service – Experienced and professional tour guides are available to plan your self-drive safari routes; guided tours are also a popular option for your African safari adventure.

For more about our range of world-leading safari vehicles visit our website.

SafariRental.Reservations@avis.co.za
www.avissafarirental.co.za

Safari✦Rental
Proudly rented by **AVIS**

7

Into the Wilds

DRIVING

Driving around Botswana is exceedingly easy if you stick to the network of first-class tarred roads between the towns, but heading into the bush is a completely different proposition, which usually requires a small expedition.

Botswana's bush tracks are maintained only by the passage of vehicles, and aren't for the novice, or the unprepared. However, if you've been to Africa at least once or twice before, perhaps including a driving trip around South Africa or Namibia, then such trips can be a lot of fun provided that you realise that you're embarking on an adventure as much as a holiday.

To explore the more rural areas and remote parks on your own you'll need a fully equipped 4x4 vehicle, stocked with food and water for your trip. Depending on where you are going, some form of back-up is often wise. This might be a reliable satellite phone, a radio (and the know-how to use it), someone tracking your schedule – with frequent call-in points so they can look for you if you don't turn up on time – or the security of travelling in convoy with at least one other vehicle.

Having assessed all the dangers, those who do this kind of trip often get addicted to the space and the freedom; it can be really rewarding and tremendous fun!

For general information on driving in Botswana, see page 151.

EQUIPMENT AND PREPARATIONS

Fuel Petrol and diesel are available in all of the larger towns, but supplies at fuel stations outside Maun and Kasane can be erratic, so it is wise to fill up frequently. For travel into the bush you will need long-range fuel tanks, and/or a large stock of filled jerrycans. (Only use metal jerrycans for fuel; plastic containers are highly dangerous.)

It is essential to plan your fuel requirements well in advance, and to carry more than you expect to need. Remember that using the vehicle's 4x4 capability, especially in low ratio gears, will significantly increase your fuel consumption. Similarly, the cool comfort of a vehicle's air conditioning will burn your fuel reserves swiftly.

Spares Botswana's garages generally have a comprehensive stock of vehicle spares – though bush mechanics can effect the most amazing short-term repairs, with remarkably basic tools and raw materials. Spares for the more common makes are easiest to find; most basic Land Rover and Toyota 4x4 parts are available. If you are arriving in Botswana with an unusual foreign vehicle, it is best to bring as many spares as you can.

Navigation See the section on *Maps and navigation*, pages 145–8, for detailed comments. There are several good maps designed for visitors that are widely available, while survey-style maps may be obtained from the Department of Surveys and Mapping in Maun and Gaborone. It's wise to take a GPS (pages 147–8), though learn how to use it before you arrive and never switch your brain off and rely on it totally.

COPING WITH BOTSWANA'S ROADS Wherever you are driving in Botswana, no matter what the road surface, you should always be prepared for animals wandering on to the road and for pot-holes.

Tar roads Botswana's network of tar roads is gradually being extended. Although these roads are generally very good, don't be lulled into complacency; pot-holes do occur, with potentially devastating consequences if hit at speed.

Gravel roads There aren't many good gravel roads in Botswana – most are either good tar, or basic bush tracks. However, the few gravel sections can be very deceptive. Even when they appear smooth, flat and fast (which is not often), they still do not give vehicles much traction. You will frequently put the car into small skids, but with practice at slower speeds you will learn how to deal with them. Gravel is a less forgiving surface on which to drive than tar. The rules and techniques for driving well are the same for both, but on tar you can get away with sloppy braking and cornering which would prove fatal on gravel.

In addition to animals wandering on to the road and pot-holes, be prepared for sand-traps, or an unexpected corner. It is verging on insanity to drive over about 80km/h on any of Botswana's gravel roads. Other basic driving hints include:

- **Slowing down** If in any doubt about what lies ahead, always slow down. Road surfaces can vary enormously, so keep a constant look-out for pot-holes, ruts or patches of soft sand that could put you into an unexpected slide.
- **Passing vehicles** When passing other vehicles travelling in the opposite direction, always slow down to minimise both the damage that stone chippings will do to your windscreen, and the danger in driving through the other vehicle's dust cloud.
- **Using your gears** In normal driving, a lower gear will give you more control over the car – so keep out of high 'cruising' gears. Rather stick with third or fourth, and accept that your revs will be slightly higher than they normally are.
- **Cornering and braking** Under ideal conditions, the brakes should only be applied when the car is travelling in a straight line. Braking while negotiating a corner is dangerous, so it is vital to slow down before you reach corners. Equally, it is better to slow down gradually, using a combination of gears and brakes, than to use the brakes alone. You are less likely to skid.

Driving at night Outside of the main towns, **never** drive at night unless it's a matter of life and death. Both wild and domestic animals frequently spend the night by the side of busy roads, and will actually sleep on quieter ones. Tar roads are especially bad as the surface absorbs all the sun's heat by day, and then radiates it at night – making it a warm bed for passing animals. A high-speed collision with any animal, even a small one like a goat, will not only kill the animal, but will cause very severe damage to a vehicle, with potentially fatal consequences. And in the bush, even on main roads, the danger of startling elephants is very real.

DRIVING TECHNIQUES You want a high-clearance 4x4 to get anywhere in Botswana that's away from the main arteries. However, no vehicle can make up for an inexperienced driver – so ensure that you are confident of your vehicle's capabilities before you venture into the wilds with it. You really need extensive practice, with an expert on hand to advise you, before you'll have the first idea how to handle such a vehicle in difficult terrain. Finally, driving in convoy is an essential precaution in the more remote areas, in case one vehicle gets stuck or breaks down. Some of the more relevant ideas and techniques include the following.

When and how to use a 4x4 Firstly, read your vehicle's manual. All makes are different, and have their quirks, and so you must read the manual before you set off. Note especially that you should **never** drive in 4x4 mode with fixed (or 'locked') differentials on tar roads. Doing this will cause permanent damage to the mechanics of your vehicle.

When you do encounter traction difficulties, stop when you can and put the vehicle into 4x4 – usually setting the second 'small' gearstick to '4x4 high' is fine for most situations.

If you're driving an older vehicle, check if the front two hubs of your vehicle have, at their centre, knobs to turn. (This is the case with many of the older Toyotas, though most newer vehicles have 'automatic' hubs.) If so, you'll need to turn these to the 'lock' position – a fact forgotten by many novices that causes untold trouble for them, and endless smug amusement for old Africa hands.

When you're past the problem, using 2x4 will lower your fuel consumption, though many drivers will use 4x4 the whole time that they're in the bush. Remember to reset your hubs to 'free' before you drive on tar again.

Driving in sand If you're in 4x4 and are really struggling in deep sand, then stop on the next fairly solid area that you come to. Lower your tyre pressure until there is a small bulge in the tyre walls (having first made sure that you have the means to reinflate them when you reach solid roads again). A lower pressure will help your traction greatly, but increase the wear on your tyres. Pump them up again before you drive on a hard surface at speed, or the tyres will be badly damaged.

If you have your own vehicle, and thus have a choice, there are tyres designed specifically for driving in sand, so it may be worth considering these – although bear in mind that the sides will bend more easily than those designed for tarmac surfaces, so you'll not want to use these for long distances on the tar.

Where there are clear, deep-rutted tracks in the sand, don't fight the steering wheel – just relax and let your vehicle steer itself. Driving in the cool of the morning is easier than later in the day because when sand is cool it compacts better and is firmer. (When hot, the pockets of air between the sand grains expand and the sand becomes looser.)

If you do get stuck, despite these precautions, don't panic. Don't just rev the engine and spin the wheels – you'll only dig deeper. Instead stop. Relax and assess the situation. Now dig shallow ramps in front of all the wheels, reinforcing them with pieces of wood, vegetation, stones, material or anything else which will give the wheels better traction. Clear sand from beneath the chassis as, even on high-clearance vehicles, this could be the root of the problem. Then lighten the vehicle load (passengers out) and – if possible – push. Don't let the engine revs die as you engage your lowest ratio gear. That probably means using '4x4 low' rather than '4x4 high'. Use the clutch to ensure that the wheels don't spin wildly and dig themselves further into the sand.

Sometimes rocking the vehicle backwards and forwards will build up momentum to break you free. This can be done by the driver intermittently applying the clutch and/or by getting helpers who can push and pull the vehicle at the same frequency. Once the vehicle is moving, the golden rule of sand driving is to keep up the momentum: if you pause, you will sink and stop.

Grass seeds in the Kalahari After the rains, the Kalahari's tracks are often knee-high in seeding grass. As your vehicle drives through, stems and especially seeds can build up in front of and inside the radiator, and get trapped in crevices underneath the chassis. This is a major problem in the less-visited areas of the Kalahari. It's at its worst from March to June, after the rains, and in the areas of the great salt pans, the CKGR, and the tracks around Tsodilo and the Aha Hills. The main tracks around Chobe and Moremi are used relatively frequently, and so present less of a problem.

The presence of long grass on the tracks causes a real danger of overheating (see below) and fire. First, the build-up of seeds and stems over the radiator insulates it. Thus, if you aren't watching your gauges, the engine's temperature can rocket. It will swiftly seize up and catch fire. Second, the grass build-up itself, if allowed to become too big, can catch fire due to its contact with the hot exhaust system underneath the vehicle.

There are several strategies to minimise these dangers; best apply them all. First, before you set out, buy a few square metres of the tightly woven window-meshing gauze material used in the windows of safari tents. Fix one large panel of this on the vehicle's bull-bars, well in front of the radiator grill. Fix another much closer to it, but still outside of the engine compartment. Hopefully this will reduce vastly the number of seeds reaching your radiator.

Second, watch your vehicle's engine-temperature gauge like a hawk when you're travelling through areas of grassland.

Third, stop every 10km or so (yes, really, that often) and check the radiator and the undercarriage for pockets of stems and seeds. Pay special attention to the hot areas of the exhaust pipe; you should not allow a build-up of flammable material there. Use a stick or piece of wire to clean out any seeds and stems before you set off again.

Overheating If the engine has overheated then the only option is to stop and turn it off. Stop, have a drink under a tree, and let it cool. Don't open the radiator cap to refill it until the radiator is no longer hot to the touch. Even then, keep the engine running and the water circulating while you refill the radiator – otherwise you run the risk of cracking the hot metal by suddenly cooling it. Flicking droplets of water on to the outside of a running engine will cool it.

When driving away, switch off any air conditioning (as it puts more strain on the engine). Open your windows and turn your heater and fan full on. This may not seem pleasant in the midday heat – but it'll help to cool the engine. Keep watching that engine-temperature gauge.

Driving in mud This is difficult, though the theory is the same as for sand: keep going and don't stop. That said, even the most experienced drivers get stuck. A few areas of Botswana (the road from Rakops to the CKGR's main gate is legendary in this respect) have very fine soil known as 'black-cotton' soil, which becomes impassable when wet.

Push-starting when stuck If you are unlucky enough to need to push-start your vehicle while it is stuck in sand or mud, there is a remedy. Raise up the drive wheels, and take off one of the tyres. You should have a hi-lift jack with you, and know how to use it.

Then wrap a length of rope around the hub and treat it like a spinning top: one person (or more) pulls the rope to make the axle spin, while the driver lifts the clutch, turns the ignition on, and engages a low gear to turn the engine over. This is a very difficult equivalent of a push-start, but it may be your only option.

Rocky terrain There's not much of this in northern Botswana – but you will find some in the southeast. Have your tyre pressure higher than normal and move very slowly. If necessary, passengers should get out and guide you along the track to avoid scraping the undercarriage on the ground. This can be a very slow business.

Crossing rivers and other stretches of water The first thing to do is to stop and check the river. You must assess its depth, the type of riverbed and its current flow; and determine the best route to drive across it. This is best done by wading across the river (though in an area frequented by hippos and crocodiles this is not advisable). Beware of water that's too deep for your vehicle, or the very real possibility of being swept away by a fast current and a slippery riverbed.

If everything is OK then select your lowest gear ratio and drive through the water at a slow but steady rate. Your vehicle's air intake must be above the level of the water to avoid your engine filling with water. It's not worth taking risks, so remember that a flooded river may subside to safer levels by the next morning.

Driving near big game The only animals which are likely to pose a threat to vehicles are elephants – and generally only elephants which are familiar with vehicles. So, treat them with the greatest respect and don't 'push' them by trying to move ever closer. Letting them approach you is much safer, and they will feel far less threatened and more relaxed. Then, if the animals are calm, you can safely turn the engine off, sit quietly, and watch as they pass you by.

If you are unlucky, or foolish, enough to unexpectedly drive into the middle of a herd, then don't panic. Keep your movements, and those of the vehicle, slow and measured. Back off steadily. Don't be panicked, or overly intimidated, by a mock charge – this is just their way of frightening you away. For detailed comments, see the boxes on pages 274 and 276–7.

BUSHCAMPING

Many 'boy scout' type manuals have been written on survival in the bush, usually by military veterans. If you are stranded with a convenient multi-purpose knife, then these useful tomes will describe how you can build a shelter from branches, catch passing animals for food, and signal to the inevitable rescue planes which are combing the globe looking for you – while avoiding the attentions of hostile forces.

In Africa, bushcamping is usually less about survival than comfort. You're likely to have much more than the knife: probably at least a bulging backpack, if not a loaded 4x4. Thus the challenge is not to camp and survive, it is to camp and be as comfortable as possible. With practice you'll learn how, but a few hints might be useful for the less experienced.

WHERE YOU CAN CAMP In national parks, there are strictly designated campsites that you should use, as directed by the local game scouts. These must be pre-booked or you are unlikely to be allowed entrance.

Outside of the parks, if no campsites are designated, you should ask the local landowner, or village head, if they are happy for you to camp on their property.

If you explain patiently and politely what you want, then you are unlikely to meet anything but hospitality in most areas of rural Botswana.

CHOOSING A SITE Only experience will teach you how to choose a good site for pitching a tent, but a few general points, applicable to any wild areas of Africa, may help you avoid problems:

- Avoid camping on what looks like a path through the bush, however indistinct. It may be a well-used game trail.
- Beware of camping in dry riverbeds: dangerous flash floods can arrive with little or no warning.
- In marshy areas camp on higher ground to avoid cold, damp mists in the morning and evening.
- Camp a reasonable distance from water: near enough to walk to it, but far enough to avoid animals which arrive to drink.
- Give yourself plenty of time before it gets dark to familiarise yourself with your surroundings.
- If a lightning storm is likely, make sure that your tent is not the highest thing around.
- Finally, choose a site which is as flat as possible – you will find sleeping much easier.

CAMPFIRES Campfires can create a great atmosphere and warm you on a cold evening, but they can also be damaging to the environment and leave unsightly piles of ash and blackened stones. Deforestation is a major concern in much of the developing world, including parts of Botswana, so if you do light a fire then use wood as the locals do: sparingly. If you have a vehicle, consider buying firewood in advance from people who sell it at the roadside – or collect it in areas where there's more wood around.

If you collect it yourself, then take only dead wood, nothing living. Never just pick up a log: always roll it over first, checking carefully for snakes or scorpions.

Experienced campers build small, highly efficient fires by using a few large stones to absorb, contain and reflect the heat, and gradually feeding just a few thick logs into the centre to burn. Cooking pots can be balanced on the stones, or the point where the logs meet and burn. Others will use a small trench, lined with rocks, to similar effect. Either technique takes practice, but is worth perfecting. Whichever you do, bury the ashes, take any rubbish with you when you leave, and make the site look as if you had never been there. (See *Appendix 3,* page 543, for details of Christina Dodwell's excellent *An Explorer's Handbook: Travel, Survival and Bush Cookery.*)

Don't expect an unattended fire to frighten away wild animals – that works in Hollywood, but not in Africa. A campfire may help your feelings of insecurity, but lion and hyena will disregard it with stupefying nonchalance.

Finally, do be hospitable to any locals who appear. Despite your efforts to seek permission for your camp, you may effectively be staying in their back gardens.

USING A TENT Whether to use a tent or to sleep in the open is a personal choice, dependent upon where you are. In an area where there are predators around (specifically lion and hyena) then you must use a tent – and sleep completely inside it, as a protruding leg may seem like a tasty take-away to a hungry hyena. This is especially true at organised campsites, where the local animals are so used to humans that they have lost much of their inherent fear of man.

Outside game areas, you will usually be fine sleeping in the open, or preferably under a mosquito net, with just the stars of the African sky above you. On the practical side, sleeping under a tree will reduce the morning dew that settles on your sleeping bag. If your vehicle has a large, flat roof then sleeping on this will provide you with peace of mind, and a star-filled outlook. Hiring a vehicle with a built-in roof-tent is a perfect solution for many, though it can take time to pack when wanting to rush off on an early-morning game drive.

CAMPING EQUIPMENT FOR BACKPACKERS If you are taking an organised safari, you will not need any camping equipment at all. If you're hiring a 4x4, then it's best to hire one here with all the kit. However, for those backpacking, there is very little lightweight kit available in Botswana. Most of the equipment is designed to be sturdy, long-lasting and carried around in vehicles. So buy any lightweight kit before you leave home, as it will save you a lot of time and trouble once you arrive. Here are a few comments on various essentials.

Tent During the rains a good tent is essential in order to stay dry. Even during the dry season one is useful if there are lion or hyena around. If backpacking, invest in a high-quality, lightweight tent. Mosquito-netting ventilation panels, allowing a good flow of air, are essential. (Just a corner of mesh at the top of the tent is *not* enough for comfort.) Don't go for a tent that's small; it may feel cosy at home, but will be hot and claustrophobic in the heat.

I have had the same 'Spacepacker' tent for many years, but sadly they are no longer manufactured. It's a dome tent with fine mesh doors on either side that allow a through draught, making all the difference when temperatures are high. The alternative to a good tent is a mosquito net, which is fine unless it is raining or you are in a big-game area.

Sleeping bag A lightweight, three-season sleeping bag is ideal for Botswana most of the time, though probably not quite warm enough for the very coldest nights in the Kalahari. Down is preferable to synthetic fillings for most of the year, as it packs smaller, is lighter, and feels more luxurious to sleep in. That said, when down gets wet it loses its efficiency, so bring a good synthetic bag if you are likely to encounter much rain.

Ground mat A ground mat of some sort is essential. It keeps you warm and comfortable, and it protects the tent's groundsheet from rough or stony ground (do put it underneath the tent!). Closed-cell foam mats are widely available outside Botswana, so buy one before you arrive. The better mats cost double or treble the cheaper ones, but are stronger, thicker and warmer – well worth the investment.

Therm-a-Rests, the combination air-mattress and foam mat, are strong, durable and also worth the investment – but take a puncture repair kit with you just in case of problems. Do watch carefully where you site your tent, and try to make camp before dark. My trusty Therm-a-Rest deflated badly one night in the Kalahari, sleeping near the Mamuno–Buitepos border. Breaking camp the next morning, I lifted the mat to find a large scorpion in its burrow immediately beneath the mat.

Sheet sleeping bag Thin, pure-cotton or silk sheet sleeping bags (or sleeping bag liners) are small, light and very useful. They are easily washed and so are normally used like a sheet, inside a sleeping bag, to keep it clean. They can, of course, be used on their own when your main sleeping bag is too hot.

Stove 'Trangia'-type stoves, which burn methylated spirits, are simple to use and light, and cheap to run. They come complete with a set of light aluminium pans and a very useful all-purpose handle. Often you'll be able to cook on a fire with the pans, but it's nice to have the option of making a brew in a few minutes while you set up camp. Methylated spirits are cheap and widely available in Botswana, even in rural areas, but bring a tough (purpose-made) fuel container with you as the bottles in which it is sold will soon crack and spill all over your belongings.

Petrol- and kerosene-burning stoves are undoubtedly efficient on fuel and powerful – but invariably temperamental and messy. Gas stoves use pressurised canisters, which are not allowed on aircraft.

Torch (flashlight) This should be on every visitor's packing list – whether you're staying in upmarket camps or backpacking. Find one that's small and tough, and preferably water- and dust-proof. Headtorches leave your hands free (useful when cooking or mending the car) and the latest designs are relatively light and comfortable to wear. Consider one of the new generation of super-bright LED torches; the LED Lenser range is excellent.

Those with vehicles will find that a strong spotlight, powered by the car's battery (perhaps through the socket for the cigarette lighter), is invaluable for impromptu lighting.

Water containers For everyday use, a small two-litre water bottle is invaluable, however you are travelling. If you're thinking of camping, you should also consider a strong, collapsible water bag – perhaps 5–10 litres in size – which will reduce the number of trips that you need to make from your camp to the water source (ten litres of water weighs 10kg). And to be sure of safe drinking water, consider taking a bottle with a filter (page 167).

Drivers will want to be self-sufficient for water when venturing into the bush, and so carry several large, sturdy containers of water. If you're driving a vehicle specially kitted out for camping, ensure that the water tank is full at the outset.

See pages 144–5 for a memory-jogging list of other useful items to pack.

ANIMAL DANGERS FOR CAMPERS Camping in Africa is really very safe, though you may not think so from reading this. If you have a major problem while camping, it will probably be because you did something stupid, or because you forgot to take a few simple precautions. Here are a few general basics, applicable to anywhere in Africa and not just Botswana.

Large animals Big game will usually not bother you if you are in a tent – provided that you do not attract its attention, or panic it. Elephants will gently tiptoe through your guy ropes while you sleep, without even nudging your tent. However, if you wake up and make a noise, startling them, they are far more likely to panic and step on your tent. Similarly, scavengers will quietly wander round, smelling your evening meal in the air, without any intention of harming you.

- Remember to use the toilet before going to bed, and avoid getting up in the night if possible.
- Scrupulously clean everything used for food that might smell good to scavengers. Put these utensils in a vehicle if possible; if not, suspend them from a tree, or pack them away in a rucksack inside the tent.

- Do not keep any smelly foodstuffs, like meat or citrus fruit, in your tent. Their smells may attract unwanted attention.
- Do not leave anything outside that could be picked up – like bags, pots, pans, etc. Hyenas, among others, will take anything. (They have been known to crunch a camera's lens, and eat it.)
- If you are likely to wake in the night, then leave the tent's zips a few centimetres open at the top, enabling you to take a quiet peek outside.

Creepy crawlies As you set up camp, clear stones or logs out of your way with great caution: they make great hiding places for snakes and scorpions. Long moist grass is ideal territory for snakes, and dry, dusty, rocky places are classic sites for scorpions.

If you are sleeping in the open, it is not unknown to wake and find a snake lying next to you in the morning. Don't panic; your warmth has just attracted it to you. You will not be bitten if you gently edge away without making any sudden movements. (This is one good argument for using at least a mosquito net!)

Before you put on your shoes, shake them out. Similarly, check the back of your backpack before you slip it on. Just a curious spider, in either, could inflict a painful bite.

WALKING IN THE BUSH

Walking in the African bush is a totally different sensation from driving through it. You may start off a little unready – perhaps even sleepy for an early-morning walk – but swiftly your mind will wake. There are no noises except the wildlife, and you. So every noise that isn't caused by you must be an animal; or a bird; or an insect. Every smell and every rustle has a story to tell, if you can understand it.

With time, patience and a good guide you can learn to smell the presence of elephants, and hear when a predator alarms impala. You can use ox-peckers to lead you to buffalo, or vultures to help you locate a kill. Tracks will record the passage of animals in the sand, telling what passed by, how long ago, and in which direction.

Eventually your gaze becomes alert to the slightest movement; your ears aware of every sound. This is safari at its best: a live, sharp, spine-tingling experience that's hard to beat and very addictive. Be careful: watching game from a vehicle will never be the same again for you.

WALKING TRAILS AND SAFARIS One of Africa's biggest attractions is its walking safaris – which bring people back year after year. However, because of the danger involved, the calibre and experience of guides when walking is far more important than when driving. Anyone with a little experience can drive you around fairly safely in a large metal vehicle, but when you're faced with a charging elephant you need to be standing behind a real expert to have much chance of survival.

Even if you're on safari with an armed guide who is experienced with dangerous big game, walking will always present more danger than driving. This is simply because humans are more vulnerable on foot than they are when encased by a vehicle. However, major problems and injuries are few and far between – well within the limits accepted by most travellers who opt for 'adventurous' holidays across the world.

Walking guides I am not confident that Botswana has progressed well towards the implementation of rigorous minimum standards for guides who lead walking safaris. Zimbabwe has for many years led the field, with a really tough training course leading to the exalted status of 'pro guide'; in many ways this is Africa's 'gold standard' of guiding.

Zambia has adopted an alternative, but also very safe, system requiring an armed scout and an experienced walking guide to accompany every walk. The scout controls the problem animal, the guide controls the group of people. It's rarely necessary to fire even a warning shot, and injuries are exceedingly rare.

However, Botswana, like South Africa, has minimum standards which I think are too low for walking guides. Thus, in my opinion, the term 'qualified guide' in Botswana doesn't mean that I should necessarily feel safe going walking with them. Thus it's mostly up to the individual safari operation to make sure its guides are experienced.

A handful of operations (Linyanti Bush Camp and its sister camps, the Footsteps operation near Shinde, Motswiri, and the Selinda Reserve, spring to mind) take their walking very seriously, understand the issues, and put safety at the top of their agenda. I'm confident to go walking with such operations.

The rest are a mixed bag; some use good guides, others I've been out with I felt were actually dangerous. One good rule of thumb is the presence of a rifle. If your guide *doesn't* carry one, then I certainly wouldn't walk with them to anywhere where we were likely to see any dangerous game. (The converse doesn't apply though; carrying a rifle does not make an inexperienced guide safe.)

Often you'll see advertising for camps in the Okavango with comments along the lines that your guide is 'a man of the swamps, completely at one with his environment'. This is doubtless true, but doesn't imply that this same guide automatically has the foresight, command and communication skills to look after frightened foreigners while avoiding game in a dangerous situation. Knowing how to save himself is different from controlling a small group, and saving *them* from a nasty end.

Thus my advice is that if you want to do much walking in Botswana, go to one of the places that really concentrate on walking safaris. The rest of the time, stick to canoes, boats and driving. Only go walking with guides who are armed, know how to use their guns, and you have discussed the issues with and satisfied yourself that they have sufficient experience for you to be safe.

Etiquette for walking safaris If you plan to walk then avoid wearing any bright, unnatural colours, especially white. Dark, muted shades are best; greens, browns and khaki are ideal. Dark blue tends to attract tsetse flies, so best to avoid that if you can. Hats are essential, as is sunblock. Even a short walk will last for 2 hours, and there's no vehicle to which you can retreat if you get too hot.

Binoculars should be immediately accessible – one pair per person – ideally in dust-proof cases strapped to your belt. Cameras too, if you decide to bring any, as they are of little use buried at the bottom of a camera bag. Heavy tripods or long lenses are a nightmare to lug around, so leave them behind (and accept, philosophically, that you may miss shots).

Walkers see the most when walking in silent single file. This doesn't mean that you can't stop to whisper a question to the guide; just that idle chatter will reduce your powers of observation, and make you even more visible to the animals (who will usually flee when they sense you).

With regard to safety, your guide will always brief you in detail before you set off. S/he will outline possible dangers, and what to do in the unlikely event of them materialising. Listen carefully: this is vital.

Face-to-face animal encounters Whether you are on an organised walking safari, on your own hike, or just walking from the car to your tent in the bush, it is not unlikely that you will come across some of Africa's larger animals at close quarters. Invariably, the danger is less than you imagine, and a few basic guidelines will enable you to cope effectively with most situations.

First, don't panic. Console yourself with the fact that animals are not normally interested in people. You are not their normal food, or their predator. If you do not annoy or threaten them, you will be left alone. No matter how frightened you are, you'll probably run slower than whatever is worrying you. So don't try to run; think your way out of the tight spot.

If you are walking to look for animals, then remember that this is their environment, not yours. Animals have evolved within the bush, and their senses are far better attuned to it than yours. To be on less unequal terms, remain alert and try to spot them from a distance. This gives you the option of approaching carefully, or staying well clear.

Animals, like people, are all different. So while we can generalise here and say how the 'average' animal will behave, the one that's glaring at you over a small bush may have had a really bad day, and be feeling much grumpier than normal.

Finally, the advice of a good guide is far more valuable than the simplistic comments noted here – though a few general comments on some potentially dangerous situations might be of use.

Buffalo This is probably the continent's most dangerous animal to hikers, but there is a difference between the old males, often encountered on their own or in small groups, and large breeding herds.

The former are easily surprised. If they hear or smell something amiss, they will charge without provocation – motivated by a fear that something is sneaking up on them. Buffalo have an excellent sense of smell, but fortunately they are short-sighted. Avoid a charge by quickly climbing the nearest tree, or by sidestepping at the last minute. If adopting the latter, more risky, technique then stand motionless until the last possible moment, as the buffalo may well miss you anyhow.

The large breeding herds can be treated in a totally different manner. If you approach them in the open, they will often flee. Sometimes though, in areas often used for walking safaris, they will stand and watch, moving aside to allow you to pass through the middle of the herd.

Neither encounter is for the faint-hearted or inexperienced, so steer clear of these dangerous animals wherever possible.

Black rhino Until 2003, there were no black rhino left in Botswana, but at the end of that year four animals were reintroduced into the heart of Moremi, and others have followed. Sightings remain exceptionally rare, but if you are both lucky enough to find one, and then unlucky enough to be charged by it, use the same tactics as you would for a buffalo: tree climbing or dodging at the last second. (It is amazing how even the least athletic walker will swiftly scale the nearest tree when faced with a charging rhino.)

Elephant Normally elephants are only a problem if you disturb a mother with a calf, or approach a male in *musth* (state of arousal), so keep well away from these. In some areas of Africa, lone bulls can be approached quite closely when feeding, but in Botswana this usually results in problems. If you get too close to any elephant it will scare you off with a 'mock charge': head up, perhaps shaking – ears flapping – and trumpeting. Lots of sound and fury. This is intended to be frightening, and it is. But it is just a warning and no cause for panic. You should just freeze to assess the elephant's intentions. When it's stopped making a fuss, back off slowly. Don't run.

There is no easy way to avoid the charge of an angry elephant, so take a hint from this warning and move away.

When an elephant really means business, it will usually put its ears back, lower its head, and charge directly at you. This is known as a 'full charge' and they don't stop. It is one of the most dangerous situations in Africa. Then you probably have to run – but elephants are much faster than you, so think while you run. Aim to get behind an anthill, up a tall tree, or out of the way somehow.

See also the boxes on pages 274 and 276–7 for more details of this behaviour with reference to vehicles.

Lion Tracking lion with a top guide can be one of the most exhilarating parts of a walking safari. Sadly, they will normally flee before you even get close to them. However, it can be a problem if you come across a large pride unexpectedly. Lion are well camouflaged; it is easy to find yourself next to one before you realise it. If you had been listening, you would probably have heard a warning growl about 20m ago. Now it is too late.

The best plan is to stop, and back off slowly, but confidently. If you are in a small group, then stick together. Never run from a big cat. First, they are always faster than you are. Second, running will just convince them that you are frightened prey, and worth chasing. As a last resort, if they seem too inquisitive and follow as you back off, then stop. Call their bluff. Pretend that you are not afraid and make loud, deep, confident noises: shout at them, bang something. But do not run.

John Coppinger, one of Africa's most experienced guides, adds that every single compromising experience that he has had with lion on foot has been either with a female with cubs, or with a mating pair, when the males can get very aggressive. You have been warned.

Leopard Leopard are seldom seen by those on foot, and would normally flee from the most timid of lone hikers. However, if injured, or surprised, then they are very powerful, dangerous cats. Conventional wisdom is scarce, but never stare straight into the leopard's eyes, or it will regard this as a threat display. (The same is said, by some, to be true with lion.) Better to look away slightly, at a nearby bush, or even at its tail. Then back off slowly, facing the direction of the cat and showing as little terror as you can. As with lion, loud, deep, confident noises are a last line of defence. Never run from a leopard.

Hippo Hippo are fabled to account for more deaths in Africa than any other animal (ignoring the mosquito). Having been attacked and capsized by a hippo while in a mokoro, I find this very easy to believe. Visitors are most likely to encounter hippo in the water, when in a boat or mokoro. (See the section on hippo on page 52.)

However, as hippos spend half their time grazing, they will sometimes be encountered on land. Away from the water, out of their comforting lagoons, hippos are even more dangerous. If they see you, they will probably flee towards the water – so the golden rule is never to get between a hippo and its escape route to deep water. Given that a hippo will outrun you on land, standing motionless is probably your best line of defence; if you must run, then head away from water or try to put a large, solid obstacle between you and the animal.

Snakes Most snakes are really not the great danger that people imagine, and will flee when they feel the vibrations of footsteps; only a few will stay still. The puff adder is probably responsible for more cases of snakebite than any other venomous snake in Botswana because, when approached, it will simply puff itself up and hiss as a warning, rather than slither away. This makes it essential always to watch where you place your feet when walking in the bush.

Similarly, there are a couple of arboreal (tree-dwelling) species which may be taken by surprise if you carelessly grab vegetation as you walk. So don't.

Spitting cobras are also encountered occasionally; they will aim for your eyes and spit with accuracy. If one of these rears up in front of you, then turn away and avert your eyes. If the spittle reaches your eyes, you must wash them out immediately and thoroughly with whatever liquid comes to hand: water, milk or even urine if that's the only liquid that can be quickly produced. See also pages 169–70.

Black mambas are another particularly dangerous snake, and although they will usually flee from people, there are occasional reports of large individuals being very aggressive.

BOATING

Trips on motorboats and mekoro are very much an integral part of a safari trip to northern Botswana – they're both very different, and both a lot of fun. Almost no operators use the paddle-yourself Canadian-style canoes that are popular elsewhere in Africa (Motswiri, Selinda Explorers and Selinda Adventure Trail are perhaps the exceptions that prove this rule).

BY MOKORO In *Lake Ngami and the River Okavango* (see *Appendix 3,* page 539), the explorer Charles John Andersson describes a mokoro used by him on Lake Ngami in the early 1850s:

The canoe in which I embarked (and they are all somewhat similarly constructed) was but a miserable craft. It consisted of the trunk of a tree, about 20 feet long, pointed at both ends, and hollowed out by means of fire and a small hatchet. The natives are not at all particular as to the shape of the canoe. The after part of some that have come to my notice, would form an angle of near forty-five degrees with their stem! Nevertheless, they were propelled through the water by the Bayeye (my boatmen were of that nation) with considerable speed and skill.

The 'appointments' of the canoe, consist of a paddle and a pole, ten to twelve feet in length. The paddle-man sits well in the stern, and attends mostly to the steering; while his comrade, posted at the head of the canoe, sends her along, by means of the pole, with great force and skill.

The natives, however, rarely venture any distance from the shore in their frail skiffs.

Local inhabitants of the Okavango still use mekoro like this, but for visitors it's more usual to have simply a single poler standing up at the stern and propelling the craft with a long pole. It's very like the punting done at some universities in Britain; a gentle form of locomotion best suited to shallow waters.

Only certain trees are suitable for making mekoro; they must usually be old, straight and strong. Jackalberries (*Diospyros mespiliformis*), sausage trees (*Kigelia africana*) and kiats (*Pterocarpus angolensis*) are favourites, while occasionally African mangosteens (*Garcinia livingstoneii*) and rain trees (*Lonchocarpus capassa*) are also used. The wood used to make the poles to propel them is less crucial, though these are often made from silver-leaf terminalia trees (*Terminalia sericea*).

The last few decades have seen a mushrooming demand for mekoro, which began to deplete the older specimens of these species in some areas. Fortunately, fibreglass mekoro, that look very similar, are now being made, and are used by almost all safari camps today. If you are given a wooden craft, check with your camp that when it's no longer usable, they intend to replace it with a fibreglass version. The Delta can't afford to lose more of its oldest trees!

BY MOTORBOAT Motorboats are used on the rivers, and in the deeper channels and lagoons of the Okavango. They can be a lot of fun, although – used carelessly – their noise and (especially) their wake can do a lot of damage, so be sensitive to the dangers and don't encourage your guide to speed. (It can be a good idea to state this from the outset.) You'll often see much more by going slowly anyhow.

Interesting variations on this theme include the small, double-decker boat used at Kwara, which affords views out over the top of the papyrus beds, and a similar set-up at Lagoon Camp, which is ideal for sundowner cruises.

THE MAIN DANGERS It's tempting to fret about dangerous animals in Africa, but it's foolish to get paranoid: animal injuries on safari are rare. With common sense and a little knowledge, boat and mokoro trips are generally very safe, although nobody should discount the very real dangers posed by hippos and crocodiles. Canoes and mekoro are more vulnerable than chunky aluminium motorboats – just as walkers take slightly more risks than those on safari in robust 4x4 vehicles.

Hippo are strictly vegetarians, and will usually attack a mokoro only if they feel threatened. Your poler is usually standing up, so he has the best vantage point for spotting potential dangers ahead. It's helpful if you're either silent, or making so much noise that every animal in the bush can hear you approaching!

During the day, hippopotami will usually congregate in deeper water. The odd ones in shallow water, where they feel less secure, will usually head for the deeper places as soon as they are aware of a nearby mokoro. Avoiding hippos is then generally a case of steering around the deeper areas, and sticking to the shallows. This is where the poler's experience, knowing every waterway in the area, is invaluable.

Really large and deep channels and waterways are seldom a problem, as the hippos can avoid you provided that you make enough noise so that they know you are around. Shallow floodplains are also fairly safe, as you'll see the hippo in advance, and avoid them.

Problems usually occur when mekoro use relatively small and narrow 'hippo trails', where hippos can submerge but can't get far enough away. Then there's a danger of accidentally approaching too close, inadvertently surprising a hippo, and/or cutting it off from its path of retreat to deeper water. Then the hippo feels cornered and threatened, and may even attack. Occasionally camps will send mekoro out in small groups, with an armed guide in the lead mokoro; though this is the exception rather than the rule. In practice, incidents happen so rarely, and yet so fast, that I'm unsure if this would really give much real protection.

Hippo attacks are not common, but do happen and can have very serious consequences. An angry hippo can overturn a mokoro without a second thought, biting at it and/or its occupants. Once in this situation, there are no easy remedies.

Crocodiles may have sharp teeth and look prehistoric, but are of little danger to you … unless you are in the water – or very close to the edge. Then the more you struggle and the more waves you create, the more you will attract their unwelcome attentions. Very occasionally this could become an issue when a mokoro is overturned by a hippo; you must get out of the water as soon as possible, either into another canoe or on to the bank.

When a crocodile attacks an animal, it will try to disable it, normally by getting a firm, biting grip, submerging, and performing a long, fast barrel-roll. This will disorient the prey, drown it, and probably twist off the limb that has been bitten. In this dire situation, your best line of defence is probably to stab the reptile in its eyes with anything sharp that you have. Alternatively, if you can lift up its tongue and let the water into its lungs while it is underwater, then a crocodile will start to drown and will release its prey.

I have had reliable reports of a man surviving an attack in the Zambezi when a crocodile grabbed his arm and started to spin backwards into deep water. The man wrapped his legs around the crocodile, to spin with it and avoid having his arm twisted off. As this happened, he tried to poke his thumb into its eyes, but with no effect. Finally he put his free arm into the crocodile's mouth, and opened up the beast's throat. This worked. The crocodile left him and he survived with only a damaged arm. Understandably, anecdotes like this about tried and tested methods of escape are rare.

MINIMUM IMPACT

When you visit, drive through, or camp in an area and have 'minimum impact' upon it, this means that the area is left in the same condition as – or better than – when you entered it. While most visitors view minimum impact as being desirable, do spend time to consider the ways in which we contribute to environmental degradation, and how these can be avoided. Most of these points apply to any areas of rural Africa.

DRIVING Use your vehicle responsibly. If there's a road, or a track, then don't go off it – the environment will suffer. Driving off-road can leave a multitude of tracks that detract from the 'wilderness' feeling for subsequent visitors. Equally, don't speed through towns or villages: remember the danger to local children, and the amount of dust you'll cause.

HYGIENE Use toilets if they are provided, even if they are basic long-drop loos with questionable cleanliness. If there are no toilets, then human excrement should always be buried well away from paths, or groundwater, and any tissue used should be burned and then buried with it.

If you use rivers or lakes to wash, then soap yourself near the bank, using a pan for scooping water from the river – making sure that no soap finds its way into the water. Use biodegradable soap. Sand makes an excellent pan-scrub, even if you have no water to spare.

RUBBISH Biodegradable rubbish can be burned and buried with the campfire ashes. Don't leave it lying around: it will look very unsightly and spoil the place for those who come after you.

Bring along some plastic bags with which to remove the rest of your rubbish, and dump it at the next large town. Items that will not burn, like tin cans, are best cleaned and squashed for easy carrying. If there are bins, then use them, but also consider when they will next be emptied, and whether local animals will rummage through them first. For this reason, it's probably best not to use the bins at most national parks' campsites; better to carry out all your own rubbish to the nearest town.

HOST COMMUNITIES While the rules for reducing impact on the environment have been understood and followed by responsible travellers for years, the effects of tourism on local people have only recently been considered. Many tourists believe it is their right, for example, to take intrusive photos of local people – and even become angry if the local people object. They refer to higher prices being charged to tourists as a rip-off, without considering the hand-to-mouth existence of those selling these products or services. They deplore child beggars, then hand out sweets or pens to local children with outstretched hands.

Our behaviour towards 'the locals' needs to be considered in terms of their culture, with the knowledge that we are the uninvited visitors. We visit to enjoy ourselves, but this should not be at the expense of local people. Read *Cultural guidelines*, pages 108–9, and aim to leave the local communities better off after your visit.

LOCAL PAYMENTS If you spend time with any of Botswana's more rural communities, perhaps camping in the bush or getting involved with one of the community-run projects, then take great care with any payments that you make.

First, note that most people like to spend their earnings on what they choose. This means that trying to pay for services with beads, food, old clothes or anything else instead of money isn't appreciated. Ask yourself how you'd like to be paid, and you'll understand this point.

Second, find out the normal cost of what you are buying. For example, most community campsites will have a standard price for a pitch. Find out this price before you sleep there. It is then important that you pay about that amount for the pitch – not less, and not too much more.

As most people realise, if you try to pay less you'll get into trouble – as you would at home. However, many do not realise that if they generously pay a lot *more*, this can be equally damaging. Local rates of pay in rural areas can be very low, and a careless visitor can easily pay disproportionately large sums. Where this happens, local jobs can lose their value overnight. (Imagine working hard to become a game scout, only to learn that a tourist has given your friend the equivalent of your whole month's wages for just a few hours' guiding. What incentive is there for you to carry on with your regular job?)

If you want to give more – for good service, a super guide, or just because you want to help – then either buy some locally made produce (at the going rate), or donate money to one of the organisations working to improve the lot of Botswana's most disadvantaged. See pages 158–60 for ideas, but also consider asking around locally; you'll often find projects that need your support.

Many lodges and camps assist with community projects, and will be able to suggest a good use for donations. Increasingly they're becoming more involved in the welfare of their surrounding communities, which is something you can encourage.

Part Two

THE GUIDE

8

Maun

This once-dusty, sprawling town has been the start of expeditions into the wilds since the turn of the century, and it is now the safari capital of the country. Maun's elongated centre is dotted with modern shops and offices, and its suburbs – until recently dominated by traditionally built, thatched rondavels – glint in the sun reflecting off tin-roofed houses.

In the 1980s, everywhere and everything here seemed geared towards the tourism bonanza. Maun had a rough-and-ready frontier feel, as contemporary cowboys rode into town from the bush in battered 4x4s. Its focal points were the camps north of town – Island Safari Lodge, Crocodile Camp, Okavango River Lodge – and the old Duck Inn opposite the airport.

Then, as Maun became the administrative centre for the northern and western parts of Botswana, government departments moved here *en masse*. The town's roads became sealed tar, rather than pot-holed gravel tracks, which opened the door to an influx of saloon cars from the rest of the country. Finally the tourism product itself changed. The pendulum swung away from last-minute budget trips bought in Maun, to upmarket safaris booked in advance from overseas. The new breed of visitors just change planes here; they seldom spend more than a few hours at Maun Airport.

However, for those who are driving themselves, Maun remains a centre to get organised, and perhaps a place to look at what cheaper safari options are available. It also offers an increasing number of activities to interest those who may find themselves with time on their hands between flights, or who are stopping over here before or after a safari.

GETTING THERE AND AWAY

Maun is 950m (3,100ft) above sea level, and however you are travelling, it is fairly easy to reach.

BY AIR
Scheduled services Maun is well connected by scheduled domestic and international flights, although you can expect frequent changes to the timetables. Air Botswana connects with Johannesburg and Gaborone daily. Their service to Kasane is limited to Tuesday and Thursday only.

Flights with Airlink between Maun, Johannesburg and Cape Town operate daily in each direction.

✈ **Air Botswana** [202 E2] Airport Av; ✆ 368 8400; www.airbotswana.co.bw. It's generally easier to reconfirm flights & make further arrangements at their main reservations office,

near the corner with Sir Seretse Khama Rd, than at the airport.
✈ **Airlink** ✆ 686 5230; www.flyairlink.com

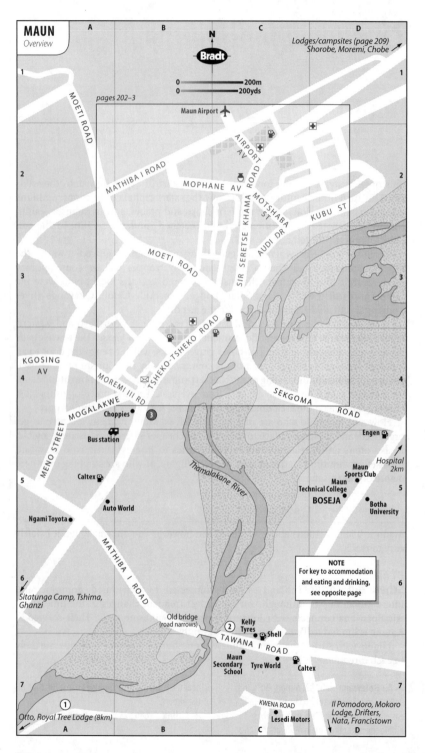

N

Bradt

Lodges/campsites (page 209)
Shorobe, Moremi, Chobe

0 ———————— 200m
0 ———————— 200yds

pages 202–3

Maun Airport ✈

MOETI ROAD

MATHIBA I ROAD

MOPHANE AV

AIRPORT AV

SIR SERETSE KHAMA ROAD

MOTSHABA ST

AUDI DR

KUBU ST

MOETI ROAD

TSHEKO-TSHEKO ROAD

KGOSING AV

MOREMI III RD

MOGALAKWE

MENO STREET

Choppies ●

③

Bus station

Caltex ⊡

Auto World ●

Ngami Toyota ●

MATHIBA I ROAD

Thamalakane River

SEKGOMA ROAD

Engen ⊡

*Hospital
2km*

Maun
Sports Club ●

Maun
Technical College ●

BOSEJA

● Botha
University

Old bridge
(road narrows)

② Kelly
Tyres

⊡ Shell

Maun
Secondary
School ●

Tyre World ●

Caltex ⊡

TAWANA I ROAD

Sitatunga Camp, Tshima,
Ghanzi

NOTE
For key to accommodation
and eating and drinking,
see opposite page

①

Otto, Royal Tree Lodge (8km)

KWENA ROAD

Lesedi Motors ●

Il Pomodoro, Mokoro
Lodge, Drifters,
Nata, Francistown

Charter airlines Maun also has a number of air charter companies, where you can hire light aircraft for private flights and transfers. These can sometimes be economical if you have four or five people travelling together. I include these and their contact details not because you ever need to book your own flights between the camps; you don't: that's always done for you by the camps concerned, or your tour operator back home. However, you may want to contact them in case of emergency, or to organise a pleasure flight over the Delta, or even to charter a plane somewhere fairly unusual for the day – like the Tsodilo Hills!

MAUN *Overview*
For listings, see pages 205–15

⊖ **Where to stay**
1 Jump Street Chalets.....A7
2 Maun Lodge...................C6
Off map
    Drifters...........................D7
    Mokoro Lodge..............D7
    Otto................................. A7
    Royal Tree Lodge.......... A7
    Sitatunga Camp............ A6
    Tshima........................... A6

✕ **Where to eat and drink**
3 Dine Inn..........................B4
Off map
    Il Pomodoro..................D7

Note that booking inter-camp flights through the camps is invariably cheaper than chartering them directly with the airlines. For rough guidance, a five-seater plane (six if you include the pilot!) and an hour's flying time costs around P4,650 (US$465). These basic prices will usually vary very little between the various companies. For details of scenic flights, see page 220.

✈ **Air Shakawe** [202 C2] Mathiba I Rd; ☏ 686 3620; e bookings@airshakawe.com; www. airshakawe.com.

✈ **Delta Air** [202 E1] Mathiba I Rd; ☏ +27 (0)823 556910; e info@footsteps-in-africa.com; www.footsteps-in-africa.com/delta-air. Delta Air has a close association with Footsteps in Africa & usually operates transfers for their camps; they do not usually deal directly with the public.

✈ **Helicopter Horizons** [202 C2] Apollo Hse, Mophane Av; ☏ 680 1186; m 7173 6913; e info@ helicopterhorizons.com; www.helicopterhorizons. com. The only company operating helicopter flights over the Delta.

✈ **Kavango Air** [202 D1] Maun Airport; ☏ 686 0323; m 7130 5112; e aggie@kavangoair.com; www.kavangoair.com

✈ **Mack Air** [202 D1] Natlee Centre, Mathiba I Rd; ☏ 686 0675; e reservations@mackair.co.bw; www.mackair.co.bw. Mack Air maintains a good reputation as a reliable, high-quality air charter company which doesn't have ties to any camps. They have 6-, 8-,10- & 14-seater planes, with the smaller ones (which allow everyone a window seat) also used for scenic flights.

✈ **Major Blue Air** [202 D2] Natlee Centre, Mathiba I Rd; ☏ 686 5671; e info@majorblueair. com; www.majorblueair.com. Major Blue has operated camp transfers & scenic flights in 3-, 5- & 7-seater planes since 2010. See ad, page 229.

✈ **Moremi Air** [202 D1] Maun Airport; ☏ 686 3632; e info@moremiair.com; www.moremiair. com. Based upstairs in the main airport building, & linked with Kwando Safaris, this is another charter specialist. Their fleet of aircraft is geared to both passenger transfers & scenic flights.

✈ **Safari Air** [202 D1] Mathiba I Rd; ☏ +27 (0)113 943 873; e info@desertdelta.com; www.desertdelta. com. Located in the Ker & Downey Botswana complex at the corner of Motshaba St & Sir Seretse Khama Rd. The company operates transfers to the lodges associated with Desert & Delta Safaris.

✈ **Wilderness Air** [202 E1] Mathiba I Rd; ☏ 686 0778; e airinfo@wilderness-air.co.bw; www. wilderness-air.com. Owned by Wilderness Safaris, Wilderness Air organises virtually all the flights in Botswana for clients to Wilderness camps, making them the biggest 'small' airline here. In an emergency, if they're not available on the number above, try getting hold of them via Wilderness Safaris (page 225).

Maun Airport [202 D1] On the north side of town, Maun's airport is just a stone's throw from many of the local safari operators, and equally close to a number of bars, restaurants, shops and other facilities.

Following construction of a longer runway to facilitate the arrival of larger planes, there are also long-standing plans to construct a new terminal building, though no date has yet been set for this. For now, the airport remains small and somewhat chaotic, and while this can result in long and frustrating queues, its size prevents some of the hassle you find at larger hubs.

Alongside a couple of check-in desks downstairs is a bureau de change, though rates are not the greatest. Bidvest car hire has a presence here, as does Botswana Tourism, where various leaflets are on display. There's also a desk for Okavango Air Rescue (page 166).

Upstairs, there's still a post-office counter, but the café has been closed for some time; try Cappello or Pizza Plus (PPCC) just outside the airport gates, or seek out better options just a little further afield.

The airport itself has no reliable left-luggage facility, but if you're passing through to visit camps in the region by light aircraft, most safari companies will collect any spare baggage from you, store it offsite and return it to you as you leave.

DRIVING OR HITCHHIKING Ignoring the odd tiny bush track, there are only three significant roads linking Maun with the rest of the country:

Northeast towards Kasane Routing right through Chobe National Park, it's about 360km of bush and thick sand (accessible only by 4x4) northeast to Kasane. For details of this track, through Shorobe to Moremi and Chobe, see *The road north of Maun: to Moremi and Chobe*, at the end of this chapter.

receiving medical attention, washing clothes, or doing creative activities. As few of the children have an evening meal at home, a snack is served before they leave.

During the school holidays the centre tries to introduce the children to new experiences, such as going into the Delta to see the wildlife or going on camping trips into the pans. In a country whose major attraction is its wildlife, most of these youngsters have never seen an elephant, or indeed been near the national parks. There are also life-skills sessions, when agencies such as the police, government social workers and NGOs dealing with child-related issues address adolescents on comprehensive sexuality education, juvenile delinquency, drugs and alcohol abuse.

As well as working with the younger children, Bana Ba Letsatsi also runs a successful youth programme for those over 18, offering training in plumbing, carpentry, hospitality or cooking. On completion, the charity works hard to gain them work experience and ultimately employment.

Bana Ba Letsatsi receives no funding from the government, so donations and sponsorship are much appreciated (and can be made through the website). So, too, are offers of help: the charity welcomes skilled volunteers, preferably for at least six months, but all expenses need to be covered by the volunteer. And if you find yourself with room in your luggage, perhaps you could take something for the Sunshine Children: they would welcome the normal family basics, such as underwear, T-shirts or shorts; plasters and hygiene materials; footballs; pens and pencils. Just phone ahead or – if time isn't on your side – you could drop items at the Ker & Downey office opposite the airport, or call Ruth Stewart at Travel for Impact (m 7230 7694), whose office is further down the same road. How much more rewarding than putting children on the streets in the first place.

Southwest towards Ghanzi and Namibia
It's about 285km of good tar road to Ghanzi and around 210km further to the Namibian border at Mamuno. If you're hitchhiking, consider catching a bus or taxi to the Maun Sports Complex (page 219), about 2.5km beyond the Ngami Toyota garage, or walking this far out as it'll get you beyond most of the local traffic.

East towards Nata and Francistown
Nata is about 305km due east along the normally tarred A3, which divides Nxai Pan and Makgadikgadi Pans national parks. Although the road was badly damaged during the rains of 2017, reconstruction was underway by the end of the year, so a good tar road should be completed before long. The road crosses the 24-hour police and veterinary control post north of Makalamabedi. Note that you cannot take any red meat through this checkpoint if you're heading east.

If you're hitching from Maun, then at least cross to the south side of the Thamalakane River as far as the Caltex service station, on the corner of Sekgoma Road and Tawana I Road. Then, if you prefer, continue for a few kilometres south, towards Mokoro Lodge (page 208), where the road starts to bend west and you should be beyond the outskirts and the majority of the local traffic.

BY BUS Maun's smart new bus station on Tsheko-Tsheko Road [198 A5] replaced its chaotic predecessor close to the local market a few years ago. Street vendors were quick to take advantage of the concrete shelters, selling drinks from colourful coolboxes to thirsty travellers, but otherwise there are few amenities.

MAUN CENTRE

Lodges north of Maun (page 209)
Shorobe, Moremi, Chobe

Chelford Plaza

Lolie Pharmacy
& Medical Clinic
Beef Boys

KORO ST

Ngami
Centre
Spar
First National

Engen

Wilderness Air
Delta Air

New Mall/
Maun Shopping
Centre

Medi-Help
Clinic

Kwando
Safaris

Ker & Downey

Desert & Delta

LEKUKARA DRIVE

KUBU STREET

African
Arts &
Images

Safari Air

AIRPORT AVENUE

Dept of
Surveys &
Mapping

Air Botswana

Kavango Air

Sanctuary
Retreats

Bushman
Crafts

Mack Air

Nhabe

Kana Jang?

MOTSHABA ST

Maun Airport

Natlee Centre

Stanbic

Wilderness
Safaris

Belmond
&Beyond

Time Travel

NARE CIRCLE

MOPHANE AV

Belmond

KHAMA ROAD

Avis/Budget

Kalahari
Kanvas

Under One
Botswana Sky

Power
Station

Great
Plains

Apollo
House

Air Shakawe

Jacana Enterprises
Motovac
Sense of Africa

N

Bradt

0   200m
0   200yds

202

Maun GETTING THERE AND AWAY

8

203

For listings, see pages 205–15

Where to stay

1 Airport Hotel.................B2
2 Riley's Hotel.................D6

Where to eat and drink

   Barcelo's (see Ngami
   Centre).....................F2
3 Bimbo's.......................B8
4 Capello........................D1
5 Choice..........................C7
6 Debonairs Pizza...........C7
7 French Connection......D3
8 Hilary's.........................D2
9 KFC...............................B7
10 Nando's........................C7
11 PPCC.............................D1
12 Tandure l.....................A3
13 Tshilli Community
   Farmstall.....................E3
14 Wax Apple...................E2

There are regular departures for the major destinations, stopping at most of the larger towns on the way. The first buses leave at around 05.30, then regularly through the morning, but do check times beforehand, and arrive early. Larger bus companies include JNG Express (↘ *391 6629*), Golden Bridge Express, Seabelo Express (↘ *395 7078; www.seabelo.bw*) and AT & T Monnakgotla Travel & Tours (↘*399 5913, 393 9788;* m *7211 1250*).

Francistown   5½hrs, P160 one-way; departures between 06.30 & 09.30
Gaborone   10½hrs, P170 one-way; departures between 05.30 & 11.00
Ghanzi   3½hrs, P65 one-way; departures at 07.30, 08.30 & 15.30
Shakawe   7hrs, around P100 one-way, depending on the company. Departures between 05.30 & 16.30.

To reach **Kasane**, hop on a bus towards Francistown and change at Nata.

ORIENTATION

Finding your way around Maun is relatively simple. Though the town straddles the Thamalakane River, most places of interest are on the northern side. Here there are two focal points: the airport area, and the area around Riley's Garage. For the purposes of distances in this guide, we have taken Riley's Garage as the centre of Maun.

MAPS If you want to head anywhere 'off-piste' in Botswana's bush, then there are several options. The Shell maps, by Veronica Roodt, have become the standard references for most travellers, and are sold in some curio shops and garages in Maun. More specific are:

Ngami Data Services [202 C2] Apollo Hse, Mophane Av; ↘686 0581; e nds@ngami.net; www.nds-printingbotswana.com. An impressive & detailed range of maps & guides of Botswana's towns, national parks & areas of interest can be printed to order on site & in the size you require. They also have prints of historic maps, the earliest of which is from the 1500s, which make for a great souvenir.

Department of Surveys & Mapping [202 E2] Airport Av; ↘686 0272; ⊕ 07.30–12.45 & 13.45–16.30 Mon–Fri. Sells more traditional survey maps at a range of scales.

TOURIST INFORMATION Botswana Tourism [202 C2] (*Apollo Hse, Mophane Av;* ↘ *686 1056, airport* ↘ *686 3093;* e *maun@botswanatourism.co.bw;* ⊕ *07.30–18.00 Mon–Fri, 09.00–14.00 Sat*) has an office close to the airport, and another within the airport building.

The local newspaper, *The Ngami Times* (*www.ngamitimes.com*), is published weekly at P5, and is useful for details of local sports and entertainment. It's available from outlets across town, including the shop at Riley's Garage.

GETTING AROUND

If you're around the centre, between the airport and Riley's, then walking is feasible, though it can be hot. Otherwise, you'll need some form of transport, most of which operates out of the bus station [198 A5] on Tsheko-Tsheko Road. All public transport vehicles, including taxis, have blue number plates.

A **taxi** out to one of the camps to the north of town will cost from P60 (or more if there's a long sand track involved), depending on your negotiating powers. If it's a shared taxi – when the driver stops to take another lift at the same time – you can expect to pay considerably less, though not as little as one of the locals. Taxis have their telephone numbers displayed on the doors, and can be pre-booked. If in doubt, ask someone you know or your accommodation in Maun for a reliable contact number, as these tend to change all too frequently.

Small **combis** ply frequently between the back of the new bus station and the outlying suburbs. Typically, vehicles leave only when full, but they will drop you on request. Fares are fixed at just a few pula – from the bus station out to Audi Camp, for example, costs about P4.

In theory there are ten clearly defined routes, with numbers painted on the front of the vehicles, but some have not been operational for many years. For the visitor, the most useful routes are as follows:

Route 1   Airport, & north as far as Audi Camp
Route 5   Maun Lodge
Route 7   Letsholathebe II Memorial Hospital

Hitchhiking is also viable on the main arteries in and around town during daylight hours.

VEHICLE HIRE

Avis/Budget [202 C2] Mathiba I Rd; 686 0039; m 7583 6018; e avismun@botsnet. bw, botswanares@avis.co.za; www.avis.com; 08.00–17.00 Mon–Fri, 08.00–14.00 Sat, noon–18.00 Sun. For a fully equipped 4x4 contact Avis Safari Rental (27 11 392 5202; e safarirental. reservations@avis.co.za). See ad, page 178.

Bidvest [202 D2] Natlee Centre, Mathiba I Rd; 686 3728; m 7133 1114, 7629 8122; www. bidvest.co.za; 08.00–19.00 Mon–Fri

Europcar [202 D2] Natlee Centre, Mathiba I Rd; 686 3366; www.europcar.co.za; 07.30–17.00 Mon–Fri, 08.00–noon Sat, 16.00–18.00 Sun

Maun Self Drive 4x4 686 1875; e info@ mckenzie4x4.com, info@botswanaselfdrive4x4. com; www.maunselfdrive4x4.com. Also trading as McKenzie Self Drive 4x4, they offer fully equipped

camping vehicles with suggested itineraries & the promise of a breakdown service as back-up.

Travel Adventures Botswana 686 1211; m 7481 4658, 7668 7162; e website@ traveladventuresbotswana.com; www. traveladventuresbotswana.com. Toyota Hilux twin cabs or Land Cruisers can be rented as they are, or kitted out with everything you'll need for a camping safari into the national parks.

Wild Wheels Matlapaneng Ward; 684 0064; e info@wildwheels4x4.com; www. wildwheels4x4.com; 08.00–17.00 Mon–Fri, 08.00–13.00 Sat. Offering fully camping-equipped 4x4 vehicles & 24/7 breakdown support, Wild Wheels was established by the Reed Family, owners of Letaka Safaris (page 226). They will also advise on self-drive itineraries. See ad, 3rd colour section.

WHERE TO STAY

Just as Maun has changed in the last decade or two, so have the places to stay. In the 1980s, the few camps on the northern side of town felt like outposts in the wilderness. Places like Crocodile Camp, Island Safari Lodge and Okavango River Lodge had the atmosphere of oases of comfort. They seemed like remote lodges and often, when the water was high enough, mokoro trips would start from the banks of the Thamalakane River beside the lodge, to pole adventurers into the Delta.

Now, although many visitors are still drawn to the riverside establishments, times have changed. Better roads and more neighbours have made these camps feel less isolated and more a part of Maun. Less water in the river has for many years put an end to mokoro trips starting in Maun (although since the floods of 2009, transfers have been made by motorboat). Whereas visitors (especially backpackers) used to stop for at least a night in Maun, now many simply transit briefly through the airport to fly in to a safari camp.

Yet while these established old camps have lost much of their atmosphere, they may still be more interesting than some of the rather bland hotels that have sprung up to serve the business market. In addition, a handful of small-scale ventures have breathed new life into the accommodation scene: most recently a clutch of small self-catering establishments and one or two excellent B&Bs. Many others, though, are basic and functional, and too far outside the centre of town to be of interest to tourists.

Establishments in Maun are normally open throughout the year. If you're driving yourself, do be aware that signposts for some establishments only face south, so keep a watchful eye out for any pre-booked accommodation.

HOTELS AND LODGES
The distinction between hotels & lodges is more one of style than of substance. While some, such as Mokoro Lodge, feel more like a hotel, Royal Tree Lodge is definitely more of a lodge in style & approach. Note that some, such as Island Safari Lodge & the Sedia Hotel, also have excellent campsites.

Royal Tree Lodge [off 198 A7] (10 tents, 2 chalets) 680 0757; e info@royaltreelodge.co.bw; www.royaltreelodge.com; ✪ TREELO 20°03.896'S, 23°22.881'E. About half an hour from Maun, the former Motsentsela Tree Lodge is set on a 2km² game farm, a pleasant halfway house between the town & the bush. All profits from the lodge go towards the work of Love Botswana Outreach Mission.

Most visitors are collected from the airport & stay just 1 night. Self-drivers, who will need a 4x4 to negotiate the lengthy & in places very sandy track, will be given directions & the gate code at the time of reservation; you cannot just turn up. As a guide, leave Maun on the road to Francistown, taking the 1st turning right at the Caltex garage into Kwena Rd (signposted to Land Rover & the lodge). Just before the tar road becomes a dirt track, turn left through a residential area & follow the signs more or less straight for about 8km until you reach a large sign for the lodge. Go right here, leading to a locked gate; beyond, a track to the lodge leads through the reserve, stocked with giraffe, zebra, kudu, springbok, impala, oryx, eland & ostrich.

The elongated central building combines a well-designed bar, lounge & dining area, all under thatch. Meals are taken at a communal table, or outside on an extensive deck shaded by trees. Winding sandy paths lead to a small pool,

& on to large Meru-style tents on stilts, which are dotted among the trees. Each is accessed from a veranda through a solid door, with mesh windows allowing a through breeze. Inside, set on a varnished wooden floor, large twin beds with copious cushions recline under a central ceiling fan. Behind, the open-plan bathroom features a dbl vanity unit, a clawfoot bath & semi-private toilet, & outside is a well-screened open-air shower. The 2 honeymoon suites follow a different mould; spacious & stylish, these are solid-walled affairs with AC, tiled floors, gecko-printed white drapes & a couple of armchairs. Their bathrooms with deep bath & outside shower are modern yet entirely in keeping, & sliding patio doors lead to a small veranda at the back.

A series of marked walking trails wends through the grounds & down to the river, affording opportunities to watch game or check out the birds; to date, some 400 species have been identified here. Riders of all abilities can take to the saddle on the reserve (US$45/hr), which is the Maun base for Ride Botswana (page 227), while those interested in the mission's work can ask to visit the orphanage, or even volunteer their time for a few hours or more. Further afield, mokoro trails can be organised, as can day trips to Moremi Game Reserve with the lodge's own guide. *US$320–368 FB, inc transfers from Maun; sgl supp't US$90.* $$$$$

Thamalakane River Lodge [off map 209] (18 chalets) Shorobe Rd; 686 4313; m 7534 6314; e res@thamalakane-lodge.com; www.thamalakane-lodge.com; ✪ THAMAL 19°53.362'S, 23°33.412'E. Opened in 2007 as Lehututu Lodge, this riverside hotel, some 19km north of the town, has one of the most attractive settings in Maun. During my most recent stay they informed me that they are also planning to build 6 extra rooms sometime in 2018.

Paths wind through the gently sloping site to the chalets, family chalets & honeymoon suite, all set in well-tended gardens & facing the Thamalakane River, although some are quite close together. Stone walls, steeply thatched roofs, tiled floors & ceiling fans help to mitigate the sun's rays, & each chalet is smartly decorated with traditional touches. All guests may use the pool, which is set in a grassy clearing & shaded by large trees, & in-room massages can be organised, as well as activities in & around Maun.

Popular locally is the restaurant, an open-sided thatched building that spills on to a tree-shaded terrace by the river. With options from steak & seafood to pizzas & vegetarian dishes, there's plenty of choice, but if you are not staying at the lodge you will need to make a reservation. **$$$$–$$$$$**

🏠 **Cresta Maun Resort** [map 209] (83 rooms & suites) Shorobe Rd; ☏ 686 3455; e resmaun@cresta.co.bw; www. crestahotels.com/hotels/cresta-maun-2. Maun's latest hotel is 12.5km from the centre of town. Under the same ownership as Riley's, but newer & smarter, it has a rather clinical, formulaic feel. Each of the rooms has AC, flat-screen TV with DSTV services & a tea/coffee station, while the larger suites have a separate lounge area. Somewhat bizarrely, the standard rooms come with a shower in the bedroom, but the suites have a more standard bathroom, complete with a bath. With its pool, gym, cocktail bar & conference rooms the Cresta Maun is very much an international-style hotel. That said, if you want a comfortable, relatively economical place to stay & don't mind being a little out of town, this could be a good option. **$$$–$$$$**

🏠 **Maun Lodge** [198 C6] (128 rooms, 12 chalets) Tawana I Rd, Boseja; ☏ 686 3939; e reservations@maunlodge.co.bw; www. maunlodge.com. Massive expansion in 2013 transformed this established place on the banks of the Thamalakane River into Maun's largest hotel. A reliable stopover, it is popular with overland groups & independent travellers alike. If some of the rooms are a little lacking in character, the main areas are pleasant & the staff are welcoming. Rooms come with twin beds, tea/coffee-making facilities, AC, TV, phone & a safe as standard,

but vary in shape & style, with either a shower or bath en suite. The thatch-&-brick chalets are particularly good value, & each has its own parking space. More expensive options overlook the river, including 2 family chalets & the presidential suite.

The open-air Boma & Riverview bar are nice spots to spend an evening, with the bonus of live music some evenings. As well as a range of light meals, there's an extensive buffet that includes grills, vegetarian options & some local dishes: perfect if you don't want to venture out. To keep you cool, there are 2 separate swimming pools, for adults & children. **$$$–$$$$** exc b/fast (P165 pp).

🏠 **Riley's Hotel** [203 D6] (51 rooms) Tsheko-Tsheko Rd; ☏ 686 0204; e resrileys@cresta.co.bw; www.cresta-hospitality.com. Riley's has always been more of an institution than a hotel. It was founded when Harry Riley arrived in Maun, in 1910. Initially he simply built an extra rondavel next to his own, suitable for 1 visitor. It had no bed, just reed matting on the floor. A few years later he joined the 2 rondavels together, building a simple dining room between them, & soon he was running Maun's first hotel. In his book *The Lost World of the Kalahari*, Laurens van der Post described Riley's in the 1950s as a 'remarkable little hotel which he [Harry Riley] had founded for the odd, intrepid traveller who had been determined enough to cross the desert, as well as for the score or so of Europeans patient & courageous enough to make Maun the unique outpost of life that it is today'.

Now those first buildings form part of the manager's house, & Riley's is owned by the Cresta group. Today's visitor will benefit from a central location on the main street, a pool & pool bar, surrounded by lawns with tables under thatched umbrellas, a children's play area & a gym. The rooms (including 10 suites with a balcony & lounge) have dark-wood contemporary furniture, AC & DSTV. Best are those upstairs, whose high thatched ceilings go a long way to keeping them cool. The modern restaurant (**$$$**) is a tad soulless, but service & food are good, & you can opt to eat outside where you'll be entertained after dark by an orchestra of frogs in the nearby Thamalakane River. **$$$**

🏠 **Airport Hotel** [202 B2] (40 rooms) Mathiba I Rd; ☏ 686 5454; e reservations@ airporthotelmaun.com; www.airporthotelmaun.

com. This 2-star hotel catering for the business market couldn't be more handy for the airport. En-suite rooms are rather stark & functional, with a dbl bed, AC, TV, kettle, fridge & safe – in short, all that you need, but nothing more. There's a bar & restaurant, & free Wi-Fi throughout, but the rather clinical feel isn't helped by a leopard skin draped over a couch in the lobby. **$$$**

⌂ **Island Safari Lodge** [map 209] (12 chalets, 6 rooms, camping) Sir Seretse Khama Rd; ☎ 686 0300; m 7211 2008; e enquire@africansecrets. net; www.islmaun.com. Island Safari Lodge was a well-established hub when I first visited Maun in 1988. It stands in 116ha beside the western bank of the Thamalakane River, about 12km north of Maun, under a forest canopy dominated by tall sycamore figs (*Ficus sycomorus*). Coming from Maun you take a well-signposted left turn just before the river, pass through the security gate, then follow a track for almost 2km through old riverine forest (perfectly navigable for 2x4 vehicles).

Accommodation is in twin-bedded thatched chalets, set among lawns & indigenous vegetation close to the river. All have AC, sisal flooring, TV, tea/coffee facilities, & en-suite shower – & folding chairs outside from which to contemplate the sunset. 2 chalets are wheelchair accessible. Further back is a block of 6 'standard' rooms, some of which adjoin making them a good choice for families or groups travelling together. The shady campsite has 2 ablution blocks, & there are dedicated spaces for overland trucks around the perimeter.

Landscaped gardens lead down to the river, where meals are served in the long bar/restaurant (⊕ 06.00–22.00) with sports TV for entertainment, & free Wi-Fi. Cooling off is easy, with a small pool close to the restaurant, & a far larger one by the campsite. Further afield, the lodge can organise boat trips at US$16/hr pp (based on 4 people), as well as day trips to Chief's Island, NG32 & Moremi, mokoro excursions & helicopter scenic flights. **$$$** *Camping US$9.50 pp.*

⌂ **Sedia Hotel** [map 209] (24 rooms, 5 cottages, camping) Sir Seretse Khama Rd; ☎ 686 0177; e sedia@info.bw; www.sedia-hotel.com. The wide-fronted Sedia, with its cream & ochre walls & deep-red blinds, occupies extensive grounds just 6km from the airport, & is well signposted from the main road. Once dubbed the 'Sedi Motel', it has improved & expanded since the early 1990s. Now, although not quite as costly

as Riley's or Maun Lodge, it has a livelier, more colourful atmosphere.

In the foyer, adorned with traditional African wall-hangings & large wooden animal carvings, you will find a couple of soft chairs & cool drinks to welcome you on arrival. Most of the rooms are laid out along 2 wings facing into the hotel's gardens, each with its own outside entrance. Bright ethnic colours adorn twin or dbl beds, en-suite bathrooms incorporate a bath with shower, & each room has AC, ceiling fan, tea/coffee station, TV & phone. Closer to the river, larger 1- & 2-bedroom cottages boast a fridge & kitchenette (but no oven or cooking facilities), AC, lounge with TV & a shady veranda.

At the back of the hotel, set among gardens with large lawns, is one of the area's best swimming pools, which is now exclusively for hotel & campsite guests. The surrounding decking is a popular venue for dining or just for a drink, while the more formal restaurant comes into its own in the winter. There is also a bar with a pool table, & a separate children's playground.

Beyond the lawns, a large & sprawling campsite leads down to the Thamalakane River, where campers share 5 well-kept showers & toilets. There is plenty of tree shade for your own tent, or you can organise a pre-erected dome tent for around P300 each. The option to park next to your tent is particularly useful as the campsite isn't well fenced, & despite the presence of a nightwatchman, the security didn't seem that tight when I last stayed here. (With good locks on the room doors, this isn't a problem for those staying in the hotel.)

The hotel is the base for Afro Trek (page 227), who operate a variety of budget safaris & mokoro trips. **$$–$$$** *Camping P70 pp.*

⌂ **Mokoro Lodge** [off 198 D7] (36 rooms) ☎ 680 0551; m 7699 1256; www.mokorolodge. com; ✪ MOKLOD 20°01.646'S, 23°26.255'E. Out of town on the Nata road, 3.4km from Riley's, this simple motel is set back from the road, with good security. Twin & dbl en-suite rooms are fairly basic but have all the essentials, plus AC, DSTV, a kitchenette & a no-nonsense bathroom. This is perhaps more geared toward local business travel but would make a reasonable & economic place to spend the night if you're passing through. More important for self-drivers is the covered parking space next to the room. There is also a restaurant on site & a new pool next to the main parking area. **$$** *exc b/fast.*

For listings, see pages 205–15

Where to stay
1 Audi Camp
2 Cresta Maun
3 Crocodile Camp
4 Island Safari Lodge
5 Maun Garden Studio
6 Maun Rest Camp
7 Okavango River Lodge
8 The Old Bridge
    Backpackers
9 Peo Luxury Apartments
10 Queness Inn

11 Rivernest Cottages
12 Sedia Hotel

Off map
    Discovery B&B
    Thamalakane
      River Lodge

Where to eat and drink
13 Marc's Eatery
    Motsana (see Motsana)

Discovery B&B,
University of Botswana,
Sexaxa Cultural Village,
Thamalakane River Lodge,
Shorobe, Chobe NP, Moremi GR

Hambukushu
Cultural Village

Matlapana
Baskets

African
Bush Camps

Motsana

Police

Sir Seretse Khama Road

Thamalakane

Shorobe Road

Shell/ATM

Maun centre

Hospital

N

Bradt

0 ————— 1km
0 ————— 1 mile

Crocodile Camp [map 209] (15 chalets, camping) Shorobe Rd; m 7560 6864; e sales@ crocodilecamp.com; www.crocodilecamp.com. On a site sloping down to the river some 15km north of town, Croc Camp is universally known as one of the old institutions of Maun. The camp was closed for refurbishments in late 2017, & they looked fairly extensive, but we anticipate that the camp will reopen in 2018. Prior to this, lack of maintenance was taking its toll on the once-impressive en-suite twin-bedded chalets, set at the top of the site, & on the older, en-suite chalets. Near the car park, a separate campsite with a modern ablution block is set under a few shady camelthorn (*Vachellia erioloba*) trees. Some pitches benefit from individual water & power supplies, & overland trucks have their own discrete area. The camp's thatched bar, overlooking the Thamalakane River, was a great place for a sundowner, & the swimming pool set in shaded lawns dotted with tables & chairs made a good spot for families. Less appealing was the restaurant (🕘 06.30–22.00), tucked away from the river. A range of activities can be booked, including motorboat & mokoro trips starting from the camp.

B&BS AND SELF-CATERING As Maun benefits from an increasing range of shops, cafés & restaurants, self-catering has been added to the accommodation mix, alongside a small selection of pleasant B&Bs. Often such establishments are too far off the beaten track for visitors, or too far from somewhere to eat, but those included below fulfil both of these needs.

Maun Garden Studio [map 209] (1-bedroom studio) ✆ 686 0254; e margaretcpalmer@gmail.com. Situated in picturesque gardens on the banks of the Thamalakane River, this is a great option for those who would prefer not to stay in a traditional hotel or lodge. The large, open-plan studio bungalow, 7km from the airport, has its own kitchenette & en-suite bathroom, & is primarily a self-catering option. However, b/fast is included, served on a terrace overlooking the gardens & river. For other meals, owner Margaret Palmer is happy to help with suggestions & reservations for restaurants around Maun. The studio feels more like a holiday home than a B&B & with secure parking & an inviting pool (which, like the gardens, are shared with the Palmers), guests could easily spend more than the customary 1 night here. **$$$**

* **⌂ Otto** [off 198 A7] (2 rooms) **m** 7436 6049; **e** darrylfreeman06@gmail.com. About 6.5km from Riley's Garage, on the banks of the Thamalakane River, Otto is an entirely self-sufficient, exclusive-use, self-catering eco-guesthouse – so you will need to bring your own drinking water. Constructed from rammed earth by the owner, Darryl Freeman, the emphasis here is on sustainable building techniques while providing a high level of comfort & a relaxing environment. The main house has an open-plan kitchen, dining area & lounge, & a separate bathroom. To one side is a large en-suite master bedroom complete with outdoor shower & bath overlooking the river & gardens. Outside is a deck, firepit & unique moat-cum-plunge pool. Separate from the main house is a second building affectionately called 'The Shack', which houses a 2nd en-suite bedroom. Darryl is happy to help with taxis, excursions & restaurant reservations, & she will often call in to check how guests are doing & to tend to the garden, but guests are essentially left to their own devices. This would best suit those with their own transport – but pre-booking is essential; you cannot just turn up. **$$$** *exc b/fast.*

⌂ Discovery Bed & Breakfast [map 209] (9 chalets) Shorobe Rd; **m** 7244 8298, 7436 0198; **e** discoverybookings@gmail.com; www. discoverybedandbreakfast.com. A taste of Botswana's culture comes to life in this quiet, attractively planted complex, about 15km north of the airport down a 300m track to the west of the main road. Individual wood-framed rondavels, painted inside & out in patterns of browns, ochres, deep reds & greens, are set on a sandy plot around a firepit, in the form of a traditional village. Inside are twin or dbl beds of rustic wooden poles swathed

in mosquito netting, with bedside lights, a toilet & basin behind a reed screen, & private showers under the stars; some also have a small veranda. A family chalet has a dbl bed & a set of bunks, ideal for 2 (young) children. The reception area doubles as a homely b/fast room, & there's a small pool at the back. A small Wi-Fi area/coffee shop (⏱ *15.30–18.00*) serving cappuccinos, iced coffees & freshly baked cakes may open only in peak season, depending on demand. Evening meals are no longer available, but there are several options nearby, & activities can happily be arranged. **$$–$$$**

⌂ Rivernest Cottages [map 209] (10 rooms) Sir Seretse Khama Rd; **** 684 0400; **m** 7149 2623; **e** rivernestmaun@gmail.com; www. rivernestcottages.com. The name 'cottages' does little to describe this pleasant but unassuming place, set on a compact plot just off the main road, with free Wi-Fi throughout. Built around a small pool, each of its 5 modern chalets incorporates 2 rooms, which have their own lounge area, TV & kitchenette, & an en-suite bedroom with a dbl or twin beds. Guests can relax at the bar with a drink, & meals can be brought in by arrangement. **$$–$$$**

⌂ Jump Street Chalets [198 A7] (10 chalets) Boseja Ward; **** 686 4688; **m** 7407 5553; **e** jumpstreetchalets1@yahoo.com; www. jumpstreetchalets.co.bw. Set in pleasant gardens in a relatively quiet spot, Jump Street Chalets are further from Maun's main roads than some other establishments. The en-suite thatched chalets are clean & comfortable, with DSTV & a mini-fridge, & a family room also has a small kitchenette. The main area consists of a reception, a pool & the thatched Linyanti bar & restaurant catering for all meals. Wi-Fi is available throughout. Jump Street is the base for Wild Ridge Bush Trail Safaris, who offer trips of 1–21 days around Botswana & surrounding countries. **$$**

⌂ Peo Luxury Apartments [map 209] (10 rooms) Sir Seretse Khama Rd; **** 684 1244; **m** 7597 9050; **e** info@peoapartments.co.bw; www.peoapartments.com. Opened in 2014, & possibly changing its name to Peo Luxury Lodge, this set of rooms is around 9km north of the airport. Geared to self-catering, each en-suite room has cooking facilities, varying from a stove & a fridge in the standard rooms to full private kitchens in the more expensive options. Outside are a decent-sized pool, raised b/fast deck & boma area, where meals from the on-site restaurant are served (weather permitting). Activities, including a w/end package, can also be arranged from here. *P800–1200* **$$** *exc b/fast.*

🏠 **Queness Inn** [map 209] (8 rooms) 📞 684 1000; m 7441 4337; e quenessinnmaun@gmail. com; www.quenessinn.com. On the less busy southern side of the Thamalakane River, this self-catering option with impressive rooms can feel a little out of the way, despite being only 6km from Riley's. 6 en-suite dbl rooms, organised around a verdant courtyard garden, have DSTV, Wi-Fi, a well-equipped kitchenette & AC; 2 family rooms have a separate lounge with sofa bed. There is also an outdoor braai area & secure on-site parking. **$$**

CAMPING AND BACKPACKING

Although many of Maun's hotels, lodges & camps offer camping as well as their normal rooms, one of the dedicated campsites is often a better bet – although the sites at both the Sedia Hotel & Island Safari Lodge are also well worth consideration.

Most of the campsites are north of Maun, on the road to Shorobe, with the furthest – Okavango River Lodge – 15km out of town. They're the obvious places to stay if you arrive in your own vehicle, but if you don't have transport, most will provide a pick-up/drop-off service into town at a price. Alternatively, a taxi from town will cost you around P60, or you can take a Route 1 combi for around P4. These pass up & down the main road near the camps throughout the day.

🏕 **Audi Camp** [map 209] (camping, 10-bed house) Shorobe Rd; 📞 686 0599; e info@audisafaris. com; www.okavangocamp.com. While standards elsewhere tend to fluctuate, Audi Camp remains one of Maun's constants. It's clean, friendly & well cared for, with the whole multi-level site securely fenced & patrolled at night by security guards. The camp is well signposted about 12km from the centre of Maun on the road north to Moremi & Chobe.

At the top of the complex is a sandy campsite under mopane trees, with a basic camper's kitchen, & ablutions in an intriguingly designed circular block that has open-air showers & hot water. Pitches with power have their own braai & water supply. Bring your own tent, or rent one of their pre-erected tents on solid bases: either 8 bare dome tents with camp beds & no linen (bedding can be rented), or small Meru tents (4 en suite) with beds & linen, as well as electric lights & fans. Firewood & ice are available, as

is a laundry service. If you don't fancy sleeping under canvas, try a room in the 4-bedroom riverside house, which has its own kitchen & bathroom.

The camp has a large thatched bar, & a restaurant area on a lower level which serves meals & snacks all day, from toasted sandwiches to steaks & vegetarian options. Down again, & near the river, is a large & very popular swimming pool. A great little shop sells a range of curios, while almost opposite is Motsana 'village', which incorporates a café & puts on occasional cultural events. The camp itself is also the base for Audi Camp Safaris (page 227). *Camping P80 pp, power point P80/night; dome tent P160/200 sgl/dbl, Meru tent P380/530, en suite P660/795, house P2,300, or P570 dbl. Transfer from town P150/vehicle.*

🏕 **Maun Rest Camp** [map 209] (12 tents, 4 rooms, camping) Off Sir Seretse Khama Rd, Maun; 📞 686 2623, 686 3472 (with answerphone); e reservations@maunrestcamp.com; www. maunrestcamp.com. Management of this quiet, spacious campsite on the river has been taken over from owners Simon & Joyce by The Old Bridge Backpackers (page 212), who were making extensive changes in late 2017. Find it by heading 7km north of the airport on the road to Chobe & Moremi.

The campsite has 12 individual pitches, of which 5 are next to the river, each with its own powerpoint, braai, water tap & picnic table. Trees shade 2 clean, brick-built ablution blocks, equipped with 4 separate showers, loos & basins plus laundry tubs & dishwashing sinks, & copious hot water from a gas geyser. For those without a tent there are twin-bedded Meru tents with electric lights & carpets, & chairs at the front. Of these, 4 share ablutions, while the others (4 on the river) are being converted to en suite. There are also 4 dbl rooms in a basic 'backpackers' house, so you can opt for more solid accommodation. A bar & restaurant for guests is under construction. This is likely to be similar to that at The Old Bridge, which is barely 2mins' walk away – so finding somewhere for a drink or dinner before then shouldn't be a problem. *Camping P100/80 pp riverfront/off river, tent P330/400 pp sgl/dbl, room P370/450.*

🏕 **Okavango River Lodge** [map 209] (camping, 8 tents, 6 chalets) Shorobe Rd; 📞 686 3707; e info@okavango-river-lodge.com; www. okavango-river-lodge.com. Opened in the late 1970s, this rustic lodge stands on the Thamalakane River, about 15km north of Maun. Leading down to the river under shady acacia trees, its campsite has a thatched gazebo with tables & benches, & an old ablution block. Set further back are basic en-suite chalets with nets, fans & twin, dbl or family accommodation, while on the other side of the site, twin-bedded tents with electric fans & lights share their own ablution facilities.

Central to the lodge is its lively bar, which can be heaving at w/ends. A bar menu promises a variety of tasty bites, from b/fast or toasted sandwiches to T-bone steaks; the food is good, & service is both prompt & friendly. The small pool is popular with campers & diners, but their quirky Sun cricket matches, which used to be played on the floodplain opposite camp, have now been relocated thanks to the (otherwise welcome) rise in river levels. The lodge offers a number of activities including a full-day boat trip to Chief's Island (*P1,250 pp, 3–4hrs, inc lunch, based on 4 people*), & mokoro trips of varying lengths on the Boro River in NG32. For details, see page 220 – & note that if you don't have a tent or camping kit, you can hire them from the lodge. Other activities can be booked at the lodge's travel desk. *Camping P110pp; tent P190/320 sgl/dbl; chalet P340/480/640 sgl/dbl/family, all exc b/fast.*

⚊ The Old Bridge Backpackers [map 209] (camping, 8 dorm beds, 8 tents) Off Sir Seretse Khama Rd; ☎ 686 2406; e info@maun-backpackers.com; www.maun-backpackers.com. 10km north of town & tucked down a well-signposted but rather pot-holed lane by the river bridge, 'The Bridge' is Maun's best backpacker hang-out by some way. Owned by David, one of the original partners in Livingstone's Jungle Junction, it was opened in 2005 on a shady site close to the old pole bridge (now a national monument). At this point the river flows permanently, & at low water hippos & crocodiles can be seen in front of the camp, while fruit bats are attracted by a large sycamore fig tree. The area used to be a vegetable garden; now, around 400 trees have been planted around the site, which offers some lovely walks with good birding.

Alongside space for independent campers, there are 8 pre-erected walk-in tents, each under a canopy with dbl or twin beds. 5 are en suite & have private verandas overlooking the river. There are also simple dome tents with 2 mattresses & bedding, & a block of individual 'dorm' beds that are useful if it's too wet to camp. All share clean, reed-screened showers & toilets that are open to the stars. A well-used pool table sits alongside the large, thatched central area, where the latest sports are on TV, & tables & chairs are set out under the trees. Food is available all day, from a full b/fast to a range of pasta dishes & pizzas from the wood-fired oven (*from P65*); there's also a self-catering kitchen. A small pool & Wi-Fi add to the facilities.

This is a relaxed outfit, young & friendly, with no shortage of activities. From the camp itself, you can depart on day trips to Moremi or Chief's Island or multi-day self- or fully catered mokoro safaris run by their own in-house operator, Old Bridge Tours & Safaris (page 227). *Camping P80 pp; dome tent P150 pp; walk-in tent P330/400 sgl/dbl, en suite P480/580 sgl/dbl.*

SOUTH AND WEST OF MAUN

⚊ Drifters Maun Camp [off 198 D7] (10 tents, camping) Chanoga; m 7230 4472; e drifters@drifters.co.za; www.drifters.co.za. Some 32km south of Maun, towards Nata, the local base of the overland safari company, Drifters, has 5 camping pitches as well as 10 Meru tents with twin beds, including 4 that are en suite. If you're heading south, it's well worth considering a night here. Take the tar road from Maun towards Nata & Francistown, then just beyond the village of Chanoga turn right down a signed sandy track of approximately 1km to the camp (you'll need at least a high-clearance vehicle for this). Here you'll find a wide riverfront location with grassy lawns, where the thatched bar & restaurant, exclusive to those staying on site, are attractively decorated with wall hangings & baskets. As well as a volleyball court there is a small pool, but the greatest attraction is the Boteti River, which when flowing (& it has been for several years), attracts numerous waterbirds – including flamingos, pelicans & knob-billed ducks. Camping is on a small, tree-shaded site, with an ablution block & hot water. *Camping P130 pp, tent P595/990 sgl/dbl, inc b/fast.*

⚊ Sitatunga Camp [off 198 A6] (12 chalets, 10 tents, camping) ☎ 680 0380/1; e bookings@deltarain.com; www.deltarain.com; ✦ SITAT 20°04.476'S, 23°21.296'E. Within a secure complex, Sitatunga remains a popular choice for overlanders, but for independent campers pre-booking is almost essential. To get there, head southwest from Maun towards Ghanzi, before turning off the main road about 12km from Riley's Garage. The lodge is about 2km from the main road down a sandy track although it is accessible by 2x4.

The large campsite lies under trees, with pitches well spread out; each has a standpipe & power point & shares basic but clean ablutions. Best of the accommodation are the 10 en-suite Meru tents. These are quite spacious, with mosquito nets cladding the twin beds, a tea station, an electric fan, & outdoor showers. Brick-walled, canvas-roofed chalets feel a little dark & cramped by comparison, albeit with AC & a ceiling fan. There's a handy laundry service, & firewood is sold at P25 per load.

Following a fire some years ago there's no self-catering kitchen, but braai facilities are available & the likes of burgers & pizzas are served in a large, airy bar area ($\oplus$ 11.00–late). For a spot of activity there's a pool by the bar, with a 2nd pool close to the chalets, & a volleyball court. *Camping P110 pp, tent P180 pp, chalet P650 pp (both 2 people max).*

✳ 🏠 **Tshima Bush Camp** [off 198 A6] (4 tents) m 7484 2079; e info@tshimabushcamp.

com; www.tshimabushcamp.com; ⊕ TSHIMA 20°11.449'S, 23°14.430'E. Also on the Ghanzi road, some 30km southwest of Maun, Tshima is run by Dutch husband & wife Bas & Anita. It's a friendly, low-key spot in 30ha of land bordering the Nhabe River, where marked walking trails make exploring easy. The occasional elephant crosses through camp, but for many birding is the draw: the previous owners identified around 350 species here.

Facing into the bush, Tshima's smart walk-in tents have twin beds under mosquito nets, & a modern en-suite bathroom. Each has a table & chairs on the veranda, plus its own picnic bench, so b/fast – brought to your tent in a basket each morning – can be both relaxed & private. In the evening guests can enjoy a 3-course dinner (*P250*) under the stars. Bas & Anita can help to organise excursions into the Delta, Moremi Game Reserve, Nxai Pan National Park & elsewhere. With easy 2x4 access from the tarred road, Tshima is a tranquil place for a spot of R&R, but note that you cannot just drop in: reservations are essential. **$$$**

✗ WHERE TO EAT AND DRINK

Maun's hardly a town for fine dining, though the demise of the long-standing Sports Bar leaves a big hole, but there are several reasonable venues, including some of the hotels and camps,. There are also numerous fast-food places, including KFC [203 B7], Nando's [203 C7], Debonairs [203 C7], Bimbo's [203 B8], Barcelo's [202 F2] and more. Expect a decent burger to cost upwards of P60 – and remember that you're in a country which counts beef as one of its main exports.

Of the hotels, pick of the bunch is the riverside restaurant at **Thamalakane River Lodge**, where the pizzas and setting are worth the journey – although if you are not staying at the lodge, be sure you make a reservation. While **Maun Lodge**, the **Sedia Hotel** and **Riley's** have competent if uninspiring formal restaurants, their open-air offerings are far more appealing. Of these, **The Boma** at Maun Lodge is relaxed and quite rustic, while eating by the pool at the back of the **Sedia** can be fun with a good atmosphere. Of the campsites, **Okavango River Lodge** is generally a good bet, as well as being arguably the town's most frequented watering hole – especially at weekends.

Individual restaurants and cafés add variety to the mix, some specialising in breakfast and lunch, and others open in the evening. Many are within walking distance of the airport, and most are licensed, with vegetarians well catered for almost everywhere.

For **traditional food**, the restaurants at both Riley's and Maun Lodge can oblige, but beat a path to Choice, or the Dine Inn [198 B4], and you're likely to be the only tourist in sight. Or close to the airport, pop out at lunchtime to one of the street stalls just opposite Capello; a satisfying serving of pap and stew will be yours for just P30–35.

✗ **Capello** [202 D1] Natlee Centre, cnr Airport Rd & Mathiba I Rd; ✆680 1277; ⊕ 07.00–23.00 daily. Almost directly opposite the airport

Capello is an obvious if slightly unimaginative option for travellers. It's one of a number of franchise restaurants to try their luck in Maun, with an extensive international-style menu. But don't expect fine dining; the vibe is more nightclub/bar than restaurant. $$–$$$$

✗ **Il Pomodoro** [off 198 D7] Nata Rd; m 7438 7590; ⏰ noon–21.00 Mon–Sat. Under new ownership, the former Chaplin's bistro is now an out-&-out Italian restaurant, offering great pizzas, pasta & antipasti. Come for the food, rather than the ambience or location (on an industrial estate, about 2km south of the Caltex fuel station); if the talk of moving closer to the town centre comes to fruition, it's likely to give this a very different vibe. $$–$$$$

✗ **French Connection** [202 D3] Mophane Av; ☎680 0625; ⏰ 08.30–17.00 Mon–Fri, 08.30–14.00 Sat. This licensed café/restaurant quite close to the airport is run by Marie & George, a couple of Swiss/Dutch origin, & is highly rated. With seating outside under mopane trees, or inside for inclement weather, it's well screened from the road, with off-road parking. The wide-ranging menu ranges from wraps & fresh salads to Moroccan-inspired mezes, meat *koftas* & *pastillas*. B/fasts, served until noon, include an innovative vegetarian version featuring ratatouille & rösti. As an aside the restaurant also sells secondhand books in aid of a charity that spays & vaccinates village dogs around the Delta. $$

✗ **Hilary's Coffee Shop** [202 D2] Off Mathiba I Rd; ☎686 1610; ⏰ 08.30–16.00 Mon–Fri, 08.30–noon Sat. Close to the airport, Hilary's has been serving since about 1995, & remains one of the more interesting & reliable places to eat during the day in Maun. Well-shaded tables are outside among mopane trees & pot plants. Hilary & her staff make everything on the premises, from mayonnaise & salad dressing to bran muffins; the home-baked whole-wheat bread is to die for, & with a little advance notice can be made to order for a camping trip. Expect the best home-cooked b/fasts in Maun, tasty wholesome lunches, including sandwiches & salads, daily specials & amazing desserts & cakes. $$

✗ **Pizza Plus Coffee and Curry (PPCC)** [202 D1] Cnr Airport Rd & Mathiba I Rd; ☎680 0925; m 7272 8318; e ashok12345@gmail.com; ⏰ 08.00–22.00 daily. Directly opposite the terminal building, PPCC has branched out from its successful venture in Kasane & is undeniably a convenient place to get a drink & use the Wi-Fi. The menu is extensive & somewhat eclectic with a selection of all-day b/fasts, pizzas, burgers & curries. Reports suggest that the curries can be good but the pizza & burgers rather disappointing. $$

✗ **Marc's Eatery** [map 209] Nunga Conservation, Sir Seretse Khama Rd; m 7400 2955; e marcseatery.business.site; ⏰ 08.00–18.00 Mon–Fri, 08.00–15.00 Sat. The place on everyone's lips at the time of research, in late 2017, Marc's had only just opened & we weren't disappointed. The food was excellent & the ambience buzzing, despite only being open for lunch (last orders 1hr before closing). The à la carte menu of sandwiches, salads, pasta dishes & burgers is supplemented by a changing specials board & the restaurant is licensed. There are now plans to open for 1 evening a week.

The associated small deli sells, among other things, a range of homemade sauces & spice mixes, perfect for taking on camping trips. With a little advanced notice (either in person or by phone/Facebook) you can also order a take-away b/fast & lunch. $–$$

✗ **Motsana** [map 209] Shorobe Rd; ⏰ 08.00–18.00 Mon–Fri, 08.00–15.00 Sat. The licensed café at Motsana 'village' is a quirky spot for b/fast or lunch, or even just an ice cream, with free Wi-Fi & a whole range of shops to add to the attraction – there's even a beauty salon here. Thu night is cinema night, when they're also open for dinner. $–$$

✳ ✗ **Tandurei Indian Kitchen** [202 A3] Village Complex, Moeti Rd; ☎680 0227; m 7684 9440, 7420 9086, 7113 7333; www.tandurei. com; ⏰ 10.30–22.30 daily. A number of Indian restaurants have popped up in Maun over the last couple of years, & this one comes up to scratch. An owner-run establishment with a sister restaurant in Francistown, it's a little out of town, but the design of the building is quirky, with an old air-rescue plane mounted on the roof. Most importantly the food is authentic & tasty & the portion sizes just right. $–$$

✳ ✗ **Tshilli Community Farmstall** [202 E3] cnr Sir Seretse Khama Rd & Motshaba St; ☎684 0940; ⏰ 07.00–20.00 Mon–Fri, 07.00–17.00 Sat, 07.00–16.00 Sun. The low-key Tshilli (pronounced 'chilli') is a fresh new addition to the café scene in Maun, & is proving deservedly popular – both as a take-away or in comfy seating in their shaded courtyard, with free Wi-Fi. Along with an all-day b/fast, the menu has plenty of choice for lunch or an early dinner, from hoisin pulled duck & spaghetti bolognese to coconut prawn curry, various snacks

& desserts. A wide range of hot & cold drinks includes the best iced coffee in Botswana! A canopy at the back shelters a dedicated ice-cream stall, La Mexicana. $–$$

✖ Wax Apple [202 E2] Airport Av; ✆ 686 0559; ◷ 07.30–17.30 Mon–Sat. Sometimes known as The Red Monkey this colourful & laid-back café is a useful find near the airport. It serves good coffee as well as a selection of wraps, toasted sandwiches,

salads & cakes. There is also Wi-Fi on site & a small curio shop & gallery. $–$$

✖ Choice [203 C7] Old Mall, Tsheko-Tsheko Rd; ◷ 07.30–22.00 daily. For a hearty helping of traditional food, join the lunchtime queues at Choice. It feels rather like a fast-food joint, with modern wooden tables & benches, but the buffet features a range of Botswana specials, including oxtail, rice & greens. $

ENTERTAINMENT AND NIGHTLIFE

With the closure of the only nightclub, Trekkers, and the ever-popular Sports Bar, Maun's nightlife is even more limited than in the past. That said, the lively bars at Okavango River Lodge and The Old Bridge Backpackers are doing their best to fill the void – and both are good spots to unwind after time in the bush.

If you're in town on a Thursday evening, it's worth checking to see if there's a film showing at Motsana 'village' [map 209] (*Shorobe Rd*). With its funky Moorish architecture and dark walls, it looks like an imposing fortress from the outside, but step through the gate and you're greeted by a large stage which every Thursday evening at 19.30 hosts a semi-open-air cinema. Seating is in the licensed café, so it's all very relaxed.

For something different and a little more cultural travellers can attend the weekly poetry night held at the Kana Jang? café at the Nhabe Museum every Wednesday from 19.30.

SHOPPING

Most shops are open Monday to Friday around 08.00–17.00, and Saturday to midday or thereabouts, with supermarket hours considerably longer. Note that locals have warned of a problem with opportunistic theft both near the airport and around the market, so watch your bags in these areas in particular.

FOOD AND DRINK You can buy most things here that you'll find in a supermarket in Europe or North America, although you may need to look around and brand names may be different. The choice (especially of fresh fruit and vegetables) may not be as varied and it is always worth bringing items linked to specific dietary requirements with you. Several of the **supermarkets** are on Tsheko-Tsheko Road to the south of Riley's Garage. These include Maun's oldest, Shoprite [203 C7] (*Tsheko-Tsheko Rd*), and its more recent rivals: Spar [203 B7] (behind Nando's) with a second branch in the Ngami Centre [202 F2]; and Choppies, near the bus station [198 B4] (◷ *08.00–20.00 daily*), with a smaller branch in New Mall [202 E1]. Most are open daily from 08.00 until about 19.00 or 20.00 midweek, but close earlier on Saturday and (particularly) Sunday.

If you're just after **bread**, try Dainty Bakes on Tsheko-Tsheko Road [203 C7], while for **vacuum-packed meats**, a good alternative to the supermarkets is Delta Deli at Riley's Garage [203 D7], or Beef Boys on Sir Seretse Khama Road near the airport [202 F2] – where you can order what you want in advance ready to pick up as you head out of town.

Supermarkets don't sell **alcohol**, so to stock up on beer and wine you'll need to go to one of the liquor stores around town. One of the better ones is Bateman's in Chelford Plaza [202 G1] (◷ *10.00–18.00 Mon–Fri, 10.00–14.00 Sat*); otherwise one of the branches of Liquorama is a good bet.

You'll find lots of small stalls and local sellers around Maun, including near the bus station. It's certainly worth checking out for the odd pile of fruit and vegetables, but also expect for more offbeat foods, like mopane worms in season, and an assorted range of bootleg CDs and secondhand items.

SOUVENIRS, CRAFTS, BOOKS AND CURIOS There's no shortage of places that sell curios in Maun, and virtually every camp in Botswana has a small curio shop. Thus it pays to shop around, particularly for books and crafts. It's also well worth seeking out individual workshops, or places where the work of local craftspeople is available. For several things under one roof, try Motsana 'village' [map 209], where there's a curio shop, Textures, and a gallery of local art and photographs.

African Art & Images [202 E1] Maun Airport; ☎686 3584, 686 0825. At this upmarket gift shop cum gallery inside the airport gates, take your pick from high-quality African art, carvings, baskets, jewellery & some beautiful photographs & prints – with correspondingly high price tags.

Bushman Craft Shop [202 D1] Maun Airport; ☎686 0025, 686 0339; e gentrade@info.bw; ⏱ 08.00–17.00 daily. Just inside the airport gates, this convenient shop sells a very good range of books, postcards, crafts, curios & safari clothes. Barely a minute's walk from the check-in desks, it's perfectly situated to dash out to while you're waiting for a plane.

The Craft Centre [202 C2] Power Station, Mophane Av; ☎686 3391. This small workshop sells local crafts including pottery, textiles, paper products & paintings – much of it handmade on the premises.

Jazella's [202 D2] Natlee Centre, Airport Av; ☎686 1900; ⏱ 07.00–18.00 daily. Jam-packed full of jewellery, bags, wall hangings, books & much, much more, Jazella's is just opposite the airport.

Matlapana Baskets [map 209] Sir Seretse Khama Rd; ☎680 1255; m 7227 1422, 7191 3303; e tkushonya@gmail.com. Award-winning master weaver Thitaku Kushonya sells baskets from her workshop about 8km north of Maun Airport. This showcases not only her work but that of women whom she has empowered by teaching them basket weaving. Look for it on the right-hand side as you head north out of Maun on Sir Seretse Khama Rd, just behind a small general store; if you reach the bridge you have gone too far. Do pay her a visit: her work is excellent &, whether you are looking for a souvenir or to learn a little more about basket weaving, you are unlikely to be disappointed. To have a go at basket weaving yourself & to learn more about the Hambukushu tribe, consider a visit next door to Hambukushu Cultural Village (page 219).

Textures [map 209] Motsana 'village', Shorobe Rd; m 7144 6036. A classy find in a quirky environment, Textures is an Aladdin's cave of curios, jewellery & feminine clothes, well sited next to a popular café.

CAMPING EQUIPMENT Most visitors bring their own camping equipment, or are booked on trips which include it. For those on budget trips, some of the tour operators hire out their kit for the duration of your trip. However, if you need to buy anything, or you need some of your own kit repaired, then there are a few specialist options.

Jacana Enterprises [202 B3] Mophane Av & opposite Parkview Shopping Centre, Boseja; ☎686 1202; e jacana@btcmail.co.bw; www. jacanaent.com; ⏱ 08.00–16.00 Mon–Fri, 09.00–13.00 Sat. An unexpected find in Maun, Jacana has safari clothing, camping equipment, torches, knives, a range of maps, GPS equipment, & lots more. It also has an exhaustive (& somewhat quirky) website!

Kalahari Kanvas [202 C2] Mathiba I Rd; ☎686 0568; e kalkanvas@botsnet.bw; www. kalahari-kanvas.com; ⏱ 09.00–17.00 Mon–Fri, 09.00–noon Sat. From its beginnings in 1986 as a tiny tent-repair company, Kalahari Kanvas has burgeoned into a major manufacturer of tents & equipment for the safari industry, with another office in Kasane. They still offer a tent-repair service & also hire out an amazing range of kit by the day, from a knife, fork & spoon set, to a 2-person, 2.4m x 2.4m dome tent, or a double-canvas bedroll with 75mm-thick mattress, a blanket, 2 pillows & 2 sheets. It's best to book stuff in advance, & deposits are required, proportional to the items hired; credit cards are accepted. Note that all kit must be returned to this office.

PAAM [202 E2] New Mall, Sir Seretse Khama Rd; ☏ 686 0992. Despite the name (the acronym stands for Pan African Ammunition Manufacturers), PAAM specialises in the outdoors generally, with fishing gear, camping kit & safari clothing.

CLOTHES Several of the camping equipment outlets also stock safari gear, and for last-minute safari purchases you could try the Bushman Craft Shop (see opposite), but for basic tops and trousers, you'd probably do better at one of the more general clothing stores: PEP next to Shoprite [203 C7], JB Sports in New Mall [202 E2], Mr Price opposite KFC [202 B7] or Woolworth's in the Ngami Centre [202 F2]. More specialist than any of these, with a good range of safari clothes, sports clothing and boots, is:

West Sports [203 D7] Riley's Garage, Tsheko-Tsheko Rd; ☏ 686 0483

OTHER PRACTICALITIES

For most visitors these days, Maun is above all a place to restock, refuel and get organised.

BANKS AND MONEY The main **banks** – Stanbic [202 D2] (*Natlee Centre, Mathiba I Rd*), First National [202 F2] (*Ngami Centre*), Barclays [203 B7] (*Tsheko-Tsheko Rd*) and Standard Chartered [203 B7] (*Old Mall*) – have ATM machines that accept Visa and, less frequently, Mastercard, so this is usually the easiest, quickest and cheapest way to get pula. It's worth noting that not all Visa cards will work in all ATMs, so if one fails it is worth trying another before contacting your bank. Alternatively, with your passport and a little time spent in queues, you can cash travellers' cheques or obtain a manual cash advance on a credit card at any of these three.

Bureaux de change generally offer a quicker service and longer hours. Most conspicuous are the branches of Sunny's, which charges no commission: one next to Riley's [203 D7] (⊕ *08.00–17.30 Mon–Fri, 08.00–13.30 Sat*) and the other by the First National Bank [202 F2] (*Ngami Centre;* ☏ *686 0919;* ⊕ *08.00–18.00 daily*). Better rates may prevail at Open Door by Riley's Garage [203 D7] (☏ *686 3150;* ⊕ *07.30–16.00 Mon–Fri, 08.00–16.00 Sat, 09.00–16.00 Sun*), but this is against a commission of around 4%, so check both and do your sums first. There is also a small kiosk in the airport building, which although convenient may not offer the best rates.

COMMUNICATIONS

Telephone Local SIM cards can be purchased at various outlets along Tsheko-Tsheko Road, including the Mascom office [203 C7] Old Mall, Orange [203 C7] in the Agora Projects building, Old Mall, and Cell City near Shoprite [203 C7].

Post and courier The post office [203 B8] is on Tsheko-Tsheko Road, south of Barclays Bank.

DHL [202 G1] Chelford Plaza, Sir Seretse Khama Rd; ☏ 686 1207; & [202 D1] Natlee Centre, Mathiba I Rd, opposite the airport; ☏ 686 1207

GARAGES AND VEHICLE SPARES There are several fuel stations in Maun. While in theory they take credit cards, don't rely on this; if the machine isn't working, you'll have to pay cash in pula.

If you're passing through and heading off into the bush then Maun is the best place to make sure your 4x4 is in tip-top condition, with plenty of spares. Places that may be able to help are usually open Monday to Friday and Saturday morning, and include:

Auto World [198 A5] Tsheko-Tsheko Rd; ✆686 3890; m 7157 9222. Spares for most major makes of vehicle.
Delta 4x4 [off 198 A6] ✆686 4572. Just south of Maun Sports Complex on the Ghanzi road, Delta offers vehicle repairs, 4x4 hire & vehicle recovery in the Delta & Kgalagadi.
Kelly Tyres [198 C6] Tawana I Rd. Located between Maun Lodge & the Shell garage.
Lesedi Motors [198 C7] Kwena Rd; ✆686 0884, 686 1694. Specialist in Land Rover parts, servicing & repairs.
Maun Motors Nata Rd; ✆686 0138
Motovac [202 B3] Mophane Av; ✆686 0872. The local branch of the spares & accessories chain.

Ngami Toyota [198 A5] Tsheko-Tsheko Rd; ✆686 0252. Maun's Toyota dealer also has spares & a bodyshop. They will repair all makes of vehicle, not just Toyotas.
Riley's Garage (Shell) [203 D7] Tsheko-Tsheko Rd; ✆686 0203; e parts@rileys.co.bw. In the centre of town, next to the famous old hotel, Riley's has a 24hr fuel station, as well as a workshop, & a shop (Autozone) carrying a range of spares, tyres & batteries.
Trans World Motors [off 198 D7] Francistown Rd; ✆686 0656; m 7211 6010/2; e transworldmotors@gmail.com. About 1km beyond Caltex. Offers mechanical repairs, as well as a 24hr breakdown service.
Tyre World [198 C7] ✆686 0107

Should the worst happen, and you **break down** in the bush without back-up, then help is at hand:

Mechto ✆686 3913; m 7130 3788

You could also try Trans World Motors and Delta 4x4 (above), who both offer a recovery and breakdown services.

HEALTH Maun's modern Letsholathebe II Memorial Hospital [off 198 D5 and map 209] (*Disaneng Rd;* ✆687 9000) is located to the east of the town. If you're coming from Shorobe or one of the lodges to the north, then continue straight over at the roundabout before the bridge rather than heading into town; it's clearly signposted.

There are also a couple of good private clinics and a dentist:

✚**Delta Dental Clinic** [203 A8] Moremi III Rd; ✆686 1023, 686 4224

✚**Prime Health Medical Centre** [203 C6] Old Mall, 458 Tsheko-Tsheko Rd; ✆686 1411, 686 2999; m 7131 4224

Pharmacies Pharmacies are usually open normal shopping hours, but most have an emergency number for calls out of hours.

✚**Okavango Pharmacy** [203 C7] Letsego Bldg, Old Mall, Tsheko-Tsheko Rd; emergency ✆686 0043

✚**Portsway Pharmacy** [203 C6] Old Mall, Tsheko-Tsheko Rd; ✆680 0857
✚**Taurus** [203 C7] Tsheko-Tsheko Rd; ✆686 3340

Opticians It makes sense to bring spare glasses and contact lenses with you, but if you do come unstuck, try:

✚ **Opticals Botswana** [203 C7] Old Mall, Tsheko-
Tsheko Rd; ☎ 686 1742; e sales@opticalsbostwana.
com; www.opticalsbotswana.com

WHAT TO SEE AND DO

Maun is really much more of a place to get organised than a destination in its own right. Those visitors who do stay for more than one night tend to use the town as a launching point for day trips (to book these, see the operators listed on pages 223–7) and aren't generally looking for activities in or around the town. If you do have time to kill, here are a few suggestions; which include the opportunity to try your hand at basket-weaving.

IN MAUN With the demise of Maun Educational Park, there's little in town to delay visitors, bar a couple of low-key cultural attractions, though exploring the river is a pleasant way to spend an afternoon, and horseriding is an added option. If you've time on your hands, you could check out what's on at the large **Maun Sports Complex**, which lies about 2.5km southwest of Riley's Garage on the road towards Ghanzi. It's used for political rallies as well as sports matches, with details published in the local newspaper, *The Ngami Times*.

Nhabe Museum [202 E3] (*Sir Seretse Khama Rd*) More of a gallery than a museum, this small venue has periodically changing exhibits that often showcase the art of local students. A small collection of artefacts includes musical instruments and hunting tools. '*Nhabe*', incidentally, is from the Bushman word for the sound of cattle pulling their feet out of the mud, now more usually rendered as '*ngami*'.

Hambukushu Cultural Village [map 209] (*Sir Seretse Khama Rd;* ☎ *680 1255;* m *7227 1422, 7191 3303;* e *tkushonya@gmail.com; P300/3hrs*) Next door to Matlapana Baskets (page 216) and under the same ownership, this is a great place to spend an afternoon. Thitaku Kushonya will take you on a 3-hour journey around a replica of a traditional Hambukushu village. Among other things you get to try your hand at basket weaving and to take home what you produce; to play traditional Hambukushu games; to learn how food was traditionally sourced and grown; and even to try on some traditional clothing. It is certainly worth ringing ahead or dropping in the day before to pre-book a tour.

Sexaxa Cultural Village [off map 209] (*Shorobe Rd; contact Lesego on* m *7502 5870; www.sexaxa-village.com;* ⊕ *daily; P200 pp*) For a hint of Botswana's traditional way of life, pay a visit to this cultural village, 18km north of Maun on the Shorobe road; it's clearly signposted to the left. The village is designed to give visitors an idea of Bayei culture, urban style – as opposed to the rural culture depicted at Shandereka Cultural Village near Moremi (page 403). If you're just dropping in, don't hold your breath; it's far better to book ahead. Generally visits are around 2½ hours but additional time and even a traditional meal can be negotiated.

Thamalakane River Boat trips along the Thamalakane River are a great way to while away an hour or two, keeping an eye out for birds. Costs vary, but P660 per hour for a four-seater boat is a good indication. Contact Afro Trek (page 227) or perhaps Okavango River Lodge (pages 211–12). If **birding** is the primary appeal, it may be worth contacting the local branch of BirdLife Botswana (☎ *686 5618;* m *7465*

4464; e *birdlifemaun@botsnet.bw; www.birdlifebotswana.org.bw*) to see if one of their members would be prepared to guide you along the river for an hour or two.

Horseriding Riding for all levels can be organised through Jen Weimann at African Animal Adventure Safaris (page 227). Typically rides are along (and sometimes in!) the Thamalakane and Boro rivers. Hard hats are available. All abilities of rider are also welcome by Ride Botswana (page 227) at Royal Tree Lodge, where you could find yourself riding among zebra, giraffe and other wildlife.

FURTHER AFIELD

Scenic flights Short flights over the Delta in light aircraft or helicopters are offered by several companies (page 199). Most people tend to book for 45 minutes then regret it; an hour is a better bet. Rates are usually quoted per person, and vary depending on the company, fuel costs and the number of people in the aircraft. As an indication, you can expect to pay from around P5,795 per hour (US$580) for a five-seater. Helicopter trips are more expensive at around US$220 per person for 45 minutes, for up to three people, with each person having a window seat and their own headset. Note that all flights are subject to P100 airport tax per passenger, which is not always included in the rates.

Mokoro trips Perennially popular are mokoro trips into the Delta, lasting from one to three days. Typically you'll leave Maun by motorboat between 07.30 and 08.30, depending on where you are staying, reaching the launch site 15km upstream in about 45 minutes, and returning in the evening by about 17.00. When the river was dry, and vehicle transfers took around 2 hours each way, a single-day trip hardly seemed worth the effort, but a shorter boat transfer changes the dynamics considerably.

Almost all these trips are run by the same community trust, the OKMCT (see box, see opposite), but can be booked only through an affiliated tour operator; you cannot book direct or drive yourself in. However, although the polers, mekoros and areas being offered by the various competing companies in Maun are all exactly the same, prices vary according to the individual company. As an indication, Audi Camp charges P930 (US$93) per person for a day trip, in which you will need to provide everything yourself, with a single supplement of P100 (US$10) per day. For an overnight trip, with two days on the water, expect to pay around P1,480 (US$148) if you're prepared to take all your own food and equipment, or P2,720 (US$272) per person for a catered trip. Extending this to two nights/three days will cost around P1,950/3,630 (US$195/363). Prices for self-catered trips from Okavango River Lodge and The Old Bridge Tours and Safaris are slightly lower. A trip very like this, from Island Safari Lodge, was my first view of the Okavango and, while it has its limitations, I'd still regard it as remarkably good value.

Moremi Game Reserve Several tour operators offer trips into Moremi, costing from around US$230 per person for a day trip (minimum 2 people), to US$750 per person for a three-night all-inclusive trip for four people travelling together. Typically such trips include a guide, park fees, camping equipment, meals and transfers, but most exclude drinks.

Lake Ngami About 90km west of Maun, Lake Ngami is very accessible as a half- or full-day trip from Maun if you have your own transport – but do ascertain first whether or not there's water in the lake. For details, see pages 424–5.

If you're heading out on a mokoro trip from Maun, the chances are that you'll be going into the NG32 concession managed by OKMCT (✆ 686 4809, 686 5210; m 7534 1813; e info@okmct.org.bw; www.okmct.org.bw). This community trust was set up to ensure that, in line with Botswana government policy, income generated by tourism directly benefits the community.

An agreement has been made with the communities in this concession to co-ordinate mokoro trips on the Boro and Santantadibe rivers, providing valuable income for those who work as polers and guides. Guide polers and unqualified polers are paid according to an agreed scale, with the balance of fees payable made up of the concession entrance fee. The polers provide their own mekoros and food. Visitors (or tour operators) usually bring all their own food and camping kit.

Government rules limit the numbers of visitors into the concession, and hence the impact of tourism. No more than 30 mekoro are allowed on each river system at any one time. Trips start at, and return to, one of five launch sites on the Santantadibe and Boro rivers: Boro (the most regularly visited), Ditshiping, Xharaxao, Xuoxao and Daunara. Each fibreglass mokoro takes two people, with a qualified guide poler accompanying every group of up to eight people. The rest of the mekoro are usually poled by locals from the various villages who don't have this qualification. Polers work on a rota basis to ensure that income derived from their work is fairly distributed throughout the community. Trips often include short walks on the islands. Indeed, when I last took a trip here, the poler appeared to have arranged our route to visit friends on various islands.

Essentially, OKMCT is responsible for the mokoro trails in the concession itself, but bookings and transfers to and from Maun are handled by individual tour operators, among them Afro Trek, Audi Camp, The Old Bridge Tours and Safaris and Okavango River Lodge. Operators book slots for trips on a first-come, first-served basis; they also pay the freelance polers and guides from the community directly. OKMCT rates are fixed, but transfer rates charged by tour operators will reflect their individual styles and costs.

Okavango Guiding School (OGS) (✆ 680 0115; e ogs@wildguides.org; www. guidetrainingcourses.com) Visitors looking for a wildlife experience with a difference and to gain a recognised qualification in guiding can take part in one of the three main courses offered by the OGS, which vary in length from one to four weeks. Set up in 2003 to train guides in wildlife and ecology, it is based at Kwapa Camp in the Okavango Delta, with students staying in en-suite 3m x 3m tents with bush toilets and bucket showers.

Courses include two- or four-week options on the Nature Guide Course and the Trails Guide Course, with prices from US$3,253 for 14 nights. Skills include poling a mokoro, tracking wildlife, rifle handling and safely approaching big game on foot. All courses are taught by licensed guide trainers.

A shorter one-week Bush Skills Course, which is tailored to international travellers, could easily be incorporated into a self-drive or lodge experience. Although you do not gain a qualification, you are likely to take away many skills and a deeper understanding of the bush, as this course includes many of the practical and theoretical highlights from the lengthier Nature Guide and Trails Guide courses. Participants also help to benefit one aspiring local guide, who receives sponsorship from the school and joins students for the duration of the course.

Maun WHAT TO SEE AND DO

8

Although the majority of those passing through Maun are pre-booked on an all-inclusive trip, this is also the best place for independent travellers and those without plans to get organised. If it all seems rather overwhelming, there are just a few points to remember.

ORGANISING A TRIP INTO THE NATIONAL PARKS If you are organising your own trip, note that you can no longer go into the national parks without proof of a confirmed reservation for your campsites or other accommodation (unless you plan just a day trip). Provided that you have confirmation, it is possible to pay entrance fees on the gate but they can also be paid in advance at one of the Department of Wildlife and National Parks (DWNP) offices (see below).

For details of the system, and of the companies who operate the individual campsites, see pages 131–3.

National parks campsite operators Most of the campsite operators have offices in Maun, and unless you have everything in writing beforehand, you may need to visit more than one of them to confirm your bookings, so do allow plenty of time. That said, both SKL and the Xomae Group are in theory prepared to do the legwork for you – though it's wise not to bank on it.

Department of Wildlife & National Parks (DWNP) [203 E5] Audi Dr; ✆686 1265; e dwnp@gov.bw; ⏰ 07.30–16.30 Mon–Sat, 07.30–noon Sun

Kwalate Safaris [202 F2] Above FNB, New Mall, Sir Seretse Khama Rd; ✆686 1448; e kwalatesafari@gmail.com; www.kwalatesafaris.com; ⏰ 08.00–16.30 Mon–Fri, 08.00–14.00 Sat

SKL [203 E5] Winela Complex, 823 Sir Seretse Khama Rd; ✆686 5365/6; e reservations@sklcamps.co.bw, sklcamps@btcmail.co.bw; www.sklcamps.com; ⏰ 08.00–17.00 Mon–Fri, 08.00–13.00 Sat

Xomae Group [202 E2] New Mall, Sir Seretse Khama Rd; ✆686 2221; m 7386 2221; e xomaesites@bctmail.co.bw; www.xomaesites.com; ⏰ 07.30–17.00 Mon–Fri, 08.00–13.00 Sat

If you'd rather have independent help, then contact one of the travel agents, who can act as a sort of one-stop shop, arranging anything from a scenic flight to setting up your whole trip, including national parks, transport and accommodation. Finally, there are the tour operators and safari companies, whose role is to organise your safari, usually using their own suppliers – which may include their own lodges and aircraft.

TRAVEL AGENTS Maun may seem to the uninitiated to be full of travel agents, but many of the companies you see are in fact tour operators (see opposite) who own and run camps and safari companies. However, if you look hard there is a handful of normal travel agents who (generally) know the local safari industry well, and can help you choose a trip. They are especially useful if you arrive in Maun without any arrangements and want to book a budget trip immediately. In such cases, booking through one of these agents will cost you exactly the same as booking directly with the camp or safari company.

The caveats to this are, firstly, that none is well prepared for booking a range of the top-end lodges at short notice; there's very little demand for this. Secondly, some will have their own favourite camps or operators – so do ask them to be exhaustive about researching the options for you before you make a decision. Also ask them to make very clear if anyone associated with them has any links with the camps or trips that they're suggesting to you. (This shouldn't necessarily put you off booking – but you ought to know!)

Liquid Giraffe [map 209] Nunga Conservation, Sir Seretse Khama Rd; ☏ 680 1054; m 7175 6413; e info@liquidgiraffe.com; www.liquidgiraffe.com
Safari Essence ☏ 686 1344; m 7230 9099; e passion@safari-essence.com; www.safari-essence.com. Sister company to Endeavour Safaris.
Sense of Africa [202 C3] Eagle Hse, Mophane Av; ☏ 686 0822/3; e info@senseofafrica-botswana.com; www.senseofafrica.com. This very good, independent travel agent, previously called Travel Wild, is a friendly, helpful & efficient one-stop

shop for what to do in & around Maun, short trips into the Delta, & longer holidays in Botswana. They also have offices in Namibia, Kenya, Uganda & Tanzania.
Tete Travel & Tours [202 E2] New Mall, Sir Seretse Khama Rd; ☏ 686 3239; m 7147 1908; e tetetravel@bbcmail.co.bw
Time Travel [202 D2] off Mathiba I Rd; ☏ 686 1007, 686 1466; e info@timetravelafrica.com; www.timetravelafrica.com

TOUR OPERATORS AND SAFARI COMPANIES

Looking at the length of this list – which is by no means comprehensive – you'll realise that Maun is the safari capital of Botswana. Listed below alphabetically, followed by specialist mobile, horseriding and camping/canoeing operators, these safari companies range from large operators with many camps through to tiny outfits which are little more than a guide and a vehicle. Since prices change regularly, these have not been included – although for an indication of the costs of, say, a mobile safari, see page 142.

While many of the larger operators have staff in Maun as well as booking offices overseas, the smaller operations may take days, or even weeks, to answer communications – sometimes because the whole team is out of the office and on safari.

Larger safari groups
For the sake of completeness, also included here are a few companies that operate from towns other than Maun.

&Beyond [202 C2] off Mathiba I Rd; ☏ 686 1979, reservations ☏ +27 11 809 4300; e contactus@andbeyond.com; www.andbeyond.com. Formerly Conservation Corporation Africa, &Beyond is a leading company committed to high quality, including good food & impressive standards of guiding, with a tracker & guide on every vehicle. Of 29 lodges throughout East & southern Africa, they have 4 in Botswana's Okavango Delta: Nxabega, Sandibe, Xudum & Xaranna. They also offer 2 semi-permanent tented camps – Savute Under Canvas & Chobe Under Canvas – & a 10-day 'expedition', taking in the Okavango, Moremi, Chobe & Victoria Falls.
African Bush Camps [map 209] Sir Seretse Khama Rd; ☏ +27 212 016 787, emergency ☏ +263 772 126986; e info@africanbushcamps.com; www.africanbushcamps.com. Despite ABC operating a handful of camps throughout northern Botswana: Linyanti Bush Camp, Linyanti Ebony

& Footsteps across the Linyanti, as well as Khwai Tented Camp and Khwai Leadwood, there is no longer an office in town (the nearest is in Victoria Falls). ABC also offers scheduled safaris to areas that include Nxai Pan National Park, combining tented & lodge-based accommodation.
Belmond [202 C3] Mophane Av; ☏ 686 0302, reservations ☏ +27 21 483 1600; e safaris@belmond.com; www.belmond.com. Part of the global group that runs hotels & lodges around the world, including the famous Venice–Simplon Orient Express train, Belmond have 3 upmarket lodges in Botswana: Savute Elephant Camp, Khwai River Lodge & Eagle Island Camp. Specifications in each are comparable to top hotels, very much belying their 'tent' status.
Desert & Delta Safaris [202 E2] Sir Seretse Khama Rd; ☏ 686 1559, 686 1243, reservations ☏ +27 11 394 3873; e info@desertdelta.com; www.desertdelta.com. This established operator, which recommends that their lodges be booked through a tour operator, runs Chobe Game Lodge, Chobe Savanna Lodge, Savute Safari Lodge, Camp Moremi, Camp Okavango, Xugana

Island Lodge, Camp Xakanaxa & Leroo La Tau. A sister company, Safari Air, operates a charter air service, enabling integrated access to each lodge. Desert & Delta also runs 11-day guided mobile safaris around Botswana, in co-operation with the affiliated Chobe Explorations. With just 2–6 participants, each trip operates between Victoria Falls or Livingstone & Maun, taking in the Chobe River, Savute, Moremi, the Okavango Delta & Makgadikgadi Pans National Park.

Footsteps In Africa +27 61 419 5064; m +27 82 355 6910; e info@footsteps-in-africa.com; www.footsteps-in-africa.com. This Maun-based company is responsible for the marketing & reservations for a selection of independent lodges across Botswana including, among others, Deception Valley Lodge & the Lodges of Botswana portfolios. They are also closely linked to Delta Air (page 199).

Great Plains Conservation [202 C3] Mophane Av; +27 87 354 6591, emergency +27 79 284 5945; e res.manager@greatplainsconservation.com, www.greatplainsconservation.com. Great Plains operates Selinda Camp, Zarafa Camp, Zarafa Dhow Safari, Selinda Explorers Camp, the Selinda Adventure Trail & Duba Plains Camp. The company is very focused on raising the bar in standards of environmental & social responsibility &, while by no means the only one with this remit, is certainly one of the most proactive in marketing its part in 'conservation tourism'.

Ker & Downey Botswana [202 E2] cnr Airport Av & Sir Seretse Khama Rd; 686 1282, 686 1418; m 7577 5300; e info@kerdowney.bw; www.kerdowneybotswana.com. Ker & Downey are 2 of the oldest names in the Delta. Back in 1945, Donald Ker & Syd Downey founded a hunting safari company in Kenya, to be joined in the mid 1950s by Harry Selby – who started their Botswana operations in 1962. Around 1979, they bought Khwai River Lodge as a photographic camp, & in 1985 the photographic company Ker, Downey & Selby was split off from the hunting company, Safari South. Today it's known simply as Ker & Downey Botswana, & runs Okuti, Kanana, Shinde, Shinde Enclave, Footsteps Camp & its most recent addition, Dinaka. Each camp provides a different experience, with varying costs.

Kwando Safaris [202 E2] Airport Rd; 686 1449; e info@kwando.co.bw; www.kwando.co.bw. Based in Maun, Kwando is a small, independent operator running 1st-class camps in Botswana. Lagoon & Lebala are primarily dry-land camps beside the Kwando River in NG14, while Kwara & Little Kwara have a full range of dry & wet activities, on the north side of the Delta. Further south are Nxai Pan Lodge within the national park of the same name, & Tau Pan Lodge in the Central Kalahari Game Reserve. All are different, but all operate game drives with both a tracker & a guide – a real advantage when it comes to tracking predators. Their focus is on enthusiastic wildlife spotting rather than excessive frills in camp, although their camps are of a high standard.

Lodges of Botswana [202 C2] 686 1154; e info@lodgesofbotswana.com, info@footsteps-in-africa.com; www.lodgesofbotswana.com. This Maun-based company was established by the late Peter Sandenbergh, who was one of the first to see the area's potential for backpacking tourism as well as the more usual upmarket variety. Today the company owns & runs 3 camps in NG27B: Delta Camp, Oddballs' & Oddballs' Enclave. They have particularly close links with both Delta Air & the Bushman Craft Shop.

Natural Selection +27 21 001 1574; e enquiry@naturalselection.travel; www.naturalselection.travel. Founded in 2016 by a group of safari operators with considerable combined experience, Natural Selection has taken on 3 camps in the Makgadikgadi (Jack's, San Camp & Camp Kalahari), along with Meno a Kwena & 3 others in the Khwai area (Hyena Pan, Sky Beds & Sable Alley), with the aim of taking over the sales & marketing while allowing these camps to keep their individuality.

Sanctuary Retreats [202 E3] Motshaba St; reservations +27 11 438 4650; e reservations.safrica@sanctuaryretreats.com; www.sanctuaryretreats.com. Part of the Abercrombie & Kent group, Sanctuary Retreats operates 4 lodges in Botswana: Chobe Chilwero, Chief's Camp, Stanley's Camp & Baines' Camp, as well as Sussi & Chuma in Livingstone.

Uncharted Africa +27 11 447 4407; e res1@unchartedafrica.com; www.unchartedafrica.com. Owners of Jack's Camp, San Camp & Camp Kalahari (all of which should be booked through Natural Selection), as well as Planet Baobab. Also operate mobile safaris throughout northern Botswana.

Under One Botswana Sky [202 C2] Mathiba I Rd; 686 0023, 625 0336; e reservations@gunns-camp.com; www.underonebotswanasky.com. From its base, near the airport, this is the operation behind: Rra Dinare, Mma Dinare, Pom Pom, Gunn's & Moremi Crossing in the Delta; Chobe Safari Lodge & Chobe Bush Lodge in Kasane as well as Nata Lodge. Safari itineraries can be tailormade to include some or all of the properties.

Wilderness Safaris [202 C2] Mathiba I Rd; 686 0086, reservations +27 11 257 500; e enquiry@wilderness.co.za; www.wilderness-safaris.com. Started by safari guides Colin Bell, Chris MacIntyre (not this book's author!) & Russel Friedman in Botswana in 1983, this has since grown into one of the subcontinent's leading safari operators, working throughout southern Africa. From their office in Maun, they also market Botswana's largest selection of safari camps. These are mostly in private reserves & include DumaTau, King's Pool, & Savuti Camp in NG15; Vumbura Plains & Little Vumbura in NG22; Kwetsani, Jacana, Jao, Tubu Tree, Little Tubu & Pelo in NG25; Chitabe & Chitabe Lediba in NG31; Mombo, Little Mombo & Xigera in the Moremi Game Reserve; & Kalahari Plains in the CKGR. Marketed as 'adventures', 'classic', or 'premier', their style, standard & prices vary, yet Wilderness effectively sets the baseline for high-quality camps in Botswana, by which other operators tend to be measured. Wilderness advises travellers to book their camps through a tour operator.

Wilderness also owns the flight company, Wilderness Air, & offers non-participatory mobile safaris, which aim to recreate the atmosphere of an unhurried exploratory journey, operating primarily in private concession areas. Departures are guaranteed with a min of 2 guests (max 8).

Mobile safari specialists
See also *Camping, boating, canoeing & budget safaris*, pages 226–7.

Barclay Stenner Safaris m 7126 9874, 7227 8404; e john@barclaystenner.com; www.barclaystenner.com. John Barclay & James Stenner have been running tailor-made mobile safaris all over Botswana for a number of years & they accompany every trip. Their fun & informative safaris usually head into the Okavango Delta, Chobe, Makgadikgadi Pans & Central Kalahari, & also visit the Ju/'hoansi Bushmen of the Kalahari. Options range from basic mobile camping to

luxurious offerings with Persian carpets, Egyptian cotton sheets & fine cuisine.

Bush Ways Safaris 686 3685; e safari-res@bushways.com; www.bushways.com. Established in 1996, Bush Ways operates scheduled mobile safaris lasting 7–18 days as well as tailor-made tours. Itineraries cover Chobe, Moremi, Nxai, Makgadikgadi & the CKGR, as well as Victoria Falls, the Caprivi Strip & some parts of Zambia. Travellers can opt for semi-participation or fully serviced camping trips, which are run even with just 1 participant, or lodge-based safaris, with no hidden costs or 'kitty' requirements. French & German translators are provided on selected safaris. Bush Ways also owns Sango Safari Camp & Khwai Guest House in Moremi, & Chobe Elephant Camp.

Capture Africa 686 1200; e Hildrene@captureafrica.net; www.captureafrica.com. Brian & Hildrene Gibson founded their mobile-safari operation in 1997. Theirs is a flexible approach, with different styles of tents to cater for a variety of travellers, including children of all ages. They specialise in private tailor-made luxury safaris with specialist guides.

Drumbeat Safaris 686 3096; m 7141 9684; e drumbeat@drumbeatsafaris.com, drumbeatsafarismaun@gmail.com; www.drumbeatsafaris.com. Established in 1996, Drumbeat is still run by its Dutch co-founder Annelies Zonjee, who organises fully inclusive comfortable & luxury mobile safaris throughout northern Botswana, as well as lodge-based safaris & helicopter trips. Mobile safaris are always private (min 2 people) so you won't be sharing – a real plus for families. Guests stay in walk-in tents, usually in private campsites within the parks, & travel in game vehicles, with the equipment & staff either trailed behind or transported separately.

Embrace Safaris m 7427 6153; e reservations@embracesafaris.com; www.embracesafaris.com. Owned & run by Alistair Wilmot, son of well-known safari guide Lloyd Wilmot, this was formerly Wilmot Safaris. Private 4–7-night mobile trips feature comfortable, en-suite tents with dbl or twin beds, bucket showers & bush toilets. Trips normally depart from Maun & include Moremi, Khwai & Savuti as well as Okavango Delta. All safaris are tailormade & privately guided safaris can be organised. See ad, page 196.

Endeavour Safaris 686 0887; e info@endeavour-safaris.com; www.endeavour-safaris.

com. Based on the premise that everyone should have the chance to visit & experience Botswana's wilderness, Mike & Silvia Hill's safari operation caters for a range of budgets, from privately guided mobile safaris to luxury fly-in lodge options & boat safaris in the Delta. Where Endeavour really scores, however, is in its safaris for families (with no age restrictions); & for disabled & senior travellers, including guests with mobility issues, or hearing & visual impairments (just be sure to let them know your needs & the extent of your disability). The company's modified Land Cruiser & mobile camp are maintained & operated by specially trained staff.

Harkness Safaris m 7289 3736/26; e enquiries@harkness-safaris.com; www. harkness-safaris.com. Andrew Harkness's safari operation caters for up to 12 guests in dome or walk-in tents, with en-suite long-drop loos & bucket showers. Trips are tailormade but usually start in Maun & finish in Kasane or Victoria Falls, taking in Moremi, Khwai, & the Savuti & Chobe River areas of Chobe National Park. The CKGR can be included in any itinerary.

Karibu Safari ✆686 1225, reservations +27 11 954 3941; m 7696 8395; e karibubots@info.bw; www.karibu.co.za. Karibu offers 'comfort' mobile safaris taking 4–17 days, with set departures. Some include Namibia & Botswana; others incorporate lodge accommodation. Tailor-made itineraries are possible in the low season.

Letaka Safaris ✆680 0363; e info@ letakasafaris.com; www.letakasafaris.com. Brothers Brent & Grant Reed, of the 6 part *Safari Brothers* television series, set up Letaka in 2000, focusing on set-departure trips in Moremi & Chobe, as well as to Makgadikgadi & Nxai pans. These, including specialist birding & photography trips, are all led by a team of high-quality guides. You'll stay in walk-in tents with gauze windows, solar-powered lights & an en-suite long-drop loo & bucket shower – with hot water brought to your tent on request.

Masson Safaris ✆686 2442; e massonsafaris@ gmail.com; www.massonsafaris.net. This small family operation runs mobile photographic safaris, both scheduled & tailormade, concentrating on game & birdlife, with a general appreciation of Botswana's more remote areas (they're especially keen on the great salt pans, Tsodilo & the Central Kalahari). Ewan Masson, who has been guiding

in Botswana for 30 years, leads most trips. Expect walk-in dome tents, complete with linen, washstand, reading light & a private chemical flush loo. Game drives are taken in extended, open safari vehicles (max 8 guests).

Penduka Safaris ✆+264 61 239643; m 7130 0215; e info@pendukasafaris.com; www. pendukasafaris.com. Started in 1963 by Izak Barnard, Penduka is one of the oldest mobile operators in southern Africa. Today it's run by Izak's son Willem & his wife Sally, who offer both scheduled & tailor-made safaris throughout Botswana, Zambia & Namibia. All are fully inclusive & fully serviced, using spacious tents with en-suite bush bathrooms, & custom-built vehicles to maximise game viewing & to suit the tough road conditions.

Roger Dugmore Safaris ✆686 2427; e rdsafaris@ngami.net; www. rogerdugmoresafaris.com. Owned & run by Roger Dugmore, this small company runs private mobile tented safaris & specialised photographic expeditions around Botswana's national parks & wilder areas of the desert & Okavango Delta, including quadbike expeditions to Makgadikgadi Pans. Safaris are guided by Roger, who likes to take time for guests to get to know each area.

Safari & Guide Services (SGS) ✆680 1444; e reservations@sgsafrica.com; www.sgsafrica. com. Established in 1986, & now based in Maun, SGS Africa organises customised mobile safaris of different styles throughout northern Botswana, as well as a variety of activities & lodge-based itineraries.

Wilderness Dawning Safaris m 7230 8855/85; e reservations@wildernessdawning.com; www. wildernessdawning.com. This reliable small operator offers scheduled camping safaris of 10, 11 & 14 days with experienced Batswana guides. Trips, for 4–10 guests, are non-participation & are spent entirely in the national parks with the exception of the Victoria Falls, & (for 1 trip) a couple of nights on the //Kabbo houseboat (pages 414–5) on the Okavango at Shakawe. The houseboat can also be booked independently of a safari tour.

Camping, boating, canoeing and budget safaris

African Wildlife Safaris Shorobe Rd; ✆686 2353, 680 0587; m 7163 7250, 7182 5999; e info@african-wildlife-safaris.com; www.african-wildlife-safaris.com. Previously called Naga Safaris, owned & run by local Batswana, this friendly outfit was established in 2001. It offers mobile camping safaris either with their own guides & cooks or fully self-catered into various Botswana parks as well as the Victoria Falls. Camping equipment is available for hire.

Afro Trek ✎686 0177/ 686 2574; e sedia@info.bw; www.afrotrek.net. Based at the Sedia Hotel (page 208), Afro Trek offers 1–3-day mokoro trips, 4x4 game safaris & short trips in & around Maun. There are also 14-day mobile safaris, to include Victoria Falls, with set-date departures (max 9 people).

Audi Camp Safaris ✎686 0599; e info@ okavangocamp.com; www.okavangocamp.com. The safari operation based out of Audi Camp (page 211) organises budget trips into Moremi & the Delta, from mobile camping safaris to drive-in mokoro trips. They also venture to Nxai Pan & the Central Kalahari. Typically, trips require 2 people min & include meals, park fees, vehicle, guide & camping equipment, with travellers expected to bring their own drinks & sleeping bags, & muck in with all camp chores. Your own luggage can be stored at base.

Khwai Development Trust [map 317] Apollo Hse, off Mathiba I Rd; ✎686 2365; e khwai@ btcmail.co.bw; www.khwaitrust.co.bw; ⊕ 07.30–16.30 Mon–Fri, 08.00–12.30 Sat. This is where you book the campsites in NG19 that are run by the trust & can organise an escort guide.

Old Bridge Tours & Safaris ✎686 2406; e info@africansafarisbotswana.com; www. africansafarisbotswana.com. Based out of Maun Rest Camp (page 211) & The Old Bridge Backpackers (page 212), they offer day trips to Moremi & Chief's Island, self- or fully catered mokoro safaris up to 4 days, & set-departure mobile safaris, at varying levels of comfort, up to 7 nights. Tailor-made safaris can also be arranged. As well as Moremi & Chobe, they cover the Central Kalahari, Nxai Pan, Makgadikgadi, Tsodilo Hills & even Drotsky's Caves.

Okavango Still ✎686 5547; e info@ okavangostill.com; www.okavangostill.com. Specialist boating safari operators, Okavango Still organises camping trips across the Delta, moving between island campsites on motorboats. Most trips start from Maun & range from 2 nights to their longest – an 8-night 'trans-Okavango' trip which involves an initial flight to Seronga, on the Panhandle, returning right through the Delta.

Horseriding specialists

African Animal Adventure Safaris m 7336 6461; e AAASafaris@gmail.com, jen@ africananimaladventures.com; www. africananimaladventures.com. In addition to local rides, Jen Weimann offers overnight horseriding trips in the Ngamiland region, perhaps along the Boro River or on the edge of the Delta, as well as further afield to the Makgadikgadi Pans.

African Horseback Safaris ✎686 1523; e reservations@africanhorseback.com; www. africanhorseback.com. Specialist horseriding safaris based out of Macatoo Camp on the western side of the Delta, in NG26. See pages 373–4.

Okavango Horse Safaris ✎686 1671; e safaris@okavangohorse.com; www. okavangohorse.com. See page 388.

RAW Botswana See *Motswiri*, page 304.

Ride Botswana m 7248 4354, 7167 1608, 7679 9883; e info@ridebotswana.com; www. ridebotswana.com. As well as riding for all levels at their Maun base at Royal Tree Lodge, Ride Botswana offers horseriding safaris for experienced riders in the Makgadikgadi Pans & Okavango Delta.

Rides on the Wild Side m 7178 4973; e rides@ ridesonthewildside.com; www.ridesonthewildside. com. Dany Hancock has brought together her experience of mobile & riding safaris to market riding holidays throughout the world. Botswana options include the Okavango Delta (for experienced riders) & – for beginners or the less experienced – the Makgadikgadi Pans, with plenty of opportunity to customise a trip.

THE ROAD NORTH OF MAUN: TO MOREMI AND CHOBE [map 310–11]

FROM MAUN TO MOREMI GAME RESERVE Leave Maun heading northeast, passing the airport turn-off on your left. After about 10km you'll reach a roundabout with a right turn to the hospital, and a left to Shorobe. Take this left turn, passing lodges that include Crocodile Camp and Okavango River Lodge. It's a good tar road, but beware of travelling too fast as you'll find domestic animals on many stretches.

Just under 40km out of Maun you'll pass through the sizeable village of **Shorobe**. The village is 53km south of Moremi Game Reserve's South Gate, and marks the northern limit of the tar road between Maun and Moremi or Kasane. Drive slowly through here as you can usually expect plenty of goats and people wandering on the road. Dotted through the village are a few small shops which sell soft drinks and very basic supplies. Otherwise, the one place that may be worth checking out is Shorobe Baskets, housed in a substantial building at the northern edge of the village.

From Shorobe, a wide gravel road leads after about 19km to the veterinary control fence, or the 'buffalo fence' as most people know it. While this stretch of the road has been regraded, it remains very slow going, so it's important to drive with care.

Just 2km after the vet fence, a left-hand turning is signposted to Moremi Game Reserve, bringing you after a further 32km to the reserve's South Gate. For comments on this road, see page 333.

WHERE TO STAY Until recently, the only place to stay that's actually on the road to South Gate was Kaziikini Campsite, although there's a national park campsite at South Gate itself. Now, however, a couple of camps around Shorobe make it possible to break the journey, whether overnight or just for a meal.

Mochaba Crossing [map 311] (7 chalets, 10 tents, camping) ✆ 683 0304/5, 684 0490; e reservations@mochabacrossing.com; www. mochabacrossing.com; ✪ MOCHCR 19°46.883'S, 23°38.550'E. Some 30km north of Maun, & 3km south of Shorobe Village, Mochaba opened in late 2015, & makes a useful stopover – for a drink, a meal or overnight. The barn-like restaurant (◷ 07.30–18.00; $–$$) serves à la carte meals from b/fast & burgers to sandwiches & steaks, & a 3-course set dinner (P195). Facing across the bush towards the Thamalakane River, neat ochre-painted chalets under thatch are set in well-maintained lawns. They're nicely finished, with twin or dbl beds (or 4 beds), a tiled shower & toilet, a fridge, kettle & AC, but more than a little pricey. Spotless if cramped en-suite tents line the edge of the dusty campsite, while smaller tents – still with fans & electric lights – share the open site & (clean) ablutions with other campers.

A tree-shaded pool, & Wi-Fi throughout, make it good value for campers. $$$–$$$$. Camping P150 pp.

Duncan's Camp [map 311] (8 dome tents, camping) ✆ +27 11 954 5363; e savannahrain@ info.bw; www.duncanscamp.com. Down a sandy 5km track to the west of the road, Duncan's is signposted nearly 7km south of the Mowana Gate. Bring your own camping gear, or use their dome tents, with both self-catering & catered options available with advance notice. All meals must be pre-booked, as must activities, which include game drives, guided walks & mokoro trips. Tent P475 pp, camping P170 pp.

Δ Kaziikini Campsite [map 311] (4 rondavels, camping) NG34 Reserve; ✪ KAZIIK19°35.394'S, 23°48.144'E. About 28km from South Gate, the community-run Kaziikini & adjacent Shandereka Cultural Village are set just off the road. For details, see page 403.

CONTINUING TO CHOBE If you're heading straight to Chobe, follow the directions on page 227 for Moremi, but after the buffalo fence continue straight ahead instead of turning left for South Gate. This leads, after about 24km, to the village of **Sankuyo** [map 311]. There's little to delay the passing motorist here, beyond a shop, a couple of bars and a school, but the village is the base for the Sankuyo Tshwaragano Management Trust, which operates in the small NG33 concession. As well as Kaziikini Campsite and Shandereka Cultural Village (see above), the trust owns Santawani Lodge (page 404).

Continuing north from Sankuyo, you'll reach a slightly obscure left turn after 13km. Ignore this and after a total of 30km, you'll come to Mababe Village. From the village, where the road bears northwest, continue for another 3km to a junction.

Turning right here will lead after a final 7km to Chobe's Mababe Gate (⊕ MABGAT 19°06.182'S, 23°59.119'E).

Had you taken the obscure left turning after Sankuyo (at ⊕ MORCUT 19°29.050'S, 23°55.111'E), you would be driving due west along the Moremi cutline before it joins up with the road between Moremi's South and North gates. Veronica Roodt says that this is a legitimate way to access North Gate, but it is not a route that we have driven, so we would welcome any feedback from readers.

Where to stay A number of lodges lie close to the road leading north to Chobe: two in the drier NG43, which lies to the east of Sankuyo; the second in the neighbouring NG41, which shares its northern and western boundaries with Chobe National Park. For details of both the lodges and the reserves, see pages 404–5.

Mankwe Bush Lodge [map 311] (8 tents, camping) NG43 Reserve. On the edge of the concession, Mankwe is to the west of the road, about 7km north of Sankuyo.

Mogotlho Safari Lodge [map 311] (13 tents) NG41 Reserve. Set on the Khwai River near Mababe Village, Mogotlho is a further 20km north of Mankwe. ★★★

Tuskers [map 311] (6 tents) NG43 Reserve. East of the road beyond the Mowana Gate. ★★–★★★

Maun   THE ROAD NORTH OF MAUN: TO MOREMI AND CHOBE

8

229

KASANE & THE NORTHEAST

NOTE
For accommodation
listings, see pages 251–2

Livingstone

Victoria Falls
Victoria Falls

ZAMBIA

ZIMBABWE

Zambezi

Zambezi NP

Kazuma Pan NP

Kazungula
Bridge under
construction

Kazungula

Lesoma
Valley

Senyati
Safari Camp

Chobe Bush
Camp

Elephant
Valley Lodge

Kasane Forest
Reserve

Camp Kazuma,
Touch of Africa Safari Lodge,
Pandamatenga,
Elephant Sands, Nata

Impalila
Island

Chobe

Kasane

Sedudu
Gate

Sedudu
Island

Chobe
Game Lodge

Puku Flats

Nantanga

Ngwezumba
Pans area

BOTSWANA

Chobe National Park

Zambezi

Ihaha
Campsite

Chobe

Ngoma Gate

Ngoma

Ngoma Bridge
(Customs &
Immigration)

NAMIBIA
(Caprivi Strip)

Baobab
Ngoma
Muchenje
Chobe Elephant
Muchenje Campsite

Chobe

Kachikau

Chobe Forest
Reserve

Savuti

Savuti

Katima Mulilo

N
Bradt

25km
15 miles
0

9

Kasane and the Northeast

KASANE

The administrative centre of Chobe District, Kasane is on the surface just a small town in the northeast corner of Botswana. It lies on the southern bank of the Chobe River, a few kilometres from its confluence with the Zambezi – where the borders of Zambia, Zimbabwe, Namibia and Botswana meet at a point. Thus, while the town is of limited interest in itself, it is an important gateway: to the Chobe National Park; to Victoria Falls in Zimbabwe and Livingstone in Zambia; to the road across Namibia's Caprivi Strip; and to the small charter flights which ferry visitors between the various lodges in northern Botswana.

Construction of a new bridge over the Zambezi River at this point is bringing change to the area, with the neighbouring town of Kazungula gaining something of the air of a border settlement. Along with shopping developments and fuel stations, several small guesthouses are springing up to service the increasing and anticipated level of passing trade. There is even a set of traffic lights (locally known as a robot) – albeit designed to control access to the new fire station.

If you're just passing through the area, it's quite likely that you'll come via Kasane, if only on a transfer bus. And if you've organised your own travelling then you're likely to want to stop here, to refuel and refresh before continuing. But for many people, Kasane is a relaxing place to stay for a couple of days and to take advantage of its proximity to Chobe National Park, affording opportunities of boat cruises and game drives into the park.

GETTING THERE AND AWAY
Self-drive and hitchhiking
To/from Nata and Francistown From Kasane it is about 316km of tarred road to Nata, and 506km to Francistown. For hitchhikers this road is easy by Botswana's standards – make an early start from Francistown and you can expect to reach Kasane by nightfall. For details of the road between Kasane and Nata, see page 252.

To/from Zimbabwe
Kazungula There is an excellent tarred road from Zimbabwe to the Kazungula border (⏰ 06.00–20.00) and across into Botswana. This means that one of Africa's biggest attractions for visitors, Victoria Falls, is a day trip away from Kasane – and, more notably, that Chobe can be visited as a day trip from the Falls.

About 2km after entering Botswana at the substantial immigration office, there's a T-junction. The right turn is for the ferry to Zambia only; left leads you immediately past a disease-control post. Here your vehicle will be driven through a puddle of insecticide and you'll be asked to stamp your shoes on an impregnated mat. You'll also be checked to make sure that you're not importing banned animal products – like fresh meat, milk, bones or skins (all part of Botswana's zealous efforts to protect their national herd from diseases). Less than 2km later there's a right turn to Kasane, while straight on leads to Nata and Francistown. This is about 12km east of Kasane town.

If you're on an organised trip, it's very easy to have a road transfer arranged for you between Kasane and Victoria Falls town. It'll take about 2 hours, and cost US$45–70 per person, one-way. Note, however, that you'll need a visa for Zimbabwe, which will set you back a further US$50.

Pandamatenga About 93km south of Kasane, and 223km from Nata, this is one of the country's few arable-farming areas. It's easily distinguished by the prominent grain silos, which tower over the surrounding sorghum and maize fields. The small border post with Zimbabwe (⊕ *08.00–17.00*) is less than 50km from Robins Camp, deep in the heart of Zimbabwe's Hwange National Park, so it can be a convenient way to drive between Chobe and Hwange.

To/from Zambia While transfers from Livingstone Airport are easily arranged and relatively inexpensive (about US$45–70 per person one-way), the Zambian government charges US$50 per person for a visa. Thus, unless you're rushing through, it's well worth an overnight stop in Livingstone, giving you the opportunity to visit Victoria Falls before heading on to Kasane. The journey from Livingstone to the border takes about 50 minutes along a straight, tarred road of about 65km, running parallel to the Zambezi.

Kazungula About 2km from the disease-control post (page 231) is a substantial vehicle ferry over the Zambezi (⊕ *06.00–18.00*) to the village of Kazungula in Zambia. It gets very busy on both sides of the river, with large lorries, local traffic and numerous pedestrians jostling to board, so allow an absolute minimum of 2 hours and plenty of patience to get through all the paperwork for the short crossing. This is particularly important in the afternoon, if you want to be sure of crossing that night. The chaos is generally greater on the Zambian side, where access to the harbour, hampered by narrow gates, is frequently gridlocked, whereas in Botswana the lorries tend to form an orderly – if very long – queue; one evening we counted a tailback of more than 60 trucks stretching for 1.5km, with drivers waiting for up to three weeks to cross.

It's not surprising, then, that a road bridge across the Zambezi at this point has been mooted for many years, and slowly it is coming to fruition. That said, although work on the bridge started in 2014, completion is likely to take at least until 2019, so there's still time to experience the colour – and hassle – that make the ferry crossing so interesting.

Foot passengers can get to the border by combi from behind the bus station in Kasane (*P3.50*), or by taxi from the same place (*about P40*). The passenger fare across the river is just P2, but vehicle fares are based on size; expect to pay about US$30 for a Land Cruiser. Those taking a car into Zambia will also be liable for tax and insurance, costing around US$20, in addition to any customs fees payable.

If you want to hitch across to Zambia, try standing where the Zimbabwean and Zambian roads fork, thus hitching on both of them. The disease-control post makes a perfect hitchhiking spot to get into Kasane or to head for Nata, as vehicles have to stop here anyway.

Sesheke Heading west on the Zambian side, it's about 130km to the small town of Sesheke, the gateway to Zambia's Western Province. The tar road crosses the Zambezi at a superb new bridge, currently one of only six to span the width of the Zambezi anywhere along its length (the others are at Chirundu, Tete, Livingstone and Katima Mulilo, with a footbridge at Chinyingi mission) – although another is under construction in Mozambique, and work on the latest bridge, at Kazungula, is well in hand. Sesheke can also be reached painlessly on good tar roads via Ngoma and Namibia.

To/from Namibia Ngoma (page 266) is the location for a bridge across the Chobe, and a border with Namibia (⊕ *07.00–18.00*). It's about 51km from the centre of Kasane by good tar road, or rather more if you take the scenic riverside route (4x4 essential) through Chobe National Park. From Ngoma, it's a further 69km of good tar to the main town of Namibia's Caprivi Strip, Katima Mulilo.

By bus Kasane's bus station [234 C3] is on Chilwero Road, behind the Shell garage in the centre of town. Buses leave Kasane for Francistown every day at around 06.00, 11.30 and 13.00 (*5hrs; P112*). If you want to get to Maun, there are two choices. Either take the slow overnight bus, leaving at 21.00 and getting to Maun at around 06.00 the following morning (*P136*), or hop on to a bus towards Francistown, then change at Nata (*P70*) on to a bus coming the other way. To get your ticket, you'll need to arrive at least half an hour early. Operators include W Khanda Express (\241 6471, 392 3267). There are other buses later in the day, but these don't depart until they are full, and a slower night bus that's slightly cheaper.

Regular minibuses and small combis ply between Kasane and Nata, linking on to both Francistown and Maun, with fares on a par with the larger buses.

To get to Kazungula for the ferry across to Zambia, or to cross into Zimbabwe, pick up a combi up the hill from the bus rank; the fare is around P3.50. Alternatively, take a taxi from the same point for around P20.

By air Kasane (airline code BBK) is traditionally a busy gateway for the light aircraft that taxi visitors around the camps of northern Botswana, but its scheduled traffic is gradually beginning to pick up, too, with regular international as well as domestic flights.

Flights between Kasane and Johannesburg are operated daily by Airlink (\625 2354), and four times a week via Gaborone by Air Botswana [234 B2] (*Main Mall;* \625 0161), on Monday, Wednesday, Friday and Sunday in each direction. Air Botswana also has two direct flights a week to Maun, on Tuesday and Thursday and on Sunday via Gaborone. Most travellers coming through Kasane will also pass through Victoria Falls or Livingstone, whose airports have frequent flights to/from Harare and Johannesburg. Do note, however, that you will need to pay US$50 for a visa in both Zambia and Zimbabwe. In theory, there is also the option to buy a KAZA visa in Lusaka, Livingstone and Victoria Falls, at US$50 per person, which covers you for travel in both Zambia and Zimbabwe, along with day trips to Botswana, but in practice these are not always available. The 90-minute road transfer between Kasane and Victoria Falls or Livingstone costs around US$45–70 per person, or you could charter a plane – albeit at exceptionally high cost.

Kasane Airport [234 C6] Bright, shiny and modern, the new Kasane International Airport is set on a ridge just a couple of kilometres west of the town.

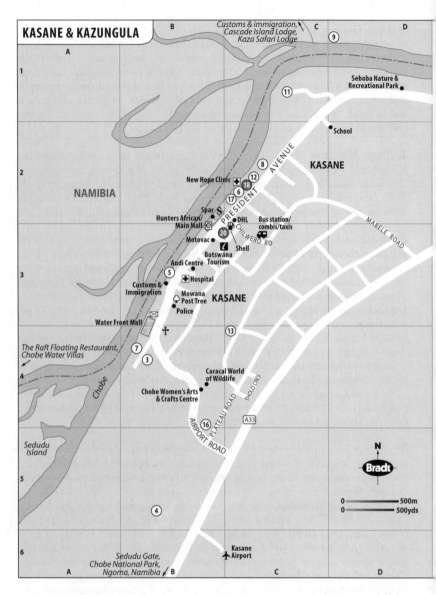

KASANE & KAZUNGULA

Customs & immigration,
Cascade Island Lodge,
Kaza Safari Lodge

NAMIBIA

KASANE

Seboba Nature &
Recreational Park

School

New Hope Clinic

PRESIDENT AVENUE

Spar
Hunters African/
Main Mall
DHL
Bus station/
combis/taxis
Motovac
CHILWERO RD
Shell
Botswana
Tourism
Audi Centre
Hospital
Customs &
Immigration
Mowana
Post Tree
KASANE
Police
Water Front Mall

MABELE ROAD

The Raft Floating Restaurant,
Chobe Water Villas

Chobe

Caracal World
of Wildlife

THO-LO CRES

Chobe Women's Arts
& Crafts Centre

Sedudu
Island

AIRPORT ROAD

PLATEAU ROAD

A33

N

Bradt

0   500m
0   500yds

Kasane
Airport

Sedudu Gate,
Chobe National Park,
Ngoma, Namibia

To find it, follow President Avenue nearly to its western end, then – just before Chobe Safari Lodge – turn left up the good tarred Airport Road. After 1.4km you'll meet the main road to Ngoma at a T-junction. Turn right here and less than 1km further you'll see a left turning clearly signposted to the airport. A taxi to or from town should cost about P40.

There are desks at the airport for Air Botswana, Airlink and Botswana Tourism (*625 2211*), as well as for the car-rental agencies. There's a bureau de change here, too, and even a VIP – well 'WIP' – lounge, with other slots awaiting occupants such as curio shops or cafés. It seems that the planners are anticipating a rosy future for the little town.

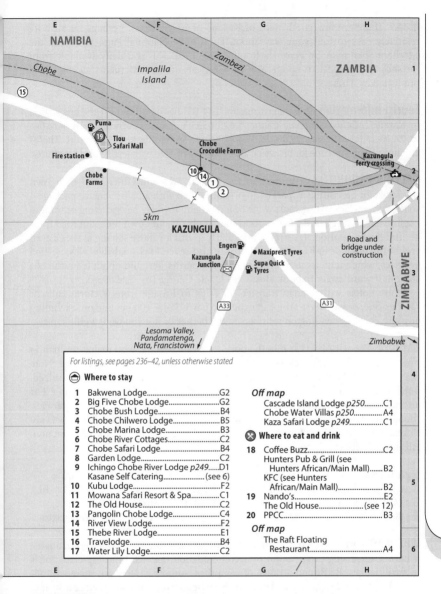

For listings, see pages 236–42, unless otherwise stated

Where to stay

ORIENTATION Kasane is a fairly linear town, spread out along President Avenue, which shadows the Chobe River as it meanders from east to west, forming the boundary with Namibia. Most of the visitors' lodges stand on the river's southern bank, accessed by short side-roads, but others are further downstream, in the Kazungula area.

A second tar road runs parallel to the town and the river to reach the border with Namibia at Ngoma. This actually cuts inland through the Chobe National Park, though isn't usually of interest for game viewing. Another tar road, which offers the only 2x4 access to the rest of Botswana, heads southwards towards Nata and the rest of the Eastern Corridor area.

Maps There are few good maps of Kasane or its environs, perhaps because it's relatively easy to find your way about. For Chobe National Park, you need the excellent Shell map, by Veronica Roodt (page 146). This is usually available from the shop at Chobe Safari Lodge, as is the Chobe National Park map/souvenir guide published by Tinkers.

Tourist information Botswana Tourism [234 B3] has an office near the bus station in Kasane (*Madiba Shopping Centre;* ✆ *625 0555;* e *kasane@botswanatourism.co.bw;* ⏰ *07.30–18.00 Mon–Fri, 09.00–14.00 Sat*), with a second desk at the airport. There's certainly plenty of scope for browsing along shelves packed with leaflets and brochures.

GETTING AROUND Most visitors to the Kasane area will either have their own transport, or be visiting as part of an organised trip with an all-inclusive package – so the general lack of transport won't be a problem. If you're backpacking or want to explore alone, you'll find a few minibuses that ply up and down the main road from behind the bus station. These are particularly useful for those staying at the eastern end of the town or in Kazungula. There are also several taxis, labelled Kasane Taxi Services, which tend to congregate near the supermarkets and uphill from the bus station. If you'd prefer to book ahead, try Uncle George (m *7144 0055*).

Many hotels will arrange transfers or trips to Kasane from Victoria Falls or Livingstone, or vice versa. You can expect to pay US$40–100 per person, excluding any visa costs, depending on numbers and whether or not you want a guide.

Car hire For self-drive car hire the options are increasing, with major companies now based at the airport and open for both incoming and outgoing flights. Note that it'll usually be cheaper to make a reservation and pay outside Botswana (indeed, outside of Africa), rather than turn up here and take the rate at the counter. For an indication of rates, see pages 128–9. For fuel, there are three 24-hour garages, though the Shell garage in the centre of town is no longer reliable. Better bets are Puma at Tlou Safari Mall, next to Shoprite, and Engen at the Kazungula Junction. All three accept credit cards.

🚗 **Avis/Budget** ✆ 625 0144; www.avis.co.za; ⏰ 08.00–13.00 & 14.00–17.00 Mon–Fri. Accepts Visa, Mastercard & Amex.
🚗 **Bidvest** ✆ 625 1148; m 7407 7400;

e vouchers.ka@bidvestcarrental.co.za; www.bidvestcarrental.co.za; ⏰ 08.00–17.00 Mon–Fri, 08.00–14.00 Sat (but meets all flights)
🚗 **Europcar** ✆ 625 0730; www.europcar.com

 WHERE TO STAY For such a small town, Kasane – and the neighbouring Kazungula – have a surprising proliferation of accommodation options, from top-class hotels to small lodges, B&Bs and a range of campsites. Almost all, though, share that all-important riverside location, and unless otherwise stated, are usually open year-round.

When planning where to stay in this area, do consider all the options. If you're just passing through Kasane, it might make sense to stay outside the national park, as listed below, since accommodation here tends to be a little cheaper than those in the park, and you may also save a few days' park fees. Be aware, though, that the further they are from the park entrance, the longer it will take before you are in a wildlife environment. If you're visiting the Kasane area specifically to see northern Chobe, and can afford one of the lodges in the park or near Ngoma (pages 271–3), then you might be better there. For those with their own transport, or seeking more of a bush feel with a lower price tag, a third option could be the Lesoma Valley (pages 251–2).

Lodges and hotels

⌂ **Chobe Chilwero Lodge** [234 B5] (15 chalets) Contact Sanctuary Retreats (page 224). This erstwhile delightful small bush lodge, now owned by A&K under their highly exclusive Sanctuary Retreats brand, feels akin to a British country house in the bush. Set high above the river, it looks out over the Chobe's floodplains from behind a relatively discreet electric fence – which doesn't deter visitors such as bushbuck, baboon & banded mongoose. Along with impressive standards of construction & design come tasteful décor (fully refurbished at the end of 2017) & many beautiful African artefacts that create something of the feel of an ethnological museum.

An imposing entrance hall leads through to the elegant lounge, where a small ante-room has an excellent selection of books, magazines & games, & a discreetly covered TV. Much effort goes into the food here; the salmon served at lunch was, quite simply, perfect. The service is impeccable – but friendly – & the wine cellar extensive. Large, solidly built guest 'cottages' topped with thatch & cooled by AC are inviting in their own right, each with a canopied bed, free-standing bath, indoor & outdoor showers, hammock, & an individual table & chairs set in lawns dotted with mature trees. Even more substantial is the honeymoon suite where privacy runs to its own plunge pool, & a private guide & vehicle. Practical souls will welcome the binoculars & field guides supplied in each chalet, Wi-Fi throughout the lodge, & even a business centre, but more hedonistic beings will make for the landscaped pools (with showers, toilets & sunbeds) or the seriously stylish spa (at extra cost, although a 15min foot massage is included for all guests). Offering Africology & Thalgo products, it has a spa bath, hydrotherapy, plunge pool, & treatment rooms that include one in a treehouse. And then there's the classy shop . . .

The lodge may not offer a real wilderness experience, but it is just a 5min drive from the Sedudu Gate into Chobe, where knowledgeable, enthusiastic guides lead game drives, largely in the eastern part of the riverfront; the high-quality 4x4s take up to 6 guests. There are afternoon boat cruises, too, in small, single-decker boats – or their own double decker, which is also used for lunches & teas. Fishing trips, & day trips to Victoria Falls in Zimbabwe, are available at additional cost. *From US$530 pp 6 Jan–Mar & Nov–20 Dec*

to US$1,020/1,530 pp sharing/sgl 15 Jun–Oct & 21 Dec–6 Jan, inc FB, most drinks, activities, park fees, laundry; exc premium wines, spa, transfers. ★★★–★★★★★★

⌂ **Chobe Marina Lodge** [234 B3] (66 rooms) ✆625 2221, reservations ✆+27 87 740 9292; e res1@chobemarinalodge.com; www.aha.co.za/ chobemarina. There's no mistaking this upmarket resort, with its deep-red & ochre buildings that feel instantly at one with its luxuriant gardens. Built across a narrow creek, with extensive tree shade, it was opened in 2002 in direct competition with Mowana Safari Resort & Spa. The spacious tiled & thatched entrance opens on to dark wooden decking, from where walkways fan out to restaurants & the bar, a curio shop, in-house tour company, private jetty, & a large infinity pool with its own bar overlooking lawns along the river.

Rooms, including 1 adapted for paraplegics, range from individual chalets at the back, each divided to create a honeymoon suite, a standard suite & a dbl room, to rather small dbl 'suites' & more dbl rooms closer to the river, & – best value by far – the surprisingly spacious 'studios'. All have tiled floors, TV, AC, fan & safe, a bath & separate shower, & a private balcony.

The hotel has 2 dining options: informal eating above the pool, or the 1st-floor Commissioners Restaurant, where à la carte or buffet meals are served in AC comfort or on a balcony overlooking the river. There's free Wi-Fi & a 100-seat conference room, but if relaxation is more your thing, try a massage in the Kwa Maningi spa.

Activities, here as elsewhere, focus on the river, with well-guided river cruises in intimate 16-seater boats, fishing trips, & of course game drives. Returning by river to the rhythm & vitality of traditional dancers performing above the jetty is an occasional highlight not to be missed. **$$$$$**

⌂ **Bakwena Lodge** [235 G2] (15 rooms) ✆625 2812; m 7530 6344, 7599 8956; e reservations@chobebakwena.com; https:// chobebakwena.com. This new lodge, opened in 2013, may not be far from the road, but the first thing that hits you is a sense of tranquillity. It's a heavily wooded site, right on the river, where the thatched lounge, dining & bar area is decked out with cane & wooden furniture, softened by cream & green fabrics & lampshades made from traditional fishtraps. It's all very understated & natural. There's an enticing eco-pool here, too, & a firepit by the river, while higher up, a viewing area looks across to Impalila Island. Accommodation is split between rooms along the river, & others built on high stilts among the trees. All have both indoor & outdoor showers, & a private veranda, with AC in the treetop houses, but just fans in the river rooms, which benefit from a cooling breeze. There are guided bicycle tours & village walks from the lodge, while excursions into Chobe National Park, using their own vehicles & boats, allow extra time for the 25min journey so you'll still enjoy a full 3hrs in the park. *US$393.50/533.50 pp sharing/sgl May–Oct, US$335.50/450 Nov–Apr, inc FB, most drinks, activities, park fees, laundry, local transfers. Min stay 2 nights.* ★★★

🏠 **Mowana Safari Resort & Spa** [234 C1] (108 rooms) ☎ 625 0300; e resmowana@cresta.co.bw; www.mowanasafarilodge.net; central reservations ☎ 391 2431; e reservations@cresta.co.bw. The Botswana flagship of the Cresta group, Mowana was conceived on a grand scale. Well designed, airy & spacious, it makes imaginative use of wooden decking, with an old baobab tree at its heart. Dbl & twin en-suite rooms, along with 8 suites, 12 family rooms & 2 rooms for paraplegics, are attractively finished with river views, & offer everything that you'd expect from a top international hotel, including remote-control AC, fan, phone, fridge, TV & safe.

Overlooking the river are 2 restaurants & 2 bars. The main restaurant has both an à la carte menu & a set-price buffet. Above it, the open-sided upstairs bar/lounge catches the breeze, with a warming wood fire for winter evenings. Less formal is the outside bar & restaurant located above a large, modern pool with separate children's pool. Guests will also appreciate the smart curio shop, an internet room & free Wi-Fi throughout. But talk of the town is the extensive riverside spa, whose treatment rooms, sauna, jacuzzi & pool share a lovely setting; even the gym has a certain appeal!

For the business visitor there are conference facilities for up to 100 people, but most are more interested in the game drives & boat cruises (*US$36, exc park fees*) that venture into Chobe National Park from the hotel's own jetty. In case that's not enough, there's also a tennis court & a 9-hole golf course, as well as evenings of traditional African culture. **$$$$$**

🏠 **Kubu Lodge** [235 F2] (11 chalets, camping) ☎ 625 0312; m 7126 5000; e reservations@

kubulodge.net; www.kubulodge.net. About 9km from the centre of Kasane, Kubu stands on a sloping site beside the river, clearly signposted from the main road. Privately owned & run, the lodge has been part of Kasane for many years & remains friendly, personable, & immaculately kept.

Kubu's square thatched chalets are substantial wooden buildings raised off the ground with steps up to a veranda at the front, set under shady trees in lush green lawns sloping down to the river. Each is well furnished with rugs on the wooden floors, wood & metal furniture & a dbl & sgl bed – or 3 sgls. Mosquito nets, screened windows & a fan keep the bugs at bay, there's a compact en-suite bathroom, & a coffee machine provides a touch of luxury.

Overlooking the river, a solid wooden building with screened windows houses the restaurant, with tables spilling out on to the veranda & a cosy mezzanine area above. A buffet lunch is around P200, & the set 4-course dinner, changed daily, P300. Lower down are a braai area & boma, then a swimming pool surrounded by lawns. A large shop offers a variety of curios, cards & a few books.

A few mins' walk from the lodge, Kubu's campsite is popular with private campers, though its 7 large dusty pitches, each with a braai stand, offer limited shade at the end of the dry season, when the trees are bare. Toilets & hot showers are clean & functional, & there's a small plunge pool (campers may not use the lodge pool). Part of the campsite slopes down to the river so though the road is lit, it's wise to take a torch if you eat at the restaurant in the evening.

Game drives & boat cruises run morning & afternoon, & fishing trips can be organised too. While the jetty at the lodge is used for cruises up the confluence of the Chobe & Zambezi, visitors heading for the Chobe River in the national park are transferred by road to a jetty in Kasane. The extensive grounds feature a marked nature trail, with helpful notes & a map on hand. *Camping US$18 pp. No children under 4.* ⊕ *Closed mid-Jan–Feb.* **$$$$$**

🏠 **Chobe Bush Lodge** [234 B4] (42 rooms) President Av; ☎ 625 0336; e reservations@chobebushlodge; www.chobebushlodge.com. Opened in 2014, this sister to Chobe Safari Lodge (see opposite) lies slightly up the hill to the back, with views towards the national park. The lofty thatched buildings & rather hotel-like rooms share a family likeness, but there it ends. An injection of contemporary chic here, manifested in sharp lines offset by muted greys, & beautiful tree-themed murals in the main area, creates a very different, more urban feel.

Bush Lodge has its own small infinity pool that flows silently into a 2nd pool below. A rather classy restaurant serves lunch & dinner à la carte, & there's also a big airy bar, a shop & an activity centre, along with Wi-Fi throughout. For a change of scene, and views of the river, guests are welcome to use all the facilities of the bigger lodge (& vice versa), from the pool & the restaurants to the grounds themselves, & activities are common to both. **$$$$** *exc b/fast (US$16–28 pp).*

🏠 **Garden Lodge** [234 C2] (8 rooms) 714 President Av; \ 625 0051; m 7164 6064; e reservations@oshaughnessys.org; www. thegardenlodge.com. This small, friendly lodge, 5km from the national park, is relaxed, personal & well designed: a welcome change from the more corporate style of the larger lodges. Unobtrusively tucked behind secure gates, it has a tranquil setting with attractive gardens. From the lofty central area, combining lounge & dining areas, & flanked by a semi-covered pool, a shaded terrace looks across an expanse of lawn towards the river. Upstairs, a rustic wooden balcony is an ideal spot for a drink while watching the river, or an intimate dinner. It's popular with the resident barn owls, too. En-suite twin or dbl rooms are bright, light & cool: kitted out in natural fabrics, with cane chairs & tiled floors, AC, ceiling fans & kettle. Each looks towards the river from its own balcony, or from a terrace leading on to the lawn; views from upstairs rooms – which include a couple of 2-storey family rooms with twin beds up a narrow staircase – are particularly good. A separate, rather dark chalet lacks a river view, but is completely detached with a private veranda. The lodge offers game drives, & boat cruises from its own jetty at the end of the garden. *US$275/400 pp sharing/sgl DBB May–Nov, US$215/320 Dec–Apr, inc local transfers. No children under 4.* **$$$$**

🏠 **River View Lodge** [235 F2] (10 chalets, 1 house) \ 625 0967; m 7126 5000; e info@riverviewlodgechobe.com; www. riverviewlodgechobe.com. Don't be put off by the unattractive entrance, or the rather utilitarian look of the painted brick chalets, for this is a friendly, well-organised & intimate lodge with an enviable

riverside location. There are plenty of trees, too, to the delight of the local bushbaby population, but hippos & crocs are deterred by a discreet electric fence. Twin, dbl & family chalets benefit from AC & fans, tea & coffee stations & mosi nets over the beds, with local artefacts adding zest to the overall décor. There's also an attractively laid-out self-catering house for up to 4 people, though most guests dine in the central area (*dinner US$20 pp*). A lounge shelter & firepit complete the picture, & there's Wi-Fi throughout. As well as the standard boat cruises & game drives into the park (*US$50 pp*), there are bikes for guests to use with or without a guide so you can explore the local area. For self-drivers, secure parking is a bonus. **$$$$**

🏠 **Chobe Safari Lodge** [234 B4] (81 rooms, 8 rondavels, camping) President Av; \ 625 0336; e reservations@chobesafarilodge; www. chobesafarilodge.com. On a spacious site overlooking the river, on the western fringes of town, Chobe Safari Lodge is the oldest of Kasane's camps. Its wide lawns, well shaded by mature trees, attract warthogs, families of banded mongoose & numerous birds. Although it is the closest lodge to the national park for boat trips, this proximity makes little difference if you're driving, since the entrance to the park is several kilometres by road.

The impressive reception, lobby, lounge, activity centre & restaurant shelter under a huge, open-sided thatched structure whose heavy rafters are an occasional playground for vervet monkeys. In front, a sparkling crescent-shaped pool is surrounded by loungers & tables beneath the trees, making this an attractive lunch venue; the burgers are said to be excellent & buffets at lunch & dinner (*US$28/36*) are very popular. Other facilities include a very well-stocked shop, a proper spa that's open to all, Wi-Fi access throughout, & 2 bars, with the Sedudu bar at the campsite a favourite place for sundowners.

There's a good choice of accommodation, in 2 price bands. At the top end, the modern 'river' rooms & slightly larger, predominantly dark-wood 'safari' rooms have twin or dbl beds, en-suite shower & bath, AC/fan, TV, safe, kettle & phone, plus a balcony or veranda overlooking lawns to the river. 'Standard' rooms, & the lodge's original rondavels, now have AC, TV & safes, as well as braai stands. For a party of 4, the family rooms are particularly good value. Meanwhile, the campsite by the river changes little, though it has acquired a few pre-erected tents over the years. It is still popular with overlanders, & now independent campers may pre-book too.

Game drives (US$42 pp, plus park fees) depart daily at 06.00 & 15.00, while well-guided boat cruises (US$38) leave at 15.00. For something a little more intimate you can explore the river between 07.00 & 14.00 in a small motorboat with a driver (US$104/2hrs, max 6), or go fishing (US$106 pp/2hrs inc tackle, max 3). Other excursions include Victoria Falls (US$217 with a guide, exc visa), & a Namibian village walk (US$42). $$$–$$$$ exc b/fast (US$16–28 pp). Camping US$15/11 adult/child.

🏠 **Pangolin Chobe Lodge** [234 C4] (14 rooms) Contact Pangolin Photo Safaris, page 248. New in Jul 2018, this contemporary lodge sits above the town, just a short drive from the airport & close to Chobe park gate for an early start. Given its ownership, it comes as no surprise that it is geared to the needs of photographers – who can start with the sunset view from the lodge towards the Chobe floodplains, & draw inspiration from the wildlife photos adorning the walls. The facilities include an editing area, & excursions in Pangolin's customised boats & 4x4 vehicles – though for non-photographic guests there are also more conventional means of transport.

Back at the lodge, the en-suite bedrooms are built on 2 storeys, & come with AC, twin or dbl beds, & a balcony sharing the view, along with a big desk & lots of space for camera gear. Balancing the rooms, & featuring the same clean design lines, the main area incorporates a dining room & pool terrace at ground level, with a bar & editing space above. US$195 pp Nov–Mar, US$395 Apr–Oct, inc FB, drinks, activities, park fees. ⊕ All year. ★★–★★★

🏠 **Water Lily Lodge** [234 C2] (10 rooms) President Av; ✆625 1775, 625 2709; e waterlily@ btcmail.co.bw. Owned by Monica Kgaile, 'quite a character' according to one local, Water Lily Lodge looks like a giant cream-washed rondavel built around a central fountain. Nicely presented en-suite rooms overlook the river, with doors on to the garden or a small balcony. Inside are twin beds & mosquito nets, plus AC, TV, safe, desk, fridge & kettle.

Meals can be taken in the attractive restaurant or outside on a thatched terrace alongside a convivial bar & a small, kidney-shaped pool. The à

la carte menu ($$) focuses on fresh fish (including excellent bream), steaks & chicken dishes & local cuisine, as well as lighter lunches. Boat cruises, game drives & day trips to Victoria Falls are on offer through their own tour company. $$$

🏠 **Travelodge** [234 B4] (66 rooms) Plateau Rd; 625 0625, 625 0828; e fom.kasane@ travelodge.co.bw; www.travelodge.co.bw. There's no missing the corporate lime green & grey of this new hotel, which is geared largely to the conference market. That said, it's pretty close to the airport, so could offer a practical bed for the night if you arrive late or are leaving early. Small but innocuous rooms have the standard hotel fittings, including a TV, safe, kettle & fridge, & there's a pool in neat lawned gardens. $$$

Guesthouses, B&Bs and self-catering

🏠 **Chobe River Cottages** [234 C2] (6 rooms) President Av; ✆625 2863; m 7553 2117; e bookings@choberivercottages.com; www.choberivercottages.com. Opened in 2013, this secure set-up is smart & airy, with modern apartment-style rooms adorned with evocative aerial photographs. Stroll past the small free-form pool (with separate baby pool), & the warthogs pulling at the grass beyond, & you'll come to a high viewing deck above the river.

From the large kitchenette off the lounge area (which would put many a home kitchen to shame) to the twin or dbl bedrooms with AC & ceiling fans, it's all exceptionally well equipped & thought out. There's a sofa bed in the lounge for an extra couple of guests, & the veranda even has a giant mosi-net curtain so you can sit out in privacy & comfort after dinner cooked on your own BBQ. If you don't fancy self-catering (& Spar is just a short walk away for supplies), then Coffee Buzz is on hand for b/fast & lunch, with the Old House for an evening meal. $$$ exc b/fast.

🏠 **The Old House** [234 C2] (10 rooms) 718 President Av; ✆625 2562; e reservations@ oldhousekasane.com; www.oldhousekasane.com. This popular restaurant offers B&B in modern but unpretentious twin, dbl or family rooms with AC & en-suite showers. The complex is wheelchair-accessible, as is one of the rooms. For amenities, there's free Wi-Fi, secure parking, a plunge pool & a very good gift shop – & of course the relaxed, pub-style bar & restaurant. The normal range of activities can be organised, including sunset river cruises. **$$$**

🏠 **Kasane Self Catering** [234 C2] (2 cottages) President Av; ✆ 625 0114; m 7553 2117; e trish@chobeselfcatering.com; www.chobeselfcatering.com. Under the same ownership as Chobe River Cottages, & almost adjacent, these 2 cottages have an entirely different style & atmosphere. Each has a leafy porch & chairs looking out to the tranquil, verdant gardens of Trish Williams's home, a haven for birds (including several endemics) that showcases her profession as a landscape gardener. In the bedrooms – a twin & a dbl – handmade patchwork quilts lend a homely touch to dark-wood traditional furniture, yet there's AC to keep the temperature down, a kitchenette with all that you could need for self-catering, & a private BBQ area. Here, as at Chobe River Cottages, there are safes, secure parking & free Wi-Fi. The same practical comments apply, too, & guests may use the neighbouring pool & riverside viewing deck – though a private deck & pool will be added here in 2018. **$$** *exc b/fast.*

Chalets and camping
As well as these 2 options, there are excellent campsites at both Chobe Safari Lodge & Kubu Lodge. Note that some of the campsites in Kasane will not accept advance bookings from individual campers (as against overland groups), so in high season it's a good idea to arrive early.

🏠 **Big Five Chobe Lodge** [235 G2] (38 chalets, camping) ✆ 625 2272; m 7652 7355; e reservations.big5chobelodge@gmail.com. The former Toro Safari Lodge, just 600m from the turn-off towards Kasane from Kazungula, had a welcome facelift from new owners in 2015, bringing it up a notch in terms of creature comforts. Despite this, & the riverside location, it's hard to inject personality into the neat rows of small, square chalets – though those at the front, with a river view, are nicely placed, & rooms in the 'enclave' are slightly larger, & cooler. Screened doors from a brick veranda lead into each of the

thatched chalets, which now have tiled floors, with fans, AC, TVs, kettles & en-suite showers. Behind these a level, grassy campsite hosts both overland groups (on a separate site) & independent campers, who benefit from 22 neat pitches with power points, a fireplace & – a big bonus – private ablution facilities, including hot showers. Shade, in the form of immature trees, is growing rapidly. In the wide-fronted central area, open to the river, solid wood furniture gives an air of permanence to the lounge & dining area (where there's Wi-Fi), & separate riverside bar, & there's a pool tucked away too. Activities include boat cruises (from the jetty at Chobe Marina) & game drives; fishing & Victoria Falls trips can also be organised. **$$$** *Camping P200 pp.*

🏠 **Thebe River Lodge** [235 E1] (31 rooms, camping) ✆ 625 0995; e reservations@theberivsafaris.com; www.theberivsafaris.com. This long-established, family-owned site is about 5km from the centre of town, adjacent to the new Puma fuel station. The base for Thebe River Safaris (page 248), it is well run, & retains something of the feel of a popular backpackers' lodge, yet was almost entirely rebuilt in 2008. Simple, clean, modern rooms are all en suite, with twin beds (plus 1 family room), mosi nets, tea & coffee facilities, & ceiling fan. Most are built in a thatched block around a courtyard, but some are in a row behind – & are rather dark.

The campsite is usually occupied by overlanders or travellers taking a trip with Thebe – whose activities are some of the most affordable in Kasane. Bookings are not accepted from independent campers, who take pot luck, & in high season the site may be full. Each of the campsite pitches has its own shaded gazebo & braai stand. The restaurant & bar have moved to the back of the site following a fire in 2017, but there's still a small pool nearer the river, & there are plans for a new, more exclusive lodge by the river. Transfers/day trips can be arranged to & from Victoria Falls & Livingstone (*day trip P960 pp*). **$$$** *exc b/fast (P100). Camping P115 pp.*

✕ **WHERE TO EAT AND DRINK** Between them, Kasane's hotels and lodges offer a range of restaurants, some of them very good, and most visitors choose to eat in their place of accommodation.

For something more relaxed, seek out the Old House, or PPCC next to the fuel station, which majors on good Indian cuisine. For a more local flavour, there's the restaurant at Water Lily Lodge. And if you're craving fast food, Kasane can oblige in the form of KFC, close to Spar [234 B2], or Nando's in Tlou Safari Mall [235 E2], next to the Puma garage.

✗ **The Raft Floating Restaurant** [off 234 A4] Contact Flame of Africa (page 247); ⊕ 11.00–15.00 daily. Anchored to the riverbank on the Namibian side of the Chobe River, opposite Sedudu Island, The Raft is popular with safari groups. A 15min boat ride upstream from Kasane, it serves a 2-course lunchtime buffet including a braai (BBQ) with salads, & a dessert. *US$40 pp inc transfers.* $$$$$

✗ **Hunters Pub & Grill** [234 B2] Hunters African Main Mall, President Av; ✆625 1087; ⊕ 08.30–21.30 Mon–Thu, 08.30–02.00 Fri–Sat, 10.00–21.00 Sun. Despite its café feel, Hunters is a licensed restaurant with a broad menu that takes you from b/fast through light lunches to dinner. Options include game, & local dishes such as *seswaa* at lunchtime. $$–$$$

✗ **The Old House** [234 C2] President Av; ✆625 2562; ⊕ 06.30–21.30 daily. This relaxed old favourite is a popular place, with pub-style tables & sports TV for the latest on the rugby field. Food – focusing on the likes of burgers, steaks, salads & pizzas – is served under cover or on a wooden deck

facing the garden, where you can wander down to the river. If you're coming in the evening, it's best to book. $$–$$$

✗ **Coffee Buzz** [234 C2] 721 President Av; m 7131 8956; www.thecoffeebuzz.co.za; ⊕ 07.30–15.00 daily. Bettina Kelly's pleasant, fan-cooled café does a good b/fast, as well as coffee & cakes, milkshakes & a range of lunch dishes. The menu, dubbed 'German-African' cuisine, includes 2 daily specials – 1 vegetarian & 1 non-veg: perhaps lentils, spiced carrots & feta salad, or Chobe bream & chips. Guests may relax in the small garden & use the pool, & it's worth checking out Bettina's colourful mosaics, too. $$

✗ **PPCC** [234 B3] Next to the Shell garage; ✆625 2237; m 7272 8318; ⊕ 09.00–22.00 Mon–Sat, 11.00–21.00 Sun. Although PPCC stands for Pizza Plus Coffee & Curry, this central spot is popularly known as 'the Indian', & has an excellent reputation. Eat inside or out on the small, shaded terrace set back from the road. A take-away service is handy for anyone self-catering. $$

SHOPPING
Food and drink Most accessible for travellers are the town's **supermarkets**: Spar, which is opposite the Shell garage [234 B2], Choppies at both Water Front Mall [234 B3] (⊕ *07.30–19.00 Mon–Fri, 07.30–18.00 Sat, 08.00–17.00 Sun*) and Kazungula Junction [235 G3] (⊕ *08.30–19.30 Mon–Sat, 14.00–19.30 Sun*), and the new Shoprite in Tlou Safari Mall at the Kasane turn-off [235 E2]. Between them you'll find pretty well everything you'll need for a camping trip.

While supermarkets themselves are not licensed to sell **alcohol**, Spar has its own off-licence, Tops (⊕ *10.00–19.00 Mon–Fri, 10.00–18.00 Sat*), on the parade in front of the supermarket, while at the Water Front Mall there's the Jacaranda Bottle Store with similar hours.

Crafts, gifts and books These are the domain of the gift shops at the various hotels along the river, with Chobe Safari Lodge [234 B4] among the best.

It's also worth checking out the various craft shops in the parade behind Spar [234 B2], and the mosaics at Coffee Buzz [234 C2]. For locally made baskets and other crafts, try the shop at Seboba Nature and Recreational Park [234 D1], or the Chobe Women's Arts and Crafts Centre (see opposite). And do browse the market stalls around the Shell garage area; lengths of colourful local fabric make excellent gifts – or tablecloths – for around P40.

Buzzadi Trading [234 C2] Coffee Buzz, President Av; m 7131 8956, 7134 6036; ⊕ 08.00–16.00 Mon–Sat. Highlights of the gift shop at Coffee

Buzz are Bettina Kelly's mosaics, from small & discreet to great big mirror frames that make a real statement.

Chobe Women's Arts & Crafts Centre [234 B4] Airport Rd; ⏰ 10.00–16.30 daily. Based next to the Caracal World of Wildlife, this is a co-operative of 30 or so women who get together to make traditional baskets & to teach their skills to others. In theory, the women work *in situ*, so that visitors can watch them weave, & perhaps meet the person who created 'their' basket; in practice, opening hours are a little erratic.

Gecko Gift Shop [234 C2] Old Hse, President Av; ⏰ 08.00–17.00 daily. This colourful Aladdin's cave of gifts, jewellery & textiles is found at the Old House – so you can combine browsing with a spot of lunch or a drink.

Clothes and equipment

Several shops in the Spar complex opposite the Shell garage [234 C3] and at Kazungula Junction [235 G3] sell everyday tops, trousers and shoes, so there's likely to be something that will fit the bill. For items of safari clothing, you'll probably do better at the shops in the larger hotels.

OTHER PRACTICALITIES

Banks and bureaux de change

Kasane is an obvious spot for changing money, with a couple of banks plus several ATMs, including at the Puma and Engen fuel stations. You can also get cash against a card in the banks. I still have memories of changing money at Barclays [234 B2] (⊕ KASANE 17°47.97'S, 25°09.015'E) in 1988 when it occupied a small, picturesque thatched rondavel; now its home is a modern, architect-designed building opposite the Shell garage.

If you're planning to change currency, it's normally quicker to go to one of the town's bureaux de change, where rates are only slightly lower than at the bank, queues are shorter, and opening hours are considerably longer. While working out how much cash to change, note that park fees are best paid in pula, so bear this in mind if you're intending to drive yourself through the national parks.

$ Open Door Bureau de Change [234 B3] Water Front Mall; ☏ 625 2088; ⏰ 07.30–18.00 Mon–Fri, 08.30–16.00 Sat, 09.00–16.00 Sun. Internet P15/30mins. Also behind Spar [234 B3] (Hunters Africa Main Mall) & at Kazungula Junction [235 G3].

$ UA Exchange Branches inside Choppies stores at both Water Front Mall [234 B3] & Kazungula Junction [235 G3].

Communications

Post and courier Kasane's main **post office** [235 G3] (⏰ *08.00–16.00 Mon–Fri, 08.30–noon Sat*) moved to Kazungula Junction in 2017. A second, smaller office [234 B3] (⏰ *08.00–16.00 Mon–Fri, 08.00–11.00 Sat*) remains in the town, just down from Water Front Mall. You can also get stamps at Kasane Computers, in the Audi Centre [234 B3] and from shops in the big hotels.

DHL [234 C3] Next to Shell garage; ☏ 625 0069

Internet Internet cafés in Kasane come and go, as does their signal. Most reliable is:

🌐 Kasane Computers [234 B3] Audi Centre; ☏ 625 2312; www.kasanecomputers.com; ⏰ 08.00–17.00 Mon–Fri, 08.00–13.00 Sat.

P14/30mins. They'll also download your digital photos on to a memory stick – a great back-up in case of memory-card disasters.

Telephone Local SIM cards can in theory be purchased at many outlets, including Orange at the Spar complex and Cell World at Kazungula Junction. Particularly efficient is the Mascom office tucked almost out of sight next to Choppies at Water Front Mall [234 B3], and open normal shopping hours.

Health Kasane's **hospital** [234 B3] (\0800 600898) is on the main road towards Chobe Safari Lodge. The town also offers a couple of private clinics, along with a dentist and a pharmacy.

⊞ New Hope Private Clinic [234 C2] President Av;\625 1733; m 7199 3199
✚ Pharma Africa [234 B3] Audi Centre;\625 1502, emergency m 7322 8502; ⊕ 08.30–18.00 Mon–Fri, 08.00–14.00 Sat, 10.00–noon Sun. Good consulting pharmacy.

✚ Prime Health [235 G3] Kazungula Junction; \625 1548, m 7267 2140, 7227 3902; ⊕ 08.00–19.00 Mon–Fri, 09.00–13.00 Sat. Small pharmacy with a polyclinic offering X-ray & laboratory facilities with links to a doctor, paramedic & MRI.

Photography To download photos to a memory stick, try Kasane Computers (page 243), who also sell memory sticks, camera memory cards, batteries and even cheap cameras.

Vehicle repairs and equipment If you're unlucky enough to break down, Kasane's not a bad place to do so, as it's used as a supply base by some of the safari operators. Certainly if you're heading across Chobe and Moremi you should make sure your vehicle's in tip-top shape before you head off.

Motovac Behind the Shell garage [234 B3] & at Kazungula Junction [235 G3];\625 0848; ⊕ 08.00–17.00 Mon–Fri, 08.00–13.00 Sat, 09.00–13.00 Sun. Sells spares for most major
makes, including Land Rover, Nissan & Toyota.
Supa Quick Tyres [235 G3] Kazungula;\625 2636. Opposite Engen garage.

WHAT TO SEE AND DO
In Kasane Attractions in Kasane itself are limited to a handful of relatively low-key wildlife and recreational operations. There is, though, the rather quirky **Mowana Post Tree** [234 B3], in the grounds of the police station, but still accessible to the public. Over the years, this venerable old baobab, with its capacious hollow trunk, has served variously as a gaol, a mail collection point and – in the 1960s – as a recruitment station for men going to work in the South African mines. The connection was one of logistics, since the mail, the prisoners and the miners were all transported in the same vehicles.

Seboba Nature and Recreational Park [234 D1] (⊕ *year-round: May–Sep 07.00–17.30, Oct–Apr 06.00–18.00; P50 pp*) Opened in 2014, and beautifully sited above a short stretch of rapids on the Chobe River, Seboba is an ambitious community project that received considerable funding from Botswana's tourist office, with a view to involving the community in the tourism sector and fostering their traditional heritage. The whole site is wheelchair accessible.

Three years on, it feels as though the project has lost its way, with tourists tending to come only for pre-booked events. This is a shame, as the park has so much to offer: a cultural village, a lovely riverside boardwalk, and a large auditorium for performances of dance, music and drama – which is somewhat underused.

In the centre of the site, a high mound known as Commissioner's Kop affords a tantalising vantage point over the rapids, while almost back at ground level, a partially raised 1km walkway runs parallel to the river, punctuated by a couple of small observation 'hides'. At the end of the walkway, you're rewarded with a picnic site set up with shaded benches, tables and barbecue stands, as well as toilets. For the visitor, one of the unspoken advantages of the site is the opportunity to go for a walk – something that is all too rare while on safari!

The village has traditional homesteads from four tribes hailing from the Chobe area: Banambiya, Basubiya, Basarwa and Batawana. At the traditional kgotla, or meeting place, each tribe in turn nominates a chief for group discussions, and perhaps visits from a witch doctor and other key members of the community. To round off a visit, the curio shop showcases the work of local basket weavers, thus encouraging the development of traditional skills among future generations.

Caracal World of Wildlife [234 B4] (*Airport Rd;* ✆ *625 2392;* e *caracal@ btcmail.co.bw; www.caracal.info;* ⊕ *09.00–16.00 daily; standard tour P35 pp; behind scenes tour P65*) Formerly known as Chobe Snake Park, then the Caracal Biodiversity Centre, this is a great place to see some of Botswana's smaller indigenous fauna. From mambas, cobras and boomslangs you'll move on to other, harmless snakes, along with bushbabies, chameleons, raptors, vultures and banded mongooses. These last are the subject of a research project by CARACAL (the Centre for Conservation of African Resources: Animals, Communities and Land use; *www.caracal.info*) into why the animals are contracting a new strain of (non-human) TB.

A standard tour, lasting between 45 minutes and an hour, introduces visitors to the diet, physical characteristics and habits of the various inhabitants of the centre. More hands on is the 'behind the scenes' tour, lasting an extra half an hour or so, when you also get to hold some of the more benign snakes. A visit here is worth combining with the Chobe Women's Arts & Crafts Centre (page 243), which occupies an imposing thatched building at the entrance.

Chobe Crocodile Farm [235 F2] (✆ *625 0430;* ⊕ *08.30–12.30 & 14.30–16.00 Mon–Sat; P50/30/20 adult/child 12–16/child 5–10*) Kasane's crocodile farm, down a quiet lane close to Kubu Lodge, is a particularly good place to take children, with tours during which you can see the eggs, hatchlings and larger creatures. Do phone ahead, though; opening hours can change.

Spa treatments Kasane isn't bad on the pampering front. Though spas at the likes of Chobe Chilwero are exclusive to lodge guests, those at some of the bigger hotels are open to non-residents as well.

Kwa Maningi [234 B3] Chobe Safari Lodge; m 7155 9522; ⊕ 09.00–17.00 daily. Options at this small spa range from pedicures & manicures to waxing & tinting, & their 'signature' treatments: a traditional African foot wash & the 45min Hakuna Matata, combining massage, cleansing & sun protection.

Mowana Safari Resort & Spa [234 C1] ✆ 625 0300; www.crestamowana.com. With 4 treatment rooms, a sauna, steam room, hot tub & serene infinity pool, this is a place for serious self-indulgence, backed by Clarins products. There's the option of open-air sessions, too, overlooking the river, & a double treatment room for couples.

Other activities In Kasane, Mowana Safari Resort & Spa [234 C1] (see above) has a **tennis** court, **gym** and nine-hole **golf** course that are open to all. Although the local branch of Birdlife Botswana (✆*625 2392; www.birdlifebotswana.org.bw*) does not currently organise **birdwatching** excursions, recommended birding guides in Kasane include Spokes Ntswabi at Classified Safaris (✆ *625 0194; www.classifiedsafaris.com*) and Peace Shamuka at Last Eden Safaris (m *7177 0324, 7123 3235; http://last-edensafaris.com*). In town, look out around dusk for bat hawks hunting above residential areas for Mozambique free-tailed bats on the wing.

Several tour operators run **fishing** trips on the Chobe and Zambezi rivers, in search of bream and tigerfish. And **canoeing and mokoro** trips on the Chobe River can be organised from the western side of the park (see page 270 for details).

Chobe National Park (⊕ *year-round: Apr–Sep 06.00–18.30, Oct–Mar 05.30–19.00; P120/day, vehicle P50/day*) Visitors to Kasane can easily explore the park's northern area from a game-drive vehicle or from the river – with the latter being one of the region's top attractions. Excursions can be organised either through your lodge, or directly with one of a handful of small local safari operators (see opposite), or – for game drives – you can drive yourself. Costs for boat cruises and game drives vary considerably according to the operator, the style and the number of participants, but average around US$30–40 per person for each activity, plus park fees.

River trips Boat cruises range from ten-seater motorboats to double-storey boats taking 40 or more people on a champagne breakfast. Most last around 3 hours, but Flame of Africa (page 247) have a triple-decker boat, the *Chobe Explorer*, which operates full-day excursions (*US$135 pp;* ⊕ *10.00–sunset*) around Impalila Island and into the national park for up to 26 passengers. Up top there are shaded sunloungers, with more seating on the middle deck, and a restaurant, toilets and showers below. The cost includes a barbecue lunch as well as tea and coffee.

The game viewing from the river can be surprisingly good, especially in the later afternoon during the latter half of the dry season. Large numbers of elephants are virtually guaranteed, and often whole herds will cross the river from one side to the other.

Some of the lodges/operators will send you out on a private little boat with a driver and a coolbox. The small boat gives you a lot more flexibility in what you concentrate on, and how long you stop somewhere, as it's just a question of requesting what you want to do from your driver/guide. It's certainly my favourite way to see the Chobe riverfront area, and probably remains one of my favourite safari experiences in Africa. It can be magical.

Because of the number of lodges in the area, the river can become quite full of boats at times, so if you want a quieter experience, try and arrange for a boat at the crack of dawn. Most of the cruises don't leave until 09.00, so you'll have the river almost to yourself for a few hours – apart from the occasional Namibian fisherman in a mokoro (there's no fishing allowed in the national park from Botswana).

Game drives Organised game drives generally head west straight into the national park, and then cover the game-drive roads and loops around the riverfront area (see *Chapter 10* for more details of these areas). If you're organising a trip with a local company, remember to compare the various options available, asking how long the drive is, and how much of that time it takes to get to the park gate and back. Typically trips last about 3 hours. Generally the lodges further east will spend more of this getting to and from the park than those further west, but in some cases they build in extra time to allow for the longer journey. Either way you're going to find yourself mostly around the eastern side of the riverfront area, where traffic densities are relatively high.

The national park allows driving only in daylight hours, so lodges that advertise night drives are conducting these outside the park, in areas where big game is much more limited.

National park permits Self-drivers should note that the Sedudu Gate into Chobe National Park (↘625 0235) is one of the busiest of the national-park gates, and hefty queues can be anticipated, especially between June and October. Thus do allow plenty of time, or – if an early start is important – pay your fees the night before. Although technically these can be paid in pula, US dollars, sterling, rand or by Visa or Mastercard, in reality it's best to stick to pula or – if the machines are working – to a card. There is some discrepancy about other currencies, and even when they are accepted, the rate of exchange can be very poor. For those planning to camp, there is a handy kiosk here manned by staff from SKL (↘625 0113; ⊕ 08.30–17.00 daily), who run the Savute and Linyanti campsites within Chobe National Park, and Kwalate Safaris, who operate Ihaha campsite, also in Chobe, along with Xakanaxa and Maqwe (South Gate) in Moremi. For more details, see page 131.

Technically, independent drivers are not allowed into the park until after 10.00, allowing the tour operators to get in first, though it's hard to ascertain if this is enforced. In practice, access times probably depend on how busy the gate is on a given morning.

Further afield Most of the lodges and tour operators in Kasane can organise trips further afield, including mokoro trips close to Ngoma, village walks across the river in Namibia, and excursions to Victoria Falls in Zambia or Zimbabwe – the last with or without a guide.

Tour operators, safari companies and travel agents
Because overland truck companies that are not officially registered in Botswana can't use their own vehicles in the park, there's a strong market in Kasane for day trips into Chobe. Most of the hotels and lodges organise these for their own guests, but some welcome outsiders too, and there are also several independent companies. There is also a handful of mobile safari operators based in Kasane.

For those all-important national park bookings, make your way to Chobe National Park's Sedudu Gate (see above).

African Odyssey [234 B3] Chobe Marina Lodge; ↘625 0500, 625 2270; e botsreservations@bots. wildhorizons.co.zw; www.wildhorizons.co.za. Offers game drives, river cruises, fishing & various guided trips & walks.

Big Sam [234 C3] President Av; nr Shell garage; ↘625 0947; e bshreservations@gmail.com. Recommended locally, Big Sam offers reliable & affordable boat cruises & game drives (*P250 pp*) & Victoria Falls trips (*P450 pp*).

Cars & Guides [234 C2] President Av, between Old Hse & Garden Lodge; ↘625 1286; e carsandguides@gmail.com. Locally run & well recommended, the name speaks for itself. Trips to Victoria Falls P450 pp.

Flame of Africa [234 C3] President Av, nr Shell garage; ↘625 2248, 625 2235; e kasane@ flameofafrica.com; South Africa ↘+27 31 762 2424; e foaweb@flameofafrica.com; www.

flameofafrica.com. The owners of Kaza Safari Lodge, Cascade Island Lodge & The Raft Floating Restaurant (page 242) also offer most excursions in the Kasane area. These include full-day trips on their triple-decker boat (page 246).

Gavin Blair Safaris m 7562 2440; e gbs@ gavinblairsafaris.com; www.gavinblairsafaris. com. This small, personal outfit leads tailor-made safaris throughout Botswana, Zimbabwe & Namibia, all guided by Gavin himself, who has more than 30 years' guiding experience. Options include lodge, fly-in, walking & canoeing safaris.

Janala Tours & Safaris [234 C2] President Av; ↘625 1775, 625 2709; e janala@btcmail.co.bw. This tour company linked to Water Lily Lodge offers some of the more affordable trips into the national park, as well as safaris further afield.

Kalahari Tours & Safaris [234 C2] President Av, next to Coffee Buzz; ↘625 0880; e info@kalahari-tours.net; www.kalaharichobe.com. This is the place for day trips & a range of short camping safaris into Chobe National Park.

Malachite Safaris `625 1537; m 7468 5154; e malachitesafaris@gmail.com; www.malachite-safaris.com. Reggie specialises in canoe trips on the Chobe River (page 270). He also offers game drives & boat trips.

Pangolin Photo Safaris m 7642 9758; e info@pangolinphoto.com; www.pangolinphoto.com. The ultimate tour company for photoholics – from beginners to experienced – Pangolin uses custom-built vehicles & boats with swivelling tripods, with DSLR cameras & telephoto lenses supplied. They also run Pangolin Chobe Lodge, Pangolin Khwai Camp, the *Pangolin Voyager* riverboat, & a mobile camp. See ad, page 70.

Thebe River Safaris [235 E1] `625 0995; e reservations@theberiversafaris.com; www.theberiversafaris.com. As well as running a popular campsite & lodge, Thebe organises its own realistically priced game drives & boat cruises into the national park. It is also the base for a mobile-safari operation, tailormade & set trips around northern Botswana. It's led by Jan, Annatjie, Jannie & Louis van Wyk, & sister Franci, who pitch trips as 'budget, middle or luxury' – depending on how much effort/cash you are willing to expend.

AROUND KASANE

Although technically on Namibian soil, there are several lodges on the northern side of the Chobe River that use Kasane as a base. Many of their visitors come through Kasane, and their activities feature trips on the river beside the park.

One of these – Chobe Savanna Lodge – stands on land directly opposite the national park, hence I'll cover this, along with various riverboats, in *Chobe National Park*, pages 268–9. Three others lie northeast of Kasane, on Impalila Island, and a fourth, Chobe Water Villas, is just north of Sedudu Island, so these are discussed below. For more details of the Impalila area, and the rest of Namibia's Caprivi Strip, see one of my other guidebooks: *Namibia: The Bradt Travel Guide*.

IMPALILA ISLAND AREA Around Kazungula is the confluence of the Chobe and the Zambezi. The Zambezi flows relentlessly to the sea but, depending on their relative heights, the Chobe either contributes to that, or (occasionally) reverses its flow and draws water from the Zambezi. Trapped between the two rivers is a triangle of land, of about 700km², which is a mixture of floodplains, islands and channels that link the two rivers. This swampy, riverine area is home to several thousand people of Namibian nationality, mostly members of Zambia's Lozi tribe. (The main local languages here are Lozi and Subia.) Most have a seasonal lifestyle, living next to the river channels, fishing and farming maize, sorghum, pumpkins and keeping cattle. They move with the water levels to higher, drier ground as the waters rise.

The largest island in this area, Impalila Island, is at the far eastern tip of Namibia, home to around 2,500 people living in some 25 small villages. It gained notoriety during the 1980s as a military base for the South African Defence Forces (SADF), as it was strategically positioned within sight of Botswana, Zambia and Zimbabwe. It still boasts a 1,300m-long runway (✆ 17°46.48'S, 025°11.23'E) of compressed gravel, used today by charter airlines to bring visitors to the lodges, but the barracks are now a school, serving most of the older children in the area.

If you transfer to the island from Kasane, you'll have to clear customs and immigration for both Botswana and Namibia on arrival and departure. Fortunately, as borders go, the **customs and immigration post** on the island (⊕ 07.30–16.30) is fairly laid-back and informal.

Flora and fauna The area's ecosystems are similar to those in the upper reaches of the Okavango Delta: deep-water channels lined by wide reedbeds and rafts of papyrus. Some of the larger islands are still forested with baobabs, water figs, knobthorn, umbrella thorn, mopane, pod mahogany, star chestnut and sickle-leaved albizia, while jackalberry and Chobe waterberry overhang the rivers, festooned with creepers and vines.

Large mammals are scarce here, and most that do occur swim over from Chobe. Elephants and buffalo sometimes swim over to Namibia, and even lions have been known to take to the river in search of the tasty-but-dim domestic cattle kept there.

Even when there are no large mammals here, the birdlife is spectacular. Large flocks of white-faced ducks congregate on islands in the rivers, African skimmers nest on exposed sandbanks, and both reed cormorants and darters are seen fishing or perching while they dry their feathers. Kingfishers are numerous, from the giant to the tiny pygmy, as are herons and egrets. However, the area's most unusual bird is the unassuming rock pratincole with its black, white and grey body, which perches on rocks within the rapids and hawks for insects in the spray.

Where to stay
Visitors to the island arrive either by air at the small airstrip, or by boat from Kasane. Supplies for the lodges are normally brought in by boat from Kasane or Katima Mulilo. Because of their location, none of the lodges here can organise game drives in Chobe; they're limited to boat trips. Prices are quoted in US or Namibian dollars.

✳ 🏠 **Ichingo Chobe River Lodge** [234 C1] (8 Meru tents) 📞 +27 21 715 2412; e enquiry@ zqcollection.com; www.zqcollection.com. Originally the brainchild of Dawn & Ralph Oxenham, Ichingo occupies a secluded site on the south of Impalila Island, overlooking the quiet backwaters of some of the Chobe River's rapids, a world away from busy Kasane just across the water. Now within the same fold as the *Zambezi Queen & Chobe Princess* riverboats (pages 268–9), it has seen some changes, but fortunately, the new owners have retained the atmosphere of this lovely old lodge. Instead, they have focused on creature comforts such as AC, king-size beds (or large twins) & larger bathrooms in the walk-in tents, colourful cushions in the lounge area, & a smart new plunge pool with attendant loungers overlooking the rapids.

Each of the tents is set high above the flood levels – important in a location where the rise & fall of water is up to 2m. En-suite showers are in a solid structure at the back, & there's a balcony at the front, with views of the water through the vegetation, dominated by the water-tolerant waterberry trees (*Syzygium guineese*), & the orange-fruited mangosteen (*Garcinia livingstonei*). Meals are taken around a large wooden table in the thatched dining area/bar/lounge that fronts on to the river.

The lodge makes a super base for birdwatching, fishing (popular with families) & game viewing

from their fleet of little boats along the Chobe River, & for fly-fishing in the rapids. There are also visits to a local Namibian village & walks to a giant baobab. *Rates in South African rand R4,950/6,435 pp sharing/sgl inc FB, most drinks, activities, transfer from Kasane Airport/Immigration Office.* ⊕ *All year.* ★★★

🏠 **Kaza Safari Lodge** [off 234 C1] (8 chalets) Contact Flame of Africa, page 247. Situated on the northwest of Impalila Island, overlooking the Zambezi's Mambova Rapids, the former Impalila Island Lodge served in many ways to bring the island to people's attention. Now under new ownership, it was being refurbished in late 2017, but retains much of the appeal of the original.

Kaza has a peaceful location, about 45min by boat from Kasane (or a shorter boat trip to the south of Impalila Island followed by a 10min drive). The large thatched bar/dining area & comfortable lounge, built around a huge baobab, is open to the breeze, though can be sheltered when it's cold. The pool deck has reclining loungers, umbrellas, & a great view of the river.

Each of the wooden chalets has glass sliding doors (backed by gauze screening) on to a wooden veranda, overlooking the rapids. Inside, much is made of polished local mukwa wood, with its natural yellow & brown colours, especially in the front where there's lots of storage. A full curtain of mosquito netting separates this from twin beds or a king-size dbl, with direct access from there to the en-suite bathroom. AC is being introduced, & there's Wi-Fi in the main area.

Along with half- or full-day game drives into Chobe there are boat cruises taking in lunch at the Raft Floating Restaurant (page 242), sunset cruises & fishing excursions. Back on land, you can walk to a local village from the lodge, take an oxcart to a 2,000-year-old baobab or explore by bike with a guide. *US$350/455 pp sharing/sgl, inc FB, most drinks, laundry & activities. No children under 7.* ⏱ *All year.* ★★★

🏠 **Cascade Island Lodge** [off 234 C1] (8 chalets) Ntwala Island; contact Flame of Africa, page 247. The former Ntwala Island Lodge, which was extended & substantially rebuilt in 2017 to double its accommodation, is now available only for group tours. The location is beautifully secluded: a cluster of islands within the Mambova Rapids, reached from a natural reed-fringed harbour. Long wooden walkways lead to the main area, facing the rapids, & on to the chalets – both old & new. The 4 new chalets are more contemporary in construction & style, & closer together than the older ones. That said, they're all pretty spacious, & all have a bath, inside & open-air showers & separate loo, & a private plunge pool set into a deck above the water. The colour scheme, in neutral shades of grey, continues into the main area, where oversize wildlife photos dominate the décor & wooden & cane chairs invite relaxation by the river. A fleet of aluminium boats is at the ready for guests to explore the quiet backwaters, indulge in a spot of fishing, or take in a sunset cruise. ⏱ All year.

SEDUDU ISLAND AREA The precise boundary between Namibia and Botswana in this area has been defined to follow the deepest channel of the Chobe River – a definition which works well for most river boundaries. However, the Chobe splits into many streams, whose strengths and depths seem to gradually alter over the years.

Sedudu Island (or Kasikili Island, as it's called in Namibia) is a very low, flat island which covers about 3.5km² when the waters are low, but shrinks to a much smaller size when it is flooded. It's used mainly for grazing cattle.

Both Botswana and Namibia have claimed that the island belongs to them. In the 1990s, it was occupied by the Botswana Defence Force (BDF) who built several watchtowers on it – chunky structures towering over the island's grassy plains, and cunningly disguised with variegated military-pattern netting. In early 1995, both Botswana and Namibia agreed to put the issue before the International Court of Justice (ICJ) in The Hague, and in 1996 they both agreed to abide by its eventual judgement.

Botswana argued that the northern channel was the main river channel, while Namibia maintained that southern channel was the larger one. Finally, in December 1999, the ICJ pronounced that the border should 'follow the line of the deepest soundings in the northern channel of the Chobe River around Kasikili-Sedudu Island'.

That said, the court also diplomatically ruled that 'in the two channels around Kasikili-Sedudu Island, the nationals of, and vessels flying the flags of, the Republic of Botswana and the Republic of Namibia shall enjoy equal national treatment'.

For visitors, this means that game-viewing boats from both countries are allowed on both sides of this tiny, troublesome patch of floodplain!

🏠 **Where to stay** There's just one lodge in this area, on the northern banks of the Chobe River as it skirts Sedudu Island. This is also the location of the Raft Floating Restaurant (page 242).

🏠 **Chobe Water Villas** [map 263] (16 chalets) 📞+264 66 253602, reservations 📞+264 61 431 8001/2; e chobe.res@ol.na; www. chobewatervillas.com. Looking across to Sedudu Island from Namibia's Kasika Conservancy, & nearer to the park than any of Impalila Island's lodges,

Chobe Water Villas opened in 2017 on the site of the old King's Den. Guests usually arrive by boat from Kasane, clearing Namibian immigration at Kasika. Almost all the staff are from one of the local villages.

Subtle greys & orange highlights underpin a design inspired by aspects of Namibian culture, giving the feel of a contemporary art installation: seemingly every part of the main structure is symbolic. In the classy restaurant, for example, 'rain' chimes sound like thunder when stirred by the breeze. There's plenty of practical input, too, from the library (with steps) & the cleverly screened buffet area to 2 bars – 1 for those included in the rates, & 1 for premium drinks. For the warmer months, there's an infinity pool mirroring the Chobe River, & a table (just one!) set in a shallow pool of water. For cooler evenings, tables morph into gas fireboxes & firepits materialise riverside. With Wi-Fi throughout & sports TV in a small meeting room, the outside world isn't far away either. There's even a 'conversation pit'!

The impressive thatched chalets stand on stilts at the water's edge, their balconies (with telescopes) offering almost unbroken views from wooden sunloungers, as if from the prow of a ship. To add to the sense of seclusion, 4 of them are on the 'honeymoon island', reached across a bouncy suspension bridge. Inside, all is calm & orderly, with the same contemporary styling, a king-size bed & comfortable sofa, ceiling fan (no AC), Nespresso machine, complimentary minibar, & a great big bathroom with a separate shower & bath. Power is supplied by a combination of solar panels & generator, with inverters for lights at night.

Game drives & river cruises in & around Chobe National Park are included in the rates; other options, such as village tours & trips to Victoria Falls, can be organised at extra cost. *From US$525/630 pp sharing/sgl Dec–Jun to US$843/1,050 Jul–Nov, inc FB, most drinks, activities, transfers from Kasane Immigration Office; exc laundry. No children under 13.* ⊕ *All year.* ★★★–★★★★★

LESOMA VALLEY Some 20km from Kasane, the tranquil Lesoma Valley (also spelled Lehsoma or Lisoma) lies to the east of the main Kasane–Nata road, in the Kasane Forest Reserve. It also sees a reasonable amount of game, especially in the dry season when elephant are regular visitors to the camps' waterholes, along with various antelope and the occasional predator. For those seeking a more affordable option away from the bustle of Kasane, this area could be worth considering.

Where to stay

Elephant Valley Lodge [map 230] (20 tents) 620 0054/5; m 7403 7717, reservations +27 11 568 2799; e res@anthology.co.za; www. evlodge.com; ⊕ ELEVAL 17°51.193'S, 25°14.585'E. Under new ownership since 2014, & now a sister camp to Kazidora in the Delta, Elephant Valley Lodge is set in secluded surroundings some 7km from Kazungula Junction. From here, drive south until you get to the 1st telegraph wire that crosses the road, then turn immediately left down a 1.8km sand track to the lodge. Guests without a 4x4 can arrange to be picked up at the junction.

At the entrance, a low, dark reception area, with a curio shop & internet facility, leads through to the main bar, lounge & separate restaurant, all under thatch with an open deck. But the lodge comes into its own at the front, where comfortable seating raised up on wooden decking overlooks a good-size floodlit waterhole, which regularly attracts elephant & buffalo. There's a new infinity pool here, too, set with double hanging chairs & wicker loungers. At the back, nicely appointed walk-in tents, on concrete plinths, are well spaced on a shaded grassy site, some around a 2nd pool. Each has coir matting on the floor, with twin beds under a single mosi net, a desk, kettle, safe, fan & electric points. It all feels well appointed, but unpretentious. While the location is an attraction in itself, game drives & boat cruises can be organised in Chobe NP too, a drive of about ½hr. **$$** *From US$425–445 pp Nov–Apr to US$545–570/708.50–741 pp sharing/sgl May–Oct, inc FB, local drinks, activities, park fees.* ⊕ *All year.* ★★★–★★★★★

Chobe Bush Camp [map 230] (9 chalets) Contact Water Lily Lodge, page 240; ⊕ WLBBC 17°52.770'S, 25°14.114'E. We have yet to visit this camp, just south of Senyati, but it's under the same ownership as Water Lily Lodge in Kasane, and we would expect it to share the same standards. Thatched, en-suite chalets are built on high stilts either individually and the others in a group of 4. These overlook the waterhole, as does a game-viewing hide. Excursions are operated by Water Lily's own tour company. *P838/1,350 pp sharing/sgl, inc FB & activities; exc park fees.* ★−★★

Ⓐ Senyati Safari Camp [map 230] (8 chalets, camping) m 7188 1306, 7531 5288; e senyatisafaricamp@gmail.com; www.senyatisafaricampbotswana.com; ✆ SENYAT 17°52.331'S, 25°14.167'E. Some 10km from the Engen garage at Kazungula, & well signposted from the tar road down a 1.8km sandy track (there's separate 2x4 access too), Senyati has something of a backpackers' vibe. The place is entirely self-catering, though they do sell meat,

ice & firewood, & there's a big bar (🕐 *17.00 daily*) looking down on to the camp's waterhole. Rustic chalets with AC, simple kitchens & BBQs are dotted around the site, some attractively thatched, others (more spacious) built of brick under tin roofs. These sleep 4–10 people, with bedding supplied. For the 19 private camping pitches, each with its own toilet, shower, braai & electricity point, you'll need to bring all your own kit, including tents. Don't miss the subterranean bunker positioned by the waterhole, offering some great ground-level photo opportunities of wildlife coming down to drink. There's also a small new pool at the back, free Wi-Fi in the evenings, & a laundry service available. Game drives, fishing & Victoria Falls trips can be organised, the last in Senyati's own 23-seater bus. **$$–$$$** *exc b/fast; camping P200 pp. No credit cards.* 🕐 *All year.*

SOUTH OF KASANE

Kasane is ideally situated for those driving into Botswana's national parks. The road south to Maun via Chobe and Moremi is covered in *Chobe National Park*, pages 290–1. For Kasane to Nata, read on.

KASANE TO NATA The long, straight, tarred A3 road from Kasane to Nata covers some 316km. For self-drivers it is effectively the gateway from Kasane to the Makgadikgadi Pans and the Central Kalahari Game Reserve, as well as south to Francistown and Gaborone. It's also increasingly popular with truck drivers, particularly at night, so be aware of this if you're unlucky enough to find yourself travelling after dark.

Between Kasane and Pandamatenga was until recently a minefield of pot-holes, but repairs have now been largely completed and it's once again a generally good surface. That said, aside from the occasional stopping area, the road is relatively narrow, so it's not ideal if you're looking for a picnic spot.

Though the journey is not terribly interesting scenically, the road forms a corridor between the unfenced Chobe National Park and Hwange National Park over the border in Zimbabwe. As a result, the area sees a fair amount of wildlife, especially elephants, throughout the year – which for drivers means exercising considerable caution. As with most roads in rural Africa, driving at night is asking for trouble – especially as grey elephants are well camouflaged against the grey tarmac.

At the Ngwasha veterinary checkpoint, about 64km north of Nata, you can expect stringent checks for prohibited goods, specifically any form of red meat. Staff regularly confiscate meat from self-drive vehicles, so unless you're prepared to cook it at the roadside, it's not worth taking the risk. You may also be asked to get out of your vehicle and sanitise not only the shoes you're wearing but also those in your luggage in a foot trough, so it makes sense to keep all footwear easily accessible.

🏠 **Where to stay** Places to stay along this road [off map 230] are listed on pages 253–4 from north to south. Most are geared to those stopping overnight rather than being destinations in their own right, and some have camping facilities. As

BOTSWANA DEFENCE FORCE
Tricia Hayne

Many, if not most, young boys in Botswana, when asked what they'd like to do when they grow up, will respond that they'd like to join the army. If that shows the esteem in which the Botswana Defence Force is held, it gives no indication of the short history that underpins the organisation.

In 1966, when Botswana gained independence from Britain, the country had no military presence. Money was tight, and the best that the government could muster was a paramilitary unit within the police force. At the time, this seemed all that was necessary.

However, despite Botswana's stability, the capacity of this small force was soon swamped by the knock-on effect of anti-colonial struggles along its eastern, southern and western borders. The increasingly violent conflict in Rhodesia saw both refugees and freedom fighters seeking a safe haven in Botswana, but the Rhodesian security forces were swift to follow their dissident population, and the fighting spilled indiscriminately on to Botswana's soil. At the same time, the country's western borders were threatened by similar cross-border skirmishes from South West Africa (now Namibia), then suffering under the apartheid regime of South Africa. To compound the problem, security forces in South Africa itself were crossing into Botswana in their hunt for anti-apartheid activitists. Thus, Botswana – and its citizens – were threatened on every side, and the police force was increasingly unable to cope.

It was against this background in 1977 that the Botswana Defence Force was formed. Initially a body of just 600 men, incorporating the police paramilitary unit, it fell under the command of the deputy police commissioner, with Seretse Khama Ian Khama (now Botswana's president), as his deputy.

The new force was soon to come under intense pressure. Only a few months later, on 27 February 1978, reports were received of a Rhodesian military presence just inside Botswana's northeastern border, near Kasane, apparently intent on flushing out anti-government guerrillas from Rhodesia. The BDF responded, only to drive straight into an ambush. In total, 15 members of the force were killed in the incident – the first of the BDF's soldiers to die in action. A memorial to the men who died lies on the road leading down to Lesoma Village (◈ LESOMA 17°54.528'S, 25°13.470'E).

By the end of the 1980s, Khama himself was in command of the army. Today the BDF is over 12,000 strong, with many of its officers trained in the USA. In addition to internal responsibilities, which include vital anti-poaching patrols in Botswana's national parks, the force is involved in international peacekeeping duties as part of SADC and UN forces.

---

the northern part of the road is sandwiched between Chobe and Hwange national parks, the area benefits from the wildlife that roams freely between the two. Thus, at least during the dry season, you could see a fair amount of game, including elephant, giraffe, zebra, tsessebe, sable and possibly wild dog.

For details of places to stay in Nata, see pages 484–6.

🏠 **Camp Kuzuma** (6 suites) m 7223 4449, 7586 1842; e reservations@campkuzuma.com; www.campkuzuma.com; ◈ CAMKUZ 18°20.409'S, 25°29.203'E. Founded in 2011, Camp Kuzuma looks & feels more like a lodge in the Delta. It lies in its own concession just inside the Kazuma Forest Reserve. To find it, turn left off the main road about 65km from Kazungula, on to the cutline towards the Zimbabwean border, then it's a further 3km to the camp.

The elevated main area overlooks a large waterhole frequented by elephant; there's a pool & deck at the front; & inside are a well-stocked bar, coffee machines, open-plan lounge & dining area. It's all very light, stylish & breezy. Well-spaced canvas suites, including a family suite, are accessed along elevated wooden walkways. King-size beds (or twins) form the centrepiece, with bedside tables & 2 chairs. A stone partition at the head of the bed separates the bedroom from the bathroom, with twin basins, twin indoor showers, an outdoor shower, a claw-footed Victorian bathtub – & of course a flush loo.

A spa, with a private area for massages overlooking the bush, will appeal to those looking for a little pampering, while activities include morning, evening & night game drives & guided walks. Further afield, sunset cruises & day trips to Chobe National Park & Victoria Falls can be arranged at extra cost. *US$632/948 pp sharing/sgl Mar–Apr & Nov, US$742/1,094 May–Oct, inc FB, local drinks, activities, laundry, transfers; exc spa. No children under 10.* ⊕ *Mar– Nov.* ★★★–★★★★★

🏠 **Touch of Africa Safari Lodge** (7 chalets) m 7165 6340, 7438 9191, 7346 1733; e touchofafricabotswana@gmail.com, info@ touch ofafrica.tv; www.touchofafrica.tv; ✪ TOASL 18°30.163'S, 25°36.256'E. Some 100km south of Kazungula, & 5km north of the turning to Pandamatenga, this family-run lodge to the east of the road makes a good stopover. Lawns dotted with lemon trees surround the buildings & a small pool. Comfortable en-suite thatched chalets, each painted a deep orange, are kitted out with both a dbl & a sgl bed, ceiling fan, mosquito nets, & a table & chairs on the shaded veranda. Power is supplied by generator. B/fast & dinner from an à la carte menu are served in the central dining area, which encompasses a bar & lounge. Both self-drive or guided game drives (*the latter P300 pp*) & guided walks (*P200 pp*) can be organised. **$$$** *exc b/fast (P95) & VAT.* ⊕ *All year.*

▲ **Elephant Sands** (14 chalets, camping) m 7344 5162; e bookings@ elephantsandsbotswana.com; www. elephantsands.com; ✪ ELESAN 19°44.935'S, 26°04.265'E. This simple but welcoming campsite is clearly signposted 7km south of the vet fence, or 53km north of Nata. For details, see page 486.

For details, see page 486.

UPDATES WEBSITE

You can post your comments and recommendations, and read feedback and updates from other readers online at www.bradtupdates.com/botswana.

10

Chobe National Park and Forest Reserve

Chobe National Park takes its name from the Chobe River, which forms its northern boundary, and protects about 10,700km² of the northern Kalahari. Its vegetation varies from the lush floodplains beside the Chobe River to the scorched area around the Ghoha Hills, dense forests of cathedral mopane to endless kilometres of mixed, broadleaf woodlands. And then there's the beauty of the newly flowing Savuti Marsh. This is classic big-game country, where herds of buffalo and elephant attain legendary proportions, matched only by some exceptionally large prides of lion.

Much of the park is devoid of water in the dry season, and most of it is inaccessible, so this chapter concentrates on the four main areas of Chobe that are accessible: the Chobe riverfront, Ngwezumba Pans, Savuti and the Linyanti. It also covers the Chobe Forest Reserve, a populated enclave almost surrounded by the park.

BACKGROUND INFORMATION

HISTORY The Chobe's original inhabitants were the Bushmen, followed by the Hambukushu, Bayei and Basubiya. The 1850s saw David Livingstone pass through the area, on his way to seeing the Victoria Falls, and a succession of big-game hunters seeking trophies and ivory. The area was first protected as a game reserve in 1961, and then proclaimed a national park in 1968, which was none too early.

Despite this distant trophy-hunting past, the game density in some areas of the park remains remarkable, ensuring the park's continued popularity. Simply driving a few kilometres along the Chobe riverfront in the dry season is demonstration enough, as you'll be forced to halt frequently to allow game to wander slowly across the road, or to watch herds coming down to drink from the river.

However, perhaps more than any of Botswana's parks, Chobe has felt the impact of tourism. In the 1980s, park fees were low and the few basic campsites were full. Rubbish became a problem, solitary game viewing was almost impossible and the animals became habituated to people. While Chobe has never been busy by East African standards, its three or four basic public campsites and simple network of game-viewing roads couldn't cope with so many visitors.

Fortunately, around 1987, the government started to implement a policy of 'high-cost, low-density' tourism. Park fees went up and the numbers of visitors dropped. The situation has now changed. With regular increases in these park fees the flood of visitors through the park has turned into more of a moderate flow. Once again, most of the park feels like a wilderness area. Even the 'honey pot' of the northern Chobe riverfront area isn't quite as busy, though the proximity of Kasane's lodges and campsites ensures that it's never going to be that quiet either.

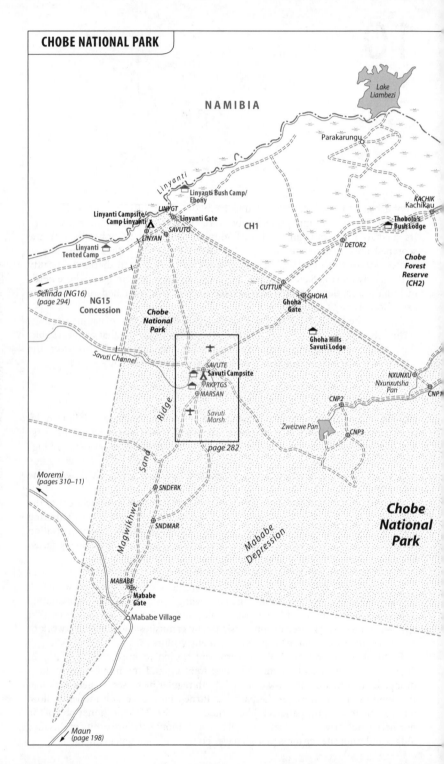

CHOBE NATIONAL PARK

NAMIBIA

Lake Liambezi

Parakarungu

Linyanti

Linyanti Bush Camp/
Ebony

LINYGT

Linyanti Campsite/
Camp Linyanti

Linyanti Gate

SAVUTO

LINYAN

CH1

KACHIK
Kachikau

Thobolo's
Bush Lodge

DETOR2

Linyanti
Tented Camp

*Chobe
Forest
Reserve
(CH2)*

*Selinda (NG16)
(page 294)*

NG15
Concession

*Chobe
National
Park*

CUTTUR

GHOHA

Ghoha
Gate

Savuti Channel

Ghoha Hills
Savuti Lodge

SAVUTE
Savuti Campsite

RKPTGS

MARSAN

*Savuti
Marsh*

NXUNXU
*Nxunxutsha
Pan*

CNP1

CNP2

Zweizwe Pan

CNP3

page 282

*Moremi
(pages 310–11)*

SNDFRK

*Chobe
National
Park*

SNDMAR

*Mababe
Depression*

MABABE

Mababe
Gate

Mababe Village

*Maun
(page 198)*

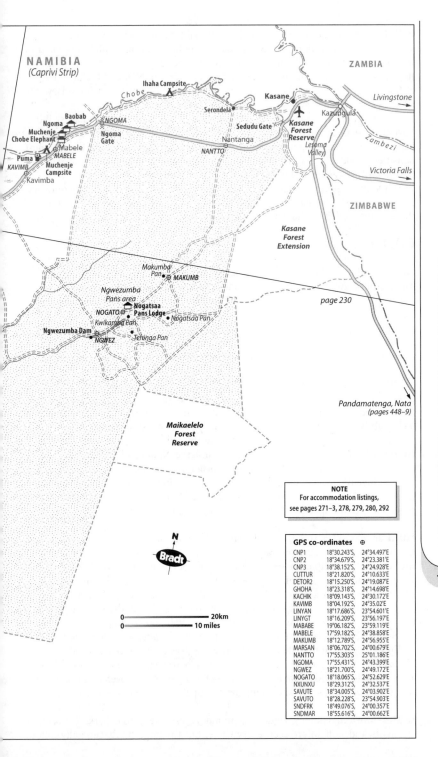

NAMIBIA
(Caprivi Strip)

ZAMBIA

Chobe

Ihaha Campsite

Kasane

Livingstone

Serondela

Baobab

NGOMA

Ngoma

Chobe Elephant

Sedudu Gate

Kazungula

Zambezi

Muchenje

Ngoma
Gate

Nantanga

Kasane
Forest
Reserve

Mabele

MABELE

NANTTO

Lesoma
Valley

Victoria Falls

Puma

KAVIMB

Muchenje
Campsite

Kavimba

ZIMBABWE

Kasane
Forest
Extension

Makumba
Pan

MAKUMB

Ngwezumba
Pans area

NOGATO

Nogatsaa
Pans Lodge

Nogatsaa Pan

page 230

Kwikamba Pan

Ngwezumba Dam

NGWEZ

Tchinga Pan

Pandamatenga, Nata
(pages 448–9)

Maikaelelo
Forest
Reserve

N

Bradt

NOTE
For accommodation listings,
see pages 271–3, 278, 279, 280, 292

GPS co-ordinates	⊕	
CNP1	18°30.243'S,	24°34.497'E
CNP2	18°34.679'S,	24°23.381'E
CNP3	18°38.152'S,	24°24.928'E
CUTTUR	18°21.820'S,	24°10.633'E
DETOR2	18°15.250'S,	24°19.087'E
GHOHA	18°23.318'S,	24°14.698'E
KACHIK	18°09.143'S,	24°30.172'E
KAVIMB	18°04.192'S,	24°35.02'E
LINYAN	18°17.686'S,	23°54.601'E
LINYGT	18°16.209'S,	23°56.197'E
MABABE	19°06.182'S,	23°59.119'E
MABELE	17°59.182'S,	24°38.858'E
MAKUMB	18°12.789'S,	24°56.955'E
MARSAN	18°06.702'S,	24°00.679'E
NANTTO	17°55.303'S,	25°01.186'E
NGOMA	17°55.431'S,	24°43.399'E
NGWEZ	18°21.700'S,	24°49.172'E
NOGATO	18°18.065'S,	24°52.629'E
NXUNXU	18°29.312'S,	24°32.537'E
SAVUTE	18°34.005'S,	24°03.902'E
SAVUTO	18°28.228'S,	23°54.903'E
SNDFRK	18°49.076'S,	24°00.357'E
SNDMAR	18°55.616'S,	24°00.662'E

0 ———— 20km
0 ———— 10 miles

Chobe National Park and Forest Reserve   BACKGROUND INFORMATION

10

257

GEOGRAPHY The geography of Chobe National Park and adjacent Forest Reserve, and indeed most of northern Botswana, is one based on an undulating plain of Kalahari sand that slopes very slightly from the northwest down to the southeast. Its altitude varies from about 950m at Linyanti, to around 930m at Ihaha and 942m at Savuti. In many ways its most defining feature is its northwest boundary: the Chobe–Linyanti river system.

On the ground, Chobe's geographical features are subtle rather than striking. Various vegetated sand dunes and sand ridges occur, including the large Magwikhwe Sand Ridge. Natural pans are dotted throughout the park, reaching their highest densities around the Nogatsaa and Tchinga areas, and also the Zweizwe area east of Savuti. Only occasional rounded hills break the Kalahari's flatness.

While the region is bounded by great rivers, within this area there are only dry, or at least very seasonal, watercourses. The Savuti Channel is the most famous of these – and until 2009 that hadn't flowed since 1982.

GEOLOGY See pages 3–11 for a comprehensive overview of Botswana's geological past. Here it's enough to note that by around three million years ago the Kalahari's longitudinal dunes had formed, channelling rivers south and east into the Limpopo. Then, around two million years ago, a tectonic shift blocked this drainage, leaving the rivers feeding a superlake in the heart of Botswana – Lake Makgadikgadi. Geologists think that the level of this fluctuated in time, but that it reached as far as the Savuti area. Compelling evidence for this are the great sand ridges in the area and the presence of smooth, wave-washed pebbles and boulders – for example those found on the southern side of the Ghoha Hills.

FLORA AND FAUNA Trying to describe Chobe as a whole without any comment or subdivisions would be very misleading. Unlike some of Africa's national parks, Chobe is best considered as a handful of totally different areas, each with a different feel, slightly different vegetation and distinct populations of animals.

Later in this chapter, I'll treat separately the wildlife highlights of the **Chobe riverfront**; the variation to be found around the **Ngwezumba Pans**; the unique situation around **Savuti**; and the isolated corner of the park that reaches northwest to the **Linyanti**. In passing, I'll also mention the circumstances of the populated Chobe Forest Reserve enclave. Meanwhile, here I'll try to give a brief overview, and cover some of the species which are found throughout the park.

Flora In general, across the whole park you'll find many similarities. Near any of the permanent rivers the vegetation is varied, with a large number of tree and bush species. It's classic riparian forest – as occurs throughout southern Africa.

Away from water, Chobe has fairly thick and sometimes thorny bush with relatively few open areas. Much of this is Kalahari sandveld, often with a high proportion of acacias and species that love deep sand, like the silver terminalia (*Terminalia sericea*). Some of Chobe, especially in the south, is covered with mopane woodland, containing almost exclusively *Colophospermum mopane*.

The main exceptions to this are a few areas of (geologically) recent alluvial deposits, like Savuti Marsh, which look totally different. Here you'll find the skeletons of various acacias and leadwoods (*Combretum imberbe*) on open plains covered in couch grass (*Cynodon dactylon*) – the latter being the principal attraction to the area for zebra.

Fauna Most of Chobe's wildlife is found across the whole park. Occasional elephants and buffalo are seen everywhere, but the large herds generally follow a highly seasonal pattern of migrations. These are principally dictated by the availability of water.

As the dry season progresses, all the small clay pans in the bush (and particularly the mopane woodlands) dry up. Then the elephants and buffalo start to form larger herds and migrate to the permanent waters of the Chobe and Linyanti rivers. These gather in their thousands by the rivers, having come from as far away as Zimbabwe's Hwange National Park. Then, as soon as it rains and the small pans in the bush start to fill with rainwater, the animals move away again and disperse.

Many of the park's animals will follow a smaller-scale, less noticeable version of this type of seasonal migration to the water, and this is what makes the game viewing in Chobe so remarkable towards the middle and end of the dry season.

At any time of year, Chobe's big game includes blue wildebeest, Burchell's zebra, impala, kudu, tssesebe, giraffe, impala, common duiker, steenbok, warthog, baboon and vervet monkey throughout the park. Eland, sable and roan antelope also range across the park, but are relatively scarce, just as they are elsewhere in southern Africa.

Lion and spotted hyena are very common, and are generally the dominant predators, while leopard, cheetah and wild dog all occur, though are seen much less frequently. Both side-striped and black-backed jackal are present – though the former are found more in the north of the park, and the latter in the south. Brown hyena probably occur, though rarely, in the drier parts of the south, though they don't seem to co-exist happily with a high density of lion or spotted hyena.

Cape and bat-eared fox are found here, though again the Cape fox prefers the drier south. I once had a particularly good sighting of a whole family of bat-eared foxes in the middle of the open plains on Savuti Marsh, early in the morning on a cold September day. There are a variety of mongooses found here; the most often seen of these are probably the banded and dwarf species, both of which are social, and very entertaining to watch.

Serval, caracal, aardwolf and aardvark are found all over the park, though are only occasionally seen due to their largely nocturnal habits. Pangolin are found here too, though they're very rarely seen.

If you have the chance to take any night drives in areas adjoining the park (no night drives are allowed inside the park), then you've a good chance to spot scrub hares, spring hares, lesser bushbabies, porcupines, genets (small-spotted and large-spotted), civets, African wildcats and honey badgers.

AN UNEASY ALLIANCE

Co-operative relationships between mammals and birds are unusual, but the honey badger enjoys two. Its association with the greater honeyguide is well known. This small bird uses a distinctive song to lure the honey badger to a bees' nest, whereupon it feasts on the grubs after the badger has ransacked the nest and had its fill of honey.

Less well known is the honey badger's association with the pale chanting goshawk. This relationship is of no benefit to the badger, since the goshawk – or sometimes a pair of them – simply follows the bigger predator around as it digs and forages for prey, and pounces on any rodent or reptile that slips past. The badger may have the last laugh though, since goshawk eggs and nestlings are among its 59 different prey species that have been recorded in the Kalahari.

Though white and black rhino would occur here naturally, as they should throughout northern Botswana, it's likely that by the early 1990s they had all been wiped out through poaching. There were then occasional reports of individual sightings – but a viable breeding population had been destroyed. The return of rhino to Botswana was initiated in 2001, when a number of white rhino were reintroduced into the Moremi Game Reserve, and more have been added in the intervening years. Although numbers remain small, they are increasing, and are gradually spreading out – with wandering rhinos now occasionally turning up in Chobe and even Magkadikgadi. Black rhino, too, have been reintroduced, though they are very rarely seen.

Birdlife More than 450 species of birds have been seen in Chobe – too many to even try to list here. Therefore I'll cover the birding highlights in the separate sections concerning the specific areas within the park. Note that the summer migrants generally arrive around October and leave again in March.

WHEN TO VISIT Noting the general comments made on pages 113–120, you'll generally find a wider variety of bird species here in the wet season, many of which will be in their breeding plumage.

The movement of the animals is rather more complex. Most of Chobe's larger herbivores migrate with the seasons, to find water to drink and pastures new. These movements are, to a large extent, predictable, so bear them in mind as you plan your trip to maximise your chances of good game viewing.

Like most of Africa's game migrations, the principle behind this one is simple. The animals stay close to the permanent sources of water during the driest months, then they disperse into the forests and (especially) the open grasslands at the start of the rains to take advantage of the fresh grazing and browsing. In northern Botswana, this means that game becomes more and more prolific near the permanent watercourses – the Chobe, the Linyanti, and the edges of the Okavango – as the dry season wears on. Then as soon as the rains come, many animals head south and east into the interior's forests and plains (especially the Makgadikgadi area and Nxai Pan). This gives the vegetation beside the rivers a little time to recover, so that when the dry season returns the animals will again find some grazing near the water.

The finer details of this are more complex, and slightly different for each species. Zebra, for example, have been the focus of a research project which tracked them using radio transmitters and a microlight aircraft, based in Savuti. This study suggested that they spend the rainy summer, from November to about February, in the Mababe Depression – venturing south to Nxai Pan, and then following the Boteti River down to around Tsoe, before heading across to the Gweta area and back north to Nxai Pan.

In March and April they pass through Savuti for a few months, where they foal. This makes a particularly good foaling ground as rich alluvial deposits from the old Savuti Channel have left the area with mineral-rich soil supporting particularly nutritious grasses. A few months later, as dryness begins to bite around July, they move again towards the Linyanti for the dry season. Finally in late October and November, they return to the Mababe area as the rains begin and the grasses start to sprout.

Similarly, Sommerlatte (see *Appendix 3*, page 541) studied elephant movements in the park in the mid 1970s. Though clearly movements have changed since then, he found that the highest wet-season concentrations were around the Ghoha Hills, the eastern side of the Mababe Depression, and the mouth of the Ngwezumba River (the Nogatsaa/Tchinga pans area).

For the visitor, this means that the game in the dry season is best in the river areas. In the wet season, and just afterwards, the interior pans are definitely worth a visit. Savuti is unusual in that, remarkably, it has good game all year, but is especially interesting around April/May and November.

GETTING ORGANISED

As with most of Botswana's wilder areas, there are basically three ways to visit Chobe: on a fly-in trip, staying at the lodges and camps; on a mobile-safari trip, organised by a local safari operator; and on a self-drive trip with all your own equipment and food.

Only self-drive visitors really need to do much of their own planning, and they should take everything they'll need to live on (including supplies of water) between Maun and Kasane. Chobe is often combined with Moremi on such a trip – which, taken at a relaxed pace, typically takes about ten days. You should stock up on food, fuel and supplies before you leave. There are a few small local shops in the villages of the Chobe Forest Reserve, but otherwise there's nothing available on the whole route, and certainly no fuel.

Although it's only about 300km between Maun and Kasane across Chobe, a lot of the driving is in second gear and permanent 4x4, so prepare for fuel consumption that's perhaps two or three times your normal tar-road consumption. In addition to long-range fuel tanks, it's wise to carry at least one if not two additional jerrycans of fuel.

The park entrance gates are open 06.00–18.30 from April to September, and 05.30–19.00 from October to March. Park rules prohibit cars on the roads between sunset and sunrise, and it would be extremely foolish to attempt to drive after dark anyway, so be careful to plan your journey to give plenty of time. The speed limit in the park is 40km/h, though you'll be very unlikely ever to get near this on the deep sand tracks which are the park's roads.

ORIENTATION Though the maps make Chobe National Park look complex, it's really very simple. In the northeast corner is Kasane, and in the southwest corner the road leaves for Maun and Moremi. Most visitors drive in on one side, and exit the other – and in the middle all roads lead to Savuti. There are concessions and camps around the national park, particularly along the Linyanti River, but in terms of orientation, work on this basis!

North of Savuti there's a 'direct' road that links it to Kasane via the Chobe Forest Reserve and the Chobe riverfront area. Then there's an indirect route that travels to Kasane via the Nogatsaa Pans area in the forested heart of the park. Most visitors choose one of these routes; see pages 273–8 for a discussion of their relative merits in various seasons. In all the above I use the word 'road' loosely – to mean two adjacent tyre tracks in the sand. You need a high-clearance 4x4 for a trip to Chobe, and lots of time.

Maps There is really only one map of Chobe that is worthwhile for normal navigation and that's the Shell map of Chobe National Park, by Veronica Roodt. The main map itself is fairly small, but it has a good inset of the game-viewing tracks of the Chobe riverfront area, and also aerial photograph backdrops for first-rate insets of the area around Savuti and Nogatsaa. Veronica's map of Savuti is especially good for navigation!

BOOKING AND PARK FEES If you're flying into organised camps, then your park fees will probably already be included in the price of your safari. If you're driving into Chobe, you'll need to have booked all your campsites in advance. You'll then need to present confirmation of your campsite bookings at the park gates before you can purchase your permit to enter. See pages 131–3 for details of how this works, and a scale of the fees.

CHOBE RIVERFRONT

Perhaps the park's greatest attraction is its northern boundary, the Chobe River. In the dry season animals converge on this stretch of water from the whole of northern Botswana. Elephant and buffalo, especially, form into huge herds for which the park is famous. In November 1853, David Livingstone passed through the area and described the river:

> though the river is from thirteen to fifteen feet in depth at its lowest ebb, and broad enough to allow a steamer to ply upon it, the suddenness of the bending would prevent navigation; but should the country ever become civilised, the Chobe would be a convenient natural canal.

Fortunately that kind of civilisation hasn't reached the Chobe yet – there are no canal boats to be seen – and today's traveller must make do with 4x4s or the small motorboats that weave along the river, among channels still ruled by hippos.

FLORA AND FAUNA HIGHLIGHTS The Chobe River meanders through occasional low, flat islands and floating mats of papyrus and reeds. These islands, and beside the river, are always lush and green – and hence attract high densities of game. Beside this the bleached-white riverbank rises up just a few metres, and instantly becomes dry and dusty. Standing on top of this are skeletons of dead trees, sometimes draped by a covering of woolly caper-bushes.

In several areas this bank has been eroded away, perhaps originally where small seasonal streams have joined the main river or hippo tracks out of the water have become widened by general animal use to access the floodplains. Here there are often mineral licks, and you'll see herds of animals in the dry season coming down to eat the soil as well as drink from the river.

Flora On the bank beside the river the vegetation contains many of the usual plants found in riparian forest in the subcontinent. Yet despite this it has a very distinctive appearance, different from that of any other African river – and this difference is perhaps largely due to the sheer volumes of game, and especially elephants, that visit it during the dry season.

The main tree species found in this riverine forest include Natal mahogany (*Trichilia emetica*) – which isn't found in the rest of Botswana – plus Rhodesian teak (*Baikiaea plurijuga*), large feverberry (*Croton megalobotryus*), umbrella thorn (*Vachellia tortilis*), knobthorn (*Senegalia nigrescens*), raintree (*Philenoptera violacea*), African mangosteen (*Garcinia livingstonei*), bird plum (*Berchemia discolor*), jackalberry (*Diospyros mespiliformis*) and the odd sausage tree (*Kigelia africana*).

Because of the intense pressure from elephants, you'll often see the still-standing remains of dead trees which have been ring-barked by elephants, with the termite-resistant skeletons, probably leadwoods (*Combretum imberbe*), being particularly noticeable.

These riverside forests can seem quite denuded towards the end of the dry season, which many naturally blame on heavy grazing by the game. Clearly this has

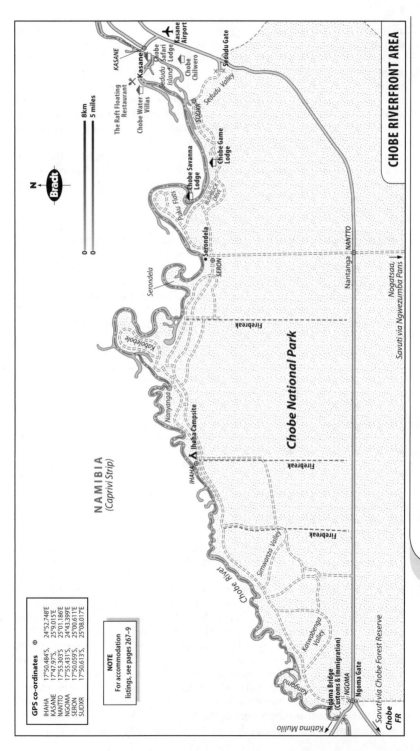

GPS co-ordinates ⊕

IHAHA	17°50.484'S,	24°52.748'E
KASANE	17°47.97'S,	25°9.015'E
NANTTO	17°55.303'S	25°01.186'E
NGOMA	17°55.431'S,	24°43.399'E
SERON	17°50.059'S,	25°00.611'E
SUDXR	17°50.613'S,	25°08.017'E

NOTE
For accommodation
listings, see pages 267–9

NAMIBIA
(Caprivi Strip)

N

Bradt

0 ——————— 8km
0 ——————— 5 miles

The Raft Floating
Restaurant ✕
Chobe Water
Villas ▢
⊕ SUDXR

KASANE
✕ **Kasane** 🛩 Kasane Airport
Sedudu ▢ Chobe Safari Lodge
Island 🏨
Chobe 🏛
Chilwero
⊕ Sedudu Gate
Sedudu Valley

Chobe Savanna Lodge ▢
Chobe Game Lodge 🏨

Puku Flats

BUSHBUCK DRIVE

Serondela ●
⊕ SERON

Serondela

Kabbulebole

Nanyanga

Firebreak — — — — Firebreak

Ihaha Campsite ⛺
⊕ IHAHA

Firebreak — — — —

Simwanza Valley

Chobe River

Kaswabenga
Valley

Kangoma
Valley

Ngoma Bridge
(Customs & Immigration)
⊕ NGOMA
✕ Ngoma Gate

Katima Mulilo ←

Chobe
FR

← Savuti via Chobe Forest Reserve

Chobe National Park

Nantanga **NANTTO**
⊕

Nogatsaa; ↓
Savuti via Ngwezumba Pans ↓

CHOBE RIVERFRONT AREA

10

263

an impact here, but commercial logging took place along this riverside before and during World War II and also took its toll of some of the larger trees.

Despite this, several different types of bushes thrive here. Buffalo thorn (*Ziziphus mucronata*) and knobbly combretum (*Combretum mossambicense*) are common, though Chobe's most distinctive bush must be the remarkably successful woolly caper-bush (*Capparis tomentosa*). This sometimes grows into a dense, tangled shrub, but equally often you'll find it as a creeper which forms an untidy mantle covering an old termite mound. Sometimes you'll even find it covering the crown of dead trees, or draped continuously over a series of bushes.

If you're out game viewing with a local guide, then ask him or her if they know of any local medicinal uses for the woolly caper-bush. The plant has very strong antiseptic qualities, and both Palgrave and Roodt (see *Appendix 3*, pages 542–3) report that this is one of the trees most widely used in Africa for its magico-medicinal properties.

Fauna The game densities along the Chobe riverfront vary greatly with the seasons, but towards the end of the dry season it is certainly one of Africa's most prolific areas for game. It is an ideal destination for visitors seeking big game. Elsewhere in the dry season you'll find fascination in termites or ground squirrels, but here you can find huge herds of buffalo, relaxed prides of lion, and perhaps Africa's highest concentration of elephant – huge herds which are the hallmark of the area.

One of the main attractions of the boat trips on the Chobe is that large family groups of elephants will troop down to the river to drink and bathe, affording spectacular viewing and photography. You'll find these here at any time of day, but they're especially common in the late afternoon, just before sunset.

When it's very dry you'll also find elephants swimming across the river at night to raid the relatively verdant crops and farms on the Namibian side, often coming back to Botswana during the day when the villagers feel more confident to emerge and scare them.

If you are not floating but driving, then be careful. Read my specific comments on driving near elephants, pages 274 and 276–7, and err on the side of caution. Most of Chobe's elephants are in family groups containing mothers with calves. They can be sensitive to any perceived threat, so keep a respectful distance from them. This can be especially difficult when you see licensed guides driving closer, but you should still keep your distance. Their experience, and general coolness in case of elephant aggression, will allow them to do relatively safely what would be dangerous for you to attempt.

If you find your car surrounded by elephants, then try to relax. Virtually all of Chobe's elephants have seen lots of vehicles before, and so are unlikely to get too upset. Don't panic or rev your engine; just sit quiet and still until the animals have passed. Ideally switch off your engine – but this is not for the faint-hearted.

The riverfront itself offers the best chance in Chobe to see hippos, crocodiles and the odd sunbathing leguvaan (water monitor). While there, also look out for the delightful Cape clawless and spotted-necked otters, which make their homes in the riverbank.

Perhaps the riverfront's most talked-about antelope is the Chobe bushbuck. This is a localised race, or perhaps a subspecies, of the bushbuck (*Tragelaphus scriptus*) which has wide distribution within sub-Saharan Africa, from the edge of rainforests to the edges of the Kalahari and throughout the eastern side of southern Africa. Their coloration exhibits a lot of regional variation, and there is certainly a distinctive race that occurs only in this Chobe riverfront area – with brighter coloration and clearer markings than are found in the rest of southern Africa.

Bushbuck are small, attractive antelope which usually occur singly or in pairs. Only the males have horns, which are short and spiralled. They are well camouflaged, with a red-brown coloration, like the soil, and a covering of white spots that blend into the shadows of the riverside's thick vegetation. They will freeze if disturbed, and there are reliable reports of lions and hyena passing within 10m of a plainly visible bushbuck and not noticing it. Only if disturbed will they bolt for cover as a last resort.

Another antelope often noted here is the puku (*Kobus vardonii*) – which some sources claim is rarely seen. This is true, but only if you've never been to Zambia, where puku are arguably the most common antelope. South of the Chobe they probably occur only in this Chobe riverfront area, and especially around the aptly named 'Puku Flats' peninsula of the floodplain.

The red lechwe (*Kobus leche*) is another water-loving antelope that is resident here, and is easily confused with the puku at first glance. Look closely and you'll see that the lechwe's underparts are much lighter, their coats seem less shaggy, and the males' horns larger. Also notice that when they run, lechwe tend to hold their heads close to the ground, while puku normally run with their heads held much higher. This makes identifying them from a distance easier – and soon you'll realise that red lechwe are usually the most common antelope on Chobe's floodplains.

Waterbuck and reedbuck are also usually found in wetter areas, and so are seen around Chobe riverfront and Linyanti but not elsewhere in Chobe. Roan are also found here, but are fairly scarce, as befits an antelope that is sought after by private game areas and is expensive to buy. Finally, the beautiful sable antelope are common nowhere, but I've seen large and relaxed herds here on several occasions. Being specialist grazers, they are more commonly found in the wooded south of the riverfront, though as sable and roan usually drink during the middle of the day, you will quite often see a small herd near the riverfront road, between Ngoma and Kasane.

Birdlife From a boat on the main river in the park you're likely to spot numerous beautiful kingfishers (pied, giant, some malachite and the occasional half-collared), with the pied seeming to be particularly numerous, perching on reeds by the river, or hovering to hold their eyes static above the river's surface. You'll also see plenty of reed cormorants and darters, various bee-eaters, hamerkops, wire-tailed swallows, a high density of fish eagles and even African skimmers (November–March only; the best place to see them is probably near Hippo Pools, beside Watercart Drive).

The fringes of the islands and floodplain are particularly good for birding, being home to many storks, herons, geese, egrets and a wide variety of lapwings (blacksmith, long-toed, crowned, wattled and, of special interest, white-crowned). Particularly unusual and worth seeking are rufous-bellied and white-backed night herons, slaty egrets, brown firefinches and wattled cranes. On the Puku Flats, look out for rosy-throated longclaw, black coucal and coppery sunbirds.

For a totally distinct environment attracting several different species, head downstream and out of the park, to the shallow rapids dotted with rocks, which are adjacent to Impalila Island on the Chobe and Zambezi rivers. (The Chobe's are the Kasane Rapids, while those on the Zambezi are known as the Mambova Rapids.) In the dense waterside vegetation before the rapids look out for the shy finfoot, while around the rapids themselves there's a thriving population of rock pratincoles.

If you have the chance to explore the Kasai Channel (which connects the Zambezi and Chobe rivers), then do so. Technically you'll need to cross into Namibia, so this trip is probably easiest to undertake from one of the lodges on Impalila Island (pages 249–50). Here you'll find small lagoons beside the main channel covered in waterlilies, and bird species that include the uncommon lesser and purple gallinules, lesser jacanas and moorhens, pygmy geese and African rails. On the edge of these, in the adjacent reeds and papyrus beds you'll probably hear (if not see) chirping cisticolas, greater swamp warblers and swamp boubous.

Back inside the park, in the band of forest back from the river, you'll find many drier-country species, including coucals (Senegal and coppery-tailed), oxpeckers, sunbirds (you can find coppery sunbirds here, too), rollers (look out for the racket-tailed), hornbills, flycatchers, weavers, shrikes, spurfowl and francolins. Large flocks of helmeted guineafowl seem particularly visible, and are especially fond of loitering along the tracks in front of vehicles. Or so it seems! Even the main tar road throws up interesting sightings; look out for ground hornbills and red-crested korhaans.

There's a tremendously wide range of raptors here, from the ubiquitous fish eagles perching on dead trees overlooking the river, through to the huge martial eagles patrolling the drier woodlands. Other resident eagles include the uncommon western banded snake eagle, black-breasted and brown snake eagles, bateleur (also known as short-tailed eagle), tawny, long-crested, Ayres' and African hawk eagle. These are joined in the summer by migrant eagles, including steppe and Wahlberg's eagles, and all year by many species of falcons, goshawks, harriers, kites and even the rarely seen bat hawk. The area has good numbers of white-backed vultures, often seen around a kill, but the vulnerable lappet-faced, white-headed and hooded vultures are also present.

ORIENTATION The southern bank of the Chobe River is slightly raised above the river, perhaps 3–4m high. Below this is a fairly level floodplain of short green grass and reeds, through which the river follows a very meandering course, roughly west to east, with many switchbacks, loops and adjacent old lagoons.

High on the bank is the main riverfront track, which is wide but for the most part sandy. This leads from Kasane to the Ngoma Gate fairly directly. Looping off from this are game-viewing tracks. Most of those on the north side drop down to the floodplains, and then loop around by the river. Those few heading off south usually follow straight firebreaks into the dry woodlands that make up the bulk of Chobe behind the thin band of riparian forest.

You can't get lost, provided that you don't cross to the south of the main road. Head east and you'll reach Kasane; west and you'll find Ngoma.

The game densities are generally at their best between Kasane and Ihaha, although the density of vehicles is also high here. When you head west past Ihaha, towards Ngoma, you'll find an increasing number of Namibians herding cattle on the floodplain areas across the Chobe River. Game densities in the forest reserve are significantly lower than those in the park, but you do have better chances of spotting some less common species like sable and roan antelope.

For details of the roads between Kasane and Savuti, see pages 273–8.

Ngoma border post (⊕ 06.00–18.00) At the westernmost point of the Chobe riverfront is the Ngoma Gate (⊕ NGOMA 17°55.719'S, 24°43.665'E), which marks the boundary between Chobe National Park and Chobe Forest Reserve. Turning northwest towards the river at this point brings you to the border post at Ngoma, where on the Botswana side is a mid 1990s building perched high above the river by a venerable old baobab, complete with picnic benches. On the other side of the river, Namibia has a more imposing office next to the tarred bridge, about 2km further on. Both are efficient, pleasant and generally quiet. As with many borders, don't be alarmed if you see the odd soldier wandering around with a gun, and don't even think about taking any pictures near the bridge without permission.

From the border, it's signposted 57km to Kasane, 65km to Kazungula, 115km to Savuti and 362km to Nata. Over in Namibia, the conversion of the 69km stretch of gravel road between the Ngoma border and Katima Mulilo has now been completed, meaning that you can now drive from Kasane into Namibia and right across the Caprivi Strip on a good tar road.

WHERE TO STAY Many people visit the Chobe riverfront while staying in or around Kasane (pages 236–41 and 249–50), or possibly from a base at Ngoma (pages 271–3). Generally the options inside Botswana's parks are more expensive, but they have better locations. Within northern Chobe, there are only two permanent choices: the basic public campsite at Ihaha or the stylish Chobe Game Lodge. There is also a semi-mobile operation, Chobe Under Canvas, while the river itself hosts several safari boats, including the *Zambezi Queen* and the three *Chobe Princesses*. On the opposite side – technically in Namibia – there is another lodge, which I've included here as it is directly opposite Chobe, and is primarily used to visit the park (though you need to clear customs in each direction; ⊕ 07.30–16.30). All these options must be pre-booked; you cannot just turn up, even at the campsite. For other lodges on the Namibian side of the river, but closer to Kasane, see pages 249–52.

Chobe Game Lodge [map 263] (40 rooms, 4 suites) Contact Desert & Delta Safaris, pages 223–4; lodge ✆ 625 0340; www.chobegamelodge. com; ✪ CHOBGL 17°50.850'S, 25°05.083'E. Opened in 1972, about 9km from the park's Sedudu Gate, this is the largest lodge in any of Botswana's national parks. Occupying a sloping site above the river, it seems in some ways like just another luxury hotel, yet its design is unusual, with tribal antiques in slightly exotic surroundings, which blend together very well.

Each of the comfortable rooms is set slightly into the bank with a barrel-vaulted ceiling & french windows on to a balcony or small veranda overlooking the river, about 60m away. The style is cool yet colonial: cream-screed floors are dotted with Persian-style rugs, the furniture is solid Rhodesian teak with comfortable chairs, & *punkah-punkah* ceiling fans (as well as AC) combine with Indian marquetry to add a touch of the orient. Smart en-suite bathrooms, fully replaced in 2014–17, now have a bath, separate rain shower & twin basins beneath Indian-framed mirrors. Large suites come equally well furnished but with a 2nd bedroom, & the honeymoon suite boasts a small, private infinity pool. When Elizabeth Taylor & Richard Burton chose this as a romantic place in which to be remarried & spend their honeymoon in 1975, it was something of a PR coup!

An extensive wide riverside walkway, entirely accessible by wheelchair, makes it possible to take a stroll, then enjoy a drink or a meal at one of several intimate seating areas along the way, with one eye on the plains below. The food is good, with a buffet for b/fast & lunch, & a more leisurely à la carte dinner served by candlelight. In the main building, a rather womblike bar downstairs contrasts with the more masculine upstairs bar, complete with full-size billiard table & a terrace overlooking the river. A library with TV & computers (there's free Wi-Fi throughout), an attractive pool, a gym (fortunately with AC), a small treatment room, & a big, colourful curio shop add to the facilities.

Activities, led by an all-female guiding team, comprise morning & evening game drives, mid-morning boat cruises, & a sunset cruise on arrival. These are taken in newly acquired vehicles & boats that are largely electric powered, lowering the impact of activities on the environment. Guests may also tour behind the scenes & discover other ways in which the lodge gained its high-level eco-credentials; it's fascinating! *Std room from US$560 pp Jan–Mar & Dec to US$995/1,293 pp sharing/sgl Jul–Oct, inc FB, local drinks, laundry, activities, park fees; exc spa, premium drinks.* ⊕ *All year.*
★★★–★★★★★

✳ **Chobe Under Canvas** (5 tents) Contact &Beyond, page 223. Like its sibling Savute Under Canvas (page 288), this is effectively a mobile camp that moves every 5 days between private campsites along the Chobe riverfront (although never with guests on site). Guests are collected from Kasane Airport, with a 1hr transfer to the camp. No self-drivers are allowed into camp, so those with their own vehicle should leave it in Kasane & transfer from there. Accommodation is in en-suite twin or dbl tents, with battery-powered lamps, an open-air bucket shower (hot water on request) & a separate flushing toilet. A communal tent offers shelter for drinks, dining or just relaxing with a book. With game drives in the morning & afternoon, & boat cruises along the river, there's plenty to keep guests occupied until a traditional bush dinner, served under the stars. *From US$560 pp sharing Feb–Mar to US$895 Jul–Oct, inc FB, most drinks, activities, laundry. No children under 12.* ☺ *Feb–Dec.* ★★★–★★★★★

🏠 **Chobe Savanna Lodge** [map 263] (13 chalets) Contact Desert & Delta Safaris, pages 223–4; ✪ CHOBSL 17°49.838'S, 25°03.198'E. The smaller sister lodge of Chobe Game Lodge was refurbished in 2017, but remains tastefully traditional in style. It stands in the private Kasika concession on the Namibian side of the river, facing west over the Puku Flats, with superb views across a quiet stretch of the river & its floodplains. The main 2-storey thatch-&-timber building houses a lounge, library & dining room, while outside are a plunge pool, a wooden sundeck & an open boma for evening fires – with a new dining shelter under construction in 2017. En-suite brick-&-thatch suites have AC, overhead fans, minibars & tea/coffee-making facilities, plus fully tiled bathroooms with separate showers & baths, & small balconies that take in the view.

Activities major on game viewing & fishing by motorboat, as well as sunset cruises. There are also nature walks along the river & trips to one of the local villages. *US$428 pp Jan–Jun & Nov/ Dec, US$645/839 sharing/sgl Jul–Oct, inc FB, local drinks, laundry, activities, park fees.* ☺ *All year.* ★★★

🏕 **Ihaha Campsite** [map 263] (10 pitches) Contact Kwalate Safaris, page 132; ✪ IHAHA 17°50.484'S, 24°52.748'E. About 35km west of the Sedudu Gate, Ihaha is the only campsite for private visitors within northern Chobe. If you're taking the riverfront road from Kasane you'll come to a signpost close to 3 sharp turns in the road, which effectively form a square around the gate. For all the imposing entrance, Ihaha has changed little under privatisation. Large pitches run parallel to the river, some with almost unlimited views across to the Namibian plains, though not

all have good tree shade. It's not terribly pretty, but the ground is firm & sandy underfoot, & it's a great spot to while away the hours watching the abundance of waterbirds by the river, or herds of impala & zebra grazing among the cattle on the other side. 2 modern ablution blocks, with hot water courtesy of solar panels, are reasonably clean, & each pitch comes with a water supply & BBQ – of sorts. *US$40 pp, exc park fees, bed levy.* ☺ *All year.*

Safari boats
Several safari boats cruise on the Zambezi & Chobe rivers, as well as into the contiguous wetlands of Namibia's Caprivi Strip. As Namibian-registered vessels, they are permitted to cruise the waters of the Chobe when the national park is closed & all Botswana-registered vessels must leave, so offer a unique opportunity to watch game & experience the tranquillity of the river after dark & at sunrise.

🚤 **Zambezi Queen** (14 suites) ☏ +27 21 715 2412; e enquiry@zqcollection.com; www. zqcollection.com. The *grande dame* of Chobe's riverboats, the 42m *Zambezi Queen* moves slowly between 2 mooring points on the Chobe River over 2 or 3 nights – with cruises departing from Kasane on Mon, Wed & Fri. Up on deck there's a pool & various areas for relaxing in the shade or soaking up the sun, & at night a telescope beckons guests to explore the heavens. In the lounge areas, AC assures cool comfort, while from the adjacent restaurant you can spot animals at dusk as they approach the water. A well-stocked bar is popular, too! There's mosquito screening throughout, including in the individual suites which feature sliding doors to private balconies & river views from the beds.

Passengers are ferried by tender boats to watch game & birds around the national park, with fishing (in season) for tigerfish or bream & visits to a Namibian village a further option. *2 nights (dep Mon & Wed) R14,970–21,420 pp sharing, 3 nights (dep Fri) R22,455–32,130 inc FB, most drinks, activities, transfer from Kasane Airport/Immigration Office; exc community development levy R95 pp/ night; sgl supp't 30%; rates in South African rand.* ☺ *All year.*

🚤 **Chobe Princess** (4–5 cabins) ☏ +27 21 715 2412; e enquiry@zqcollection.com; www.zqcollection.com. More intimate & more wide-ranging than the *Zambezi Queen*, the 3

SERONDELA

For years the only campsite in northern Chobe was at Serondela (✧ SERON 17°50.059'S, 25°00.611'E), sprawling along the riverside about 17km west of Kasane. The local animals had lost their fear of man, and all the dangerous big game seemed to make a point of regularly sauntering through camp. Over the years, ignorant tourists had taken to feeding some of the animals and the baboons, particularly, became a menace – aggressive, adept at stealing food if you turned your back for a second, and even able to open zips on unguarded tents.

On one occasion a lone male bounded on to the tailgate of my 4x4, snatching a packet of biscuits in its jaws from a food box, and sprinted off – all in a matter of seconds while I and a companion were a few steps away at the front of the vehicle. Before leaping up into the back it knew that we'd seen it and were coming back to chase it, but also knew that it was faster and so continued. It was obviously very well practised at this sort of smash-and-grab raid.

Further, Serondela was relatively close to the eastern side of the park, so it added considerably to the density of traffic in the peak times for game viewing: dawn and dusk. So for several reasons the site was closed in the late 1990s and superseded by the new Ihaha site. Today it is used by safari groups and self-drivers as a tranquil riverside picnic site, complete with benches and tables, and even toilets.

Chobe Princesses – with 4 or 5 cabins – cruise some 50km of the Chobe River, mooring at points as far west as Serondela over 2 or 3 nights. The en-suite cabins are smaller than on the *Queen*, but similarly well appointed, with AC & big picture windows, so you can sit & watch wildlife from your cabin, as well as on deck. This is the chance for total relaxation with a drink, or in the on-board plunge pool, but for more involvement tender boats are available for fishing, game viewing or birdwatching with an experienced guide, & there is also the opportunity to visit a Namibian village. *2 nights (dep Mon & Wed) R11,550–14,220 pp sharing, 3 nights (dep Fri) R17,325–21,330, inc FB, most drinks, activities, transfer from Kasane Airport/Immigration Office; exc community development levy R65 pp/night; sgl supp't 30%; rates in South African rand.* ⊕ *All year.*

Pangolin Voyager (5 cabins) Contact Pangolin Photo Safaris, page 248. Launched in 2015, this is the ideal boat for keen photographers, who will appreciate the specialist tender boat that comes complete with rotating chairs & swivelling tripods. That said, there are 3 other small boats to ensure that those who want to go fishing or birdwatching or simply to enjoy the river don't miss out. En-suite cabins, on the lower deck, have twin beds (or a dbl), fans & gauzed windows that allow the breeze to circulate. Above you'll find a lounge, communal dining table & braai area, while up top is largely open to the elements, giving great views over the river & national park. Note, though, that if you want the services of a photographic tutor, you'll need to book this in advance, at extra cost. *US$295 pp Nov–Mar, US$495 Apr–Oct, inc FB, most drinks, activities, transfers from Kasane.* ⊕ *All year.*

WHAT TO SEE AND DO Game viewing and birdwatching are the main activities on the Chobe riverfront; walking and night drives are not allowed. Most visitors explore along the floodplains beside the river, which offers relatively easy game viewing, even without a guide.

If you're driving yourself and have a little time to spare, don't ignore the roads away from the river on the western side of this riverfront section, particularly the Kaswabenga and Simwanza Valley roads, as well as the firebreaks marked

10

on Veronica Roodt's maps of Chobe. The landscape here is broken country with rocky hillsides and gullies: classic leopard country and very different from anything else you're likely to see in Chobe. You'll often find surprisingly good concentrations of game here in October, despite its apparent distance from the river, because the game tends to rest in the shade of the forest on its way to and from the water.

Two recent additions to activities in this area are canoeing and mokoro trips (*around US$25/hr pp*). Both are conducted on the river on the western fringes of the park, near Ngoma, but participants may be collected from Kasane as well as from lodges within and to the west of the park. Do remember that you'll be sharing your space with both hippos and crocs, so make sure that your guide has given serious thought to the safety aspects of such a trip.

Malachite Safaris \ 625 1537; m 7468 5154. Trips of 1½hrs & 2½hrs in 2-seater Canadian canoes with a guide are operated along the western channels of the Chobe River.

Thaoge Polers Safaris m 7314 3466; e clongwani@gmail.com. Run mokoro trips just below Ngoma Safari Lodge.

THE CAPRIVI STRIP

As you look across the Chobe River – and indeed the Linyanti – from Botswana you're looking into Namibia's Caprivi Strip, but how did the land come to belong to Namibia in the first place? On the map, the Caprivi Strip appears to be a strange appendage of Namibia rather than a part of it. It forms a strategic corridor of land, linking Namibia to Zimbabwe and Zambia, but seems somehow detached from the rest of the country. The region's history explains why.

When Germany annexed South West Africa (now Namibia) in 1884, it prompted British fears that they might try to link up with the Boers, in the Transvaal, thus driving a wedge between these territories and cutting off the Cape from Rhodesia. Out of fear, the British negotiated an alliance with Khama, a powerful Tswana king, and proclaimed the Protectorate of Bechuanaland – the forerunner of modern Botswana. At that time, this included the present-day Caprivi Strip. Geographically this made sense if the main reason for Britain's claim was to block Germany's expansion into central Africa.

Meanwhile, off Africa's east coast, Germany laid claim to Zanzibar. This was the end game of the colonial 'scramble for Africa', which set the stage for the Berlin Conference of July 1890. Then these two colonial powers sat down in Europe to reorganise their African possessions with strokes of a pen.

Britain agreed to sever the Caprivi from Bechuanaland and give control of it to Germany, to add to their province of South West Africa. Germany hoped to use it to access the Zambezi's trade routes to the east, and named it after the German Chancellor of the time, Count George Leo von Caprivi. In return for this (and also the territory of Heligoland in the North Sea), Germany ceded control of Zanzibar to Britain, and agreed to redefine South West Africa's eastern border with Britain's Bechuanaland.

At the end of World War I the Caprivi was reincorporated into Bechuanaland, but in 1929 it was again returned to South West Africa, then under South African rule. Hence it became part of Namibia – where it is now largely incorporated into the Zambezi Region.

CHOBE FOREST RESERVE

Chobe Forest Reserve is an enclave largely surrounded by Chobe National Park. To the northwest of it are seasonal marshes, Lake Liambezi and, eventually, Namibia.

The reserve, and the area to the northwest of it – concessions known as CH1 and CH2 – were long designated respectively for photographic safaris and community-managed hunting, but since the ban on commercial hunting in January 2014, this has changed.

The traditional photographic area in CH1, beside the Linyanti River, is the location of Linyanti Bush Camp and its sister camp. However, as the flora and fauna here are essentially the same as in the Linyanti Concession, we have included these camps in the Linyanti chapter (pages 300–1).

Most visitors simply pass through the southern corner of CH2 between Kasane and Savuti (see *Western route: via the riverfront,* pages 275–8, for details of this drive). Yet for those visiting the riverfront, the lodges near Ngoma are well worth consideration, not least as Chobe's game-drive loops become quieter as you move west from the Kasane area to Ngoma.

WHERE TO STAY [map 256] There are now four lodges here in the forest reserve, although the fourth – Baobab Safari Lodge – is run for the exclusive use of groups. All are worth considering as alternatives to those in the Kasane area, as well as potentially convenient stopovers. The lodges are set high on a ridge overlooking the Chobe River floodplain and are normally reached by road from Kasane, taking about an hour for the transfer. The new campsite is lower down the hill, so closer to the Chobe floodplain.

In 2018, a new boat jetty was opened in the park, upstream from the Ihaha Campsite so away from the busy Kasane area. This is for the exclusive use of Ngoma Safari Lodge, Muchenje Safari Lodge and Chobe Elephant Camp, each of which has a light, pontoon-style boat for seasonal sunset cruises, breakfast or lunch on the river, and birding.

Ngoma Safari Lodge (8 chalets) lodge 620 0108, reservations +263 213 284 3211; e aatreservations@saflodge.co.zw; www.africaalbidatourism.com; ◈ NGOMSL 17°56.513'S, 24°42.558'E. More or less adjacent to Muchenje, Ngoma opened in 2011. Its dining tables, bar, umbrella-shaded terrace, rock-style pool & firepit are all strategically placed on different levels to make the most of panoramic views over the floodplain below. It's light, airy & stylish (don't miss the beaded chandeliers!), yet retains a strong sense of place combined with more than a hint of tradition. As for practicalities, there's Wi-Fi throughout, & a spotting scope helps you to keep an eye on the game in the distance.

Well spaced along the ridge are split-level chalets, which soak up the view from individual patios with sunloungers, & tiny plunge pools that are the envy of the local elephant population. There are outside showers, too, while inside are contemporary bathrooms with twin basins, a bath & separate loo. On a lower level, the beds – lit by good lights & enveloped by mosquito nets – face the plains through full-length glazed windows, & cool drinks, tea & coffee, & *biscotti* are on hand to help while away the afternoon. 2 rooms can be converted into triples. Although the room nearest the central area has no steps, so is more suited to those with limited mobility, note that the paths are quite rough.

Typically, guests spend their 1st day on a short game drive either to the river below the lodge or into Chobe National Park, with their 2nd full-day trip taking in a game drive through the park, lunch, & a cruise on the Chobe River. Walks & night drives in the forest reserve, leisurely cruises on their own boat, & mokoro trips are further options. You could even do a (very long) day trip into Savuti. See ad, 3rd colour section. *From US$565 pp Jan–Mar & Dec to US$975/1,219 Jul–Oct, inc FB, most drinks, activities, laundry, park fees, Kasane/Kazungula transfers. No children under 10.* ☺ *All year.* ★★★–★★★★★

10

🏠 **Muchenje Safari Lodge** (10 chalets)
📞 620 0013–15; m 7164 6017; e info@
muchenje.com; www.muchenje.com; ✪ MUCHEN
17°57.115'S, 24°42.361'E. Perched on the
escarpment overlooking the floodplain, Muchenje
was built in 1996 by Matt & Lorna Smith, who
have owned & run it ever since. It's a comfortable,
traditional lodge with a strong sense of hospitality
& a good team of staff. To get there, follow the
signs from the T-junction at Ngoma towards
Mabele & Savuti; the turning to Muchenje is just
3km along on your right.

Well-spaced thatched chalets are comfortably
furnished with a dbl or twin beds surrounded by a
walk-in mosquito net. Each has a modern en-suite
shower & toilet, AC & ceiling fan, electric lights, &
a veranda with a view. Discreetly tucked away is a
honeymoon (or family) chalet – it sleeps up to 4 –
with a 2nd storey, a large bath tub, & an absolutely
private veranda set to one side.

At the heart of the lodge, a wide, solid, stone
building under a high thatched roof forms a
crescent above the plain, making the most of the
setting. Here you'll find a large table for communal
dining, a lovely curved central bar with plenty of
seating, & a small clothes/curio shop. Above the
bar is a game-viewing platform which, along with
a big new pool, shares that impressive view. And in
the evening, bush dinners can be arranged in their
private boma.

Activities at Muchenje are many & varied; if you
want to be busy all day, you can be! Game drives
into the national park use an area that tends to be
more private than around Kasane, as less traffic
reaches this far west. Bush walks (with armed
guides) in the forest reserve are also offered, as is
birdwatching on the river. Those staying 2 nights
or more – which includes most guests – can opt
for a full-day safari taking in a midday boat cruise
along the Chobe (thus avoiding the afternoon
'boat rush'), followed by a picnic lunch in the bush
& a game drive back through the park. Their new
boat will allow a more open & convivial style of
boat trip, too, & if you'd like to visit a local village
school, your guide may introduce you to his family
& show you round. *From US$435 pp Jan–Mar to
US$725/1,110 Jul–Oct pp sharing/sgl, inc FB, local
drinks, activities, laundry, Kasane transfers.* ⊕ *All
year.* ★★★–★★★★★

🏠 **Chobe Elephant Camp** (12
chalets) 📞 686 3763; e reservations@
chobeelephantcamp.com; www.
chobeelephantcamp.com; ✪ CHOBEC
17°56.840'S, 24°42.055'E. A sister camp to Sango
Safari Camp (page 320), the newest lodge in this
area opened in 2013, with magnificent views
across the Chobe floodplains. Its turning off the
tar road is at the same point as Muchenje Safari
Lodge (see left), from where it's signposted down
a 600m sand track.

With a view to mitigating the effects of a harsh
climate & the impact on the environment, the
entire lodge has been constructed of sandbags –
while a pool helps guests to cool off in the heat.
It's an understated, relaxed place, focusing on the
setting rather than on the frills, though with AC,
inside & outside showers & king-size beds in the
rather rustic chalets (2 of them suited to families),
creature comforts are not lacking. The cavernous
lounge, dining & bar area, reached from the
chalets along gravel paths, is open on 3 sides, its
few walls whitewashed to create something of a
farmhouse effect. Meals, though, are often taken
outside, where there's a warming firepit that's lit in
the evenings. Staff are friendly & welcoming, & the
guiding – on game drives, boat cruises & sunset
cruises on their own boat – is good. Guests may
also explore the river from a mokoro or canoe, or
take part in cultural visits to a local village. *From
US$335 pp Jan–Mar & Dec to US$495/650 Jul–Oct
pp sharing/sgl, inc FB, local drinks, activities, park
fees, laundry, transfer from Kasane. Self-drive
US$280–390/545 pp sharing/sgl inc FB, local drinks.*
⊕ *All year.* ★★★

🏠 **Baobab Safari Lodge** (8 chalets)
✪ BAOBAB 17°56.615'S, 24°43.319'E. About 3km
inside the Chobe Forest Reserve, this stone-&-
thatch camp is run by Wilderness Safaris for group
trips, with no independent guests accepted. The
central building combines dining, bar & lounge
areas, while along the ridge sit individual chalets
with pitched canvas roofs, each with twin beds
& an en-suite bathroom. As you would expect,
activities focus on game drives & boat cruises in
the national park.

🔺 **Muchenje Campsite &
Cottages** (3 cottages, camping) m 7500 7327;
e bookings@muchenjecampsite.com; www.
muchenjecampsite.com; ✪ MUCHCC 17°57.261'S,
24°40.658'E. New to the Muchenje area in 2015,
this family-owned-&-run spot is particularly well
placed for those heading to or from Savuti (there's

even a fuel station almost adjacent!), as well as those looking to explore the western side of the riverfront on a budget. Some 7.2km from the Ngoma border post, & just off the tar road, it's geared entirely to self-catering travellers, with home-grown vegetables for sale, bread to order, & a small shop selling meat, firewood & ice. There's Wi-Fi reception here, too, & a small pool nearby. The cottages, each with a dbl bed & a sleeper couch, can sleep up to 4, & have tiled patios with table & chairs & a braai, proper kitchenettes, AC, & outside showers. For campers, there are

10 individual & very separate pitches – some looking across the floodplains – sharing 6 private (& spotless) showers & toilets. 2018 will see the addition of 3 permanent walk-in tents, backed by a beautiful baobab tree. These will share ablutions with other campers, but will have their own small kitchenettes, braai facilities & private verandas, with twin beds & electric lights inside. It's a well-thought-out place with a real understanding of the market. Activities can be organised on request. *Cottage P900 per cottage; camping P170 pp, both exc bed levy.* ⊕ *Closed Feb.*

LIAMBEZI AREA

This large, shallow lake is located between the Linyanti and Chobe rivers. When full, it covers some 10,000ha, although since 1985 it has been much drier, and frequently something of a dustbowl – until the exceptional rains of 2009. Thus for many years, people and cattle have populated its bed rather than hippos and crocodile.

Lake Liambezi's main source of water used to be the Linyanti River. However, even in recent years of good rain it failed to fill the lake after filtering through the Linyanti Swamps (which themselves are very dry). Even despite good water levels in the Kwando-Linyanti system in the 2011–12 rainy season, it didn't break through as far as Liambezi. As a result there has been a trend towards less and less water in the lake and the marshes around it, and more villages. By 2014, however, for the first time in many years Lake Liambezi had a few inches of water in it, due to good rains, a recovery of the Bukalo Channel from the northeast, and possibly some flow-back from the Chobe River.

DRIVING FROM KASANE TO SAVUTI

There are two routes through Chobe National Park between Kasane (✦ KASANE 17°47.97'S, 25°09.015'E) and Savuti. Certainly the shorter is the western route, which is about 172km from Kasane to Savuti, via the Chobe Forest Reserve, and can take in the Chobe riverfront drive (pages 275–8) if you have time. The alternative is the eastern route, which is about 207km long. This stays within the park and passes through the Nogatsaa Pans area. Both have their own appeal – and their own challenges.

The western route is arguably the more beautiful, especially if you drive along the riverfront, but the eastern route is generally quieter, and has a particularly scenic stretch running parallel to the Ngwezumba River. Note that in the wet season, you're recommended to use the western route. Firstly, it's probably slightly more frequented by vehicles. Secondly, you'll find it particularly easy to get stuck in the clay soils found around the pans (both Nogatsaa/Tchinga and further south at Zweizwe). That said, if you do brave the pans route, the birding can be particularly good at that time of year.

Don't imagine that the western route is always easy at that time. Most of this is fairly thick sand and you'll often be crossing fossil dunes with woodland on the crests and scrub or grasslands in the valleys. Veronica Roodt (see *Appendix 3*, pages 542–3) reports that there's a patch where water sometimes gathers just south of the Ghoha Hills. So beware of problems there after heavy rains.

DRIVING NEAR ELEPHANTS: AVOIDING PROBLEMS

Elephants are the only animals that pose a real danger to vehicles. Everything else will get out of your way, or at least not actively go after you, but if you treat elephants wrongly there's a chance that you might have problems.

To put this in perspective, most drivers who are new to Africa will naturally (and wisely) treat elephants with enormous respect, keeping their distance – simply out of fear. Also in the more popular areas of Chobe or Moremi, where the elephants are habituated to vehicles, you'd have to really annoy an already grumpy elephant for it to give you trouble.

To give specific advice is difficult, as every elephant is different. Each is an individual, with real moods and feelings – and there's no substitute for years of experience to tell you what mood they're in. However, a few basics are worth noting.

Firstly, keep your eyes open and don't drive too fast. Surprising an elephant on the road is utterly terrifying, and dangerous for both you and the elephant. Always drive slowly in the bush.

Secondly, think of each animal as having an invisible 'comfort zone' around it (some experts talk of three concentric zones: the fright, flight, and fight zones – each with a smaller radius, and each more dangerous). If you actively approach then you breach that zone, and will upset it. So don't approach too closely: keep your distance. How close depends entirely on the elephants and the area. More relaxed elephants having a good day will allow you to get within 25m of them, bad-tempered ones that aren't used to cars may charge at 250m! You can often approach more closely in open areas than in thick bush. That said, if your vehicle is stationary and a relaxed, peaceful elephant approaches you, then you should not have problems if you simply stay still.

Thirdly, never beep your horn or flash your lights at an elephant (you shouldn't be driving yourself at night anyhow!). Either is guaranteed to annoy it. If there's an elephant in your way, just sit back, relax and wait; elephants always have right of way in Africa! The more sound and fury – like wheelspins and engine revving – the more likely that the elephant will assume that you are attacking it, and this is especially the case with a breeding herd.

Finally, look carefully at the elephant(s):

- Are there any small calves around in the herd? If so expect the older females to be easily annoyed and very protective – keep your distance.
- Are there any males in musth around? These are fairly easy to spot because of a heavy secretion from penis and temporal glands and a very musty smell. Generally these will be on their own, unless they are with a cow on heat. Such males will be excitable; you must spot them and give them a wide berth.
- Are there any elephants with a lot of seepage from their temporal glands, on the sides of their heads? If so, expect them to be stressed and easily irritable – beware. This is likely to have a long-term cause – perhaps lack of good water, predator pressure or something as random as toothache – but whatever the cause, that animal is under stress, and so should be given an extra-wide berth.

EASTERN ROUTE: VIA THE PANS For the eastern route, you need to take the tar road from Kasane towards Ngoma, away from the river. About 18km beyond the Sedudu Gate into the park, you'll reach a crossroads (⊕ NANTTO 17°55.303'S, 25°01.186'E). A right turn, north, would take you to the riverfront road in the Serondela area. Left, signposted to Nogatsaa 50km, and Photha 78km, leads you within 1km to the Nantanga Pans, and on to the only road south through Chobe National Park.

About 23km from the tar road you'll come to a fork. Here you can take either route, as they join up at a clear junction by Makumba Pan (⊕ MAKUMB 18°12.789'S, 24°56.955'E) about 12–14km further on. If you bear right at the fork, then you'll need to turn right at this junction; if you've taken the left fork, then continue straight on at the junction. Some 13km from the junction (at ⊕ NOGATO 18°18.065'S, 24°52.629'E), there's a left turn towards the new Nogatsaa Pans Lodge, which is actually on the edge of Kwikamba Pan. For Savuti, continue straight on here, skirting the complex of roads around Nogatsaa and Tchinga pans towards a crossroads close to Ngwezumba Dam (⊕ NGWEZ 18°21.700'S, 24°49.172'E). At this point, follow the signpost straight on to Savuti, following the dry bed of the Ngwezumba River, with occasional vistas opening up through the trees. After about 31km you pass some solar panels on the left, then a further 2km brings you to a small track on the right (at ⊕ CNP1 18°30.243'S, 24°34.497'E), which leads after almost 4km to Nxunxutsha Pan (⊕ NXUNXU 18°29.312'S, 24°32.537'E), at the southernmost point of the Chobe Forest Reserve. If you were to take this track, and bear left around the edge of the pan, you'd find yourself on a track going uphill towards two beautiful baobab trees. This leads almost immediately on to the cutline between Chobe Forest Reserve and Chobe National Park, and after another 33km of relatively straightforward driving to the Ghoha Gate into the park (⊕ GHOHA 18°23.025'S, 24°14.732'E).

To continue to Savuti, however, ignore the turning towards Nxunxutsha Pan, and continue broadly southwest (to ⊕ CNP2 18°34.679'S, 24°23.381'E). From here the road takes a more southerly direction, leaving the riverbed behind. About 7km later, where the road splits (⊕ CNP3 18°38.152'S, 24°24.928'E), take the right turn leading southwest through the pans. After a further 11km the road turns west and finally northwest towards Savuti. This track enters Savuti by the south side of Qumxhwaa Hill (Quarry Hill) and joins the western route from Kasane just north of the channel.

The total distance from Kasane to Savuti along the eastern route is about 207km, and it takes 5 or 6 hours to drive in the dry season. An advantage is the possibility of a midway stop at the Ngwezumba Pans (pages 278–80), although scenically this route lacks the beauty of the Chobe River.

WESTERN ROUTE: VIA THE RIVERFRONT Taking the western route you have a choice of ways to start. If you're in a hurry, or starting late in the day, then drive the 57km to Ngoma from Kasane on the tar. Alternatively, and much more enjoyably, meander along the riverfront road (pages 262–71), which passes Serondela and Ihaha before joining up with the end of the tar road at Ngoma near the border post (pages 266–7). Both routes are a little over 50km, but whereas the tar road will take about an hour (the speed limit is 80km/h), the river route will take several, depending on how much you stop to watch animals or take photographs.

Whichever route you take, you'll reach the park gate at Ngoma, where you may be required to sign the register and possibly also to walk across a disinfectant mat while the wheels of your vehicle are sprayed to prevent the spread of any disease. Then you should take a left turn, heading roughly southwest, and signposted as

10

the B334 to Mabele (12km), Kachikau (37km), Parakarungu (67km) and Savuti (110km). This is now tarred all the way to Kachikau, making the first part of the journey – through the **Chobe Forest Reserve** (pages 271–3) – very straightforward. On a practical note, a new fuel station opened in 2017 some 7km south of Ngoma, a boon for anyone heading into or out of Savuti.

About 11.5km from the border post, you'll pass a big baobab and a large sign proclaiming **Mabele**. You'll still be able to see the Chobe floodplain off to the right, but with little game on it. Mabele General Dealer (⊕ MABELE 17°59.182'S, 24°38.858'E), on the right before the football pitch, is the best shop in town, though it's still very limited. The vegetation is mostly acacia species here, with lots of umbrella thorn (*Vachellia tortilis*), but the scenery becomes less inspiring.

Some 25km from Ngoma you come to **Kavimba**, whose landmark two baobabs stand guard on each side of the road (⊕ KAVIMB 18°04.192'S, 24°35.020'E). This is the location of the Kachempati Basket Weavers Co-operative (☏625 0339; ⊕ 08.00–17.00 daily) – so if you're interested, it may be worth asking around for their craft shop. Then a little over 10km later you'll reach the sprawling town of **Kachikau** (marked on some maps as Kachekabwe), where you can buy a limited range of drinks and foodstuffs. There's also a forestry camp here, and the smart, well-built Liswaani Community School. In the centre of town (⊕ KACHIK 18°09.143'S, 24°30.172'E) there's a right turning signposted to Setau, a small settlement in the communal area to the north of the forest reserve, near Lake Liambezi.

Just beyond Kachikau, some 92km from Kasane, the tar road comes to an abrupt halt, reverting almost instantly to deep, sandy tracks. Having passed a bottle store and Chobe Craft Centre on the left, this leads after some 10km to the turn-off point for those driving themselves to Thobolo's Bush Lodge, about 3km west of this road

DRIVING NEAR ELEPHANTS: FACING A CHARGE

If you get into a hair-raising situation with elephants, then you've probably not kept your distance. The key was prevention, and you failed. Now you must keep cool, with your logic ruling your fear. A few words here are inadequate – you need experience – but I'll outline some basics.

If you are unexpectedly surrounded by peaceful elephants when your vehicle is stationary and switched off, don't panic. Don't even start the engine, as that would startle them. Just sit there and enjoy it; there's no real cause for concern. Only when they've passed and are a distance away should you start up. When you do start: never start and move off simultaneously, which will be interpreted as the vehicle being very aggressive. Instead start up quietly, wait a little and then move.

More often a situation occurs when one from the herd will be upset with you. In that case you've approached too closely. (The key was to keep your distance – remember?) Then an annoyed elephant will usually first mock charge. This normally first involves a lot of ear flapping, head shaking and loud trumpeting – mock charges are often preceded by 'displacement activities', and the animals often show uncertainty about charging. The individual then runs towards you with ears spread out, head held high, and trumpeting loudly. This is terrifying, especially if you're not used to it. But be impressed, not surprised; elephants weigh up to 6,000kg and have had several million years to refine this into a really frightening spectacle.

However terrifying, if you stand your ground then almost all such encounters will end with the elephant stopping in its tracks. It will then move away at an (for details, see page 278). The country around here is rolling vegetated dunes, which means lots of corrugations and deep, deep sand. Plenty of leadwood trees are around, so beware of punctures (especially if you've reduced the pressure in your tyres for the sand). The long, strong, leadwood spines will cause punctures in even the sturdiest of 4x4 tyres.

Continuing southwest, the next 40km towards the national park are, quite simply, challenging. The final 16km or so can be particularly hard going, with many a vehicle getting bogged down in the sand. To avoid this, you can take a right fork towards Linyanti, as indicated by the signpost at ⊕ DETOR2 18°15.250'S, 24°19.087'E, rather than the left fork (signposted to Savuti). This leads to a point on the cutline (⊕ CUTTUR 18°21.82'S, 24°10.633'E) which is about 7.7km northwest of the gate. Thus you just need to turn left along the cutline to return to the main track, and turn right to the gate. Although you'll still encounter plenty of sand on this route, it's not as thick as the more direct alternative. (For anyone heading in the opposite direction, from Savuti to Kasane, you would simply turn left up the cutline immediately after exiting the gate, and then take a right turn (⊕ CUTTUR) just after the end of a band of mopane trees.)

Either way, about 80km from Ngoma you'll arrive at the impressive Ghoha Gate (⊕ GHOHA 18°23.025'S, 24°14.732'E), which marks the end of the forest reserve, and the start of Chobe National Park. If you were to turn right here, then this (very rough and sandy) cutline would lead you along the cutline to the Linyanti Gate, on the Linyanti River just east of Linyanti Campsite, and to the camps run by African Bush Camps.

Savuti, however, is a further 28km to the southwest, so you'll need to sign in at the gate, produce your camp reservations and pay your park fees.

angle, with its head held high and turned, its back arched, its tail raised, and the occasional head-shake. Often you'll find the 'teenagers' of the herd doing this – testing you and showing off a bit.

However, if you flee or back off rapidly during such a mock charge, the elephant will probably chase your vehicle, perhaps turning a mock charge into a full charge (see below). So, before you move, make very certain that you have a swift escape route, and that you can drive faster than the elephant can run. (In deep sand, you can forget this.)

As a fairly desperate measure, not normally needed, if the elephant is really getting too close, then increasing the revs of your engine – commensurate with the threat – will encourage the animal to stop and back down. Don't beep your horn, don't rev up and down, but do steadily press your accelerator further down as the elephant gets closer. (I've never needed to do this; it's overkill for most mock charges.)

However, if you're really unfortunate then you'll come across an upset or traumatised animal, or one that really perceives you as a threat and that makes a full charge. This is rare – expected only from injured elephants, cows protecting calves, males in musth and the like. Then the individual will fold its ears back, put its head down, and run full speed at your vehicle. I'm pleased that I've never faced one of these, but if you do then your only option is to drive as fast as you can. If you can't get away then I'd try revving, as above, matching its threat with your engine's noise. But I'd also start praying – this is a seriously dangerous place to be.

As you enter the national park you'll see the Ghoha Hills on your left in the distance. A few kilometres later you'll pass the first of the hills, which is dotted with baobab trees, and now topped by the new Ghoha Hills Savuti Lodge. The road inside the park is generally a little less sandy than that outside, although it does cross the northern edge of the Magwikhwe Sand Ridge just south of the hills.

About 25km after the entrance gate you'll pass a sharp-angled right turn, which leads to Savuti airstrip, and a couple of kilometres further on you'll reach a new bridge over the usually dry Savuti Channel, almost next to Savuti Campsite. Although this route is shorter (about 172km in total) and the first part at least is more spectacular than the eastern route described on page 275, the southern section in particular is generally more difficult and time-consuming to drive.

 ## Where to stay

Thobolo's Bush Lodge [map 256] (12 chalets, camping) m 7327 9665; e thobolosbushlodge@gmail.com; http://thobolosbushlodge.com; ⊕ THOBOL 18°12.273'S, 24°23.519'E. Geared exclusively to the self-catering market, this new lodge opened in Aug 2016 is well placed for those travelling between Kasane or Ngoma to Linyanti or Savuti – or wishing to explore areas of Chobe & the Linyanti River on a professional game drive (*US$150 pp, inc park fees & lunch, min 4*). You'll find it signposted from both Kachikau, where you go to the end of the tar, then turn right for a further 3km to the lodge, & at the Ghoha Gate, where you turn north for 19.6km from the cutline (at ⊕ CUTTUR 18°21.82'S, 24°10.633'E).

The man behind the lodge is Mike Gunn, who has been influential in Botswana's tourist industry since the early 1980s. Having founded, and sold, camps on the Khwai River and (Gunn's Camp) in the Delta, he has turned his attention to an old hunting concession – & Thobolo's is the result. Constructed on 2 storeys, the main area has a traditional cash bar & lounge overlooking Barangwe Pan, which is pumped with water in the dry season, & a shop & reception area below that also sells firelights, etc, for campers. Meals are available on request (*b/fast US$12, dinner US$20*), but each well-screened chalet also boasts its own kitchen with table & chairs. There are 2 en-suite twin bedrooms, too, & a private upstairs viewing area. The whole lodge is run on solar power, with high-quality insulation & ceiling fans to cool the rooms, & glazed windows with screens to keep out the bugs. A separate campsite shares the views over the waterhole. *Self-catering US$325 (2 people); camping US$40 pp.* ⊕ *All year.*

NGWEZUMBA PANS

About 70km south of the Chobe River, and reached along the eastern route described on page 275, lies a large complex of clay pans surrounded by grassland plains, mopane woodlands and combretum thickets. There are well over a dozen individual pans: Nogatsaa, Gxlaigxlarara, Tutlha, Tambiko, Kabunga, Kwikamba and Phoha, to name but a few, and all hold water after the rains. This makes them a natural focus during the first few months of the year, when the animals tend to stay away from the permanent waters of the Linyanti and Chobe rivers.

If any of the water pumps here are working consistently then the pans are likely to attract wildlife during the dry season too. Should you be planning to head this way in the heart of the dry season, it's worth asking first at one of the gates into the park if the pumps are working.

FLORA AND FAUNA HIGHLIGHTS With water there, the pans are excellent in the dry season. Early in the dry season they're quite likely to hold water anyway – so taking the eastern route certainly makes sense around May–August. Once the natural water dries up, the pumps are vital. With water in the late dry season you can expect herds of Chobe's game interacting; it's a place to just sit and watch for hours.

Curiously, perhaps the area's most notable game doesn't need permanent water and so is found here all year. This area is perhaps the only place in Botswana where oribi antelope occur naturally. These small, elegant grazers are orange-red above, white underneath, have a dark circular scent gland under their ears and a short bush tail with a black tip. Only the males, which are very territorial, have short, straight horns. They are usually seen in pairs, or small groups, feeding in the open grasslands during the morning or late afternoon. If startled they will often emit a shrill whistle before bounding off at a rapid rate with a very jerky motion.

This is also the only area of Chobe where you've any real chance of spotting gemsbok (or oryx). This is the dominant large antelope species in the parks south of here, but it's relatively unusual to see them in Chobe. These pans, together with the complex around Zweizwe, are also probably the park's best place to spot roan antelope, which never thrive in areas of dense game but seem to do well around here.

For birdwatchers, the pans, and especially the larger ones like Kwikamba Pan, can be superb during the rains. Expect a whole variety of aquatic birds passing through including Egyptian and spur-winged geese, lesser moorhen, red-knobbed coot, red-billed and Hottentot teal, African pochard, dabchick and even the occasional dwarf bittern or whiskered tern. The large grassland plains here also attract grassland species such as yellow-throated sandgrouse, harlequin quail, croaking cisticola and, occasionally, Stanley's bustard.

WHERE TO STAY There used to be two campsites here, at Nogatsaa – which was a great place for watching the game coming to bathe and drink, and still has a tall hide, and the very basic Tchinga (alias 'Tshinga' and 'Tjinga'). Now those have gone, leaving only private campsites in the area, which are exclusive to licensed Botswana tour operators running mobile safaris. The arrival of a new lodge here in 2017 has once more opened this little-visited area of Chobe to independent exploration.

Nogatsaa Pans Lodge [map 257] (12 chalets) reservations +27 63 613 9144; e reservations@ghohahills.com; www.ghohahills. com; ⊕ NOGATP 18°19.324'S, 24°53.207'E. Opened in late 2017, the sister lodge to Ghoha Hills Savuti Lodge brings new life to this little-visited area of Chobe. The location is stunning, right on the edge of the large, open Kwikamba Pan, which is pumped to retain water all year round – to the relief of the resident wildlife, from elephant & hippo to sable antelope & lion. At present, guests arrive by road, a transfer of about 3hrs from Kasane, or 2hrs from the Ghoha Gate into Savuti.

The lodge itself is smart, almost minimalist in tone, yet from the exterior its thatched main area & tented chalets blend in well with the environment. Arranged around the pan, the chalets are huge, though some are more private than others. They're entered through sliding glass doors off a big veranda, but large gauze windows with roll-down blinds & a floor fan help the air to circulate. Inside, the lines are simple & uncluttered, against a backdrop of cream canvas-lined walls,

& distressed white wooden floors. A king-size bed (or twins) takes centre stage, backed by a plain desk. To one side are twin sinks & a storage area, with both inside & outside showers & the toilet tucked out of sight. In the family suite, 2 bedrooms are separated by a lounge area with a sofa bed to take an extra child, & the bathroom at the back. By day, you can stroll to the main area along the sand path behind the chalets, but after dark you will be driven to & from your room; wildlife in this completely open camp is an ever-present danger.

In the open-plan main area, the wood & thatch gives a warmer yet still contemporary & stylish feel, with muted greys & browns mirroring the grey bark of a big shady jackalberry tree, & cowhides dotted across teak floors. Meals are taken either individually or as a group, as guests prefer. At the front, an expanse of wooden decking plays host to an infinity pool & attendant loungers, with a firepit below, & a separate bar topped by a stargazing deck & telescope. Activities follow a typical safari day, with morning & afternoon game drives to explore the nearby pans & around the dry

10

bed of the Ngwezumba River. *From US$395/514 pp sharing/sgl Dec–mid-Jan to US$695/904 Jul–Oct, inc FB, local drinks, activities, laundry, current park* *fees; exc transfers. No children under 4.* ⊕ *Mar–mid-Jan.* ★★★–★★★★★

GHOHA HILLS

Most people pass through the Ghoha Gate on their way to Savuti with scarcely a glance at the two hills that give this area its name. That's not unreasonable, given the game-rich areas further south, yet the hills are notable for providing the only high ground for some distance – and also offer a vantage point for a new lodge.

Many years ago the area was inhabited by the Basubiya, and rocks by the turning to the lodge indicate that there was once a well here. The predominant vegetation is Zambezi teak, scattered across deep tracts of Kalahari sand. The thickets provide a perfect hiding place for steenbok, and offer good camouflage for giraffe, which in turn are stalked by waiting lion, but the game is very skittish.

GETTING THERE Most visitors fly in to Savuti airstrip, followed by a 40-minute transfer to the lodge, but it's possible to be transferred by road from Kasane. For self-drivers, the turning is signposted to the left just 7km from the Ghoha Gate, then it's a further 1.8km to the lodge, culminating in an unexpectedly steep and rocky track.

WHERE TO STAY

 Ghoha Hills Savuti Lodge [map 256] (11 chalets) ☎319 0662, 620 0001, reservations ☎+27 63 613 9144; e reservations@ghohahills.com; www.ghohahills.com; ⊕ GHOHAL 18°26.175'S, 24°13.122'E. Opened in 2012, this smart lodge is perched on a hill above the plains, facing east to catch the sunrise. Entirely Batswana owned, it is set in its own private concession within the national park, with an exclusive 60km network of game-viewing tracks. From a viewing deck at the lodge, you can observe 2 waterholes, one of them overlooked by a well-shaded hide which makes a perfect spot for a sundowner. While pre-booked helicopter trips over Savuti can be organised, most guests spend their time on a full-day game drive to the Savuti Marsh, taking in some rock paintings *en route*. The journey takes at least an hour each way, so exploring the area around camp is often restricted to the evening of arrival or the early morning. Thus, while the lodge is quite a way from Savuti, it may best be considered as a satellite from there, rather than as a destination in its own right.

High standards have been set for the buildings here. As if marching up the hill, huge en-suite tented chalets, including 2 family suites, have either twin beds or a king-size dbl. In front, a giant gauze panel feels like a living cinema screen with the plains as backdrop, & at the back are a separate toilet & shower. It's unfortunate that the access road runs behind the chalets, but the addition of new front-facing verandas has made a big difference to their privacy. Up again you'll come to an extensive central area, like a big thatched tithe barn, stylishly set on several levels with apron decks looking over the plains. Well-prepared meals are usually served at private tables, but if guests wish to eat together, or with their guide, this can be arranged. There's the option of private dinners on the deck below, too, where a pool is set among the rocks & there's a warming firepit for winter evenings – or stargazing; the manager is trained to use the lodge's telescope. Crowning the hill is a new gym, its view shared by the treatment room in the equally new spa. *From US$475/618 pp sharing/sgl Dec–Mar to US$920/1,196 Jul–Oct, inc FB, local drinks, activities, laundry, current park fees; exc transfers. No children under 4.* ⊕ *All year.* ★★★–★★★★★

SAVUTI

Unlike most game-viewing areas, Savuti isn't just about animals. Its game can be great, but that's only half the story. To understand the rest, and discover some of its spirit, you must dig into its history – from the geological past, to the first humans and then the European hunters, 'explorers' and conservationists – and learn of the reputation of some of its famous characters. Savuti seems to have more stories linked with it than all the other game areas in Botswana combined. So seek these out before you come, as only then will you really appreciate why Savuti has a legendary quality about it.

HISTORY The key to the area's attraction is the mysterious Savuti Channel, which is often dry (as it has been for a large part of the last 35 years) but sometimes – as between 2009/2010 and 2014 – inexplicably flows. Its journey starts in a lagoon at the southern tip of the Linyanti Swamps. When it flows, it meanders a little south and then eastwards until it enters the national park.

Continuing east, it flows through a wide gap in the Magwikhwe Sand Ridge (in former times, its flow probably formed this gap); this is the place usually referred to as Savuti. From here the channel turns abruptly south, and spills out into the Mababe Depression, a huge flat area which was once the bed of an ancient lake (see pages 3–5 for more details), and formed the flat expanse of the Savuti Marsh.

At its peak, with the channel and marsh full, it must have been like a vast drinking trough over 100km long, penetrating the heart of the dust-dry northern Kalahari. It's no surprise that it attracted huge quantities of game and, in turn, whatever people were around at the time.

San/Bushmen The early hunter-gatherers certainly had settlements here, evidenced by at least five sites in the hills around Savuti containing rock art. Archaeologists link these paintings with those in the Tsodilo Hills, and with the traditions of people of the Okavango.

A few of these sites are known to the guides at some of the lodges here, so if you are staying at one then request for your guide to take you to see them. Despite park regulations about walking, at least one of these sites now has a clear signpost to it. However, you need to think very carefully before trying this on your own – given not only the park's rules, but also the high density of lion, leopard, buffalo and elephant in the area.

Early explorers There are many reports of this area from the early European explorers – fascinating if only to look back and see what they recorded of Savuti. In June 1851, when Livingstone passed through here, the marsh was a 'dismal swamp' some 16km long, fed by both the Mababe (now called Khwai) River, which spilled over from the Okavango system, and also by the 'strongly flowing' Savuti Channel.

Chapman also crossed the channel around 1853, when he recorded it as dry. When the great white hunter, Frederick Courtney Selous, came in 1874, the channel was full and flowing into the marsh. However, when Selous came back in 1879 he noted that the channel had partially dried out, and no longer fed the marsh. Mike Main, in his excellent book on the Kalahari (see *Appendix 3,* page 543), concludes that sometime in the 1880s the channel dried up.

Modern history The channel seems to have remained dry until a heavy rainy season, 1957–58, when it began to flow strongly once again. This continued until 1966, when it dried up once more. It then flowed from 1967 to 1981, when it seemed permanent and enhanced the area's reputation as a top game destination.

In the 1970s, Lloyd Wilmot started a camp here, Lloyd's Camp, which was to put both Lloyd and Savuti on the map. Lloyd is, in fact, the son of one of the

10

SAVUTI AREA

GPS co-ordinates ⊕
MARSAN	18°06.702'S, 24°00.679'E
RKPTGS	18°35.245'S, 24°04.402'E
SAVELE	18°34.207'S, 24°03.269'E
SAVSAF	18°33.927'S, 24°03.441'E
SAVUTE	18°34.005'S, 24°03.902'E

Linyanti Campsite

Ngoma, Kasane

S a n d   R i d g e

✈ Savuti airstrip

NOTE
For accommodation listings, see pages 287–9

Khlaxhlane Pan

Qumxhwaa (Quarry) Hill

Savute Safari Lodge
SAVSAF ⊕
Camp Savuti
SAVELE ⊕ ⊕ *SAVUTE*
Savuti Campsite
Savute Elephant Camp

Small Qumxhwaa (Quarry) Hill

Damagosera (Kudu) Hill ▲

Nogatsaa, Tchinga

Savuti Channel

Tanxhwaa (Sable) Hill ▲
RKPTGS ⊕
● **Rock paintings**

S a n d   R i d g e

Tsohxhwaa (Bushman) Hill ▲

Sexaxamba Pan

N
Bradt

0 ————— 3km
0 ————— 2 miles

MARSAN ⊕
Leopard Rock ▲ ▲ *Twin Hills*
Kwando Pan

● **Old airstrip**

M a g w i k h w e   S a n d

Motsibi Island

Savuti Marsh

SAND-RIDGE ROAD

MARSH ROAD

Mokgweba Island

↓ Mababe Gate

Okavango's famous crocodile hunters, Bobby Wilmot, and has many sisters, most with strong connections in the area. A safari here was always offbeat. Lloyd built up a reputation for empathy with the game, and a total lack of fear for his own safety when dealing with it. Everyone who visited came away with stories of remarkable animal encounters, and Savuti's reputation grew.

However, the channel's flow was gradually reducing and, in 1982, it ceased to flow completely. Gradually the water shrank into a few remaining pools, and then they dried up too. With them went the fish, hippos, crocodiles and all the other creatures that had lived there. During this time Lloyd was frequently photographed kneeling or lying in front of a thirsty elephant, excavating sand from a hole in the bottom of the channel until he reached water. This sad time was well chronicled in a video, *The Stolen River*, by Dereck and Beverly Joubert. It's also one of the main subjects of Clive Walker's book, *Savuti: the Vanishing River* (see *Appendix 3*, page 544).

Nobody really knows why it stopped, as nobody understood why it started again after almost 80 years of dryness. Explanations range from changes in the paths used by the Linyanti's hippos to tectonic shifts; see Mike Main's book, *Kalahari*, for a more detailed discussion. That the channel flowed once more between 2009 and 2014 is thus of considerable note.

Even with the channel dry, Savuti remains a classic area for game. Experts observe that the soil here is especially good, and the grazing particularly rich. Furthermore, there are now several permanent waterholes in the area. The oldest, near the centre of Savuti, is pumped by the national park, while two others are in front of the two lodges in the area. A further two are towards the bottom of the marsh, on opposite sides of it – and these try to attract the game, and especially the elephants, away from the centre of Savuti which has been so heavily impacted by game over the years.

ORIENTATION The (normally dry) Savuti Channel starts from the Zibadianja Lagoon, at the southern tip of the Linyanti Swamps, and flows through the Linyanti Reserve, before entering the national park about 35km away. Heading east, it cuts through a wide gap in the Magwikhwe Sand Ridge, around which are a number of low, rounded hills – the Gubatsaa Hills. This area, about 54km due east of the lagoon, is known as Savuti – and aside from the years between 2009 and 2014 – has been dry for much of the past 35 years. From here, the channel spreads out into the Mababe Depression, forming a large marshy area covering about 110km², and known as the Savuti Marsh.

Maps There are numerous small, winding sand roads around Savuti, relatively few landmarks and very few signs on the tracks. It's easy to become disoriented. If you want to explore the area in detail, you should have with you Veronica Roodt's excellent Chobe map (see page 146), and preferably also a GPS. This and other maps are often available at the park gates, but it's wise not to rely on it.

FLORA AND FAUNA HIGHLIGHTS
Flora Savuti's habitat is a mostly undistinguished thick thorny scrub, with camelthorn (*Vachellia erioloba*) and silver terminalia (*Terminalia sericea*) making up much of it, though there are also large areas of mopane (*Colophospermum mopane*). You'll also find substantial stands of shaving-brush combretum (*Combretum mossambicense*) and Kalahari appleleaf (*Philenoptera nelsii*), and it's perhaps the most westerly area where you can find the lovely paper-bark albezia (*Albezia tanganyicensis*). Dotted all over the drier parts of the area are landmark baobab trees (*Adansonia digitata*); their ability to survive being ring-barked is essential to survival here.

The main contrast to these wooded areas is the Savuti Marsh. Here, the dry areas of the marsh are covered with a variety of perennial grasses that stand above the (geologically) recent alluvial deposits of the channel. These grasses are tolerant of the slightly higher salinity levels present, and some are particularly nutritious and a great attraction for the game when there's moisture about. With the recent floods, part of the marsh is once more underwater, with an attendant change in the vegetation in those areas.

Here you'll also see the skeletons of dead trees, still standing in the flat grasslands and newly flooded marsh areas. These were mostly camelthorns, umbrella thorns (*Vachellia tortilis*) and leadwoods (*Combretum imberbe*) which are thought to have seeded and grown up between the 1880s and the 1950s, when the marsh was dry. Then when it flooded in the late 1950s they were drowned – though the hard, termite-resistant wood still stands.

On the southern side of the marsh you can see the bush gradually starting to invade the grasslands again, with the distinctive, low 'round mounds' of candle-pod acacia (*Vachellia hebeclada*) leading the aggressors.

Fauna At the heart of the park, Savuti sees most of the park's species (pages 258–60), with the normal exception of the Chobe bushbuck and the water-loving species – though with the return of the water, reedbuck and waterbuck may well make their way back.

Whereas when the channel was dry, much of the interest was concentrated around the three remaining waterholes, now there is plenty of water to be found. Either way, there is invariably a lot of game. Lion are frequently found lying around, and big herds will pause as they approach, or wait until their thirst overcomes their fear.

Savuti's elephants are notable for a number of old bulls that live in the area permanently, and are often individuals known to guides who have spent a lot of time in the area. These are augmented by large breeding herds which pass through. Whenever it's dry you can be sure that there's action and jostling for drinking positions at waterholes and along the channel.

In recent years, at least one of the local lion prides has grown so large that they will kill elephants to satisfy their hunger – traumatising the local elephants in the process. (The Khwai River area in Moremi has a similar phenomenon.)

Spotted hyena have always been numerous and very noticeable at Savuti. In the late 1980s and early 90s they would appear at the campsite, skulking around the bins, as soon as the sun set. After dark, and when people had gone to sleep, they'd pick up anything that they could carry, and eat anything small enough to crunch up – including, I was once assured, a glass lens from a 35mm camera! My aluminium camping cooker was stolen by a hyena once at Savuti, and still bears the scars of its strong jaw.

S M Cooper (see *Appendix 3*, page 540) studied the clan sizes here in 1986–88, and found that there were five territorial clans in the area, and a number of transient animals passing through. The clans each averaged about 18 adult females, six males, five of unknown sex and ten cubs under two years of age – so around 39 members of each clan. They tend to prey on reliable, low-density resident game species like impala and warthog throughout the year, and augment this by feasting on the herds as they pass through the area, especially the new-born zebra foals.

Despite the presence of so many lion and hyena, leopards also do well here, perhaps helped by the presence of the rocky kopjes which make a perfect habitat for them. Daryl and Sharna Balfour have some lovely shots of leopard at Savuti in their book on Chobe (see *Appendix 3*, page 544).

Once, when driving with one of Lloyd's guides (who shall remain nameless), we realised that there was an early-morning commotion in the air, and followed this to a young female leopard that had *just* killed an impala. The guide knew that she had a cub nearby to feed. However, our vehicle's approach had, unwittingly, frightened the leopard off her kill, and soon after we arrived so did a hyena – which proceeded to claim the prize.

Such was the maverick nature of Lloyd's Camp that this guide simply jumped out of the cab, grabbed the hindquarters of the impala, and started upon a tug of war with the hyena for the carcass. Spurred on by this, and the realisation that the cub would otherwise miss a meal, I joined in. Eventually we won the carcass and hauled it up on to a low branch hoping that the leopard would reclaim it.

But nature, once upset, isn't so easily put right. As we pulled back from the scene the hyena returned, stretched up on its hind legs, and plucked the impala from the branch with ease. Others swiftly joined it, devouring it within minutes. The leopard had already given up and disappeared, perhaps in disgust.

In the wet season there are still movements of buffalo, zebra and wildebeest which come on to the marsh to graze, though the huge herds of buffalo that used to come when the channel last flowed have now stopped coming. In his guide to Botswana (see *Appendix 3,* page 543) in 1968, Alec Campbell describes the scene on the marsh at that time:

Here the Savuti Channel carries water from the Linyanti … forming a marsh about a meter deep. From June to December huge herds of buffalo visit the marsh to feed in the surrounding scrub mopane and one can see as many as 6,000 daily. Out on the flats which surround it on the southern and western sides are herds of bull elephants, wildebeest, impala, giraffe, tsessebe and sometimes large numbers of zebra. Lion are also quite common.

Cow elephants with their young spend much time in the taller mophane to the east of the marsh but come down to drink in the afternoon. Hippopotami and waterbuck are to be seen in the Channel especially near the mouth where it enters the marsh.

Numbers now probably don't match what was seen then, though April–May is still the prime time for zebra and wildebeest herds to pass through, usually foaling as they go. The precise timing of this is heavily dependent upon the local rainfall patterns.

The kori bustard (*Ardeotis kori*) is one of the world's heaviest flying birds, weighing up to 17kg, and – despite a wingspan of 2.8m – it is a reluctant flyer, needing a good run-up to get airborne. On the ground, these stately birds strike conspicuous figures, and are often seen around the pans, either picking their way hesitantly across the grassland in pairs, one at least 100m from its partner, or resting in the midday shade of an acacia.

Kori bustards often associate with game herds, whose trampling hooves disturb the locusts, beetles, reptiles and other small creatures on which they feed. In turn, they sometimes provide a similar service for the carmine bee-eater (*Merops nubicoides*). This dazzling bird arrives from central Africa in October, and spreads out across the grassland in large flocks. Its usual hunting technique is to hawk for insects – particularly bees – in acrobatic sorties from a fixed perch, such as an anthill or bush, and return to the perch to dispatch and swallow the catch. In open grassland, where fixed perches are in short supply, a kori bustard provides an ideal mobile alternative.

In fact the bustard goes one better than a bush by actively stirring up food for the bee-eater, which snaps up whatever it can catch around the bigger bird's feet before settling again on its back. Bee-eaters are not known to try this trick from the backs of mammals, yet the bustard remains surprisingly tolerant of its passengers, and sometimes two or more of them will hitch a ride.

The dry season can witness large numbers of tsessebe move on to the marsh area to graze. Occasionally, at the end of the dry season, oryx have been known to appear at the south end of the marsh, but they are very uncommon this far north. Always you'll find groups of giraffe in the acacia woodlands on the edge of the marsh and all over the area.

Finally, if you're anywhere around the hills in the area, then P C Viljoen (see *Appendix 3*, page 541) notes that several klipspringer were spotted here on the Qumxhwaa Hill (Quarry Hill) in 1978 and 1979. This has since been confirmed by several reliable sources – including Tricia and Bob Hayne in 2005. Their existence here is remarkable, as the nearest other significant klipspringer population is probably in Zimbabwe's Hwange National Park, about 130km to the east.

Birdlife The list of bird species found in Savuti runs to over 300 species, but some of the more unusual include the Marico flycatcher, crimson boubou, capped wheatears, pennant-winged nightjars (only during the summer, October–January; look especially on the roads at dusk) and Bradfield's hornbill.

In addition, when you're in areas of acacia woodland then keep a look-out for racket-tailed rollers and the spectacular displays of the male broad-tailed paradise whydahs in breeding plumage (February–April).

On Savuti's open areas you'll find the occasional secretary birds, Stanley's bustard, and plenty of the larger kori bustards. The Balfours' coffee-table book on Chobe (see *Appendix 3*, page 544) has a wonderful picture of a carmine bee-eater using the back of a kori bustard as a perch from which to hawk around for insects. Kori bustards are Africa's heaviest flying birds, but heavier still is the flightless ostrich, which can sometimes be seen here. During the summer, Abdim's and white storks congregate in numbers on the marsh.

GETTING THERE It's a day's drive from either Kasane or Maun to Savuti, so most guests at the lodges fly in to Savuti's airstrip (which can take planes as large as a DC3). Visitors to the campsite usually arrive driving their own fully equipped 4x4s, complete with all their supplies. For details, see *Driving from Kasane to Savuti*, pages 273–8, and *Driving from North Gate (Khwai) to Savuti, Chobe NP*, page 322.

WHERE TO STAY Savuti's two luxury camps, its campsite and a new mid-range lodge are all close to each other. All face on to the Savuti Channel, and all are near the bridge over the channel, just to the north of the marsh. Note that the small Savuti Camp, though on the Savuti Channel, is in the private Linyanti Concession west of Savuti: nowhere near the marsh, nor in the area that has, historically, been known as 'Savuti'. For details, see page 299.

Stay in the area for long and you'll hear of the legendary Lloyd Wilmot and his famous Lloyd's Camp; this became something of an institution here, but has sadly now closed. Allan's Camp and Savuti South were opened here (by Gametrackers) and subsequently closed – only to be combined and rebuilt as Savute Elephant Camp (see below).

Because they are in the national park, the lodges here are not permitted to conduct night drives, or to drive off-road, so all activities concentrate on 4x4 game drives during the day – usually with the option to visit local Bushman paintings on request.

Savute Elephant Camp [map 282] (12 chalets) Contact Belmond, page 223; ✪ SAVELE 18°34.207'S, 24°03.269'E. Situated close to the Safari Lodge, Elephant Camp is set to reopen in Jun 2018 following major refurbishment. The camp's traditional style, though, will remain largely intact, as will the footprint of its big tented chalets. Raised on large wooden platforms, each of these faces west over the Savuti Channel, with safari chairs & a comfy day bed on the veranda from which to peruse the wildlife. The tents – which will be clad with a new, high-insulation material – are lined with cream canvas, softened by stylish fabrics in muted colours. Along with polished wooden floors & twin ¾-size beds (or a dbl) under a four-poster mosquito net, the solid furnishings include a sleeper couch suitable for a child, an additional sofa & a writing desk. The AC/heating units & ceiling fan can, like the room's lights, be used day & night, & there's an intercom system in case of emergency. Behind the wooden headboard are twin basins, a bath, large mirrors & plenty of storage space, with polished hardwood doors opening on to a separate flush toilet, & a very private outside shower that's easily big enough for 2.

Paved paths under acacia trees link the rooms with the camp's bar, lounge & dining room, a big, open-sided construction that leads down to an extended terrace, & down again to a long, narrow swimming pool surrounded by decking overlooking the channel. When it's dry, a waterhole is pumped here, attracting elephants to jostle in the water below you, & guests will be able to witness these interactions close up from a new low-level hide. The lodge emphasises the quality of its à la carte meals, served on the terrace or in the dining area, with traditional evenings held in the stockaded boma. With a spotting scope on the terrace, Wi-Fi throughout & a discreet library with a guest computer & satellite TV, Elephant Camp combines 21st-century mod cons with the elegance of yesteryear. It's very similar to its sister camp, Khwai River Lodge (page 319), with which it shares a professionalism marked by friendly service. *From US$970 pp Jan–Mar & mid-Nov to Xmas to US$1,470/2,205 pp sharing/sgl Jul–Sep, inc FB, local drinks, activities, laundry.* ⏰ *All year.* ★★★★–★★★★★

Camp Savuti [map 282] (5 tents) Contact SKL, page 132. This relatively traditional camp was opened on a large, sandy site next to the main campsite in 2010. Set up on wooden platforms, its Meru-style tents have verandas overlooking the (usually dry) Savuti Channel. With twin/dbl beds, AC, en-suite corner baths, flush toilets & open-air showers, they're fairly large & well finished – but note that one of the chalets is literally adjacent to one of the campsite pitches, so is not as private as you might expect. And on the privacy front, you may be sharing your early-morning & afternoon game drives with campers, with up to 8 people on a vehicle. Steps lead up to the chalets & to the open-fronted central area, whose pole-walled sides under a canvas roof help to keep it airy & cool.

With decorative ropework & handmade baskets, it's attractively designed, combining a large bar & dining area at the back with plenty of seating. By the channel, a simple wooden platform provides the option for dining under the stars. *US$685 pp, inc FB, local drinks, activities, laundry, park fees, airstrip transfer.* ☺ *All year.* ★★★★

※ 🏠 **Savute Safari Lodge** [map 282] (12 chalets) Contact Desert & Delta Safaris, pages 223–4; ✪ SAVSAF 18°33.927'S, 24°03.441'E. Savute Safari Lodge opened in 1999, right next to the site of the old Lloyd's Camp, so the local wildlife is exceptionally relaxed with people – to the point that lions have occasionally been found sleeping on the paths between rooms. (There's a discreet electric fence around the lodge &, as with most wildlife camps in Botswana, guests are always escorted by the staff if walking around the camp after dark.) Here, as at the Elephant Lodge, most visitors arrive by plane.

While the design of the lodge is akin to that of a small hotel, the atmosphere is warm, welcoming & very professional. From grounds dotted with tall trees, white giraffe statues welcome visitors to the main area, where a hi-tech fireplace takes centre stage among the sofas, & stools surround a proper bar. With glazed windows & sliding doors, it feels both solid & contemporary. Above, a library – with a computer for guests' use – looks over the trees, ideal for an hour or so's birdwatching. There's a dining area with wooden chairs & tables, but weather permitting, lunch & dinner are usually served on a lower terrace with a firepit & a view of the channel, where water is pumped in the dry season. As a result, elephants regularly congregate here, especially in the afternoons, & you may well spot lions or even giraffe coming to drink too. Sharing the view are sunloungers lining a shaded pool. A curio shop has a range of handicrafts, jewellery, books & clothing.

Large, light, airy chalets, similar in size to those at Elephant Camp, are mostly of wooden construction, with high thatched roofs & raised, polished decking. Glass sliding doors backed by mesh mosquito screens form one entire wall, affording a spectacular view of the channel from 8 of the rooms, or their large verandas, while the others look over the bush. White-tiled bathrooms feel a little out of kilter, but that aside, the soft neutral décor blends well with contemporary design & furnishings, including a comfortable 2-seater couch & armchair. Twin or dbl beds with quality linen are surrounded by a walk-in

mosquito net, below a ceiling fan; there's no AC, but the design of the chalets helps to moderate the excesses of the climate. Electricity is supplied by a generator, backed up by battery power at night.

The guides here when I have visited were keen on wildlife & enthusiastic about finding it. With notice at the time of booking, private guides can be arranged for a whole day. *US$560 pp Jan–Mar & Dec, US$720 pp Apr–Jun & Nov, US$995/1,293 pp sharing/sgl Jul–Oct, inc FB, local drinks, laundry, activities, park fees.* ☺ *All year.* ★★★– ★★★★

🛖 **Savute Under Canvas** (5 tents) Contact &Beyond, page 223. The khaki canvas of this mobile camp may not look inspiring, but this operation takes glamping to a whole new level. Like Chobe Under Canvas (pages 267–8), it is based at private campsites, but here exclusively within the Savuti area. Most guests stay for 2 or 3 nights, but the maximum is 5; in order to protect the environment from damage, the entire camp is moved every 5 days to a new site. Thus the large en-suite tents, proper twin or dbl beds with truly comfortable bedding & good bedside lights, bucket showers & flushing toilets are packed up, along with the central tent, which serves as a dining area & bar, & the selection of field guides that are on hand for you to peruse. 2 game drives a day enable you to explore the area, returning in time for brunch or a starlit dinner. The food, from the most basic of kitchens, is extremely good (do ask to look 'backstage'), & the service is excellent. *From US$500 pp sharing Jan–Mar to US$755 Jul–Oct, inc FB, most drinks, activities, laundry. No children under 12.* ☺ *Part of Jan.* ★★★–★★★★

🛖 **Savuti Campsite** [map 282] (14 pitches) ✆620 0218; contact SKL, page 132; ✪ SAVUTE 18°34.005'S, 24°03.902'E. Savuti's newly privatised campsite is now fronted by an impressive DWNP office & entrance gate, but remains a wonderful place to camp. The site is unfenced, but an ingenious circular wall surrounding the ablution block is designed to be elephant-proof. Smaller animals like cats can easily get out over the wall, but not easily get in. The toilets, showers & laundry areas themselves, with solar-heated water & electric light, are certainly cleaner than of yore.

Many of the numbered pitches sit under old camelthorn trees (with pitch No 1 being particularly good), but shade is very limited in the wet season, when the trees have no leaves. Each has its own braai stand, & a water tap ingeniously encased in concrete to prevent elephants from pulling the pipes to access the clean water (they would often make such an effort for clean water, rather than drinking from the dirty waterhole!). The size of the site, & the distance between the pitches, is such that some campers even drive to the ablution block after dark. Others opt for the proximity & shade offered by the reserve pitches closer to the block. Visibility is good, with not too much undergrowth, though it can be very dusty & there may be the low whine of a generator in the background.

A basic shop (⊕ 11.00–noon & 15.00–19.00) stocks biscuits, tinned goods, beer, wine, basic toiletries & sometimes firewood – oh, & boot polish! – but don't rely on it; you should still aim to bring in everything you need. Game drives can be organised through Camp Savuti (pages 287–8) at US$85–95, depending on the season.

Alongside the elephants for which Savuti is famed, the camp has almost nightly visits from spotted hyenas which, I once discovered, can carry away a full rucksack at high speed, despite being pursued. They will steal & eat anything, from a camera lens to a bar of soap, so leave nothing outside. Then sit back after dinner, turn off your lights, & shield your eyes from the fire. Now, when your vision has adjusted to the dark, shine around a powerful torch. With a little patience you should be able to pick out the ghostly green eyes of hyena, just beyond your firelight. (But beware of shining a torch accidentally at a passing elephant. They don't like this at all!) If you do have any hyena problems, remember that they will push their luck, but are essentially cowardly animals. Chase them & they will run, sometimes dropping their spoils. Just be very careful of what else you might run into during the chase! US$50 pp, exc park fees. ⊕ All year.

WHAT TO SEE AND DO Game viewing and birdwatching are the main activities at Savuti, and there's always something going on – though you might have to look quite hard for it at the end of the dry season. Driving at night is not allowed, but often the wildlife will come quite close enough if you just stay in your campsite/lodge and keep looking around you. There are also some interesting rock paintings on Tsonxhwaa (Bushman) Hill, signposted from the road at (⊕ RKPTGS 18°35.245'S, 24°04.402'E).

DRIVING SOUTH FROM SAVUTI

TO THE MABABE GATE From the DWNP office at Savuti Campsite, it's a drive of about 66km along the direct route south to the Mababe Gate, though you can add another 7km if you take the scenic marsh road. About 5km south of the campsite, just before the hill known as Leopard Rock, the track splits two ways. This junction (⊕ MARSAN 18°06.702'S, 24°00.679'E) is shown very clearly on Veronica Roodt's Chobe map. Along this short stretch, you'll see a couple of signs pointing to the left stating 'rock paintings'.

At the junction, the left-hand track is the **marsh road**, signposted to Savuti Marsh and following its western side. More scenic than the sand-ridge road, it's often a particularly good area for giraffe due to the high number of acacia trees around. In the dry season, it's also a much easier drive, albeit very rutted in parts, but it's a bad route to choose during the rainy season, as you will almost certainly get stuck.

The right fork is the **sand-ridge road**, which heads west of the marsh, and is the more direct route towards the Mababe Gate and Maun. Taking this you will come to another fork after about 25km (⊕ SNDFRK 18°49.076'S, 24°00.357'E), where you bear left for the old sand-ridge road, or right for a dull but relatively straight transit road which now bears the 'sand-ridge' name, and eventually bears left before reaching the gate. The old sand-ridge road is named for the Magwikhwe Sand Ridge, which you'll cross about 26km south of Savuti. Don't expect this to be too obvious, as the ridge is little more than a wide, vegetated sand dune. You will climb slightly to get on to it, and drop slightly to come off – and in between the driving is more difficult than normal as your vehicle's tyres will sink deeper into the sand.

10

Both the marsh road and the old sand-ridge road meet up again at ⊕ SNDMAR 18°55.616'S, 24°00.662'E, about 20km north of the Mababe Gate: the old sand-ridge road takes 37km to reach this from the junction, and the marsh road about 44km. A sign here reads: Khwai 45km, North Gate 54km and Maun 133km. Around here the road becomes more difficult during the rains. In contrast to Savuti's relatively lush vegetation, there is little ground cover, and only low stunted mopane trees to protect the soil from the extremes of the elements. The road's fine earth is hard-baked when dry, and very slippery when wet.

On reaching the Mababe Gate (⊕ MABABE 19°06.182'S, 23°59.119'E; ✆620 0219), you sign out of (or into) Chobe National Park, by presenting your park permit.

CONTINUING TO MOREMI GAME RESERVE AND NORTH GATE From the Mababe Gate, a wide new gravel road leads all the way to North Gate, passing through Khwai Village on the way. While this is much faster than the old route, it misses out on the stunningly beautiful valley of the Khwai River (pages 315–16) where, after the unrelenting dryness of southern Chobe in the dry season, the lily-covered waterways and shady glades under huge spreading umbrella thorns (*Vachellia tortilis*) are completely magical.

The new road is not difficult to find, but there are a couple of junctions that can be confusing. Almost immediately south of the Mababe Gate, the road forks, with a green block indicating Moremi to the right; straight on is for Maun directly. Continuing towards Moremi, you'll come after 4km to another green block (⊕ TOKHW 19°07.719'S, 23°58.078'E). Ignore the signpost right to Khwai, but continue straight ahead for a further 3.5km. At the T-junction, turn right on to the new transit road between Mababe Village and North Gate.

The new road crosses NG18, the Khwai Community Development Trust concession, so you cannot drive off route without a permit. Close to the board proclaiming the trust's ownership, you'll see a signpost to the left to their two Magotho campsites, but otherwise it's an uneventful drive to the Khwai River. You will, though, come to a turning north along this road (at ⊕ SEROTO 19°04.317'S, 23°50.071'E), signposted to Seronga. Beware of this, as it would lead you astray through private concessions towards Selinda.

Continuing to North Gate, the road turns sharply to the left then comes to a new bridge. From here, it's a further 6.5km to North Gate (⊕ NOGATE 19°10.394'S, 23°45.092'E). First, though, you'll go across (or around) another river, pass through Khwai Village, and finally cross a pole bridge over the Khwai River. In 2017, heavy flooding made the river crossing almost impassable, but a detour was signposted around this to the east. If warning logs are laid across the road, do not pass as the river is deceptively deep even for large 4x4s.

CONTINUING TO MAUN Going straight on at the Mababe Gate fork will lead you much more directly and quickly to Maun, reaching Mababe Village (also known as Kudumane) on the new gravel road, after about 10km. Here you'll take a right turn, passing through Sankuyo, the veterinary fence, and then Shorobe, before a final stretch on the tar to Maun. (See page 333 for the latter part of this route – and if you have a GPS then set it for ⊕ MAUN at 19°58.508'S, 23°25.647'E to keep you in roughly the right direction!)

If your destination is Maun, then don't imagine that travelling through the edge of Moremi (on the direct road from North Gate to South Gate) is a quick option. It'll take a good 6 or 7 hours to reach Maun this way. You'll have some slow, heavy driving across the sand ridge, and will be liable for an extra set of park fees for

Moremi (even if you have already paid some for the same day in Chobe). However, if you have pre-arranged a few nights in Moremi, then do take this road and don't miss the chance to stop off. It offers a completely different experience.

🔺 **Where to stay** There are three clear accommodation options along the route towards Maun: two lodges and a community campsite. Close to Mababe Village you'll spot a right turn to **Mogotlho Safari Lodge** (page 405), then a little over 20km further south there's another right turn to **Mankwe Bush Lodge** (page 405). Further south again, **Kaziikini Campsite** (page 228), and Shandereka traditional village, lie some 4km east of the road, in the direction of South Gate.

LINYANTI

The Linyanti River acts as a magnet for game during the dry season, just as its continuation, the Chobe, does further north. Although a few kilometres of the river fall within Chobe National Park, this section tends to be dominated by some very thick reedbeds and vegetation, so can be a disappointing area for wildlife. In addition, reaching this area requires a considerable side-track from the established Moremi–Savuti–Ihaha route across Chobe, so it has tended to get few visitors in the past.

East of the park along the river is the CH1 photographic concession, which is the location of Linyanti Bush Camp and Linyanti Ebony (pages 300–1). To the west is NG15, the Linyanti Concession (pages 295–9), which has several good camps, the nearest of which is Linyanti Tented Camp. And in the middle, within the national park, are Linyanti Campsite and the new Camp Linyanti. Visitors driving themselves are restricted to the national park area and CH1; access to the camps within the Linyanti Concession is permitted only on a fly-in safari.

Note that despite there being a track marked on the maps from Seronga towards the Linyanti, this is not a practical one to use to get here from the west. First, neither private self-drive vehicles nor mobile operators are allowed to drive through the private concessions between the Linyanti and Okavango. Second, you cannot at present cross the Selinda Spillway. And third, even with a GPS, navigation would be a complete nightmare!

FLORA AND FAUNA HIGHLIGHTS This area has a very similar ecosystem to that of the Chobe riverfront (pages 262–6), although the vegetation beside the water here seems to have many more large trees and to be in a more natural state. Because Chobe's Linyanti riverfront is sandwiched between two private concession areas, it's a relatively limited size for game drives. You'll usually see large numbers of elephant at the end of the dry season, but this small stretch of the park is seldom quite as rewarding as the Chobe riverfront area, where the game is much more 'tame'. The presence to the east of an area where hunting was until recently still practised probably hasn't helped to relax the game, although things have improved considerably in that area. West of Linyanti is the private Linyanti Reserve, which is an excellent area with a long stretch of beautiful riverfront and some very good game (pages 295–9).

GETTING THERE AND AWAY Linyanti Campsite and Camp Linyanti (and therefore Linyanti Bush Camp and Linyanti Ebony; pages 300–1) can be approached along deep, sandy tracks either on the transit road direct from Savuti (about 40km) or along the cutline from the Ghoha Gate (totalling 43km). If you're coming from Kasane, follow the directions for Savuti (see *Driving from Kasane to Savuti*, pages 273–8) until you reach the cutline, where instead of turning left for the Ghoha Gate, you turn

10

right towards the Linyanti River. From here it's a slow-going 28km to the Linyanti Gate (✦ LINYGT 18°16.209'S, 23°56.197'E), where you'll need to present your permit before proceeding to the campsite or lodge, just 5km to the southwest.

From Savuti, drive over the new bridge across the Savuti Channel and on to its north bank, and then turn left, heading northwest. Within 1km or so, you'll approach a T-junction, and take a left heading westwards. This crosses the sand ridge (though you may not notice this!) and about 3km later there are two left turnings. Ignore these. Follow the road around to the right, heading in a more northerly direction.

The first few kilometres of this drive is relatively easy, but after this there's about 30km of trickier driving – very deep sand and tougher going, especially one 3km stretch that will test your driving skills (and your vehicle) to the maximum. The scenery is gently rolling dunes, with many flatter areas of low mopane. Visiting one October, I found large numbers of elephants on the road north. Towards the river there was also a pall of dust and woodsmoke hanging over the woods, which was clearly coming from fires raging across the river in Namibia, though in the same month a few years later, the air was clear.

For those doing this journey in reverse, the transit road is signposted from just inside the gate. Note, however, that the roads around Linyanti Campsite are very confusing to navigate, so be particularly vigilant in finding the right track south from here. The correct turning is at ✦ SAVUTO 18°18.228'S, 23°54.903'E, where there's a motley collection of signs at a clear crossroads. Driving through in October 2013, we inadvertently took the cutline road south from Linyanti, ending up at the (then flowing) Savuti Channel before we realised our mistake. Be warned!

WHERE TO STAY Until 2013, drive-in guests to this area of Chobe National Park were limited to camping with their own equipment at the national parks' Linyanti Campsite, but with privatisation came the introduction of the permanent Camp Linyanti. Just outside the park, some 10km to the north, are the camps run by African Bush Camps. As these share much of the same landscape as those in the Linyanti Concession, I have covered them in that chapter (pages 300–1).

Camp Linyanti [map 256] (5 tents) Contact SKL, page 132. Opened next to the campsite in 2013, & under the same management, Camp Linyanti was being revamped in 2017. Its main area, right on the river, is complemented by expanses of wooden decking, & was always well placed to make the best of the picturesque setting. The thatched chalets, though, were originally small & very cramped, but these are being both enlarged & remodelled. The result, while still very rustic, is a real improvement – affording river views from the beds through mesh-fronted wooden doors, a reasonable amount of space to move around, &

showers both inside & out. *US$600 pp, inc FB, local drinks, activities, laundry, park fees; exc transfers.* ⏲ *All year.* ★★★★

Å Linyanti Campsite [map 256] (5 pitches) Contact SKL, page 132; ✦ LINYAN 18°17.686'S, 23°54.601'E. About 40km from Savuti, this is a beautiful little site, close to the river & very quiet, with an acceptable standard of cleanliness. Its pitches share a small ablution block, but there's no drinking water – although filtering & treating river water to drink would be possible in an emergency. Activities can be organised through Camp Linyanti, above. *US$50 pp, exc park fees.* ⏲ *All year.*

WHAT TO SEE AND DO Game drives, walks, mokoro excursions and boat trips can be organised at Camp Linyanti for all visitors – campers and lodge guests alike. In addition to the 7km of accessible riverfront, new game-drive routes have been opened in this corner of the park. Next to the riverbank, there are plenty of reedbeds, which can be a delight for birdwatchers, and the water is home to countless hippo. I've come across the occasional person who absolutely adores this section of the park.

11

Linyanti, Selinda and Kwando Reserves

Almost parallel to the Okavango, the Kwando River flows south from Angola across the Caprivi Strip and into Botswana. Like the Okavango, it starts spreading out over the Kalahari's sands, forming the Linyanti Swamps. Also like the Okavango, in wetter years this is a delta, complete with a myriad waterways linking lagoons: a refuge for much wildlife. It's a wild area, much of which is on the Namibian side of the border, in the Mamili National Park, where it's difficult to access. A faultline channels the outflow from these swamps into the Linyanti River, which flows northeast into Lake Liambezi, and thence into Chobe.

Both the Kwando and the Linyanti rivers are permanent, so for the animals in Chobe and northern Botswana they are valuable sources of water. Like the Chobe and Okavango, they have become the ultimate destination for migrations from the drier areas across northern Botswana – and also sought-after safari destinations, especially in the dry season.

In recent years this area, between the Chobe National Park and the Okavango Delta, has been split into three large concessions – Kwando in the north, Linyanti in the east, and Selinda in the middle. In some ways these are similar, as each encompasses a large area of mopane woodlands and smaller, more prized sections of riparian forest and open floodplains on old river channels. Look at the locations of the camps and you'll realise that much of the interest lies in these floodplains and riparian forests – diverse habitats rich in species.

Away from the actual water, two fossil channels are also worthy of attention: the Savuti Channel and the Selinda Spillway. Both offer contrasting and interesting wildlife spectacles.

BACKGROUND INFORMATION

HISTORY The Kwando River has its headwaters in Angola, from where it flows south across Namibia's Caprivi Strip, forming one boundary between Namibia and Botswana. Progressing over the Kalahari's sands, it is thought that once – around one or two million years ago – it continued southeast, probably through the course of the present-day Savuti Channel, into the Mababe Depression to swell the vast Lake Makgadikgadi (see pages 3–11 for more on the geological history of the region). Then, at some point in the last million years, tectonic shifts raised up a faultline running northwest which effectively 'captured' this river, and diverted it along the fault to flow into the Chobe and Zambezi rivers, thus creating what we now call the Linyanti River.

LINYANTI, SELINDA, KWANDO AREA

KEY

Private concession

GPS co-ordinates ⊕

CUTTUR	18°21.820S,	24°10.633E
DETOR2	18°15.250S,	24°19.087E
LINYAN	18°17.686S,	23°54.601E
LINYGT	18°16.209S,	23°56.197E
MARSAN	18°06.702S,	24°00.679E
OKAV16	18°40.219S,	23°29.856E
OKAV22	18°43.931S,	23°46.320E
SAVBRI	18°34.979S,	23°33.018E
SAVUTO	18°28.228S,	23°54.903E

NOTE

For accommodation listings, see pages 298–9, 300–1, 302–4, 306–7

Bradt

N

0   20km
0   10 miles

top   Many of the camps in northern Botswana benefit from cool waterside locations (SS)

above left   The best of Botswana's safari lodges boast a very high level of luxury (SS)

above right   Innovative sunshades help mitigate the extremes of the Kalahari climate (SS)

below   Camping in Botswana's national parks can feel exceptionally remote (BH) pages 131–3 above   Riding safaris are a great, non-intrusive way to see the Okavango's resident wildlife (SS) pages 372–4

left   A walking safari provides the ultimate adrenalin rush, but it's important to stay safe (AVZ) page 120

below   A scenic flight gives an entirely different perspective on grazing buffalo (TH) page 220 *above*   Travelling by mokoro is a very unobtrusive way to explore the tranquil waters of the Okavango (SS) pages 191–2

below   Game drives in the Okavango Delta give guests an exceptional view of wildlife, including herds of elephant (JG)

above   The iconic baobab — here in the Makgadikgadi Pans — is known as the 'tree of life' (HT/S) page 465

left above   Waterlily (*Nymphaea nouchali caerulea*) (TH) page 352

left below   Flame lily (*Gloriosa superba*) (TH)

below   During the rains the desolate Makgadikgadi Pans come to life, with migrating herds of zebra and wildebeest (JG) pages 465–6 *above*   Considered to be the highest point in the Kalahari, the Tsodilo Hills rise above the surrounding desert (RF) pages 427–36

right   The Central Kalahari Game Reserve is Africa at its most remote (JG) pages 491–510 *above left*   A Hambukushu woman fishing with a woven basket (SS) page 102

top right   Colourful fabrics hang from a roadside stall in Kasane (TH)

above right   Traditionally Botswana's main carbohydrate, sorghum is pounded and then made into porridge of different consistencies (SS) page 154

below   Guiding visitors around the Kalahari helps the San retain the hunting and gathering skills that have been honed over millennia (SS) pages 91–100

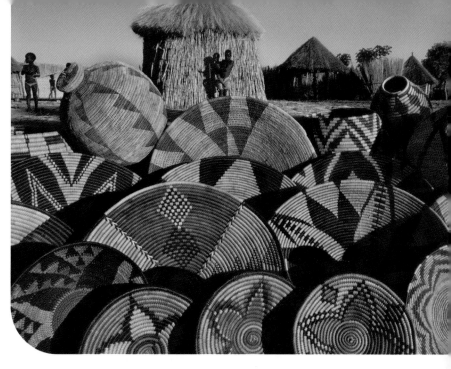

above Baskets are hand woven for use in the home, as well as for decorative purposes (SS) page 110

below The rhythmic clapping and singing that accompany a trance dance build to a crescendo as the night wears on (SS) page 95 *above*   The rarely visited Gcwihaba Caves are part of a labyrinth of underground passages (SS) page 445

below   Sporadically inhabited for about 60,000 years, the Tsodilo Hills feature some of the world's most impressive rock art (TH) pages 427–36

Around the same time, a parallel fault – the Thamalakane Fault – is also thought to have halted the Okavango's course, trapping it and ultimately silting it up to form an inland delta. As the gradients in this part of the northern Kalahari are very small indeed (1:4,000 is typical of the gradient in the Okavango Delta) the routes taken by these watercourses are very susceptible to the tiniest tilts in the earth's surface. As an aside, these faults probably mark the most southerly extent of Africa's Great Rift Valley.

Like the trapped Okavango, silting gradually allowed the Kwando/Linyanti river to spread out into a small inland delta, forming what we call the Linyanti Marshes today.

There is one further geographical feature of note in this area: an ancient river course known as the Magwegqana (spelled in various ways) or Selinda Spillway. This splits off from around the Okavango's Panhandle area, and heads northeast, entering the Linyanti River system just north of the Zibadianja Lagoon. This doesn't seem to be the obvious product of any local faultlines – although it does roughly follow the line of the Linyanti–Gumare Fault. It's either some form of overflow from the Okavango Delta, or perhaps an ancient river course, or both. Either way it's highly visible from the air, and on the ground offers a rich and open environment for game.

GEOGRAPHY The geography of the various parts of this area follows on directly from its geological history, and can easily be divided into four types of environment.

Firstly, there are the Linyanti Swamps, composed of river channels, lagoons, reedbeds and banks of papyrus. Secondly, adjacent to these is a narrow belt of riparian forest that lines these waterways – on the northern edge of the Linyanti Reserve, and the eastern edge of Kwando.

Thirdly there are two intermittent rivers, the Selinda Spillway and the Savuti Channel. Although both were dry for a number of years, both have flooded annually since 2009. There are similarities as well as differences between them, most notably the sheer width of the spillway as it approaches the Linyanti Swamp compared with the relatively narrow Savuti Channel.

Finally, and common to all the concessions, are large areas of dry woodland dominated by large stands of mopane trees, which cover most of the three areas but are usually of least interest to the visitor on safari.

LINYANTI CONCESSION (NG15)

The Linyanti Concession covers 1,250km² of the northern Kalahari, dominated by large areas of mopane woodlands. However, its northern and western edges are bounded by the waters of the Linyanti River, complete with a string of lagoons and marshes. Adjacent to this is a narrow band of highly varied riparian forest which is the focus of most safari activities.

Cutting from west to east, through the southern part of the concession, is the bed of the Savuti Channel. A dry sand river during the 1990s and early 2000s, where a number of waterholes would attract game during the dry season, the channel started flowing once again in 2008. In 2017, it continued to flow through 2–4km of the concession, reviving the lush, riverine woodland along its banks, which in turn attracts a range of wildlife.

GETTING ORGANISED
Getting there and away Getting to any of the camps in the Linyanti Concession is simple: you fly. Wilderness Safaris (who run all four camps) include light-aircraft

11

flights in their trips into these camps, and it's very easy to fly here from Maun, Kasane, or another camp in northern Botswana. The airstrip (page 300; ⊕ DUMAIR 18°31.948'S, 23°39.264'E) is equidistant between DumaTau and Savuti Camp.

Logistics at all these camps are worked out well in advance, and everybody who arrives must have a prior reservation (most made months earlier). No self-driving visitors are allowed into the area, even those with reservations. So if you drive in, you can expect to be escorted off the property and pointed in the direction of a public road!

When to visit Note the general comments made on pages 113–20, and then also the specific comments made for the Chobe riverfront, on pages 262–6 – because the Linyanti's riverfront has broadly the same kind of game movements as that area. In short: game concentrates around here when it needs the water, and spreads out when it can easily drink elsewhere.

This means that the game will be better when it's drier, although you'll find a wider variety of bird species here in the wet season, many of them in their breeding plumage.

FLORA AND FAUNA Until commercial hunting was outlawed throughout Botswana in 2014, the Linyanti Reserve was technically a 'multi-purpose concession', where both photographic safaris and hunting were allowed. However, Wilderness Safaris – who have been running the reserve for more than 15 years – has always focused exclusively on photographic tourism, thus reducing the negative impacts of hunting on the animal populations.

Flora As with the animals, in many ways the vegetation here is very similar to that of the Chobe riverfront area, though it generally seems in much better condition. It's thicker, older and more lush – though perhaps that is simply the result of much less logging by humans and slightly less pressure from the animals.

In the dry season there is usually at least 1km of open ground between the slightly raised riverbank, dotted with mature riparian forest, and the actual waters of the Linyanti. Most of this is open grassland, which this will flood occasionally at times of very high water in the river system. In this area you'll find some smaller bushes, like russet bush-willows (*Combretum hereoense*) and Kalahari star apples (*Diospyros lycoides*) – the latter also known as toothbrush bushes after a surprisingly effective use for their thinner branches. (You may also hear this called the blue bush.)

Beyond the floodplain, and up the riverbank, you'll find classic riparian forest with plenty of tall species like knobthorn (*Senegalia nigrescens*), raintree (*Philenoptera violacea*), leadwood (*Combretum imberbe*), jackalberry (*Diospyros mespiliformis*), African mangosteen (*Garcinia livingstonei*) and some marvellous spreading sycamore figs (*Ficus sycomorus*). There are some woolly caper-bushes (*Capparis tomentosa*) in the lower vegetation, but fewer of them than you'll notice beside the Chobe.

Inland, far from the river, is dominated by mopane (*Colophospermum mopane*), though there are also mixed areas, notable for their Kalahari appleleaf (*Philenoptera nelsii*), wild seringa (*Burkea africana*), and others in the areas of deeper sand, like old watercourses. Baobabs (*Adansonia digitata*) are dotted around sporadically.

The area around Savuti Camp is very much like this dry woodland, interlaced with sandy fossil riverbeds, while along the narrow Savuti Channel itself you'll find more open grassland.

Fauna All year round you're likely to see impala, kudu, giraffe, reedbuck, steenbok, warthog, baboon and vervet monkeys throughout the area. Lion and spotted hyena are common, and generally the dominant predators, while leopard are often seen in the riparian forest and can be the highlight of night drives.

Cheetah occur, but not very frequently, and may have moved out of the area. Wild dog usually stay near their dens from around June to September (with July and August being the most reliable time for them), and then range widely over most of northern Botswana. Wild dog sightings on the reserve were reportedly consistent in 2017, with four packs being spotted regularly, one of which is believed to have denned between Savuti and DumaTau, and a second north of King's Pool. (As an aside, dens in wild areas like this are not easily located, even when wild dogs have a presence in the vicinity.)

Blue wildebeest and Burchell's zebra are present all year, although around May they will arrive in larger numbers, remaining within reach of the water until just before the rains begin in around November–December, when they normally head southeast towards Savuti Marsh. Elephants and buffalo follow a similar pattern, with small groups around all year, often only bulls, but with much larger breeding herds arriving in June–July and staying until December. During this time you'll regularly find very large herds of both buffalo and elephant, hundreds strong. Sable and roan antelope are regularly seen from June to December, congregating at waterholes around midday in herds up to 25 strong. Tsessebe occur, but are uncommon. Eland are very rare here, and gemsbok don't occur this far north.

Waterbuck are permanent residents, especially towards the northeast of the concession. This is one of relatively few areas of Botswana where they're found. Keep a look-out around King's Pool and Linyanti Tented Camp, particularly at the interface between the mopane woodlands of the interior and the riparian forest by the river. Sitatunga are occasionally sighted from boat trips on the river and from the deck of Linyanti Tented Camp.

Side-striped and black-backed jackal are around, the latter reaching the extreme northern edge of its distribution here (so it isn't common). Bat-eared fox are regularly seen; the area around King's Pool airstrip seems to be a particular favourite. Mongooses, especially banded and dwarf, are always around, and even bushpig are resident at DumaTau.

Serval, caracal, African wildcat and aardwolf occur. Before the channel started flowing in 2009, Savuti Camp had a notably excellent record of sightings for these, especially serval. Sightings have since been less frequent, but they still sometimes occur. Aardvark are occasionally seen, with one local expert reporting that they used to be spotted frequently in the riverine forest near the Zibadianja Lagoon.

When you're out on night drives, you've also got a chance to see scrub hares, spring hares, lesser bushbabies, porcupines, genets (small-spotted and large-spotted), civets and honey badgers.

Birdlife In the riparian woodlands, birds of particular interest include wood owls, swamp boubous, brown firefinches, white-rumped babblers and collared sunbirds. Of particular note is the beautiful Schalow's lourie, a local race of the Knysna lourie found in this region.

There are numerous summer migrants, including carmine bee-eaters that nest here in their hundreds. There are several colonies in the area, including one between King's Pool and DumaTau, where there used to be a hide. Carmines tend to arrive around September and leave by March–April. Some appear to have learned to follow vehicles down the Savuti Channel, catching the crickets that jump away from the moving wheels. Others use the kori bustards, which frequent the channel, as moving perches. Other summer visitors include the thick-billed cuckoo and the

11

narina trogon. And in 2017, a Ross's touraco was resident in the King's Pool area for a month, an extremely rare visitor!

The raptors are well represented. Bateleur and fish eagles are probably the most numerous, but you're also likely to spot African hawk, and tawny, martial and black-breasted snake eagles. Gymnogenes are relatively common. When the first rains come in December, migrants like Wahlberg's and steppe eagles seem notably attracted to the first flush of green in the Savuti Channel – hence December to February can be a particularly good time here.

Throughout the year, western banded snake eagles are also sometimes seen, though they're not common, along with giant eagle owls, bat hawks (look out on the edge of the forest, by the river, in the evening) and the occasional Pel's fishing owl.

On the water there's a host of different species, though some of the marshes and lagoons within the Linyanti Concession can be difficult to access. (For mokoro and boat trips, consider the camps operated by African Bush Camps in the CH1 concession, pages 300–1.) Some of the more unusual residents include slaty and black egret, rufous-bellied heron, painted snipe, long-toed lapwing, African rail and wattled crane. African skimmers usually nest here in September, with Zibadianja Lagoon, among others, being a favourite spot for them.

⌂ WHERE TO STAY

All four camps within the Linyanti Reserve are owned by Wilderness Safaris (page 225). They range from the substantial comfort of King's Pool to the much more simple bushcamp style of Linyanti Tented Camp, and are listed here from north to south. All cater exclusively for fly-in visitors and none will accept visitors who want to drive in.

⌂ King's Pool [map 294] (9 chalets)
⊕ KINGSP 18°26.276'S, 23°42.415'E. Luxury is the keyword here – for King's Pool is one of Botswana's top 3 or 4 lodges & one of Wilderness's flagship camps. It overlooks the Linyanti River & the swamps beyond from a position in the very centre of the reserve, almost 18km northeast of DumaTau & a similar distance from Linyanti Tented Camp.

Each of the well-spaced rooms, which include a 2-bedroom family unit, is effectively like an individual villa, on high wooden decking under a thatched roof. Extensive & stylish, they're pole framed with canvas-&-gauze wall panels, & a soundly constructed bathroom, with separate toilet. Leather armchairs, teak furniture with rich fabrics in neutral colours, & a large bed under a mosquito net give a solid, conservative feel. Big folding doors lead to a deck with a small plunge pool & a *sala* – think exclusive thatched gazebo with day bed – overlooking the Linyanti River.

You could justifiably just chill here & watch game on the river – & many visitors do – though for the energetic, each room comes supplied with an exercise mat & weights. The central area, while not particularly cosy, is well appointed with leather chairs & extensive decking, while outside there's an open-air boma for meals under the stars. On the edge of camp there's a swimming pool &, separately, a hide for game viewing (though it's questionable if this offers better game viewing or birdwatching than is already possible from the balconies of the chalets).

Activities are mainly 4x4 game drives, day & night. These concentrate on the riverine forest areas beside the water &, when dry, the wide grassy floodplains between the river's water & the high bank. Short walks are also possible, & when the water levels are high enough (around Apr–Aug) there's a double-decker boat for gentle sundowner cruises – with sleepouts on board a further option.

A couple of small game hides allow guests to get close to wildlife, especially elephants, hippo & waterbirds. Both double as a lovely setting for lunch, with one a great option for dinner *à deux*. *From US$1,060/1,330 pp sharing/sgl Jan–Mar to US$2,245/2,975 Jun–Oct, inc FB, most drinks, activities, park fees, laundry; exc transfers.* ⊕ *All year.* ★★★★★

⌂ DumaTau [map 294] (10 tents)
⊕ DUMATA 18°32.217'S, 23°33.917'E. At the western end of the Linyanti, overlooking the Osprey Lagoon from

its southeastern shore, DumaTau is east of the source of the Savuti Channel. Its location between 2 elephant corridors means that pachyderm sightings are almost guaranteed, especially in the dry season (Jun–Oct), & the camp's elevated design permits elephants to get very close without any awareness of spectators just metres away.

The camp was rebuilt completely in 2012. Its luxurious en-suite tents, 2 designed for families, are raised on wooden platforms, & have hot showers (both indoors & outside) washbasins & flush toilets. There is a central dining room, bar & lounge, & a small plunge pool for afternoon dips. Activities centre around 4x4 game drives, day & night, which visit the riverine forest beside the Linyanti, as well as the drier areas along the upper reaches of the Savuti Channel & the mopane forest between. Short walks are sometimes possible, & when water levels are high, a boat can be used on the lagoon & in nearby waterways. Guests staying 3 nights or more may pre-book (at no additional cost) a sleep out on the reserve's covered star deck at the source of the Savuti Channel (with a guide in a tent not too far away). The deck has a sunken lounge, a flush toilet & handbasins – & superb views. *From US$985/1,290 pp sharing/sgl mid-Jan–Mar to US$1,780/2,315 Jun–Oct, inc FB, most drinks, activities, park fees & laundry; exc transfers.* ⏰ *All year.* ★★★★–★★★★★

🏠 **Savuti Camp** [map 294] (7 tents) ✪ SAVUTI 18°35.834'S, 23°40.412'E. Savuti Camp stands beside the Savuti Channel, about 42km due west of the Savuti Marsh – the area within the Chobe National Park that's commonly known as 'Savuti' (pages 280–9). It's about 13km as the eagle flies from Zibadianja Lagoon.

The camp's Meru-style tents, 1 designed for families, are raised up on individual wooden decks with a veranda, under the cool shade of a large thatched roof. All have en-suite showers, toilets &

washbasins with hot & cold water. Raised wooden walkways lead to a dining room & bar/lounge area under a thatched roof, a star deck & small pool.

Activities concentrate on 4x4 game drives by day & night, although walks are also possible, & there are several elevated hides to visit. Until the heavy rainfall of 2008–09, the waterhole in front of the camp was the only source of water in the dry season for miles around. Hence the camp had a justified reputation for lion & elephant – & witnessed a surprisingly high concentration of serval on night drives. Now it appears that the dry periods are back, & the few kilometres of water here attract large herds of game & their attendant predators. *From US$745/1,010 pp sharing/sgl mid-Jan–Mar to US$1,545/2,010 Jun–Oct, inc FB, most drinks, activities, park fees & laundry; exc transfers.* ⏰ *All year.* ★★★★–★★★★★

🏠 **Linyanti Tented Camp** [map 294] (5 chalets) About 10km southwest of Chobe's Linyanti Campsite (page 292), & not to be confused with Linyanti Bush Camp, this is an old-style safari camp, far from the interior-designer chic found elsewhere. With a maximum of 8 guests, it is often used by set-departure fly-in groups, & families or small groups of friends. Wood-framed, canvas-walled chalets have replaced the original tents, but it still offers modest comforts in place of plush luxuries. Each chalet has functional features such as a wardrobe, bedside table with reading lamp & dressing table with mirror, along with an en-suite hot shower, washbasin & flushing toilet. Together with the dining & bar area, which nestles beneath an open & slightly elevated timber-&-canvas structure, they all overlook the Linyanti River. There's a pool here, too, and a new woodpile hide close to an elephant path with views over the river. Activities are limited to day & night game drives in the camp's concession & day trips further afield. Rates quoted only as part of a group trip. ⏰ *All year.*

LINYANTI ENCLAVE (CH1)

Just to the east of Chobe National Park's Linyanti Gate, this concession shares a very similar environment to that of the Linyanti Reserve, although the riverside camps here offer water-based activities as well as game drives. Note that the unrelated Linyanti Campsite and Camp Linyanti lie within Chobe National Park, so are covered in that chapter (page 292).

GETTING THERE Whereas camps within the Linyanti Reserve are exclusively for fly-in guests, those in CH1 can also be accessed by self-drivers – although all guests must have a prior reservation; you cannot just turn up here.

By air Guests arriving by air at one of African Bush Camps' properties are flown to Saile airstrip, from where it's a pleasant half-hour game drive to Linyanti Bush Camp and Linyanti Ebony.

By road Self-drivers can approach the Linyanti River camps from one of two directions, both involving significant stretches of deep sand. From Kasane, the best option is to drive towards Chobe National Park's Ghoha Gate, as described under *Driving from Kasane to Savuti*, on pages 273–8, but then to turn right along the cutline; this is outside the park, so you don't need to pay park fees. Some 36km from the Ghoha Gate you'll reach the Linyanti Gate, where you turn right. From here, it's just over 4km northeast along the river to Linyanti Bushcamp. Approaching from Savuti, you could either head north to the Ghoha Gate, then continue along the cutline as above, or take the direct if little-used route to the Linyanti Gate as described on pages 291–2, then continue north for a further 4km or so to the camps.

WHERE TO STAY African Bush Camps (page 223) operates two very open camps here: Linyanti Bush Camp and the adjacent Linyanti Ebony. For every guest, US$10 per night is paid (at no extra cost to the guest) into the African Bush Camps Foundation. This in turn ploughs the money back into the fields of education, conservation, community infrastructure and empowerment, so your visit is having a direct benefit on the wider community.

For the simpler and unrelated Linyanti Campsite and Camp Linyanti, both sharing a river frontage but within Chobe National Park, see page 292.

Linyanti Bush Camp [map 294] (6 tents) ⊕ LINYBC 18°14.804'S, 23°57.514'E. This fundamentally traditional camp on the edge of the Linyanti Marshes opened in 2007. It's comfortable & attractive, yet the surrounding bush is almost entirely unmanicured, a feeling enhanced by sand paths & a very open outlook facing the marshes. Large, walk-in tents, which were upgraded in 2017, have big gauze windows & new wooden decks to take in the view. The tents themselves are smarter than of old, without compromising the setting. Solid twin ¾ beds or a king-size dbl sit on wooden floors, along with other dark-wood furniture & a homely sofa. There's a basin, solar-heated shower & flush toilet en suite, a floor-standing fan/cooling unit, & decent bedside lights.

The camp has a deliciously cool splash pool surrounded by a stockade to keep out elephants, & an old logpile hide serves as a backdrop for traditional dinners. There's a rather quirky curio shop, too, whose wares include baskets made by a ladies' co-operative at realistic prices. Typically you'll enjoy an early-morning b/fast round the campfire, or dine at a long table on the deck or in the open-sided canvas shelter, where comfortable chairs invite relaxation.

Activities are led by top-class guides & are very flexible; guests are welcome to do 3 or even more activities a day if they wish. Along with day & night game drives, mokoro excursions & walking, these include a magical ½hr helicopter flight across the marshes & wooded hinterland, followed by a game drive back to camp. When the water is high enough, usually around Dec–Aug, a shaded pontoon boat makes for leisurely cruising along the channels. *From US$580 pp Jan–Mar & Dec to US$905/1,106 pp sharing/sgl Jul–Oct, inc FB, most drinks, activities, park fees, laundry; exc transfers. No children under 7.* ⊕ *All year.* ★★★–★★★★

Linyanti Ebony [map 294] (4 tents) Adjacent to Linyanti Bush Camp, & very similar in style, Ebony works as a stand-alone camp that's ideal for small groups or families. With this in mind, it has 1 elevated family tent, sleeping up to 5 in 2 interconnecting en-suite rooms, of which 1 has a bath with a view. This tent is reached from the main area along a wooden walkway that incorporates a small splash pool, whereas sand paths lit by paraffin lanterns lead to the other tents. These are set on low wooden decking, & are not unlike those at Bush Camp, though 1 has its own bathtub. The mess tent is open to the front, its deck shaded beneath a mature ebony tree, & with a traditional firepit facing the marsh. Activities follow an identical format to those at its sister camp, with the same vehicles & guides, but Ebony has its own kitchen. *Rates as Linyanti Bush Camp.* ⊕ *All year.* ★★★–★★★★

SELINDA CONCESSION (NG16)

Selinda covers a long swathe of 1,350km², including a large section of the Magwegqana or Selinda Spillway, the often-dry waterway that links the Okavango to the Linyanti Swamps. However, after a period of close on 30 years, the Spillway is again flowing all the way from the Okavango Delta to the marshes of the Kwando and Linyanti, transforming the landscape into a mosaic of savannah and wetland.

Most of the reserve's camps are in the far east of the concession, in a very open area where small tree-islands stand amid large dry plains. The western side of the concession is largely thick combretum and mopane forest; here, the old Motswiri Camp, once used for hunting, has been totally refurbished for photographic safaris.

FLORA AND FAUNA
Flora The area around Selinda and Zarafa camps is the wide mouth of the Magwegqana or Selinda Spillway – which is largely composed of open floodplains dotted with small palm islands. The spillway floods only very rarely, as now, but when it does it clears, or kills off, many small trees and bushes on the plains, leaving only flat marshes and grasslands behind.

Until 2009, these areas were gradually being colonised by 'pioneer species' of invading bushes, among them the wild sage (*Pechuel-loeschea leubnitziae*), which covered large areas of the spillway with its aromatic grey-green foliage, and the candle-pod acacia (*Vachellia hebeclada*). With the return of the water, these plants are likely to be cleared.

Dotted around this area are small, slightly raised 'islands' of trees. These have been here for decades, and can survive the periodic flooding – though see the comments on pages 9–11 if you're curious as to how such 'islands' are formed. The trees found on these tree-islands are typical in many ways of those in the riparian forests, though with the addition of lots of real fan palms (*Hyphaene petersianna*). Some are tall trees, many are only bush-sized, but all help to make Selinda's environment a particularly attractive one. Among the other tree species here, African mangosteens (*Garcinia livingstonei*) seem particularly common and lush, their branches all apparently flung outwards, as if a green bomb had exploded inside.

Fauna As in the Linyanti and Kwando reserves, there's a population of resident game here, which is swelled from about June onwards by the arrival of large numbers of game which move into the reserve for its proximity to the permanent waters of Zibadianja Lagoon and the Kwando–Linyanti river system.

Permanent game includes impala, red lechwe (on the east side near the lagoon), kudu, tsessebe, giraffe, reedbuck, steenbok, warthog, baboon and vervet monkeys. Lion and spotted hyena are common, and there are good sightings of leopard, usually around the larger tree-islands. The very open country is certainly good for cheetah, and though I've never seen them myself, I do get regular reports of them here.

Over the years, Selinda has been one of Botswana's better reserves for wild dog; the pack known locally as the 'Selinda pack' have denned at various locations in the area in most years for some time now. Although wild dog do range over the whole of northern Botswana, if you want any chance of seeing them then you'll need a place where your guide can drive off-road, to stick with them as they hunt, and where there's lots of dry, open grassland with not too many trees, so that the driving is relatively free of obstacles. This narrows your choice down to a few of the private reserves, but would certainly include Selinda, Mombo, Vumbura, Kwara, Linyanti, the area around the Khwai River, and the southern side of Kwando. I don't wish to imply here that you won't see dogs elsewhere; you will. However, if I were going out specifically to look for dogs, then I'd start in these areas. On one visit I followed them hunting for over an hour. As they sped across the open ground, they would frequently run through the small palm-islands to try and flush out any game hiding there. To keep up with them, we'd drive around the islands, and wait for them to come out on the other side again.

Herds of wildebeest and zebra arrive around May, staying here until just around November–December. Elephants and buffalo follow a similar pattern with individuals being seen all year, and larger breeding herds arriving around June–July and staying until December. Eland, sable and roan occur, but none of them is common.

Side-striped jackal, bat-eared fox and various mongooses are resident, as are the more nocturnal serval, caracal, African wildcat and aardwolf. Night drives will usually locate scrub hares, spring hares, lesser bushbabies, genets (small-spotted and large-spotted), civets, sometimes honey badgers or porcupines, and – rarely – aardvark.

Birdlife Virtually all of the birds typical of riparian woodlands in the neighbouring Linyanti and Kwando reserves (pages 297–8 and 306) also occur in the tree-islands of Selinda. In addition to this, the reserve is noted for good sightings of collared palm thrush, plus species of open grasslands like ostriches, secretary birds, kori bustards, red-crested korhaans, various sandgrouse and both common and (from November to March) harlequin quails. The family of coursers is well represented here – with the uncommon bronze-winged and three-banded varieties occurring as well as the more widespread Temminck's and double-banded coursers.

During Botswana's summer months the birding is at its best, with all the European and central African migrants in residence. Then, black coucal, carmine bee-eaters, and flocks of Abdim's and white storks can be seen, along with African skimmers fishing on the surface of the lagoons, while raptor concentrations are always good.

GETTING THERE AND AWAY Now that the spillway is flowing, the Selinda Reserve is effectively cut off from Maun and Kasane by rivers, so all visitors arrive by air, rendering redundant the detailed directions for self-drivers that appeared in earlier editions of this guide. The flight takes about an hour from Maun or Kasane, and is very easily organised by the camp or your tour operator. There's an airstrip situated halfway between the Selinda and Zarafa camps, less than 5km from either of them.

WHERE TO STAY All the camps in the Selinda Concession, except Motswiri, are now run by Great Plains Conservation (page 224), but the pioneer here was Linyanti Explorations.

Linyanti Explorations started in Botswana in 1976 as the small, owner-run operation which founded Chobe Chilwero (selling it in 1999), and they solidified their reputation with the superb, simple camps of the Selinda Reserve. Over the years, as ownership of Botswana's safari camps became concentrated into fewer companies, and many of those camps have opted to prioritise luxury, Linyanti Explorations dared to be different. It stayed simple, concentrating on its wildlife and guiding – and hence was always a firm favourite of mine!

In 2006, the company was bought by Great Plains Conservation, which is backed by Dereck and Beverly Joubert, famous wildlife film-makers and photographers. They stopped the (controlled) hunting that took place in the west of the reserve, and spent a lot of money upgrading and rebuilding the two camps. They also refurbished Motswiri (page 304), a former hunting camp which stands in a lovely spot beside the Selinda Spillway in the far west of the concession – and is now leased to RAW Botswana, who specialise in riding and walking safaris. (I was lucky enough to drive from Selinda to Motswiri during the high flood of 2006. Then the spillway flooded completely, nearly linking the Linyanti and Okavango systems for the first time in many years; three years later, in 2009, the link was made.)

More recently, the company added Selinda Explorers camp to their portfolio. Two simple tented camps in the western section of the reserve, Lechwe Island and Ketumetse Trails camps, have been demolished. In their place, Great Plains has introduced the Selinda Canoe Trail, which traverses the reserve from west to east.

Like most of Botswana's high-quality camps, bookings for all these must be made in advance and virtually everyone flies in. Great Plains encourages travellers to book through good overseas tour operators that specialise in Africa.

🏠 Zarafa [map 294] (4 tents) ⊕ ZARAFA 18°35.17.5′S, 23°31.544′E. Once Botswana's smallest permanent camp, the former Zibadianja Camp was renamed in 2009 to reflect a complete rebuild, taking it right upmarket. The new camp, constructed along a well-vegetated forest about 2km southeast of the original, overlooks the floodplains of the Zibadianja Lagoon. It remains tiny, but the huge tents (each almost 100m²), top service & food put this in the bracket of one of Botswana's best camps. Set among the trees, each tent (more like a marquee in style) is an individual suite with a large deck, a separate lounge with comfortable chairs, & its own plunge pool. Both indoor & outdoor showers are complemented by a copper bath, & there's even a copper-hooded fire for warmth in the winter months. Conversely, there's a unique cooling system above each of the beds for the warmer months.

Mirroring the style of the suites is the main dining & lounge area, with an expansive deck for outdoor dining. Power for the whole camp is derived entirely from solar panels – claimed to be an African first for such a luxury camp.

Activities at Zarafa, & the team's enthusiasm for them, mirror those at Selinda, with the addition of a motorised pontoon which traverses the lagoon in front of camp. The guiding when I last visited was up to its usual high standards. *From US$1,410 pp mid-Jan–Mar to US$2,800/4,200 pp sharing/sgl mid-Jun–Oct, inc FB, most drinks, activities, park fees, laundry; exc transfers.* ⊕ *All year.* ★ ★ ★ ★ ★

🏠 Selinda Camp [map 294] (9 tents) Contact Great Plains (page 224); ⊕ SELIND 18°31.897′S,

23°31.354′E. Standing on the edge of the Selinda Spillway, the reserve's main camp has been extensively refurbished over the years. Substantial walk-in tents, including one for families, are constructed on raised wooden decks under thatched canopies. Each has comfortable twin or dbl beds, & an en-suite bathroom with shower, washbasin & flush toilet at the back, as well as an egg-shaped stand-alone bath. The tents are decked out with furniture from all over Africa, including colonial-style desks & lamps made from Maasai gourds. Electricity for fans, water heaters, etc, is provided by solar power.

The camp's main building is a towering thatched structure, its horseshoe shape containing a bar (often self-service) & a comfy lounge, with many of the pieces painted by wildlife artist Keith Joubert. Meals are served both indoors & under the stars, where the candlelit dinners are marvellously atmospheric. There's also a reading area, an artefacts store, & a walk-in wine cellar. Outside are a small plunge pool for when it's hot, & a boma area with central campfire for cool mornings & evenings.

The team remain enthusiastic about their activities, which concentrate on 4x4 game drives in the morning & afternoon/evening. The former can start very early in the morning (a good sign of commitment to their game spotting!), the latter eventually becoming spotlit night drives. In addition, short walks can be organised, often as part of a drive, & during the winter months canoeing & boating are on offer. Hides across the reserve offer good spots to relax during an afternoon siesta. *From US$820 pp Mar to*

11

US$1,740/2,610pp sharing/sgl mid-Jun–Oct, inc FB, most drinks, activities, park fees, laundry; exc transfers. ⊕ *All year.* ★★★★–★★★★★★

🏠 **Selinda Explorers** [map 294] (4 tents) ⊕ SELEXP 18°30.686'S, 23° 25.913'E. About 90mins' drive west of Selinda & Zarafa, on the banks of the Selinda Spillway, this is the most recent addition to the concession. It is designed very much in the style of a classic mobile camp, albeit in a static setting, with canvas the fabric of choice & an open-sided main area shaded by large jackalberry trees. Uniquely for northern Botswana, Selinda Explorers may be reserved only as a whole, so is ideal for a large group of friends or a family. The atmosphere really comes to life as the sun goes down, when the camp is lit entirely by paraffin lanterns & a campfire. Although there's no electricity, cameras & other devices can be charged through an inverter system powered by the game-drive vehicle batteries.

Guests stay in large, Meru-style tents, with more than enough space to stand up & walk around in. Each is simple but well decorated with twin beds, or a dbl, & some nice touches such as a decanter of port or cognac on a night stand. The bathroom is open to the night sky, with canvas walls for privacy. There's no running water, but hot & cold water are delivered to your tent on request, & the 'flush toilet' has an external tank, filled regularly with water from the spillway.

Although game drives are an option, activities focus on getting out of the vehicle & into the bush on foot, or exploring the spillway by canoe, always accompanied by experienced armed guides. *From US$790 pp Mar to US$1,200/1,800 pp sharing/sgl 15 Jun–Oct, inc FB, most drinks, activities, park fees, laundry; exc transfers.* ⊕ *Mar–Oct.* ★★★★–★★★★★

🔺 **Selinda Adventure Trail** High wet-season rainfall across southern Africa between about 2008 & 2011 resulted in increased water levels that have been almost unprecedented in the last 30 years. Since then, the waters of the Selinda Spillway have been ideal for canoeists, leading to this canoe & walking safari, with weekly departures Jun–Aug.

The 4-night trip, for 2–8 participants, starts midway along the spillway, running east to Selinda & Zarafa camps for about 45km, with stops to explore the banks on foot. Usually, 2 participants share a Canadian canoe, although these can accommodate 3 people if fitness is an issue. At night, fly-camps are set up along the riverbank, with a cook on hand to prepare the evening meal. Starting or ending the trip with a night at Selinda or Zarafa is encouraged. *4-night safari US$3,600 pp sharing, inc FB, most drinks, activities, park fees, laundry; exc transfers.* ⊕ *Jun–Aug.* ★★★★

🏠 **Motswiri** [map 294] (5 tents) ☎ 686 0244; www.rawbotswana.com; ⊕ MOTSWI 18°46.00'S, 23°02.05'E. In the face of increasing levels of luxury in much of Botswana, Motswiri is refreshingly simple. It lies about 70km or 4hrs' drive from Zarafa, on the far western side of the reserve, which has until recently been virtually unvisited for photographic safaris.

The camp, set under leadwood trees, benefits from fantastic views over the Selinda Spillway. Its split-level tented main area, all chunky wood with rustic chairs & tables, allows comfortable, sheltered dining even during the rains. A sandy path leads past a small pool with a deck & sunloungers to the Meru-style tents, which are modified slightly with proper wood-framed doors & timber poles. Inside are a dbl or twin beds (which one of my colleagues commented was the most comfortable he had ever slept in!), hessian floor covering, & an en-suite bathroom with both indoor & open-air showers & plenty of hot water. Lighting via a battery system allows for charging of batteries too.

Motswiri focuses almost exclusively on horseriding & walking safaris, while – when water levels permit – boating & a spot of fishing are a great way to occupy an afternoon. Motswiri also has the use of a small, semi-permanent fly-camp which guests can either walk or ride to, spending a night or two exploring this section of the spillway by boat, on horseback & on foot. *From US$670 pp early Jan–Mar & mid-Nov–mid-Dec to US$895 mid-Jul–Oct, inc FB, most drinks, activities, park fees.* ⊕ *All year.* ★★★★

KWANDO CONCESSION (NG14)

On the northern edge of Botswana, bordering Namibia across the Kwando River, the Kwando Concession covers an enormous 2,320km² of very wild bush. It's one of Botswana's larger wildlife concessions. Beside its eastern boundary, formed by the river, is a narrow belt of riverine forest. In the south this opens out into some large tree-islands and open floodplains. There are two photographic camps on this productive eastern side.

The vast western part of the concession includes huge tracts of thick mopane woodland. Here, far from the river, there was until recently a seasonal hunting camp.

GETTING ORGANISED
Getting there and away Like most of Botswana's private concessions, Kwando is reached by a short flight from Maun, Kasane or one of Botswana's other camps. There are two main airstrips in the concession: one near Lagoon (Kwando airstrip), and the other near Lebala. Both the camps here work out their logistics well in advance. Trips are always pre-arranged, and they don't welcome drop-in visitors, nor ever really get any.

Thus virtually nobody would consider self-driving into these camps, even by prior arrangement. However, if you did then you'd pre-arrange your visit with the camps and take the transit route north through Selinda. It's about 14km in a straight line from Selinda to Lebala, and a further 30km by road from there to Lagoon.

When to visit Game viewing revolves around the reserve's riverfront on the Kwando River and its adjacent riverine forest. Thus note the comments made on pages 113–20, and also the specific comments made for the Chobe riverfront area, on pages 262–6. The Kwando's riverfront has broadly similar game movements to the Chobe or Linyanti riverfronts. In short: game concentrates around here when it needs the water, and spreads away again when it can easily drink elsewhere.

This means that the game viewing improves as the land dries out. Then buffalo and elephants move into this area from the west and south and zebra and wildebeest move in from the great plains of the Chobe. Later, when it rains, so the animals will move away – although birdwatchers will find more of interest in the wet season when there's a greater variety of bird species, many in breeding plumage.

FLORA AND FAUNA
Flora Kwando's environment and ecosystems are similar to those of the Linyanti and Selinda reserves. The north of the reserve is most like the Linyanti Reserve, in that it's dominated by the presence of the river, which runs on its eastern border in a roughly straight line. Adjacent to this is a band of riverine forest, characteristically rich in its variety of trees. These include African mangosteen (*Garcinia livingstonei*) – which remind me of a bomb exploding, as all the stems grow out straight from the top – jackalberry (*Diospyros mespiliformis*), sausage tree (*Kigelia africana*), leadwood (*Combretum imberbe*) and knobthorn (*Senegalia nigrescens*).

As you move further south in the reserve, around Lebala Camp, you're getting into the northern side of the Magwegqana or Selinda Spillway, and here the riverine forest opens out, becoming a mosaic of open areas covered in low bushes and grasses. These open areas are often dominated by wild sage (*Pechuel-loeschea leubnitziae*) and interspersed with patches of forest, which become smaller and more island-like as you move further south.

These forest patches and islands contain many of the same riverine tree species, and you'll also find marula trees (*Sclerocarya birrea*), occasional baobabs (*Adansonia digitata*) and increasing numbers of real fan palms (*Hyphaene petersiana*), plus many camelthorns (*Vachellia erioloba*) and the invasive candle-pod acacia (*Vachellia hebeclada*).

11

Further south still, the land becomes even more open as you approach the reserve's southern boundary and the Selinda Reserve.

Fauna Like the Linyanti and Selinda, Kwando's resident game is augmented in about June by migrant game which arrives here from the drier areas south and west, attracted by the permanent waters of the Kwando River.

Common species found here include impala, red lechwe, kudu, tsessebe, giraffe, steenbok, warthog, baboon and vervet monkeys. Roan, sable and common duiker also occur, but not frequently. Lion, leopard and spotted hyena are common, while cheetah are rarely seen. Hippo and crocodiles frequent the river, along with the playful spotted-necked otters.

Herds of wildebeest and zebra are resident from about May to December. Elephants and buffalo follow a similar pattern with individuals around all year, and larger breeding herds arriving around June–July and staying until December. These large herds are particularly common near the river during the dry season, and the elephants seem to have a penchant for aggression if approached too closely. When one of the camp's guides was driving, he would refer to them nonchalantly as 'cheeky' animals; but driving myself through the area once I found it much more nerve-racking. They reacted completely differently from the relatively passive elephants found in the busier parts of Chobe and Moremi.

Kwando is also a good reserve for seeing wild dog, especially in the dry season, helped by Kwando Safari's policy of actively 'tracking' animals across the bush, and having both a tracker and a driver/guide on each of its vehicles. In 2016, wild dog were regularly seen denning near both Lagoon and Lebala camps.

Highlights of the night drives here include Selous' mongoose, genets and aardwolf – along with more usual sightings of scrub hares, spring hares, bushbabies, genets, civets, honey badgers and porcupines.

Birdlife The birdlife here is almost identical to that of the Linyanti Reserve (pages 297–8), with plenty of variety. I particularly remember a huge colony of carmine bee-eaters that we seemed to have discovered by accident when stopping on a drive for a 'sundowner' drink.

Sacred and hadeda ibis are particularly common in the waterways, while rarer residents include slaty and black egrets, and rufous-bellied herons.

 WHERE TO STAY Both the camps here are owned and run by Kwando Safaris, who are based in Maun (page 224).

Lagoon [map 294] (8 tents) ✛ LAGOON 18°12.980'S, 24°24.790'E. Overlooking the Kwando River, Lagoon is the more northerly of Kwando's 2 camps in the riparian forest belt. It stands amid tall, mature forest that includes some fine marula (*Sclerocarya birrea caffra*) & jackalberry (*Diospyros mespiliformis*) trees.

The whole camp was rebuilt in early 2011 & remains in very good shape. Large chalets set on stilts along the river are designed to maximise the views from both the veranda & each area of the interior. The front walls are made entirely of gauze, & this, together with a ceiling fan over the bed,

ensures that everything is light & breezy. In the split-level interiors, there's a comfortable seating area at the front, a dbl or twin beds set higher up, & an en-suite bathroom with a stand-alone tub & outdoor shower.

The food at Lagoon is good, served buffet-style in a thatched dining room facing the river. The bar is largely self-service, & an extensive curio shop has local handicrafts & some useful books. The lounge area has comfortable armchairs, a small library & various board games. Game frequently wanders into camp & on one visit an old bull elephant came within touching distance of the dining room as we ate brunch, in search of some tasty morsels in the tree above. It was very relaxed, apparently oblivious to the general fuss that it was causing.

Lagoon Camp has a plunge pool for the hotter months, but its main activities are 4x4 game drives & boating excursions, usually 1 early in the morning, & the 2nd in late afternoon, which usually turns into a night drive as the light fades. With a tracker accompanying every drive, & a maximum of 6 people per vehicle, there's a willingness to drive cross-country & actively track coveted game, such as big cats & wild dogs. The guides are enthusiastic about their big game, & sometimes positively zealous in their tracking of it. For gentle sundowner cruises (subject to water levels) there is a 2-storey floating pontoon-type boat on the river, & if you're keen on fishing, you can try your hand at spinning for tigerfish & bream.

Lagoon's atmosphere is laid-back, friendly & not at all regimented – mealtimes are usually adjusted around game-viewing times, rather than vice versa. A slight minus is that the tents are quite close together (although all have canvas blinds that can be closed). *From US$662 pp Dec–Mar (exc Xmas) to US$1,343/1,673 pp sharing/sgl Jul–Oct, inc FB, most drinks, activities, park fees.* ⊕ *All year.*
★★★★–★★★★★

✳ 🏠 **Lebala** [map 294] (8 tents) ⊕ LEBALA 18°24.760'S, 23°32.540'E. Lebala is in a very different location; the name means 'open space', which is appropriate as there are lots of plains around it. It's just 14km from Selinda, & yet 26km (measured in a straight line) from Lagoon – so

it's no surprise that its environment is close in character to that of Selinda, but quite different from the area around Lagoon.

The camp's substantial & custom-designed tents, rebuilt in 2008, are on raised decking made of polished Zimbabwe teak. Sliding doors lead to a very large bedroom, with 2 ¾-size beds & solid but simple teak furniture. Screened 'shadecloth' walls mean that wildlife can be watched from your room, with curtains & blinds to control the level of light. Outside is a large private veranda for sitting out, with a few chairs & a table. Canvas room-divisions separate the bedroom from the 'entrance hall', where there is a spot to put suitcases, a hat-&-coat stand, a large wardrobe & a writing desk. The large bathroom has a stand-alone claw-footed bath, his & hers washbasins & a separate toilet, while outside is a dbl shower. (Hot water comes very efficiently from individual gas geysers.)

Teak walkways wind from the tents to a thatched dining area, where good meals are served. Adjacent is a comfy lounge & bar area, with a modest library of books, & one side open to the plains around. There's a campfire for the cooler months, & a plunge pool for the warmer ones.

Activities concentrate on 4x4 game drives & walking. As at Lagoon, the guides always drive with a tracker & will actively seek the game. Last time I visited, I arose late one morning, only to learn that wild dog had sprinted through camp just before sunrise. *From US$662 pp Dec–Mar (exc Xmas) to US$1,343/1,673 pp sharing/sgl Jul–Oct, inc FB, most drinks, activities, park fees.* ⊕ *All year.*
★★★★–★★★★★

BOTSWANA ONLINE

For additional online content, articles, photos and more on Botswana, why not visit www.bradtguides.com/botswana?

12

The Okavango Delta – Moremi Game Reserve

Much of what is covered in this section – especially concerning flora and fauna, and when to visit – is applicable to the Okavango as a whole. Therefore I've covered this information here in detail, and made reference to it elsewhere where appropriate. The map of the Delta in the first colour section relates to the whole area.

Remember that Moremi and its surrounding reserves are separated only by lines on a map; their ecosystems blend together seamlessly. Birds and animals move without hindrance across almost the whole of the Okavango, Linyanti and Chobe regions. Thus all the country covered in *Chapters 12–16* is really one continuous area dedicated to wildlife. The enormous size of this, and the diversity of ecosystems that it contains, are two of the main reasons why the wildlife of northern Botswana is so spectacular.

Although seasonal flooding is the lifeblood of the Okavango Delta, between 2009 and 2011 the area experienced the biggest floods in over 20 years. Normally seasonal or even dry rivers are flowing, roads and dykes have been swamped, and camps have found themselves underwater. Even in the south and east of the Delta, the Gomoti has flooded all the way to Shorobe and there is contiguous water between the Gomoti, Santantadibe, Thamalakane and Boro systems. All this in turn impacts on the wildlife, and is a tremendous boost to the area's ecology. For the visitor, minor inconveniences are offset by a greater concentration of game on the islands, and increased opportunities for water-based activities.

BACKGROUND INFORMATION

HISTORY In his *Travels and Researches in South Africa* (see *Appendix 3*, page 540), David Livingstone recounts what he was told by the local people near Lake Ngami in 1849 about the origin of a river there:

> While ascending in this way the beautifully-wooded river, we came to a large stream flowing into it. This was the Tamunak'le. I enquired whence it came. 'Oh, from a country full of rivers – so many no one can tell their number – and full of large trees.'

However, within 100 years of Europeans finding this 'country full of rivers', its environment and wildlife were under threat. In an exceedingly far-sighted move, the Batawana people proclaimed Moremi as a game reserve in 1962, in order to combat the rapid depletion of the area's game and the problems of cattle encroachment.

NG22

Duba
Expeditions

NG23
Duba Plains

Little Vumbura,
Vumbura Plains

Moanachira
Lagoon   Xugana

Xugana
Lagoon

NG21

Kwara,
Little Kwara

Ngoga

Footsteps   Shinde

Camp Okavango

GCODIK

Jao

Gcodikwe
Lagoon

NG25

Mombo &
Little Mombo

Kwetsani

Pelo

Jacana

Tubu Tree,
Little Tubu

Jao Camp

Chief's

Chief's Island

Xigera

M o r e m i

Xo Flats

Abu Camp,
Seba Camp

Nxabega

Xudum

Macatoo

Kanana

Eagle Island   Oddballs'

Moremi
Crossin

NG26

NG27A

Delta Camp   Gunn's
Camp

S a n d v e l d
T o n g u e

Pom Pom

NG27B

Xaranna

Mokolwane

Xudum

NG30

Kujwana

NOTE
For accommodation listings,
see pages 332, 336, 341–3

NG29

KEY

	GPS co-ordinates ⊕			
Tar road	1BRIDG	19°17.099'S, 23°23.531'E	MOGSGT	19°25.412'S, 23°36.755'E
Gravel road	3BRIDG	19°14.368'S, 23°21.430'E	MOGTO	19°23.594'S, 23°32.972'E
Main 4x4 track	4BRIDG	19°15.128'S, 23°24.173'E	MORCUT	19°20.050'S, 23°55.111'E
Other 4x4 track	CAMPMO	19°11.322'S, 23°24.489'E	NOGATE	19°10.394'S, 23°45.092'E
Vet cordon fence	GCDDIK	19°09.731'S, 23°14.507'E	SEROTO	19°04.317'S, 23°50.071'E
Game reserve	MABTO	19°09.643'S, 23°57.932'E	SOGATE	19°25.548'S, 23°38.733'E
Concession boundary	MAGOTO	19°05.596'S, 23°52.284'E	XADRY1	19°12.944'S, 23°37.087'E
	MOGPIC	19°28.811'S, 23°32.153'E	XADRY2	19°14.573'S, 23°31.234'E

NG20

NG18

page 317

Chobe National Park

Seroto SEROTO

NG19

Sable Alley

Machaba

MAGOTO

Mababe Gate

MABTO

Moanachira

Xakanaxa Lagoon

CAMPMO

Camp Moremi, Xakanaxa, Okuti

NOGATE

Khwai Campsite

Mababe Village

Khwai

Third Bridge

3BRIDG

XADRY1

Mogotlho Safari Lodge

NG41

Mboma Island

4BRIDG

1BRIDG

XADRY2

page 325

Mopane Tongue

MORCUT

Xini Lagoon

MOGTO

South Gate Campsite

Mankwe Bush Lodge

G a m e   R e s e r v e

Mogogelo Loop

MOGSGT

SOGATE

South Gate (Maqwee)

Sankuyo Village

MOGPIC

Sandibe

NG34

NG43

NG31

Gomoti Tented Camp

NG33

Chitabe & Chitabe Lediba

Santawani

Kaziikini Campsite

Tuskers Bush Camp

Qorokwe Camp

Rra Dinare

Baines

Mma Dinare

Stanley's

Gomoti Plains

Mowana Gate

NG32

Duncan's Camp

Santantadibe

Veterinary fence

Mochaba Crossing

Shorobe

N

Bradt

0 ————— 15km
0 ————— 10 miles

Maun

Ninabe

Ghanzi

Nata (*pages 448–9*)

Savuti
(*pages 256–7*)

Initially Moremi consisted mainly of the Mopane Tongue area; then in the 1970s the royal hunting grounds of Chief Moremi, known as Chief's Island, were added. In 1992, the reserve was augmented by the addition of a strip of land in the northwest corner of the reserve, between the Jao and Nqoga rivers. This was done to make sure that it represented all the major Okavango habitats, including the northern Delta's papyrus swamps and permanent wetlands which had not previously been covered.

As an aside, this is often cited as the first reserve in Africa that was created by native Africans. This is true, and recognises that the native inhabitants were the prime movers here, rather than the colonial authorities. However, beware of ignoring the fact that Africa's original inhabitants seemed to co-exist with the wildlife all over the continent without needing any 'reserves', until Europeans started arriving.

GEOGRAPHY Moremi Game Reserve protects the central and eastern areas of the Okavango Delta. It forms a protected nucleus for the many wildlife reserves/concessions in the region. Physically Moremi is very flat, encompassing extensive floodplains, some seasonal, others permanent, numerous waterways and two main land masses: the Mopane Tongue and Chief's Island.

Its area is defined in some places by rivers, although their names and actual courses are anything but easy to follow on the ground. Its northern boundary roughly follows the Nqoga–Khwai river system, while its southern boundary is defined in sequence by the Jao, Boro and Gomoti rivers.

It's worth noting that since the middle of the last century it seems that the western side of the Delta (specifically the Thaoge River system) has gradually been drying up. As this has happened, an increasing amount of water is entering the Moanachira–Khwai river system, on the eastern side of Chief's Island – helping to raise water levels around the Khwai River area, and increase the incidence of flooding on the roads there.

FLORA AND FAUNA The ecosystems of Moremi Reserve are among the richest and most diverse in Africa. Thanks to generally effective protection over the years, they have also been relatively undisturbed by man. Now with wildlife tourism thriving around the park as well as in the private concessions, we can be really optimistic about its future. The regime of conservation supported by money from benign tourism is gaining ground. One such success story is the reintroduction of rhino into Moremi: the first to be sent back into the wild areas of northern Botswana since poaching wiped them out.

Flora There are over 1,000 species of plants recognised in Moremi, yet large tracts of the reserve are dominated by just one: mopane (*Colophospermum mopane*). This covers the aptly named Mopane Tongue and parts of Chief's Island. Because the park has had effective protection for years, and the soils are relatively rich but badly drained, much of this forest is beautiful, tall 'cathedral' mopane – so called for the gracefully arching branches which resemble the high arches of a Gothic cathedral. You'll often find large areas here where there are virtually no other species of trees represented.

Beside the many waterways you'll find extensive floodplains, and some lovely stretches of classic riparian forest with its characteristically wide range of tree and bush species.

Laced through the areas of mopane you'll also find open areas dotted with camelthorn trees (*Vachellia erioloba*), and sandveld communities following the sandy beds of ancient watercourses, dominated by silver terminalia (*Terminalia sericea*), wild seringa (*Burkea africana*) and Kalahari appleleaf (*Philenoptera nelsii*). You'll find much, much more detail on this vegetation in Veronica Roodt's essential *Trees and Shrubs of the Okavango Delta* (see *Appendix 3*, page 542, for details).

Fauna Moremi protects as dense and diverse a population of animals and birds as you'd expect to find in one of Africa's best wildlife reserves. With the reintroduction of rhino, you can see all the big five, and a lot more besides.

Elephant and buffalo occur here year-round in large numbers, and you're likely to see blue wildebeest, Burchell's zebra, impala, kudu, tsessebe, red lechwe, waterbuck, reedbuck, giraffe, common duiker, bushbuck, steenbok, warthog, baboon and vervet monkey throughout the park. Eland, sable and roan antelope also range across the park but are less common, as they are elsewhere in Africa. Sitatunga live deep in the swamps.

Lion, leopard, cheetah and spotted hyena all have thriving populations here. Moremi is central to wild dog, which range widely across most of northern Botswana.

Both side-striped and black-backed jackal occur, though the latter are more common. Brown hyena probably occur, but relatively rarely and only in the drier areas with lower densities of the other large predators. Similarly, bat-eared fox are found, though not so commonly as in Botswana's drier areas. There is a wide variety of mongooses to be found, including the banded, dwarf, slender, large grey, water and Selous' mongoose. Meanwhile in the water, Cape, clawless and spotted-necked otters are often glimpsed though seldom seen clearly.

Serval, caracal, aardwolf and aardvark are found all over the park, though are only occasionally seen due to their largely nocturnal habits. Pangolin are also found here, and seem to be slightly less rare than in other areas of their range.

Although night drives aren't allowed within the reserve itself, some of the camps near North Gate will finish their afternoon drives outside the park, and hence do short night drives back to camp. Then you have a chance to see scrub hares, spring hares, lesser bushbabies, porcupines, genets (small-spotted and large-spotted), civets, African wildcats and honey badgers. Black-and-white-striped polecats are also nocturnal, though very seldom seen.

Until 2001, rhino had been absent due to poaching, though in November of that year the first white rhino were reintroduced into the Mombo Concession, in northeast Moremi, with black rhino following a couple of years later. Although they're now free to roam, several have remained on Chief's Island.

Birdlife Moremi boasts over 400 bird species, a great variety, which are often patchily distributed in association with particular habitats; though visiting any area, the sheer number of different species represented will strike you as amazing.

Although there are no birds that are truly endemic to Botswana, the Okavango is a hugely important wetland for many species, among which are a number of rarities worth noting. Top of the Okavango's list of 'specialities' is the slaty egret. Expect to find this in shallow, reedy backwaters and pans. Besides the Okavango, this rare egret is only resident in the quieter corners of the Chobe and Linyanti rivers, and the Bangweulu Wetlands in Zambia. To identify it look for its overall slate-grey colouring, except for its lower legs and feet which are yellow, as are its eyes and some of its face, while the front of its neck is a rufous red. (The less uncommon black egret lacks the yellow on the legs and face, or the rufous neck.)

Much easier to spot are magnificent wattled cranes which can be seen in the Delta fairly readily, usually in pairs or small groups wandering about wet grasslands or shallow floodplains in search of fish and small amphibians and reptiles.

For keen birdwatchers, other specials here include brown firefinch, lesser jacana, coppery-tailed coucal, Bradfield's hornbill, pink-throated longclaw and the inconspicuous chirping cisticola.

WHEN AND HOW TO VISIT See pages 113–20 for more general comments on the whole of northern Botswana, and note that the best times to visit are dependent upon how you intend to visit, exactly which camps you are visiting, and why.

Flying in If you're flying into a camp in Moremi or the Delta then the season won't make much difference to the access. The Okavango's camps used to close down during January and February, but now most keep open throughout the year, despite being much quieter during the green season (December to March).

In terms of vehicle access to the various game-viewing areas from your camp, the rains are typically less of a concern than the flood, the peak of which usually lags behind the rains by several months (depending on how far up the Delta you are). However, generally there will be the most dry land from about August to January.

Driving in If you're driving yourself into Moremi, it's important to understand that only a restricted area of the reserve will be accessible to you, and the wet season will make this access even more difficult. As the rains continue, their cumulative effect is to make many of the roads on the Mopane Tongue much more difficult to pass, while it simply submerges others. Thus only the experienced and well equipped need even think about driving anywhere through Moremi between about January and April.

Most visitors who drive themselves come to Moremi in the dry season, between around May and October. Then the tracks become increasingly less difficult to navigate, although even then there are always watercourses to cross. As with all national parks, the speed limit in the park is 40km/h, with no vehicles allowed on the roads between sunset and sunrise.

Flora and fauna The flora and the birdlife are definitely more spectacular during the rains. Then the vegetation goes wild, migrant birds arrive, and many of the residents appear in their full breeding plumage. So this is a great time for birders and those interested in the plants and flowers.

The story with the animals is more complex. In most of Moremi there is water throughout the year. Higher water levels here simply means less land area available for animals that aren't amphibious. However, around the edges of the Delta, animal densities are hugely affected by the migration towards the water from the dry central areas of the country.

Thus game viewing generally gets better the later in the dry season that you go … although this trend is probably less pronounced in the centre of the Delta than it is at the edges.

Activities The water levels will affect the activities that you can do while here. In some areas mokoro trips are possible only for a few months every year, when water levels are high enough. Similarly, the game drives from a few of the camps are generally possible only when water levels are low enough.

Costs The cost of some camps in the Okavango varies with the season. This depends very much on the company owning/marketing the camps, but in general you can expect July–October to be the period of highest cost, December–March to be the time of lowest cost, and November, April, May and June to be pitched somewhere in the middle.

GETTING ORGANISED

Orientation Moremi Game Reserve covers a large tract of the centre of the Okavango Delta, and a wide corridor stretching east to link that with Chobe National Park.

At the heart of Moremi is a long, permanent island, Chief's Island, oriented from southeast to northwest. At about 60km long and around 10km wide this is the largest island in the Delta, and it's usually cut off from the mainland by waterways and floodplains. Within the eastern side of Moremi is a triangular peninsula of dry land covered (mostly) in mopane trees, known as the Mopane Tongue.

Between and around Chief's Island and the Mopane Tongue, Moremi is a mosaic of rivers, lagoons, floodplains and small islands which slowly and gradually change with the passage of time.

Maps Once again, Veronica Roodt's definitive map of Moremi Game Reserve (pages 145–6) can't be recommended too highly for visitors to Moremi, and is essential for anyone planning a self-drive trip there.

Booking and park fees If you're flying into an organised camp, then park fees will probably already be included in the price that you've paid. If you're driving in you'll need to have booked all your campsites and paid all your park fees in advance; see pages 130–3 for details of how to go about this, and a scale of the fees. On arrival at the park gate, you'll need to present your confirmation documents confirming that you have pre-booked your campsites, and paid your park fees, before you are allowed to proceed.

Opening hours (⊕ *Apr–Sep 06.00–18.30, Oct–Mar 05.30–19.00*) As with other national parks, Moremi's opening hours vary with the season, roughly corresponding to 'dusk 'til dawn'. You're not allowed to drive in the park outside of these hours.

THE MOPANE TONGUE

Within eastern Moremi, the dry triangle of the Mopane Tongue juts into the Delta from the east, between the Khwai and Mogogelo rivers. Each side of this is about 40km long, and roughly marking the corners are the campsites of South Gate (Maqwee), North Gate (Khwai) and Xakanaxa – a reminder that this is the only area of Moremi that is accessible for visitors driving themselves.

Aside from the riverine forest which lines its edges, most of the interior of this peninsula is covered in forests of mopane, including many stretches of very mature and beautiful forests.

KHWAI RIVER AND NORTH GATE (KHWAI) Near the northeastern edge of Moremi, the northernmost waterways of the Okavango gradually narrow to form the Khwai River, which – along with various channels – is spanned by several wooden pole bridges. The tracks beside the river and around the floodplains are often stunning in their beauty, and prolific in their wildlife. It's a spectacular area, and especially so if approached from the dusty heartlands of Chobe during the dry season.

While this stretch of the Khwai River falls within the community-run NG19 concession, I have included it here as it falls naturally on the route between Chobe and Moremi, and thus – especially for self-drivers – it feels more logical. Most of the lodges here conduct their activities along the river, although some do occasionally go into Moremi. The downside of that is that it can get quite busy around key sightings.

Flora and fauna highlights

Flora All along the edge of the Khwai's floodplain you'll find some of the region's most beautiful, mature riverine forest. Stunning trees, tall and old, abound, including a large number of camelthorn (*Vachellia erioloba*) and some almost pure stands of leadwood (*Combretum imberbe*). There are also patches of acacia woodlands, usually standing on sandy patches of ground between the river valley and the mopane woodlands of the Tongue's interior.

Fauna The Khwai area seldom fails to deliver some very impressive wildlife spectacles when visited in the dry season. This is perhaps to be expected, as it marks the boundary of the Okavango's waters that flow east and north – and so is the closest drinking water for large numbers of thirsty animals in southern Chobe during the late dry season.

I've had some particularly good leopard sightings here, seeing the cats lounging around in shady trees during the day, usually on the edge of the riverine forest. Mixed areas of broken woodlands and open areas is classic leopard territory, and because it's been protected for so long, many of the residents are very relaxed in the presence of game-viewing vehicles. Well suited to this environment, too, are wild dogs, which denned close to the river in 2013 and have since been regularly seen with their pups. Other prolific predators include spotted hyena, which have had a den nearby for several years.

As well as the almost ubiquitous impala, you're likely to spot kudu and waterbuck in this environment, and you probably have a better chance than in most places of seeing the normally elusive roan antelope, which regularly come down to the river to drink.

Birdlife Khwai's birdlife is varied, like the habitats found here, though with only a narrow channel of water in the dry season, you'll usually have to search elsewhere for large numbers of the more aquatic species. That said, even in the dry season you will find storks (saddle-billed and marabou) and wattled cranes pacing around the open areas in search of fish, frogs and reptiles to eat.

Khwai does have a reputation, especially towards the end of the dry season, for having a very high density of raptors – with which I can concur. I've been closer to a martial eagle here than anywhere else, and had a lovely sighting of a marsh harrier hunting, and both bateleur eagles and giant eagle owls seem particularly common. So as you drive along, keep glancing into the sky and checking the tops of trees for the distinctive outline of a perched raptor.

Orientation It's relatively easy to orient yourself here, although since the opening of the new transit road, most self-drivers simply pass through this area, glimpsing the Khwai River only from the bridge. The Okavango's waters approach from the west down the Khwai River. To the west they're flanked by floodplains, loops, meanders and lagoons, but gradually travelling east this valley narrows and concentrates the river water into a small channel.

Central to the whole area is the bridge at North Gate (now more commonly called Khwai), which spans the channel. South of this is Moremi Game Reserve, and north are the small settlement of Khwai Village (home to 500 people), the

KHWAI RIVER AND NORTH GATE (KHWAI) AREA

KEY

Gravel road
Main 4x4 track
Other 4x4 track

GPS co-ordinates ⊕
KHWAIR 19°09.052'S, 23°47.543'E
NOGATE 19°10.394'S, 23°45.092'E

NOTE
For accommodation
listings, see pages 318–21

N

0 _____ 3km
0 _____ 2 miles

Khwai Community Concession (NG18)

NG19

Mababe Gate,
Chobe NP

Khwai

Magotho 1
Magotho 2

Xwara
Pan

Chobe,
Maun

Lepapana Pans

Tongue

Makgapha Pan

Machaba/
Little Machaba

Jeremotsaa Pan

Big
Qonimotshaa Pan

Xhlu-oro Pan

Khwai
River Lodge

Xhleba Pan

Small
Qonimotshaa Pan

Khwai
airstrip
⊕ KHWAIR

Motswiri Pan

Moremi Game Reserve

Mopane

Kaunga Pan

Khwai
Tented Camp

Sango

North Gate
(Khwai)

South Gate (Maqwee)

Khwai
Guest House

Khwai
Village

Khwai
Campsite

NOGATE

Pole bridge

Khwai Development
Trust

Khwai Leadwood
Under Thatch

No access

Sable Alley

Sagogama Pan

Seolo Pan

Kgaba Pan

Samahundu
Pool

Xakanaxa

Baobab
tree

Dombo
Hippo Pool

Oqu
Ledibo

community-controlled concessions of NG18 and NG19 (pages 349–51), and the area's airstrip. Access to the area along the river is from the village of Khwai.

Getting organised There are a few small shops in Khwai Village, a welcome sight if you've been driving for several days and supplies are running low. Most sell just a few cans and soft drinks, but ask around and you might find potatoes and other fresh vegetables, and even fresh bread. There are also baskets for sale.

On the edge of the village, near the bridge across to North Gate, is the office of the Khwai Development Trust. The small NG19 concession, which stretches north of the Khwai River bordering Moremi, and east to Chobe National Park, is owned and managed by the community of Khwai Village. Here the people have formed the trust, originally funded at least in part by auctioning off their hunting quota to various organisations (though hunting is no longer allowed in Botswana). Unusually in the private concessions, self-drivers are allowed to explore this area, on payment of a concession fee of P145 per person per day (this is included if you are camping at one of the trust's campsites), but it is not permitted to drive beyond the concession boundaries into NG18 and towards the Linyanti and Selinda reserves.

The trust's office (683 0271/2; e khwai@btcmail.co.bw; www.khwaitrust.co.bw; 07.30–16.30 Mon–Fri, 08.00–12.30 Sat) is where you pay your concession fees, but note that their campsites (Magotho 1 & 2) must be pre-booked through their Maun office (page 227). While there is no requirement to have a guide, you can pick up a community 'escort guide' here, or organise one in Maun. Their role is simply to show you the routes, which is valuable in an area where it's surprisingly easy to get lost, but they are not trained wildlife guides. There is no charge for their services, as they are paid by the trust – though a tip is normally expected – but if you'd like the guide to stay with you at one of the trust's campsites (page 321), you will need to provide all his/her food and drink.

You can also book cultural tours from Khwai (*P2,000/group*), which will include the opportunity to visit Khwai Village, talk to the villagers about the culture of the Khwai Bushmen, and watch a performance of dancing and singing.

Getting there

By air Most visitors to the lodges arrive at the airstrip (◈ KHWAIR 19°09.052'S, 23°47.543'E), which is close to Khwai River Lodge. This is a short hop from Kasane, Maun or any of the other airstrips in the region. There are no facilities at the airstrip; it's just a flattish section of low grass with a windsock next to it.

By road If you're driving into the Khwai area from Savuti, Xakanaxa, South Gate or Maun, see the directions given on pages 322–3, and simply follow them in reverse – or check out the individual 'getting away' sections for these places.

🏠 **Where to stay** The erstwhile three lodges here were at one time reduced to one, Khwai River Lodge, but since then accommodation in this area has burgeoned. All the lodges listed here, like the guesthouse and the trust's two campsites, lie on the north side of the river, between Chobe National Park and North Gate, but only the lodges lie on the river itself. The national park's campsite is across the river at North (Khwai) Gate.

Note that all the lodges and campsites must be pre-booked; you are likely to be turned away if you simply roll up.

Khwai River Lodge [map 317] (15 chalets) Contact Belmond, page 223; ⊕ KHWAIL 19°08.860'S, 23°48.019'E. I've very fond memories of the original Khwai River Lodge, with understated little bungalows among the leadwood trees on the edge of the floodplain. It was one of the Okavango's oldest lodges, & full of character. Now all that remains is the basic structure of its old office, which has been transformed into a deliciously cool Africology spa (in-room massages are also possible). Around this, an opulent lodge was built in the late 1990s to the same design as that originally used for Savute Elephant Camp (page 287) – & with similarly excellent levels of service.

Set among neat grassy lawns, the central area is slightly raised on a timber platform & topped by an enormous thatched roof. A fireplace forms the focus of the lounge, with comfy couches & a small library. There's a bar to one side, & to the other a dining area where candles illuminate wooden tables for stylish table d'hôte dinners. In front, a wide area of decking sports a telescope for scanning the shallow river valley, while a 2nd sits on a raised observation deck – a good spot for a private dinner. On a lower level are a firepit, for convivial evening drinks, & a big swimming pool. To keep tabs on the outside world there's Wi-Fi throughout, and a discreet internet lounge has a satellite TV, a film library, & even yoga mats. Activities focus on early-morning & late-afternoon game drives, with night drives after dinner if requested.

The lodge's large (18m x 6m) tented rooms – far too opulent to be called tents – are built on high timber platforms under thatch, & well spread out along the river valley. From a wide veranda, with a hammock & wicker chairs overlooking the river, glass sliding doors reveal polished wooden floors, rugs & good-quality wooden furniture with muted fabrics. Four-poster-style mosquito netting surrounds the twin ¾-size beds, usually pushed together, as well as bedside tables & battery-powered lamps. Above, an AC unit & ceiling fan fight a valiant if sometimes losing battle to keep the room cool. Separate rooms at the back of the room house the toilet & 2-person shower, while a suite also has an outside shower & private plunge pool. *From US$1,220 pp Jan–Mar & mid-Nov–Xmas to US$1,970/2,955 pp sharing/sgl Jul–Sep, inc FB, local drinks, activities (exc spa), laundry.* ⊕ *All year.*
★★★★★

✳ **Little Machaba** [map 317] (4 tents) reservations ☎ +27 82 579 5249; e enquiries@ machabasafaris.com; www.machabasafaris.com. Opened in 2016, Little Machaba is a few hundred metres south of Machaba Camp, around a corner & overlooking a wide bend of the Khwai River. The builders didn't change a successful formula, & so the feel, layout & facilities of the tents is very similar to those of Machaba, albeit perhaps slightly smarter & more contemporary in their choice of colours.

It's smaller than Machaba, with just 4 tents, 2 of which are family units. These each have a central lounge area between 2 bedrooms, which share a bathroom with indoor & outdoor showers. In-room massage, charged separately, is available from the resident therapist. Little Machaba's main area is very similar to that of its sister camp, albeit a little smaller. It, too, is furnished with plump cushions on the big armchairs, & assorted books & help-yourself drinks. One side opens on to a wide veranda with relaxing chairs.

Most activities here are game drives, but walking safaris are an option, as are mokoro trips when the water is high enough; the boat station is 30mins' drive from camp. *From US$615 pp mid-Jan–Mar to US$1,130/1,808 pp sharing/ sgl Jun–Oct, inc FB, activities, most drinks, park fees, laundry. No children under 12.* ⊕ *All year.*
★★★–★★★★★

Khwai Tented Camp [map 317] (6 tents) Contact African Bush Camps, page 223; ⊕ KHWAIT 19°15.178'S, 23°77.110'E. Set in a grove of feverberry trees some 1.5km from Khwai Village, Khwai Tented Camp opened in 2008, but has since moved: in 2012, & again in 2017, to this new location on a tributary of the Khwai River. Small & intimate, it combines the simplicity of an old-style safari camp with more modern creature comforts. Its walk-in Meru tents have twin or dbl beds, solar-powered lights, a writing desk, comfortable chair & hanging space, plus an en-suite bathroom with twin basins & separate cubicles housing a flush toilet & shower. The tented communal area, finished with a long refectory-style table & homely seating, is a convivial place to relax over a meal or a drink – while in front the firepit on a raised deck adds another focus.

Activities are fairly flexible, from walking safaris & 4x4 game drives (day & night), to mokoro trips when the water is high enough,

& visits to Khwai Village, which benefits from the camp in many ways. Most visitors arrive by air, self-drivers are welcome on the same basis – which includes doing all activities with the camp's staff. *From US$580 pp Jan–Mar & Dec to US$905/1,106 pp sharing/sgl Jul–Oct, inc FB, local drinks & activities. No children under 7.* ⊕ *All year.* ★★★–★★★★★

🏠 **Khwai Leadwood under Thatch**
[map 317] (6 chalets) Contact African Bush Camps, page 223; ⊕ KHWAIL 19°16.631'S, 23°73.448'E. Khwai Leadwood Under Thatch is the reincarnation of the old Tsaro Elephant Lodge, which was taken over by African Bush Camps in 2016. It has since been refurbished to a good standard & is now a well-priced & family-friendly base from which to explore the Khwai area & Moremi.

Set back among sycamore & leadwood trees within the Khwai River floodplain, the camp has 4 standard & 2 family chalets, all with solid walls, thatched roofs & private verandas. Inside, stone floors make the chalets feel cool & there are twin or dbl beds with bedside tables & lamps, a writing table & some comfy chairs. One chalet has a low mezzanine bedroom & lounge below with a warming fireplace for the winter months. En-suite bathrooms have basins, a shower & a flush toilet. The family chalets are similar but larger, with 2 bedrooms & 2 bathrooms. Activities here include 4x4 game drives (day & night), walking safaris, mokoro trips when the water is high enough & visits to Khwai Village. ⊕ *All year.* ★★★– ★★★★

🏠 **Machaba Camp** [map 317] (10 tents) reservations ✆ +27 82 579 5249; e enquiries@ machabasafaris.com; www.machabasafaris.com; ⊕ MACHAB 19°07.371'S, 23°48.820'E. Delightfully positioned on a wide, shallow stretch of the river frequented by elephants & hippos, Machaba opened in Mar 2013 on the site of the old Machaba Camp. It's a welcoming, hospitable camp that strikes a good balance: comfortable & attractive while still at one with the environment.

At the heart of Machaba, 2 open-fronted tented wings spread from the entrance. One is furnished with armchairs & sofas, its tables dotted with books, magazines & sweets, its walls adorned with maps. In the other, tables set with white linen are backed by a buffet. And in front, directors' chairs surround a warming firepit by the river. It's the kind of place that invites conversation.

The attention to detail runs through to the spacious tents, reached along sandy paths beneath shady trees, & accessible by those with limited mobility. Spacious & uncluttered, these are a twist on the traditional safari camp, their floors dotted with rugs, their metal basins in pairs beneath hanging mirrors, & their en-suite 'bucket' showers boasting hot running water. In 2 family tents, a central lounge separates 2 bedrooms which share a bathroom & outside shower. In-room massage is offered at extra cost by the resident therapist.

At the far end of the site is a secluded circular pool, a real draw during the heat of the day; no doubt elephants would be attracted too, should the river ever dry out! Even the curio tent (including baskets made by the staff) is appealing rather than simply functional. Game drives are the backbone of activities here, but walking safaris are an option, & mokoro trips (some distance away) when the water is high enough. The guiding is both good & personable, & if you'd like to see behind the scenes, just ask. *From US$545 pp mid-Jan–Mar to US$995/1,592 Jun–Oct pp sharing/sgl, inc FB, activities, most drinks, park fees, laundry. No children under 12.* ⊕ *All year.* ★★★–★★★★★

🏠 **Sango Safari Camp** [map 317]
(6 tents) Contact Bush Ways Safaris, page 225; e reservations@sangosafaricamp.com; www. sangosafaricamp.com; ⊕ SANGO 19°09.826'S, 23°45.771'E. Opened in 2010, Sango is that rare find: an old-fashioned camp that focuses on safaris rather than frills. It's set back from a shallow section of the river, just a short drive from Khwai Village. Self-drivers (who must pre-book all meals & activities), should turn off the road just metres north of Khwai Guesthouse (⊕ 19°09.578'S, 23°45.594'E), from where a track leads to the camp.

Squashy cushions bring comfort to the airy mess tent, which is open to the view, & dinner is often taken under the stars. Guests stay in traditional en-suite tents, set along sandy paths on low varnished wooden decks with small verandas. Each is well thought out, with proper twin or dbl beds flanked by bedside tables & lights & surrounded by mosquito netting. A fan is welcome in the heat of summer, as are the outside shower & the small pool, complete with shaded loungers. Game drives are at the heart of Sango's activities, with afternoon drives continuing after sunset on the way back to camp, & night drives on request. Even at camp you can take in the action on the river, perhaps from the camp's tall observation hide. There are also nature walks with an armed guide, mokoro trips on a tributary of the Khwai, & village tours – which may include the opportunity to watch basket weavers at work. *From US$350 pp Jan–Mar & Dec to US$630/850 pp sharing/sgl Jul–Oct, inc FB, activities, most drinks, park fees, laundry; exc transfers. Self-drive rates available, exc activities, park fees.* ⏲ *All year.* ★★★

🏠 **Khwai Guest House** [map 317] (6 chalets) Contact Bush Ways Safaris, page 225; www. khwaiguesthouse.com; ⊕ KHWAIG 19°09.505'S, 23°45.662'E. On the edge of Khwai Village as you're coming in from Mababe, the former KLLK Guesthouse is now under the same ownership as Sango Safari Camp. It's a welcoming but very low-key spot, popular with self-drivers & plugging a big gap in the market. While we miss the colourful murals that once adorned the exterior walls of the cool thatched chalets, the upgrade in beds (5 twins, 1 dbl) & bedding beneath wrap-around mosi nets is a big plus, as are the semi-open-air shower & separate toilet. The new circular mess tent is a convivial place for meals or to while away the siesta hours. Options are flexible, from a fully inclusive package to B&B or DBB with additional meals (*US$17/25 lunch/dinner*) on request, & game drives from US$60 pp. **$$$–$$$$$** *From US$270 pp to US$325/380 pp sharing/sgl inc FB & activities; exc drinks.* ⏲ *All year.* ★★–★★★

🅰 **Khwai (North Gate) Campsite** [map 317] (10 pitches) ☎ 683 0082; contact SKL, page 132; ⊕ NOGATE 19°10.394'S, 23°45.092'E. Khwai is situated on a lovely site to the south of the Khwai River, immediately on your left as you enter Moremi at North Gate. Its pitches are dotted

amid tall woodlands, some along the river, where fireflies put on a mesmerising display as night falls, & the grunts of hippos form the bass notes to the general cacophony from baboons & spurfowl. There are good, clean ablution facilities, & each site has a braai stand of some description with a firepit & waste bin. In the past, monkeys here could be a menace, openly stealing from our vehicle as we stood close by, though it was hard not to laugh at their brazen theft.

Look out for especially impressive specimens of sickle-leaved albizia (*Albizia harveyi*). Their fine leaves & flattened seedpods might look like acacias, but trees of the albizia family don't have thorns. You'll also find a few huge sycamore figs (*Ficus sycomorus*), easily spotted because of their yellow-orange bark & a tendency for parts of their wide trunks to form buttresses. Old Africa hands will avoid camping directly under a fig tree, though, as their fruits are sought after by everything from baboons & bats to elephants – any of which can make for a messy tent in the morning, & a very disturbed night's sleep. *US$50 pp, exc bed levy & park fees.* ⏲ *All year.*

🅰 **Magotho Campsites** [map 317] (15 pitches) Contact Khwai Development Trust, page 227. Reached from a turning south off the main transit road between Mababe & North Gate (at ⊕ MAGOTO 19°05.596'S, 23°52.284'E), these 2 campsites – Magotho 1 (8 pitches) & 2 (7 pitches) – are set beneath mature camelthorn trees. Neither has any facilities at all, not even toilets, so you will need to bring everything with you, including all water, & take everything out. Note that campsites must be pre-booked, & that the trust's other 2 campsites, Sable Alley & Matswere, are reserved for operators so are not open to the public. *P300 pp.* ⏲ *All year.*

What to see and do Wherever you stay, however you travel, your activities during the day will largely focus on game drives, as walking and night drives are forbidden by park rules, and the Khwai is too shallow and narrow for safe boating. Mokoro trips, however, are possible on several nearby channels – and offer a tranquil opportunity to explore the river up close.

Game-viewing roads and loops spread out on both sides of North Gate, to the west and east. Most stick close to the Khwai River, either exploring the river's floodplain or the adjacent band of riverine forest. You'll need Veronica Roodt's map of Moremi (page 146) to get the best from these, as they're not shown on the main map of Botswana.

One particularly attractive loop within the game reserve, almost 14km west of North Gate and signposted 'Hippo Pool', leads to a large, shallow lake where hippos wallow in the permanent water. At one end of the pool is a tall bird hide, with a toilet at the base, so you can leave your vehicle and spend time in the heat of the day observing waterbirds such as Egyptian and spur-winged geese, knob-billed and white-faced ducks and woolly-necked storks.

Getting away from North Gate

Driving from North Gate (Khwai) to Savuti, Chobe NP This route used to be very confusing, but the opening of a new gravel road running parallel to the old sand tracks near the Khwai River has simplified it considerably. On the downside, the route no longer takes you along the stunningly beautiful Khwai River, which is now largely the preserve of the lodges dotted along its banks (pages 318–21).

From the park entrance at North Gate (✸ NOGATE 19°10.394'S, 23°45.092'E), cross the pole bridge over the Khwai River, and follow the road through Khwai Village, then over (or around) another small river to a new steel bridge (✸ STEELB 19°07.564'S, 23°45.840'E). A little over 2km from here, the road turns sharply to the right, then continues uninterrupted all the way to Mababe Village. For the Mababe Gate into Chobe National Park, turn left about 35.5km from North Gate (✸ MABTO 19°09.643'S, 23°57.932'E), then follow that road for about 7.5km. At the gate, stop and sign in before continuing roughly north towards Savuti.

About 20km north of the Mababe Gate, the road splits. Both forks lead to Savuti. The right fork is the **marsh road**, which is more scenic, but can be very rutted and bumpy during the dry season, with great views of the marsh. It is certainly going to be the worse of the two during the rainy season, when you'd be wise to take the left fork, the more direct if less interesting, **sand-ridge road**. This stays closer to the Magwikhwe Sand Ridge, climbing on to it at one point.

After about 37km on the sand-ridge road, or 44km on the marsh road, these routes converge (✸ MARSAN 18°36.078'S, 24°03.678'E) beside Leopard Hill Rock, which is about 5km south of the heart of Savuti.

Driving from North Gate (Khwai) to Xakanaxa This route is really very straightforward – although the introduction of a 'dry' route to avoid the oft-flooded sections on the old road has changed things a little in recent years. Start from the park's entrance at North Gate and follow the road southwest towards South Gate for about 1.2km. Here you'll find a substantial right turn signposted to Xakanaxa, heading in a more westerly direction. Follow this for almost 20km until you come to another junction (at ✸ XADRY1 19°12.944'S, 23°37.087'E). Turning right here would lead you after a further 24km straight to Xakanaxa, mainly through old, established mopane woodlands. This route, however, has been frequently closed and at best very wet since the unusually high floods of 2009, so if you're planning to take it, do ask advice from the staff at the gate before you set off.

Turning left, however, leads on to a more circuitous but considerably more predictable 'dry route' that heads southwest for 12km before joining up with the main route from South Gate (✸ XADRY2 19°14.573'S, 23°31.234'E). From here, it's a further 11km or so northwest to the new Xakanaxa Gate (✸ XAKGT 19°11.865'S, 23°25.865'E).

The real joy of this journey comes from the numerous side-loops that detour to the right of the road. If you feel lost, remember that heading west and south will generally keep you going in the right direction. Heading north will go deeper into the detours and usually bring you back to the Khwai River. While the 'dry route' itself is less rewarding, you will pass several of these loops during the first 20km stretch from North Gate, so you won't be missing out.

NEGOTIATING THE ROADS AROUND XAKANAXA

While the new road has done much to alleviate the problems of getting from North Gate to Xakanaxa, tracks along the old route, and indeed off-road, can get pretty waterlogged. When I drove this route in 1999, most of the loops were fine. A few – often those marked as 'seasonal roads' on Veronica Roodt's map of Moremi – were tricky and required one to cross quite deep water in the vehicle. The scenery on the road around Qua Lediba (*lediba* is the local word for 'lagoon'), particularly looking out west towards the Xuku floodplain, was very beautiful as we meandered between the dappled light of the forest and open lagoons.

However, west of Qua Lediba, the road became progressively more difficult, with deeper and deeper stretches of water to cross. Several times we forded water across the road, until one large pool stopped us. Forest to the left and lagoon to the right. There was no easy way around. The track was flat sand; solid not slippery. Vehicle tracks had been this way recently – a good sign.

As we considered our next move, two large trucks, run by a mobile-safari operator, approached and drove across, showing us the depth; we crossed safely. We avoided the next pool, but in a third the vehicle lurched alarmingly to the right – my passenger falling across me as I drove. The Land Rover didn't blink though and pulled us through. Nerve-racking when alone, such puddles are more fun with a party of two vehicles, as then one can pull the other out of difficulty if necessary.

Back on the main road, heading west we found a drift, where the road had been washed away. Various alternatives circled off left, finding shallower, but more slippery, places to cross. The water at the main road was deeper, but the substrate was more solid. On the whole, a safer bet.

Drivers with reservations at the campsite or one of the lodges should sign in at the gate before proceeding, but if you're camping at Third Bridge, their paperwork is handled at the campsite.

Driving from North Gate to South Gate and Maun This is a very straightforward route, on a very straight road. From North Gate's campsite you simply follow a substantial track for about 30km, which heads southwest, directly towards South Gate (⊕ SOGATE 19°25.548'S, 23°38.733'E).

To continue to Maun, see *Driving from South Gate to Maun*, page 333. Alternatively, and thus avoiding park fees, you could follow the first part of the instructions under *Driving from North Gate (Khwai) to Savuti, Chobe NP*, page 322. Instead of turning off for the Mababe Gate, continue on the gravel road as far as Mababe Village, where you turn south on to the road to Sankuyo, Shorobe and ultimately to Maun.

TIP OF THE TONGUE: XAKANAXA AND BEYOND One corner of the Mopane Tongue's triangular peninsula juts towards the centre of Moremi, and at the end of the tip is Xakanaxa Lagoon. Beyond it, on three sides, is the Delta's maze of channels, floodplains, lagoons and islands. A few of the larger, closer islands, such as Goaxhlo and the large Mboma Island, are accessible via simple pole bridges. Beyond this, Moremi becomes inaccessible without a boat: that's the realm of the small, fly-in safari camps.

12

The patchwork of environments found here is typical of the inner reaches of the Delta. It's also phenomenally beautiful, and one of the most reliably good areas for wildlife on the subcontinent. Expect extraordinary densities of game and birdlife and, as it's been protected for years, the animals are generally very relaxed.

For the self-driving visitor, the game and scenery here are as good as they get in Botswana – don't miss this area.

Flora and fauna highlights Picking out the wildlife highlights for an area like this, and trying to point out what's special, is virtually impossible. There's usually something special around every corner. It's not that you'll see different things here than you will elsewhere in Moremi, or even Botswana; it's just that you'll see them all in a very small area.

Orientation The main route from North Gate to Xakanaxa roughly follows the northern edge of the Mopane Tongue. Similarly, the main road from South Gate to Third Bridge roughly follows the southern edge of the Tongue. This section covers the area around and between Xakanaxa and Third Bridge.

In Veronica Roodt's map of Moremi (page 146) there are some detailed insets of the road layouts around this area, so make sure that you buy a copy of this before you get here. You'll also find plenty of useful references and background information on the reverse of the map.

Getting there
By air Virtually all lodge visitors arrive and leave via Xakanaxa airstrip, which is easily linked with any of the other airstrips in the region.

By road For details of self-drive access, see *Driving from South Gate (Maqwee) to Xakanaxa* (page 333) and *Driving from North Gate (Khwai) to Xakanaxa* (pages 322–3).

 Where to stay There are three long-established camps and one campsite, all clustered on the edge of the Xakanaxa Lagoon, a huge expanse of water that is fed by the Moanachira River. This can be traced upstream, passing close to Camp Okavango, Shinde and Xugana, although access to these isolated water-based camps is no longer permitted by boat. A second campsite lies a little further away, at Third Bridge, at the foot of Mboma Island. It's also possible to camp on one of the islands northwest of here, and the addition of a remote island camp has widened the options further. All must be pre-booked; you cannot just turn up, even at the campsites.

Activities throughout focus on game drives in Moremi and boat trips on the lagoons – though the latter are best seen as sunset cruises, with the occasional sighting of elephant or kingfishers, rather than wildlife-viewing excursions.

Note that because of the particularly high game densities here, and the relaxed, fearless nature of the animals, walking around within camp can be an experience at times. While the lodges at Xakanaxa are surrounded by discreet electric fences to deter elephants, other wildlife can get through – so guests here, as at most lodges in Botswana, are escorted to and from their rooms after dark. The campsites, though, are completely open. Lion, hyena, leopard, buffalo, wild dogs and elephants all wander through very frequently – so be careful when you are walking around, especially after dark.

XAKANAXA

N

Bradt

0   5km
0   3 miles

*Channel to Xugana, Shinde,
Kwara, Camp Okavango*

Xhobega Lagoon

Xobega Island Camp ▲

GCODIK ⊕

Xhamu Lagoon

Gcodikwe Lagoon

Gcodikwe Campsite ▲

Gcodikwe Campsite ▲

Salvinia Lagoon

Moanachira

Xakanaxa Lagoon

Okuti ⊕
Boat Station

Xakanaxa Campsite ▲ ▲

Camp Xakanaxa
Camp Moremi
CAMPMO ⊕

*Nchunga
(Dead Tree)
Island*

*Gcoxhio
Lagoon*

*Gcoxhio
Island*

⊕ XAKGT
Xakanaxa
Gate

Xakanaxa airstrip ✈

*Kia-Oro
(Paradise) Pools*

Gcma-oro Pool

*Nyondambesi
Lagoon*

North Gate (Khwai) →

North Gate (Khwai) →

XADRY2 ⊕
South Gate (Maqwee) →

M o p a n e   T o n g u e

Botelele Pool

4BRIDG ⊕
Fourth Bridge

Dobetsaa Pans

Maya Pool

*Gcoxhio
Lagoon*

Monxa Bridge
(small poles) ⋈

Third Bridge
Third Bridge
Campsite ▲
3BRIDG ⊕

Lechwe Pans

Lebala Pan

Tsau Pan

*Magwexhlana
Pools*

Second
Bridge ⋈

2BRIDG ⊕
First Bridge

1BRIDG
⊕

B o d u m a t a u

Bodumatau
Bridge ⋈

*Bodumatau
Lagoon*

South Gate ⊕ →

M b o m a   I s l a n d

Mboma Lagoon

MBOMAT ●
Mboma Boat
Station ●

KEY

════	Main 4x4 track
-----	Other 4x4 track
⊕	GPS co-ordinates

NOTE
For accommodation
listings, see pages 324–8

GPS co-ordinates   ⊕

1BRIDG	19°17.099'S,	23°23.531'E
2BRIDG	19°17.003'S,	23°22.553'E
3BRIDG	19°14.368'S,	23°21.430'E
4BRIDG	19°15.128'S,	23°24.173'E
CAMPMO	19°11.322'S,	23°24.489'E
GCODIK	19°09.731'S,	23°14.507'E
MBOMAT	19°11.574'S,	23°17.126'E
XADRY2	19°14.573'S,	23°31.234'E
XAKGT	19°11.865'S,	23°25.865'E

🏠 **Camp Moremi** [map 325] (12 tents) Contact Desert & Delta Safaris, pages 223–4; ✦ CAMPM 19°11.322'S, 23°24.489'E. The furthest southwest of the 3 camps here, Camp Moremi is set under huge old trees where natural papyrus & ferns nod over lawns cropped short by hippos. A lot of other animals venture into camp, too, though elephants are kept at bay by discreet strands of electrified wire around the perimeter. Closed for rebuilding at the end of 2017, this old camp was set to reopen in May 2018 with what is promised to be a 'modern twist' on a traditional camp.

At the heart of the new camp will be a series of decks raised up in a marvellous old jackalberry tree (*Diospyros mespiliformis*), with superb views over the lagoon. Accessed along a gradually ascending boardwalk, these will variously house the reception area & curio shop, seating & dining areas, & the bar – with a view to creating greater privacy for guests than was possible in the old rather angular structure.

Back at ground level, paths will fan out to the small pool, with umbrella-shaded sunbeds on a wooden deck, as well as the firepit, viewing deck, boat station & the new tented rooms.

The camp's old rooms felt almost like suites, & it's reasonable to assume that that sense of space will remain in the new canvas structures. These, including a large family room, will be slightly elevated on wooden decks & will of course have en-suite bathrooms.

Activities concentrate on morning & afternoon game drives, & motorboat trips around the lagoons & waterways. As Camp Moremi & Camp Xakanaxa are owned by the same company as Camp Okavango & Xugana (pages 357–8) in the Delta, it's a good idea to combine several nights in each of the 2 locations, sticking to game drives here, & switching to motorboat & mokoro trips there. *From US$560 pp Jan–Mar & Dec to US$995/1,293 pp sharing/sgl Jul–Oct, fully inc.* ⊕ *Closed mid-Jan–mid-Feb.* ★★★–★★★★★

🏠 **Camp Xakanaxa** [map 325] (12 tents) Contact Desert & Delta Safaris, pages 223–4; ✦ XAKANA 19°10.973'S, 23°24.567'E. Less than 1km northeast of Camp Moremi, Xakanaxa is the oldest of Moremi's camps, established in the 1960s. From its hunting & fishing origins it became a photographic camp in 1988, & – despite refurbishment in 2014 – its intrinsic character remains intact. The camp is solidly built in a

beautiful location overlooking the lagoon, with plenty of natural shade. Its raised, thatched dining area is memorable for a long, 18-seater table, made from reclaimed old railway sleepers. There's a separate lounge/bar with leather sofas, a circular area built out over the water with chairs around a central fire, & another apron with an infinity plunge pool. A 2nd, much larger & more secluded pool is tucked behind the curio shop.

The solid wood furnishings run through to the comfortable Meru-style tents, which stand on wooden decks beneath canvas shadecloths, their verandas facing the lagoon. Turkish-style rugs & a fan top the floors, & a child bed can be added to 2 of the tents if required. At the back, screened by poles & reeds, are a hot shower, handbasin & flush toilet. 4x4 game drives & boat trips are offered morning & evening. *From US$560 pp Jan–Mar & Dec to US$995/1,293 pp sharing/sgl Jul–Oct, fully inc. No children under 9.* ⊕ *All year.* ★★★–★★★★

🏠 **Okuti** [map 325] (7 rooms) Contact Ker & Downey Botswana, page 224. Sandwiched between Camp Xakanaxa & the boat station, Okuti occupies quite a tight spot among shady trees overlooking the lagoon. Although opened in the early 1980s, it was completely rebuilt in 2007. The result is an ingenious triumph of design over space – all barrel-vaulted ceilings & soft curves, with sand-coloured walls, an extensive circular deck that is partially open to the lagoon, & a pool enclosed by rough wooden stakes in the style of a rural *kraal*. The domed entrance, with shelves of books, opens on to the dining area & a separate lounge, where there's a help-yourself bar & a computer for guest use (though no Wi-Fi). From here, long wooden walkways are punctuated by huge, almost tunnel-like rooms shaded by great swathes of canvas. Twin or dbl beds & comfortable chairs sit beneath reed-lined ceilings, & mesh sliding doors reveal an (unshaded) veranda over the lagoon. Every room has indoor & exceptionally private outdoor showers, which in the 2 family chalets are shared by 2 bedrooms, while the honeymoon suite boasts an outdoor bath. Activities concentrate on well-guided 4x4 game drives with no more than 4 on a vehicle (except on request), & motorboat trips on the lagoon from their own jetty. With a curio shop that offers locally made baskets, it all adds up to a well-run & friendly camp in a good location. *From US$530* *pp early Jan, Mar & Dec to US$1,010/1,295 pp sharing/sgl Jul–Oct, inc FB, local drinks, activities, laundry; exc transfers.* ⊕ *Mar–early Jan.* ★★★– ★★★★★

Å Xakanaxa Campsite [map 325] (8 pitches) Contact Kwalate Safaris, page 222; ⊕ XAKCMP 19°11.026'S, 23°24.986'E. To the east of Okuti, Xakanaxa Campsite stretches along this tip of the Mopane Tongue, almost adjacent to Xakanaxa Boat Station. On arrival, campers should sign in at the smart DWNP Xakanaxa Gate (⊕ XAKGT 19°11.865'S, 23°25.865'E) which is 3km southeast of the campsite. The site's roughly marked pitches, some only just off the dirt road (though there's no traffic to speak of), blend into one long camping area lining the river. Along with 2 new ablution blocks that are reasonably well maintained, water taps are dotted around the site, with a motley selection of tables, benches & braai stands of varying quality.

I've always loved these sites, & on one Sep visit the purple hanging flowers of the Kalahari appleleaf (*Philenoptera nelsii*) were in full force, reminding me of small jacaranda trees. However, as with Third Bridge, this is an area of particularly dense game, so as you move about the campsite, keep your eyes open for animals at all times. *US$40 pp, exc park fees, bed levy.* ⊕ *All year.*

Å Third Bridge Campsite [map 325] (9 pitches, 5 en-suite tents) Contact Xomae Group, page 222; ⊕ 3BRIDG 19°14.368'S, 23°21.430'E. Third Bridge is about 8km in a straight line from Xakanaxa Campsite, although by road it's about 18km, depending on the route used. Despite their relative proximity, if you're camping in the area for 4–5 nights, then ideally try to split your time between the 2 sites. Third Bridge is well located for visiting Mboma Island, & is a more open site, with plenty of tree shade. It used to be my favourite site in Moremi but with privatisation its inherent character as a wilderness destination has been compromised. Now – with an ostentatious DWNP gate to greet you on the 'dry' route from Xakanaxa, a clutch of staff houses & 2 large (clean) ablution blocks – it's lost its old allure.

That said, the old pole bridge has missed out on the upgrade, & parts are slowly sinking into the mud. You'll see that the water's crystal-clear as it passes over the sandy bottom of the narrow waterway, & people used to bathe here often, but despite the apparently impenetrable stands

of papyrus, there have been regular attacks by crocodiles; hence the plethora of notices warning you against swimming.

The site itself is sprawling, with pitches spread out across 2 almost distinct areas. It's notable for some attractive large feverberry trees (*Croton megalobotrys*) & a particularly fine sausage tree (*Kigelia africana*). Third Bridge is also known for a troop of very cheeky baboons, who have developed stealing food into a form of sport. So what's good practice anywhere is vital here: lock everything away when you're not using it, & make sure any rubbish is securely fastened in the cage provided. When we last stayed, there wasn't a baboon in sight, but don't bank on it. There was, though, a bearded lioness that strolled through the camp.

The new regime has brought bonuses in the form of Wi-Fi in the office, a credit-card machine, & a shop selling a motley selection of goods from beer, baskets & even beef to tinned foods, charcoal & firewood, though don't rely on them; it's still best to arrive fully equipped. Morning & afternoon game drives can be organised from the site costing P300–700 pp for around 4hrs, depending on numbers (min 2, max 10), or P1,100–1,500 pp for a full day – though bring all your own food & drink. There are also motorboat trips (*P600/hr up to 9 people*) from the camp's own boat station (page 329). *Camping US$50 pp, self-catering tent US$100/150 pp sharing/ sgl, all exc park fees.* ⊕ *All year.*

Å Gcodikwe campsites [map, 325] Contact Xomae Group, page 222. Camping on the nearby Gcodikwe (or Gcadikwe) Island, just northwest of Mboma Island, must – like Third Bridge Campsite – be organised in advance. You'll find 2 sites here, in the area of the Gcodikwe Lagoon, unimaginatively known as Gcadikwe 1 & Gcadikwe 2. Access to the island from Third Bridge boat station takes about 3hrs, though if water levels are low you'll go from Mboma. Normally you need to bring in all your own equipment, food & water – & bring out all your rubbish; there are no facilities whatsoever on the island (& that includes toilets). It's possible, though, that fully catered trips may be available on request. *Self-catered US$85 pp per night, plus P3,500 for the boat & driver/guide per night; fully catered around P3,000 pp/night (min 4), inc FB , activities & boat transfer, exc drinks.*

🏠 Xobega Island Camp [map 325] (10 tents) 📞 +27 21 712 5284/5; e reservations@

12

sundestinations.co.za; www.xobega.com;
⊕ XOBEIC 19°10.221'S, 23°12.304'E. Access to
Xobega (Xhobega) Island is by a 1½hr boat ride
from Xakanaxa Boat Station, or alternatively from
Mboma Boat Station. The set-up here is simple,
befitting an undeveloped island: small, walk-in
tents with basic twin beds & solar lighting; en-
suite (hot) bucket showers, canvas washbasins
& chemical toilets; open-sided dining & lounge
shelters, with hammocks & a central campfire.
There are boat cruises & mokoro trips morning &
late afternoon to explore the lagoon & its varied
birdlife, including a heronry, but largely this is
about escaping to an (almost) private island. See
ad, 3rd colour section. *From US$295 Dec–Mar to
US$395 Jul–Oct, inc FB, activities, park fees, boat
transfers; exc drinks. No children under 12.* ⊕ *All
year.* ★★–★★★

What to see and do

Until recently, self-drive visitors here conducted their own game drives, or perhaps took a boat trip for a few hours from one of the lodges. Now, more organised water activities are available for independent visitors too.

Self-drive There's a lot of exploring to do in this area, which is veined with game-viewing loops and tracks. So take your time – and be aware that after heavy flooding some previously navigable tracks might be impassable. Drive around slowly, and stop frequently. There are a number of specific areas that you might aim for, or just end up at.

Floodplain roads The network of tracks to the west of the main track between Xakanaxa and Third Bridge is probably the most rewarding in Moremi for game. Many are also very beautiful, lined with glassy pools that attract considerable numbers of both game and birdlife.

Goaxhlo Island and Pan Also known as Dead Tree Island, you'll recognise it by the number of skeletal trees that surround the pan of open water. Like those at Savuti, these were killed by drowning – when the channels changed and inundated the area. Most are mopane trees, and because of their resistance to termites, and semi-submerged state, they're decomposing very, very slowly indeed. This is quite an eerie sight, and photographers will find plenty to inspire them, especially if there are any animals present. Keep a particular look-out for the graceful pink spoonbills that breed here.

Dobetsaa Pans Take a left in a southerly direction, perhaps 1km after crossing Fourth Bridge on the way to Third Bridge, and you'll find a short loop leading down past a few very scenic pans. Veronica Roodt comments that this is 'one of the few places in Moremi where the African skimmer can be seen'. But even without the skimmers it's a good birdwatching spot with some very open pans.

Mboma Island West of Third Bridge is a large, long island, circled by a loop road which stretches for about 50km around it. There's a spur to this at the north end, and a short cut back to Third Bridge halfway round. It's worth spending a day here, as Mboma's environments are varied and beautiful, though different from the floodplain loops nearer to Xakanaxa. I've had great sightings of cheetah on the northern side of the island, and the south is said to be a popular haunt of buffalo herds.

Boat trips I'd recommend that you take at least one trip by boat or mokoro on to the lagoons and waterways of Moremi. It's usually worth the cost, unless you're due to be going on to a camp with water-based activities. But remember that boat fuel is costly to buy and transport, and that you're in a very remote location, so these trips aren't cheap.

All the drivers are qualified guides, in as much as they can name the various birds and plants that you'll see, but their understanding of what you want may not tie up with yours. For this reason, do explain your objectives clearly before you set out, even to the lodge guides, or you may find yourself being driven at breakneck speed from one side of the lagoon to the other, watching a hastily named bird rise up in fright at the approaching roar of the engine, or veering away from the occasional pod of hippo. And do ask questions – your driver may well know the answers.

Aside from the lodges at Xakanaxa, three boat stations hold the exclusive rights to take boats on to the lagoons, although effectively there are four operators involved. This exclusivity is in part to help prevent the spread of *Salvinia molesta*, or Kariba weed, an invasive plant that is posing a serious threat to Botswana's waterways (see box, page 17). You'll need a hat, suncream and drinks, but little else except, of course, a camera. It is reasonably safe to leave a vehicle parked at either place.

There's little or no shade on most of the boats, so the best times to venture out are early morning, or in late afternoon, culminating in sunset over the lake. A couple of hours is really the ideal; less than that and it'll seem rushed so you'll miss out on the gentle beauty of the place. In theory there's no need to book, but the number of boats is limited so it makes sense to give them advance warning.

Xakanaxa Boat Station Ngami Marine; ☎ 686 0364; e nm@info.bw; ⏰ dawn–dusk; ◈ XAKABT 19°13.098'S, 23°22.247'E. Literally adjacent to the campsite at Xakanaxa, this enterprise – signposted as Okavango Boating – offers trips on to the lagoon from 4 boats, including a double decker (*P670/US$67 per hr for up to 16 people*), a 12-seater (*P580/hr*) & an 8-seater (*P520/hr*). If you ask around at the campsite, you may well find someone to share a boat, thus cutting costs.

Impala Tours & Safaris ☎ 686 3440; m 7233 5544, 7331 0210. A little further along the lagoon from Xakanaxa Boat Station, east of the campsite, a 2nd outfit offers similar trips but with a smaller range of boats, all at P540/hr.

Third Bridge Boat Station Contact the Xomae Group, page 222. Based at Third Bridge Campsite, this relative newcomer has 3 9-seater boats costing P600 (US$60)/hr per boat. Typically you'll go out for 2–3hrs morning or afternoon, taking a slow cruise from the campsite & exploring 3 lagoons. Game drives are also available (see campsite, page 327).

Mboma Boat Station ☎ +27 72 523 2796; e reservations@wildsideafrica.net; www. wildsideafrica.net. The most established of Moremi's boat stations is at the far northwest tip of Mboma Island, about 1hr's drive (15km) from Third Bridge, or 3hrs (63km) from South Gate. The turn-off from the main loop road is at ◈ MBOMAT 19°01.574'S, 23°17.126'E, with the station about 1.5km west of there. Both 6- & 9-seater Motorboats with a driver can be hired by the hour (*6-seater: P750, 9-seater P900*), or by the day (*6-seater P3,500, 9-seater P3,850*). The longer trips usually leave between 08.00 & 09.00, & return between 15.00 & 16.00. Sometimes they'll stop for lunch (bring your own) on one of the islands on the lagoon. For a more leisurely trip, you can go out on a mokoro with an experienced poler (*P195 pp/hr for up to 2 people*).

Gcodikwe Lagoon and heronry Gcodikwe (or Gcadikwe, Gcudikwa) Lagoon (◈ GCODIK 19°09.731'S, 23°14.507'E) is one of the Okavango's largest and most famous lagoons. A huge, almost circular oxbow lagoon encompassing several large tree-islands, it is reachable only by boat: a trip of about 90 minutes from Xakanaxa. It is perhaps best visited from one of the lodges just outside the park, the best being Kwara (6km northeast), Shinde (11km northwest) or Camp Okavango (15km west) – though you can double all these 'straight-line' distances to allow for meandering through the waterways.

The 'islands' are made up mainly of water-fig trees and a little papyrus growing in shallow water. Over the millennia these have accumulated a mass of bird guano and detritus under them to raise their levels and grow. Now they're large, but still isolated from any predators that are not aquatic. Hence they have become a vital breeding ground for the Okavango's waterbirds. For a few years, the heronry was much smaller than it used to be, partly because of disruption to the breeding birds caused by elephant, which come here to feed in the early summer. By 2017, however, it was back to its former glory.

Thousands of birds come to this heronry to breed, including herons, egrets, storks, ibises, cormorants and many others. Most of the nest-building activity starts around August, and breeding seems to be timed so that the chicks hatch around October and November, when water levels are low and fish are easier to catch. Certainly when I last visited in late February, there were only a few birds around.

Watch carefully and you'll see that the larger, more robust species like marabou and yellow-billed storks tend to nest in the canopy of the trees, while the smaller, more vulnerable species can be found within the trees. Also keep an eye out for water snakes and leguvaans, which come here in search of chicks.

Getting away from the Mopane Tongue

Driving from Xakanaxa to North Gate (Khwai) It's about 44km to drive directly from Xakanaxa to North Gate; just head east from the Xakanaxa Gate (✛ XAKGT 19°11.865'S, 23°25.865'E). However, ask advice from the camp's office before you set off as if this road is blocked by high water levels, you will need to take the 'dry' route to the south. For details, see pages 322–3.

Driving from Xakanaxa to South Gate (Maqwee) Many would travel from Xakanaxa to South Gate via Third Bridge, using the route described in the next section, as the scenery's more varied and, in the dry season, I'd expect the game to be better – especially around the Mboma Island area.

However, the most direct route is along a track that heads southeast from near the western end of Xakanaxa's airstrip, taking about 42km to reach South Gate. The route is generally good, even when it's wet, apart from a number of clay pans which can be sticky.

Driving from Third Bridge to South Gate (Maqwee) I always find the tracks around Mboma Island confusing, but to reach South Gate you set off west on to Mboma Island from Third Bridge. Keep bearing left when the road forks and after 3–4km you'll be travelling south. The road then bends east, south and even west until you reach another pole bridge which is known, rather unimaginatively, as Second Bridge (✛ 2BRIDG 19°17.003'S, 23°22.553'E).

Crossing this, you'll then head southeast towards another pole bridge referred to as (surprise!) First Bridge (✛ 1BRIDG 19°17.099'S, 23°23.531'E). From here it's an uncomplicated drive southeast to South Gate, with most of the trip through mopane woodlands – which in turn conceal any number of elephants.

If time is on your side, consider a detour off the main track. There's a short, easy loop off to the south of the road, about 12km before the gate; it's clearly marked on Veronica Roodt's map of Moremi (page 146). Characterised by flat, open plains, dotted with anthills and small pans, this is a great place to look out for storks, with large numbers of marabou in particular when we visited at the end of the dry season. Don't worry if you miss the connection with the main road at the picturesque Xini Lagoon, which isn't at all clear on the ground when it's dry; the track links up almost seamlessly with the main road to South Gate, and the woodland landscape, just a couple of kilometres further on.

Very close to here, at ⊕ MOGTO 19°23.594'S, 23°32.972'E, is a turning towards a new and promising series of tracks, signposted to Mogogelo Hippo Pool and Black Pools. The loops here are clearly marked, running around and across floodplains, shallow pans and areas of woodland. An added and unexpected bonus in the heat of the day is a picnic site (⊕ MOGPIC 19°28.811'S, 23°32.155'E), with benches and tables set out in a beautiful shady grove of trees looking out on to a floodplain. If exploring at the end of the dry season, when most of the pools had dried up, was somewhat disappointing, Veronica Roodt claims that the area supports 'vast numbers of game'. Certainly all the signs were there, imprinted in the mud across numerous shallow depressions – and at the neighbouring Xini Lagoon, the scene was like something out of a picture book of African wildlife. If you follow the loops in an easterly direction, you can rejoin the main track about 4km west of South Gate at ⊕ MOGSGT 19°25.412'S, 23°36.755'E.

SOUTH GATE (MAQWEE) South Gate (⊕ SOGATE 19°25.548'S, 23°38.733'E), also known as Maqwee Gate, is usually treated as a transit stop by most visitors as it's in the midst of fairly unexciting mopane forest, with a small campsite sheltered among the trees.

Having described it as unexciting, this may just be my failure to really get to know the area well. I've only stayed here for three individual nights, one during each of three different trips (always at the start or the end of a trip across Chobe and Moremi). However, on one of those occasions, just as I was getting up, about half-a-dozen wild dogs gently jogged through the camp and into the forest. I don't think our roof tent has ever been packed away so rapidly – but try as we might, tracking them was a waste of time, with park rules forbidding off-road driving in Moremi!

On another trip I found a whole pack of wild dogs lounging on the road a few kilometres south of South Gate, in the NG33/34 concession area. They posed for photographs just a few metres from my vehicle for 20 minutes or so – totally unconcerned with our presence. So perhaps, especially in the earlier months of the year, South Gate warrants a closer look and more than just an overnight stop.

Flora and fauna highlights

Flora Around South Gate the trees are almost all mopane (*Colophospermum mopane*), with their distinctive butterfly-shaped leaves. Tall, undamaged specimens can reach 18m in height, when they're known as 'cathedral' mopane for their gracefully arching branches. In neighbouring areas, where the nutrients are not as plentiful or the trees have been damaged by elephants, this same species grows much lower – and is known as 'stunted mopane'. In both you'll find their leaves hanging down and tending to fold together during the heat of the day, leaving little shade underneath.

This tremendously successful tree is one of the commonest species in the hot, dry areas of the subcontinent. It's notable for its tolerance of poorly drained, alkaline soils – and often occurs in areas where there's a lot of clay. Driving in mopane country during the rainy season usually involves negotiating lots of sticky, clay-filled mud-holes.

For the camper, the mopane wood is a dark-reddish colour, hard, heavy and termite-resistant. Thus even long-dead pieces won't have been completely eaten by termites. It burns exceedingly well, smelling sweetly and producing lots of heat. You're no longer allowed to collect firewood in Moremi, but it's worth seeking out outside the park. (Turn each piece over, looking under it carefully for snakes and scorpions, before picking it up.)

Fauna With relatively dense forests this area can seem devoid of wildlife. But don't be mistaken; it isn't. Because the soil in mopane forest areas is often very poorly drained, it's dotted with small pans – temporary shallow ponds – during and shortly after the rains. This allows most of the big-game species to leave the over-populated areas beside the watercourses and disappear into these huge areas of forests.

Elephant, zebra, impala, kudu, tsessebe, common duiker, bushbuck, steenbok, eland, roan warthog, baboon and vervet monkey can all be found here, as can lion, leopard, cheetah, spotted hyena, wild dog and many of the smaller mammals. But you will have to look much harder here for them than on the open floodplains and beside the watercourses where they congregate during the dry season.

What you are guaranteed to see at any time of year are lots of bush squirrels (*Paraxerus cepapi*), which are so common in mopane woodlands that they're often known as 'mopane squirrels'. See pages 13–14 for more details.

Birdlife The high density of small rodents in mopane woodlands, especially bush squirrels, means that it's a good place for small raptors which hunt from perches (rather than the air). These include barn owls, smaller hawks and kestrels, and even martial eagles.

Meanwhile two species here are very common. The small, black-and-white Arnot's chat appears in pairs or small groups, often hopping about the ground or lower branches in search of small insects – memorably described by a friend on first sight as 'little flying zebras'. There's also the red-billed hornbill, which seems to be everywhere with its heavy flap-flap-flap ... glide ... flap-flap-flap ... glide ... style of flight. Remember Rowan Atkinson's performance as the hornbill in Walt Disney's *The Lion King* and you'll never be able to watch one again without smiling.

Orientation Navigating around South Gate is very straightforward, with just five clear roads: one to Maun via the veterinary checkpoint; another to North Gate; one to Third Bridge, which stays close to the southern side of the Mopane Tongue; and a fourth to Xakanaxa which cuts through the heart of the Tongue. The fifth, now closed to self drivers, leads to Santawani Lodge (page 404). There are now several game-drive loops quite close to the gate in Moremi; for details, see *Driving from Third Bridge to South Gate (Maqwee)*, pages 330–1.

Getting there For directions to South Gate, see *Driving from Xakanaxa to South Gate (Maqwee)*, *Driving from North Gate to South Gate and Maun* and *Driving from Third Bridge to South Gate (Maqwee)* on pages 330, 323 and 330–1 respectively.

 Where to stay There's only one place to stay:

⚑ South Gate (Maqwee) Campsite [map 311] (10 pitches) Contact Kwalate Safaris, page 132. Immediately next to the park gate, where campers should first book in, this campsite stands among shady mopane trees, with the constant buzz of cicadas for company. Pitches around the edge of the site are both larger & more private than the others, but each has its own table & benches. The site boasts the new ablution blocks that have been installed across many of Botswana's parks, with solar-heated water – though the old facilities remain as a reminder of how it used to be! *US$40 pp, exc park fees, bed levy.* ☉ *All year.*

Getting away from South Gate
Driving from South Gate (Maqwee) to Third Bridge Take the most westerly exit from the campsite and the route is very easy. After about 24km you'll pass a right turn, marked by an old green cement block. One side of this notes that

Mboma and Third Bridge are off to the left. There are no indications where the right turn goes, though it actually leads around the east side of the Bodumatau Lagoon.

Keeping on the main road (to the left), you'll then pass, in order, First Bridge (⊕ 1BRIDG 19°17.099'S, 23°23.531'E) and Second Bridge (⊕ 2BRIDG 19°17.003'S, 23°22.553'E), before finally reaching the campsite at Third Bridge (⊕ 3BRIDG 19°14.368'S, 23°21.430'E). Note that when we last drove this route, in late 2013, Second Bridge was impassable, and the Third Bridge has partially collapsed, though it was still possible to drive across.

Driving from South Gate (Maqwee) to Xakanaxa The more scenic route is to follow the directions to Third Bridge, opposite, then continue southwest to Fourth Bridge (⊕ 4BRIDG 19°15.128'S, 23°24.173'E) and thence to Xakanaxa. The 'new' bridge is already in poor repair, but the old one is still passable, and in the dry season it's possible to drive to the side. From there proceed broadly northeast to the Xakanaxa Gate (⊕ XAKGT 19°11.865'S, 23°25.865'E), where you turn west for the campsite and lodges. You can navigate through this labyrinth of game-viewing loops using Veronica Roodt's map, or by sticking to the main track, setting your GPS for Xakanaxa, and then keeping slightly east of the direct-line direction.

However, if it's late in the dry season and you've plenty of time, then you may want to take a detour around the Bodumatau Lagoon, which avoids Third Bridge completely. (This track is marked as 'seasonal' on most maps, and is much less reliable than the main track, especially when wet.) In that case, take the right turn at the green concrete block that is about 24km from South Gate. It's 16km to the Bodumatau Bridge from here, then a further 13km to Fourth Bridge. One local operator refers to the first part of this road after the green concrete block as 'Elephant Alley', for its winding road through dense mopane is often frequented by elephants. Drive carefully.

Alternatively, there's a shorter, alternative route marked on the Shell map. Head towards North Gate from South Gate for about 300m, then turn left for 10km to the Kudu Flats, where you bear left again and follow the road all the way to Xakanaxa. The final part of this ties up with the 'dry' route from North Gate to Xakanaxa.

Driving from South Gate to North Gate (Khwai) A very direct, straight road leads about 30km north-northeast from South Gate to North Gate (⊕ NOGATE 19°10.394'S, 23°45.092'E). There are no game-viewing loops off this road.

Driving from South Gate to Maun Leaving the park from South Gate, after a few hundred metres there's a well-signposted fork. For Maun, take the main fork to the left, along a wide but badly rutted gravel road that is painfully slow going. The right fork leads into NG33 and the wild-dog research station near Chitabe (page 400), but this road is now closed to self-drivers.

Heading towards Maun, to the right lies the NG33 concession, while to the left is an area managed by the community, NG34. Both are good wildlife areas, but because the land and the wildlife are managed, technically the road you are on is a 'transit route', and you are not allowed to stop and camp. The nearest place to camp is the community-run Kaziikini site (page 403).

After a further 17km you'll reach the sizeable village of **Shorobe** (pages 227–8). Roadside vendors sell cold drinks, and there's a craft studio on the east side of the road, but little else to tempt the passing traveller. From here the road to Maun is tarred, passing the University of Botswana. The total journey from South Gate to the Engen garage, which is the first fuel station in Maun, is about 90km.

Aside from the Mopane Tongue, the only way to access any of the rest of Moremi is from one of the small private safari camps with access only by air. There are three main camps within Moremi: Mombo and Chief's Camp at the north end of Chief's Island, and Xigera right on the western edge. These are described in the following pages.

However, there are a number of camps, such as those in NG19 near North Gate (pages 318–21), which stand just outside the edge of the park, but conduct some of their activities within the park. These include the camps in NG21 (Camp Okavango, Shinde and Xugana Island Lodge – pages 356–8) and the old camps along the south end of the Boro River in NG27B (Oddballs' Camp, Delta Camp, Gunn's Camp and Eagle Island Camp – pages 382–4).

Because these two areas are very different I'll subdivide this concession into two sections: one covering Xigera's area, and the other concentrating on Mombo and Chief's Camp.

XIGERA If you had to stick a pin on the map in the centre of the Delta, you'd probably put it near to here. The Xigera (pronounced 'keejera') area is within the boundaries of Moremi Reserve, near its western border and technically in Moremi's only private concession area, NG28.

Concession history Look at an old map of the Delta and you'll realise that the western boundary of Moremi used to be further east than it is now. Then the Xigera and Mombo areas were part of the NG28 concession and outside the park. Xigera was originally built in 1986 by Hennie and Angela Rawlinson, two well-known Maun residents, at a place that Hennie called 'Paradise Island'.

Then, in 1992, Moremi was expanded westwards and northwards. This was done in order to bring under its protection all the major Okavango habitats, as until then none of the northern Delta's papyrus swamps or permanent wetlands had been included. This expansion swallowed up NG28, including the Xigera and Mombo areas. Thus these camps now occupy prime sites within Moremi Game Reserve.

In 1998, the Rawlinsons renewed the lease for another 15 years and shortly after, the camp was completely demolished, and rebuilt from scratch a short distance away. Now, however, the lease is wholly owned by Wilderness Safaris (page 225).

Flora and fauna The area around Xigera is one of the Delta's few truly deep-water experiences. (Jedibe, when it was open, used to deserve this accolade. It really was surrounded by apparently endless papyrus swamps, with only the odd island. Camp Okavango, Kwara, Xugana and Shinde could also lay claim to have deep-water experiences to some extent.)

Here at Xigera you're very close to the Jao River, which feeds the Boro and is one of the Okavango's major waterways.

Flora Spending much of your time on the water, you're probably going to be particularly aware of the aquatic grasses and sedges. Of these the graceful, feathery papyri (*Cyperus papyrus*) are perhaps the most striking, and certainly one of the most interesting (see box, opposite).

In shallower sections you'll also find large areas of common reeds (*Phragmites australis*) and the tall miscanthus grass (*Miscanthus junceus*). There are also a few lovely stands of pure water fern (*Thelypteris interrupta*) on the edges of some of the channels and lagoons.

PAPYRUS

The graceful, feathery papyrus is a giant sedge which dominates large areas of the Okavango. It grows in areas of permanent swamp in thick floating mats, unmistakable for its feather-duster heads that sway in the breeze. At first it's perhaps surprising that such vigorous, lush, emerald-green vegetation thrives here with apparently few nutrients available from the clear water or the poor Kalahari sands beneath.

The secret lies in a number of remarkable adaptations. Firstly, papyri have nitrogenous bacteria between their scale-leaves which 'fix' nitrogen from the air into a form that the plants can use. Secondly, they photosynthesise using a special 'carbon-4' pathway, thus making more efficient use of the sun's energy than most plants.

With these adaptations, plus water and sunshine, papyri are among the fastest-growing plants in the world. You'll quickly see another factor that helps them here if you cut a stem of papyrus (preferably a dying one!). Observe that although thick and strong, it's very light. So the plant is committing relatively little energy or materials to raise such a tall, strong stem.

In fact papyri store most of their energy in long, thick rhizomes which form part of the tangled floating mat. From this base, their shoots can rise up to about 2.5m high, and yet typically have a life cycle of only three months. Within this they grow swiftly to maturity, flower and die – leaving a tangle of brown, dead stems near water level. The nutrients from these old stems are withdrawn back into the rhizome, ready to power the birth of another shoot. This rapid recycling of nutrients is another of the keys to the plant's lush, vigorous growth.

On the islands you'll find the normal trees of the Delta, including a good number of confetti trees (*Gynmosporia senegalensis*). The English name for these comes from the small, scented white flowers which come out around May–June, and then fall underneath the tree in large enough quantities to be scooped up.

Fauna   This isn't a bad area for big game (the most dominant cat being the leopard), but that's not why I'd go to Xigera. If you're staying at Xigera then remember that the bridge across the channel, linking the camp on one island with the main vehicle track to the airstrip on the other, isn't only used by people. Many other animals find it convenient, especially at night. Spotted hyenas cross it almost religiously every night, lion regularly and leopard occasionally too. Monkeys and baboons play on it during the day. Look underneath at the fish in the clear water and you may even see the odd spotted-necked otter fishing for bream.

On the larger island elephants are often in evidence, sometimes in substantial herds of 50 or so, and when I was last here the floodplain beyond my tent's veranda was dotted with lechwe. On game drives you've a good chance of spotting impala, tsessebe and even wild dogs.

As you'd expect for the environment, the Xigera area has one of the highest densities of sitatunga antelope in the Delta. These lovely creatures are notoriously difficult to spot, but gliding around silently in a mokoro probably offers you the best chance possible – just keep your eyes wide open and your mouth tightly shut!

On one occasion here recently, an eminent guide was leading a number of mekoro, trying to get as close as possible to a sitatunga. When the antelope made a break to get away, it jumped directly over one of the mekoro.

12

Birdlife Given the environment of large areas of permanent papyrus and swamp vegetation, plus some islands, this is a good camp for seeking the more water-dependent birds in the Delta.

Notable among these are the African skimmers, which usually arrive at Xigera Lagoon around September or October. About 20 pairs of these incredible birds have been noted here in recent years; if they're new to you then take a few moments to watch one of them through binoculars. You'll see it using the most amazing flying skills to place its lower mandible in the lagoon at a fixed depth, and steadily scythe through the water. Then periodically you see the bill snap shut with its catch of an unfortunate small fish. This is compulsive viewing, even if you never normally look at anything smaller than a lion; an incredible fishing technique.

While floating around you can expect to see assorted kingfishers, herons, egrets and other waterbirds. Included in this list, if you're lucky, will be purple (but not lesser) gallinules, lesser jacanas, moorhens, lesser moorhens and green-backed herons. It should be a good area for bitterns (including the dwarf and little), though I've never seen one here.

Other unusual birds that enthusiastic ornithologists should look out for include chirping cisticolas, tawny-flanked prinias, palm swifts and Pel's fishing owl, all of which are regularly sighted here.

When to visit Because the focus at Xigera is more on the environment and birdlife than game per se, this area can be visited any time of the year.

Getting there and away Only pre-booked guests may visit this area, flying in to Xigera's own airstrip (⊕ XIGAIR 19°23.155'S, 22°44.618'E). Note that there's no practical dry-land access from here to Mombo, Chief's Camp or the nearby Nxabega, and that driving in isn't an option.

Where to stay Although there are two camps here, one – Xigera Mokoro Trails – is predominantly visited as part of a set mobile itinerary. For most visitors, Xigera is the only option. Both camps are run by Wilderness Safaris (page 225).

✴ 🏠 **Xigera Camp** [map 310] (9 tents)
Sited on Paradise Island, Xigera opened in 2000. If you've never been to the Delta, then simply conjure up an image of a luxurious safari camp in the heart of the swamps, enveloped by a green, tropical lushness: you've probably come close to visualising Xigera.

Xigera's tents are widely spread out on one fringe of the island along 800m of raised boardwalks that stretch as far as a small lagoon that seems to attract good game. Constructed of part wood, part canvas, each is raised on a wooden deck a few metres above the island floor. The front, with 2 large sliding doors & huge gauze windows, is easy to open up for good views & airflow, the latter assisted by an efficient, free-standing, antique-style electric fan. The camp is fully solar powered, with constant 220V electricity supplied to the chalets, & a back-up generator.

Inside, along with dbl or twin beds enclosed in a walk-in mosquito net, are a writing desk, large trunk & easy chairs. Behind the bed is a bamboo screen & towel rack, a dressing table, twin basins, an inside flush toilet & separate shower. Through the tent's rear door is a blissful outdoor shower. One of the tents is designed for families, with 2 tents linked by an internal passage.

Overlooking a perennial channel, & the footbridge across it, is the camp's comfortable thatched dining room, bar & exceedingly cosy lounge. Close by, the camp has a good-size curio shop selling materials, jewellery, postcards, film, T-shirts & a few hats. There's also a small plunge pool, filled with water pumped from the Delta. This may seem superfluous in such an environment, though clearly litigious-minded visitors aren't encouraged to find 'safe' places to swim in the Delta itself.

LIFE IN PAPYRUS SWAMPS

Papyrus swamps are in many ways a difficult habitat. Below the waterline, little light penetrates the floating mat of dead, tangled stems and rhizomes. The constant decomposition of dead papyrus stems means much organic debris, and water which is acidic and low in oxygen. With no light, there's no chance for algae or any other higher plantlife.

Above the waterline the stems form a dense, tangled mass. The stems themselves are fibrous, difficult to digest and very nutrient-poor. Combined with a floating base that can't support any weight, this makes life here almost impossible for most larger animals. Only the specially adapted sitatunga antelope is at home here.

For animals as small as rats and mice, the situation isn't so bad. They don't generally stay in the papyrus beds, but they are light enough to make forays there, supported by the floating mat and individual stems. Greater cane rats are the largest of these, growing up to about 80cm on a diet of papyrus shoots, reeds and other vegetation. Although they swim well, they normally live in small family groups in burrows on permanent dry land, leaving these at night to forage in the reedbeds and papyrus.

A few birds also use the papyrus for shelter and nesting, including several species of weavers, the red-shouldered widow and red bishop bird – which will tear the feathery umbels of the papyrus as material to weave their intricate nests. Many more will come into papyrus areas to hunt for fish or insects, and there will be very few trips here when you won't see at least a few malachite and pied kingfishers.

Like Jao (page 367), Xigera feels like one of the Okavango Delta's most tropical, slow & romantic camps. It offers a great water experience, though I'd suggest that most visitors spend only 2 nights here, rather than 3 or 4 that might be the norm at a camp with more emphasis on game activities.

From US$680/930 pp sharing/sgl 11 Jan–Mar to US$1,120/1,460 Jun–Oct, inc FB, most drinks, activities, park fees & laundry; exc transfers. No children under 6. ⊕ All year. ★★★★– ★★★★★

Activities Motorboat trips and mokoro excursions have always been the main activities from Xigera, but their team has located a good area for game drives, and has come up with a way of stationing vehicles on the larger islands there. So usually, water levels permitting, it's now possible to drive there too.

Thus from about May until October, while the water is high, you boat to the game-drive vehicles, and then drive from there. Then it's possible to do motorboat trips as well as mokoro trips directly from the camp.

However, between about November and May, the water level is lower and it's then possible to keep the vehicles near camp and drive directly from there, though the motorboats have to be stationed in deeper water a short distance north of camp, and are reached by mokoro.

A recent change of regulations means that catch-and-release fishing is now permitted, except during the closed season of January and February. Xigera keeps a limited supply of basic angling gear.

Because the camp is within Moremi Game Reserve, night drives and off-road driving are not allowed. Short walks are conducted, but the guides are not allowed to carry rifles.

12

MOMBO AND CHIEF'S CAMP Mombo and Chief's share a concession within Moremi, but they are about 25km apart – which is a long way in the Okavango. Hence, unless they want to cross paths, you'll never normally see vehicles from one camp in the other camp.

Concession history Since the mid 1980s, the rights to run Mombo were owned by Jao Safaris (now defunct). They subleased this to many safari companies including Ker & Downey, Bonadventure (who were one of the main tour agencies when I first visited Maun in 1987) and, lastly, Wilderness Safaris. During this time, and especially in the last few years, it gained a first-class reputation for game.

When Jao Safaris' lease expired in 1998, there was clearly going to be very stiff competition for this area. Because it was recognised as such a prime area, the Land Board (ie: the government body responsible) allowed for two sites to be put up for tender, at opposite ends of the concession. Some 29 companies entered. There was tremendous competition: the best proposal and overall management plan would win.

Eventually two bids were accepted, one from Wilderness Safaris and another from A&K (whose Botswana operation is now called Sanctuary Retreats). Each needed to promise the government the highest possible revenue, as well as the best (that is, most sustainable and productive) management plan.

To achieve this, they both arrived at the obvious solution: each built one of the country's most upmarket camps, and attached an appropriately high price tag to it. It was the only way to make financial sense with such high concession fees. Thus the new, much more luxurious Mombo came into being, near the old Mombo site, and Chief's Camp was built south of that, on the northwestern side of Chief's Island. The tender process had maximised the government's revenues, and pushed part of the area's tourism a step further upmarket.

If plans afoot come to fruition during the lifetime of this edition, as seems likely, then we can expect Chief's Island to be subdivided into a few more wildlife concessions, to allow in a few more camps. If so, this will be part of the government's push to increase revenue, while still trying to retain their high revenue and exclusive approach to tourism.

Flora and fauna highlights

Flora The environments found here aren't unique in the Delta, but they are old, established, and have long been protected – and so are basically pristine and undisturbed.

Perhaps the most interesting, and certainly the most photogenic, habitats here are the shallow floodplains which surround the northern end of Chief's Island. (It's such a distinctive landscape that an image of it has remained deeply ingrained in my mind since my first visit here, in the mid 1990s.)

Looking at the whole Delta, you'll realise that this area is very close to the permanent swamps at the base of the Panhandle. Because of this, the floods here are more regular and predictable than they are lower down the Delta. This regular seasonal flooding has created a very photogenic environment of short-grass plains, among which are a number of tiny islands fringed by dense, feathery stands of wild date palms (*Phoenix reclinata*). For me, this is the quintessential Delta landscape – and it's sufficiently open to be excellent for game viewing.

(Away from the Okavango Delta, the only place that I've seen which is similar to this in southern Africa is the Busanga Plains of northern Kafue, in Zambia. Again, these are consistently flooded every year, and have very little disturbance.)

Go back on to the dry land of Chief's Island and you'll find a range of more familiar landscapes and floral communities. Across southern areas of the island (albeit not visited on game drives) are some areas of impressive, tall 'cathedral' mopane (*Colophospermum mopane*), often a popular retreat for game during wetter months.

Running through this you'll find lines of Kalahari sandveld, reflecting the locations of old, long-dry watercourses. Here you will see sand-loving species like the silver cluster-leaf (*Terminalia sericea*), the Kalahari appleleaf (*Philenoptera nelsii*), perhaps some camelthorn (*Vachellia erioloba*) and umbrella thorns (*Vachellia tortilis*), and the odd leadwood tree (*Combretum imberbe*).

Where the land meets the water, there are bands of classic riverine forest including fine specimens of raintree (*Philenoptera violacea*), sausage tree (*Kigelia africana*), jackalberry (*Diospyros mespiliformis*), African mangosteen (*Garcinia livingstonei*), figs (mostly *Ficus sycomorus*) and some wild date palms (*Phoenix reclinata*). Throughout the area's forests you'll occasionally find huge old baobab trees (*Adansonia digitata*) – which probably have lived long enough to see the environment change around them!

Fauna The game in this area is at least as dense as anywhere else in the Okavango, and probably more so as a result of historic peat fires on the north of Chief's Island releasing nutrients *en masse* into the ecosystem. Because the area's a private one, the game viewing is just about the best you'll find in southern Africa. It's dense, varied, and good sightings of predators are virtually guaranteed.

See *Flora and fauna* at the start of this chapter for more extensive comments on Moremi as a whole; in this particular area impala, tsessebe, zebra and giraffe are usually the most numerous of the larger herbivores – although warthogs are remarkably common. (So numerous that they have become a major prey species for both lion and leopard.) Elephant and buffalo are resident here in good numbers, with more individual animals seen during the rains, and generally larger herds recorded as the dry season progresses.

Zebra populations are far denser than elsewhere in the Delta. Herds of red lechwe are common in the flooded areas when the water's high, but they rarely venture into the drier parts of the reserve. Kudu and wildebeest also occur, as do the occasional reedbuck and steenbok; sable and roan are usually never seen here.

Though the majority of the Delta's usual line-up of nocturnal animals do occur, without taking night drives most are difficult to spot. The exception seems to be honey badgers, porcupines and spring hares, which are sometimes seen around the camps at night. In 2017, Mombo was also regularly visited by a civet in the evenings.

The area has a justified, first-class reputation for excellent predator sightings. Spotted hyena are probably the most successful large carnivore in the area, though lion are also common – as they are in many areas of the Delta. And cheetah, very much at home among the sprinkling of slightly raised date palm islands and termite hills that make ideal look-out posts, have become more widespread with at least 12 individuals known to be in the area in 2017.

There are good numbers of leopard around – although their appearances during the day are relatively limited. Originally Mombo, and this area, built its reputation on some of Africa's best sightings of wild dog – largely because of a very large and successful pack of about 40 dogs that denned here for several years in the mid 1990s. With this pack in residence, visitors were virtually guaranteed amazing sightings, and the area's dry open floodplains proved marvellous for following the animals as they hunted. Then that pack broke up, as is the usual process when the alpha female dies, but two other packs now operate in the area, so sightings remain pretty good.

Finally, a real good-news story for this area, and the Delta as a whole. Both black and white rhino used to occur here naturally, but by the early 1990s they had been

12

RETURN OF THE RHINO

Until the middle of the 20th century, the white rhino was common in northern Botswana, while the less populous black rhino was still holding its own in the area around the Kwando and Chobe rivers. However, protection was inadequate, and with illegal hunting spurred on by the value of rhinoceros horns on the world market, the animals' presence was increasingly threatened. By 1992, the area's population of black rhino had been wiped out, declared 'locally extinct', and white rhino numbers were down to a critical 19. The future looked bleak.

In response, an anti-poaching operation was set up by the Department of Wildlife and National Parks (DWNP), backed by the Botswana Defence Force (BDF). As a result, the remaining white rhino were removed to wildlife sanctuaries so that they could be protected until the time came when they could safely be released back into the wild.

Then, in 2001, in a collaborative venture between Wilderness Safaris (*www.wilderness-safaris.com*) and the Botswana Government's DWNP, the Botswana Rhino Reintroduction Project was born. Under its auspices, four white rhino were initially reintroduced on to Chief's Island in 2001: two females and two males. Since then, many more animals have been reintroduced, and a healthy population of white rhino is now firmly established both in the Moremi Game Reserve and elsewhere in the Delta.

Next it was the turn of the black rhino. Almost two years after the project started, in November 2003, four black rhinos were released to roam in the Delta for the first time in well over a decade. This initial population also bred and since then, further significant reintroductions of animals from South Africa and Zimbabwe in 2014 and 2015 have bolstered this breeding nucleus and helped build up numbers here as a meaningful conservation initiative.

As both species gain ground, and without being constrained by fences, some are moving away. With the aid of tracking devices, these migrations are being carefully monitored. The Wilderness Safaris Rhino Reintroduction Project also carries out detailed ecological and behavioural studies of the reintroduced black and white rhino populations with a view to gaining a greater understanding of the distances travelled by both species, the importance of individual habitats, and their preferred choice of vegetation. In turn, this will provide key information for their protection into the future.

Support from the government and private stakeholders, including the DWNP's Anti-Poaching Unit, the involvement of the BDF and a zero-tolerance approach to poaching, means that the Delta's new rhino population has remained relatively unscathed, but poaching elsewhere in Africa has reached epidemic proportions. In South Africa, more than 6,000 rhino have been killed for their horns in just a decade. In an attempt to counter the very real threat of extinction, two concerned tour operators, Great Plains and &Beyond, have joined forces to found Rhinos without Borders (*www.rhinoswithoutborders.com*), whose remit is to move 100 rhinos out of South Africa into the relative safety of Botswana. At a cost of US$45,000 per rhino, it's an expensive mission, but the first animals were successfully translocated in 2017, and more are following.

For the wildlife visitor, the news is positive: for the first time in 25 years, rhino are again being spotted in Botswana. Finally, the big five are reunited.

exterminated by poaching. At last, in 2001, the first white rhino were brought back into this area. Over the next few years more were released on to Chief's Island and they have been breeding well – with increasingly frequent sightings in Moremi. With the success of the white rhino reintroduction, the focus shifted in 2003 to returning the black rhino to the Okavango Delta as well. See box, opposite – but note that although both species are present, sightings of the black rhino remain rare.

Birdlife At the heart of the Delta, and with a large and diverse area of dry land and floodplains, this area of Moremi gets periodic visits from virtually all of the birds in the Delta, so singling out a few to mention here is inevitably a flawed process.

However, top of the list for a special mention are the vultures, attracted by the game densities and predator activity. Most numerous are the white-backed, hooded and lappet-faced vultures – though you'll also find a surprising number of white-headed vultures. Palm-nut vultures occur, too (usually frequenting the real fan palms), though they're not common.

Also attracted by the game are both kinds of oxpecker – though yellow-billed (which feed on the backs of hippos) seem more common than the red-billed variety.

As happens everywhere in the Delta, when the waters recede, isolated pools of fish are left behind. As these gradually dry up the fish become more and more concentrated, attracting the most amazing numbers of predatory birds. Pick the right day (usually one between about May and October) and the right pool, and you'll be entertained for hours by large concentrations of pelicans, saddle-billed storks, marabou storks, black egrets, grey and Goliath herons to name but a few. It's an amazing sight. In other receding pools you'll find congregations of pelicans or, in those which aren't so frantic, painted snipes can be seen if you look hard (or have a good guide!).

The short-grass floodplains here suit wattled cranes, which are often found in numbers, and on the drier plains watch for secretary birds and kori bustards. The latter occasionally have carmine bee-eaters using their backs as perches. In plains with longer grass you may be able to spot an African crake, while ostriches are very rarely seen (perhaps because there are too many large predators).

On the water look for pygmy geese and dwarf jacanas in the quieter areas, along with many species of more common waterbirds. There's often a good number of the relatively rare slaty egrets about too.

When to visit Because the focus here is firmly on game viewing, the dry season is the obvious time to visit. That's when the game is at its most visible and most dense. That said, from July to October the camps (especially Mombo) have substantial 'high-season supplements', which can make the costs at other times of the year seem very attractive.

If you decide to come at a less popular, and cheaper, time then remember that Chief's Island is a large, permanent island with its own large, permanent population of game. Thus you'll still see some first-rate game even if the game viewing isn't quite as good as it would have been during October.

Getting there and away Only pre-booked guests flying in visit this area, as there is no practical dry-land access to Chief's Island. Driving here isn't an option. Each camp has its own airstrip on Chief's Island; Mombo's airstrip is at ✈ MOMBOA 19°12.680'S, 22°47.510'E.

Where to stay Both Mombo and Chief's are top-of-the-range camps in one of southern Africa's very best game areas – though Mombo is a notch above Chief's and the game viewing arguably slightly better in the Mombo area. Both come at a high cost – though Chief's hasn't been around long enough to build up quite the same reputation that Mombo has. However, note that some safari purists contend that elements of the clientele who visit this camp are attracted more by the image of the camp rather than the reality of the game viewing, which can be to the detriment of the atmosphere at times.

⌂ **Mombo Camp** [map 256] (9 tents) Contact Wilderness Safaris, page 225. This is the flagship Wilderness Safaris' camp in Botswana, one of their 4 'premier' camps (the others are Jao, page 367; Vumbura Plains, page 362; & King's Pool, page 298) & is one of the most expensive photographic camps in Botswana. Raised on wooden decking high off the ground, beneath tall shady trees, the camp was completely rebuilt in 2017. While many of the original features, such as the iconic wooden front doors into the tents, have been retained, others have been recycled – so old floors now do service as wood panelling & even b/fast counters. New to the camp are private plunge pools for each tent, & multi-layered, insulated roofs designed to mitigate the effects of the climate, & the camp is now 100% solar powered.

The main area, incorporating a comfortably furnished lounge/bar, overlooks wide floodplains. A long polished wooden table for candlelit dinners sits in the dining area, with one side open to the decking via roll-down blinds. A couple of smaller areas, one of them alfresco, extend the dining options, while traditional dinners are sometimes served in the large boma. At the front, a campfire surrounded by deckchairs is a good place to gather for after-dinner drinks.

Mombo's 'tents' – 5 to the east of the main area, & 4 to the west – remain very large. Made of canvas supported by wooden poles, they're connected by raised wooden walkways. Mombo's iconic wooden doors open to reveal in each suite a sitting room with a bar unit, a separate bedroom with twin or dbl beds, & a bathroom with a dressing area, indoor & outdoor showers & a bathtub. Copper cladding evinces the 'old Mombo' feel, along with vintage leathers, natural oak & antique brass finishings, & décor is designed to reflect local artwork & legends. At the front of each tent, sliding wooden louvred doors backed by separate gauze doors, open on to an extended deck, where a small private plunge pool has been added overlooking the floodplain. You'll also find a table, chairs & a lounger are shaded from the sun by the canvas roof. On one side is a thatched sala, or small gazebo, with a mattress & cushions, which makes a nice shady spot from which to watch game. Even the area beneath the decking seems to be a popular evening spot for buffalo. *From US$1,930/2,610 pp sharing/sgl 11 Jan–Mar to US$2,955/3,845 Jun–Oct, inc FB, most drinks, activities, park fees, laundry; exc transfers.* ☺ *All year.* ★★★★★

⌂ **Little Mombo** [map 256] (3 tents) Continuing along the decking, past a gym, spa & lap pool, is Mombo's tiny sister camp. Although adjacent to the main camp, Little Mombo operates as a separate entity. Its tents have the same design as those of its neighbour, & its main lounge/dining/bar area is similarly furnished, though smaller. Little Mombo has its own outdoor boma, plunge pool & communal sala – as well as individual ones for the rooms. *Rates as for Mombo, above.* ☺ *All year.* ★★★★★

⌂ **Chief's Camp** [map 256] (12 tents) Contact Sanctuary Retreats, page 224. About 25km from Mombo, just off the western side of Chief's Island, this is the pride of Sanctuary Retreats' operations in Botswana.

Chief's was completely rebuilt in 2016, to stunning effect. The main area is raised on decking where its high thatched roof covers a large, open-plan area. This encompasses a reception desk, lounge & a well-stocked bar, with new wooden coffee tables & both leather & cloth sofas, & a dining room with a number of tables. Here guests tend to dine with their own guide, who is generally allotted to you when you arrive (you usually stick with the same guide & take all your drives with him/her). When last visited, Chief's food was outstanding, & accompanied with an impressive selection of wine.

Outside this dining/lounge area, an expanse of wooden decking acts as a veranda, where you can sit in the shade of large jackalberry (*Diospyros mespiliformis*) & marula (*Sclerocarya birrea*) trees. An 8m-long swimming pool is surrounded by loungers & a small sala. Those with a passion for shopping might seek out the efficient shop stocked with books, T-shirts & some stylish curios.

Chief's secluded 'pavilion' tents are set on each side of the main area, & reached from a simple sand path that is lit at night by electric hurricane lamps. All are slightly raised off the ground on decking, & have private verandas overlooking the plains (which usually flood around Jun–Aug, when the water may come all the way up to the lodge). Each tent has a wooden door & polished wood floor, with very stylish & extremely modern décor. Beside the twin or dbl beds, Adjustable coil lamps attached to a wooden headboard flank the twin or dbl beds. There's an open wardrobe, a couple of chairs & tables, a stone-decorated chandelier & a ceiling fan, powered by 24hr electricity (110/220V). The bathroom, adjacent to the main body of the tent, is bright & open, with proper partition walls, twin washbasins beneath a large mirror. Doors lead out to a massive open-air shower, separated by the sliding glass doors of a large indoor shower. The toilet is behind a wooden door – completing the impression that this is the bathroom of a plush hotel rather than a safari camp.

Set at the far end of the tents is Chief's dedicated spa – one of only 3 in the Delta. Small but well equipped, it offers treatments including massages, facials, manicures, body scrubs & wraps – all of which can be experienced from a deck overlooking the floodplain. *Pavilion from US$1,180 pp 6 Jan–Mar to US$2,815/4,926 Jul–Aug & 21 Dec–6 Jan, inc FB, most drinks, activities, park fees, laundry; exc transfers.* ⊕ *All year.* ★★★★★

Activities Game drives are the main activity at Mombo and Chief's camps, though both are constricted to some extent by the park's rules. Night drives and fishing are not currently allowed.

Chief's Camp also offers mokoro trips, subject to water levels. When the floods arrive, up to 70% of Chief's Camp's network of roads becomes covered in water, and mokoro trips can start off right at the lodge.

12

13

The Okavango Delta – Private Reserves around Moremi

In his book *Lake Ngami and the River Okavango* the Victorian-era explorer and trader Charles John Andersson wrote:

> On every side as far as the eye could see, lay stretched a sea of fresh water, in many places concealed from sight by a covering of reeds and rushes of every shade and hue; while numerous islands, spread over its whole surface, and adorned with rich vegetation, gave to the whole an indescribably beautiful appearance.

For modern visitors the Okavango Delta has lost none of its beauty – something that was internationally recognised in 2014, when it was designated the 1,000th UNESCO World Heritage Site. However, finding reliable information on the various areas from brochures can be as challenging as Andersson's expedition. This chapter aims to demystify these areas, and to identify some of the strengths and weaknesses of the areas and their camps.

Here I will cover all of the private reserves around the Okavango and the main camps within these. But before you read any of my comments, here are a few general observations on the chapter:

- I've covered the reserves in the order of their concession numbers, from NG12 to NG43.
- There are virtually no fences between these areas, so the game flows freely between them, and won't always be where I suggest it is.
- Remember that differences in environment and game can be as great within a reserve as they are between one reserve and its neighbour. Despite this, some trends are evident, which I've tried to draw out.
- The marketing leaflets of the reserves usually claim that every animal/bird is found in their particular areas – particularly the 'sexy' ones like wild dogs and Pel's fishing owls! There is some truth in this, in that virtually all the animals/birds do occur in all the reserves. However, I've tried to get behind the spin with a realistic assessment of what you're most likely to see, and where you're most likely to see it. I've tried to make my comments reflect realistic probabilities, but they can't be definitive.
- I've made comments largely from my own first-hand experience, informed when in these areas by guides and experts. Occasionally, I have used reliable local sources. That said, I have not spent a year in each reserve, so my observations have been snapshots from the times that I've visited, augmented

OKAVANGO'S PRIVATE RESERVES CAMPS & LODGES

NG14

Lagoon

Linyanti Campsite/
Camp Linyanti

Linyanti Bush
Camp/Ebony

CH1

Linyanti
Tented Camp

*Chobe
Forest
Reserve*

Ghoha Gate

King's
Pool

Ghoha Hills
Savuti Lodge

NG15

DumaTau

Sayuti Campsite
& Lodges

Selinda
Explorers

Selinda
Zarafa

Savuti
Channel

*Zweizwe
Pan*

Veterinary
gate

NG16

Savuti
Camp

*Chobe
National
Park*

NG12

Motswiri

NG20

NG18

Sky Beds

NG22

Little Vumbura,
Vumbura Plains

Hyena Pan

Xugana

NG21

Kwara,
Little Kwara

Footsteps

Shinde

Sable Alley

NG19

Camp
Okavango

Pangolin Khwai
Camp

Khwai
Village

Khwai River
Lodge

Mababe Gate

Gcoverega

Third Bridge
Campsite

Mababe Village
(Kudumane)

NG41

Camp Moremi,
Xakanaxa,
Okuti

Khwai
Campsite

North Gate
(Khwai)

Mogotlho

Chief's

Moremi Game Reserve

Mopane Tongue

Chief's

*Chief's
Island*

South Gate
Campsite

Mankwe

Eagle
Island

Sandibe

South Gate
(Maqwee)

Sankuyo
Village

Delta

Gunn's

NG31

Chitabe

Gomoti
Tented Camp

**NG
33**

NG34

Tuskers
Bush Camp

Oddballs'
NG27B

Moremi Crossing

Santawani

Kaziikini
Campsite

NG43

Xaranna

Baines'

Stanley's

Rra Dinare

Qorokwe

Mma Dinare

gate

Mowana
Gate

Xudum

NG32

Gomoti
Plains Camp

NG30

Kujwana

Shorobe

Khurunxaraga Gate

Xaraxau

Sakapane

NG44

NG47

NG35

NG46

Matsibi
Gate

Kudum Gate

Maun

Matlapaneng

NG49

NG45

Drifters

Tsibogolamatebele

Tshima

Nengwa

Veterinary
gate

Nata

Tikaseolo

Komana

Tatamoge

Motopi

Matima

NG37

Makgalo

Makalamabedi

Dorokae

Senagom

CT8

Toteng

Veterinary
gate

13

Mogapelwa

NG38

NG39

Khwebe Hills

> **NOTE**
> For accommodation listings, see
> pages 348–9, 349–51, 353–4, 356–8,
> 362–3, 367–9, 371–2, 373–4, 377–8,
> 382–4, 387–8, 390, 394–5, 397–8,
> 402–3, 404, 405

by comments from my team of Botswana experts and the travellers who visit with my travel company. They don't pretend to be comprehensive, systematic surveys, but I do believe that they're broadly representative.

- Under each reserve I've tried to cover the basics of the wildlife and the practicalities. This has necessitated some repetition, but it's a reflection of the fact that there are more similarities between the various reserves in the Delta than there are differences.

MAPULA AND KADIZORA (NG12)

Outside the buffalo fence, north of Vumbura and Duba Plains, the Magwegqana or Selinda Spillway starts in an environment similar to southeast Vumbura – though generally NG12's islands are bigger and its vegetation more established. In the south are good game viewing and extensive mopane woodlands; last time I was in the area, two cheetah left Vumbura heading north to hunt in NG12.

Several villages stand on this concession's northern boundary, including Seronga, Beetsha (Betsaa), Eretsha (Eretsa), Gunotsoga (Ganitsuga) and Gudigwa. In 2003, the area received its first visitors, thanks to an exciting project to create the Delta's first upmarket, community-run 'cultural camp', Gudigwa. Sadly, the impact of two bushfires in 2003 took its toll, however, although the camp was reopened in 2006, a further fire and irresolvable issues with the community mean it has now shut down with little hope of reopening.

In the same concession are Mapula Lodge – which opened at about the same time – and Kadizora Camp, which opened its doors in 2014.

FLORA AND FAUNA HIGHLIGHTS The NG12 concession is bisected by the Okavango's main buffalo fence, which is punctuated by gates to allow access, but is reasonably effective in controlling the flow of larger game from one side to the other. Both Mapula and Kadizora are just north of the buffalo fence, so are able to operate on both sides.

Wildlife on both sides of the fence reflects the variety of habitat in this area, though it is more prolific to the south. Zebra and giraffe are common, as are a range of antelope, from red lechwe and waterbuck to impala, wildebeest and kudu. These in turn attract the predators, including leopard and lion, but also wild dog, which den here regularly. Buffalo and elephant are permanent residents. The birdlife, too, is exceptionally varied. This is a good place to spot the endangered wattled crane, as well as carmine bee-eaters, and the African paradise flycatcher.

GETTING THERE AND AWAY Visitors to all lodges in NG12 arrive by air. The trip takes 40 minutes from Maun, and costs around US$225 per person each way.

WHERE TO STAY

 Mapula Lodge [map 346] (9 chalets) ☎ 686 3369; e mapulalodge@btcmail.co.bw; www. mapula-lodge.com. Occupying a stunning position on the edge of seasonal floodplains, Mapula Lodge overlooks a permanent lagoon complete with a large contingent of resident hippos. Batswana owned & run, it has a relaxed, homely atmosphere, with many of its staff drawn from nearby villages. A comfortable open-sided lounge & dining area under thatch extends to a large deck in the shade of an ancient African ebony, & beyond to a sunlounger placed enticingly at the end of a long jetty. More loungers around a small pool are an inviting spot to relax in the afternoon, while the bush bar comes into its own as the sun dips below the horizon. Solidly built chalets are raised up on private decks fronting the lagoon, with views from the bedroom bathroom & (very good) outside shower. Activities focus on day & night game drives on both sides of the buffalo fence (the range covered depending on flood levels, but drives can be quite long), as well as boat trips (when water levels permit), mokoro excursions & guided walks. Often, vehicles go out with a guide & tracker. That said, on one visit here we experienced guiding that was poor to the extent of being dangerous.

We've looked at Mapula several times over the years, & while there's considerable potential here, we can't currently recommend this lodge. *From US$462 pp Jan–Mar & Dec to US$835/1,085.50 pp sharing/sgl Jul–Oct, inc FB, local drinks, activities, laundry. No children under 8.* ⊕ *All year.* ★★★– ★★★★

🏠 **Kadizora Camp** [map 346] (13 rooms) 📞 +27 11 568 4264; **e** res@anthology.co.za, sales@anthology.co.za; www.kadizoracamp. com. Opened in 2014, Kadizora lies some 15km northwest of Duba Plains in the remote north of the Okavango Delta. Following a recent revamp the camp now has 9 'luxury' & 4 'standard' rooms, each with either twin beds or a dbl, & all en suite. The larger tented 'luxury' rooms are built on low wooden platforms, their polished wooden floors adorned with rugs & each with a writing desk & small lounge area. In the bathroom you'll find his & hers basins, a shower, bath & separate toilet.

In the sprawling main area, 2 communal tents are set on a large wooden deck surrounding a central firepit. These house a lounge & a bar/dining area, although weather permitting meals are often taken on the deck. There is also a small pool. Activities include hot-air balloon safaris, mokoro trips, safari game drives & bush walks. *US$400/615 pp sharing/sgl Jan–Apr & Nov–Dec, US$550/1,150 May–Oct, inc FB, local drinks, activities, laundry.* ⊕ *All year.* ★★★

KHWAI PRIVATE RESERVE (NG18)

On the southern edge of the small NG19 concession, where hunting has long been illegal, you'll find a collection of lodges benefiting from the beautiful frontage along the Khwai River. These are managed by the community-run Khwai Development Trust, and for the sake of continuity, I've described them in *Chapter 12* under North Gate, on pages 318–21.

The larger NG18 area, which stretches north to the Linyanti Concession, east of Kwara and west of Chobe, is a private concession. For many years, the only time that I'd been here was when driving on the 'transit route' between Moremi and the Linyanti and Selinda reserves, a route that is no longer passable. The interior of this concession appeared to be fairly monotonous mopane, but there were signs of game around. Now, however, there are three newly refurbished camps which allow travellers to experience this relatively unexplored area.

FLORA AND FAUNA HIGHLIGHTS This was for many years a hunting concession, so the game here is still quite skittish, albeit becoming gradually more habituated to vehicles. Wild dog pass through the area frequently and there are good numbers of leopard and lion. Elephants and particularly zebra seem to be prolific too. During 2017, there were dogs denning not far from Sable Alley, and sightings were good.

GETTING THERE AND AWAY Most guests at lodges in the reserve arrive by air into an airstrip built in 2012. From there it's just a 10-minute drive to Sable Alley, an hour's drive to Hyena Pan and a further 30 minutes on to Sky Beds.

🏠 **WHERE TO STAY** New to this concession is Sable Alley (formerly Banoka Bush Camp), along with Sky Beds and Hyena Pan. All three are marketed by Natural Selection (page 224).

🏠 **Pangolin Khwai Camp** [map 347] (7 tents) Contact Pangolin Photo Safaris, page 248. Set to open in Mar 2018, Pangolin Khwai adds to the portfolio of this specialist photo safari operator. The camp's large thatched communal area overlooks an expanse of grassland. In the centre,

13

in front of the bar, is a sunken lounge firepit, with a seating area to one side, & a long table for group dining to the other. Slightly raised off the ground, the en-suite tents sit on wooden decking with a veranda for afternoon siestas – or checking on the morning's haul of photos. Activities include game drives, night drives & mokoro excursions. *From US$395 pp Jan–Mar to US$795 Jun–Oct, inc FB, most drinks, activities, park fees; exc transfers.* ⊕ *All year.* ★★★–★★★★★

🏠 **Sable Alley** [map 347] (12 tents) Overlooking a deep, lily-lined lagoon connected to the Khwai River, the former Banoka Bush Camp reopened in May 2017 following complete renovation.

The open main area, set on stilts overlooking the river, is vast – so even when camp is full you can be as social or as reclusive as you wish. As soon as you enter the building, there are steps leading down to a protruding sundowner spot with camp chairs & a firepit. To one side is a large, newly built pool with changing facilities & fresh towels. In the main area itself, the lounge leads through to a well-stocked bar with a variety of gins, & plenty of places to chill out with a drink, & a dining area where meals may be taken communally or at individual tables. Beyond this, a sunken deck brings you down closer to the lagoon. Sandy pathways lead to the tents, including 2 family tents, which are also raised on stilts. From each veranda, timber-framed, mesh sliding doors open to reveal twin beds, or a dbl. A tall wooden headboard separates the bedroom from a wardrobe, his & hers basins, a large shower that opens on to an outdoor shower with views over the lagoon, & a toilet in a separate cubicle.

Early in the season, around Apr/May, the mopane around the lodge is quite dense, so game drives can be quite uneventful at first, but a short distance away the landscape opens up into wide pans & some attractive riverine scenery. Walking in these more open areas is a real treat, & there are also mokoro & boat trips on offer – as well as the option to spend a night at Sky Beds (see opposite).

Sable Alley combines well with many camps & makes a great private reserve alternative to the Khwai area. *From US$560 pp Jan–May to US$840/1,200 pp sharing/sgl Jun–Oct, inc FB, most drinks, activities, park fees, laundry; exc transfers.* ⊕ *All year.* ★★★–★★★★★

🏠 **Hyena Pan** [map 347] (8 tents) The recently refurbished Hyena Pan is set deep in mopane woodland overlooking Hyena Pan itself. This is one of the few permanent water sources in the area, & at the end of the dry season (Sep–Oct) attracts a variety of game, including elephant, buffalo, wild dog, lion & leopard. As a result of heavy rains in 2016 & 2017, the water came right up to camp.

The main area sits about a metre off the ground under a high thatched roof, sharing the view of the pan with the firepit below. The dining area, dominated by a long communal table, leads on to a lounge area with comfortable sofas & armchairs, with more seating under canvas by a small infinity-style plunge pool. The small, quirky bar is made out of an old log, & the whole area is adorned with local artefacts, old suitcases & fun ornaments. Scatter cushions & an eclectic mix of furniture add splashes of vibrant, ethnic colour.

Reached along wooden walkways & sandy paths, the large Meru-style tents have twin beds, or a dbl. Wooden headboards screen the en-suite facilities behind, which include a large mirror, flushing toilet & shower. The tents are not overly luxurious but are comfortable, & attractively furnished with touches of colour & unusual light fittings. The combination of thick mopane in this area & relatively unexplored terrain means that game drives are often conducted in the Khwai Community Concession (NG19). For Sky Beds, see below. *From US$395 pp Jan–May, to US$595/895 Jun–Oct pp sharing/sgl, inc FB, most drinks, activities, park fees, laundry; exc transfers.* ⊕ *All year.* ★★★

🏠 **Sky Beds** [map 347] (4 platforms) Acting as a fly-camp, Sky Beds can be booked as an excursion from either Sable Alley or Hyena Pan; it cannot be booked independently. The camp is made up of 2-tier raised platforms, each set about 70m from the edge of a permanent waterhole and roughly 50m apart. At the top is an open bedroom where you sleep under the stars, with a mosquito net depending on the season. The area below, with an enclosed shower & flushing loo, also provides a private changing area. Hot water is pumped up from a little generator when needed. An additional platform serves as the bar, affording good 'sundowner' views over the pan, & simple but convivial meals are taken near the fire around a long camp table. It's a rustic camp that offers something totally different so would be a great choice for the more adventurous. A variety of game, such as elephant, buffalo, roan, kudu, wild dog & lion, frequents the waterhole, which is at its best Aug–Oct.

From US$395 pp Jan–May to US$595 Jun–Oct, inc FB, most drinks, activities, park fees; exc transfers; min 2 people. ☺ *All year.* ★ ★ ★

KWARA (NG20)

The Kwara Concession covers a huge 1,750km², in the middle of the Delta's northern edge. It's bounded to the north by Selinda (NG16), to the west by Vumbura (NG22) and to the east by Khwai Private Reserve (NG18). On the south side, the reserve is adjacent to Moremi Game Reserve and the small enclave of NG21 (which includes Camp Okavango, Xugana and Shinde). This location means that the reserve spans the transition from deep-water areas on the extreme north of the Delta, through very large areas of open floodplains, many of which are dry for much of the year, to the substantial dry areas of its northern section.

CONCESSION HISTORY Kwara has been an established safari camp since the mid 1990s. It was initially privately owned and run, before being operated first by Bird Safaris, then by Ker & Downey, with the marketing taken on by Wilderness Safaris. In 1999, the camp was taken over by the Kwando Safaris team, who bought the rights to the concession in about 2008.

Since then, there have been just two camps here: Kwara and Little Kwara. Now, as I write in early 2018, change is on the horizon; the existing camps are looking old, and Kwando Safaris has permission to build more camps in this concession. The current plan is to build smarter replacements for Kwara and Little Kwara on a nearby site called 'Splash', to open at some point in 2018. Then when those are running smoothly, the aim is to demolish and rebuild both Kwara and Little Kwara.

FLORA AND FAUNA HIGHLIGHTS Kwara Reserve is very large, and covers a wide spectrum of environments from deep-water lagoons and thick papyrus to dry-country scrub and mopane woodlands. Therefore, trying to describe here any dominant species of plants or animals is at best inconclusive, and at worst completely misleading.

These are a few general notes on what you're likely to find here, plus observations of what I have found most interesting on my visits over the years.

Flora South of the camp lie the permanent swamps; a true deep-water environment. You'll find large stands of both papyrus and phragmites reeds, often with waterberry and water-fig trees dotted among them. Look down in some of the deeper main channels and you'll find the water opaque, heavy with sediment.

However, in most of the lagoons and the slower channels you'll be able to see right to the Kalahari sand at the bottom, and any water creatures or plants there. Among the mass of weeds, ask your guide to point out the delicate web of stems belonging to one of the Okavango's many species of bladderwort (*Utricularia* species). These usually form a submerged tangle of green, hair-like stems with tiny, thin leaves. Dotted among these are numerous small 'bladders' which, when touched by a small invertebrate like a mosquito larva, can suck the animal in and capture it. The bladder then digests the animal, and in the process gets valuable nitrogen, which is in very short supply in the mineral-impoverished waters of the Okavango.

Much easier to locate, floating on the surface of the lagoons, you'll find the fan-shaped, serrated leaves of the water chestnut (*Trapa natans*). This is often found on the edges of the lagoons, and is interesting not so much for its white flowers, but for the horned seedpod which it forms. The barbs on this will latch on to the fur or skin of animals, as an aid to dispersing its seed. Their large size suggests that the area's numerous hippo are involved.

Move away from the water, north of camp, and you'll start entering the drier parts of the Kwara Reserve. You'll see that between the dry and wet, there's a transition zone where the bush is a mixture of ancient tree-islands surrounded by plains that were once flooded. The tree-islands were once more distinct, and surrounded by true floodplains, but as this area has dried out, the vegetation on the plains has grown and blurred the distinction between plains and tree-islands. Similarly, the salt deposits that are often found at the heart of the tree-islands have dissipated.

Like many areas on the edges of the Delta, this is in the extremely slow process of change. This zone was once wet, and now its landscapes and vegetation are very, very gradually reverting to landforms and vegetation of the drier areas – a process that will take millennia to complete. Here you'll find most of the Delta's usual species of trees, from African mangosteens to jackalberries, and both real fan and wild date palms. Plus a few species more often seen in the drier areas of Chobe, like Kalahari appleleaf (*Philenoptera nelsii*) and silver cluster-leaf (*Terminalia sericea*).

Fauna In the drier areas, Kwara's dominant antelopes appear to be tsessebe and impala, with very healthy populations of reedbuck, kudu and giraffe. You'll also find wildebeest, zebra, bushbuck, warthog and steenbok, plus a liberal sprinkling of elephant and the odd herd of buffalo. On the floodplains around camp, lechwe are also common, while deep in the papyrus there are sitatunga, though these are not often seen.

When I first visited this area in 1996, most of the reserve was still in the grip of hunting, with dismal game viewing and a bleak outlook. The few game drives I went on yielded remarkably little. Antelope would flee at 500m, and we had almost no sightings of big game. Since then, the wildlife situation has changed immeasurably and photographic camps have been run successfully in the area by Kwando Safaris for some years. This is an interesting reflection of what's been happening in northern Botswana in the past ten to 15 years, as areas that had been used for hunting have been supplanted by photographic camps. Now that commercial hunting has been banned, even more areas are opening up.

Large areas of this concession are open and dry for most of the year and Kwando Safaris' approach is to track the big predators actively wherever possible. So now all the big cats – lion, leopard and cheetah – are around and regularly seen, and it's a particularly good area for seeing wild dog. I made one visit here a long time ago (around 2010) in February, which is usually a very difficult time for spotting predators. But despite the thick, green vegetation the guide and spotter managed to locate a pack of wild dogs and track them for several miles across the bush until we caught up with them as they killed an impala.

Birdlife As with the range of animals, the birdlife is inevitably varied. About 6.5km southwest of Kwara is Gcodikwe Lagoon. This is within Moremi Game Reserve, but Kwara is the nearest camp to it, so makes a good base for visits here. (See the more comprehensive notes on pages 329–30 about Gcodikwe, but note that within a boat ride you'll find one of the region's most important breeding colonies of storks, egrets, herons and spoonbills.) It is at its busiest between September and November, but there are always a few birds there.

Elsewhere in Kwara you'll find a good range of the usual species found in and around the Delta. The more common residents include reed cormorants, darters, African and lesser jacanas, malachite, pied and giant kingfishers, pygmy geese, fish eagles and marsh harriers. Meanwhile the coucals are particularly well represented, with Senegal, coppery-tailed and (in summer) even black coucals all seen. More unusual sightings include fulvous duck, swamp boubous, black and slaty egrets, black-crowned and white-backed night herons, and the occasional migrant osprey.

In the drier areas north of the permanent waterways, some of the more common residents include blacksmith lapwings, red-billed spurfowl, double-banded sandgrouse, lilac-breasted rollers, yellow-billed hornbills, Meyer's parrots, fiery-necked nightjars, palm swifts, white-rumped babblers, red-eyed and Cape turtle doves, black-crowned tchagras, Heuglin's robins and black-breasted snake eagles. More unusual sightings might include western banded snake eagles, Dickinson's kestrels (often perching on palm trees), red-necked falcons, bat hawks, swallow-tailed bee-eaters, red-billed helmet shrikes, brown-throated weavers and wattled cranes.

WHEN TO VISIT As with much of the Delta, the big game here is invariably more prolific during the dry season; and although many of the birds breed between December and March, Gcodikwe is generally at its most spectacular before then. That said, visiting in February still allowed me some first-class game viewing, including wild dog, as noted above. So don't write off the green season as a universally lousy time for game: it just takes a bit more tracking down then.

GETTING THERE AND AWAY Kwara can be reached by road from Shinde, or by boat from the Xakanaxa area, but in practice virtually all visitors arrive by air at the small airstrip a short distance from camp. Like most camps in the Okavango, you can't just drop in here, and even if you could the camp wouldn't welcome you. It's essential to pre-book your visit.

WHERE TO STAY This concession is owned by Kwando Safaris (page 224) who run all of the camps here, as well as sister camps in NG14, Lebala and Lagoon (pages 306–7); Nxai Pan Camp in Nxai Pan National Park, and Tau Pan Camp in the

Central Kalahari. At the time of writing, there are only two camps here, Kwara and Little Kwara, but this will change during the lifetime of this book.

Kwara [map 347] (8 tents) Kwara stands on a small tree-island amid floodplains. Most of its tents, measuring 3.5m x 7m x about 2m high, are raised on teak decks with good views over the surrounding plains & lagoons. Lined in a light-green canvas, to help make them brighter inside, they have large windows of traditional insect-proof mesh. The wardrobe, luggage rack, bedside tables, chairs & beds are all of solid teak, standing on a polished floor dotted with rugs. The bathroom, in a separate part of the tent, includes twin washbasins, a flush toilet, & an inventively designed large shower that's enclosed but surrounded by a screen that's partially open to the outside. The honeymoon suite (No 8) also has a free-standing bath.

Slightly raised up on decking beneath a large jackalberry tree (*Diospyros mespiliformis*), Kwara's thatched bar-lounge & dining area is cosy & comfortable. It overlooks a shallow lagoon that often attracts good numbers of game. The camp's food is good & the bar well stocked, as you'd expect. Nearby there's a swimming pool set into wooden decking & lined by sunloungers, & a raised look-out hide where you can spend the middle of the day reading or taking in the view. There's also a gift shop. Kwara shares a fairly informal approach with its sister camps, Lagoon & Lebala, which are all designed slightly differently. While each aims to provide a very comfortable camp, the accent is firmly on the activities & the guiding rather than ever more creature comforts. *From US$620 pp Jan–Mar & Dec to US$1,090/1,420 pp sharing/ sgl Jul–Oct, inc FB, activities, park fees.* ☺ *All year.*
★★★–★★★★★

Little Kwara [map 347] (5 tents) Although Little Kwara is only 2km or so from Kwara, it is constructed very differently. Built in 2006 on a tree-island, its tents are raised on high wooden decks, with canvas walls & ceilings into which large mosquito-gauze windows have been set, all with roll-down flaps. Polished wooden flooring, twin ¾ or king-size beds, & some solid furniture set the tone, while behind a large bedhead is the dressing area. Each tent has its own en-suite bathroom complete with bath, & indoor & partially covered outdoor shower. To the front, a large sliding door of gauze leads to a private veranda set amid the trees.

Sandy paths lead to the spacious main lounge overlooking the lagoon, & a well-stocked bar area where guests can help themselves. Low wicker tables, trendy sofas & proper armchairs with comfy cushions all add to the sense of a tastefully designed camp. To the side is a restaurant area, & there's also a curio shop.
Activities are of the same high standard as those at Kwara, with trackers as well as guides on every vehicle. *From US$662 pp Jan–Mar & Dec to US$1,343/1,673 pp sharing/sgl Jul–Oct, inc FB, activities, park fees.* ☺ *All year.* ★★★– ★★★★★

ACTIVITIES Kwara is big on activities, and has a wider range available through the year than many camps in the Delta. Game drives and night drives are the norm, and the camp boasts that there are never more than six guests on a vehicle with a guide and tracker. Together with very knowledgeable guides, this makes the game-viewing experience here among the best in the Delta, and certainly better in the green season than most dry-land camps. Much of this is due to their willingness to actively track the game, heading off-road and into the bush at the slightest sign of something interesting.

On the water, the varied terrain means that motorboat and mokoro trips are possible all year, and the camp also has a double-decker pontoon-type boat. Climbing on top of this in the papyrus-lined channels is magical, and will give you a completely different view of the waterscape.

XUGANA, CAMP OKAVANGO AND SHINDE (NG21)

This concession is relatively small by Botswana's standards, but shares a long southern boundary with Moremi Reserve, and was devoted to photographic safaris long before the hunting ban. To the north, NG21 adjoins the Kwara and Vumbura concessions.

Within the reserve, the activities are primarily water-based, although Shinde also offers game drives, and its sister camp, Footsteps, specialises in walking safaris as Footsteps Across the Delta.

FLORA AND FAUNA HIGHLIGHTS NG21 is adjacent, and in many ways very similar, to the southern parts of the neighbouring Kwara Reserve, NG20. Thus read my comments on the flora and fauna there (pages 351–3) for a complete picture. That said, a greater proportion of NG21 Reserve is permanent swamp, as it has several large, permanent rivers flowing through it. The Moanachira passes through, heading east to feed the Gcodikwe Lagoon, before flowing into the Xakanaxa Lagoon. This in turn forms the source of the Khwai River that eventually reaches to the far eastern corner of the Delta.

A less clear channel, the Mborogha, flows southeast almost to Chief's Island where it ultimately feeds into the Gomoti and Santandibe rivers, both important watercourses of the lower Delta (though in the last few decades there seems to have been a change of flow between these two major rivers, from the Mborogha to the Moanachira).

In *Okavango: Jewel of the Kalahari* (see *Appendix 3*, page 544), Karen Ross notes that the eastern rivers, the Moanachira and Mborogha, carry far more water today than they did 100 years ago. So with all these waters concentrated into NG21 it's perhaps not surprising that it's an area where you'll find plenty of deep-water lagoons and channels.

Most of NG21 Reserve has too much water to be one of the Delta's prime game-viewing areas, but in the dry area around Shinde you'll still find good densities of game, including impala, red lechwe, tsessebe and giraffe. Lone bull elephants are around for most of the year, while the breeding herds migrate here from the dry interior towards the end of the dry season.

Kudu, sable and buffalo are infrequently seen. Sitatunga, while common in the areas of thick papyrus, are rarely sighted – though one of the guides at Shinde seems to be particularly adept at spotting them from motorboats and mokoros. NG21 is also a good place to look for water-based mammals like the very common hippo and the more elusive spotted-necked otters.

The dominant predators are lion and hyena, with leopard and wild dog also found here. In some years, a pack of wild dogs has been regularly spotted around Shinde and Footsteps, sometimes moving between here and Kwara.

WHEN TO VISIT While game viewing under the clouds of the green season can be quite rewarding, most people need at least dryness and preferably a blue sky and tropical sun to appreciate the magic of boating through the Okavango.

During a visit to Camp Moremi during the green season, the weather one morning was glorious. This prompted the enthusiastic manager to ask me why Expert Africa sends relatively few visitors to the Okavango between January and March. 'It's almost empty of visitors and often the weather's superb,' he beamed. Later that day the clouds drew in and it rained on and off for 36 hours, foiling any ideas I had about photography for the rest of my stay. Hence I'd advise that water-based camps like Xugana and Camp Okavango are best visited during the dry season.

GETTING THERE AND AWAY All guests pre-arrange their trips here, and fly in to the camps' own airstrips, which are all nearby. Camp Okavango's (⊕ CAMPOA

13

19°07.720'S, 23°05.930'E) is a short walk behind the camp, and from the air you'll realise that it takes up most of the very small island on which the camp is situated!

Shinde's airstrip (⊕ SHINDA 19°07.070'S, 23°09.180'E) is a 5-minute drive northeast of the camp. Xugana's (⊕ XUGAIR 19°02.200'S, 23°05.710'E), too, is very close and northwest of the camp.

Guests heading for Footsteps arrive at Shinde by plane, then have a leisurely 1½-hour transfer. This varies but will sometimes involve a game drive, followed by a short river crossing by mokoro, and a final drive to camp.

🏠 **WHERE TO STAY** Of the four camps in this area, the two water camps, Camp Okavango and Xugana, are both owned and marketed by Desert & Delta Safaris (page 223). The others, Shinde and Footsteps, are run by Ker & Downey Botswana (page 224).

✳ 🏠 **Shinde** [map 347] (8 tents) Contact Ker & Downey Botswana, page 224. The long-established Shinde – owned by Ker & Downey since the early 1980s – stands in a tree-shaded spot in the heart of NG21, about 6km east of Camp Okavango, 12km west of Kwara & 8km southeast of Xugana. It's a well-run camp, refurbished in 2015, with a long-serving team of staff & a very flexible approach. The camp is set on a picturesque channel that feeds the Moanachira River, so with land-based as well as water activities, there's plenty of choice; if you have the energy to do 3 activities in a day, then that can be accommodated.

Shinde's lounge & dining areas are built on several levels, rising towards an unusual bowed canvas roof that's a little like an old ox-wagon. Down below, guests can help themselves to drinks from the bar, & peruse the collection of baskets made by the staff, before gathering round the firepit before dinner. Set well away, beyond a discreet electric wire fence designed to deter elephants from coming into camp, is a sheltered pool with sunloungers & views across the plains.

Approached along open, sandy paths, & sharing the view, are traditional, walk-in tents – 3 of them forming the distinct Shinde Enclave. The tents are built on raised wooden platforms protected by large shadecloths that also shelter a porch with a couple of comfy chairs. Inside are twin beds (or a king-size dbl), their crisp white linen offset by neutral canvas, dark-wood furniture & traditional wall hangings. Bedside lights sit on wooden trunks, Persian rugs dot the wooden floors, mesh windows allow the air to flow freely, & a separate room behind the bed houses an en-suite shower, basin & flush toilet.

Families or groups of up to 6 seeking a more exclusive set-up can book the Shinde Enclave, which comes with a dedicated waiter & guide, & has its own bar, firepit, dining area & lounge, & a small deck overlooking an expanse of papyrus & reeds dotted with palm islands. *From US$530 pp Mar & Dec to US$1,130/1,485 pp sharing/ sgl Jul–Oct, inc FB, most drinks, activities, park fees, laundry; exc transfers. No children under 10 at Shinde; no children under 7 at Shinde Enclave.* ◷ *Mar–early Jan.* ★★★–★★★★★★

✳ ⅄ **Footsteps Camp, home to Footsteps Across the Delta** [map 347] (3 tents) In operation since 1998, Footsteps is – along with Selinda Explorers & Linyanti Bush Camp (pages 304 & 300) – one of the few operations in the Delta that focus strongly on walking safaris. It's an intimate, semi-permanent camp & the standard of guiding is excellent.

As with any good walking safari, numbers are small; Footsteps takes a maximum of 6 guests at a time. Its small, twin-bedded tents, lit by paraffin lanterns, have en-suite bathrooms complete with flushing toilets & bucket showers. One of the tents can be converted to sleep a family of 5. It's all very rustic, with dinner usually eaten under the stars & wildlife regularly roaming through. Yet despite the camp's remote location & rudimentary facilities, the standard of food is good, with plenty of fresh fruit & vegetables, newly baked bread each day, & a well-stocked bar. If you'd like to take a look 'backstage', they're very happy to show guests around.

The days largely revolve around walking (always with an armed guide & back-up guide), but it's very flexible. Typically you can expect 2 walks each day: one of 3–4hrs in the early morning, & a 2nd, shorter walk combined with a game drive in the late afternoon, allowing you to explore further afield. Mokoro trips & fishing are also possible when the water is high enough.

Footsteps is one of the bases for Ker & Downey's Young Explorers safari (see box, page 117), for which the camp is always booked exclusively. Otherwise children under 16 are not accepted here. *From US$530 pp Mar & Dec to US$740/930 pp sharing/sgl Jul–Oct, inc FB, drinks, activities, laundry; exc transfers. No children under 16 except for Young Explorers.* ☺ *Mar–Nov.* ★★★–★★★★

🏠 **Xugana Island Lodge** [map 347] (8 chalets) Though it's been periodically reinvented, with the latest refurbishment in 2017, Xugana is one of the Delta's older camps; it is said to have been started as a hunting camp as early as the 1960s, probably by Henry Selby (of the hunting company Ker, Downey & Selby). Subsequently, in the early 1980s, it was bought by a local businessman, David Hartley, as a private family retreat. This eventually became more commercial &, along with its sister camp, Tsaro Elephant Lodge (now closed), was marketed under the banner of Hartley's Safaris until they were bought by Desert & Delta Safaris in 2000.

One of the few things that hasn't changed about Xugana over the years is its location on the banks of a forested island beside a large, deep lagoon: a spectacular site. It's about 7.5km north of Camp Okavango (yet the most direct route by boat covers about 16.8km of waterways). For many years Xugana used the lagoon itself as a swimming pool, suspending a crocodile-proof wire cage in the lagoon for bathers to cool off in. While environmentally admirable, some of the camp's less enlightened guests found this pool's occasional murkiness off-putting, so a new swimming pool was built among the landscaped lawns at the centre of camp. These are dotted with natural vegetation, with everything protected from hungry elephants by an electric fence. (The old pool was renovated & converted into a floating deck, used for special occasions, the odd alfresco dinner & sundowners.)

The camp's open-sided lounge, bar & dining areas under thatch are set back slightly from the jetty, facing the water. In good weather, most meals are taken on the spacious deck overlooking the lagoon, shaded by fig & leadwood trees, & with a fireplace perched above the water. A good small curio shop sports a fair selection of local books & wildlife guides, plus T-shirts, handicrafts & postcards.

Xugana's chalets are built of reed & thatch, raised up on wooden decking, with twin beds or a dbl under a large, walk-in mosquito net. Each has a ceiling fan under its high ceiling, operated by the camp's generator during the day. There's a 12V lighting system in the rooms for use at night. The bathrooms are en suite with a walk-in hot shower, flush toilet & washbasin, & outside, facing the lagoon, is a private wooden deck with a pair of canvas safari chairs. Water is heated by solar power. *From US$560 pp Jan–Mar & Dec to US$995/1,293 pp sharing/sgl Jul–Oct, fully inc.* ☺ *All year.* ★★★–★★★★

🏠 **Camp Okavango** [map 347] (11 suites, 1 family suite) On the south side of this concession, Camp Okavango was originally on the west side of Nxaragha Island amid floodplains, lagoons & waterways. However, during a complete rebuild in 2016 the camp was moved forward, changing the aspect to overlook floodplains & channels. It's a measure of the meandering geography of the Delta's waterways that although its sister camp, Camp Moremi, is only about 33km away as the egret flies, the most direct route by boat (coincidentally, via the Gcodikwe Lagoon) is slightly over 60km.

'Camp O', as it's usually known, was started by an American woman, Jessie Niel, in the early 1980s, & was swiftly followed by Camp Moremi. She ran & marketed them as a pair under the banner of Desert & Delta Safaris until, in the mid 1990s, the operation was taken over by a group called Chobe Holdings, associated with Chobe Game Lodge & AfroVentures – though the name was kept.

Despite being quite large by Okavango standards the whole camp is built on raised platforms with the suites & main area linked by wooden walkways. For seclusion during the day, there's a raised viewing hide that is built into a sausage tree (*Kigelia africana*) & 3 knobthorn trees (*Senegalia nigrescens*) near the end of the jetty. It's a nice spot to relax with comfy chairs & the view over the papyrus & reeds might interest patient birdwatchers. However, the infinity pool (which overlooks the same floodplain), & the sundeck probably make better places to relax.

Wooden walkways lead to the spacious suites, each with twin or dbl beds, crisp linen, tea &

13

coffee station, lounge area & deck complete with sunloungers. The en-suite bathrooms come with hot his & hers showers, his & hers washbasins & a flush toilet.

Although the camp focuses on boat & mokoro trips, bush walks on the islands are possible, though see my comments on walking trips in Botswana (pages 187–91) before you set off. Camps like this which concentrate on water activities tend to have a slower pace than those which also offer game drives; you'll have more time just to relax. *From US$560 pp Jan–Mar & Dec to US$995/1,293 pp sharing/sgl Jul–Oct, fully inc.* ⏰ *All year.* ★★★–★★★★

ACTIVITIES Xugana, Camp Okavango and Shinde all operate motorboat excursions to explore the lagoons, plus mokoro trips to visit the areas of shallower water nearby. Often the mokoro trips are combined with walking on the islands, though these are usually led by an unarmed guide, so read my comments on walking (pages 188–91) before you depart. Note that if you're keen to visit Gcodikwe Lagoon then Camp Okavango or Shinde are much nearer to it than Xugana.

Both water activities are primarily for birdwatching and for learning about the general environment rather than for game viewing, though it's also possible to go fishing (for bream and tigerfish normally) from the motorboats.

In addition to these water activities, both Shinde and Xugana offer 4x4 game drives day and night (with a maximum of four guests per vehicle at Shinde), and at Shinde you can also take part in walks accompanied by an armed guide and tracker. However, those serious about walking would be better off spending a few nights at their specialist sister camp, Footsteps Camp (pages 356–7).

VUMBURA AND DUBA PLAINS (NG22 AND NG23)

Immediately north of Moremi's Mombo Concession, the Vumbura and Duba Plains reserves (NG22 and NG23) share many similarities of game and landscape with Mombo. This northern area of the Delta is one of my favourites, but because of the similarity between Vumbura and Duba, if you are planning a trip to this area then it's best to include only one of them in your itinerary.

Vumbura is a varied reserve, and the areas through which you drive are often very pretty. Much of its landscape consists of wide-open plains with tiny islands – almost a cliché of the Okavango. Vumbura's game is notably diverse, so most visitors will see a wide range of antelope and have a good chance to spot the less common predators.

Duba Plains, to the west of Vumbura, is visually similar but with larger open plains. It doesn't quite have Vumbura's diversity of game, though this is improving, but the big attraction here has been as a long-standing venue for battles between large herds of buffalo and sizeable prides of lion. Thus, it has often provided a very impressive spectacle of big game, particularly during the drier months of April to October. In the wet season (November to March), when the buffalo are fitter from eating the lush grass, the lions focus more on lechwe and warthog.

Both camps can access water activities, Vumbura for the whole year, although the areas aren't quite so picturesque as, say, the Jao Flats. There are no mekoro trips from Duba Plains.

CONCESSION HISTORY Until around 1997 this was a hunting area, but then Wilderness Safaris started Vumbura, Little Vumbura and Duba Plains camps.

For several years there were two small, seasonal hunting camps running in the northeast of the Vumbura Concession (one of which was on the site of Kaporota). These had closed by 2001 and both areas are now used solely for photographic safaris.

THE ANATOMY OF A COMMUNITY PARTNERSHIP

Though 'community-based natural resource management' is recognised as one of the main strategies for achieving sustainable development in the rural areas of Botswana, really good examples of it are few and far between. Wilderness Safaris have a strong track record with successful community projects in other countries, like Damaraland Camp in Namibia, and here in Botswana their flagship community project is the Vumbura and Duba concessions. The camps in these private reserves or concessions started in 1997 when the safari company and their partners made an agreement with the community to which the government had given management of concession areas NG22 and NG23. Great Plains continues to liaise and work with the local communities in much the same way that Wilderness still do.

The community, in this case, consists of five villages to the north of the Okavango Delta: Seronga, Eretsha, Beetsha, Gudigwa and Gunitsungwa. The villagers had to set up a trust, with a fully constituted board to represent all the villages and people of the area in their dealings with the government, the Land Board and the safari companies. The ten-person board is made up of two elected people from each of the five villages. Wilderness Safaris/Great Plains Conservation pay a six-figure US-dollar lease fee each year to the board (this is a lot of money in rural Botswana). The board decides how to use that money for the benefit of the community. Further, as part of the deal, the two safari companies have to employ at least 118 people from the villages (though they actually ended up giving jobs to around 150), and to deliver on a number of community projects. These projects have resulted in the setting up and supporting of a number of secondary cottage industries in the villages, like basket weaving and vegetable gardens; in addition they have sponsored an inter-village football tournament; helped with transport problems; and set up village shops, mortuaries, etc.

Perhaps the most difficult issue about this kind of agreement for any safari company is the short duration of the leases; the community can swap their safari company after the first year if it wishes to, then again after the second year, the fifth year and the tenth year. Given the huge investment in infrastructure and the long-term nature of the marketing, this is difficult for most safari companies to contemplate. Sixteen years into the project, the safari companies are slowly starting to reap the benefits of a stable, long-term relationship with the community as their partner. Equally, guests to these camps know that their safari is actively benefiting both the communities in the area, and thus, in turn, the local wildlife.

In 2012, Duba Plains split from Wilderness Safaris and is now owned and managed by Great Plains Conservation, along with its sister camps in the Selinda Reserve (pages 302–4). Dereck and Beverly Joubert, the wildlife film-makers, are closely involved with this venture, while Vumbura and Little Vumbura are still very much a part of Wilderness Safaris.

As is increasingly the case with reserves in Botswana, both Duba and Vumbura have an element of local community involvement. Five local villages – Seronga, Eretsha, Beetsha, Gudigwa and Gunitsungwa – have some control over the concession, and derive considerable benefit from its success. Most of the staff for the camps come from these villages too, so there's a flow of revenue from these

13

camps back to the communities by way of wages (see box, page 359, and comments on NG12 on page 348).

FLORA AND FAUNA HIGHLIGHTS Both these reserves are broadly similar in character, although Duba Plains (as you might expect) has more extensive open plains, whereas the plains at Vumbura are often partially flooded, and they're broken up by more islands, including many small palm islands.

Flora Much of these concessions consist of very beautiful, open floodplains dotted with islands, many of which are tiny. The vegetation of the larger islands is dominated by many of the Okavango's usual tree species, including raintree (*Philenoptera violacea*), leadwood (*Combretum imberbe*), African mangosteen (*Garcenia livingstonei*), jackalberry (*Diospyros mespiliformis*), sausage tree (*Kigelia africana*) and sycamore fig (*Ficus sycomorus*).

You'll also find knobthorn trees (*Senegalia nigrescens*), although relatively few of them, and some particularly large, wonderful specimens of feverberry trees (*Croton megalobotrys*), named after the anti-malarial properties of the seeds and the bark. (These properties had been known to local African residents for centuries, but were brought to the attention of a wider audience by an article in the medical journal, *The Lancet*, in 1899. Apparently there has still not been any detailed research on these medicinal properties.)

Among the main bushes that you'll find here are the Kalahari star apple (*Diospyros lycioides lycioides*), which is often also called the blue bush, for its overall bluish tinge, or the 'toothbrush bush', as its roots can be peeled and used as a toothbrush. (Veronica Roodt reports that on using it 'at first my mouth burned and I became extremely worried when my whole mouth turned yellow. The result, however, was remarkable – white teeth and fresh breath.') Another very common bush in this area is the evergreen magic gwarri bush (*Euclea divinorum*), also sometimes known as the 'toothbrush bush' for the use of its branches. Both these bushes produce dyes that are used in Botswana to colour palm leaves for weaving baskets.

In the northeast of Vumbura there are some fine acacia woodlands, while as you travel west from Vumbura into Duba you'll find more and larger open floodplains, slightly less thick wooded islands, and more clusters of the wild date palm (*Phoenix reclinata*).

As well as the drier areas, there are many small channels near the Vumbura camps, and some open, lightly reeded lagoons. The channels are lined intermittently with a mixture of papyrus and common reeds, and periodically open out on to floodplain areas. Scenically the areas near these camps don't quite match up to the sheer beauty of the Jao Flats, as there are very few feathery real fan palms or lily-covered lagoons.

Fauna When I last visited, I was very impressed by the varied line-up of antelope that I saw in the Vumbura Reserve in a few days. Unlike many of the areas further from the heart of the Delta, there wasn't just a high density of one or two species, to the virtual exclusion of the rest.

Species that you can expect to see here include tsessebe, impala, lechwe, kudu, zebra, wildebeest, giraffe, warthog and steenbok. Sable are seen fairly often, especially near the airstrip. Waterbuck are common; Vumbura is one of the few places within northern Botswana where you'll find good numbers of them. Duiker, reedbuck and bushbuck are seen infrequently, while roan antelope are rare, though have been seen occasionally in the late dry season. I know of just one (February) sighting of sitatunga in Vumbura.

Wild dogs regularly den here, and one year I was lucky enough to be able to watch a beautiful pack with pups at its den, situated in the mopane woodlands on the east side of the Vumbura. However, in this thick band of mopane woodland it wasn't possible to follow them when they moved off.

Cheetah are also resident, though like the rest of the smaller game they will move through the buffalo fence and out into the huge NG12, to the north. In the dry season, when many of the open floodplains are dry, the open environment is perfect for cheetah, rather like Mombo and parts of Selinda, so it's a particularly good area in which to seek them.

Leopard are occasionally seen on night drives, and on a recent visit I had a great sighting with a fresh kill on one of the small islands. Lion and spotted hyena are both relatively common. Both black-backed and side-striped jackals occur here, though the black-backed are seen much more regularly.

Moving westwards, Duba Plains is noted not only for its huge open plains, but has long had a reputation for high concentrations of buffalo, and particularly for lion–buffalo interactions. Larger herds of buffalo usually congregate in the Delta during the dry season, though in recent years they have been seen in Duba less, and spend more of their time to the north and towards Vumbura . When present, these usually attract the attention of the larger lion prides which have more experienced hunters, and lion have always been very much the dominant predator in the Duba Plains area. The converse of this is that in the past, Duba hasn't had quite the same balance of species, or the diversity, that you often find in Vumbura. Wild dog, cheetah and impala have been largely absent, while very good populations of lechwe have diverted the lions' attention, along with reedbuck, bushbuck, waterbuck and kudu. And the area is curiously popular with warthogs! Spotted hyena are flourishing, despite the sizeable prides of lions, and side-striped jackals are seen fairly frequently, but black-backed are largely absent.

In recent years, we've seen a reduction in the number and size of the buffalo herds, and far fewer lion–buffalo interactions, but a rise in the number of other species, from cheetah to recently reintroduced rhino.

Birdlife The birdlife here is as varied as you'll find in any area of the Delta with a good mix of dry and wet environments. Certainly in one afternoon of very casual bird spotting on the river from Vumbura you can expect to find a range of kingfishers (malachite, pied and giant), jacanas, several species of egrets (including slaty), black-winged stilts, open-billed storks and reed cormorants. In addition, the open floodplains with short grass seemed to attract very good numbers of various waders plus saddle-billed storks, glossy and sacred ibises, spoonbills and – relatively unusually – pelicans. Over several previous trips the quality of birdlife has been particularly impressive. As well as large numbers of common species, we spotted comparative rarities such as the pink- (or rosy-) throated longclaw, wattled crane and Stanley's bustard. Pel's fishing owls can also be found in the area, and in both 2006 and 2010 (albeit just for a day), the waterlogged plains of the Duba Concession played host to a very unusual sight in the Delta: flamingos.

WHEN TO VISIT As elsewhere in the Delta the big game is more diverse and prolific during the dry season, although the birdlife is generally better between December and March. Driving around the reserve can be more difficult then, as there's usually a lot of water around and many roads are submerged. To deal with this problem, vehicles at Duba Plains have been modified to be higher off the ground.

13

GETTING THERE AND AWAY All the camps here accept only pre-booked guests who fly in. Driving isn't possible without permission – and permission is never given (though it would be only a few hours' drive from Seronga, if you knew the way!). Note that each camp has its own separate airstrip. Vumbura's (VUMAIR) is at ✪ 18°57.504'S, 22°49.063'E, and Duba's (OMDOP) at ✪ 19°01.039'S, 22°41.059'E.

WHERE TO STAY The two Vumbura camps are marketed by Wilderness Safaris (page 225): Little Vumbura as a 'classic' camp, and Vumbura Plains one of their 'premier' camps. Duba Plains and Duba Expeditions are the domain of Great Plains Conservation (page 224), who have made significant changes to the camps.

Vumbura Plains [map 347] (7 rooms north, 7 rooms south) This camp falls into the 'seriously posh' bracket: a contemporary lodge in the bush, split across 2 sites: Vumbura Plains North, which incorporates 2 family rooms, & Vumbura Plains South. Although these are linked by a walkway, they have separate central areas & management, so feel like 2 camps, softening what could otherwise be a slightly corporate effect. Vumbura Plains South has a newer feel as much of it was rebuilt after a fire in Jun 2016.

Modern in design, each of the large, square rooms (emphatically not tents) features light-coloured wood & its own sizeable private deck with plunge pool & a small sala, lit by soft spotlights. In the big open area, voluminous white net curtains slide on ceiling rails, acting as room dividers, & practical items such as wardrobes are cleverly concealed along one side. One quarter of the room houses a square sunken lounge with low seating & soft cushions; another part features a free-standing shower on a concrete slab with a view through the large windows (or shower curtains for privacy) – & there's a another completely outdoor shower too. It's all quite unexpected & very different from a typical safari camp.

For families, Vumbura Plains has a big plus: 2 private family suites, each having a completely separate en-suite room for children (from age 6). Linking the 2 rooms is a private deck with 3 enclosed sides, which means that – unusually – children can be slightly independent of their parents.

At the heart of each camp, set beneath indigenous trees overlooking the plains, is a wooden platform sheltered by a roof supported by poles. When it's raining or blowing a gale, wooden slatted blinds protect guests from the worst of the elements, but during the dry season, this makes for dining or relaxing almost alfresco, with

a cool through breeze. As elsewhere, the décor is contemporary & quite fun: shaggy, long-pile rugs, plenty of soft comfortable sofas & modern *objets d'art*. The stylish mode of the camp extends to meals, which are served to a table set with sparkling cutlery & crystal glasses. A cappuccino maker is on hand throughout the day, & the bar is particularly well stocked.

The service is friendly & staff try very hard to meet the high standards set by the camp. Activities include the usual 4x4 safaris, walking & boats/mekoro trips. There's also a well-stocked curio shop between the camps – & shared by guests at both.

I have found camps like this, Mombo & Chitabe attract some of the company's more ambitious & keen guides, who certainly rank among the best in the company. *From US$1,040/1,300 pp sharing/sgl Jan–Mar to US$2,520/3,280 Jun–Oct, inc FB, activities, park fees, laundry & most drinks; exc transfers.* ⊕ *All year.* ★★★★★

✳ **Little Vumbura** [map 347] (6 tents) Although less than 2km from its larger sister camp, Little Vumbura (✪ LVUMBU 19°00.070'S, 22°51.710'E) feels quite separate, perhaps because it's on a small island & always approached by boat. The camp is set beneath a large waterberry tree (*Syzygium cordatum*), & the open sides of its canvas structure (which can be rolled down) are shaded by dense surrounding stands of wild date palms, a couple of fig trees (*Ficus sycomorus*) & an assortment of jackalberry trees (*Diospyros mespiliformis*). This all gives the very comfortable feeling that the camp has been built from within the vegetation, & you're cocooned in a small, tropical hideaway.

Following extensive refurbishment in early 2017, the new dining area & bar are set on decking about 1m off the ground & linked, via a 50m jetty, to the launch area for the boats. There's a small shop stocked with books, materials, local baskets

& African curios, a plunge pool, & a firepit set in a wonderful open hexagonal section of decking that extends into the reeds & is used for dinner, drinks & stargazing.

The walk-in tents, 1 designed for a family, stand on low platforms. Inside, they're spacious & comfortable, their bedrooms leading on to a lounge area, & with an en-suite shower, washbasin & toilet. A few paces away is a more natural open-air shower, with a view of the floodplains. *From US$995/1,290 pp sharing/sgl Jan–Mar to US$1,830/2,379 Jun–Oct, inc FB, activities, park fees, laundry & most drinks; exc transfers.* ☻ *All year.* ★★★★–★★★★★

✳ 🏠 **Duba Plains** [map 346] (5 tents, 1 suite) Of all the 'usual' fly-in camps in the Delta, Duba Plains is one of the most northern. It is north of Moremi Game Reserve, a 5min flight west of Vumbura. Reopened in Mar 2017 after a complete rebuild, Duba Plains is now a very smart camp, though it's still fairly small. The main area is built on raised decking under a high canvas roof around a large jackalberry tree. Leather armchairs & a couple of sofas are set around a large wooden chest which doubles as a coffee table; a library area features an extensive selection of wildlife-related books; & beyond a large wooden dining table is a well-stocked wine cellar. Outside, a large deck with a firepit affords plenty of room for alfresco dining with a fantastic view over the floodplains.

Duba's impressive tents, with mosquito-proof gauze windows, are linked by bush paths, & raised on decks to give good views of the plains. Each has a big veranda with a plunge pool sunk into the railway-sleeper decking, & a canvas-shaded area with a table & 2 chairs. The tents are some of the largest I have seen, with mosquito nets around the beds, a living room & a large open-plan bathroom (but separate toilet), & smart, tasteful décor accentuated by extensive use of wood.

Because of its location near the Panhandle, Duba is one of the first camps in the main Delta to be flooded. From about May to the end of Aug the shallow-water plains around it usually have enough water for mokoro trips. *From US$1,410 pp 11 Jan–Mar to US$2,800/4,200 pp sharing/sgl 15 Jun–Oct, inc FB, most drinks, activities, park fees, laundry; exc transfers.* ☻ *All year.* ★★★★★

🏠 **Duba Expeditions** [map 346] (5 tented rooms) This relatively new camp will be relocated in early 2018 to the north of the concession. The main area sits on light wooden decking under a sweeping canvas roof, & is open at the front & back. The 'campaign' style of furnishing is common to all the Great Plains properties, featuring lots of leather, brass & dark-red rugs. Here that translates into 2 comfortable leather sofas & a couple of armchairs around a wooden coffee table & a large communal dining table, perfect for social dinners. On the open decking, a cauldron-style firepit is surrounded by more seating & some reclining chairs – which are great for stargazing.

The airy tented rooms are spacious & very much in keeping with the main area. With their own private veranda, & en-suite facilities that include double vanities & indoor shower, they also have plenty of mod cons. *From US$820 pp 11 Jan–Mar to US$1,740/2,610 pp sharing/sgl 15 Jun–Oct, inc FB, most drinks, activities, park fees, laundry; exc transfers.* ☻ *All year.* ★★★★–★★★★★

ACTIVITIES The Vumbura camps have year-round access to deep permanent water, so boat trips are possible all year, with opportunities to fish if you wish, and mokoro excursions a further option. Boating at Duba Plains, however, is dependent on water levels, and there are no mekoro here. All the camps also have 4x4 game drives day and night (though night drives are sometimes restricted when flood levels are very high, between May and August). Short walks are also offered by these camps, though I would generally go to a specialist walking camp if I wanted to do much walking.

COMMUNITY AREA (NG24)

Currently this is the only one of the Delta's photography-specific areas (ie: hunting is not allowed) which has no proper safari operation in it. Until about 1999 this was the location for Jedibe Camp, which had long been run by Wilderness Safaris and was one of their earliest photographic camps in the Delta.

I visited Jedibe in about 1996. It was located deep within a maze of deep-water channels and papyrus, and the main activity there was exploring on motorboats. This was superb fun (although motorboats are probably the most expensive activity to run for any camp, given their thirst for fuel!) as the boats could reach some stunning areas of the most beautiful floodplains, as well as exploring the papyrus-lined channels of the main rivers. Mokoro trips, incorporating walks on the islands, were also possible but usually of secondary interest.

However, in 1999, Jedibe's lease came up for tender – which means a reopening of negotiations between the government, the community (the Okavango Jakotsha Community Trust) and anyone who is interested in taking responsibility for the area's lease.

Since Jedibe was built, many new mixed land-and-water camps had come into existence in the Delta, and proven very successful. Furthermore, their range of game drives and water activities was wider than Jedibe's options. This left Jedibe looking less commercially attractive, with a very specific, limited niche as a deep-water camp in permanent papyrus, running mainly (inherently costly) motorboats. Jedibe's northerly location, far from Maun, meant expensive transport links and running costs too.

These factors all made Jedibe less commercially viable, at a time when the local community was expecting to get more for the concession. As a result no agreement could be made.

If you do visit this area, then don't go for the animals. Although there are animals on the islands, this is a deep-water area and you should treat any game sightings as a bonus. Instead come for the bird and water-life. Expect lots of deep, fast-flowing channels and endless banks of papyrus, which periodically open out on to spectacular floodplains.

 WHERE TO STAY The small Makwena Camp on the edge of the reserve, accessed from Etsha 6 on the Panhandle road, folded some time ago, and despite an application to build a 12-room lodge on the site, with a further tented camp at nearby Majamboroka, neither has yet materialised. Perhaps with the completion of the bridge at Mohembo (page 411) this concession might open up again, but for the time being visiting options are limited.

JAO, KWETSANI, JACANA, TUBU AND PELO (NG25)

Close to the Panhandle, west of Moremi, NG25 is a particularly beautiful concession covering about 600km² of the upper Okavango Delta. Most of this is a fairly wet environment, with extensive floodplains, especially around the Jao Flats, though there is a substantial drier section, where Tubu Tree Camp is situated, to the west of the reserve. The annual flood generally reaches this reserve around April or May, instantly expanding the area of the floodplains.

FLORA AND FAUNA HIGHLIGHTS The area around Jao and Jacana feels very much like most people's image of the Okavango: watery and terribly picturesque. It's a lovely environment, one that is mirrored at Kwetsani when the flood arrives. While the game diversity in the area might not quite match some of the areas further east yet, lechwe and lion are generally common and those alone will keep most people entertained. That said, visiting on one occasion in April, we didn't see a single lion; and conversely, in 2017, we did see an unusually large number of sitatunga.

The birding is also good, with enough diversity of habitat to mean that you'll find most Delta species here if you look hard enough. I've had great luck in the past here with gallinules and pink-throated longclaws.

Hundu Island, the area around Tubu Tree Camp on the western side of the concession, is much drier and totally different from the eastern part of the reserve where the three older camps are situated. Historically this area had a reputation as a good place to see leopard, but since the arrival of small prides of lion, leopard sightings have been less frequent.

Flora The reserve's most memorable area must be the beautiful Jao Flats, a series of huge open floodplains, dotted with tiny islands that are often only a few metres across. These vast floodplains are covered in a mix of very sparse vegetation, much of which is the aptly named hippo grass (*Vossia cuspidata*), which has round, slender leaves, pointing periodically out of the water by up to a metre. Often these have a tiny flower spike on top, reminiscent of a minute papyrus head.

Much taller and denser are the stands of tall common reeds (*Miscanthus junceus*), and even areas of the attractive bulrush (*Typha capensis*). The latter have distinctive velvety seedheads and edible roots (which taste a little like chewing gum or sugarcane!). As you'd expect in such a watery area, the deeper parts have thick stands of papyrus.

There's usually plenty of open, shallow water around, and in the slow-flowing channels look out for water lettuce plants (*Ottelia ulvifolia*) underwater, with its wavy leaves, long trailing stems and delicate, trumpet-shaped flower held above the surface by a single air bladder.

The many small islands in the area are often little more than bases for the emergence of a ring of bushy wild date palms (*Phoenix reclinata*), and perhaps the odd real fan palm (*Hyphaene petersiana*), springing up through the centre of the low canopy, perhaps around a termite mound.

Also look out for the wild dagga plant (*Leonotis nepetifolia*), with its bright-red flowers, like baubles from a Christmas tree. These will remain standing long after they turn brown and die. There are also thickets of the uncommon magic gwarri bush (*Euclea divinorum*), which is believed by some local people to have wood with supernatural powers. Above these you'll find raintrees (*Philenoptera violacea*), woodland waterberry trees (*Syzygium guineense*) and the occasional bird plum or motsentsela (*Berchemia discolor*).

Some of the bushes on the larger islands are more typical of drier areas, including the Kalahari appleleaf (*Philenoptera nelsii*) and the Kalahari star apple (*Diospyros lycioides lycioides*), with its blueish tinge which sometimes gives it the name of 'blue bush'. Ask your guide and s/he may show you how its twigs can be used as a toothbrush!

Similarly these larger islands have bands of acacias, including the umbrella thorn (*Vachellia tortilis*). These become more prevalent as you move further east in the reserve, where you find larger islands, with thicker belts of acacia bush and areas of mopane also.

Fauna Most of the reserve around the Jao Flats is a good area for lion and superb for lechwe. The lechwe occur in large herds and will frequently startle; listen to them splash as they run across the flooded grasslands. Lion are certainly the dominant predator.

Other game is usually present in lower densities, but in the eastern section you can expect to spot blue wildebeest, zebra, small groups of tsessebe and elephants. Kwetsani, in particular, is noted for the increasingly relaxed bushbuck which seem to frequent its island. Sable and roan are virtually never seen here, but the large areas of papyrus are home to sitatunga, though as ever these take a lot of effort to see.

Lone male buffalo will pass through, especially from June onwards, and later in the dry season larger breeding herds move across the reserve. Elephants have a broadly similar pattern, and their herds get larger as the dry season progresses.

Cheetah aren't usually seen on the eastern side of the reserve until the waters have receded a long way, which means around October. Then they'll move west again as the waters rise in February. Hyena and leopard are seen occasionally but infrequently throughout the reserve and the year. Although sightings of wild dog are unusual, your best chance is in the area near to Tubu Tree where in the latter half of 2017 a pack of five adults was being seen quite regularly.

The western area of the reserve, accessed from Tubu Tree and Little Tubu, is a much drier habitat where you can expect giraffe, kudu, tsessebe and impala in the mixed acacia woodlands.

Like most of the reserves around the Okavango, Jao Reserve was previously used for hunting, which may not have been at all ethical. It is alleged that leopard were baited and snared in numbers, and hyena shot. This would have enabled the lion prides to grow with little competition, thus satisfying the demand for lion trophies – and explaining the once very high numbers of lion and relative scarcity of other predators.

Fortunately all commercial hunting was stopped here well over a decade ago, and the animal populations are returning to a more natural balance.

Birdlife This is a good reserve for birdwatching, particularly for some of the less common water-based species. During a few gentle boat rides on the eastern side of the reserve, I had good sightings of many of the commoner waterbirds, plus lesser jacanas, lesser moorhens, purple and green-backed herons, slaty egrets, white-faced whistling ducks, and both purple and lesser gallinules. (Both of the gallinules were seen in small lagoons close to Kwetsani.) The number of waterbirds peaks during September and October, notably in the channels between Jacana and Jao, while between October and November, wattled cranes are here in good numbers, too. Very occasionally, visitors are treated to the sight of African skimmers, of which there is a breeding colony near to Pelo.

Meanwhile driving in the drier areas we came across a similarly good range, and noted several flocks of Meyer's parrots, Dickinson's kestrels nesting at the top of an old palm tree, a very unusual melanistic Gabar goshawk, wattled starlings and a tree full of open-billed storks. Then, again near Kwetsani, we found some very uncommon pink-throated longclaws (a big tick!) in a wide marshy plain where they seem to be resident.

Though not too unusual, African snipes can be found here. Listen carefully around dusk, as the sun sets and darkness falls. Then, during the breeding season, the birds fly high and zoom back to the ground. Their fanned-out tail feathers make a noise like a percussion instrument – called 'drumming'.

The western side of this reserve, around Tubu Tree, should have a wider range of raptors than the east (Jao, Kwetsani and Jacana), simply because it's drier.

WHEN TO VISIT For the water activities, any time is fine as long as it doesn't rain. Hence from April to November would be my choice of time to visit. However, if you're on a serious game-viewing trip then it's better to come towards the end of the dry season where this area's diversity of species does pick up, with dry-country species like cheetah being seen here periodically.

GETTING THERE AND AWAY As with most camps, flying in here is the only option, and is almost always booked in advance. Driving in is totally impractical.

WHERE TO STAY All six camps in the Jao Reserve are marketed by Wilderness Safaris (page 225). They range from the opulence of Jao to the relative simplicity of Pelo. All cater exclusively for fly-in visitors.

Jao Camp [map 346] (9 rooms) Standing on the southeast side of the Jao Reserve, Jao is one of Wilderness Safaris' flagship 'premier' camps (the others being Abu, Mombo, Little Mombo, Vumbura Plains & King's Pool).

Approaching Jao by boat, you navigate through gentle waterways surrounded by reeds before coming to the large, 2-storey main building. It's about 30m long & 8–10m wide, with designer-inspired scraggy thatch & hints of an Indonesian longhouse. Upstairs is the dining room, where everybody usually eats around a long elegant table (handcrafted on site, apparently, using Zimbabwean rosewood); & a spacious lounge with comfy leather sofas, a chess table & stylish lamps. B/fast is sometimes served outside on the long balcony.

Down a magnificent flight of stairs there's a small library, a snug, a well-stocked wine cellar (including French & Italian vintages) & a curio shop. A few paces away from this you'll find 2 circular swimming pools & a few sunloungers amid the palms. Jao is also home to one of the few spas in the Delta, offering a wide range of treatments, including ones specifically for children.

The rooms at Jao are among the most luxurious & spacious in the Okavango region. All are on stilts, accessed by raised wooden walkways. They have one long side, facing the nearby channel, & scraggy thatch to match the central longhouse. Their position gives lots of privacy, though also makes the walk to the farthest rooms as much as 600m (less fit visitors can request chalets closer to the centre). At the side of the chalet, through a large, swivelling door, is a lounge with a huge coffee table, big comfy settee, a fridge, minibar & tea/coffee station. This is only a third of the open-plan room, which also has twin beds or a dbl under a walk-in mosquito net, with air filtered by an EveningBreeze cooling system over the bed. Light wooden floorboards are held together by wooden studs rather than nails or screws & beautifully finished with 'adzed' edges. Behind a slight partition (plus a roll-down reed blind) is a dressing area with a wardrobe (containing a safe), an old-style claw-footed bath, & 2 conical sinks placed centrally: a stylish use of space. Another partition separates this from a shower room, &

there's a sliding door to the toilet. The chalets are effectively insect-proofed, though one long side is made of gauzed or glass doors that can be folded back, concertina-style on to a full-length veranda. Outside is an open-air shower, surrounded by circular clay walls & with a view over the channel. A sala – or small gazebo under a shady thatched roof, with a mattress & cushions – makes a lovely perch to relax in the afternoon, raised far off the ground in the heart of the date-palm forest, overlooking the channel.

In short, the camp is visually impressive & exceedingly comfortable. It's an obvious choice for honeymoon couples, yet it's a large camp where guests tend to stay in their rooms rather than mix socially, so it doesn't have quite the intimacy or sociable feel of some of the smaller camps. *From US$1,155/1,460 pp sharing/sgl 11 Jan–Mar to US$2,425/3,155 Jun–Oct inc FB, most drinks, activities, park fees, laundry; exc transfers.* ⊕ *All year.* ★★★★★

Kwetsani [map 346] (5 tents) Kwetsani faces east, towards the rising sun, from a long, narrow island about 10km northwest of Jao, its larger, more opulent neighbour. (This can take 40mins if the roads are dry, or 1hr by boat.) The tents & some of the main area were rebuilt & refurbished in 2015.

The main lounge/dining room area at Kwetsani is slightly raised & stands under a high thatched roof, with one open side overlooking the plain. There's a dining table under part of this, as well as a lounge area with comfy chairs, a leather sofa & a small bookshelf. Nearby is a well-stocked bar, complete with a jackalberry tree (*Diospyros mespiliformis*) growing up through it.

The wooden decking floor extends from under the thatch on to a wide veranda, which has been built around a huge sycamore fig (*Ficus sycomorus*), a marula (*Sclerocarya birrea caffra*) & a sausage tree (*Kigelia africana*). There's usually a spotting scope standing on the deck. Nearby is a guest washroom/toilet, which not only has a tree growing up through it, but also has half of its wall cut away, affording a great view. Down a sloping walkway, almost on the level of the surrounding plains, a few sunloungers, umbrellas & chairs surround a small splash-pool, & from here, more steps lead down to a firepit at ground level, which is perfect for pre-dinner drinks.

Modern, open-plan tents with 2 ceiling fans incorporate a lounge area with a comfortable L-shaped sofa, & a desk with a couple of chairs. Further back, twin beds or a dbl are surrounded by a large mosquito net; & at the end is the bathroom – partly open plan, but with the toilet in a separate cubicle. There are both indoor & outdoor showers. At the front of the tent, large glass doors can be almost be fully folded back, allowing easy access to the spacious deck.

Kwetsani is a lovely camp, which now looks smarter & more modern than other camps in the concession. However, activities, particularly game drives, may feel limiting here, as a boat transfer is needed to reach Hunda Island & you must return on the boat before dark. *From US$985/1,280 pp sharing/sgl 11 Jan–Mar to US$1,690/2,200 Jun–Oct, inc FB, most drinks, activities, park fees, laundry; exc transfers.* ⏲ *All year.* ★★★★– ★★★★★

🏠 **Jacana Camp** [map 346] (5 tents) Although less than 4km north of Jao, Jacana is a 35min boat ride away. It stands on an island in the very beautiful Jao Flats area, & as at Jao, the density of date palms lends the feeling of a tropical island. In the last few years, water levels in the Delta have been quite high, & the area around Jacana is now permanently flooded. Consequently the camp is best for mokoro excursions, while game drives entail a 20min boat ride to reach their vehicles.

Jacana started life as a base for mokoro excursions for small escorted-group itineraries across Chobe & Moremi, then it was upgraded to one of Wilderness's 'classic' camps, though it's still much smaller than most in the Delta. The dining/bar area is a simple 2-storey structure under thatch with roll-down screens around its side. Downstairs are a neat, well-stocked bar & a small lounge/reading area with easy chairs & a sofa. Upstairs is the dining area, with a polished wooden floor & a large dining table. Behind this is a thatched hut, which they call a *hustshi*. Meals are sometimes eaten outside, near the firepit, which reminds me of eating in a traditional African kraal.

Rebuilt in 2012, the comfortable tents are raised slightly on decking to offer more space & style. From the small veranda, with directors' chairs & a table, doors slide open to reveal polished wooden

floorboards & dbl or twin beds beneath a large walk-in mosquito net, itself beneath a ceiling fan. 2 comfortable wicker chairs & a writing table invite relaxation, while practicalities are served by a basic wardrobe, some shelves, & a tea/coffee station. Another sliding door leads to a spacious, largely open-plan bathroom. A large metal-framed mirror hangs over dbl basins set into a wooden surface, & head-height wooden poles serve to section off the shower & adjacent toilet slightly.

One of Jacana's most entertaining features is the guest toilet, which features an impressive cement-moulded bowl, a pulley made in 'Heath Robinson' style to flush the toilet, & a great view.

The camp is a really good option at any time of the year for those wanting water-based activities, & is pretty good value for a couple of nights, especially towards the end of the dry season. *From US$680/885 pp sharing/sgl Nov–19 Dec to US$1,120/1,460 Jun–Oct, inc FB, activities, most drinks, park fees, laundry; exc transfers.* ⏲ *All year.* ★★★★–★★★★★★

🏠 **Tubu Tree Camp** [map 346] (8 tents) West of the other camps in the concession, & another of Wilderness Safaris' 'classic' camps, Tubu Tree first opened in 2002. The camp has the feel of a large treehouse, elevated on wooden walkways that link the tents to the main area, & with great views over seasonal floodplains. To one side is a large, simply furnished dining area; to the other, a relaxing, open-sided lounge with comfy sofas, chairs & some interesting reference books. A viewing scope enables guests to focus on the comings & goings of wildlife on the floodplains. From a quirky bar, built around the trees & with a top carved from a sausage tree, a walkway leads down to a small plunge pool & sundeck with loungers. Beyond, a firepit is the venue for evening get-togethers.

Tubu's tents – 2 of them designed for families – stand on wooden decks, each with a veranda & a couple of directors' chairs affording super vistas over the floodplains. Double or twin beds, a writing desk & a couple of soft chairs furnish the bedroom, while a divider behind the bed separates this from the en-suite shower, toilet & washbasin, plus a separate outside shower. Unfortunately, the baboons here had, in 2017, become quite bold & were periodically breaking into empty rooms to eat soap, play with shiny things & generally be a nuisance, so guests should keep medication, valuables & scented items locked in the safe.

Tubu has access to large areas of dry mopane & acacia woodlands. From around Apr–Sep, & perhaps later, mokoro trips & fishing ought to be possible, but for the rest of the year activities are generally limited to game drives & walks on Hunda Island. That said, at drier times they will often use different launch points for the mekoro to extend their seasonal use. *From US$985/1,280 pp sharing/ sgl 11 Jan–Mar to US$1,690/2,200 Jun–Oct, inc FB, most drinks, activities, park fees, laundry; exc transfers.* ⊕ *All year.* ★★★★–★★★★★

🏠 **Little Tubu** [map 346] (3 tents) Adjacent to Tubu Tree (see opposite), & with the same 'treehouse' feel, the much smaller Little Tubu was opened in 2013, & affords a more intimate & exclusive option than its bigger sister. Shaded beneath a riverine canopy & overlooking the floodplain, the elevated dining area & bar, & a raised pool, are well placed to watch the abundant wildlife. Sharing the views are Little Tubu's spacious en-suite tents, which are almost identical in design to those at Tubu Tree. There is also a honeymoon tent here, which is further away from the main area than the other chalets, offering greater privacy, & it also has a sala day bed raised among the trees. *From US$985/1,280 pp sharing/sgl 11 Jan–Mar to US$1,690/2,200 Jun–Oct, inc FB, most drinks, activities, park fees, laundry; exc transfers.* ⊕ *All year.* ★★★★– ★★★★★

🏠 **Pelo Camp** [map 346] (5 tents) Set in the centre of the concession, Pelo is the simplest camp in the reserve: a seasonal camp focusing on mokoro excursions, boating & fishing. The canvas structure incorporates a dining & lounge area set beneath jackalberry, wild date palms & mahogany trees, alongside an outdoor 'boma' area & a viewing platform on an old anthill. Modest tented rooms have twin or dbl beds, a writing desk & sofa chairs, with a basin at the back & 2 screens providing privacy for the flush toilet & shower. In front of the tent is a covered porch with safari chairs, & a bucket shower with views over the floodplain.

Pelo used to appeal to the more adventurous traveller who was happy without latter-day frills, but since its refurbishment in 2015 it has become a comfortable & intimate camp. It is not a place for those in search of dry-land activities: it opens when the flood arrives & closes when the waters recede. It's also important to realise that as Pelo is situated on an island, all activities must finish before dark; no boats are permitted on the water after sunset. On the other hand, the camp takes advantage of its westerly facing firepit & has sundowner drinks ready for your return to camp. *From US$460/600pp sharing/sgl Nov to US$715/930 Jun–Oct.* ⊕ *Mar–Nov.* ★★★– ★★★★

ACTIVITIES I would visit Jao and Kwetsani primarily for their water activities – trips by boat and mokoro – which are generally offered all year (though motorboats at Kwetsani may be restricted by water levels around October–January). That said, day and night game drives (and sometimes short walks on the islands) are also possible nearby, and will make a bonus for your stay.

Jacana is also best regarded as a water-based camp, with motorboat and mokoro trips all year, as well as game drives near camp when the water levels are not in high flood. Game drives, offered by all the camps except Pelo, are usually taken on Hunda Island, which is reached by a short boat ride. Closer to camp, Kwetsani offers slightly better game viewing than the other two.

Pelo is also all about the water – in fact, because of concession limits it has no vehicle of its own.

Tubu Tree is quite the opposite: a dry-land camp for game drives which can also arrange mokoro trips when the flood levels are high. A couple of nights at Jacana or Pelo, and a few at Tubu Tree, make a relatively inexpensive combination, at least by the standards of the Delta.

The comfortable game drives in this reserve tend to be in vehicles with three rows of three seats, of which the centre seats are often left empty. When I last went walking, the guide was a capable, experienced walking guide who gave an appropriate pre-departure safety briefing and clearly knew how to use the rifle that

13

he carried. He also escorted the mokoro trip, which I was pleased to see eschewed the easier hippo trails in favour of a more difficult, but much safer, route through a shallow floodplain. Though he's now left this reserve, I hope that the standards of safe practice which he set will remain.

ABU, SEBA AND MACATOO (NG26)

At this large concession west of Moremi, the focus has long been more on the activities than on the environment, though the addition of Seba Camp in 2007 broadened the appeal of the concession to include more conventional safaris. Abu Camp was for many years the only place in the Delta for riding elephants, and while this is no longer offered, interaction with elephants remains the focus of its activities. Macatoo Camp is one of the Delta's two centres for horseriding. A fourth, hunting camp, the relatively famous Selby's, has been closed for many years and hunting has since been banned in Botswana.

FLORA AND FAUNA HIGHLIGHTS The finer details of the wildlife in this concession tend to be eclipsed by the experience of the horses that you ride, or the elephants that you're with – hence I will make only relatively sketchy comments here on the wild fauna in this area.

However, you will find here most of the Delta's usual big game, including elephant, buffalo, giraffe, blue wildebeest, kudu, tsessebe, red lechwe, impala, zebra,

---

ABU CAMP'S ELEPHANTS

Abu Camp was named for a large bull with matching tusks, born around 1960. Probably from East Africa or the Kruger Park, Abu was taken when small to the United States, where he was used for rides at a wildlife park in Grand Prairie, Texas. He was returned to Africa in 1988, to feature in the movie *Circles in a Forest*, and moved to Botswana in 1990, where Randall Moore described him as exceptionally calm, intelligent and gentle. He appeared in many later films, including *White Hunter Black Heart* and *The Power of One*. He died in 2002, but his name lives on in 'Baby Abu', born in 2006.

At present, there are half-a-dozen elephants at the camp. Some of Abu's older elephants came from zoos in the USA, while some of the younger ones were orphans from South Africa's Kruger National Park and several were born at the camp. Under a long-term research programme that commenced in 2002, many of Abu's residents have successfully been released into the wild, although some – such as Pula and Seba – are still seen around camp. The current members of the Abu herd are:

CATHY The herd's largest adult cow was born around 1960, captured in Murchison Falls National Park, Uganda, when young, and taken to a zoo outside Toronto. In 1988, she returned to Africa with Abu. She was also involved in filming *Circles in a Forest* and came to Botswana in 1990, once filming was complete. Gentle and temperamentally stable, she is the matriarch of the herd; her influence helps keep the herd, particularly the young ones, in check.

SHIRHENI Born around 1986 and orphaned in Kruger, Shirheni moved to the camp in 1989. She lost her first calf, but her next three – Pula, Abu (baby Abu) and reedbuck, steenbok, warthog, baboons and vervet monkeys. Lion and spotted hyena are the dominant predators, with occasional appearances by leopards and wild dogs.

That said, like NG25 to the north, and NG29 and NG30 to the south, I don't think that the variation and density of game are quite up to the levels of, say, central Moremi or some of the areas on the north side of the Delta. However, rest assured that you'll still see plenty of game when visiting here.

WHEN TO VISIT Because the focus of a trip here is for most people the experience of horseriding or the interactions with elephants, it's fine as long as you avoid the rains. So visit anytime from late April or May to the middle or end of December.

GETTING THERE AND AWAY The only option for these camps is to make advanced bookings and fly in. There's an airstrip near Abu Camp which is used by this and Seba Camp, while Macatoo has a second airstrip. Driving here is not possible.

WHERE TO STAY Wilderness Safaris (page 225) operate two camps within this concession, each offering something different, but each very luxurious. The original camp, and the only one to offer elephant-focused activities, is Abu Camp. The other camp, Seba, is more akin to a regular safari lodge in the Okavango Delta – and would be a good choice for those travelling with children over the age of six. For Macatoo Camp, see pages 373–4.

Warona – have thrived, and she has proved to be a calm and doting mother. Pula and Abu have both been successfully released into the wild, so her time is now devoted to looking after Warona.

WARONA Shirheni's fourth calf, she arrived just before Christmas 2011 – her name in Setswana meaning 'for us'. When she isn't playing with Lorato or Paseka she can often be found with Cathy at the front of the herd.

PASEKA She was found hiding in the generator room of Abu's sister camp, Seba, after being injured in a hyena attack and subsequently abandoned by her wild herd. Named after the day she was found, Easter, she was taken to Abu where her wounds were treated and she was accepted by the herd. Initially Shirheni adopted Paseka, but once she became pregnant with Warona, the late Kitimetse stepped in.

LORATO Daughter of the late Kitimetse, Lorato was born in 2009, just before Valentine's Day: hence her name, which is a derivation of the word 'love'. She is a fast learner and has formed strong bonds with all of the herd's new arrivals, including her half-sister Naledi.

NALEDI The latest addition to the Abu herd – whose name means 'star' – was born to Kitimetse on a starlit night in November 2013. Sadly she was orphaned when her mother passed away just six weeks later. Drastic action was needed to comfort Naledi and save her life. She was separated from the herd to be raised by hand, but since then she moved back in with the herd and has become a firm favourite of guests and staff alike.

🏠 **Abu Camp** [map 346] (6 tents) When Ker & Downey was involved with this operation, Abu Camp stood on the site that today is occupied by Nxabega (pages 377–8). Today's Abu Camp also overlooks a lagoon but is now nestled in a grove of hardwood trees. It's an immaculately designed lodge with a price tag to match – this is one of Botswana's most expensive camps.

Raised up on teak decking, with a shaded veranda & canvas chairs, Abu's tents are among the most luxurious rooms in the Delta: all slightly different, but all very stylish. Beautifully polished teak floors are dotted with matching rugs. Spacious en-suite bathrooms feature a stand-alone shower, flush toilet, twin washbasins – & a sliding door from the shower to a claw-foot bath on the veranda. Each tent also has a small study area with a writing table & cabinets featuring old books, local artefacts & a selection of southern African rocks.

The dining area, set on an expanse of tiered, teak decking, punctuated by jackalberry trees (*Diospyros mespiliformis*) & sycamore figs (*Ficus sycomorus*), stands in front of the main lounge, which has comfy chairs & a small library. The food is good & the service attentive, as you'd expect of a camp that regularly hosts the world's glitterati as guests. Pictures, ornaments & carvings of elephants (& especially of Abu) are all over the camp.

In Dec 2016, it was announced that Abu Camp would no longer be offering elephant riding. Instead, elephant activities now focus on walking with the elephants through the bush & experiencing life as one of the herd. So while activities here are flexible, depending on both the guests & the elephants, they will usually include at least one elephant activity during your stay here. In addition, 4x4 game drives, walks &, depending on water levels, mekoro or motorboat excursions are available.

It's important to note that, in common with most safari camps in Africa, all visitors at Abu Camp are required to sign an indemnity form which, basically, absolves the camp from any responsibility for your safety while participating in a trip. And as at any camp in the bush, you accept that you're taking on certain risks to do with Africa's animals & their unpredictability that you wouldn't face sitting on the couch at home. The only difference here is that being in such close proximity to such huge, strong animals does present a greater risk than most normal photographic safaris. Although the camp prides itself on a very good safety record, & no client has ever been injured by one of the elephants in 23 years of operation, it is important to remember that elephants are unpredictable & can react in unpredictable ways. In extreme cases, the consequence could be fatal.

Although riding the elephants is no longer permitted, the elephant interaction at Abu Camp is still a once-in-a-lifetime experience. The real fascination is your proximity to these animals: being able to walk beside them as they plod along & to observe them at such close quarters, effectively as one of the herd, rather than viewing them from afar as is usual on safari. Guests may even have the opportunity to be involved in the herd's mud baths, training or veterinary care. *From US$1,892/2,555 pp sharing/sgl 11 Jan–Mar to US$2,985/3,885 Jun–Oct, inc FB, most drinks, activities & laundry.* 🕒 *All year.* ★★★★★

🏠 **Seba Camp** [map 346] (8 tents) Named after one of the original elephants in the herd, Seba Camp is also the base for research into the interaction between wild elephants & those released into the wild. It's an upmarket camp, with en-suite tents secluded among riverine vegetation overlooking a lagoon. Unusually for the Delta, Seba is quite family friendly, its 2 family rooms, with 2 interconnecting en-suite bedrooms & their own plunge pools, ideal for those with younger children. All the rooms are equipped with solid wood furniture, their décor reflecting individual Batswana ethnic groups. Central to the camp are a tasteful & comfortable living & dining area, & a pool. Guests can take day & night game drives, & mokoro trips when the water is sufficiently high. *From US$781/1,066 pp sharing/sgl 11 Jan–Mar to US$1,475/1,920 Jun–Oct, fully inclusive. No children under 6.* 🕒 *All year.* ★★★★–★★★★★

HORSERIDING SAFARIS Contact African Horseback Safaris, page 227. These riding safaris were established by British rider Sarah-Jane Gullick, who set up the operation in 1994, originally with Ker & Downey Safaris (based out of a camp called Macateer Camp). Today, the operation has been taken over by John Sobey.

The general comments on Okavango Horse Safaris (page 388) about the fascinating experience of riding through the Okavango apply equally well to this operation. Suffice to say that once you step into the saddle, most of the Okavango's resident game will treat you and your horse as a single, composite four-legged herbivore. So antelope will relax around you, and predators will give you pause for thought!

Below is some basic information for these trips. Contact African Horseback Safaris if you need more precise details as they've a lot of information about their trips that they can send.

The horses The horses are a variety of thoroughbreds, Namibian Hanovarians, Arabs and Kalahari–Arab crossbreeds ranging from 14 to 18 hands (140–180cm) high.

Tack and clothes Good-quality English- and Western-style trail saddles are supplied, each with its own water bottle. Guests may borrow half chaps; long leather boots are impractical.

African Horseback Safaris does not supply hard hats or safety helmets; you must bring your own. They suggest that riders wear their riding clothes and boots on the plane, and bring their hat and wash bag as hand luggage, in case luggage gets delayed.

Information about you

Riding ability These safaris are for experienced riders aged 12 years and over. Riders over 60 need to be 'riding fit' and strong. Trips usually involve about 4 to 6 hours in the saddle each day. Thus riders need to feel competent about keeping up with the group, and capable of riding at all paces, rising to the trot and controlling their horse at the canter. They may also be required to gallop out of trouble, so these trips do not take beginners. For safety reasons, if they think that your riding is not up to standard, you won't be allowed to ride here.

Weight limits There's a weight limit of 15 stone (210lb or 95kg) per person, above which they can sometimes make special arrangements for advanced riders.

About the trips African Horseback Safaris offers a range of safaris from three to ten nights, giving plenty of scope. Following arrival in camp, each trip starts with an introductory talk on the safari, and a safety briefing. While safaris were once timed to start and finish on Tuesdays and Fridays, guests are now welcome to choose the dates that best suit their itinerary.

The riding groups have a maximum of six to eight guests. Trips normally incorporate not only riding but also the occasional game drive, walk and night drive, while the more adventurous may opt to spend a night in the 'treehouse', sleeping high up in the tree canopy under the African night sky. Boating, canoeing and fishing are also possible sometimes, depending on water levels.

Safety Two guides accompany each riding safari, carrying a first-aid kit, rifle, radio and GPS.

🏠 The riding camp

🏠 **Macatoo Camp** [map 346] (7 tents) Renovated in 2013, Macatoo is comfortable but simple &, as with most camps, the service is of a good standard. Each of its large tents has twin beds, & an en-suite shower & toilet, while new to the camp are the 'honeymoon suite', with a bath on a raised platform & a large private deck, & a 'friends & family suite' with 2 tents linked by a walkway & viewing deck above ground level. Dinner is usually a stylish 3-course affair, served by candlelight, with high-quality food freshly prepared. There is a furnished mess tent, a small splash pool & a daily laundry service. ★★★– ★★★★

The costs From January to March, and December, rates are £475 per person per night, including all meals, drinks and activities. This rises to £580 from April to July and 1–15 November, while in the high season (July to the end of October) the cost is £670 per person. Note that prices are quoted in pounds sterling, rather than the more normal US dollars.

Air transfers to/from Maun are £195 per person, one-way. Macatoo use a cement airstrip, which is 45 minutes' drive from camp.

POM POM, KANANA AND NXABEGA (NG27A)

This large, strictly photographic concession is now effectively split between three safari companies: Ker & Downey Botswana (who run Kanana), &Beyond (who run Nxabega) and Under One Botswana Sky (who own Pom Pom).

CONCESSION HISTORY By the early 1970s there were a number of camps throughout the Delta, most of which accepted either hunting or photographic guests. One of the bigger companies involved here was Safari South, who ran many camps including Khwai River Lodge, Four Rivers Camp (near the present Kwara), Queenie, Splash, Jedibe, Machaba, Mombo, Pom Pom and Shinde.

Around 1985, Ker & Downey was split from Safari South, as a wholly owned subsidiary, to differentiate the photographic camps from those used for hunting. Ker & Downey then had four photographic camps in the Delta: Shinde, Mombo, Jedibe and Machaba.

A company called Jao Safaris owned Mombo at that time. Various contracts changed, which resulted in Ker & Downey leaving Mombo and Jedibe. (These were eventually taken up by Wilderness Safaris, in 1989.) Meanwhile, the government had designated NG27 for photographic use only, and Ker & Downey took over the running of Pom Pom, which had been another old hunting camp run by Safari South.

From 1985 Pom Pom was the only major camp here, but in 1990 they started a 'partnership' with Randall Jay Moore. Moore brought trained African elephants over from the USA to start Elephant Back Safaris (pages 370–1), and Ker & Downey built Abu Camp (page 372), on the site that Nxabega now occupies, in the north of the reserve. In 1993, I was very excited to visit Pom Pom – and to get here I took my first flight over the Delta! It was then one of Botswana's most upmarket camps, and the rest of the clientele during my stay were from America. The combination of Pom Pom and then Abu Camp was a winning one; business was good for them. (Note that throughout this time there were also a few simple bushcamps in the area, used by various operators.) However, the following year Randall Moore tendered for, and obtained, his own concession next door: NG26. This upset the apple cart, as he then built the camp that is today known as Abu Camp – thus taking away a highly profitable chunk of business from Ker & Downey.

NG27 Concession has always been subdivided. First AfroVentures (who subsequently merged with CC Africa, now &Beyond) built Nxabega Camp on the site of the old Abu Camp, in the north. Then, in 2000, Ker & Downey opened their own new camp, Kanana.

In 2001, Wilderness Safaris took over the marketing and management of Pom Pom, building a completely new small camp here, but keeping the name and location of the 'old' Pom Pom. Since then, it has again changed hands, and is now under the same ownership as Chobe Safari Lodge in Kasane.

FLORA AND FAUNA HIGHLIGHTS Travelling from south to north, the landscapes, flora and fauna change very slowly, but there are slight differences between the various parts of the reserve. Bear in mind while reading this that the similarities between the different areas are much greater than their contrasts.

Flora The NG27 Concession is in the heart of the Delta and contains most of the typical Delta environments: thickets and stands of riverine forest; more open areas of invasive bushes; and occasional floodplains.

The area around Pom Pom is very open and pretty, notable for many tiny islands amid wide open floodplains, which are often submerged between May and September. These distinct islands are often covered, or at least fringed, by real fan (*Hyphaene petersiana*) and wild date palms (*Phoenix reclinata*), and between them are large marshy floodplains. There are quite a few baobabs in the area, and the forest patches are fairly sparse.

Moving northeast to the area of Kanana, there are fewer flat, open plains and more areas colonised by expanses of wild sage. Around these are larger islands and woodland patches with plenty of the Delta's usual riverine tree species: sausage trees (*Kigelia africana*), jackalberries (*Diospyros mespiliformis*), knobthorns (*Senegalia nigrescens*), the occasional marula (*Sclerocarya birrea caffra*) and the odd raintree (*Philenoptera violacea*). (The raintree, also sometimes called the appleleaf, gets its name from the droplets which are secreted by froghopper insects as they suck the sap from the leaves. This keeps the soil beneath the tree moist, and in exceptional cases can even form pools.)

Further northwest, around Nxabega, the forests become more in evidence with large, dense lines of broadleaf forests and patches of acacia. Mixed with these are a few open plains, fringed by real fan palms (*Hyphaene petersiana*) and stands of riverine trees. In the midst of the larger floodplains you'll see occasional islands crowned with an African mangosteen (*Garcinia livingstonei*), or perhaps a large sycamore fig (*Ficus sycomorus*), growing out of an old termite mound perhaps surrounded by a few russet bush-willow bushes (*Combretum hereroense*). Some of the Nxabega's floodplains have thick coverings of hippo grass (*Vossia cuspidata*) that turn a lovely shade of orange-red around September.

Fauna The variety of game in NG27 certainly seems wider to me than that found in areas further south and west – though I feel that it's not as wide as some of the reserves on the northeast side of the Delta. Tsessebe, impala, wildebeest, lechwe, steenbok, baboon and zebra are all common and seen very regularly. Giraffe do particularly well here, they're very relaxed among the many acacia thickets, and there is a good number of resident elephants.

Lion and spotted hyena are the commonest large predators, though the mixed woodland is a perfect habitat for leopard that are numerous, though only seen occasionally. Cheetah are seen only rarely, when the reserve is at its driest (October to March); they're not at all common. Wild dog pass through periodically (as they do through most areas of northern Botswana) though not frequently. Both black-backed and side-striped jackal are common.

As with most of the Delta there's always plenty of smaller animals, too widespread to be worthy of particular comment … though I recall a great sighting of an entertaining troop of dwarf mongooses here once!

Birdlife The birding is good and very varied in this concession. Kanana has immediate access to the deep Xudum channel that is lined with a mixture of water figs, huge floating mats of graceful papyrus and anchored sections of miscanthus grass (*Miscanthus junceus*). Among the birdlife, there's a notable profusion of squacco herons. However, what is really interesting is the Kanana heronry (⊕ KANHER 19°30.02'.S, 22°51.10'E), discovered only in 2001. Like the heronry at Gcodikwe, the shallow floodplain is dotted with tree-islands, primarily of water-fig trees interspersed with papyrus and waterberry. Protected in some measure from predators, these in turn attract countless waterbirds during the breeding season, which starts in July and reaches its peak between September and December.

When found, many birds were breeding here, including yellow-billed, marabou and open-billed storks, darters, cormorants, herons and egrets, while a survey by BirdLife Botswana in 2011 confirmed the presence of vulnerable pink-backed pelicans from mid-July. How such a large heronry went 'unnoticed' for so long is a complete puzzle, but the survey concludes that it is 'the most dynamic and vibrant heronry that we have ever visited in Botswana'. However fascinating, visitors must remember the problems that disturbances can cause to the birds; don't encourage your guide to approach too close to the heronry.

Nxabega doesn't have the heronry, though one recent September over 500 open-billed storks and about 1,000 squacco herons were seen gathering to roost just a little west of Nxabega. It does, however, have a couple of very old pole bridges across small waterways in its reserve. These prove particularly attractive perching places for waterbirds that can then be seen while driving. (This is an advantage if, like me, you prefer a stationary base from which to use a camera and tripod, rather than a rocking boat.) There are lots of hamerkops, small herons, egrets (including a good number of slaty), black crakes and bee-eaters. Kingfishers are well represented; here I've got closer to photographing a diminutive malachite kingfisher than I ever have while on a boat.

Read the marketing literature for almost any camp in the Delta and you'll realise that claims for sightings of 'the elusive Pel's fishing owl' are a tedious marketing cliché. Every camp simultaneously trumpets their rarity, and yet claims you'll see one while staying there. That said, when I last visited Nxabega, one such owl was making predictable, regular appearances on one of the old bridges, and the guides advised that three pairs were regularly seen in different locations in the area. Meanwhile, I'm reliably informed that in 2002 a pair of Pel's fishing owls was seen in, and said to be nesting in, trees about 100m from camp.

Having said all that about the resident birds that associate with water, you'll find an equally good variety of drier-country birds in this reserve. On my last visit, among the eagles, I spotted tawny, bateleur, Wahlberg's and, most remarkably, a martial eagle battling with a large monitor lizard on the ground beside our vehicle, near Pom Pom. (We found both locked in combat, but at a stalemate. Eventually they disentangled themselves and the great lizard made a hasty retreat under a bush.)

Finally, on a more domestic note, the staff at Nxabega seem to have 'tamed' a pair of wild yellow-billed hornbills sufficiently for them to come along to afternoon tea on most days.

WHEN TO VISIT The area is lightly less seasonal than those further south and west, though there's still a big difference between the game densities through the seasons: they're a lot better when it's drier. As usual, the birding is as good as it gets during the wetter time of the year (December to around March).

GETTING THERE AND AWAY All of these camps work only with guests flying in, usually having made their bookings months before they travel. Driving here is not possible without permission, and is anyway totally impractical.

WHERE TO STAY The camps are totally different from one another, perhaps because they're run in different ways by different companies.

Nxabega Okavango Tented Camp [map 346] (9 tents) Contact &Beyond, page 223. Built on the site of the original Abu Camp, Nxabega is the most northerly of the camps in NG27, occupying an area of 70km². It's about an hour's drive north of Kanana (though only around 12km as the birds fly!) & 11km south-southeast of Xigera, which is in Moremi. However, for most of the year Xigera is inaccessible by land from Nxabega because of the Boro River.

Nxabega's main building is constructed on a grand scale around a huge jackalberry tree, from local timber & reeds, with a high shaggy thatched roof. Inside, it is swish but understated, with clean lines & teak-panelled walls. The large dining area stands under 2 electric candelabras & the bar is exceedingly well stocked with obscure liqueurs, imported spirits & good wines. (Unlimited house wine, beers & soft drinks are normally included in the rate, but if you want to drink their cellar of vintage wines dry, they'll charge extra!)

The large, high-quality tents are raised on wooden platforms about a metre above the

ground, with verandas overlooking the floodplain. All are well spread out, with a discreet 30–40m between them – from No 1 on the far right to the honeymoon suite, past the large swimming pool on the left. Inside, on sisal mats laid on a smooth wooden floor, twin or dbl beds are draped with quality cotton sheets, down duvets & assorted pillows. Each tent is well furnished with chairs, a dressing table, luggage rack, wardrobe & bedside lamps (powered by a solar-powered battery system). At the back of each is a small en-suite bathroom with a flush toilet, hot shower (heated by a gas geyser) & a washbasin.

Activities include 4x4 game drives, mokoro excursions & boat trips, with good catch-&-release fishing possible on the Boro River. Nxabega has been constructed with care & generally seems to be run with a higher complement of staff than most lodges (average 2 staff per guest). This gives it an air of quality. The food is particularly good, but what I appreciated more was the flexibility that visitors have over everything, from the timings of b/fast & lunch, to the scheduling of

13

activities. These are seldom regimented, & the staff make real efforts to organise activities to suit you. If you've ever wanted to do a late-night drive after dinner to look for aardvarks, or a midday boating trip . . . Nxabega is a good choice! *From US$795/1,192.50 pp sharing/sgl Jan–Mar to US$1,750/2,625 Jun–Oct, inc FB, local drinks, activities, laundry.* ☺ *All year.* ★★★★–★★★★★

🏠 **Kanana** [map 346] (8 tents) Contact Ker & Downey Botswana, page 224. Originally opened in 2000 & refurbished in 2016, Kanana stands at roughly the centre of NG27, & overlooks the reedbeds of the Xudum River. This gives the camp access to a permanent, deep-water channel for boating all year.

Accommodation is in very comfortable tents spread out to the left of the main area. These are separated by about 20m, so even the furthest room isn't miles from the centre of camp. Inside, the teak floor is covered with various rugs, & the tents are well furnished with a wooden wardrobe, luggage rack, dressing table & chairs, & plenty of thoughtful touches. Teak bedside tables have electric lights, powered like the whole camp by solar-powered batteries. Twin or dbl beds have good-quality cotton sheets & down pillows with blankets. A canvas divider separates the sleeping space from the en-suite flush toilet, washbasin & (very efficient) shower. Outside on the shaded veranda, to the front & side of the tents, there's a table & comfy chairs, & all the tents face the river from under a cover of riverine trees – jackalberries, knobthorns & sausage trees. These, & the plunge pool, are linked by sandy paths, illuminated at night by lanterns.

Kanana's main area is a U-shaped wooden building with a large tree in the centre & an alfresco dining deck, several small lounge areas (one with a small library), a bar &, down nearer the water, a 'sandpit' for fires.

Though the comfortable game-drive vehicles have been carefully thought out, with storage for binoculars & lots of space, the camp's strongest suit is its mokoro trips, often including short island walks. It's particularly convenient that when water levels are good, these can be launched directly from the side of the lodge's main area, & into the reedbeds which surround the Xudum River. There are also boat trips, including fishing for bream or catfish. A real highlight, especially around Sep–Dec when many species of birds are breeding, is a boat trip to the heronry. As with most camps, Kanana works on the basis of one long safari activity after b/fast, then siesta time after lunch, & another activity following afternoon tea, before dinner. Late-night drives after dinner are also possible. *From US$530 pp Mar & Dec to US$1,010/1,295 pp sharing/sgl Jul–Oct, inc FB, drinks, activities, laundry; exc transfers.* ☺ *Mar–Dec.* ★★★–★★★★★★

🏠 **Pom Pom** [map 346] (9 tents) ✆ 686 4436; m 7132 4404; contact Under One Botswana Sky, page 225. One of the original upmarket camps in the Delta, opened in 1985 by Ker & Downey, Pom Pom was rebuilt by Wilderness in 2001, then brought under the same umbrella as Chobe Safari Lodge in Kasane (pages 239–40) in 2005. Although it is barely 5km southwest of Kanana, a game drive between the 2 camps would take 45mins.

The camp's Meru-style tents are built on platforms & incorporate a private lounge area, a secluded veranda & a spacious interior, all overlooking a small permanent lagoon. The design is an eclectic mixture of solid wood & African furniture, including twin or dbl beds (there's also 1 family unit). Each also has an en-suite bathroom, behind a wall & partially open to the stars.

A central area under thatch brings together the dining area, bar & a curio shop; there's also a small pool. Activities include day & night drives, mokoro trips & short walks. There is the opportunity to fish, or watch game & birdlife, from a boat at all times, but only when water levels are very high can you take a boating excursion. (The main flood hits here around May, often filling the dry lagoon in a day. The area's highest water levels usually occur around Jun–Aug.) *From US$505 pp Dec–Mar to US$980/1,160 pp sharing/sgl Jul–Oct, inc FB, most drinks, activities, park fees, laundry; exc transfers. No children under 6.* ☺ *All year.* ★★★–★★★★★

DELTA, ODDBALLS', GUNN'S AND EAGLE ISLAND (NG27B)

Between NG30, NG32 and Moremi stands a fairly small photographic reserve, just off the southwest side of Chief's Island. This was the first area of the Okavango where tourism really took off in volume, and it's now very interesting to see it making the transition to smaller numbers of visitors, and more upmarket camps.

CONCESSION HISTORY A short history of the Delta and Oddballs' camps is an interesting illustration of the transition between different types of tourism mentioned previously. It started shortly after Lodges of Botswana bought Delta Camp in 1983. During their first year they not only catered to upmarket visitors, but also used the camp as a base for the mokoro trips of more budget-conscious travellers.

This mix didn't work in one camp, and so in 1984 they built a separate lower-budget camp at the other end of their island. The nickname of their first manager was 'Oddball', and so this became – tongue in cheek – Oddball's Palm Island Luxury Lodge. Oddball's marketing was astute and well targeted, portraying a relaxed, hippie hang-out where spaced-out campers could find paradise on their own island in the Delta. This became a buzzing base for budget mokoro trips in the heart of the Delta – *the* backpacker's place in the Delta, known in hostels from Nairobi to Cape Town, and beyond.

It was very successful. At first they just had showers, toilets and a (fridge-less) bar; campers brought all their own food and kit. It grew fast, eventually encompassing a shop for campers and food, as well as chilled drinks from a fully fledged bar.

When business peaked during the late 1980s and early 1990s, they had up to 120 visitors *per day* flying in, some camping for a night in the camp and others heading out on mokoro trips. Then there were no limits on how many visitors the camp could accept. The camp had a rule that every visitor had to stay at Oddball's for at least one night.

Then two things happened which changed this business. First, in July 1989, the government raised its national park fees from P10 per person per week to P30 per person per day, and then to P70 per day. Mokoro trips from Oddball's had always been to Moremi, and this increased their prices dramatically.

Second, there had long been a process of tendering for camps, whereby safari operators bid for leases to operate safari camps. In 1996, the government introduced new leases to camps in many of the Delta's reserves, insisting that safari companies not only produce large cheques for rental and royalties (per visitor), but also a 'management plan' for the reserves. These became effective in January 1997.

In drawing up these detailed management plans, the safari companies were forced to look not only at their game and environmental policies, and the sustainability of them, but also how they trained their staff, and what they were doing to help the wider community in the area. This process raised the issues of sustainability, responsible tourism and community development – and placed them in the centre of the government's decision-making process. Thus, it made them important to the safari operators.

Oddball's had started a programme of training their polers as early as 1988. Like all camps, it now insists that all of its polers have a qualification as a professional mokoro guide. The government requires that standards like these are now applied across the board for all the camps in the region.

By 1997, Oddball's alone had about 35 mokoro guides working for them. They were able to renew their leases on Oddball's and its smaller, upmarket sister camp, Delta Camp. However, the government had made a hard bargain: they had to reduce the number of visitors to a maximum combined total of 60 people at any one time. That was 40 guests at Oddball's and 20 at Delta Camp, a fraction of past numbers.

Immediately prices had to be increased in order to cover their costs from a much smaller base of visitors. In December 1999, both camps were extensively renovated;

13

economics dictated that they had to move more upmarket, charging more, to stay in business. The camp on the Oddball's site was rebuilt in much greater style, as a fully fledged upmarket camp that could command high prices. Then the names of the two camps were switched. This newly built camp on the site of Oddball's old site is now known as Delta Camp, while the older camp which was once known as Delta Camp became Oddballs' (with the apostrophe moved to reflect a change of emphasis).

Thus the 1980s camp has become an upmarket camp for the next century, while the original budget camp has been totally rebuilt and refurbished as a new luxurious camp, to standards which are now much higher than they were.

This is a textbook example of what has happened right across Botswana. Pressure from the government, using park fees and the concessions as tools of implementation, has led to lower numbers of visitors to Botswana's wild areas, and hence to more costly safaris and more upmarket lodges. For their money visitors now get a much more exclusive experience, with mokoro guides who have more training and better skills than before – and are paid better as a result.

In summary: the environment benefits, the local people benefit, Botswana's finances benefit, and even the visitors get a better experience – that is, those who can still afford to visit!

GEOGRAPHY NOTE As with the whole Delta, the floods in this area are variable and unpredictable, in both duration and timing. The flood usually arrives between March and May, and remains for an average of four months. However, hydrologists note that since the late 1980s, there was a measured decrease in the amount of water flowing down the Boro River. In the 1994–95 period of water inflow, it was estimated that the lower Boro River received little over half of its long-term average. That water flow then gradually decreased, until – due to heavy rainfall in Angola – water levels rose again, and by 2009 were back to those of the 1980s. The flood levels continued to be very impressive through 2010 and 2011, before starting to return to more normal levels in 2012 and 2013, where they remain at the time of research in 2017.

Changes in water levels could also be explained by postulating that the western side of the Delta is gradually rising relative to the eastern side. Hence the Thaoge is gradually flooding less, and the Khwai is flooding more. The Boro is fairly central to the Delta, and derives its flow from the Nqoga River (the source of the Khwai River). However, it breaks from this at a very sharp, acute angle, and hence some experts suggest that it should be considered as being influenced the same way as the rivers on the western side of the Delta.

Having said all this, some say that changes in water flows could be caused simply by a hippo changing its regular path in the higher reaches of the Delta! Whatever the cause, this reduced flow isn't necessarily good or bad for the visitor; but it is a help in understanding some of the gradual changes which are happening (over decades) to the area's vegetation.

FLORA AND FAUNA HIGHLIGHTS The Boro River and its associated floodplains dominate this reserve. A land survey in 1996 estimated that only about 4% of the whole reserve was permanent swampland, but 75% was classed as seasonally inundated swamp and grasslands. The remainder is dry land: riverine forests and grasslands on the islands. So this is a very seasonal environment, which changes annually with the floods.

Flora As noted above, there is relatively little permanent swamp here. Small patches of papyrus are found though, usually in photogenic little clumps beside the main Boro River. Look carefully and you'll also find areas of common reeds (*Phragmites australis*), Miscanthus grass (*Miscanthus junceus*), bulrushes (*Typha capensis*) and a number of floating-leafed, emergent and submerged species.

Perhaps the major feature of the area is some splendid, mature patches of riverine forests that line sections of the Boro River. Here you'll find lots of real fan palms (*Hyphaene petersiana*), often in beautiful dense stands. There's also a scattering of all the 'usual suspects' that you'd expect in riverine forest in the region, including leadwoods (*Combretum imberbe*), jackalberries (*Diospyros mespiliformis*), knobthorns (*Senegalia negrescens*), sausage trees (*Kigelia africana*), large fever-berries (*Croton megalobotrys*), woodland waterberries (*Syzygium guineense*) and occasional baobab trees (*Adansonia digitata*). However, perhaps the area's most unusual flora are the huge strangler figs (*Ficus* species, probably *thonningii*, *natalensis* or *fischeri*). There are several specimens here enveloping large leadwood trees – an amazing sight.

On the larger island, and particularly on Chief's Island (in Moremi, but visited from these camps), you'll find permanently dry forest areas. These vary from mopane woodlands in areas of clay soil, to areas of acacias where there's more sand.

In the deepest areas of sand you'll find *Terminalia sericea*, the source of the best wood from which to craft traditional mokoro poles.

Adjacent to the river are large areas of very shallow floodplains. A wide variety of grasses, sedges and herbs are found in these areas with various species of *Eragrostis*, *Imperata*, *Panicum*, *Aristida* and *Cymbopogen* being common. More than 200 plant species have been recorded here, though the floodplains are very often dotted with a sparse covering of *Imperata cylindrica*, sometimes known as 'silver spike', with long, rigid leaf spikes growing from a rhizome, some with a small 'spikelet' at the end.

Fauna Of the camps in this reserve, only Eagle Island Camp (pages 382–3) conducts game drives, and then only when it is dry enough to do so, As such, a visit here is usually much more about the ambience of the Delta than about spotting game. Come for the experience, let any game sightings be a bonus, and you'll have a good trip.

That said, there are good game densities in the area, and especially on the adjacent Chief's Island. Even from a mokoro you're likely to see hippopotami and crocodiles in the water. Elephants are frequently seen in the drier months, from May to October, wandering through the floodplains; from December to April they are around in smaller numbers.

When out walking on the islands there is a chance of much more game. The area's dominant antelope is the red lechwe, but you will also find tsessebe, impala, zebra, kudu, reedbuck, giraffe, warthog and buffalo. As the area becomes drier with time, blue wildebeest are being seen more often. Roan, sable and waterbuck remain absent from this area. When the flood is at its height, sitatunga are occasionally seen. With the reintroduction of rhino to Chief's Island, there's a very slim chance that you could bump into one of them.

The most common predators are lion, spotted hyena and side-striped and black-backed jackals. Leopard are rarely seen, but they will be relatively common as the riverine forest suits them perfectly. Wild dogs and cheetah also occur, but are rare sightings – though we were lucky enough to see a pack of some 15 dogs from Eagle Island Camp in 2017.

Birdlife Birding is an important feature of all the trips here; you'll probably spend much of your time exploring the area from a mokoro. As mentioned above, the water levels can vary hugely – in October 2002, they dropped by 15cm in just three weeks. So expect the channels and the birdlife to vary greatly through the seasons.

13

When water levels are lowest, around November to February, you may find skimmers on some exposed sandbanks. Meanwhile knob-billed ducks, long-toed and blacksmith lapwings, and saddle-billed storks are among a whole host of permanent residents. As levels rise, red-winged pratincoles gather in large flocks, and there is always a good variety of kingfishers, from giant and pied to the tiny pygmy and malachite. Woodland kingfishers – insectivorous birds which are usually seen hunting for insects in the riverine forest – appear for the summer around the end of October. They arrive with a variety of migrants, including carmine bee-eaters, aerobatic yellow-billed kites, and paradise flycatchers, the males of which have the most spectacular tails. I have also had a reliable report of black coucals in front of Delta Camp, but haven't seen them there myself.

Much of the Boro channel sees the annual catfish run (see box, page 415), and this area is no exception. If you're lucky enough to catch this then you can spot 30 species or more in a 100m stretch of waterway. Pelicans, skimmers and a wide variety of herons, egrets, storks, stilts, snipes and cormorants all appear in quantity then, to take advantage of the abundant food.

WHEN TO VISIT Though open all year, these camps rely primarily on mokoro trips and so are certainly at their best when the sun is shining and the sky blue, ie: between April and November. If you're camping out then it makes for a better trip if it's not too cold at night, so my favourite months for visiting here would be around May–early June (though those months can be cold, too) and September–October time. However, these activities heavily depend on water levels – mainly to ensure that guests and guides avoid the hippo population. On a recent visit in September the water was getting very low and all but the shortest mokoro outings had been stopped.

GETTING THERE AND AWAY It is possible to embark on a boat transfer to this area from Maun, heading up the Boro River, but this tends to be more costly and take much longer than flying, which is the usual means of transport into this concession. There are several airstrips, including Delta airstrip (⊕ DELAIR 19°31.840'S, 23°05.430'E), which is closest to both Oddballs' and Delta Camp, and, about 4km southwest from there, Xaxaba airstrip (⊕ XAXAIR 19°33.220'S, 23°03.510'E).

WHERE TO STAY Of the camps in this reserve, Delta and Oddballs' are run by Lodges of Botswana (page 224); Gunn's Camp and Moremi Crossing (formerly Gunn's Bush Camp) from their base in Maun, Under One Botswana Sky (page 225); and Eagle Island Camp by Belmond (page 223).

Eagle Island Camp [map 347] (12 tented rooms) One of the Delta's first photographic camps was built here at Xaxaba Island (unless you're fluent in one of the local Khoisan languages & used to the various clicks, this is usually pronounced 'Kakaaba', with 'Ka' as in 'cat'). Originally known as Xaxaba Camp, it was at one point bought by Lloyd Wilmot (of 'Lloyd's Camp', Savuti' & Wilmot Safaris fame) before being run for many years by Gametrackers, which became Orient-Express Safaris & is now known as Belmond. There's still a bushcamp on the same spot, known as Baboon Camp & used by wildlife researchers, but close by is this reserve's plushest camp: Eagle Island.

The camp was built to basically the same design & specification as its sister camps, Khwai River Lodge (page 319) & Savute Elephant Camp (page 287). This means large, opulent tented rooms built to high specifications on timber platforms under thatched roofs. Each has a wide veranda at the front & an outside lounge with an inviting plunge pool. They're well spread out & linked by well-lit pathways. Inside, each tent is fully furnished with polished wooden floors, rugs & luxurious furniture. The twin ¾-size beds, which are usually pushed together & can be made up as a king-size dbl, have high-quality cotton bedding, bedside tables & twin lamps, all surrounded by a mosquito net. The rooms come with many of the accoutrements of a top hotel such as a minibar, safe & AC. At the back, as well as a walk-in dressing room-cum-wardrobe, are his & hers basins, indoor & outdoor showers, a polished black bath & a separate toilet.

The expansive main area includes an open-fronted dining area, where meals are usually served individually, & a comfortable lounge area arranged around a large fireplace. There is also a curio shop, a TV room & – down a long grassy spit towards the boat station – the romantic Fish Eagle sundowner bar.

Eagle Island is primarily a camp for water-based activities – mainly mokoro trips & guided walks on the islands, plus motorboat trips during high-water periods (usually Jun–Sep). For most of the year there's also a large 14-seater 'sundowner cruiser' which can slowly coast along the main channels. Helicopter safaris – a great way to see the scenery & animals from a different perspective – are also on offer. When it becomes so dry here that there's not enough water for good mokoro & motorboat trips, game drives are also on offer. *From US$1,220 pp Jan–Mar & 15 Nov–23 Dec to US$2,470/3,705 Jul–Sep inc FB, activities, drinks, laundry.* ⊕ *All year.* ★★★★★

🏠 **Delta Camp** [map 347] (7 chalets) Owned & run by Lodges of Botswana since 1983, this camp overlooks the Boro River. In 2000, it was completely rebuilt on the site of the old Oddball's Camp. Its reed-&-thatch chalets have open verandas looking northeast into Moremi. All have an en-suite bathroom, including a shower, toilet & washbasin. There is also a treehouse in the fork of a jackalberry tree (*Diospyros mespiliformis*), reached up some steep steps. This comes complete with a small balcony with a couple of chairs & a hammock from which to look out over the channel & the wildlife beneath.

Activities centre around mokoro trips, with your guide poling the mokoro & leading walks on the islands. With a little advance notice, it's possible to go on day trips with picnic lunches. *From US$495 pp Dec–Mar to US$885 Jul–Oct, inc FB, most drinks, activities & park fees; 30% sgl supp't.* ⊕ *All year.* ★★★–★★★★★

🏠 **Gunn's Camp** [map 347] (7 tents) Situated on the Boro River, overlooking Moremi Game Reserve, Gunn's was founded & run for years by the brusque Mike Gunn. It used to be accessed as often by motorboat as by plane from Maun. In the 1980s, it ran week-long 'fitness in the wilderness' courses which, among other things, taught you how to punt your own mokoro.

Since then it has been taken more upmarket, its twin-bedded Meru tents featuring neutral colour tones, teak furniture & en-suite bathrooms with flush toilets, stand-alone bathtubs & outdoor showers. At the front of each tent is a small, enclosed lounge area with 2 comfy chairs, footstools, a desk & electric lighting. In the central dining/bar area, set across 3 levels & constructed of canvas & thatch, the upper seating area is noteworthy for excellent views across the river & floodplains. There is also a small swimming pool & a campfire.

Activities are organised in the morning & evening, usually involving mokoro trips & perhaps including a walk on one of the islands. Fishing is also possible Apr–Dec. With prior notice, overnight mokoro trips can be arranged, camping on an island with dinner around a campfire & a walk the following morning. When the channels are deep enough, motorboat trips along the Boro are also possible. *From US$375 pp Dec–Mar to US$795/975 pp sharing/sgl Jul–Oct, inc FB, most drinks, activities, park fees, laundry; exc transfers; no sgl supp't for 3 nights or more.* ⊕ *All year.* ★★★–★★★★

🏠 **Moremi Crossing** [map 347] (16 tents) The former bushcamp of Gunn's Camp (above) has been completely refurbished & renamed, drawing a definitive line under the lower-budget camping options of times gone by. Accommodation is in en-suite Meru-style tents, which include 2 family tents, all shaded by African ebony, sycamore fig & palm trees. Meals are served in a thatched central area, which also houses a bar & curio shop. This is fronted by a crescent-shaped deck that overlooks the permanent Boro channel & Chief's Island. Tucked behind is a swimming pool with a few sunloungers. The camp aims to be 100% eco-friendly, with solar power & modern waste disposal technology, though it does have a back-up generator. Activities combine mokoro trips with walks on the islands, as well as motorboat cruises & wilderness camping on nearby islands – though this option must be requested in advance. As an alternative to the flight into camp, it's possible to take a boat transfer from Maun as an optional extra (*US$125 pp, min 4 people). From US$380 pp

13

Dec–Mar to US$635/815 pp sharing/sgl Jul–Oct, inc FB, most drinks, activities, park fees, laundry; exc transfers. No sgl supp't 3 nights or more. No children under 8. ⊕ All year. ★★★

🏠 **Oddballs' Palm Island Luxury Lodge** [map 347] (15 dome tents) Southeast of Delta Camp, but beside the same Boro River, Oddballs' is still thought of as a destination in the Okavango for budget travellers, even though it's *much* more expensive than it was. For your money, you now have your own 2.4m x 2.4m (3-person) dome tent which stands on a raised wooden deck, surmounted by a roll of reeds for shade. Outside is a view over the Delta; inside are dbl or twin beds; & on its veranda a small table & stools.

Unlike the backpackers' camp of old, a stay here now includes all meals & activities. These activities focus on mokoro trips (they are one of the last camps in the Delta still to use traditional wooden mekoro), & walks on nearby Chief's Island. It is also possible to do a longer mokoro trail that usually includes a 1st & last night at Oddballs' itself, with the intervening nights camping out on islands. Most of your camping kit & food is provided on the mokoro trail, but you must bring your own sleeping bag & drinks, & you generally all muck in & cook together over an open fire. *From US$295 Dec–Mar to US$445 Jul–Oct, inc FB, most drinks, activities & park fees; exc P200 pp wilderness camping fee for mokoro trail.* ⊕ All year. ★★–★★★

✳ 🏠 **Oddballs' Enclave** [map 347] (5 tents) An upmarket offshoot of Oddballs' was built in 2009 on the other side of the same island as Oddballs'. Depending on water levels, guests will either be transferred by mokoro to camp or take a short walk from the airstrip. The enclave's 'mini-Meru' walk-in tents are fairly basic but come with twin or king-size beds with open-air en-suite bathrooms. The main area, although quite compact, is smartly decorated with a bar & lounge, a large communal dining table &, among other seating options, a fun swing chair made from an old mokoro. *From US$420 pp Dec–Mar to US$605 Jun–Oct, inc FB, most drinks, activities & park fees.* ⊕ All year. ★★★

ACTIVITIES Though these camps differ slightly in their activities, they are essentially water camps from which you take guided mokoro trips along the Boro River, and on to its associated floodplains.

Most also offer walking trips on the islands – just as camps here have for decades. These generally use the bushwise local mokoro guides, whose local knowledge can be excellent (even if their communication skills in English are more variable). They will almost never be carrying any firearms for protection (that's not allowed inside the Moremi Game Reserve), so see my general comments under *Walking in the bush* pages 187–91, for a further discussion of the safety issues raised by this approach. The exception here is Eagle Island, who will on request walk with rifles on their concession outside the reserve.

A final note of warning from a cost perspective. There is a 'wilderness camping fee' imposed by the government for visitors camping overnight within Moremi Game Reserve as part of a mokoro trip. The fee, P200 per person per day, is payable in cash on arrival, and cannot be prepaid.

XIGERA, MOMBO AND CHIEF'S CAMP (NG28)

Although technically in the NG28 concession, on the north and west side of Chief's Island, Xigera, Mombo and Chief's Camp were effectively swallowed up by Moremi Game Reserve in 1992. Thus these three private camps and their satellites are covered in *The Okavango Delta – Moremi Game Reserve*, pages 342–3.

XUDUM, XARANNA AND OHS (NG29 AND NG30)

Together these equally large concessions cover a total of about 2,500km² on the southern edge of the Delta, sandwiched between southern Moremi and the Sandvelt

Tongue. There are two operations here: Xudum and Xaranna run by &Beyond, and a specialist horseriding operation run by Okavango Horse Safaris. The reserves are so large that horseriders and safari campers are most unlikely to come across one another. Travellers should realise that these areas don't have the best game densities, but they are perfect for keen birdwatchers, and there are relatively frequent sightings of lion.

FLORA AND FAUNA HIGHLIGHTS Visiting one September, I concentrated my time in the far northern corner of the concession, close to Moremi Game Reserve – and probably its most productive area for wildlife. There the land was relatively dry, with only a few areas of floodplain, which is probably fairly typical of these areas towards the southwest edge of the Delta. Because of this location, the annual flood hits these areas relatively late – typically around the end of May or June. Then good water levels last until around the end of October or November.

Further south, around Xudum, there have been extensive changes in water levels over the last decade, which has impacted significantly on the wildlife in this area. A recent visit, in February, found the birding at its best here.

Flora Across the reserve there are lots of large, open plains covered in tall grass and interspersed with dry established thorny thickets and expanses of turpentine grass (*Cymbopogon* spp). Tall and with sharp barbs, it is widely used for thatching. Among these are dense stands of leadwood trees (*Combretum imberbe*) and knobthorns (*Senegalia nigrescens*). The latter are so numerous that their beautiful, creamy flowers combine to form a powerful perfume.

Perhaps as the result of fires in the past, there are large areas of chest-high wild sage, amid occasional 'islands', typical of the Delta, where termite mounds are dotted among African mangosteens, raintrees, marulas, sausage trees and jackalberrys. Among the larger stands of trees are umbrella thorns (*Vachellia tortilis*) and real fan palms (*Hyphaene petersiana*). But these islands of forest are relatively infrequent and quite poorly defined.

In the far north, the concession has a short boundary with Moremi: the Boro River, which is one of the Delta's best-known channels and is lined in parts by mature riverine forest.

Overall the mixed environment contains a wide variation of tree and plant species, though it doesn't have the beauty of some of the more mature, established forests or floodplain areas.

Fauna There's a good range of species here, typical of the Delta, though game densities are probably not as high as further north. They are certainly highly seasonal with animals proving scarce during the rains, and then numbers improving as the land dries out in the dry season. In the deeper waters around the Boro River, there's no shortage of hippos or crocodiles.

In the north, the dominant antelope is probably tsessebe (in one study of the Delta these made up 70% of all lion kills), though impala are also fairly common, occurring frequently in small groups. Family groups of giraffe and small numbers of zebra and wildebeest are also seen in the drier areas, along with kudu and steenbok, but rising water levels around the Xudum River over the past decade have impacted on the wildlife in this area. Populations of red lechwe and reedbuck have swollen, while those of the plains game such as zebra and wildebeest have declined. Roan, eland and gemsbok are seen very rarely, and generally only in the drier areas on the south side of the NG29 concession.

Between about December and June elephants occur in small family groups (this is typical of their behaviour in the whole region when food is plentiful). Then they tend to be most frequently found in the mopane scrub areas in the south of the concession. Later in the year, as the land dries up, they gradually coalesce into larger herds, hundreds strong, which move north and east, nearer to the heart of the Delta. Buffalo tend to occur in large herds that move through the concession in the dry season; smaller groups are seldom seen.

Of the predators, lion are by far the most common in these concessions, although numbers have reduced as the plains game moved away. Leopard are also permanent residents and, though generally shy, are increasingly seen around the new camps. I didn't see any spotted hyena on my last visit, though they're almost certainly around. Cheetah are very scarce, and generally only seen in the driest of months, around October to December. Then the grass is shorter, and there's more dry land, and so less pressure from lion. At other times of the year the cheetah tend to move away from the water, south and west out of the concession.

Birdlife The varied habitat leads to good birdwatching, and explorations both of the Boro River area and further south can be excellent. Along the river, very large flocks of red-winged pratincoles congregate on the exposed sandbanks, where the grass is cropped short thanks to the grazing lechwe. May witnesses the biggest pratincole colonies, which first appear as the Boro River begins to rise. Before that, while the sandbanks are exposed, you'll sometimes find African skimmers around. Old favourites include saddle-billed storks, knob-billed ducks, night herons, long-toed lapwings and spurwing geese. Look out, too, for the relatively uncommon lesser jacana among the more common African jacanas, and the rufous-bellied heron. With luck, you might even spot the rare blue-grey flycatcher.

In the area's drier grasslands black-bellied korhaans are highly visible, with their eye-catching courtship displays. The wild sage areas here are often burned and, immediately after this, wattled cranes arrive in numbers to dig up snails and other creatures that are exposed by fires.

Raptors which are frequently seen include various vultures, bateleur, fish and tawny eagles, both the black-chested and brown snake eagles, and the occasional martial eagle. The opportunist yellow-billed kites and steppe eagles usually start arriving for the summer in late August, and while the smaller raptors are more scarce, black-shouldered kites are often spotted (and easily recognised because they hover in mid-flight). Trees on the islands also shelter both eagle owls and the occasional Pel's fishing owl, its tawny plumage unmistakable against the dark foliage.

WHEN TO VISIT These areas on the edge of the Delta have more seasonal variation than areas further north, so the game really is significantly better later in the dry season than earlier. As with anywhere in the Delta, the wetter times of the year are better for birdwatching.

Geography note Be aware that the western side of the Delta (from the Thaoge into Lake Ngami) has been drying up since the middle of the last century. As a result of this (or vice versa) an increasing amount of Okavango's water is finding its way into the Muanachira/Khwai system, on the eastern side of Chief's Island.

Thus the floodplains of the west are gradually drying out and being invaded by flora used to drier conditions, while the drier areas of the Khwai River, and areas like Sandibe, are gradually becoming wetter.

GETTING THERE AND AWAY Access to all the camps is by light aircraft, using Pom Pom airstrip in a neighbouring concession, followed by a 45-minute transfer to Xaranna, or about 1½ hours to Xudum (times vary according to seasonal rainfall when the transfer may require driving instead of boating). Road transfers from the airstrip to the riding camps is possible only between about June and September; the alternatives are a helicopter transfer, or a 4-hour road/boat trip from Maun. Guests must have a prior reservation. No self-driving visitors are allowed into these areas, though in case of emergency, it's sometimes possible to access the camps by road – a dusty, bumpy 6 hours from Maun.

TRADITIONAL SAFARI CAMPS Following many years when the camps in this concession were caught in some form of legal limbo, two new lodges were opened in 2008 by &Beyond (page 223). Both are located in the south of the concession, so share a similar area in terms of wildlife and activities, and both have a similar commitment to high standards. Their high ratio of staff to guests allows considerably greater flexibility in choice of activities than is often the case. Rates are identical, so the choice for the visitor comes down more to one of style than substance.

🏠 **Xaranna Okavango Delta Camp** [map 347] (9 tented chalets) Spread out among mature jackalberry & sycamore fig trees, Xaranna Camp faces east across a seasonal lagoon & occupies a super birding spot. It can offer mokoro trips from camp throughout the year, as well as fishing, bush walks & game drives, with trips by motorboat an added option in the winter months, usually Apr–Sep. There's considerable emphasis on flexibility, which is a big bonus for guests.

Themed using light wood offset by green & white fabrics, with splashes of pink, the camp has the strong imprint of a designer at work. The wide, open-fronted central area, under green canvas raised on heavy poles, is divided neatly into sections at different levels. At one end is a circular boma-style area & firepit, while at the other is a comfortable lounge, with comfortable chairs & sofas, all in the hallmark green & white; there's even a green-covered Scrabble set! A good library of brown-paper-wrapped books contrasts with other volumes bound in pink & green, & monochrome photos are used to dramatic effect both on walls or under glass as tables or counters. In the centre is a round long table, while more comfortable chairs around the outside invite guests to relax with a drink. The theme continues on to the deck, & even on to the jetty where a family of white-painted hippos is in residence. A curio shop offers a range of items, from the lodge's own sarongs to beaded jewellery, baskets, candles & a few field guides, as well as clothing essentials

& even binoculars. There's a guest computer & Wi-Fi in the main area.

To each side of the main building lie spacious tented chalets, with gauze panels & coloured blinds. From the private bar at the entrance to the private pool at the back, it's clear that these are far removed from the standard safari tent. In the middle is a good-sized bedroom, its twin beds (or a king-size) under walk-in mosi nets affording a view across the channel. To one side, sharing the view, the bathroom features twin basins, a separate toilet, a free-standing bath, & showers inside & out. A narrow deck runs around the front, linking a sheltered circular day bed to the pool. It's clear that plenty of thought has gone into kitting out these rooms. As well as AC, there are fans on each side of the bed, attached to the bedposts. Camp-style hanging wardrobes contain everything from toiletries to a hairdryer & torch, & for those in need of activity, each room has its own 'gym in a basket', offering the potential for a workout after all those game drives. There's even a couch in the bathroom, with stylish sarongs as well as bathrobes & slippers, & it's possible to arrange in-room massages. Access to the rooms is by sliding doors front & back, with consequent problems of retaining heat in winter. An inverter system means that lights & fans operate at night, while a generator powers appliance (including AC) during the day.

For those who put style & service high on their agenda, this – & its sister camp, Xudum – should

13

be serious contenders. *From US$885 pp sharing Jan–Mar to U$1,820 Jun–Oct, inc FB, local drinks, safari activities, laundry. 50% sgl supp't. Children 6–12 join activities at manager's discretion.* ⊕ *All year.* ★★★★–★★★★★

🏠 **Xudum Okavango Delta Lodge** [map 347] (9 suites) Built a short distance from the older camp of the same name, Xudum is on a long, thin, wooded island towards the middle of the NG29 concession. Situated just ½hr by boat from Xaranna, or 1½hrs by road, the camp also has its own airstrip.

First impressions are monochrome & deceptively low-key. Off-white plastic chairs are drawn up to functional tables; filled tyres hanging from the roof & stacked beer cans make handy occasional tables. But make no mistake: the style guru at Xaranna is behind the set-up here, too. Flat roofs & square areas of thatch combine to create less a sense of continuity than one of unstudied homeliness. The open-plan kitchen adds a surprisingly homely touch, too, with many guests enjoying the chance to get involved. Comfy charcoal-coloured sofas, oversized black-&-white photos & individual tables for dining make this a place to relax. A curio shop holds a similar stock to that at Xaranna.

Xudum's suites are spacious & stylish, with AC, fans & good lighting. Constructed of wood with sliding meshed doors, each has a thatched upstairs sala to catch the breeze (& wonderful for alfresco nights), extensive ground-level decking with a 2nd, circular day bed tucked in the shade & a plunge pool with adjacent outside shower, all overlooking the plains. Inside, dark-wood panelling offset by brown textured blinds & mosquito nets around the king-size or twin beds lend something of the air of a 5-star hotel, with wide steps leading down to a grand bathroom, where a free-standing bath takes centre stage. (There's also a huge open-plan shower, & a separate toilet.) Mostly it avoids being ostentatious, though the dbl-length basin is a design idea too far. Individual touches include sarongs, a personal 'gym', & a cocktail shaker for the minibar, & in-room massage is available. The chalets, reached along sandy paths through the bush, are generally well spread out, 3 to one side, 6 to the other. That said, some have been built closer together, making them ideal for friends or families. For absolute privacy, choose numbers 1 or 9, out on the end.

Day & night drives & mokoro trips are on offer throughout the year, with boat cruises & walking safaris in winter only, when the grass is low & the water levels up. Catch-&-release fishing is possible Apr–Dec. The flexibility at Xaranna extends to this lodge, too, with early-afternoon activities available if requested, in addition to those during the morning & late afternoon. *Rates & children as for Xaranna, page 387.* ★★★★–★★★★★

RIDING SAFARIS Contact Okavango Horse Safaris (OHS), page 227. Provided that you are a competent rider, seeing the Okavango from horseback can be totally magical. From the point of view of most of the wildlife in the Delta, once you step into the saddle you become part of a four-legged herbivore (albeit a strangely shaped one). Thus generally they relax around you, so you can ride with herds of antelope without disturbing them, and see the environment from a kudu's-eye view. The palm islands, grassy floodplains, mopane forests and clear streams all ensure that the ground beneath you is always changing. Your horse will wade from island to island, where the going is normally quite good and firm along the edges – allowing the rider to move on at a trot and canter.

Having said all this, just as the herbivores perceive you as an antelope, so will the predators. Hence the emphasis on safety that a horseriding operation must have in this environment: it's not unusual to have to gallop to safety from a pride of lion – usually with the guide at the rear, gun in hand.

Perhaps unlike most of the other camps in this book (except African Horseback Safaris, pages 372–4), the precise details of Okavango Horse Safaris' camps are really much less important than the arrangements made for the riding activities. Thus here I'll cover briefly the basics of these safaris, before mentioning the camps and costs.

The horses OHS advises that they use full and part thoroughbred, Pure Arab, Anglo Arab, Friesian cross and Botswana Warm Bloods (American Saddle bred cross African Boerperd) horses. All are between 14 and 17 hands high, well schooled and responsive, and have fairly even temperaments.

Tack and clothes The tack used is English style as well as South African Trail saddles, and each saddle has a seat saver for comfort. Tack is of high quality and kept in good condition. An assortment of saddles is used, including well-known makes such as Albion, Ideals and Symonds. All horses go in snaffle bridles.

OHS produces specific 'clothes lists' for their trips, but they can do laundry in their camp. Like all operations, the air transfers dictate that you stick to a strict weight limit (excess can be left in Maun). Note that proper riding clothes, and clothes of bush colours, are important here. A limited assortment of half chaps and riding gloves is kept in the camp for guests' use, but it is strongly recommended that riders bring and wear their own hats.

Information about you To book a place on one of their trips, OHS will ask you for your age, weight, height and riding experience – as well as the more usual questions of your preference in drinks, specialised dietary requirements, allergies, etc. They'll also require you to fill out an indemnity form in camp before beginning your trip, a practice which is now widespread in camps throughout southern Africa.

Riding ability You must be able to ride well. This isn't a place to learn to ride, or to come if you feel at all nervous on a horse. This means being able to 'post to the trot' for 10 minutes at a time, being comfortable at all paces, and being able to gallop out of trouble. It is a great advantage if you are fit and a proficient rider. A separate programme can be organised for non-riding partners, on request, focusing on game drives, walks and mokoro trips.

Weight limit The maximum weight for any rider is 14½ stone (200lb or 90kg), and OHS insist that potential riders may be required to step on a pair of scales!

About the trips Having established that you can cope with the rigours of a riding safari, you have a choice between five-day, seven-day and ten-day safaris, which include rides between some or all of OHS's camps detailed on page 390. Two–four-night breaks are also available on request. The longer trips are normally scheduled in advance on set dates throughout the year. While this does lack flexibility, it means that you are with a group of people and can get to know each other. Generally, the best time to go is in the latter half of the dry season, between August and October.

On all trips there's a demonstration and talk at the beginning of the safari on how to handle big-game situations, as well as a familiarisation session with the tack. After that, expect to spend between 4 and 6 hours in the saddle each day, broken by refreshment stops. Typically this means that you'll have some picnic breakfasts and lunches, and also 10-minute walks every couple of hours spent in the saddle. (This acts to rest the rider by giving him/her the chance to use different muscles, and it also helps to relieve the horse from the constant pressure of a rider's weight.)

Although the focus here is firmly on horseriding, alternative activities are often possible during afternoons which are not 'day rides'. These can include game drives, birdwatching walks, mokoro rides and night drives.

Safety Riding in big-game country can be difficult, especially when a horse looks very much like an antelope to a hungry lion. Thus safety is a big issue; it's at the root of why this isn't a place for inexperienced riders. An extremely experienced guide accompanies every ride, and they do carry a .375 rifle in case of emergency.

These riding itineraries take a maximum of eight riders at once (again, for safety reasons). They will accept children, though these must be strong, competent riders (a Pony Club test pass is insisted upon). The cost for a child is the same as for an adult.

🏠 The riding camps

These aim to be comfortable and simple, and all are staffed. Three meals a day are prepared, with vehicle-supported picnic lunches and bush breakfasts. As with most camps, they emphasise fairly healthy food with fresh vegetables and salads, and bake fresh bread each day. Dinner is often a three-course affair, usually served by candlelight at a dining table beside the campfire. Lighting and power for charging of cameras is supplied by a solar system and there is even Wi-Fi at the main Kujwana Camp.

The camps are spread out over a considerable distance, with Kujwana – the company's base, where the horses are stabled – in the centre and the other permanent camp, Mokolwane, almost 20km to the southeast. All of which goes to emphasise what a large amount of ground these horseriding safaris can cover.

🏠 **Kujwana Camp** [map 347] (6 tents)
Kujwana is the company's base, & this is where the horses are stabled. It is situated on the Xudum River, on a hippo-shaped island of mature trees about 8.5km southeast of Xudum lodge.

At the heart of the camp, overlooking the river, is a raised treehouse complete with a bar & separate dining area. Lined up on one side of this main area are Meru-style tents, each on a raised deck with a shaded veranda & twin or dbl beds, a flush toilet & hot-water shower en suite. There are also 2 more spacious, riverside suites: The Hippo Cradle & The Rocking Horse. Laundry is done every day except when the camp is on the move. The camp has 220V solar power & also Wi-Fi, so it's possible to recharge camera batteries & keep in touch with the outside world! ★★★★–★★★★★★

🏠 **Mokolwane Camp** [map 346] (5 tents)
Mokolwane is the most northern of the OHS camps, barely 5km southwest of Pom Pom in the adjoining NG27A reserve. It is situated among mature trees on a small island, facing east across open plains & a tributary of the Matsebi River. In winter, when the river is full, access is by water only.

While the camp is in part a satellite of Kujwana, this is no longer its sole focus & it is included in all the 5-, 7- or 10-night set-departure itineraries. As well

as riding, guests can choose from mokoro trips, game drives & walking. Central to the camp is an open-sided green canvas-roofed dining area, built on 2m stilts beneath a mature African ebony overlooking the plain, & with drop-down sides to keep out the worst of the elements. A levelled-off termite mound under a neighbouring sycamore fig forms a convenient bar area. Sharing the view, & the height, are canvas 'treehouses', spaced out on either side along sand paths. Their sides are of half-height canvas, with drop-down clear plastic screens for extra protection. Each is accessed by wooden steps, & has twin beds (or there's 1 dbl) under mosquito nets, & an en-suite bathroom at the back that's open to the skies, with flush toilet, basin & shower; water is heated by a gas geyser. ★★★★–★★★★★★

🛆 **Fly-camp** [map 347] (6 tents) To the more remote southeast side of the reserve the fly-camp's exact location varies depending on the location of the game. Accommodation is on single stretcher beds supplied with bedrolls, cotton sheets & duvets, & surrounded by mosquito nets. The bathroom facilities include a long-drop toilet, wash stand & a bucket shower (that's the type where the bucket is filled with hot water & raised on a pulley for you by the camp staff!). ★★★★–★★★★★

The costs Unusually for Botswana, but in common with the other riding camps, prices here are quoted in pounds sterling rather than US dollars. From December to March, riding trips cost £570 per person sharing per night, including full board, drinks, guiding, riding, game drives, walks and mokoro trips, and a concession fee of US$14 per person per night. From April to mid-July and during November, the cost is £660 per person sharing per night, rising to £750 between mid-July and the end of October. Visitors who want single accommodation should add 50% to these costs, though this is usually waived if you're prepared to share a tent with another visitor. Guests staying at Kujwana can upgrade to either The Hippo Cradle or The Rocking Horse riverside suites for £70 per person per night.

The flight between Maun and the camps costs £200 per person return, or for £260 take a 25-minute scenic helicopter flight from Maun and land directly on the camp island. In addition, a bed levy of £5 per person is charged at Mokolwane towards a fund to enable children of some of the staff to attend university.

CHITABE AND SANDIBE (NG31)

NG31 Reserve covers a relatively small 360km² of the eastern Okavango Delta. However, it's a superb location which looks on a map like a bite out of the southern side of Moremi Game Reserve – between Chief's Island and the Mopane Tongue. Sandibe and Chitabe share this reserve, though generally keep to their own sides of it. Sandibe has about 160km² on the northern side, and Chitabe (with the adjacent Chitabe Lediba) occupies the southern 200km². The two camps are relatively close, about 12km apart, and they share an airstrip.

The reserve is particularly interesting as it's experiencing a period of change. The Gomoti River, which forms the northern and eastern border of the reserve, was dry from about 1984, but began to flow again in 1999, spilling on to the seasonal floodplains and dramatically increasing the amount of water in this area. Previously only about 5% of Sandibe's area had water on it; now it's closer to 50% permanent water. Around Chitabe, however, only around 10% of the area is permanently flooded, with a further 56% flooding seasonally; the rest is dry throughout the year.

FLORA AND FAUNA HIGHLIGHTS NG31 is a varied reserve: there are quite marked differences between the northern sides (east and west) and also between these two and Chitabe's area further south, even if the list of species which occur in both are broadly the same. There is a complex mix of environments in this reserve; what follows here is very much a simplification.

The most striking difference is that the northwest of the reserve is a wetter environment than the rest. Just north of this reserve, in Moremi, the Mboroga River flows south between the dry-land areas of Chief's Island and the Mopane Tongue. Forming a number of large lagoons, it splits into two channels. One branch, the Gomoti River, then forms part of this reserve's northern boundary, and all of its eastern side. The other branch, the Santantadibe River, is a deep, wide channel that leads to lots of lagoons and runs down this reserve's southwestern side.

Flora Sandibe overlooks the permanent Santantadibe River from within this watery area, in the reserve's northwestern corner. Around it there are plenty of open-water areas and floodplains, fringed by belts of riverine vegetation with a high proportion of real fan palms (*Hyphaene petersiana*). The islands here can be large, and on the largest you will find occasional baobab trees growing – an indication that they've been dry islands for a long time.

The northeastern side of the reserve, around the location of the airstrip, is a spit of dry land where the habitats seem to occur in belts. There are belts of thick mopane forest interspersed with belts of dry 'acacia thornveld', where you'll find mixed stands of camelthorn trees (*Vachellia erioloba*), umbrella thorns (*Vachellia tortillis*) and the very similar, but thornless, sickle bush (*Dichrostachys cinerea africana*); also buffalo thorn (*Ziziphus mucronata*), with its two types of thorn, which snag on any passing animal (and on clothing) and have earned it the Afrikaans name *wag-'n-bietjie*, meaning 'wait-a-bit'.

There are also bands of lower, more 'scrubby' vegetation, including classic species of deep Kalahari sand like the silver cluster-leaf (*Terminalia sericea*), and some very striking areas forested with large numbers of dead leadwood trees (*Combretum imberbe*). These trees, with their hard, termite-resistant, wood were killed by flooding when the water levels in the area changed – but will probably stand for many years, looking from the air like a river of dead trees.

Moving to the south side of the reserve, nearer to where Chitabe stands, you will find a lot of mixed forest areas with classic riverine species of trees like the large feverberry (*Croton megalobotrys*), sausage tree (*Kigelia africana*) and jackalberry (*Diospyros mespiliformis*).

Around here there are some smaller islands surrounded by shallow floodplains covered with hippo grass (*Vossia cuspida*). The deeper channels are mostly lined by phragmites reeds (*Phragmites australis*) and miscanthus grass (*Miscanthus junceus*). These are permanent channels which don't dry up, and seem to have relatively little seasonal variation; they simply spread out on to wider floodplains when the flood finally arrives (around May or June usually).

At the southern end of the reserve is a belt of soil with a high clay content, providing the perfect substrate for large stands of mopane trees (*Colophospermum mopane*), which sometimes seem so uniform that it almost appears to be a monoculture.

Fauna This reserve has a wide range of game species, dominated by impala, tsessebe, kudu and, on the floodplains, red lechwe. Zebra are fairly numerous, blue wildebeest less so, and giraffe are very common in the bands of acacia thornveld (35 were observed together at one point on the airstrip). Reedbuck, duiker and steenbok are often seen, while eland and roan are found only rarely (usually towards the south of the reserve); sable seem to be totally absent.

The sightings of buffalo and elephants here seem to follow the same broad patterns. Throughout the year there are small resident herds of both around, plus odd old bulls and small bachelor groups. However, from around June to October large breeding herds pass through. Then buffalo herds can number well over a thousand, and herds of a hundred elephants are not unknown.

The key to understanding this is to realise that when there has been rainfall, usually starting around November–December, the big herds move into the large swathes of mopane forest between the Okavango and the Kwando–Linyanti river system; that is, into the interior forests of Kwando (NG14), Linyanti (NG15), Selinda (NG16), Khwai Community (NG18) and Kwara (NG20). While there, their water needs are sustained by the seasonal clay pans which hold water. However, when these pans start to dry up, around May or June, they move back to the areas of permanent water, including this reserve.

The reserve has plenty of lion and recently they seem to have concentrated mainly on hunting buffalo.

Leopard are common here, with the mixed woodlands and floodplains being an ideal habitat for them. I've had one of my best leopard sightings in Botswana near Chitabe, and on my last trip I saw an astonishing seven leopards including three cubs in 12 hours during a stay at Sandibe. Hence I tend to regard this as one of the country's best concessions for leopard.

Cheetah stay here throughout the year, and are most frequently seen in the drier, more open eastern side of the reserve. Their populations are perhaps helped by relatively low numbers of spotted hyena.

The reserve seems to have made a name for itself for wild dog. This may partially be due to the involvement in the reserve's management of Dave Hamman, who took many of the photographs for the book *Running Wild* (see *Appendix 3,* page 544), about the 'Mombo' pack of wild dogs in Moremi.

There certainly is a healthy population of dogs here, including what is reputed to be the biggest pack in the Delta with 30-odd individuals in late 2017. They seem to like the marginal floodplains, and will flush the antelopes through plains and islands to catch them. A few years ago there were three dens in the concession, though these are usually moved from one year to the next ... so the situation is relatively unpredictable from year to year. Having said this, I'd probably choose a more open and less wooded area than Chitabe if I were specifically hoping to track down some wild dogs.

Finally, on a more unusual note, this reserve seems to have had an unusually high incidence of pangolin sightings. Many of these sightings have been on full-moon night drives, when the pangolin has been seen foraging around in the open. Aardvarks and aardwolves are also sometimes seen here at night. Perhaps this, and the pangolin sightings, is really a reflection of the camps' enthusiasm for (or at least willingness to organise) serious late-night game drives, rather than a higher density of these animals in this area per se.

Birdlife A recent survey counted 386 species in this immediate area. In general, Sandibe is the better location for waterbirds, although this is by no means exclusive. Along with many more common species, Okavango 'specials' like the Pel's fishing owl, wattled crane, slaty egret (thought to be the world's rarest heron), black coucal and black egret have been recorded.

Chitabe has a wider variation of dry-country birds, with its most common raptor being the bateleur eagle, though there are also good numbers of many other eagles including martial, brown snake, black snake, tawny and western banded snake eagles. Marsh harriers are found in the wetter areas, along with the inevitable fish eagles and even the uncommon migrant European marsh harriers. Look out for bat hawks in the late evening. Less spectacular, though almost equally uncommon, brown firefinches can certainly be found here.

WHEN TO VISIT As with the rest of the Okavango, the big game here is more diverse and prolific during the dry season, although the birdlife is generally better between December and March. That said, NG31 is in the heart of the Okavango where the water is for the most part permanent, and so these differences aren't as great here as you'll find in some of the more outlying, western areas of the Delta.

GETTING THERE AND AWAY All visitors to these camps pre-book their time and fly to the camps. NG31's main airstrip (✪ CHITAA 19°27.952'S, 23°22.443'E) is about 7km north of Chitabe and 8km east of Sandibe. This is barely 60km from Maun, making it one of the closest of the Delta's airstrips for camps. However, this doesn't usually affect the price of a trip. Wilderness Safaris, for example, usually charge a set rate for a package including time at its camps and flights to/from them. This price doesn't vary with the position of the camp within the Delta.

WHERE TO STAY There are just three choices, all very good, if very different. Chitabe and Chitabe Lediba are run by Wilderness Safaris (page 225), as part of a joint venture with Flamingo Investments which has resulted in a very loyal staff: many have been at these two camps for ten years or more. Sandibe is run by &Beyond (page 223).

Unusually for the Delta, both Sandibe and Chitabe Lediba welcome children. At Sandibe they're even given a workbook to keep them busy while teaching them about the area, and the camp staff are adept at ensuring that they don't disrupt the activities or ambience for the other guests. At Chitabe Lediba there are currently two family tents consisting of two twin-bedded en-suite rooms; in one of these the rooms are linked by an internal hallway, making it well suited for families with younger children. That said, Chitabe Lediba limits children to those aged six or over, unless the whole camp is taken over, and those travelling with under 12s must book a private vehicle.

✳ 🏠 Sandibe Okavango Safari

Lodge [map 347] (12 suites) Set in a band of thick riverine vegetation facing the Santantadibe River, Sandibe originally opened in 1998, but was rebuilt in 2014. Gone are the permanent concrete buildings, to be replaced by unique wooden structures on elevated decks – with inspiration for the curving roofs drawn from pangolins & weaverbird nests. In the rebuild, &Beyond created a luxurious, more sustainable & environmentally more efficient camp.

The main lodge resembles the upturned hull of an enormous ship. Beneath are an indoor & outdoor dining area, as well as the lounge & bar. The décor here is minimalist with plenty of white-washed wood & a muted sandy pallet enlivened by stylish highlights such as the suspended copper mokoro. From the bar a raised deck extends out toward the river, offering a serene spot for a sundowner. As at its sister camp, Nxabega, Sandibe has a well-stocked wine cellar, which is also used for private dinners. (Although good-quality house wine is included as part of your stay, the vintage wines & more esoteric, imported spirits cost extra.) There is also a small but interesting curio shop.

Sandy paths connect the central area with the large suites, which are set on sizeable wooden decks raised up on stilts. Each is clad in the same wooden tiles as the main building to create a modern, almost spherical cabin amid the trees. Inside, as in the main area, wood dominates the design of the open-plan room, complete with a cosy lounge & fireplace for the winter months. Past the dbl or twin beds enclosed in a large mosquito net are the bathroom & a walk-in dressing room, divided by an island with hanging mirrors & copper basins. A rare use of concrete at Sandibe creates a tube with a skylight at the top, forming an indoor shower, & there is also a spacious outdoor shower. Outside, a big private deck is split over 2 levels: one with a large outside sofa & the lower one with a circular plunge pool & day bed. The unique design of Sandibe coupled with elegant interior features & great game makes this an excellent choice for those looking for luxury on safari. *From US$1,140/1,710 pp sharing/sgl Jan–Mar, to US$2,350/3,525 Jun–Oct, inc FB, drinks, laundry, all activities.* ⊕ *All year.* ★★★★★

🏠 **Chitabe Camp** [map 347] (8 tents) Chitabe is set facing southwest across a channel on an old, established tree-island. It first opened in 1997, but since then has been considerably revamped, taking the camp more upmarket. In accordance with Wilderness's current policy, the entire site has step-free access throughout.

The whole camp is raised up on wooden decking under typical tall, shard trees of riverine forests, including jackalberries (*Diospyros mespiliformis*), knobthorns (*Senegalia nigrescens*) & sausage trees (*Kigelia africana*). High 2m walkways lead between the tents, the lounge & the dining areas that form the centre of the camp. Here you'll find a large central area with a bar on one side, under thatch, & a separate dining area. Scattered around the open areas of decking are tables & chairs, & a walkway leads from here down to a largish plunge pool (about 8m x 3m).

Chalets at this old favourite were completely rebuilt & enlarged in 2009. Gone are the traditional if appealing old tents, to emerge as a fully fledged luxury camp under canvas. In the words of the architect, the effect is 'overstated camping'. The designers have gone minimalist, but have taken great pains to iron out the little annoyances of many upmarket safari tents. Thus, glazed sliding doors with mesh sides lead indoors, where there are opening windows as well as gauzed panels, to maximise the flow of air. Mosquito nets run right round bedside tables & lamps as well as the twin or king-size beds & in a unique piece of design the bathroom (with twin basins, a dbl wardrobe & separate loo) can be separated from the bedroom by doors that are cleverly designed to slide into the bedhead. A 2nd, outdoor shower, enables you to watch the stars as you refresh. The tents are lined with a sand-coloured canvas that sets the tone for the neutral décor. Interior design & furnishing are similar throughout but each room has its own colour theme. *From US$985/1,290 pp sharing/ sgl mid-Jan–Mar to US$1,690/2,200 Jun–Oct, inc FB, most drinks, activities, park fees, laundry; exc transfers.* ☼ *All year.* ★★★★–★★★★★

※ 🏠 **Chitabe Lediba** [map 347] (5 tents) This smaller version of Chitabe Camp, formerly Chitabe Trails, lies just a few hundred metres away, on the other side of the same island. While the central area is very similar in design & style to that at Chitabe, with a pool & curio shop, here the tents are built on low platforms, & they're linked by lower walkways. Each tent has a solid door leading from the deck into the bedroom, where twin beds, or a dbl, are surrounded by mosquito netting under a fan, & there's a table & wicker chairs. The en-suite bathroom is part of the tent, with a shower cubicle, washbasin & flush toilet; there's also a (much nicer) outdoor shower off the deck. Ideal for families, couples or friends travelling together are 2 units in which 2 twin-bedded en-suite rooms are linked by a shared deck or hallway.

Chitabe Lediba's tents were upgraded in 2010 to match those of Chitabe Camp, but this remains a very relaxed, if now smart, camp. This is one of my favourite camps in the Delta; I often prefer the Delta's smaller, more intimate camps & the experience that I had here on my last visit was magical. *Rates as Chitabe Camp, see opposite.* ☼ *All year.* ★★★★–★★★★★

ACTIVITIES The camps differ little in their activities. All three are essentially dryland camps, which concentrate on day and evening game drives, plus – during the dry season, when the grass is low – occasional guided walks.

STANLEY'S, BAINES', GOMOTI PLAINS, QOROKWE AND BUDGET MOKORO TRIPS (NG32)

This 'multi-purpose area', covering over 1,500km², is controlled by the local communities – and perhaps because of this operations continue to change and evolve more than they do in most of the Okavango's private areas. The reserve is now split for operational purposes into three zones. The western side is home to two permanent sister camps, Stanley's Camp and Baines' Camp, which have been operating for many years, and which share the area with the Grey Matters elephant project. Further east, and close to the Santantadibe and Gomoti rivers, is the location of two new camps opened in 2017. Of these, Qorokwe, south of NG31, is close to the Santantadibe River and has a 9km stretch of Gomoti waterfront, while in the neighbouring zone, which incorporates Gomoti Plains, this river frontage is around 3km. An entirely separate area of this large zone is also used for budget mokoro trips by operators from Maun. Because these are such distinct operations, I've described them separately.

FLORA AND FAUNA HIGHLIGHTS

Flora NG32 is the concession on the other side of the buffalo fence from the relatively populated areas around Maun. It's at the southern end of the Delta, relying on the Boro and Santantadibe rivers for flooding – and last in line to receive the water. In a dry year, the floods can be very low and patchy.

This means that there are relatively few short-grass plains that are regularly flooded, but significant patches of floodplains that are only intermittently wet. These provide an ideal base for a profusion of the invasive wild sage (*Pechuel-*

The Okavango Delta – Private Reserves around Moremi STANLEY'S, BAINES', GOMOTI PLAINS, QOROKWE AND BUDGET MOKORO TRIPS (NG32)

13

loeschea leubnitziae), which covers large open areas with its aromatic grey-green foliage. Where they've had slightly longer to become established, you'll find the distinctive rounded outlines of candle pod acacia bushes (*Vachellia hebeclada*) starting to appear in these areas – as one of the first shrubs to move in it usually indicates that an area has been dry for many years. In some of these open areas where the recent floods haven't reached, you'll find a profusion of termite mounds.

Aside from this, driving around NG32 near Stanley's the vegetation seems to occur in strips, including linear expanses of riverine forest where the major tree species are leadwoods (*Combretum imberbe*), jackalberries (*Diospyros mespiliformis*), marula (*Sclerocarya birrea*) and sausage trees (*Kigelia africana*). There are relatively few areas of deep, deep sand here and not that many acacia glades, but there are some quite dense – and very attractive – concentrations of real fan palms (*Hyphaene petersiana*).

When visiting with a mokoro poler, you'll see a very different side to the area. Unless the flood has been very high, you'll probably be poling within the vicinity of the Boro or the Santantadibe. This is at the very shallowest end of the Delta, so expect large areas of miscanthus grass (*Miscanthus junceus*) and common reeds (*Phragmites australis*), plus the occasional floodplains of hippo grass (*Vossia cuspidata*). In the east of the concession, around Qorokwe and Gomoti Plains, poling is on the tributaries of the more open Gomoti and Santantadibe rivers, where vegetation is far more varied.

If you do pole up the Boro, then you'll find the environment generally gets more interesting as you continue. After a few days, you'll leave behind some of the more boring stretches of reeds, and start finding wider floodplains around you, and more lagoons. Wherever you pole, the islands on which you stop will often be classic little palm islands fringed with palms and the riverine forest.

Fauna The game densities generally get better as you head further northeast in the area, around Qorokwe and Gomoti plains, both of which are close to the Gomoti River. Certainly, the game around Stanley's and Baines' is generally quite sparse, with the exception of elephant.

Impala are probably the commonest antelope, with tsessebe a close second and red lechwe certainly dominating any areas which are flooded. Kudu, giraffe, zebra, reedbuck, warthog and occasionally wildebeest are all found here; sable, roan and waterbuck are not. Elephant and buffalo occur singly during the wetter parts of the year, and pass through in larger herds as the dry season reaches its end.

When the flood is at its height, there may be the occasional sitatunga around, but apart from a few places on the rivers, there aren't enough papyrus reedbeds to support them.

Lion are around in good numbers, and while leopard occur, they're not frequently spotted. Wild dog pass though, and sightings of them seem to increase between about October and December. However, the open wide plains where you could follow them are limited in the concession.

Cheetah are certainly around and often seen in the drier areas – on one drive here during a fairly brief visit one of this book's contributors spent a magical 25 minutes with a male cheetah as he strolled from termite mound to termite mound searching for the perfect vantage point.

In 2017, both black and white rhino were relocated into this vast concession from South Africa – and in October that year one of our contributors saw three rhino during a short two-night stay: a magical outcome given how recently Botswana had no rhino at all.

Birdlife NG32 is a classic edge-of-the-Delta reserve that has a good mix of dry-country and shallow-water bird species. The most common species include red-eyed, mourning and Cape turtle doves, which all greet the morning with a variety of gentle coos. Identify the last by their lyrical exhortations to 'work harder, work harder'.

Other birds frequently seen here include long-tailed shrikes, red-billed quelea, buffalo weavers, lilac-breasted rollers, blacksmith lapwings and long-tailed and glossy starlings. Crimson-breasted shrikes provide startling flashes of red; Meyer's parrots can often be seen as a flash of colour flying at speed.

In more open areas you'll find red-billed and Swainson's spurfowl, flocks of helmeted guinea fowl, kori bustards and occasional ostriches. Sandgrouse are common in acacia groves, as are yellow-billed hornbills, while their red-billed cousins prefer the reserve's mopane woodlands.

The floodplains support a varied cast of waders and waterbirds, including the occasional wattled cranes. This is a good reserve for raptors: bateleur (short-tailed) eagles, black-breasted and brown snake eagles are especially common, and Gabar goshawks are frequently seen.

WHEN TO VISIT Like most of the areas on the edge of the Delta, the game densities are better during the dry season than during the rains. So while from June to October is the best time to visit for game, the birdwatching is usually more interesting during the rains, from around December to March.

GETTING THERE AND AWAY For those staying at Stanley's and Baines' camps, access is by air to the nearby airstrip; you're not allowed to drive yourself.

WHERE TO STAY Of the four camps in this concession, two of them – Stanley's and Baines' – offer the opportunity for elephant interactions with Grey Matters (see box, page 399).

Baines' Camp [map 347] (5 rooms) Contact Sanctuary Retreats (page 224). Named after the Victorian painter Sir Thomas Baines, this rather funky camp in design terms was refurbished in late 2017. Linked by raised wooden walkways, the rooms are unusual in that their solid walls are built out of recycled drink cans, wire mesh & hessian, & covered in plastic; why? – it also contains elephant dung! And so that guests can see how it's constructed, a section of wall in the main area is left with just cans & wire mesh. Distressed frames surround old pictures on the walls, lampshades are of ostrich eggshell, & there's an easel in each room where guests can paint. Rather more contemporary are 'star beds', which are set four-poster style under mosquito nets, & can be rolled out on to the decking under the stars. For activities, see pages 398–9. *From US$750 pp 7 Jan–Mar & Nov–20 Dec to US$1,605/2,408 Jul–Aug & 21 Dec–6 Jan; see Stanley's (page 398) for details.* ☺ All year. ★★★★–★★★★★★

Qorokwe Camp [map 347] (9 tented suites) Contact Wilderness Safaris, page 225. Opened in Dec 2017, this new feather in the Wilderness Safaris cap is a 'classic camp', putting it in line with the likes of DumaTau (pages 298–9), Chitabe Camp (pages 394–5) and Little Vumbura Camp (pages 362–3). Built out of timber, canvas & steel, Qorokwe overlooks a lagoon, with both the suites & the main area raised on platforms 2m or so off the ground to afford views over this & the surrounding bush. Each suite has a bedroom, good-sized lounge (with a furnished deck) & an en-suite bathroom, with indoor & outdoor showers, & even a bath for cold wintry nights; a family suite also has its own plunge pool. Activities focus predominantly on both day & night game drives in open-sided game vehicles, with each guest guaranteed a 'window' seat, but nature walks, & mokoro & boat trips, will also be offered, depending on water levels. *From US$846/1,097 pp sharing/sgl 11 Jan–Mar to US$1,830/2,379 Jun–*

Oct, inc FB, local drinks, activities, park fees, laundry. ⏱ *All year.* ★★★★–★★★★★★

🏠 **Gomoti Plains** [map 347] (10 tented rooms, 1 villa) ☏ +27 82 579 5249; e enquiries@machabasafaris.com; http://machabasafaris.com/gomoti-plains. Opened in Apr 2017 under the same ownership as Machaba Camp in the Khwai area (page 320), Gomoti Plains overlooks a tributary of the Gomoti River & the floodplains beyond. It's a smart, light & airy camp, designed with solar power, low-energy appliances & sophisticated waste-disposal systems to minimise its impact on the environment.

The muted décor of beige, grey, mustard & green is underpinned by hardwood floors to create a modern feel, but it's all very relaxed & well thought out. Comfy sofas in the lounge, stylish dining tables, the narrow decking in front of camp & chairs around the campfire all share the view, as do a reasonable-sized pool & most of the tented rooms. The latter are fronted by a deck where you'll find a day bed & a couple of directors' chairs. A zipped door opens into a dbl or twin bedroom with its own sofa, good lighting, plenty of hanging space, & an en-suite bathroom with inside & outside showers & a separate toilet. For families or friends travelling together, there are 2 specially designed units of 2 tents sharing a bathroom & small lounge, & – new for 2018 – a private villa that will sleep 4 with its own chef & guide. Along with day & night game drives from camp, there are motorboat & mokoro excursions, guided walks & – back at camp – the option of a spa treatment (at extra cost) by a qualified therapist in the privacy of your own room. It all adds up to a well-designed camp in an area of very good game. *From US$615 pp 11 Jan–Mar to US$1,130/1,808 pp sharing/sgl Jun–Oct, inc FB, local drinks, activities, park fees, laundry.* ⏱ *All year.* ★★★–★★★★★★

🏠 **Stanley's Camp** [map 347] (8 safari tents) Contact Sanctuary Retreats (page 224). Originally built by a maverick local character, Alistair Rankin (the subject of a number of local bush myths – some involving mokoro trips, buffalo & uncomfortable nights spent in trees), Stanley's was completely rebuilt by Sanctuary Retreats at the turn of the century, & fully refurbished in late 2017.

The open-plan dining/lounge area sits under a large canvas tent (think of a 'big top' circus), on slightly raised wooden decking. Wildlife photos printed on oversize canvases stand out from the cream walls, with the odd woven basket or wooden carving. The sitting area takes centre stage with a couple of comfy sofas & a few leather chairs around a rather lovely, almost rustic coffee table. The 'library' is a slightly eccentric collection of novels, magazines & reference books. To the rear are the bar, & a small curio shop that also showcases baskets made by the staff. A short wooden walkway leads to a small pool with sunloungers, a couple of umbrellas & unobstructed views of the floodplains.

Dinner may be a social affair, with everybody eating together, but other meals are usually taken at individual tables. If you're staying for a few days you can request a picnic lunch, so that you can stay out in the bush all day. After dinner, there are often night drives, but otherwise guests usually retire for drinks & a chat to a small firepit in front of the big top.

The camp's tents, all raised on wooden platforms, are to one side of the main area, connected by paths through the bush. A covered deck extends from the front of each tent, with a comfy day bed & a hammock for that all-important midday siesta. Inside all is fairly cosy but comfortable, with smooth wooden floors, twin or dbl beds with electric lights mounted on the headboard, a desk with drawers & a chair, a couple of bedside tables & an old-style wooden wardrobe, & both ceiling & powerful floor-standing fans. Each tent has its own en-suite toilet & shower, complete with a wooden dresser with sink & mirror, & the usual complimentary toiletries. For activities, see below. *From US$550 pp 7 Jan–Mar & Nov–20 Dec to US$1,215/1,823 Jul–Aug & 21 Dec–6 Jan, inc FB, local drinks, activities, park fees, laundry; exc transfers & elephant trips with Grey Matters (extra US$264–466 pp per activity).* ⏱ *All year.* ★★★–★★★★★

ACTIVITIES AT STANLEY'S AND BAINES' CAMPS Activities at both camps usually revolve around 4x4 game drives and night drives, though it's normally possible to take mokoro trips for at least a few months a year – typically around June to September. The water's not consistently deep enough to run motorboat trips from Stanley's, but they are sometimes an option at Baines'.

GREY MATTERS

Doug Groves started out working with elephants in American zoos, including Washington Park Zoo and San Diego Wild Animal Park. Subsequently, in 1987, he came to Africa as the trainer of four elephants who were being returned from the US to South Africa for a film, *Circles in a Forest* – the first of many filming projects for him. As an aside, the main elephant involved in this was Abu, who went on to lead the herd at Abu Camp (NG26; see box, pages 370–1), the Okavango's only other operation that offers visitors time in the company of elephants which are not wild.

In 1994, Randall Moore and Ker & Downey went their separate ways – and almost simultaneously Ker & Downey invited Doug to Botswana, to set up and run an elephant-based tourism project. Now Grey Matters isn't linked to Ker & Downey, and instead works closely with both Stanley's and Baines' camps.

The project now has two female elephants, both orphans from culling programmes. The older of the two is **Thembi**, who was orphaned by a cull in the Kruger. Originally a very insecure calf, she's gradually become more confident. She is said to be smart and very social, and loves being the centre of attention.

The younger elephant, **Morula**, came to Doug in 1994 as a maladjusted 17 year old, lacking confidence and with a troubled background. Doug comments that she started off being exceedingly submissive to him and the other elephants, but then vented her frustrations on trees. He adds that she's gradually become more secure and relaxed here.

Grey Matters is also the base for Living With Elephants (686 3198; e info@ withelephants.org; www.withelephants.org). This not-for-profit organisation was started by Doug and Sandi Groves in 1999, aiming to secure the future of their trio of elephants (Abu has since died), and to work through various projects towards a more harmonious relationship between Botswana's elephant and human populations.

Projects undertaken include their 'Outreach programme', whereby children from Maun and nearby villages spend two days at Grey Matters, interacting with the elephants and learning about them through hands-on experience and discussions.

Elephant activities (☉ *closed 15 Jan–15 Feb*) Aside from the standard game drives and water-based trips, many guests choose to pay the extra US$327–586 per person (depending on the season) to spend a morning with Doug and Sandi Groves and their elephants at Grey Matters (see box, above).

These activities normally consist of about 4 hours in the morning – a leisurely foraging walk with the camp's elephants, which allows you to get used to observing and interacting with them at close quarters. You'll be encouraged to touch and walk with the elephants as they forage – and to view them as individuals. Riding the elephants is not part of these trips. At the end there's usually a picnic lunch in the bush.

The maximum number of guests at any one time is ten. Do note that the elephants take 'annual leave' between 15 January and 15 February, so this activity is not possible then.

BUDGET MOKORO TRIPS NG32 is the end destination for virtually all of the one- to four-day mokoro trips offered from Maun, through the Okavango Kopano Mokoro

Community Trust (OKMCT). These must be booked through a private tour operator in Maun, who will organise a road transfer into the Delta; you cannot just turn up. For full details of how to choose a trip, and what to expect, see page 220.

These trips aren't really about game, although you may see some. Relax, take a bird book and a pair of binoculars, and enjoy the experience of being poled along the waterways, and seeing some of the birdlife, and water-life, close up. My first trip into the Delta was like this – and it was enchanting. Subsequently I've seen more interesting areas of the Delta, and infinitely better game, but it's still hard to beat the sheer joy that you'll get from floating around on a mokoro in such an amazing environment for the first time.

From my experience, mokoro trips are much more fun when the sun's shining and the sky is blue; grey skies and (even worse) rain do take the edge off it. Thus best avoid January and February if you have a choice – and ideally come between about April and the end of October.

See my comments on walking (pages 187–91) before you set off on foot with your poler in search of big game – as none of these trips is likely to be led by someone that I'd describe as a professional walking guide, and none of the polers carries any guns.

SANKUYO TSHWARAGANO MANAGEMENT TRUST (NG33 AND NG34)

NG34 covers an area of about 900km², an area with good game that encompasses part of the road between Moremi's South Gate and Maun. Thus, and very unusually for the region, it's a private concession through which you can drive yourself, albeit only on the main gravel road leading into and out of the area. The concession is now divided into five zones, each run by a different operator.

BACKGROUND INFORMATION NG34 is run for the benefit of the local community, through the Sankuyo Tshwaragano Management Trust – and it's a reserve which sees more frequent changes than most. Until about 2001 it was the location for Gomoti Camp; shortly after that closed, Starling's Camp was built here. Then that morphed into Moremi Tented Camp, which again was closed. Now a new lodge, Rra Dinare, has opened on the same site, with its partner – Mma Dinare – set to join it in 2018, and things are looking up. New camps are set to open in a second zone in 2019, further improving access to this area.

Meanwhile there's long been an intermittent presence here of animal researchers, many of whom seem to have subsequently written books. Naturalist and lion researcher Peter Katz was here for several years at a camp some 2km from Starling's. His book, *Prides*, was published in 2000, and more recently the three children staying with him and his partner wrote *The Lion Children* (see *Appendix 3*, page 545).

Before that, John 'Tico' McNutt began a wild-dog research unit here in 1989, co-authoring *Running Wild: Dispelling the Myths of the African Wild Dog* (see *Appendix 3*, page 544). The project has broadened and developed since then, and now – as the Botswana Predator Conservation Trust (*www.bpctrust.org*) – conducts research into leopard, lion, cheetah and spotted hyena, as well as wild dog.

FLORA AND FAUNA HIGHLIGHTS Ancient floodplain habitats dominate large tracts of land in the reserve, with mature acacia trees and fertile grasslands, while away from the floodplain, mopane woodland comes into its own. Most of the area around the Gomoti River, where the new Rra Dinare and Mma Dinare camps are based, is an attractive combination of big open floodplains with occasional islands.

Like much of the Delta around eastern Moremi, the flood patterns here do seem to have changed recently. When Tico McNutt first came in 1989, the Mogogelo River, near Santawani, still had water in it; since then this has dried up – and despite the high floods of 2009 it is still not flowing. Yet these indications are mixed. Observe the Gomoti River, which flows seasonally, and seems to have been flooding further and better during the last few years.

With something as complex as the changes in water flows and levels in the Delta, everyone has a slightly different opinion. Perhaps one of the most pertinent comments on this was, allegedly, from local wit Willy Philips, who commented that 'the only reliable water in the Okavango is the water in the toilets'.

Flora Although parts of NG34 feature quite thick, and relatively unproductive, mopane woodlands, the floodplains that spread out from the rivers, including the western side of the reserve adjoining the Gomoti River, are much more interesting.

Even driving on the main road south from South Gate to Maun you'll get a flavour of this, as you pass through some superb stretches of open acacia savannah – where you'll find very good populations of giraffe, if you're not speeding through too fast. The dominant species here is camelthorn (*Vachellia erioloba*), though you'll also find a few umbrella thorns (*Vachellia tortilis*) and some stately old leadwoods (*Combretum imberbe*) among them. It's classic mature Kalahari sandveld – and matches many people's image of Africa. These areas run like veins through the reserve, marking out the areas of deepest sand.

Around the Gomoti River, things are different. Here you'll find plenty of lovely areas of old riverine forest, containing all the usual species including sausage trees (*Kigelia africana*), marula trees (*Sclerocarya birrea*), jackalberries (*Diospyros mespiliformis*), African mangosteens (*Garcinia livingstonei*) and sycamore figs (*Ficus sycomorus*). You'll also find knobthorns (*Senegalia negrescens*), which are immediately obvious around September and October for their creamy-white flowers and almost sickly-sweet perfume. Occasionally you'll find small islands, or patches, of these standing together.

The floodplains here come in two broadly different varieties. Those plains that still regularly flood are usually covered with short grass – a photogenic environment that's easy for game viewing. The others, which have been dry for a number of years, have often been largely covered with wild sage (*Pechuel-loeschea leubnitziae*). This classic 'pioneer species' thrives in areas that have recently been disturbed and can quickly take a hold when a floodplain dries out; it thrives in areas that have recently been disturbed. Other, slower-growing species of shrubs and trees will eventually germinate and take over these areas, though not for some years yet.

Amid all of these plains, you'll find islands, large and small. These have riverine trees and shrubs on them, including a scattering of real fan palms (*Hyphaene petersiana*) and a notably high density of knobthorn trees (*Senegalia negrescens*).

Fauna My first memory of this area was in May 1993, when I'd been driving myself through Chobe and Moremi with a friend. It had been a good trip, though we were disappointed not to have seen any wild dogs. By the time we left South Gate, in the heat of midday, we had given up trying to spot animals. We were in NG34, but didn't think of this as a wildlife reserve.

After about 14km along the main track, we slowed down to find our way blocked by a large pack of very lazy wild dogs wandering about the road, and lounging by the side of it, yet showing little interest in our vehicle. They posed for photographs, as harmless as lapdogs, for about 30 minutes until they finally wandered off

– thus providing us with one of the best game sightings of our whole trip. Only now, knowing how long researchers spend following the dogs in this area, do I understand why these dogs were so totally relaxed with our vehicle.

The commonest antelope here is probably the impala, a favourite prey of leopard and wild dog, but you'll also find good numbers of tsessebe and kudu, along with giraffe, zebra, wildebeest and warthog. Elephant are fairly common and, like buffalo, often move through here in the dry season in large herds. Roan are also seen occasionally.

Of the predators, lion are dominant although the area certainly has a permanent presence of wild dog, and there's no shortage of spotted hyena. The landscape is a good habitat for leopard, too, and they have become less shy in recent years. Cheetah occur, but aren't seen often.

Birdlife The birdlife reflects the variety that you'll find anywhere in the Delta, and obviously depends heavily on the water levels. One checklist for NG34 and the small NG33 lists 208 species, but doesn't even pretend to be exhaustive.

However, the more common birds which are most frequently seen on the Gomoti floodplain around the lodges and campsite include the long-tailed and glossy starlings (from which the former Starling's Camp took its name), plus red-eyed, Cape turtle and mourning doves; blacksmith and crowned lapwings; long-tailed and crimson-breasted shrikes; red-billed queleas; buffalo weavers; lilac-breasted rollers; and white-backed and hooded vultures. Pelicans, several species of egret, ibises and yellow-billed storks jostle for position in the pools, and wattled cranes and paradise flycatchers or whydahs are also spotted periodically.

Meanwhile in the acacia woodlands, along with the ever-present doves, you're likely to find kori bustards; large flocks of helmeted guinea fowl; red-billed and Swainson's spurfowl; southern ground and red- and yellow-billed hornbills; Meyer's parrots; double-banded, Burchell's, Namaqua and yellow-throated sandgrouse; plus the occasional Gabar goshawk, bateleur and ostrich.

WHEN TO VISIT Big-game animals are more prolific here during the dry season, as with the rest of the Okavango – although the birdlife is generally better between December and March. Because NG34 is on the southwest side of the Delta, the flood reaches it last. Also note that NG34 contains some of the closest dry-season watering points for the game that spreads out towards Nxai and Makgadikgadi during the rains. Around this, there is a much higher density of game in the dry season than the wet. That said, quite a lot of the reserve is mopane woodlands, a favourite location for animals during the rains and early dry season – so expect it to have some game around all year.

GETTING THERE AND AWAY Most visitors arrive by air into the Santawani airstrip (✪ STWAIR 19°30.621'S, 23°37.372'E) in NG33, which is about 10km from the lodges. If you're driving yourself, you can follow the main route through NG34 between Maun and Moremi Game Reserve or Chobe National Park, but driving off this route is no longer permitted without an escort. The campsite is along the road towards Moremi's South Gate. For details of these routes, see the directions under *From Maun to Moremi Game Reserve*, pages 227–8.

WHERE TO STAY With the introduction of Rra Dinare and Mma Dinare, accommodation in this reserve is looking up. As in almost all the concessions, all lodges must be pre-booked, but if you find yourself travelling between South Gate and Maun and need a space for the night, your best option is Kaziikini Campsite, which lies right on this road (opposite the cultural village of Shandereka). Alternatively, you could divert about 30km towards Mankwe Bush Lodge in NG43 (page 229).

🏠 **Rra Dinare/Father Buffalo** [map 347] (8 tents) Contact Under One Botswana Sky, page 225. Opened in May 2017 on the site of the former Starling's Camp, Rra Dinare faces the Gomoti River across the floodplains towards NG32. This stands under a huge marula tree (*Sclerocarya birrea*), around which a few smaller knobthorns (*Senegalia nigrescens*) are clustered. From its classic wood-&-thatch main area to very well-spaced tents, the camp is designed to maximise the views; thus you can watch wildlife from almost anywhere, whether that's the lounge, your tent, the open pool deck, the chairs around the firepit, or even the loo with a view. Connecting it all are lengths of high walkways – broken by the occasional wildlife 'corridor' to allow larger game such as elephant & buffalo to pass through without damaging the structure. Big airy tents with ceiling fans have an unusual lounge area at the front, off the veranda, with screened doors from there into the bedroom, & an en-suite toilet, ceramic basins & outside shower at the back. In the family tent, the bathroom is off the main room, so this wouldn't work for a group of friends. In all, twin beds (or a dbl with advance notice) are comfortable, showers are piping hot, & there's lots of seating for the siesta hours. To make you feel at home in the main area, there's a help-yourself bar, a tea & coffee station, & a constant supply of filtered water. Power comes entirely from solar panels, albeit with a generator as back up.

Game viewing in 4x4 vehicles explores both riverine & dry areas, & you can also drift down the Gomoti River in a mokoro, or take a nature walk – albeit well away from the area's buffalo; Rra Dinare is aptly named! *From US$505 pp Dec–Mar to US$980/1,160 pp sharing/sgl Jul–Oct, inc FB, most drinks, laundry, activities. No children under 6.* ⏱ *All year.* ★★★–★★★★★

🏠 **Mma Dinare/Mother Buffalo** [map 347] (9 tents) Contact Under One Botswana Sky, page 225. Just 3.5km as the crow flies south of Rra Dinare, the newest camp in the reserve is set beneath mature trees on the edge of the Gomoti River, with beautiful views across the floodplains. Opening in mid 2018, it will operate entirely independently of its partner. Nevertheless, it is very similar in design & style, albeit with 1 additional tent, & has the same facilities & activities, so guests here can expect a very similar experience. *Rates as Rra Dinare.* ⏱ *All year.* ★★★–★★★★★

⛏ **Kaziikini Campsite** [map 347] (4 rondavels, camping) ☏ 680 0664; e operationsstw@botsnet. bw; ✦ KAZIIK 19°35.425'S, 23°48.190'E. Some 28km from South Gate, Kaziikini occupies a lovely wooded setting just off the road. Its 10 camping pitches (2 with power) are large, shady & well kept, each with its own water tap & rubbish bin. These share ablutions with small, twin-bedded rondavels, though the mixed-sex facilities of the open-air ablution block offer little privacy.

There's a bar here, but if you're after a meal in the Mogogelo Restaurant, you may need to order several hours in advance, or even at the time of reservation. Locally made baskets can be purchased in reception. At a push you could use Kaziikini as a base for driving into Moremi or Chobe, but within the reserve itself, self-drive game drives can be conducted in your vehicle with a community escort (not a professional guide). Alternatively, you can take a full-day's guided game drive in their vehicle, with lunch.

Kaziikini is a pleasant spot to regroup & watch some of Botswana's more common birds, but given its location, it feels overpriced & not a place to linger. *Camping US$24 pp, rondavel US$57/75 pp sharing/sgl, exc b/fast.* ⏱ *All year.*

Shandereka Cultural Village Opposite Kaziikini Campsite, this cultural village under the same ownership was refurbished in 2017. It is set up for visitors to learn about the rural culture of the Bayei people, including hunting techniques, local medicine and traditional dancing, but it's best to make a reservation for the 2-hour tour.

SANTAWANI PARTNERSHIP (NG33)

The small Santawani Reserve, covering just 60km², is really an enclave that has been cut out of NG34. It borders Moremi, and in character is very similar to the area around South Gate and parts of NG34. In the past, this hasn't proved an easy area in which to run a stand-alone operation, and the old Santawani Safari Lodge – one of the Delta's older photographic camps – finally fell into disuse. Now, however, the presence of waterholes and some permanent lagoons has improved things no end. In 2002, together with the Sankuyo Tshwaragano Management Trust, the lodge was reopened, and in 2016, following a further two changes of management, it was taken over by Wilderness Safaris. In the east of the reserve, Sankuyo Bush Camp has been reinvigorated by Wilderness as Gomoti Tented Camp, with both camps currently used for private group bookings only.

GETTING THERE AND AWAY At present, access to the lodges is exclusively by air into Santawani airstrip (✪ STWAIR 19°30.621'S, 23°37.372'E).

 WHERE TO STAY Both lodges in the reserve are currently managed by Wilderness Safaris under their group scheme, and are not at present open to independent travellers.

🏠 **Gomoti Tented Camp** [map 311] (5 tents) This small camp set beneath shady acacia trees would be a good option for self-drivers heading into Moremi if the set-up were to change. Walk-in tents, set on low wooden decks, are entered through proper doors to reveal twin beds, reading lamps, directors' chairs, a wardrobe & en-suite toilet & shower, with a couple more chairs on the shaded veranda. In the evening, guests dine by the light of paraffin hurricane lanterns around a long table in the thatched dining area, where there's also comfortable seating. To explore the reserve there are day & night game drives & nature walks. ⊕ *All year.*

🏠 **Santawani Lodge** [map 347] (6 tented chalets) Upgraded in 2017, the lodge's Meru-style tented structures are built on shallow decks, looking out to the floodplain from small verandas with a couple of directors' chairs. Inside, twin beds with mosi nets & bedside lights are cooled by an electric fan, & there's an en-suite shower/toilet at the rear. The open, thatched dining room, bar & lounge area boasts no frills, with sand floors, bare tables & basic chairs. In front of the lodge, a small waterhole attracts good numbers of game. Mokoro trips can be arranged. ⊕ *All year.*

MABABE (NG41), AND MANKWE AND TUSKERS (NG43)

These two concessions, characterised by open savannah and scattered with large camelthorn (*Vachellia erioloba*) trees, lie to the east of the Delta. NG41 is a community concession that shares its northern and western boundaries with Chobe National Park. On its southern border is NG43, which is really a huge (3,460km²) patch of the Kalahari, east of Moremi's South Gate and south of Chobe's Mababe Gate.

This is not an area where there's easy or prolific game viewing. I include it here because it is the base for two small bush lodges, under the same ownership, which may prove very convenient stops between Maun and either Moremi or Chobe. In time, as the areas under wildlife protection effectively expand, it may even become more of a game-viewing destination in its own right. Should you wish to explore NG41, note that there is a P60 concession fee payable, and that you must have a community escort guide with you in your vehicle to show you the various game-drive routes (and make sure you don't go off-road). There is no charge for this – the escorts are not qualified guides – but they will in all likelihood expect a tip.

GETTING THERE AND AWAY Virtually all visitors travelling directly between Maun and Chobe will pass through sections of both NG43 and NG41, even if they aren't aware of it.

To reach Mankwe from Maun, head towards Chobe's Mababe Gate (that is, follow the directions to Sankuyo in *The road north of Maun: to Moremi and Chobe*, pages 227– 9). The turning to the lodge is clearly marked, 7km north of Sankuyo Village. Mogotlho Safari Lodge (✪ MOGOT 19°13.109'S, 23°57.365'E), in NG41, is about 20km north of Mankwe Bush Lodge – or some 10km before Mababe Village. For Tuskers you turn east off the road just north of the vet fence at the Mowana Gate.

WHERE TO STAY

🏠 **Mankwe Bush Lodge** [map 347] (8 tents, camping) 📞686 5787/8, reservations 📞+27 21 712 5284; **e** reservations@mankwe.com; www.mankwe.com; ✪ MANKWE 19°21.769'S, 23°53.775'E. In the northwest corner of NG43, just north of Sankuyo Village, Mankwe is set among mopane trees some 2km east of the road. The camp was rebuilt following a fire in 2016, creating a dining & lounge area beneath a large Bedouin tent overlooking the campfire, & a new pool with sunloungers is to follow. Overlooking the surrounding bush, fairly large Meru-style tents on wooden decks are simple but pleasantly furnished, with twin beds, battery-powered lights & an en-suite flush toilet, basin & gas-fired shower.

About 1.5km from the lodge, beneath camelthorn & mopane trees, are 6 private campsites, each with its own flush toilet, bucket shower & washbasin. Firewood is available, but otherwise you'll need to be fully equipped, with all your own drinking water as well as food & fuel. That said, with a couple of hours' notice, campers may eat at the lodge (*3-course dinner P265*).

You can use Mankwe as a base for self-drive day trips into Moremi Game Reserve, or take part in their organised activities. These include 3–4hr afternoon drives with a sundowner in the NG43 concession (*P525 pp, based on 4 people*), & full-day drives (*P1,400 pp*), usually into the Khwai River area. Guided bush walks & night drives are further options, along with 4x4 trails across NG43, accompanied by a local guide. *From P2,685 pp sharing DBB; camping P260 pp; exc transfers.* ⊕ *All year.*

🏠 **Mogotlho Safari Lodge** [map 347] (13 tents) 📞686 0968; **m** 0765 13917; **e** mogotlho@info.bw, reservations@deltasure. com; www.mogotlhosafarilodge.co.za; ✪ MOGOTL19°13.840'S, 23°58.696'E. Opened as a hunting camp in 2000, Mogotlho switched allegiances to a photographic lodge in 2008. It lies 2.5km east of the road, in NG41, its large central deck with a firepit occupying a lovely spot above the Khwai River, shaded by camelthorn (*Vachellia erioloba*) trees. There's a cash bar here, & behind, an extensive if rather dark lounge & dining area. En-suite tents on low plinths are set well away from the river. Day & night game drives, & bush walks, are centred on the area around the Khwai River. *US$294/440 pp sharing/sgl DBB; US$457/685 FBA, both exc bed levy & P60 concession fee.* ⊕ *All year.* ★★★

🏠 **Tuskers Bush Camp** [map 347] (6 tents) 📞+27 21 712 5284/5; **e** reservations@ sundestinations.co.za; www.tuskers.net; ✪ TUSKER 19°35.695'S, 23°55.208'E. Tuskers lies beneath mopane trees about 15km east of the gravel road. Walk-in tents with roll-down flaps have twin or dbl beds, solar-powered lights & a simple en-suite bucket shower & eco-toilet. The traditional thatched dining area, with a sandy boma & firepit for outside dining, overlooks a waterhole. Guests take part in game drives & – depending on the weather/season – walking safaris within the concession. See ad, 3rd colour section. *From US$295 pp Dec–Mar to US$395 Jul– Oct, inc FB, activities, park fees; exc drinks.* ⊕ *All year.* ★★–★★★

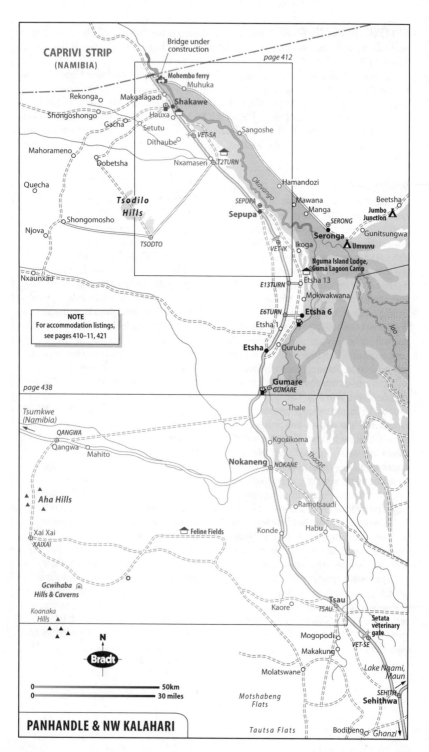

CAPRIVI STRIP
(NAMIBIA)

Bridge under
construction

page 412

Mohembo ferry
Muhuka

Rekonga
Makgalagadi
Shakawe
Shongoshongo
Gacha
Hauxa
Setutu
VET-SA
Sangoshe
Mahorameno
Dithaube
Dobetsha
Nxamaseri
T2TURN
Quecha
Hamandozi
Okavango
Mawana
Tsodilo
Hills
SEPUPA
Manga
Beetsha
Jumbo
Junction
Sepupa
SERONG
Njova
Shongomosho
Seronga
Gunitsungwa
TSODTO
VET-IK
Ikoga
Umvuvu
Nxaunxau
Nguma Island Lodge,
Guma Lagoon Camp
E13TURN
Etsha 13
Mokwakwana
E6TURN
Etsha 6
NOTE
For accommodation listings,
see pages 410–11, 421
Etsha 1

Etsha
Qurube

page 438

Gumare
GUMARE

Tsumkwe
(Namibia)
Thale

QANGWA
Qangwa
Mahito
Kgosikoma

Nokaneng
NOKANE
Thaoge

Aha Hills
Ramotsaudi

Feline Fields
Xai Xai
XAIXAI
Konde
Habu

Gcwihaba
Hills & Caverns

Koanaka
Hills
Tsau
TSAU
Kaore
Setata
veterinary
gate
N
Mogopodi
VET-SE

Bradt
Makakung
Lake Ngami,
Maun

0   50km
0   30 miles
Molatswane
SEHITH
Sehithwa

PANHANDLE & NW KALAHARI
Motshabeng
Flats
Tautsa Flats
Bodibeng
Ghanzi

14

The Okavango Panhandle and Northwest Kalahari

If much of the Okavango Delta is the preserve of the privileged few who can afford to fly in to exclusive safari camps, then the Panhandle presents more egalitarian options. Here you'll find the raw edge of Botswana's safari industry, camps on the edge of the Delta run by idiosyncratic owners or local communities – without marketing aids or slick glossy brochures. This is the Okavango's safari scene as it was 20 years ago!

Go west, into the Kalahari, and it's wilder still. Here there's almost nothing organised, yet the amazing Tsodilo Hills were declared Botswana's first World Heritage Site in 2001. Adventurers may want to dig deeper here, and explore the caverns of the Gcwihaba Hills or the remote Aha range.

THE PANHANDLE

Look at a map of the Okavango Delta and you'll see that it's shaped like a frying pan, with the main river flowing down the centre of the handle, from the northwest. Thus this area gets its name.

ORIENTATION The Panhandle's western side is very easy to access with a 2x4, as the road between Sehithwa and Shakawe is tar. Once you leave the main road and the larger settlements, however, a high-clearance 4x4 is essential to cope with the often deep sand in the area.

The track that follows the river on the eastern side is used much less, though it's not intrinsically difficult. Visitors very rarely travel along this track as the only practical access to it is via the ferry that crosses the Okavango at Mohembo, north of Shakawe. This may, however, be set to change, with construction of a new bridge over the Okavango at Mohembo underway in 2017. Although it is already behind schedule, this may well open up the hitherto less-visited eastern side of the Panhandle during the lifetime of this book.

GEOLOGY AND GEOGRAPHY All of this area is in the Kalahari, though here it's dominated by the influence of the Okavango River. This flows south into Botswana from the Angolan Highlands, having crossed Namibia's Caprivi Strip (now incorporated into the Zambezi Region). Entering Botswana, the river's gradient is very low. However, it is constrained from spreading out by steep riverbanks on either side. Underneath the sand lies a more fundamental constraint: parallel faultlines in the earth's crust that run southeast, about 10–15km apart. Thus the river meanders gradually southeast, between them, forming a series of wide, sweeping curves and the odd oxbow lagoon – but always remaining within the constraints of the banks.

Where the river's meanders kiss the banks at the edge of the floodplain, villages have sprung up: Shakawe, Sepupa and Seronga. The southern extent of the faultlines lies around Seronga, so south of here the river begins to spread wider to form the main body of the Delta.

FLORA AND FAUNA The Panhandle isn't a prime area for game viewing, so don't come here expecting masses of big game or you'll be disappointed. That said, you may catch glimpses of the occasional sitatunga or small herds of lechwe, and you're almost bound to see numerous hippo and crocodile. However, there are some first-class areas for birding, and plenty of areas with deep-water channels and lagoons.

Flora Looking from the Panhandle's banks, often all you can see is a gently swaying mass of feathery papyrus heads. Here, more than anywhere else in the Delta, the environment is polarised: there are deep-water channels, and there are the papyrus beds that surround them.

Occasionally you'll find sections of phragmites reeds and, when the waters are low, open stretches of sandbanks. Sometimes the odd day-lily (*Nymphaea nouchali caerulea*) will take hold in a quiet inlet on the edge of the channel, but mainly the vegetation here is huge expanses of floating papyrus.

Birdlife The birdlife here is as varied as anywhere in the Delta, though getting to actually see the birds that inhabit the papyrus can be tricky. Some of the more sought-after sightings would be painted snipes, rufous-bellied herons, lesser jacanas, chirping cisticolas, brown-throated weavers and coppery-tailed and white-browed coucals. Greater swamp warblers and swamp boubous can often be heard calling from the papyrus, but are less easy to spot.

The Panhandle is a particularly good area for the white-backed night heron. Look out, too, for white-backed ducks (sometimes in large numbers) perching on the sandbanks, as well as long-toed lapwings, red-winged pratincoles and, of course, the Panhandle's most acrobatic birding attraction: the African skimmer. These distinctive, black-and-white birds fly south to the Delta between about September and December. They mainly come to breed on the sandbanks of the Panhandle, which are exposed while the water is low. Gathering in small flocks, each pair excavates a shallow depression in the sand where they'll lay their eggs and raise their young.

One of the Delta's most amazing sights is to watch these birds feed. With long, graceful wings they fly fast and low, holding their elongated lower mandible just low enough to cut the water's surface. This is hollow and has sharp edges, shaped to minimise its drag in the water. When this touches a small fish near the surface, it is quickly raised against the upper mandible, trapping the fish firmly. I always marvel at their flying skill, moving their body in all directions while their bill traces a constant, steady path through the water.

Note that because African skimmers nest very near the waterline, on low sandbanks, their nests and young are very vulnerable to both predators and to damage from the wash caused by fast-moving motorboats. So boats operating in these areas should never be driven too fast.

Another spectacular migrant, better seen in the Panhandle than anywhere else in the Delta, is the carmine bee-eater. These come to southern Africa to breed, and stay from about October to March. They nest in large colonies, building their nests underground at the end of tunnels which they excavate into the side of

E6TURN	19°06.706'S, 22°16.152'E	T2TURN	18°35.834'S, 21°59.986'E
E13TUR	19°00.793'S, 22°17.356'E	TSAU	20°10.294'S, 22°27.265'E
GUMARE	19°22.242'S, 22°09.242'E	TSGATE	18°47.275'S, 21°44.856'E
NOKANE	19°39.694'S, 22°11.184'E	TSODTO	18°47.378'S, 21°44.981'E
QANGWA	19°31.868'S, 21°10.281'E	VET-IK	18°50.327'S, 22°13.756'E
SEHITH	20°28.259'S, 22°42.372'E	VET-SA	18°29.256'S, 21°55.142'E
SEPUPA	18°44.150'S, 22°10.625'E	VET-SE	20°15.775'S, 22°33.926'E
SERONG	18°48.771'S, 22°24.988'E	XAIXAI	19°52.867'S, 21°04.934'E

sandy riverbanks. You won't forget the sight of hundreds of these bright carmine-pink birds twittering around a riverbank that's holed with nests like a piece of Swiss cheese.

Above the water you'll regularly spot African fish eagles; marsh harriers and even the occasional migrant osprey are also sometimes seen. On the banks beside the waters and papyrus there's a narrow band of thick riverine forest, before the bush becomes that of the dry Kalahari. Here there's a wide variety of different birdlife – typical of any of the riverine areas in this region. Notable sightings would include the tiny brown firefinch, Bradfield's hornbill, the western banded snake eagle and Pel's fishing owl.

GETTING THERE AND AROUND

By vehicle The main tar road on the west side of the Panhandle is generally maintained to a high standard, and offers straightforward driving in a 2x4. While it was full of pot-holes in mid 2017, particularly between Gumare and Shakawe, there seems to be a concerted if slow effort to repair the surface. For anywhere else in this area, though, you really need your own fully equipped 4x4. Do note that fuel supplies along this stretch, and even as far as Maun, have historically been erratic, and despite relatively reliable fuel supplies in Shakawe, Gumare and Sehithwa in recent years, it's wise to fill up when you can.

By bus Several buses per day ply between Maun and Shakawe, starting at around 04.00, with the last departure of the day at 13.00 in each direction. The whole trip takes about 7 hours and costs a total of P100. Buses stop at the main villages on the way, turning off to the larger centres such as Gumare and Etsha 6, but near the smaller villages they just pick up and drop off passengers on the main road.

By air There are small airstrips dotted around, so if you charter a plane you can get to most places here: Shakawe, Nxamaseri, Nokaneng, Tsau and Guma Lagoon. Tsodilo Hills also has an airstrip, but you really need a vehicle while you're there to get the most out of it. This is also true for the Gcwihaba or Aha Hills, which can alternatively be accessed via the relatively new airstrip at Xai Xai.

THE EASTERN PANHANDLE Although visitors relatively rarely see the side of the Okavango's Panhandle to the east of the river, those who do usually come for the mokoro trips. These have long been run by the Okavango Polers' Trust, but other companies have now stepped into the market. For travellers who are constrained by a relatively tight budget, this is one of the few options left to see any of the Okavango.

A good gravel road runs down the eastern side of the river from Mohembo to Seronga. Between the two you'll find numerous smaller villages which survive mainly on fishing and, away from the river, a number of tiny 'cattlepost' settlements used by people tending their cattle in the interior of NG11 – which is fairly continuous cattle-ranching country.

Getting there and away

By air Seronga has an airstrip (✈ SERAIR 18°49.180'S, 22°25.020'E) that is by far the easiest and most convenient way for most travellers to access the village. Check in Maun with an operator such as Audi Camp or The Old Bridge Backpackers for details of the options.

By 4x4 The only practical way to access the eastern side of the Panhandle with a vehicle is to cross the Okavango River on the ferry at Mohembo, in the far north.

There appears on many maps to be another route, which seems to go around the eastern side of the Delta and link into Seronga from the Linyanti area, via the village of Beetsha. However, the tracks on this side have very few users and no signposts. They cross a number of different private concessions, none of which would welcome your visit: straying off designated transit routes will get you into trouble. Meanwhile, when the tracks meet villages they split and vanish. But perhaps the greatest danger is of water blocking the route. It's easy to get dangerously lost in this region and then to run out of fuel, water or supplies. There's no help at hand, so I'd strongly advise against trying to use any of these tracks.

By bus/boat Both Shakawe and Sepupa are fairly easy to access on one of the local buses that run up and down the road to the west of the river, between Shakawe and Sehithwa; getting across to the eastern side of the river is more of a challenge. The once-regular motorboat ferry between Sepupa and Seronga Boat Station (✈ SERBOA 18°49.316'S, 22°24.855'E) has been out of service for many years, but fortunately, Swamp Stop (page 418) has stepped in to fill the gap. Passengers pay P2,500 for a small boat, or P3,000 for the larger vessel (carrying up to 16 people), with boats departing from their jetty. Do note, though, that the Swamp Stop was under new ownership in 2017 and this service may be subject to change in the near future.

As an alternative, it may be possible to arrange a boat transfer with one of the lodges at Guma Lagoon (page 421), if you're staying there for a period of time. The only other option – until the road bridge is finished – is to use the vehicle ferry at Mohembo, and then hitch south down the road on the eastern bank.

Seronga Seronga (✈ SERONG 18°48.771'S, 22°24.988'E) is a sizeable village at the eastern base of the Panhandle. It's the regional centre for a number of small settlements to the east of it, along the northern edge of the Delta, as well as a focus for the people who still live in the northern areas of the Delta.

Where to stay The only viable option in this area at present offers several options. Mbiroba Camp, run for years by the Okavango Polers' Trust, seems to have disappeared off the radar.

 Jumbo Junction [map 406] (2 chalets, 10 tented rooms, camping) m 7585 6213; e reservations@jumbojunction.com; www. jumbojunction.com; ✈ JUMBO 18°49.31'S, 22°36.19'E. Situated some 28km east of Seronga on the northern bank of the lower Selinda

Spillway, Jumbo Junction has been through a period of expansion, & now has a couple of chalets, a fully serviced tented camp, an island bushcamp & a campsite that includes some permanent dome tents. The campsite takes both overland trucks &, in a separate area, independent travellers, all sharing 4 ablution blocks. Central to the camp is a large thatched bar & restaurant overlooking a permanent lagoon. Activities, all dependent on water levels, focus on mokoro trips, island walks, fishing & game drives. There is also the opportunity to go ballooning over the Delta. *Chalet US$450/585 pp sharing/sgl, tented camp US$400/520, island bushcamp US$845 pp, all inc FB, most drinks & most activites. Camping/dome tent US$25/60 pp.* ★★★–★★★★

THE WESTERN PANHANDLE

Mohembo border Mohembo – almost 16km north of Shakawe – marks the road border at the top of the Panhandle between Botswana and Namibia's Caprivi Strip. Here you'll find a neat customs and immigration area (✪ MOHEMB 18°15.700'S, 21°45.768'E; ⊕ *06.00–18.00 daily*) where the formalities are normally handled promptly and efficiently. Possibly as a result of unreliable banking services in the Panhandle and Caprivi, the authorities on the Botswana side of the border now accept card payments for cross-border fees, etc. The reliability of this facility remains to be seen, but with luck it will make the formalities smoother and easier for all involved.

Crossing the Okavango at Mohembo
For travellers wishing to cross to the eastern bank of the Okavango River, there's a (free) ferry (⊕ *06.00–19.30 daily*) a little over 3.5km south of the border. If you're driving from the border, you'll come to a T-junction, where you turn left for the ferry, or right for Shakawe. The ferry usually takes a few vehicles at a time, including the occasional small truck. Expect to find a lot of people waiting around here – some to cross, others to meet those who have crossed, or to buy and sell things.

In 2017, construction was in hand of a new 161m bridge across the Okavango River next to the site of the existing ferry crossing. Completion is expected by July 2019, thus opening up this previously under-visited area to travellers.

Shakawe
This sprawling town stands east of the main road on the northern banks of the Panhandle of the Delta, some 16km south of the Mohembo border post, and 281km north of Sehithwa. Driving into the old village used to feel like entering a maze of reed walls, each surrounding a small kraal, as the track split countless ways between the houses. The odd trap of deep sand was enough to stop you for an hour, and thus serve up excellent entertainment to numerous amused locals.

Today, however, Shakawe is a bustling little town, albeit still something of a backwater. Just a stone's throw from the tar road you'll find a significant base for the Botswana Defence Force, as you'd expect in one of the country's more sensitive border areas, and a major police station. If you have the time, take a walk along the river; sometimes there's a mokoro ferry shuttling local people to and from the eastern side of the river, full with their wares to sell or recent purchases to take back home.

Of particular importance to drivers are the filling stations (one of which advertises 24-hour service, perhaps for the trucks passing through). Barclays Bank (with an ATM) has a presence here, too, as does a branch of Choppies, while other, smaller shops and a post office are largely concentrated within the small shopping centre around the bus stop.

If you fancy a break before driving on, you could try a guided tour of **Krokovango Crocodile Farm** (✪ KROKO 18°25.817'S, 21°53.682'E; m *7230 6200;* ⊕ *08.00–17.00 Mon–Sat; P25/15 adult/child*), about 10km south of Shakawe. The farm is in an

14

MOHEMBO, SHAKAWE & TSODILO HILLS

NAMIBIA
(Caprivi Strip)

Bridge under
construction

Mohembo
border post

Mohembo
vehicle ferry

Shakawe

*Gauxa
Lagoon*

Sekondomboro

Okavango

**Drotsky's
Cabins**

DROTSK ⊕

⊕ SHAKAL

Kara Lodge

⊕ XARO

**Krokovango
Crocodile Farm**

**Shakawe
River Lodge**

*Xaro
Lagoon*

VET-SA ✕

Sangoshe

**Somachima
veterinary
fence**

*Nxadao
Lagoon*

TSVIEW ✳
Viewpoint

OLD PANHANDLE ROAD

Nxamaseri Village

**Nxamaseri
Island Lodge**

T2TURN ⊕

NXAMAS ⊕

NXTURN ⊕

page 428

*Tsodilo
Hills*

SEPUPA ⊕

Swamp Stop
Sepupa

SWAMPS

TSODTO ⊕

Thamacha veterinary fence

VET-IK ✕

**Ikoga
Gate**

Ikoga

GPS co-ordinates ⊕		
DROTSK	18°24.868'S, 21°53.120'E	T2TURN	18°35.834'S, 21°59.986'E
E13TUR	19°00.793'S, 22°17.356'E	TSODTO	18°47.378'S, 21°44.981'E
NXAMAS	18°36.426'S, 22°05.268'E	TSVIEW	18°33.830'S, 21°58.273'E
NXTURN	18°38.125'S, 22°02.797'E	VET-IK	18°50.327'S, 22°13.756'E
SEPUPA	18°44.150'S, 22°10.625'E	VET-SA	18°29.256'S, 21°55.142'E
SWAMPS	18°44.749'S, 22°11.843'E	XARO	18°25.423'S, 21°56.364'E

NOTE
For accommodation listings,
see pages 413–15, 417, 418

Gumare ↓

attractive woodland setting, with crocs at all stages of growth from hatchling to adult. They're at their most active at feeding time, usually at 11.00 on Tuesday and Friday – though the adults are not fed at all between May and July, so the first feed in August could be quite a spectacle!

Getting there and away There are good daily bus services to Maun via the rest of the western Panhandle from the centre of town. Of these, the fastest service is the Golden Bridge Express (*P100 one-way*), which departs at set times throughout the day, taking about 4½–5 hours to reach Maun. Minibuses are cheaper but very cramped and take an hour longer; they also depart only when full. Alternatively, hitchhiking is relatively easy along this road.

Self-drivers will need to allow around 4 hours to reach Shakawe from Maun. And for fly-in guests, there's the option of charter flights taking about an hour. The airstrip is to the west of the main road, just 400m off the tarmac.

Where to stay In Shakawe itself, options are many but we recommend just one. About 10km south of the town, however, are a number of water-based camps on the river catering mainly for fishing and birdwatching, and houseboats add further variety. With the increase in the number of travellers along the Caprivi Strip, trade here has picked up so you will often need to book. The options here are listed from north to south, followed by the houseboats.

Hawk Hotel (13 rooms) Shakawe; m 7352 3114; e barone@gov.bw; ⊕ HAWKH 18°21.012'S, 21°50.108'E. To find this guesthouse, follow the tar road as it goes north through the centre of town to the river, then – having turned away from the river – it's on the left after another 1.5km (& about 300m from the river in the other direction!). En-suite rooms are arranged around a small courtyard within a walled enclosure. It's hardly picturesque, but rooms are clean & come with mosi nets, a kettle & satellite TV, & 6 have AC as well. Sgl rooms have a dbl bed, but dbls are larger & worth the extra P260. There's just about space to pitch a tent here, too, & you'll be allocated a separate toilet & shower. By the pool, there's a shaded restaurant area where b/fast, lunch & dinner are served, so you won't go hungry. **$$** *exc b/fast.*

Drotsky's Cabins [map 412] (10 chalets, camping) ✆ 683 0226; m 7496 8638; e drotsky@btcmail.co.bw, drotskys@info.bw; https://drotskys.com; ⊕ DROTSK 18°24.868'S, 21°53.120'E. Almost 8km south of Shakawe you'll find a left turn off the tar road on to a sandy track. This leads east, crossing the old road up the Panhandle for about 3km to reach the extensively remodelled Drotsky's Cabins. You should be able to drive this track in a normal 2x4 car, though the sand can be very thick, so some driving skill is needed.

This once-small fishing camp is still run by Jan & Eileen Drotsky & their family, who have seen Shakawe change from a remote outpost to a thriving little town. The central area is designed like a vast log cabin on high stilts, under a thatched roof, & is approached by an almost palatial series of steps & walkways. Adorned with wrought-iron chandeliers & wood carvings, & with a separate bar under whirling fans, it may sound rather grand, but the effect is homely rather than ostentatious. The log-cabin theme continues in the large, twin-bedded en-suite chalets, also raised up on stilts; space is clearly not an issue here! AC, fans & flat-screen TVs are standard, while old-fashioned armchairs add a touch of traditional comfort, & we loved the ornate ceramic basins. Outside, perfectly manicured lawns sweep around a pool to the river beyond. The main area is entirely wheelchair accessible, as is one of the chalets. Activities focus on the river with boat cruises & fishing trips. It is also possible for self-drivers to use this as a base for the Tsodilo Hills, 65km away, although this is a long round trip.

Campers enjoy a shaded but sandy campsite with 20 pitches on the site of the original cabins, each with lights, electric points & a firepit – but watch out for the local monkey population! There are ablution blocks here, & meals can be arranged at the main camp with advance notice.

14

Drotsky's is a genuine old camp, where hospitality hasn't been learned from a manual. It can be a super lodge, & offer you fascinating insights into the area, its history & its ecosystems. **$$$** *exc b/fast; camping P200 pp.*

🏠 **Shakawe River Lodge** [map 412] (10 chalets, 4 dome tents, camping) ☏ 684 0403; **m** 7230 6822; **e** info@shakawelodge.com; www. shakawelodge.com; ✪ SHAKAL 18°26.059'S, 21°54.326'E. Known for decades as Shakawe Fishing Camp, this relatively new lodge – opened in 2013 – has risen from humble surroundings. Gone is the simple fishing camp of yore, its expansive river frontage now hosting a stylish yet very open lodge that's all neutral colours beneath a topping of smart thatch. From the entrance, you're greeted by a riverside vista of palm trees & papyrus, where basket chairs hang enticingly in the breeze. Sunloungers on a raised pool deck catch the river view, too, as do the smart restaurant & lounge. Most of the twin & king-size dbl en-suite chalets with sliding glass doors are lined up along a rather reedy section of the river, their contemporary décor enhanced by AC, TV & a bar fridge.

Downstream, the shady old riverside campsite has had a makeover, but remains relaxed & unpretentious, with 10 clearly demarcated pitches, its own bar, & spotless if well-worn showers & toilets. Campers are welcome to dine at the lodge, where an à la carte menu features a good selection of pizzas. Beside the slipway, look out for the hulk of an old houseboat, a relic of the Angolan war from the late 1970s. Apparently it was used by 32 Battalion of the South African forces, who were stationed in the Caprivi Strip, but it broke loose & drifted south, & has been gently rusting in Botswana ever since!

The lodge is clearly signposted some 2.5km east of the main road, about 5.5km north of the Somachima Veterinary Fence (✪ VET-SA 18°29.256'S, 21°55.142'E), or 11km south of Shakawe, & is accessible by 2x4. Guests have always come here to fish, especially during the peak season of Jun–Aug, & certainly fishing is still a focus; boats can be hired by the hour or day (*from P250/1,200 exc fuel*), but birdwatching, as well as day trips to the Tsodilo Hills & Mahango Game Reserve (*P800 pp/day, min 4 people*) add another dimension. *Camping P200 pp; pre-erected tent P490.* **$$$$**

🏠 **Xaro Lodge** [map 412] (8 Meru tents) ☏ 683 0226; **m** 7212 2970; **e** xarolodge@info. bw; https://drotskys.com/xaro-lodge.html; ✪ XARO 18°25.423'S, 21°56.364'E. Xaro is about 8.5km downstream from Drotsky's Cabins, its parent camp, & is usually reached from there by a 30min boat trip. It is set in 30ha on an outcrop from the mainland, in an established grove of knobthorn (*Senegalia nigrescens*), mangosteen (*Garcinia livingstonei*) & jackalberry (*Diospyros mespiliformis*) trees, while in the garden you'll find a host of succulents & cacti, banana trees & even a small baobab (*Adansonia digitata*). Originally built in the mid 1980s by Hartley's Safaris, Xaro passed through several hands until it was acquired by Jan Drotsky, whose son, Donovan, now runs the camp with his wife, Yolande. Royal, one of the marvellous staff who has been with the family for years, recalls that the lodge has always been used for fishing & birdwatching from motorboats, never from mekoro – & that's still the situation.

The origins of a beautiful, old-style Okavango camp still remain in the thatched, stone dining area with a large table in the centre & various old books on shelves in the walls, but a new bar has been introduced, & the Meru-style tents replaced. With en-suite facilities & sliding doors leading to wooden decks, 2 of these can be accessed with a wheelchair. Activities are as at Drotsky's. **$$$** *exc b/fast.*

Houseboats Moored on the river near Shakawe, several houseboats offer the opportunity to explore the western fringes of the Delta while based on the river itself. It's an entirely different approach, & may well appeal to those seeking a more relaxing trip with less of an emphasis on fishing (although fishing is still an option!). For a general overview, contact Okavango Houseboats (*www.okavangohouseboats.com*), or consider one of the following:

🚢 **//Kabbo** (8 cabins) Contact Wilderness Dawning Safaris, page 226. This 2-storey 'floating lodge', moored on the river near the Hawk Hotel (page 413), is designed to make the most of its location. On the lower deck, each en-suite cabin has sliding glass doors just above water level, while above are the dining area, bar & – for those who want to brave the African sun – sundecks.

Boating & fishing trips (catch & release) are available or – if you tire of the water – there are visits to the Tsodilo Hills, all at US$75 pp (min 2). *US$1,680/night, min 8 people, inc FB & 1 water-based activity/day; exc transfers.* Apr–Oct. ★★

🚤 **Kubu Queen** (6 berths) m 7230 6821/2; e oldafricasafaris@ngami.net; www.kubuqueen. com. From its base at Shakawe, the *Kubu Queen* is moored at a different spot each night, with tender boats so that guests can explore the river & its channels, & go fishing (except in the closed season, Jan–Feb). Nature walks on some of the larger islands are a further option. Inside, there's a lounge, bar & dining area. Each of the 2 cabins has a dbl bed, while a further 2 guests can sleep under the stars on the upper deck, where simple twin beds are set up under mosquito nets. The shower & toilet are shared, but groups are not mixed, so you won't be sharing with strangers. Another alternative for up to 12 people is to camp on one of the islands.

The boat is owned by Greg & Kate Thompson, who have worked in the safari industry in the Okavango for almost 20 years; Greg is a professional guide. *US$280 pp (min 4), inc FB, fishing, airstrip transfers; exc VAT, drinks, fuel for tender boats.* All year. ★★

THE CATFISH RUN

The amazing phenomenon of the catfish run is unique to the Okavango Delta. It happens every year, between early August and the end of November, though its timing is difficult to predict precisely.

As the water level starts to drop in the northern part of the Panhandle, it is still rising in the southern part of the Delta. The catfish runs start in the north of the Panhandle, where the lowering water levels concentrate the Delta's smaller fish – especially the relatively small churchill (*Petrocephalus catostoma*) and bulldog (*Marcusenius macrolepidotus*) – in the channels and papyrus banks.

The main predatory species involved include the sharp-toothed catfish (*Clarias gariepinus*), a hardy, omnivorous species which grows up to 1.4m in length and 59kg in weight, and the much smaller blunt-toothed catfish (*Clarias ngaensis*). These catfish hunt in packs and a 'run' starts with the catfish swimming upstream inside the papyrus banks. Here they slap their powerful tails on the surface of the water, making a noise like a gunshot, and against the papyrus, to stun the smaller fish, their prey.

Hundreds and sometimes thousands of catfish will work their way upstream like this, making the water 'boil' with their frenzy of activity. All this noise and commotion attracts an eager audience of herons, storks, egrets, fish eagles and other fish-eating birds on the banks, while crocodiles, snakes and tigerfish lurk beyond the papyrus in the deeper channels waiting to snap up anything that escapes into open water.

Although in each run the catfish swim upstream, when it's finished they pause and drift back down, subsequently rejoining other catfish and starting new runs. So as the water levels drop further down in the Delta, the location of the runs moves south also.

These runs occur in many different sizes. There will be several per day in different areas of the Delta, each covering a distance of a few kilometres before fizzling out. A couple may be longer than this, perhaps continuing for as long as two weeks and covering a lot of distance, but these are the exception rather than the rule.

Eventually, signalled by the onset of the rising waters, the catfish will themselves move out on to the floodplains and spawn.

Nxamaseri Though the small village of Nxamaseri is not a stop for most visitors, I've included this section because the surrounding area is a very interesting one, offering an insight into the attractions of the Delta that is on a par with most of the reserves further east.

The Nxamaseri Channel is a side-channel of the main Okavango River. When water levels are high, there are plenty of open marshy floodplains covered with an apparently unblemished carpet of grass, and dotted with tiny palm islands. It's very like the Jao Flats, and is one of the Okavango's most beautiful corners.

Like Guma Lagoon, further south, it's fairly easily accessible due to the presence of a lodge. If you want a real Delta experience in the Panhandle, then this should be high on your list of places to visit – though getting here requires either your own vehicle or a flight.

Flora and fauna highlights The Nxamaseri Channel is north of the point where the main Okavango River divides at the base of the Panhandle, and is a stretch of open, clear water up to about 30m wide in places. Beside the edges you'll find stands of papyrus and common reeds, while its quieter edges are lined by patches of waterlilies, including many night-lilies (also known as lotus lilies; *Nymphaea lotus*) as well as the more common day-lilies (*Nymphaea nouchali caerulea*). Look out also for the heart-shaped floating leaves, and star-shaped white or yellow flowers of the water gentian (*Nymphoides indica*).

As with the rest of the Panhandle, this isn't a prime area for game viewing. You may catch glimpses of the odd lechwe or the shy sitatunga, and you're almost bound to see hippo and crocodile, but big game is scarce. However, the channel is a super waterway for birdwatching; home to a tremendous variety of waterbirds. Without trying too hard, my sightings included many pygmy geese, greater and lesser jacanas, lesser galinules, colonies of reed cormorants, darters, several species of bee-eater and kingfisher, green-backed herons, a relaxed black crake, numerous red-shouldered widows and even (on a cloudy morning in February) a pair of Pel's fishing owls. Beside the channel are pockets of tall riverine trees and various real fan and wild date palms, whose overhanging branches house colonies of weavers (masked, spotted-backed and brown-throated). Upstream of the lodge, on the main Okavango River, there's a colony of carmine bee-eaters at a location known locally as 'the red cliffs'. This is occupied from around early September to the end of December, but is probably at its best in late September or early October (the best time for most migrant species here). While watching for birds, keep an eye out for the elusive spotted-necked otter (*Lutra maculicollis*), which also frequents these waters.

Getting there Nxamaseri (also spelt Nxamasere) Village lies about 37km south of Shakawe, or 19km north of Sepupa. From the north, follow the tar road to the Somachima Veterinary Fence (✪ VET-SA 18°29.256'S, 21°55.142'E), then after 10km you'll pass a slight rise marked by a sign as 'Tsodilo View' (✪ TSVIEW 18°33.830'S, 21°58.273'E). From here, on a clear day, you should be able to see the Tsodilo Hills to the southwest, but thick vegetation has obscured the view, and sand sprinkled with broken glass makes it a far from attractive place for a break. Less than 3km south of this viewpoint you'll pass a sign to Nxamaseri, which leads to the village of the same name. The turning to Nxamaseri Island Lodge (✪ NXTURN 18°38.125'S, 22°02.797'E) is clearly signposted almost 9km south of the village turn-off. Advanced reservations are essential; this is not a place to try and drop into unannounced. Most visitors are transferred to the lodge (✪ NXAMAS 18°36.426'S, 22°05.268'E) from the airstrip, but self-drivers leave their vehicle in the guarded parking spot by the turning, and are transferred by 4x4 vehicle and boat for the final few kilometres.

Where to stay

✴ 🏠 Nxamaseri Island Lodge [map 412]
(8 chalets) m 7132 6619; e info@nxamaseri. com; www.nxamaseri.com. Started as a fishing camp in about 1980, Nxamaseri is now back in the hands of the original owners, PJ & Barney Bestelink (who run Okavango Horse Safaris) & remains a wonderful all-round lodge justifying a stay of at least 2 days. It has been built within a thick & tropical patch of riverine vegetation. All around are knobthorn (*Senegalia nigrescens*), waterberry (*Syzygium cordatum*), sycamore fig (*Ficus sycomorus*), mangosteen (*Garcinia livingstonei*), jackalberries (*Diospyros mespiliformis*), sausage trees (*Kigelia africana*) & some of the most wonderfully contorting python vines (*Cocculus hirsutus*) that you'll see anywhere.

Ongoing refurbishment means that the strong sense of place has been retained, but with higher standards of accommodation & food. Its wide, thatched lounge/dining area is built around a couple of lofty old jackalberry trees, with an open frontage to the river: it's comfortable & well thought out, but not ornate. Wooden walkways lead to large chalets, a 2-bedroom family room sharing a bathroom & the new 'Tsodilo room'. The chalets are built of brick beneath high thatched roofs, but both the newer rooms & the family room are predominantly canvas structures. Each chalet has four-poster-style mosi nets, bedside lights powered by a generator or batteries, an en-suite shower & toilet, & a wooden deck above the river. More secluded is the spacious 'Tsodilo room', which has a private deck overlooking one of the smaller channels. This is also used as a honeymoon suite &

for guests spending a day at the Tsodilo Hills.

It is claimed that fly-fishing in the Delta was pioneered at Nxamaseri, & certainly it remains an attraction for people who fish seriously, but to this have now been added 1st-class boat trips for birdwatching, visits to a local village to watch basket making, & day trips to the Tsodilo Hills. There tends to be less emphasis on mokoro excursions, but these are also possible (& magical) when the water levels are high & there are suitable areas of shallow water nearby. Fly-fishing & lure/spinning fishing with top-quality equipment under expert guidance are possible throughout the year. That said, the very best tiger fishing months are Aug–Nov, while the best times for bream are Mar–Jun. During the first 3 months of the year the rain & new floodwaters are said to disturb the fish, which move out to the floodplains, so fishing in the channels can be more difficult. Nxamaseri's record tiger fish catch is about 10kg, though in a normal season they'd expect to have 10–15 catches over the 6kg mark. Like most Okavango lodges, Nxamaseri operates a 'catch-&-release' system, except for the occasional bream that has been damaged. They have a large, flat, barge-like boat which provides a particularly stable platform for several people fishing, & is also ideal for photography, plus a fleet of aluminium-hulled craft. *US$600/900 pp sharing/sgl Jul–Oct, US$475 pp rest of year, inc FB, most activities, fishing tackle, transfers from airstrip/road, alcoholic drinks; exc lost tackle. Day trip to Tsodilo Hills & full-day fishing US$170 pp (min 2 people). ⏀ All year.* ★ ★ ★

Sepupa (⊕ SEPUPA 18°44.150'S, 22°10.625'E)
Sepupa, sometimes spelled 'Sepopa', is 1.7km east of the main road, about 223km north of Sehithwa and perhaps 58km south of Shakawe. Here you'll find a few shops including a bottle stall and a general dealer.

Most visitors, however, are looking for Swamp Stop – either to spend the night, or to get a boat across to the eastern side of the river. The lodge is clearly signposted from the main road; just follow the access road to Sepupa Village for 1km until the pot-holed tar runs out, then turn right and continue for a further 2.5km; the track is fine for a 2x4 car.

🏠 Where to stay
For years there was only one option here, but now accommodation has being developed on the tiny Pepere Island, 2.5km long by 1km wide, and there are several houseboats moored close by.

▲ **Swamp Stop** [map 412] (12 chalets, 5 tents, camping) m 7261 0071; e res@swampstop.co.bw; https://sepopa-swampstop.com; ◈ SWAMPS 18°44.749'S, 22°11.843'E. There are big plans for this established backpackers/overland stop, which came under new ownership in 2016. For now, the original riverside campsite under trees is still there, with open pitches, power points & lighting, & an ablution block, & there's a 2nd site, at the back, where 8 neatly swept & reed-fenced pitches have their own BBQ/cooking area, firepit, power & light. Wacky metal doors in a reed enclosure surround the showers & toilets, with handbasins attractively set in an upturned mokoro, & a separate washing-up area. The occasional overlander group gets its own separate area, albeit sharing the same facilities. For those without their own camping kit, there are twin-bedded Meru tents with electric lights close to the bar & restaurant, & refurbished semi-detached chalets kitted out with AC, minibar, en-suite bath & shower & a private deck.

Adjacent to twin oval pools, the Swamp Stop's riverside bar & restaurant has an upstairs deck with views over the papyrus to the main channel of the Okavango. Down below, you can get b/fast, light meals such as sandwiches & burgers, & mains, from curry to steak – or soak up the views with a beer at the bar.

Previous owners have marketed the camp well & positioned it as one of the very few remaining bases for budget safaris into the Delta, & a springboard for getting to Seronga. Now the camp offers the main means of crossing the river, with transfers at P2,200–2,500 per boat – the latter taking up to 16 people. Locally, you can explore the river by motorboat (*from P300/hr, but bring your own fishing tackle*), or take an overnight mokoro trip to Pepere Island, with excursions to the Tsodilo

Hills also on offer. **$$$** *exc b/fast; tent P350 dbl; camping P110 pp.* ⊕ *All year.*

🏠 **Pepere Island** (11 Meru tents) Contact Swamp Stop, see above. The all-inclusive camp at Pepere Island, some 2½hrs by boat from its sister camp, the Swamp Stop, opened in 2008. It has also been bought by the new owners, so considerable change can be expected, but in 2017 things were much the same. It's a simple place, its Meru-style tents set up on wooden decks, & en-suite cabins, with shower & bath, built of timber with reed roofs. Visitors come for the activities – guided mokoro trips, game walks & birding – & the resident wildlife, which includes elephant, zebra, buffalo, red lechwe & sitatunga, as well as hippos & crocs, of course. Of the birds, top attractions are Pel's fishing owl, & the migrant carmine bee-eater. *Tent US$240 dbl FB; cabin P850 dbl, exc meals (P300 pp/day).*

Houseboats As at Shakawe, there are a few houseboats moored on the river here, affording an entirely different perspective on life in the Delta. 3 of these – the *Inkwazi, Inyankuni* & *Madikubu* – are operated by Okavango Houseboats (✆ 686 0802; e krause@info.bw; *www.okavangohouseboats.com*), & cruise between Sepupa & Seronga. If you're prepared to bring all your own food & drinks, you can hire one of these boats outright for P7,280 per day, excluding fuel & transfers, but with a crew available to prepare your meals. Alternatively, you can organise to stay on a full-board basis (*P636 pp per night, exc drinks, use of tender boats & activities;* ★).

The boats are accessible by road, but transfers from Sepupa to Seronga can be arranged at P650 pp return, while airstrip transfers are P140.

THE DELTA'S WESTERN FRINGES

Ordered from north to south, here's a brief listing of the main landmarks and villages on the road between Sepupa and Sehithwa. If it gets a little repetitive, then take that as a fair reflection of the road, which is long and well surfaced with tarmac. Most of this area has a low, wide verge of groundcover which is often cut – helping to ensure that big game can be seen before it is standing in front of you. But for all this visibility, the scenery is uninteresting.

Although you're travelling at times very close to the western edge of the Okavango Delta, the road passes through apparently undistinguished areas of bush. You may see the occasional animal, but with man and cattle as the dominant species in this area, only birdwatchers are likely to find much of interest on the drive.

SEPUPA TO ETSHA 13 The overall standard of the tar road along the western side of the Delta is generally pretty good, and while it was riddled with often large potholes in 2017, efforts to repair these were ongoing.

Ikoga Gate About 12km south of the Sepupa turn-off, or 211km north of Sehithwa, you may have to stop at the Ikoga Gate (✛ VET-IK 18°50.327'S, 22°13.756'E), which is a checkpoint on the Thamacha Veterinary Fence.

Ikoga turning About 206km north of Sehithwa, there's another turning east, this time to Ikoga.

Etsha 13 Some 32km south of the Sepupa turn-off, or 191km north of Sehithwa, is a turning (✛ E13TUR 19°00.793'S, 22°17.356'E), which leads slightly over 3km east to Etsha 13. This small village has a few basic shops, but little more. More important for visitors, it marks the access road to Guma Lagoon and Guma Lagoon Camp.

GUMA LAGOON On the western side of the Delta, at the very base of the Panhandle, Guma is a large, papyrus-lined lagoon. It is linked to the Thaoge River, the main eastern finger of the Okavango River system, by a short channel (40 minutes by boat from the camp or the lodge). Both Guma Lagoon and the main Thaoge River are excellent spots for fishing and birdwatching – a combination that, with relatively easy 4x4 access from around Etsha 13, has encouraged two very different camps to set up here. Note that during heavy rains or high water, alternative access routes to

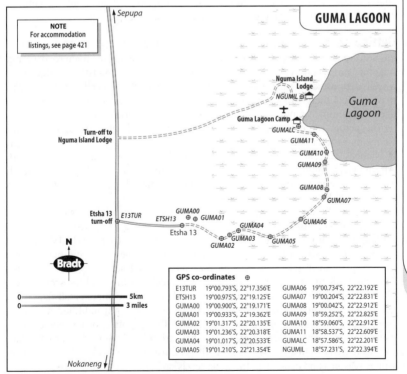

GUMA LAGOON

NOTE
For accommodation
listings, see page 421

Sepupa

Nguma Island
Lodge
NGUMIL

Guma
Lagoon

Guma Lagoon Camp
GUMALC
GUMA11
GUMA10
GUMA09
GUMA08
GUMA07

Turn-off to
Nguma Island Lodge

Etsha 13
turn-off   E13TUR   ETSH13   GUMA00   GUMA01
GUMA04
GUMA06
Etsha 13   GUMA03   GUMA05
GUMA02

N
Bradt

0   5km
0   3 miles

Nokaneng

GPS co-ordinates ✛			
E13TUR	19°00.793'S, 22°17.356'E	GUMA06	19°00.734'S, 22°22.192'E
ETSH13	19°00.975'S, 22°19.125'E	GUMA07	19°00.204'S, 22°22.831'E
GUMA00	19°00.900'S, 22°19.171'E	GUMA08	19°00.042'S, 22°22.912'E
GUMA01	19°00.933'S, 22°19.362'E	GUMA09	18°59.252'S, 22°22.825'E
GUMA02	19°01.317'S, 22°20.135'E	GUMA10	18°59.060'S, 22°22.912'E
GUMA03	19°01.236'S, 22°20.318'E	GUMA11	18°58.537'S, 22°22.609'E
GUMA04	19°01.017'S, 22°20.533'E	GUMALC	18°57.586'S, 22°22.201'E
GUMA05	19°01.210'S, 22°21.354'E	NGUMIL	18°57.231'S, 22°22.394'E

14

the camps may be put in place. These are often extremely sandy with some water crossings, and can be difficult to navigate, so a 4x4 is essential.

Flora and fauna highlights Guma isn't a place for big game; it's a deep-water environment that offers good birdwatching and fishing.

The vegetation around the lagoon is mainly papyrus, though you'll also find large stands of phragmites reeds. You'll also find the odd waterberry (*Syzygium cordatum*) and water fig (*Ficus verruculosa*), especially in the smaller channels and backwaters.

On the banks, the riverine vegetation is thick and lush. It includes plenty of wild date palms (*Phoenix reclinata*), river beans (*Sesbania sesban*) and potato bushes (*Phyllanthus reticulatus*), which are members of the euphorbia family and are not related to potatoes at all – but smell the air on a warm evening and you'll realise where their name comes from.

Also keep an eye out for large sour plum (*Ximenia caffra*), water pear (*Syzygium guineense*), jackalberry trees (*Diospyros mespiliformis*) and the occasional sausage tree (*Kigelia africana*) – one of which greets you as you enter Guma Lagoon Camp. Further from the water, you'll often find acacias: camelthorn (*Vachellia erioloba*), knobthorn (*Senegalia nigrescens*) and umbrella thorn (*Vachellia tortilis*) are the main species here. There are a few baobabs (*Adansonia digitata*) in the area, but they're not common.

The more common birds include fish eagles, many species of herons, egrets, warblers, bee-eaters and kingfishers, pygmy geese and greater and lesser jacanas. Look for red-shouldered widows in the papyrus, and reed cormorants and darters sunning themselves on perches over the water.

In the riverine forest areas you can find Heuglin's robins (white-browed robin chats), crested and black-collared barbets, green pigeons, various sunbirds and, in summer, the spectacular paradise flycatchers in breeding plumage.

Getting there and away Despite their proximity, the two lodges at Guma Lagoon are normally accessed from two separate points along the main road: Guma Lagoon Camp (and the lagoon itself) via Etsha 13, and Nguma Island Lodge, from a well-signposted turning about 3km further north. You'll need a 4x4; if you're driving a 2x4 then with prior notice the lodges can arrange to collect you at a pre-agreed location, leaving your car somewhere safe while you're at the camp.

The actual routes depend on the conditions. Signboards to Nguma Island Lodge make their access drive of 12km or so relatively straightforward. Although it changes according to the prevailing conditions, it is usually well marked. Alternatively, Nguma Island Lodge has an airstrip, or you can fly in to the small airstrip at Gumare and be collected from there. It may also be possible to fly in to Seronga, and be transferred to the lodge by boat from there.

However, the track to Guma Lagoon Camp, although marked with arrows, is very sandy and considerably more circuitous; it's easy to get lost. The first hurdle is finding the right track out of the small village of Etsha 13 (✪ ETSH13 19°00.975'S, 22°19.125'E). In theory there's a sign saying 'camp' on a telephone pole, but it's none too clear. This will take you through the village on a track going east-southeast. Gradually this turns east, then northeast, and finally north – and the scenery gets prettier, with fewer domestic animals and settlements, and more small date palm islands and open floodplains. The distance varies between 10km and 13km, and you'll need to allow around 45 minutes. As a guide, GPS waypoints for just one possible route are shown on the map on page 419. There are certainly more direct routes than this, as the whole area is criss-crossed with confusing bush tracks. However, many will be seasonal and depend on the water levels, so beware of getting stuck!

Where to stay There are only two choices at this lagoon. Though both have campsites as well as tented rooms, they are each quite different and don't generally work closely together.

Guma Lagoon Camp [map 419] (12 'cabins', camping) 687 4626; e info@guma-lagoon.com; www.guma-lagoon.com; ⊕ GUMALC 18°57.586'S, 22°22.201'E. Relaxed, friendly & popular with anglers, Guma Lagoon Camp occupies a picturesque spot with open views across the lagoon. It focuses mainly on self-drive, self-catering visitors, although meals can be provided with advance notice.

Nestling among the trees at the water's edge are en-suite 'cabins', constructed of wood & canvas on raised decks to catch the breeze. With twin/dbl beds, wooden floors, electric lights & a veranda over the lagoon, they're comfortable, but not luxurious. At the campsite, each of the 7 pitches has its own toilet, hot shower & braai pit. Guests prepare meals in the fully equipped kitchen, with pots, pans, cutlery, cooking equipment & fridge/freezing facilities, before congregating in the shaded dining/bar area with a deck extending over the lagoon. A small pool is a welcome place to cool off, perhaps after a game of volleyball.

In addition to boating & fishing (*boat hire from P295/hr, exc fuel*), there is the option of a full-day mokoro trip (*P1,190/2 people*), or staying overnight on one of the islands (*from P1,420 pp, plus P392/day for a luggage mokoro*); note that children under 12 may not take part in mokoro excursions. Camping equipment can be hired, & food/drinks organised by the camp with advance notice. Rates exclude transfers (*P107 pp*) & concession fees (*P50 pp*). **$$$** *Camping P135 pp; 4x4 transfer from Etsha 13 P115 pp one-way.* ⊕ *All year.*

Nguma Island Lodge [map 419] (13 Meru tents, 6 self-catering tents, camping) 683 0159; m 7356 0120; e nguma@dynabyte.bw; www. ngumalodge.com; ⊕ NGUMIS 18°57.231'S, 22°22.394'E. Situated on the northwestern edge of the lagoon, this lodge was opened in 2000,

& is owned & run by Nookie Randall, who has lived in the area for over 20 years with her late husband, Geoff. (Geoff played an important part in pioneering the fibreglass mekoro in the area – & thus is partially responsible for saving an enormous number of the Delta's old trees!)

It's a linear site, neatly divided into two. At one end, where the lodge is based, tents are spread out among the trees along fairly high wooden walkways & raised up on high wooden decking. Inside you'll find comfortable twin beds with percale linen & colourful cushions, chairs, a bedside table & a wrought-iron hanging unit. At the back of each tent is an en-suite shower, toilet & washbasin. Power comes from a generator, with a system of back-up batteries for the lights at night; batteries can be charged in the main area.

Walkways continue to the raised main area, so everything is above water if levels rise to a high flood. Normally the ground beneath is dry, with cool lawns dotted with date palms. A comfortable lounge, dining room & well-stocked bar are housed in a large log cabin. There's a better collection of local baskets & craftwork than in most curio shops, & some are for sale in the small shop.

At the other end of the site, but under the same cool canopy of trees, is the Delta Dawn campsite. As well as camping pitches, there are pre-erected twin tents with linen & towels provided. Ablutions are simple, with wooden-clad showers & toilets, & there are also braai stands & facilities for washing up. The campsite's bar & restaurant, however, was not open in mid 2017. (Fishermen should note that there is no freezer space.)

Activities include ½-day, full-day & overnight trips by mokoro, as well as boat trips by the hour (for up to 6 people). Fishing tackle is available for hire, & lures, etc, for sale. Other options include island walks & birding excursions. *Rates on application.* ⊕ *All year.*

What to see and do Precise activities depend on where you're staying, though boat trips are really the main draw. On the whole, the water's deep enough to limit the scope of mokoro for most of the year, and so motorboats are the vehicle of choice. If you're not a devout angler or birdwatcher, then just take a few rods and a pair of binoculars and do a little of both – it's very relaxing.

In 1969, the war in Angola (which, in many ways, was an extension of the Cold War using African proxies) displaced a large number of mostly Hambukushu people from the Caprivi area into Botswana. There they were accepted as refugees. Initially they were received at Shakawe, but eventually the plan was to move them to a new village to the south, called Etsha (pronounced 'Etsa').

However, while the refugees were at Shakawe it's said that they naturally split into 13 separate groups. So when they were moved, they naturally split into 13 villages, which spread out along the western edge of the Delta, 1km apart. They were called, somewhat unimaginatively, Etsha 1, Etsha 2, Etsha 3 and so on up to the most northerly, Etsha 13.

Now the old track that links them and runs close to the Delta has been largely superseded by the new tar highway, which takes a more direct route on the east of the old road. However, you'll still find tracks linking the two, one of which is close to Etsha 13, and another close to Etsha 6.

ETSHA 6 TO SEHITHWA

Etsha 6 About 45km south of the Sepupa turn-off (178km north of Sehithwa) there's a signposted turning (⊕ E6TURN 19°06.706'S, 22°16.152'E) to Etsha 6, which is less than 3km east of the road. For the traveller, it's a reasonable halfway point between the turn-offs to the Gcwihaba Caves and the Tsodilo Hills, but visitor accommodation is currently lacking.

Fuel is available from a Shell station in the centre of town, though don't rely on it. Opposite is a Co-op which stocks tinned food, soft drinks and basic staples like rice and maize in quantity, though there's very little fresh produce.

Turning right on to the old Panhandle road at the T-junction near here will bring you to the post office, with an internet café, though the old hand-pump fuel station here no longer exists. A further kilometre or so along the road, a craft shop run by the Botswana Council of Churches (BCC) sells very nice baskets woven on the premises, though opening hours seem erratic.

Gumare An ostentatious new 'bus rank' on the main road signals the turn-off to the east for Gumare, which lies about 146km north of Sehithwa, 37km from Nokaneng, and 77km south of Sepupa. There are both Shell and Engen fuel stations here, making Gumare one of the more reliable places to fill up along this side of the Delta.

The town itself (⊕ GUMARE 19°22.242'S, 22°09.242'E) is one of the main towns of the Panhandle area, and has clearly seen considerable investment in recent years. The roads into town are tarred, and as if vying for attention with the bus station, there's a smart branch of Barclays Bank, with a (usually working) ATM, a post office and a large Shoprite supermarket, which is great for stocking up on supplies. If you've time to spare, it may be worth seeking out the small craft shop, Ngwao Baskets (⏲ 08.00–16.00 Mon–Fri), on the road into town, where you'll find good local baskets at reasonable prices.

 Where to stay While there are several guesthouses in Gumare, most are extremely overpriced for what they offer.

🏠 **Ramorwa Guest House** (10 rooms) ✆687 4556; **m** 7169 4999; **e** ramorwaguest@botsnet.   bw; ⊕ RAMORW 19°21.770'S, 22°09.973'E. About 1.3km from the centre of Gumare, & well signposted, Ramorwa is tucked away down a quiet residential street. Small but comfortable rooms lead off a tree-shaded courtyard, a pleasant place to make use of free Wi-Fi access. With AC, TV & fridge, & a dbl bed under mosi nets, they're well equipped but not fancy. If you can't face the walk into town, you can get traditional or international-style meals here, too. **$$** *exc b/fast*.

Sexhebe Guesthouse m 7176 0038. This rather imposing guesthouse lies on the main road, just north of the turn-off to the town, but despite repeated attempts we have been unable to raise anyone to show us around. We understand that it has 3 categories of rooms, all with AC, TV & an en-suite shower. Meals are available on request, & there's Wi-Fi & guarded parking. **$–$$**

Where to eat and drink Not only does Gumare have a restaurant, it actually offers a selection. Of these the best is rather aptly considered to be Best Food, on the right as you enter the town from the main tar road, while a good alternative is the Rocla Restaurant. If all you're after is food for a picnic, there's also a good bakery in town, and a couple of grocery stores.

Nokaneng

The village of Nokaneng (⊕ NOKANE 19°39.694'S, 22°11.184'E), about 114km south of Sepupa, 109km north of Sehithwa, is marked by a radio mast amid a group of houses. There's little to detain the visitor here except a small grocery shop and a bar.

More significantly for travellers, shortly north of the radio mast is a road heading west signposted '120 to Qangwa' (⊕ QANGTO 19°39.608'S, 22°11.063'E). This leads eventually to the Namibian border, near Tsumkwe, where there's a relatively new border crossing (but check that it's open before you go). Before the border, the village of Qangwa marks the point where you can turn south and access both the Aha Hills area and, eventually, the Gcwihaba Hills and Caves. See pages 436–45 for more on these areas.

Tsau

About 180km south of Sepupa or 43km north of Sehithwa, you'll come across a turning to the village of Tsau (often written 'Tsao'), just to the east of the main road (⊕ TSAU 20°10.294'S, 22°27.265'E). Its prominent radio mast is quite a landmark, too. Here you'll find lots of small houses, though relatively little tree or vegetation cover, and a few small, general shops. Back on the main road, there's a small stall announcing 'tyre fix' – handy in an area where punctures are all too frequent.

Some 10km north of Tsau is a large banner on the side of the road (⊕ GTURN1 20°07.047'S, 22°22.291'E), marking a more southerly turn-off to the Gcwihaba Hills and Caves.

Setata Veterinary Fence Gate

About 27.5km north of Sehithwa you'll have to stop and pass through the Setata Gate (⊕ VET-SE 20°15.775'S, 22°33.926'E) in the veterinary fence. Here as at other veterinary checkpoints, campers may have their vehicles searched for red meat, which you are not permitted to take across the vet fence.

Sehithwa

Coming from the Panhandle, you'll reach a T-junction, where you meet the tarred A3. Turning left will bring you to the turn-off for Sehithwa, and on to Toteng and Maun, while right leads to Ghanzi, some 195km away. Note that the layout of this junction is not entirely clear on the 2008 Shell map.

The village of Sehithwa (⊕ SEHITH 20°28.259'S, 22°42.372'E) itself lies just south of the main A3, about 93km from Maun. There's a fuel station close to the turning that is under new ownership, so fuel supplies are considered to be more reliable than in the past. That said, it still makes sense to fill up wherever you can.

Sehithwa is a more substantial settlement than Toteng, with a couple of small guesthouses, of which one – Ditoro Guest Lodge – is 1km or so from the main road. You'll also find a few general shops and liquor stores, and a not-inconsiderable police station. Sehithwa and Toteng have a significant Herero population, and you will often pass ladies in the typical Victorian-style full-skirted dress and striking headdress.

LAKE NGAMI The existence of a great lake within the Kalahari was known to Europeans from early reports of Bakwena and Batawana people, though it wasn't reached by them until the mid 19th century. Livingstone arrived on 1 August 1849, with Cotton, Oswell and Murray, narrowly beating Charles Andersson, who set out specifically to reach it from present-day Namibia.

In his book, *Lake Ngami and the River Okavango* (see *Appendix 3,* page 539), Andersson was hugely disappointed with what he first took to be Lake Ngami. He wrote:

> At last a blue line of great extent appeared in the distance, and I made sure it was the long-sought object; but I was still doomed in my disappointment. It turned out to be merely a large hollow in the rainy season filled with water, but now dry and covered with saline encrustations.

However, he hadn't reached the lake at this stage, and after getting beyond some pans and reedbeds, and over a series of sand ridges, he finally glimpsed the water, and described the moment:

> There, indeed, at no very great distance, lay spread before me an immense sheet of water bounded only by the horizon – the object of my ambition for years, and for which I have abandoned home and friends, and risked my life.

Visiting the lake is certainly easier than it was for those first explorers, though signposting is poor, and at times it can still be very disappointing. Even after the exceptional rains of 2008–09, much of the lakeshore was lined by shoulder-high thistles, so while the lake had plenty of water, it was still far from being an attraction in its own right.

Note that although the lake is very large when full, a high rate of evaporation and a very shallow profile means that the area covered by water can vary enormously.

Getting there and away The lake's bed is surrounded by a triangle of good roads, so approaching it is in theory a matter of turning off one of these and following your nose (or, perhaps better, your compass or GPS). However, it's one of those areas where all roads seem to lead back to where you first started – often enough to Sehithwa – so while you can strike out on your own, there's a simpler way.

About 3.5km north of Sehithwa, on the main road towards Toteng and Maun, there is a clear sign to the lake pointing to the south of the road (✪ LKNGTO 20°27.021'S, 22°44.427'E). Turn down that track and after continuing straight for about 2km you should get to the lake (✪ LNGAMI 20°27.812'S, 24°45.247'E).

When to visit The pithy answer to this question is 'whenever it's full of water!' And there lies the rub; it's only worth going if there's water in the lake, but few people will have been there and be able to tell you. Your best chance of getting up-to-date information is probably from operators in Maun, and especially the pilots, because if the lake is just a wide expanse of clay, it's better to save yourself a trip.

The state of this mystical lake varies greatly, depending upon whether the Delta's flood, which has historically been Lake Ngami's main source of water, has been high enough to overflow into the Kunyere River which feeds the lake. The lake was an empty dustbowl for the late 1980s and 1990s, but then filled to a shallow depth during 2000 and 2001, and since 2009 has held a serious amount of water. So ask around to find out what's happening.

If and when it really floods, Lake Ngami comes alive with birdlife, and has been identified as one of Botswana's 'important bird areas' (IBAs). From October, the ducks, geese, waders and other northern migrants arrive, lining the muddy shores until the weather cools towards the end of April. The flamingos, both greater and lesser, don't choose their times so carefully – being found here in their thousands whenever the conditions are right for the algae on which they feed. They appear from the shore as a pink haze settled on the water's surface.

Where to stay There's nowhere official to stay near the lake, but the land is open enough to camp rough – provided that you ask permission first from the nearest local villagers. On my last visit the villagers suggested that I go a few kilometres away from the lake to avoid the mosquitoes. This was a very wise move. You'll need to be self-sufficient, of course; and don't count on finding any drinkable water.

What to see and do This is purely a birding destination, though because visitors here are really very rare there are no tracks or pathways (for 4x4s or walkers) designed for birdwatchers. All the tracks have been made to serve the villagers and their many, many cattle. All this makes getting around time-consuming and at times difficult – but if there's water here then it might be worth it.

It's worth noting that Lake Ngami has been incorporated in a new management plan for the Okavango Delta, which proposes developing tourist facilities along the Panhandle and creating a scenic route along this western side as far as the lake. If birdwatching tours start up here, perhaps with the opportunity to take a canoe out on the lake, it could be quite a draw – when the lake is full of water!

TOTENG TO MAUN

Toteng Though a significant dot on the map, Toteng (✛ TOTENG 20°21.407'S, 22°57.204'E) is little more than a road junction at the centre of a sprinkling of small cattle-farming homesteads. Once it marked the turning southwest to Ghanzi, but now that the new tarred A3 goes via Sehithwa, it's easy not to notice the place at all. If you're looking for the old road to Ghanzi, you'll find it at ✛ GH2OLD 20°21.407'S, 22°57.204'E, on the west side of the main road.

Despite its apparent insignificance, Toteng has historical importance as a centre for the Batawana; in his *The Guide to Botswana*, Alec Campbell (see *Appendix 3*, page 543) comments that: 'When they arrived in Ngamiland in 1795 they settled at Kgwebe and later moved to Toteng.' This was also one of the areas that received an influx of Herero people after their defeat at the Battle of Waterberg.

Beyond Toteng, the tar road leads in around 64km to Maun. If you're planning to stop *en route*, there's a delightful small camp, Tshima Bush Camp, about equidistant between Toteng and Maun, though you do need to have a reservation; for details, see page 213.

THE NORTHWEST KALAHARI

This area is Botswana at its most enigmatic. Here you'll find huge tracts of the Kalahari, punctuated only by isolated Bushman settlements. It's an area where you need to have a good 4x4 (or two), and for the most part you must be totally self-sufficient – travelling with all your own food, water, fuel and equipment.

It's not somewhere which will attract visitors for its game viewing or birdwatching, though you will find both game and birds. In fact, it's not an area that attracts many visitors at all. But old Africa hands are drawn here for its isolated ranges of hills. One displays a breathtaking cultural heritage of paintings, another hides a labyrinthine cave system, and a third – well … the Aha Hills are just there. On the map. In the middle of the Kalahari. Waiting to be visited.

For more information on the science and explorations of this area, interested readers are directed to numerous articles in *Botswana Notes and Records*, some of which are noted in *Appendix 3*, pages 540–3.

⌂ WHERE TO STAY You can camp at the Tsodilo Hills, the Gcwihaba Caves and the Aha Hills (see the relevant sections later in this chapter for details), but if you're looking for something that's arguably even more isolated, there is a new lodge a couple of hours' drive west of Tsau that could fit the bill.

⌂ Feline Fields [map 438] (6 suites) `686 5756; m 7222 2302; e info@felinefields. com; www.felinefields.com; ✛ FELIN 19°58.560'S, 21°48.800'E. Sometimes referred to as the 'Lodge at Feline Fields' or simply 'The Lodge', this ambitious new property is set in the bush about halfway between the main Sehithwa–Shakawe road & Gcwihaba Caves. The brainchild of Marjan Bloom & Raphael Real del Sarte, it was designed & built to be 'the perfect safari lodge', & they have gone a long way to achieving their goal. The main area is a large thatched wooden building that houses an open-fronted kitchen, where you can watch the chefs as they prepare varied & delicious meals for you to eat in the communal dining area. To one side is a library with an Apple Mac for guests to use, free Wi-Fi & seating that includes an inviting sofa swing; to the other side a well-stocked bar. Activity is key, here, with a 25m lap pool surrounded by sunloungers, a small but well-equipped 'bush' gym above the pool, an outdoor hard tennis court & a golf driving range.

The well-spaced suites come in 2 styles – thatched 2-storey pool suites, & smaller tented suites, their décor combining modern styling with safari classics & personal touches. Each of the 3 pool suites, which include free Wi-Fi & a Polaroid camera for guests to use, has a raised super-king-size bed, separate day bed, writing desk & chair, fans, a mini-fridge and an enormous en-suite bathroom with a shower, bath, his & hers sinks & a separate toilet. Upstairs, a 2nd day bed makes the most of the Kalahari views, & in front a private 4m x 6m swimming pool is set into a large wooden deck. The 3 tented suites come with twin beds or a dbl & have the bonus of an outdoor 'star bath'. Distances between the suites & the main area are such that guests are offered mountain bikes to get around. Not surprisingly, mountain biking is included in the activities here, along with golf,

tennis, horseriding, spa treatments & nature drives. The lodge's proximity to the Aha Hills, Xai Xai & the Gcwihaba Caves allows superb access to San cultural experiences, & a San guide from Xai Xai can be arranged on request to show you the caves or perform a trance dance in the Aha Hills; it is also possible to visit a San village.

Feline Fields is not a safari destination but a few days here will allow guests to indulge in relaxation & great food, & to experience a taste of San culture. *Tented suite US$890 pp, pool suite US$1,190 pp, inc FB, drinks, laundry, road transfers & most activities, exc specialised San activities & air transfers.* ⊕ *All year.* ★★★★–★★★★★

TSODILO HILLS (\ 687 8025; ⊕ 07.30–17.30; admission P50 pp; camping P130 pp/ night) Rising above the bush-covered undulations of the western Kalahari, the Tsodilo Hills consist of four hills, roughly in a line, with names from San folklore: the Male Hill, the Female Hill, the Child Hill and a smaller unnamed kopje. Highest is the Male Hill, reaching 410m above the surrounding bush, and – at over 1,400m in total – often considered to be the highest point in Botswana. The San believe that the most sacred place in the hills is near the top. Their tradition is that the first spirit knelt on this hill to pray after creating the world, and that you can still see the impression of his knees in the rock there.

The Female Hill, which covers almost three times the area of the Male, is a little to its north, but reaches only about 300m above the plain. This is where most of the main rock art sites can be seen. Then there's the Child Hill, 2km further north again, and smaller still at only about 40m high. And another 2.2km northwest of the Child is a yet-smaller kopje that is said by the San to be the first wife of the Male Hill, who was then left when he met the Female Hill.

Archaeologists say that the hills have been sporadically inhabited for about 60,000 years – making this one of the world's oldest historical sites. For only about the last millennium has this included Bantu people; for thousands of years prior to that, the San lived here, hunting, using springs in the hills for water, and painting animals (over 2,000 of them) on the rocks.

For both San and Bantu, the Tsodilo Hills were a mystical place, a 'home of very old and very great spirits' who demanded respect from visitors. As told in *The Lost World of the Kalahari* (essential reading before any visit here; see *Appendix 3,* page 542), these spirits created much trouble for some of the first Europeans to visit – and were still doing so as recently as the 1950s. Long ago it must have been, in van der Post's words, 'a great fortress of living bushman culture, a Louvre of the desert filled with treasure.'

The Tsodilo Hills remain a remarkable place, an important national monument which, in 2001, was declared a UNESCO World Heritage Site. While this should help to safeguard the hills for future generations, I can't visit without wondering what it was like when the San were here. What we regard now as the high art of an ancient people is remarkable, but it's very sad that our understanding of it is now devoid of the meaning and spirituality with which it was once imbued.

Visitors are no longer permitted to explore the Tsodilo Hills alone, but it's still worth spending several days searching out the paintings along the marked trails with a guide. However, after several visits over the years, I am left remembering

14

TSODILO HILLS

KEY

Gravel road	⎯⎯⎯⎯
4x4 track	=======
Cliff Trail	⎯ ⎯ ⎯
Rhino Trail	··········
Lion Trail	— — —
Male Hill Trail	▬ ▬ ▬ ▬

GPS co-ordinates ⊕

LITURN	18°45.538'S,	21°45.109'E
MLTURN	18°44.243'S,	21°43.575'E
SANVIL	18°48.147'S,	21°43.903'E
TSODTO	18°47.378'S,	21°44.981'E
TSOMUS	18°45.526'S,	21°44.208'E

Rhino Trail

1 Nos 2/8 up ravine and on top
2 Nos 9/10 including 2 rhino
3 No 11 whales and penguin
4 No 13 Laurens van der Post
    panel (high up)
5 Nos 14/16

Cliff Trail

A Zebra, rhino, lion
B Elephant
C Python cave
D Aardvark

Child Hill ▲

B
A C
D
Start of Cliff Trail
MLTURN ⊕

Female Hill ▲

Start of Rhino Trail/1
Museum
TSOMUS ⊕
5
4
Remains of old settlement
2
3
Cave 12
LITURN ⊕

Lion panel & start of Lion Trail

Nxamaseri →

Male Hill ▲

White Paintings shelter

Fence
Gate
Old San Village

N
Bradt
Campsite ▲
Airstrip ✈

0 ⎯⎯⎯ 1,000m
0 ⎯⎯⎯ 500yds

Campsite ▲

Main gate
TSODTO ⊕
Campsite gate

← Tshukumutshu

Fence

Hambukushu Village

San Village ⊕ SANVIL

NOTE
For accommodation listings, see pages 432–3

428

the captivating feeling of spirituality in the hills far more than simply the images of the paintings, however remarkable. I've known this to disturb some visitors profoundly; they were uneasy to the point of wanting to flee the hills, and couldn't wait to get away, while others find the hills entrancing and completely magical.

So if you come here, then do so with respect and take your time – don't just come to tick it off your itinerary and leave.

A word of warning In *The Lost World of the Kalahari*, you can read Laurens van der Post's story of his first visit to the hills: of how his party ignored the advice of their guide, and disturbed the spirits of the hills by hunting warthog and steenbok on their way. Once at the hills, his companion's camera magazines inexplicably kept jamming, his tape recorders stopped working, and bees repeatedly attacked his group – and the problems only ceased when they made a written apology to the spirits.

So perhaps the spirits here are one more reason why you ought to treat the Tsodilo Hills with the very greatest of respect when you visit them.

Folklore and archaeology The Tsodilo Hills hold a special spiritual significance for the people of the region, and are of immense archaeological value to the wider world for what can be learned about some of our earliest ancestors.

Folklore The San believe the hills contain the spirits of the dead, and that their powerful gods live in caves within the Female Hill, from where they rule the world. They believe that these gods will cause misfortune to anyone who hunts or causes death near the hills.

They have many beliefs, all specific to places within the hills. For example, there's a cave on the western side of the Female Hill that contains a permanent source of water and, the San believe, a giant serpent with spiralling horns, like a kudu. If a San guide takes you around the hills, then ask them about legends and stories associated with the places that you visit on the hills.

Meanwhile the Hambukushu people, who also live in the area, believe that God lowered man to earth at the site of the hills, and he landed on the Female Hill. For proof they point to footprints engraved into the rock, high up on the hill. However, modern sceptics claim these are simply natural marks in the rock, or suggest that they might even be the footprints of dinosaurs!

Archaeology Archaeologists think that people (*Homo sapiens* as opposed to *Homo erectus*) have occupied the area for at least 60,000 years. Estimating the age of rock paintings is very difficult, and is usually done by linking a style of painting with nearby artefacts which can be scientifically dated with precision (eg: by carbon-14 dating techniques).

However, the Tsodilo Hills have been the subject of more archaeological research than most of southern Africa's sites – so we do have an idea about the people who lived here. So far, most of the evidence unearthed dates from the Middle Stone Age period. There have been several major excavations, including ones at the Depression Shelter, the Rhino Cave and White Paintings. (See *Appendix 3,* pages 540–1, for articles in *Botswana Notes and Records* with more details. There's also a more personal view of a visit to one of these excavations in Mike Main's *Kalahari: Life's Variety in Dune and Delta*.)

Excavations at White Paintings, a site at the base of the Male Hill, indicate habitation going back at least 40,000–50,000 years. For this the archaeological team

14

excavated as deep as 7m below ground level, finding a variety of stone blades and scrapers. It's estimated that over 55% of the raw materials for these tools don't occur in the hills, and must have been brought in from outside. This at least indicates a movement of people, and perhaps early bartering or trading networks.

Excavations at the Depression Shelter certainly indicate that people were using coloured pigments here, probably for painting, more than 19,000 years ago. However, despite what you'll often read, nobody really knows exactly how the artists made their paints. Many things have been suggested, but animal fats and derivatives of plants seem the likely binding agents, probably mixed with pigments obtained largely from ash, various minerals and plant dyes. Iron oxide, in the form of ochre, seems a particularly likely mineral to have been used.

Meanwhile much more recently, about AD800–1000, specularite was being mined here intensively. This mineral was historically used for cosmetic purposes by groups within southern Africa, further emphasising the likelihood of a long-standing trade network that included the people of the Tsodilo.

The paintings The paintings at the Tsodilo Hills chart thousands of years of human habitation, and include some of the world's most important and impressive rock art. Its special nature is augmented by the realisation that these hills are 250km from the nearest other known rock art. They are totally removed from all of southern Africa's other rock paintings. Even within the hills, some of the paintings are located on high, inaccessible cliffs, with commanding views over the landscape. This was surely a deliberate part of the paintings for the people who created them – although soil erosion has probably also played its part.

Campbell and Coulson, in their excellent book *African Rock Art* (see *Appendix 3*, page 543), assert that the Tsodilo Hills 'contain some 4,000 red finger paintings composed of about 50% animals, 37% geometrics, and 13% highly stylised human figures'.

The paintings belong to several different styles and if you take the time to look closely at them will often amaze you with their detail. Although most of the animals painted are wild, Campbell and Coulson noted that there is a much higher incidence of paintings of domestic stock than at any other similar sites in southern Africa.

The human figures include many schematic men painted with erect penises. It's thought that these could be associated with the trance dance – a traditional dance of the San in which rhythmic breathing often produces an altered state of consciousness.

Geology The Tsodilo Hills are formed from metamorphic rocks that are technically known as micaceous quartzite schists. These started out as shales, probably deposited as mud on the surface of an ancient sea. Great heat and pressure in the earth changed them, and you can see the small crystals of minerals formed during this process if you look carefully.

Tsodilo's schists have particularly high mica and quartz contents, and a coarse-grained surface. Conveniently, this texture means that rocks give a good grip to rubber-soled shoes, so they're relatively easy to clamber around. In many places there are piles of boulders, and you'll often need to hop between these if you want to explore the hills.

There are a few permanent springs of water in the hills, but these are very difficult to find without a local guide. They were certainly important to the early inhabitants of the area though, as they would have been the only water sources for miles around.

Flora and fauna Unlike most destinations for visitors in Botswana, a visit to the Tsodilo Hills really isn't about looking for animals, birds or plants. The focus is much more cultural and historical. That said, don't forget that you are in a very sparsely populated area of the northern Kalahari and there is wildlife around.

On the roads that approach the hills I've been very aware of fresh elephant dung, and fleeting glimpses of occasional fleeing small buck. There are certainly kudu, steenbok and duiker here permanently, as well as leopard and probably spotted hyena.

In his 1934 book *The Mammals of South West Africa* (see *Appendix 3,* page 540), G C Shortridge records that klipspringer were found here at the hills, although I've not come across any reports of them more recently, so it seems unlikely that there is any population of them left now.

Everywhere around the hills you'll find quite a wide variety of birdlife, including the ubiquitous grey hornbills – easily heard as well as seen with their descending call of 'phe, phephee, pheephee, pheeoo, phew, pheeoo-pheeoo' (with thanks to Kenneth Newman – see *Appendix 3,* page 542 – for expressing this song so well on paper!).

Look out also for the Tsodilo gecko (*Pachydactylus tsodiloensis*), a small, nocturnal gecko with yellow and brown stripes which is endemic to these hills.

Looking at the vegetation, keep your eyes open for stands of mongongo trees (*Ricinodendron rautanenii*), which occur on the hills and sometimes in pure stands on the Kalahari's sand. These can reach 15–20m in height, and are characterised by smooth, often peeling bark on grey to light-brown stems and compound leaflets a little like the chestnut trees of Europe. After sprays of yellow flowers around October–November, they produce egg-shaped grey-green fruits from February onwards. These can be up to 3.5cm x 2.5cm in size, covered with smooth hairs. Inside these are mongongo nuts, which can be cracked open to reveal an edible kernel – one of the most important, and celebrated, foods for the San across the Kalahari. Coates Palgrave (see *Appendix 3,* page 542) comments that this is a protected tree in South Africa, and that its light, strong wood is sometimes used as a substitute for imported balsa wood.

Although large animals aren't prolific in this area, there is big game in the bush around the hills, including elephants, so drive carefully when you are in the area.

Getting there and away Access to the Tsodilo Hills was improved immeasurably around 2004 with the construction of a new route from the main Shakawe–Sehithwa road. With a relatively smooth gravel surface, it has cut down driving time during the dry season to about 40 minutes, and in so doing has completely changed the nature of a visit here. After heavy rains, however, the gravel road can become very muddy, so in those conditions you'll need to allow nearer to 2 hours for the journey. This road is normally accessible by 2x4, but when you arrive at the hills, a high-clearance vehicle may be advisable.

In the past, there were two access routes: both difficult, sandy, 4x4-only routes, taking about 2½–3 bone-shaking hours (mostly in low-range gear) to complete. Both boasted an unusual type of corrugation which made the whole vehicle bounce up and down. Drive faster than about 10km/h and you found your head hitting the ceiling. It was painful, and ensured that getting to the hills was always a long and tedious drive.

Now, however, the bush is gradually reclaiming these old routes, and only the one road in – and out – remains, starting from close to the village of Nxamaseri. The turning off the main road (✪ T2TURN 18°35.834'S, 21°59.986'E) is indicated by a large green signboard that is surprisingly easy to miss, so do keep your eyes open.

14

It's almost 15km south of the Somachima Veterinary Fence (⊕ VET-SA 18°29.256'S, 21°55.142'E), or 25km north of the turning to Sepupa. From there the track heads southwest until after 34.4km it reaches a right turning clearly signposted 'Tsodilo 5km' at ⊕ TSODTO 18°47.378', 21°44.981'E. This leads after just 0.4km to the main entrance gate to the hills (⊕ TSGATE 18°47.275'S, 21°44.856'E), kitted out in the smart green livery of the hills.

Hitchhiking I wouldn't try to walk or hitchhike here, though we know of one intrepid hiker who made it from Maun to the Tsodilo Hills in October 2013. With more animals around than vehicles, and searing daytime temperatures with little shade, his experience must have been unpleasant at best.

By air There's a bush airstrip at the hills, so it's quite possible (albeit at significant cost) to charter a plane to get you here from Maun or elsewhere in the region. However, once on the ground you'll need a 4x4 to get to the base of the hills, and to the start of the various walking trails, which would need to be organised in advance – perhaps with one of the lodges along the Panhandle if you're staying with them.

Approaching from the air you'll appreciate the hills' uniqueness within the desert, though you'll miss the excitement as they're first sighted over the treetops.

Getting organised Access to the hills is now firmly controlled, with all visitors passing through the entrance gate, where you'll pay your entrance fees. Management of the site was recently handed over to the community, and the increase in fees has been significant – but at least it is now the local people who benefit from the extraordinary heritage that is on their doorstep.

Whereas once the hills were a place to explore for yourself, preferably with a local guide, nowadays you must hire a **guide** – either at the entrance gate or by the parking area, where picnic benches are laid out in the shade. The cost varies depending on the trail (*P120–175*), so do give yourself plenty of time to investigate each of the paintings as you go; 2 hours is probably about average, but you may wish to take longer. Some of the guides are truly excellent, while others are less well qualified, so if you're genuinely interested in understanding more about the hills, it may be well to ask a few salient questions before you agree on a guide.

Next to the parking area you'll find a small **museum** (⊕ TSOMUS 18°45.526'S, 21°44.208'E) – more a series of contemplative thoughts about the hills than an exhibition of artefacts, but interesting nonetheless. This is where you'll pay for your guide, and can sometimes buy cold drinks, and a small selection of handmade jewellery. A large ablution block contains not just toilets, but showers, too – useful for sluicing off the inevitable dirt that will have accumulated if you've tackled one of the more arduous trails (though there are no towels). For the trails themselves, do wear good, strong shoes or boots, and take a hat, suncream and plenty of water. A walking pole might be a useful extra.

Most visitors spend their time on Female Hill, and may visit the Male. Without a special permit, visitors are not allowed to the Child Hill or the kopje beyond, to which there are no vehicle tracks. Ideally, plan your day to start walking as early as possible – which given that the park gates don't open until 07.30, will not be much before 08.00. Campers, though, can gain a good half an hour on this, which is well worthwhile to avoid walking in the heat of the day.

 Where to stay There has long been talk of a new tented camp opening at the hills, but for now, your options are limited to camping.

⋏ Tsodilo Hills campsites (6 pitches) Until 2013, there were several individual campsites scattered among the hills, some of them within easy walk of the paintings themselves. Then camping came under the control of the Tsodilo Community Trust, the original sites were closed, & 6 new sites created. These are corralled into one very large open area, with a rather over-the-top entrance gate (⏲ 07.00–16.30) exclusively for campers. You'll find this gate, clearly proclaiming 'Tsodilo Community Trust Campsite', at right angles to the main gate to the hills. If you're camping, you can pay both your camping (*P130pp/night*) & entry fees (*P50 pp/day*) here. There's also a craft shop to the side of this gate, though when we've visited it has been firmly closed.

Although you'll be told more or less where to pitch your tent, the pitches are only roughly demarcated, & quite far apart, so unless it's busy it's really a question of finding one that you like. 4 of them – the Mopororo (⊛ MOPORO 18°47.194'S, 21°44.406'E), Dimbo, Dimbo da diwe and Aininai sites – are only about 1km from the gate, sharing a small modern ablution block that would be fine if the goats would stay out & the local baboons weren't so intent in turning on the taps. The pitches themselves have a standpipe for water, & a firepit, so it's all fairly civilised. Wherever you camp, do be aware that you might find domestic animals around.

Having paid their entry fees along with the camping fee, campers have their own entrance to the hills – a gate in the fence (⊛ CAMPGT 18°46.653'S, 21°43.952'E) that separates the 2 parts of the site. From the ablution block to the gate it's about 2km, then a further 2.4km from the gate to the parking area. Thus as a camper, you can be at the museum & ready to start on one of the trails slightly earlier than those driving in. There's no great advantage in this except when it's very hot – when the earlier your start, the more pleasant it will be exploring the trails. *Camping P130 pp.*

The trails Visitors have the option of four trails on the hills: the Rhino Trail, the Cliff Trail, the Lion Trail and the Male Hill Trail. References to other trails, however enticing, are irrelevant: you are no longer permitted to explore beyond these guided routes. The old Divuyu Trail, for example, can be visited only by archaeologists engaged in scientific research.

In theory, guides will tailor your walk as required, taking into account both what you want to see and the level of exertion required. In practice, however, visitors

---

GUIDES OF THE FUTURE?

Some years back, before there were any organised guides to the hills, I drove to the San village of Hambukushu – which had been moved from its old location between the hills to a new location (⊛ SANVIL 18°48.147'S, 21°43.903'E) about 3.8km south-southwest of there, well away from the hills. With sign gestures and improvisation, I tried to ask for a guide. The man of the family that I was speaking to eventually sent me off with two of the children, a boy called Xashee, aged 10, and a girl called Tsetsana, aged 16.

At first I thought that I'd been fobbed off with the children, who were silent in the presence of their family. However, as soon as we got into our car to drive back to the hills, it transpired that Tsetsana was on holiday from school, and spoke excellent English. Her brother spoke much less to us, but seemed to know more of the sites with rock art. They bounded up the hills with bare feet, faster than we could in walking boots. They knew their way about very well and although we only followed on the 'standard' trails, we would have missed many of the paintings without their help.

Perhaps these children, or their friends, are among the guides who show people around the hills today.

14

are usually encouraged to take the Rhino Trail, at the north end of the Female Hill, which is the most accessible trail, and features the most well-known paintings. The best guidebook to the area is *Guide to the Tsodilo Hills World Heritage Site*, which is available from Ngami Data Services in Maun (page 204).

The notes that follow are from my own and readers' observations. I'm aware they may contain errors as well as omissions, but I hope that they'll spur other readers to explore – and perhaps send me any corrections or additional comments.

Rhino Trail *(P120/guide; approx 2hrs)* In theory this trail is marked with sequentially numbered posts, though despite walking the trail on several occasions, some of them have proved elusive, especially in the lush vegetation early in the year. In 2017, sections of the trail were closed to the public while wooden steps were being constructed to improve access to the site.

The trail starts from close to the old Squirrel Valley Campsite (⊕ SQCAMP 18°45.385'S, 21°44.248'E), a short walk from the museum and car park. The numbered posts are clearer at the end of the dry season, and the GPS references here should be a help to make sure you're in roughly the right place, but if your guide doesn't know the trail well, you may still have to search a bit to find the paintings. Note that some of the numbered posts indicate features of archaeological interest, rather than paintings, such as an old waterhole or a place where hunters would have sharpened their spears – though steps are being added in some places to improve access.

The first marker, **No 1**, sets the scene with a granite rock whose deep grooves suggest that it served for sharpening spears.

Picture 2 (⊕ PICT2 18°45.331'S, 21°44.225'E) is deeper into the ravine and higher up, at an altitude of 1,063m. There's quite a lot of steep rock-hopping to climb up this ravine at the beginning of the trail. It won't be suitable for anyone who is uncomfortable clambering around rocky slopes.

Less than 100m north-northwest of No 2, but higher up again, is **Picture 3** (⊕ PICT3 18°45.291'S, 21°44.239'E), a beautiful silhouette of a rhino that's perhaps 100cm across, with gemsbok below.

By the time you reach **Picture 5**, which includes an impressive giraffe, the trail starts to open out, and you're heading towards the centre of the Female Hill. Here **No 7** marks another spear-sharpening rock on the site of an old San settlement. It's a large, relatively flat and secluded area, where the head of the tribe and his family would have been well protected. Another grooved rock here indicates where tools were sharpened, and the geometric designs painted on the rocks suggest the presence of shaman.

Found under an overhang, **Picture 8** (⊕ PICT8 18°45.150'S, 21°44.576'E) – known as 'the dancing penises' – depicts several men in what is considered to be an initiation ceremony. It lies at an altitude of 1,102m, from where you can see the Male Hill.

Continuing downhill, you'll come to the site of a lower settlement, whose inhabitants' role was to protect the upper settlement from invasion. Here, the white domestic animals of **Picture 9** (⊕ PICT9 18°45.437'S, 21°44.723'E) were created more recently than most of the paintings – around 1,000 years ago. Their chalk-based pigments have survived the elements as they're sheltered beneath a cave overhang. Almost adjacent, the main figures of **Picture 10** consist of two rather beautifully painted rhino, for which the Rhino Trail is named. These are the most famous of Tsodilo's paintings, as they now form the logo of The Botswana Society.

Shortly, this trail joins the main track which leads west between the Female and Male hills. Detour to the right of this, and you'll find **Picture 11** (⊕ PICT11

18°45.635'S, 21°44.862'E), which appears to include a penguin and at least one whale. Arguably this is one of the pieces of evidence that indicates that the Bushmen travelled far more widely than is commonly believed, adding weight to Robert Gordon's contention in his *Bushman Myth: The Making of a Namibian Underclass* (see *Appendix 3*, page 539), that our view of the Bushman is often misguided.

This trail then leads around to **No 12** (✪ CAVE12 18°45.673'S, 21°44.842'E), a large cave at the base of the Female Hill, facing the Male Hill. Known locally as the Makena Cave, it is said to be where a woman who went missing for several months was found, over a thousand years ago. From here there's a short tunnel back to the path, where – if you look up – you'll see an extraordinary rock formation that resembles a three-dimensional map of Africa.

Following the main track north along the west side of Female Hill brings you to **Picture 13** (✪ PICT13 18°45.627'S, 21°44.436'E). Move closer to the hill here, then look up and slightly back at the hills; there, high up, you'll see what is now known as the '**van der Post panel**'. In his inimitable style, Laurens described first seeing this:

> Over the scorched leaves of the tops of the bush conforming to a contour nearby, and about a hundred feet up, was a ledge of honey-coloured stone grafted into the blue iron rock. Above the ledge rose a smooth surface of the same warm, soft stone curved like a sea shell as if rising into the blue to form a perfect dome. I had no doubt that I was looking at the wall and part of the ceiling of what had once been a great cave …
>
> But what held my attention still with the shock of discovery was the painting that looked down at us from the centre of what was left of the wall and dome of the cave. Heavy as were the shadows, and seeing it only darkly against the sharp morning light, it was yet so distinct and filled with fire of its own colour that every detail stood out with a burning clarity. In the focus of the painting, scarlet against the gold of the stone, was an enormous eland bull standing sideways, his massive body charged with masculine power and his noble head looking as if he had only that moment been disturbed in his grazing. He was painted, as only a Bushman, who had a deep identification with an eland, could have painted him.

This footpath, which follows the west side of Female Hill, heads roughly north. Very close to the path, **Picture 14** depicts rhino, warthog and several antelope. Next, less than 400m from the start of the trail, **Picture 15** (✪ PICT15 18°45.556'S, 21°44.361'E) includes lots of very clearly painted giraffe, rhino, gemsbok and other antelope on a wonderfully colourful outcrop of rock.

Finally, just before arriving back at the old Squirrel Valley Campsite, **Picture 16** includes a curious circular design – almost geometrical – that is reminiscent of a shield, the shell of a tortoise or even a wheel; this, like similar earlier paintings, is considered to be a shaman symbol.

Cliff Trail *(P175/guide; approx 3hrs)* This is at the north end of Female Hill, starting near the old Malatso Campsite, which is found by forking right at ✪ MLTURN 18°44.243'S, 21°43.575'E. You'll reach the steep base of the cliffs, about 50m away, where there's a turning circle for vehicles.

The trail circles broadly clockwise around the northern part of Female Hill, before taking a short cut back to near its start over a col.

Reader Jon Williamson walked the Cliff Trail in 2011, and sent us the following report:

The Cliff Trail is fairly similar in appearance to the Rhino Trail, but the path was not as cleared. Some points along the trail were partly obstructed by tree damage caused by elephants. The cliff paintings were as frequent as those found along the Rhino Trail, but not as grandiose: we saw impressions of lion, rhino, zebra, aardvark, elephant and scorpion, as well as some geometric shapes:

zebra	✪ 18°43.917'S, 21°43.734'E
rhino	✪ 18°43.908'S, 21°43.735'E
lion	✪ 18°43.899'S, 21°43.741'E
zebra	✪ 18 43.659'S, 21°43.810'E
elephant	✪ 18°43.669'S, 21°43.880'E
scorpion	✪ 18°43.712'S, 21°43.896'E
ardvaark	✪ 18°44.196'S, 21°43.732'E

The most exciting part of the Cliff Trail was actually just off the trail: a cave (✪ PYTHCV 18°43.863'S, 21°43.870'E) containing a rock formation shaped like a large snake. Before our trip, we had read that the earliest evidence of practised human rituals was found in a cave in Botswana, so we persuaded our guide to show it to us.

Lion Trail (*P175/guide; approx 2hrs*) This trail stays at ground level, and doesn't include any climbing. It overlaps with some of the Rhino Trail's paintings at the base of the south end of Female Hill, as well as visiting sites on the north side of Male Hill. It starts at the base of the Male Hill, reached by turning off the track between the Male and Female hills at ✪ LITURN 18°45.538'S, 21°45.109'E.

Male Hill Trail (*P175/guide; approx 2hrs*) Also known as the Summit Trail, this starts from the same place as the Lion Trail, though it eventually goes to the top of Male Hill, then back down the same route. The route has some strenuous scrambles, so good footwear and relatively good fitness are essential, but the views from the summit are well worth the effort.

Around the hills Just south of the entrance gate to the hills is a small settlement, **Hambukushu**, with some corrals for animals. Further away, on the way from the main gate to the San Village, a track heads off right, on a northwest bearing of about 305°. I've followed this for 7–8km, and it remains a good track, which I believe heads for a place called **Tshukumutshu**. I'd welcome more information on it if readers have gone further.

AHA AND GCWIHABA (*admission P60 pp; camping P30 pp/night*) Over 150km southwest of the Tsodilo Hills lies an even more remote area, populated by scattered San villages and dotted with a number of hills. This is one of the most remote areas of the Kalahari, and it attracts the most experienced bush travellers simply 'because it's there'. This is expedition territory, best reserved for those who are well equipped and bush-wise. Most go to visit the Aha Hills, straddling the border with Namibia, and the nearby Gcwihaba Hills, which contain the fascinating Gcwihaba (or Drotsky's) Caves. These are easily located and not commercialised.

In reality, though the Gcwihaba Caves are the only cave system here that's practical for most visitors to see, there are a number of others in the area which have been unearthed by local scientists in the last few decades. The locations of these are usually kept secret to avoid visitors damaging them or having a serious accident (which would be all too easy).

Geology and geography Turning east from Tsau, you'll soon start to notice the road's gentle decline. It's entering the Gcwihaba Valley, a fossil river valley which may have been an ancient extension of the Okavango Delta. Within this, a group of six low hills protrude above the sand and rise to a maximum of 30m above the surrounding valley. (Compare this with the Male Hill at Tsodilo, which reaches 410m.) About 40–50km northwest of these, the Aha Hills share a very similar geology and appearance.

All of these low hills are made almost exclusively of dolomite marble which, early in its formation, is thought to have been steeply folded, causing many of its strata to stand vertically. It's estimated to be about 800–1,000 million years old.

This rock has been weathered into a very jagged, sharp surface and many loose blocks which aren't always easy underfoot. Underneath, numerous faults and fractures split it. When weathered it appears a grey colour, but if you break it you'll find a pearly-white colour inside. There are occasional bands of muscovite in the marble, and beds of more recent limestone and calcrete.

About 15–20km southwest of the Gcwihaba are the Koanaka Hills. These are similar in geological origin, but essentially inaccessible to visitors. There has been some recent exploration of these (see *Discovery and Exploration of Two New Caves in the Northwest District*, in *Appendix 3*, page 540). One of them – called the 'blue cave' – is Botswana's largest cave complex found to date.

Formation of the caves Like many cave systems in the world, the Gcwihaba Caves have been formed by the action of acidic groundwater flowing down through the faults in the rock. This gradually dissolves the alkaline limestone over the centuries. Some of this limestone has been redeposited as stalagmites and stalactites.

That said, this simple and quite standard explanation for the cave formation doesn't entirely explain why the cave system is more or less horizontal throughout. (It has northeast and southeast entrances, and appears to have had two levels at different times.) Because of this, Cooke and Baillieul note (see *Appendix 3*, page 540) that from the size of the caves and passages, it seems likely that very large volumes of groundwater must have moved within the rock here – perhaps an underground course of the old Gcwihaba River. This would explain the sheer size of some of the caves.

For that to have been the case, the area's water table must have been much higher for at least one period historically, and probably two. After these levels had subsided, and the caves emptied of water, then stalagmites and stalactites would have been formed gradually by a trickle-through of more moderate volumes of water (eg: rainfall) through faultlines.

History Though people have occupied the area for at least 12,500 years, it doesn't seem as if the caves were used extensively. Excavations in Gcwihaba Caves (in 1969 by Yellen et al; see *Appendix 3*, page 541) did find evidence of charcoal, ostrich eggshell and bone fragments, thought to be the remnants of human occupation, but the finds were limited and there is no rock art here at all.

These caves were first brought to the attention of the outside world in June 1932 when the local !Kung people showed the cave to a farmer from Ghanzi, Martinus Drotsky. Hence for many years this was known as Drotsky's Cave. (As an aside, Martinus was the grandfather of Jan Drotsky, who runs Drotsky's Cabins, near Shakawe.)

The local !Kung refer to these hills as '/twihaba' – hence the hills, and main cave and this cave system, are now usually referred to as the Gcwihaba Hills and Caves respectively (although you'll see this spelled in a variety of ways in various publications).

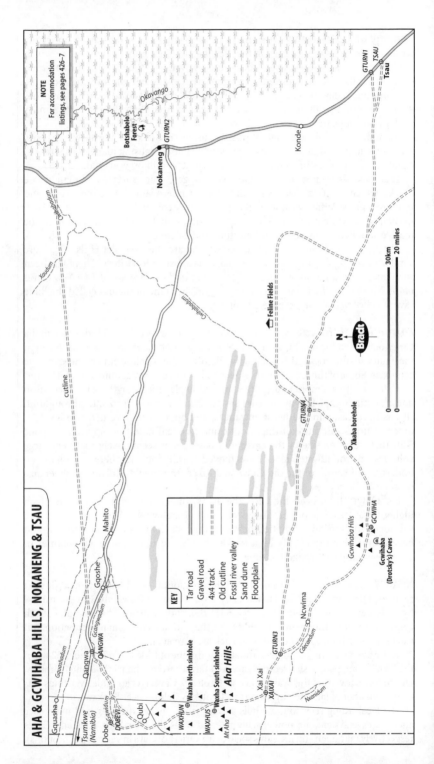

AHA & GCWIHABA HILLS, NOKANENG & TSAU

NOTE
For accommodation
listings, see pages 426–7

KEY
	Tar road
	Gravel road
	4x4 track
	Old cutline
	Fossil river valley
	Sand dune
	Floodplain

Okavango

Botshabelo
Forest

Nokaneng GTURN2

GTURN2

Konde

GTURN1 TSAU
Tsau

Ghabadodum

Xaudum

Cwihbodum

Feline Fields

Bradt

N

GTURN4

Xkaba borehole

0 ——— 30km
0 ——— 20 miles

Mahito

Gaoshe

Gquashadum

Gcangwadum

OANGWA

Qangwa

Gguashe

Tsumkwe
(Namibia)

Dobe G/gwidum
DOBEV

Qubi

WAXHUN
WAXHUS Waxha North sinkhole

Mt Aha Waxha South sinkhole

Aha Hills

Xai Xai
XAIXAI

GTURN3

Nxanidum

Ncwima

Gxcoedum

Gcwihaba Hills

GCWIHA

Gcwihaba
(Drotsky's) Caves

438

GPS REFERENCES FOR AHA AND GCWIHABA HILLS MAP (opposite)

DOBEVI	19°34.830'S, 21°04.428'E	QANGWA	19°31.868'S, 21°10.281'E
GCWIHA	20°01.250'S, 21°21.230'E	TSAU	20°10.294'S, 22°27.265'E
GTURN1	20°07.047'S, 22°22.291'E	WAXHUN	19°43.532'S, 21°03.489'E
GTURN2	19°39.577'S, 22°11.010'E	WAXHUS	19°46.643'S, 21°02.518'E
GTURN3	19°54.286'S, 21°09.418'E	XAIXAI	19°52.867'S, 21°04.934'E
GTURN4	19°57.556'S, 21°44.541'E		

The hills and caverns were declared a national monument in 1934 and the Director of the Bechuanaland Geological Survey visited the caverns with Drotsky in 1943. The first cave survey was undertaken in 1970 by a school group from Falcon College in Zimbabwe (then Rhodesia). Various scientific explorations and surveys have been done since then, including an expedition in 1991 by the British Schools Exploring Society (now BSES Expeditions).

Nowhere else in this area has had as much time or attention given to it as the Gcwihaba Caves, though the two sinkholes in the Aha Hills have been surveyed on at least two occasions.

The people The people of the area are mostly Ju/'hoansi Bushmen, together with a few Herero (Mbanderu). Because of the lung disease that swept through this area of the country and the subsequent eradication of cattle here in the late 1990s, work patterns have changed. Thus many people are employed by branches of the government, working to clear roads and similar public works.

A particularly detailed and interesting article on the community in the Xai Xai area, with details from a study there, can be found at www.kalaharipeoples.org/resources.

Flora and fauna Though visits to this part of the Kalahari are usually for caves and culture, there is some wildlife around. As with most places in the Kalahari, this area is at its most beautiful and the flora and fauna are at their most vibrant during and shortly after the summer rains (January to about April).

Flora This classic Kalahari environment is dominated by the silver terminalia (*Terminalia sericea*), identified by the silvery sheen on its blue-grey leaves and the Kalahari appleleaf (*Philenoptera nelsii*). You'll also find some bushwillows (*Combretum callinum*) and wild seringa bushes (*Burkea africana*).

Raisin bushes (*Grewia flava*) are here accompanied by sandpaper raisin bushes (*Grewia flavescens*) and the false sandpaper raisin bushes (*Grewia retinervis*). Rub a leaf of either of the latter between your fingers and you'll soon realise how they got their common names.

One tree worth noting here is the Namaqua fig (*Ficus cordata*). This is well known throughout the central highlands of Namibia and down to the Cape – but otherwise unrecorded in Botswana. Here you'll find it growing all over the hills, its roots often flattened against the rocks. Several strong specimens grow around the entrances to the Gcwihaba Caves, green and thriving even during the dry season, perhaps due to the cooler, moister microclimate in the air of the caves.

Similarly, the mopane aloe (*Aloe littoralis*) is found here and throughout Namibia, but nowhere else in northern or central Botswana. It's a striking plant with a single, vertical stem, succulent leaves with serrated edges and a flower head that branches into pointed spikes of red flowers.

All around the region you'll certainly find the Devil's claw creeper (*Harpogophytum procumbens procumbens*). Recognise it by its pinky-mauve flowers with a hint of yellow in the centre in January to March, and after that its small but wicked oval fruit that has hooks on all sides – like some tiny medieval jousting ball with grappling hooks. (This could be confused with the large Devil's thorn, *Dicerocaryum eriocarpum*, which has a brighter pink flower but a much less elaborate fruit.)

The Devil's claw is found all over the Kalahari, but has recently been in demand from overseas for its medicinal properties. Extracts of this are variously claimed to aid in the treatment of intestinal complaints, arthritis and many other ailments. Hence anywhere near a centre of population is likely to be largely devoid of these plants, but in the more remote areas of the Kalahari you'll often find it beside the sandy track.

Fauna Big game is present throughout this area, but it's relatively scarce especially near to settlements where you're more likely to come into contact with dogs and domestic stock. That said, gemsbok, springbok, eland, steenbok, duiker and kudu all occur in the area. Veronica Roodt reports seeing six very relaxed wild dog near the entrance to Gcwihaba Caves, and there are also occasional lion, leopard, cheetah and spotted hyena around. Hence there must be a reasonable population of their antelope prey – even if these seem elusive due to the relatively thick vegetation, and lack of waterholes at which they might gather and be more easily spotted.

Given the huge distances that elephant can cover, and the spoor that I've seen near the Tsodilo Hills, I wouldn't be surprised to find lone bulls wandering around during the wet season. Drivers, be warned.

If approaching this area then, while looking for big game, don't forget the smaller stuff. Small seasonal pans will fill with a noisy mélange of bullfrogs which have spent the dry season underground, attracted by the water and the number of grasshoppers and crickets around.

There's no better time to see plenty of small reptiles, from the Kalahari serrated tortoise, with its bold, geometric patterns, to the flapnecked chameleon. Around sunset, and for the first few hours after that, listen out for the *click-click* of the barking gecko, sometimes described as like rattling a box of matches. The onomatopoeic name 'Aha' is said to come from the sound made by these often-unseen residents.

Inside the Gcwihaba Caves is a different story. Some of the earlier scientists to visit the cave noted that leopard inhabited it, and found fresh spoor. Meanwhile, its name derives from the !Kung word for 'hyena's hole'. While I don't know of any more recent visitors who have come across large predators in here, you can't help but notice the bats! These can be noisy and smelly, but are otherwise harmless.

The most common species here is probably the insectivorous Commerson's leaf-nosed bat (*Hipposideros commersoni*). These are the largest insectivorous bats in southern Africa which, although they only grow to a weight of about 120g, can have a wingspan as large as 60cm. These have short, pale fawn-coloured hair all over, and black feet. Males have distinctive tufts of white fur on their shoulders. These are the bats that leave the caves in large numbers at dusk.

Also found in numbers are the tiny Dent's horseshoe bat (*Rhinolophus denti*), which weigh a mere 6g and measure about 7cm long, with a wingspan of 20cm, when fully grown. Horseshoe bats like this are identified because of complex 'nose-leaf' structures on their face between their mouths and their foreheads (used to locate their insect prey using the animal equivalent of radar).

A third common bat here is the Egyptian (also called 'common') slit-faced bat (*Nycteris thebaica*), which is easily identified by its long, rounded ears and the 'split' running down the centre of its face. They fly efficiently but relatively slowly, eat insects, and grow to about 10cm long with a wingspan of about 24cm.

Given the presence of these bats, it's quite likely that they support a small ecosystem of invertebrates in the caves. In similar caves in Namibia, several hundred kilometres to the west of here, scientists have recently also discovered small but highly poisonous spiders. So tread carefully …

Birdlife As with anywhere in the Kalahari, the birds here can either survive without drinking water, or will routinely fly long distances to find it every day. Guineafowl and red-billed spurfowl are very common, though coqui and crested francolin also occur. Sandgrouse are common, particularly the namaqua and double-banded species, though you'll also find Burchell's and, occasionally, the yellow-throated varieties. Doves are here too, with Cape turtle, laughing and namaqua species always around.

The area's LBJs ('little brown jobbies', as keen birdwatchers refer to the plethora of smaller, brown birds whose similarities tax their identification skills) include chestnut-backed finchlarks, sabota larks and penduline tits.

Larger and more visible birds, which are easier to spot and identify, include double-banded coursers, and black-bellied and red-crested korhaans. Both of these korhaans show interesting displays during the mating season. You may also come across the world's heaviest flying bird, the kori bustard, and ostriches are not unknown, though they are very uncommon.

Of the raptors, by far the commonest is the pale chanting goshawk, which is usually seen perching atop a bush, small tree or post, surveying the area. When disturbed it'll usually swoop off, flying low, to a similar perch not far away. The very similar, but slightly larger, dark chanting goshawk may also be found here, on the edge of its range. (These are distinguishable in flight, from above, as the pale variety has a white rump, whereas the dark chanting goshawk has a darker colouring and a darker, barred rump.)

Getting organised To get the best out of such an experience, you're probably wisest to come here with an experienced mobile-safari operator who – and this is vital – knows the village and villagers well. They'll also know what's possible, while the community benefits in just the same way. Operations who may be able to help include Old Bridge Tours & Safari (page 227). This will be more costly than trying to do something yourself, but probably much more satisfactory.

Alternatively you might drive yourself, with at least one fully equipped 4x4, and with all your food and water. Although water is usually available at Xai Xai Village, and basic supplies may be found both there and at Qangwa, it's better to bring with you everything that you might need.

As with any tracks in the Kalahari, and especially those that are rarely used, a major danger is fire caused by grass seeds and stems blocking up your vehicle's radiator, or collecting near its exhaust system. If you're driving here, especially during the first few months of the year, you must take steps to prevent this (page 182).

A third option would be to fly in, using the airstrip at Xai Xai, although with the exception of Feline Fields (pages 426–7) there is a lack of accommodation in the area for fly-in guests.

To explore the caves you'll need several good torches, plus extra batteries and bulbs (a fail-safe emergency back-up is essential, as there's no-one here to help you), and perhaps a lighter or matches. A large ball of string would also be handy to prevent you getting lost.

Getting there and away Two roads head west from the main Shakawe–Sehithwa road, the A35, and then loop around and join up with each other around the Aha Hills. Both are very long. The southern route is very sandy and very hard-going, while the northern route is longer, but better as far as Xai Xai. Either way, navigation is reasonably straightforward, and a 4x4 remains essential.

The northern route About 300m north of the centre of Nokaneng there's a track heading west (✿ GTURN2 19°39.577'S, 22°11.010'E). This is the longer of the two routes, but the surface is now gravel, so although it can still be heavy going, it's usually the easier option. From here to Xai Xai, you can expect the drive to take about 3–4 hours.

From Nokaneng, the road twists and turns quite a lot but after a little over 120km, or around 3 hours, you'll reach the tiny village of **Qangwa** (✿ QANGWA 19°31.868'S, 21°10.281'E), sometimes spelled 'Xangwa', or even 'Gcangwa', which supports a small shop.

From Qangwa the gravel road continues west towards Namibia, ultimately to Tsumkwe (✿ TSUMKW 19°35.507'S, 20°30.184'E). For the hills, take the track that leads southwest for over 10km to another small village, Dobe (✿ DOBEVI 19°34.830'S, 21°04.428'E). From there the track picks its way through the Aha Hills, heading due south. It passes west of the small group of hills which contain Waxhu North Cave (or sinkhole) (✿ WAXHUN 19°43.532'S, 21°03.489'E), and east of the main range of hills, within which is found the Waxhu South Cave (or sinkhole) (✿ WAXHUS 19°46.643'S, 21°02.518'E). That said, the relatively thick bush found in the area makes these caves difficult to find, even with the aid of a GPS. Finally, after about 37km, the road reaches the village of **Xai Xai** (✿ XAIXAI 19°52.867'S, 21°04.934'E).

In some literature you'll find this designated as Nxainxai, CaeCae or, more recently, /Xai/Xai. However you want to spell it, this is one of the largest villages in the area, with a population of about 300–400 Ju/'hoansi San people, and perhaps 50 Herero (Mbanderu) people, who are mostly cattle farmers. The village has a borehole, a small school, a basic health post and a few shops, as well as a recently upgraded airstrip.

From Xai Xai the route turns east, becoming the southern route described below which ultimately ends on the main road near Tsau. About 10km east of Xai Xai you pass a clear right turn (✿ GTURN3 19°54.286'S, 21°09.418'E) to the Gcwihaba Hills and Cave (✿ GCWIHA 20°01.250'S, 21°21.230'E), a distance of almost 30km.

The southern route A large banner on the side of the road some 10km north of Tsau (✿ GTURN1 20°07.047'S, 22°22.291'E) clearly marks the correct path to follow for the southern route. This is the shortest route to the hills and caves (the latter being relatively well signposted), but it can become a quagmire if there has been rain in the area.

During the dry season, the first few hours from Tsau are generally fairly easy driving, as the hard, compacted track gently descends into the fossil river valley. However, during the rains a number of wide, shallow pans hold water here, turning it into a series of connected mud-holes and a challenging route even for experienced drivers. After that, the country becomes rolling duneland with thick sand, which is slow going but not as treacherous as the mud.

About 90km from Tsau there's a left turning (✿ GTURN4 19°57.556'S, 21°44.541'E). This passes the Xhaba borehole, a satellite cattle post of Xai Xai Village, after about 26km, and then reaches the hills another 26km later. It's the quickest way to the hills. If you miss this turn-off then continue on to the main turning (✪ GTURN3 19°54.286'S, 21°09.418'E) used by the northern route (see opposite), and take a left there. This is over 150km from Tsau.

Where to stay There is a rudimentary campsite at the Aha Hills, and three sites at Gcwihaba. Since these are not signposted, it's best to contact the warden, Eric Keharara (m *7375 6518;* e *ekeharara@yahoo.com*) in advance. He can then direct you to the appropriate site – and collect your fees for camping (*P450 pp*), the concession (*P100 pp*), vehicle entry (*P50*) and entry to the site (*P100 pp*).

⛺ **Aha campsite** There is no water at this campsite (the nearest is at Xai Xai), nor any other facilities, including toilets, so it's vital that you bring everything that you need with you, & take away all your rubbish (or at least everything that cannot be burned & reduced to ash). Take a spade, so you can bury your waste deeply, & always burn your toilet paper. *P450 pp.*

⛺ **Gcwihaba campsites** There is an ablution block with showers & toilets here, but in 2017 it was very dirty & run down. So while you may be able to get water here in an emergency, we would recommend that you still take everything you might need – & bring out all your rubbish. *P450 pp.*

Aha Hills About 40–50km northwest of the Gcwihaba Hills, and visible from them, is a range of low, rounded hills: the Aha Hills. These straddle the Botswana–Namibia border, and are among the most remote and little-visited destinations in Botswana.

Like the Gcwihaba Hills, this range is made of dolomite marble that has been split by weathering into numerous faults and fractures. This presents a very jagged surface, with many loose blocks underfoot, and isn't easy to walk on.

The range covers about 245km², most of which is in Botswana, and very little of which has been properly mapped or documented. With the new access road to Xai Xai, visitors can now reach the hills from both Botswana and Namibia with relative ease.

Exploring the hills In some ways the hills are attractive simply because they're so remote. Even though there are now designated campsites, this is a place that few visitors ever get to.

Clambering around isn't as much fun here as in the Tsodilo Hills, simply because the rock surface is totally different. Instead of large boulders with an even surface and an easy grip, the Aha Hills are made of endless jagged little blocks. So if you do come here, stout walking shoes with strong soles make clambering around a lot easier.

Two sites on the Botswana side have attracted some interest, and both are sinkholes – large holes in the ground. The local people apparently know both simply as 'Waxhu', which means 'house of god'. Both can only be visited using specialist climbing/caving equipment, so don't be tempted to try and climb down. There are no mountain-rescue teams in Botswana!

Waxhu Cave (north; ✪ WAXHUN 19°43.532'S, 21°03.498'E) was first described in 1974 and is about 70m deep.

Waxhu Cave (south; ✪ WAXHUS 19°46.632'S, 21°02.518'E) is also known by some of its recent visitors as 'Independence Cave', because they first visited it on the fifth anniversary of Botswana's independence. This cave is about 50m deep.

Botswana Notes and Records (see *Appendix 3*, pages 540–1) records many more details on these sinkholes, including rough maps of them and information about the various expeditions that have explored them recently.

GCWIHABA CAVES

N

Bradt

0 — 50m
0 — 50yds

15

14

13

12

5

10

11

4

7

9

6

8

3

2

1

Gcwihaba Hills and Caves The low, rounded hills here are not the attraction, but beneath them is a labyrinth of passages and caves, some with enchanting rock formations of stalagmites, stalactites and spectacular 'flowstones' which seem like waterfalls of rock.

Some of these chambers reach up to 10m in height, while other passages are so narrow that you'll need to clamber and squeeze through. All were formed by the dissolving and depositing action of acidic water on the limestone of the rocks around, though now the caves are totally dry.

Although there is a new museum at Gcwihaba, backed by the Botswana Department of Tourism, this was very much shut when we visited in 2017, and also looked in poor repair – perhaps reflecting the low number of visitors to the area.

Exploring the caves The string that used to mark the route through the total darkness of the caves was recently removed due to disrepair and the chance of tourists getting lost, making it more important than ever that you attempt this route only with a local guide.

There are two main entrances to the caves, about 250m apart, each marked with a monument. Although there is a route between them, it's not straightforward or obvious, so getting through may tax your map-reading skills. (You won't be able to rely on your beloved GPS either, as they're useless under the rock ceilings of the caves!) There are lots of dead ends, closed-off passages and caverns to penetrate. If your curiosity flags, then remind yourself of the legend of Hendrik Matthys van Zyl, the wealthy founder of Ghanzi, who is said to have stashed a portion of his fortune here in the late 1800s.

Most of the caves are on one level, though there is a section, slightly nearer to the south entrance than the north, where several of the corridors split into two different levels, one raised several metres above the other. You can expect a considerable amount of bat guano underfoot, but at least the complete lack of natural light means that you shouldn't need to worry about snakes.

Start exploring the caves from the main (north) entrance. Here, on one of the large boulders towards the right of the main entrance hall, you'll find the inscription 'Discovered 1 June 1932, M Drotsky'.

The route starts at the lower entrance, and proceeds down an increasingly steep and narrow passageway. There's a short vertical climb down into what's been christened the 'rope pit', before you emerge up the other side on to a shelf. Then it's a bit of a squeeze before you find yourself in a large chamber.

From here the route basically climbs, though there are lots of side-passages to distract you, and part way through is where there are two different levels to the passages. You'll also come across the chambers with bats in them, deep within the cave complex, before finally emerging from the southern entrance (where there's a ledge that is now used as a roost by a resident barn owl).

BOTSWANA ONLINE

For additional online content, articles, photos and more on Botswana, why not visit www.bradtguides.com/botswana?

446

15

The Kalahari's Great Salt Pans

The great salt pans lie in the heart of the northern Kalahari, forming an area of empty horizons into which the blinding white expanse of the pans disappears in a shimmering heat-haze. In winter, dust devils whirl across the open plains; in summer many become undulating seas of grasses beneath the turbulence of the stormy skies. It is a harsh, spare landscape, not to everybody's taste, but it offers an isolation as complete as anywhere in southern Africa, and a wealth of hidden treasures for those prepared to make the effort – including Stone Age ruins and prehistoric beaches.

The wildlife is rich, but highly seasonal and nomadic. At times you'll find great concentrations of plains game, with all their attendant predators, and, in good years, spectacular breeding colonies of flamingos crowd the shallow waters of Sua Pan. At other times the stage seems empty. But even then, there is always a cast of smaller Kalahari residents behind the scenes – from coursers and korhaans to mongooses and mole-rats.

BACKGROUND INFORMATION

ORIENTATION The tarred Nata–Maun road bisects this barren region. In May 2017, the road was badly flooded and partially destroyed by an unusually wet rainy season, but rapid repairs to this major route were anticipated. To the south of the road lie the vast, dry depressions of Sua and Ntwetwe, with their scattered 'islands' of granite and fossilised dunes, fringed by grassland and acacia savannah. To its north is the Nxai Pan complex, including Nxai and Kgama-Kgama pans, now grassed over, and Kudiakam Pan, overlooked by the famous Baines' Baobabs.

Much of the region is unfenced ranching country, where wildlife has largely been supplanted by cattle. However, the fauna and flora are protected in a number of reserves. Makgadikgadi Pans National Park extends south of the Nata–Maun road, between the western shore of Ntwetwe Pan and the Boteti River. Nxai Pan National Park adjoins this to the north of the Nata–Maun road, and includes the Nxai Pans complex and Baines' Baobabs. The much smaller Nata Sanctuary, established to protect the seasonal breeding waterbirds of the Nata River delta, is situated in the northeast corner of Sua Pan. Each of these areas has its own distinct attractions and seasonal peculiarities.

GEOGRAPHY The Magkadikgadi Pans consist of an immense expanse of largely flat and featureless terrain in the north of the Kalahari. The pans themselves are located roughly between the diamond town of Orapa in the south, the village of Nata in the northeast and the Boteti rivercourse in the west. This falls away northwards towards the Mababe Depression and the Chobe–Zambezi river catchment system.

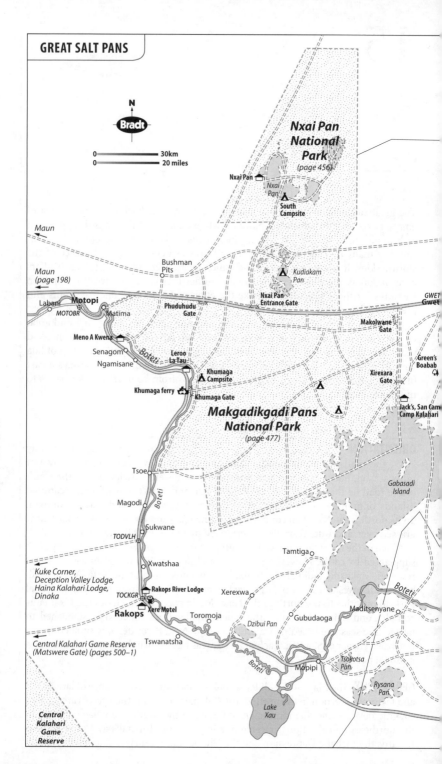

GREAT SALT PANS

Maun

Maun
(page 198)

Nxai Pan
National
Park
(page 456)

Nxai Pan

Nxai
Pan

South
Campsite

Bushman
Pits

Kudiakam
Pan

Nxai Pan
Entrance Gate

GWET
Gwet

Labani
MOTOBR
Motopi
Matima

Phuduhudu
Gate

Makolwane
Gate

Meno A Kwena

Senagom
Ngamisane

Boteti

Leroo
La Tau

Green's
Boabab

Xirexara
Gate

Khumaga
Campsite

Khumaga ferry

Khumaga Gate

Jack's, San Cam
Camp Kalahari

Makgadikgadi Pans
National Park
(page 477)

Tsoe

Boteti

Gabasadi
Island

Magodi

Sukwane

TODVLH

Kuke Corner,
Deception Valley Lodge,
Haina Kalahari Lodge,
Dinaka

Xwatshaa

Tamtiga

Rakops River Lodge

TOCKGR

Xere Motel

Xerexwa

Boteti

Maditsenyane

Rakops

Toromoja

Central Kalahari Game Reserve
(Matswere Gate) (pages 500–1)

Tswanatsha

Dzibui Pan

Gubudaoga

Tsokotsa
Pan

Boteti

Mopipi

Rysana
Pan

Central
Kalahari
Game
Reserve

Lake
Xau

0   30km
0   20 miles

N
Bradt

Pandamatenga, Kasane
(pages 256–7)

GPS co-ordinates ⊕

GWETA	20°11.434'S, 25°15.888'E
MOTOBR	20°12.723'S, 24°07.600'E
NATA	20°12.693'S, 26°10.859'E
TOCKGR	21°01.718'S, 24°22.607'E
TODVLH	20°52.202'S, 24°21.374'E

NOTE
For accommodation listings, see
pages 460–1, 471, 474–5,
482–4, 485–8, 487, 489

Sepako

Nata

Vet fence gate

Elephant Sands

NATA
Nata
Nata Lodge
Pelican Lodge

Entrance
gate

*Nata
Sanctuary*

Planet
Baobab
weta
dge
Xao

Tsigara

Makalone

Sowa Spit

Chapman's
Boabab
Tshataga

Sowa

(goods only)
Francistown

Sua Pan
(page 469)

Thabatshukudu

*Ntwetwe
Pan*

Tshwagong

*Kubu
Island*

*Kukome
Island*

Tshitane Pan

*Ntsokotsa
Pan.*

Mea

*Guguago
Pan*
*Nkokwane
Pan*
Mmatshumo

Mosu

Francistown

Orapa
(closed town)

Letlhakane, Serowe,
Khama Rhino Sanctuary

At its centre lie two huge adjacent salt pans – Sua (to the east) and Ntwetwe (to the west) – which cover an estimated combined area of roughly 12,000km². Around them are a number of smaller pans, including Nxai Pan to the north and Lake Xau to the south.

GEOLOGY To grasp the complex geology of this area, you really need a broader understanding of the way in which the whole Kalahari was formed (pages 4–6). In brief, the pans are the desiccated vestiges of the huge superlake which, several million years ago, covered most of central Botswana and moulded the landscape of the entire region. Subsequent climate change, seismic upheavals and the diversion of rivers (the details of which divide geologists) starved this lake of its water supply, shrinking it to today's flat, caustic depressions of grey clay, and withering its surrounding wetlands into arid savannah.

Today the pans generally receive no more than 400–500mm of rain annually (though the last few years have bucked that trend) and have no permanent standing water. After good rains, however, they briefly become shallow saline lakes again, fed by the seasonal Boteti River from the west – bringing the overspill from the Okavango – and the Nata River from the northeast.

FLORA AND FAUNA The plant and animal life of the region reflects its harsh climate. The plants are hardy and resilient species; the animals comprise either nomadic species that follow the rains in large seasonal movements, or specialised sedentary species adapted to arid Kalahari conditions. Populations fluctuate wildly according to rainfall. Consequently wildlife viewing is a hit-and-miss affair, depending entirely on the time of year and local conditions. However, in the right place at the right time, it can be spectacular, and the wide, open spaces make for excellent visibility.

Flora The flora of the Makgadikgadi Pans region can be graded into a loose series of zones, each determined by the soil in which it grows. At the centre lie the pans themselves: barren, windswept and devoid of any plant life. These sterile, salty dustbowls are surrounded by extensive grasslands which flourish on Kalahari sands, comprising a mixture of salt-tolerant species around the pans, coarse 'finger' grasses across the sandy plains, and nutritious 'sweet grasses' on the margins. The grasslands are punctuated with scattered trees and thickets, consisting primarily of acacia species.

Further from the pans, where the soil has a richer sand and clay mix, this acacia savannah becomes a denser bush, interspersed with other woodland trees, including various combretum and terminalia species. To the north and east, the acacias are replaced by a belt of mopane trees (*Colophospermum mopane*), which flourish on the more heavily clay soils.

To the west, the alluvial soils and hidden water table of the Boteti riverfront support a strip of dense riverine woodland. Here typical Kalahari species, such as camelthorn (*Vachellia erioloba*) and blackthorn (*Senegalia mellifera*), grow alongside riverine giants such as sycamore figs (*Ficus sycomorus*), sausage trees (*Kigelia africana*) and many of the other riverine species that are usually associated with wetter areas.

Across the region, towering real fan palms (*Hyphaene petersiana*) cluster in elegant, waving stands above the grasslands, forming extensive groves of palm woodland to the west of Ntwetwe Pan. Equally conspicuous are the scattered baobabs, which sprout incongruously around the pans and on isolated rock outcrops, each with centuries of history recorded in its swollen limbs.

Fauna Fossil evidence unearthed on the pans shows that in wetter, prehistoric times, the region supported the whole spectrum of African big game – including abundant elephant, buffalo and rhino. Today, the selection of large mammals is more limited than in the game-rich areas of Moremi and Chobe to the north and west. Rhino had disappeared altogether (though they are once more to be seen in the national park to the west), while elephant and buffalo occur only occasionally, in small numbers on the fringes.

However, the grasslands draw huge herds of grazers, which can, despite recent declines, still rival anything outside Tanzania's Serengeti for sheer numbers. Zebra and wildebeest gather in tens of thousands, supported by smaller numbers of gemsbok, eland and red hartebeest. Movements are unpredictable, but in general the highest concentrations occur in the western Boteti region during the late dry season (August–November) and further north in the Nxai Pan area during the rainy season (December–April).

Hardy springbok are impervious to drought and remain scattered across the grasslands throughout the year. In the Nxai Pans area, the mopane woodland shelters browsers, including impala (which supplant springbok where the bush thickens), kudu, sable and tsessebe. Here, giraffe are common and a few breeding elephant frequent the fringes of the northern pans.

Another pocket of diversity occurs along the Boteti River, where the thicker bush provides cover for grey duiker, bushbuck and waterbuck. Giraffe and elephant also visit this area, while the permanent pools even support a few hippos and crocodiles – emigrants from the Okavango.

A variety of predators prowls the region. Lions generally follow the game, particularly the zebra herds in the Boteti area and the winter springbok in Nxai, but seldom occur on the pans themselves. Cheetah are most often seen around Nxai Pan, while leopard frequent the denser bush of the Boteti waterfront. Spotted hyena keep to the woodland fringes in small numbers and are rarely seen, while the brown hyena – a Kalahari specialist – is found around the pans themselves.

Wild dogs are highly nomadic and, though unusual, can turn up anywhere. Here they are most often seen in the vicinity of Nxai Pan. Smaller predators include bat-eared fox, black-backed jackal, aardwolf, honey badger, African wildcat, small-spotted genet and striped polecat. Yellow mongooses are common on the grasslands, while the slender mongoose prefers acacia thickets.

Without much in the way of fruiting trees, the Makgadikgadi is not a good region for primates – except along the Boteti, where both vervet monkeys and baboons do find food and cover. However, throughout the region the lesser bushbaby, which feeds mostly on insects and acacia gum, thrives in the acacia savannah.

Other mammals of the grasslands include the ubiquitous aardvark and porcupine, and the bizarre spring hare is particularly abundant. Most smaller mammals are nocturnal, allowing them to avoid the high daytime temperatures, when a larger surface area to body ratio quickly causes overheating. On this principle a variety of rodents make their home in burrows and emerge at night, including the desert pygmy mouse, hairy-footed gerbil and Damara mole-rat (see box, page 495).

The black-tailed tree rat avoids the burning sun by hiding in tree holes, and protects the entrance to its lair with a scruffy 'nest' of twigs. At night this species can be seen scampering through the branches of a camelthorn, using its prehensile tail for added agility.

One exception to the nocturnal rule is the ground squirrel, an animal of the deep Kalahari that occurs in the sandy south of the region. This highly sociable rodent can forage in the full glare of the sun by using its tail as a parasol to cast protective shade.

Reptiles and amphibians Further down the evolutionary scale, a variety of reptiles and amphibians thrive in Makgadikgadi's arid expanses, though most pass unseen by the visitor. Acacias, with their deeply fissured bark and abundance of insect prey, provide havens for skinks and geckos above the open grassland. At ground level, the ground agama ambushes termites from a hollow at the foot of a shady bush, while the legless Kalahari burrowing skink swims just below the surface of the sand in search of beetle larvae, and is often found drowned when pans fill up overnight. In sandier areas, barking geckos emerge from their burrows on summer evenings and fill the Kalahari night with their bizarre territorial clicking calls.

Perhaps the highlight of Makgadikgadi's smaller animals is one that few have either heard of or seen: the Makgadikgadi spiny agama (*Agama makarikarica*). This is a small species of the agama family – a lizard – that's endemic to Makgadikgadi. It feeds on termites and beetles, and lives in tunnels at the base of bushes.

The acacia woodland is home to a broad cross-section of typical bushveld reptiles, including monitor lizards (both water and rock), flapneck chameleons and leopard tortoises. Snakes encountered at ground level include black mamba, snouted cobra, African egg-eater, mole snake and the ubiquitous puff adder, while

HIGH-RISE LIVING

The towers of mud built by termites, known as termitaria, are often the only points of elevation for miles across the Makgadikgadi grasslands. Not all termites build mounds – harvester termites (Hodotermitidae), which are common on Kalahari sands, leave little evidence of their underground tunnels above the surface – but those that do, the Macrotermitinae species, are responsible for one of the true wonders of nature.

Communicating entirely through pheromones, millions of blind worker termites can raise several tons of soil – particle by particle – into an enormous structure over 3m high. Below the mound lies the nest, where separate chambers house brood galleries, food stores, fungus combs (where termites cultivate a fungus that can break down plant cellulose) and the queen's royal cell. The queen produces up to 30,000 eggs a day, which means – since she lives for many years – that the millions of inhabitants of the colony are all brothers and sisters.

The whole structure is prevented from overheating by a miraculous air-conditioning system. Warm air rises from the nest chambers, up a central chimney, into thin-walled ventilation flues near the surface (you can feel the warmth by placing your hand just inside one of the upper vents). Here it is cooled and replenished with oxygen, before circulating back down through separate passages into cavities below the nest chambers. Finally, before returning to the nest, it passes through specially constructed cooling veins, kept damp by the termites. In this way, termites maintain the 100% humidity and constant temperature of 29–31°C required for successful production of eggs and young. (These conditions are exploited by monitor lizards, who seal their eggs inside termitaria for safe incubation.)

After the rains, when conditions are right, the queen produces a reproductive caste of winged males and females – known as imagos – who leave the colonies in huge swarms to mate, disperse and establish new nests. Mass termite 'emergences' are one of the bonanzas of the bush, offering a seasonal feast to everything from frogs and spiders to kites, falcons and tawny eagles.

arboreal species such as boomslang and spotted bush snake hunt chameleons and birds' eggs among the thorny tangle.

To survive this harsh habitat, many frogs aestivate below ground during the dry season. Giant bullfrogs emerge from their mud cocoons after seasonal rains to take over temporary pans in a frenzy of breeding. These frogs are so aggressive that they have even been observed snapping at lions. The much smaller rain-frogs of the *Breviceps* genus, like the bushveld rain-frog (*Breviceps adspersus*), have toughened feet, evolved for digging their burrows. They also appear with the rains, and gather at the surface during termite emergences, cramming in as many of the hapless insects as time will allow.

Invertebrates The Kalahari teems with invertebrate life. Good years bring swarms of locusts and mass migrations of butterflies to the grasslands, while countless termites demolish and carry away the dead vegetable matter that carpets the ground. Termites are fundamental to the ecology of the region. Not only do they recycle and enrich the soil, but they are also a vital prey species for everything from eagles and aardvarks to skinks and spiders.

There are 14 genera of termites, each of which has a different mode of foraging: harvester termites (Hototermitidae) nest in underground burrows, while *Odontoterms* termites of the Macrotermitinae family construct the enormous raised mounds that can be seen for miles across the grasslands – each one a miracle of air conditioning (see box, opposite).

Among a multitude of other insects are the wingless tenebrionid beetles, which scuttle rapidly across open ground on long legs and squirt a noxious fluid at attackers. More visible are the chunkier dung beetles, which swarm on strong wings to fresh animal dung, then roll it away and bury it as 'brood balls' in which their eggs are laid and their larvae mature.

On hot summer days, thickets throb with the stridulating calls of cicadas, the adults having only two weeks of life in which to mate and deposit their eggs, after up to 17 years' underground larval development.

Termites and other insects feed a host of invertebrate predators. Sand divers (Ammoxennidae) are small, fast-moving spiders that paralyse termites with their venom and bury themselves if disturbed. Golden orbweb spiders (Nephiladae) string their super-strong webs between thorn bushes to ensnare flying insects.

Contrary to popular belief, sun-spiders, or solifuges (Solifugae), are not venomous, but pursue insects at high speed across the ground and despatch them audibly with powerful mandibles. You'll often see these large arachnids running across the ground at night near campfires. Though frightening at first, they're totally harmless and don't bite people!

Not so harmless are the resident scorpions, which detect the vibrations of prey through their body hairs. As a rough rule of thumb for the nervous, species with larger pincers and slimmer tails have less powerful venom than those with smaller pincers and larger tails.

Red velvet mites are parasites on larger invertebrates and often gather in sandy areas in the early morning after rain showers, looking like tiny scarlet cushions. Another tiny parasite, the voracious tampan tick, lurks in the sand beneath camelthorn trees and, chemically alerted by an exhalation of its victim's CO_2, emerges to drain the blood from any unsuspecting mammal that fancies a nap in the shade.

Birdlife The great salt pans region offers several distinct habitats for birds. The open grasslands support typical ground-nesting, arid country species such as coursers, korhaans, sandgrouse, chats, larks and pipits. Both the world's largest bird – the ostrich – and the world's largest flying bird, the kori bustard, strike conspicuous figures in this featureless terrain, while greater kestrels, pale-chanting goshawks, marsh owls and the statuesque secretary bird are among the more common resident predators.

Any isolated stands of trees are beacons for birds: red-necked falcons breed in fan palms, while baobabs provide roosts for owls and breeding sites for hornbills and rollers. Elsewhere, typical arid woodland residents dominate the thicker scrub, including red-billed spurfowl, grey lourie, fork-tailed drongo, pied babbler, glossy starling, white-browed sparrow weaver and a wide variety of shrikes, barbets, flycatchers, robins, sunbirds, warblers, waxbills and whydahs.

Eagles, including martial and bateleur (or short-tailed eagle), roam the skies. Smaller predators such as Gabar goshawk and pearl-spotted owl hunt the thorn scrub, and vultures follow the herds across the region, hoping for casualties.

In summer the resident bird population is swelled by a huge influx of migrants drawn to the seasonal bonanza of seeds and insects. Some are non-breeding visitors that come from as far afield as Europe and central Africa. White storks (from Europe) and Abdim's storks (from East Africa) arrive wheeling on thermals to stalk the savannah; carmine and European bee-eaters hawk their insect prey just above the grass; shrikes, including red-backed and lesser grey, claim prominent territories on thorn bushes from where they ambush hapless lizards and grasshoppers.

Other more local breeding visitors include seed-eaters such as wattled starlings, doves, finchlarks, canaries – and the prolific red-billed quelea, whose flocks reach swarm proportions. Migrant raptors are lured by the brief abundance of prey, with many different species – including western red-footed falcons, steppe buzzards, yellow-billed kites and tawny eagles – congregating at mass termite emergences (see box, page 452).

After good rains, when Ntwetwe and Sua Pans turn briefly into glassy lakes, waterbirds arrive in their thousands. The shallow, saline conditions are ideal for both greater and lesser flamingos, which construct their clay nests under the blazing Kalahari sun and filter-feed on algae and brine shrimps. Meanwhile pelicans, darters, cormorants and ducks flock to the brackish waters of the Nata River delta, in the northeast of Sua Pan. Here, waders such as stilts, sandpipers and avocets forage along the shoreline, while jacanas, pied kingfishers, weavers and bishops frequent the reedbeds.

GETTING ORGANISED

Once you leave one of the few main roads in this area, you generally need to be in a self-sufficient 4x4 vehicle. Bringing along all your food and water is always a good idea, as while you will find water in some places, there is very little in the way of shops. A few towns around the pans (pages 484–9) can be good sources of fuel, but generally supplies are limited and/or intermittent.

If you're venturing off across Makgadikgadi, then you really should take at least two vehicles and have a GPS, a compass and a map; an environment of flat salt without any landmarks at all can be very disorienting, especially during a windstorm. In such a situation, breaking through the pan's crust and getting stuck can create a life-threatening situation.

MAPS The usual 'suspect' – Veronica Roodt's *Shell Tourist Map of Botswana* (page 146) – covers this area well, with a variety of useful GPS points.

If you plan on exploring a lot of the pans, then you should also get hold of a copy of the excellent *African Adventurer's Guide to Botswana*, by Mike Main (see *Appendix 3*, page 543). This has a number of carefully described routes through the area, as well as much interesting general information. However, do be aware that tracks can change, so always be vigilant.

BOOKING AND PARK FEES If you want to stay in either of the national parks then you must book ahead for a campsite. See pages 130–3, for details and fees for these national parks.

Similarly Jack's Camp, San Camp and Camp Kalahari should be booked in advance, and it is also advisable to reserve the campsite at Nata Sanctuary. That said, most of Sua and Ntwetwe pans fall outside the control of the authorities, so independent travellers can camp anywhere that appeals – though do first read the notes on safety on pages 183–7.

NXAI PAN NATIONAL PARK

Nxai Pan National Park lies to the north of the Nata–Maun road at the northern fringe of the ancient Lake Makgadikgadi basin. It is contiguous with Makgadikgadi Pans National Park, to the south of this same road. Nxai is probably the easiest area of the pans to drive yourself into, and from December to around July will also have the best game. Add in the spectacular sight of Baines' Baobabs to make a super destination for a three- to four-day self-drive trip.

Note that Nxai is usually pronounced to rhyme with 'high', unless you're familiar with the clicks of the Khoisan languages, in which case the correct pronunciation of the 'x' is actually a palatal click (ie: press tongue against the roof of your mouth, and then move down).

BACKGROUND INFORMATION
Geography The park covers an area of 2,658km², comprising Nxai Pan itself, Kgama-Kgama Pan complex to the northeast, and the Kudiakam Pan complex (including Baines' Baobabs) to the south. The baobabs were added to the original park in 1992.

The pans themselves are ancient salt lakes, ringed to the south and west with thick fossil dunes of wind-blown Kalahari sand. Today they are completely grassed over, but scattered across their surfaces are smaller pans or waterholes that fill up during the rainy season. Two of these are artificially maintained by the park authorities to provide surface water throughout the year, but the watercourses that once fed the area from the northeast have long since dried up.

The park's general topography is flat and featureless, with the famous baobabs being the most striking landmarks, and one of the higher points of elevation. To the north and east the soils become increasingly clayey, supporting the encroachment of mopane woodland and integrating with the dense mopane woodlands of the Chobe–Zambezi river catchment system.

Flora and fauna highlights
Flora The open grassland that covers the pans consists of many palatable 'sweet' grasses (eg: *Themeda* spp), which sustain the large herd of grazers that invade the area in summer. These grasslands are studded with 'islands' of acacias, consisting mostly of candle-pod acacia (*Vachellia hebeclada*). This is easily recognised from around October to March, as its seedpods stand upright, like candles. Other

15

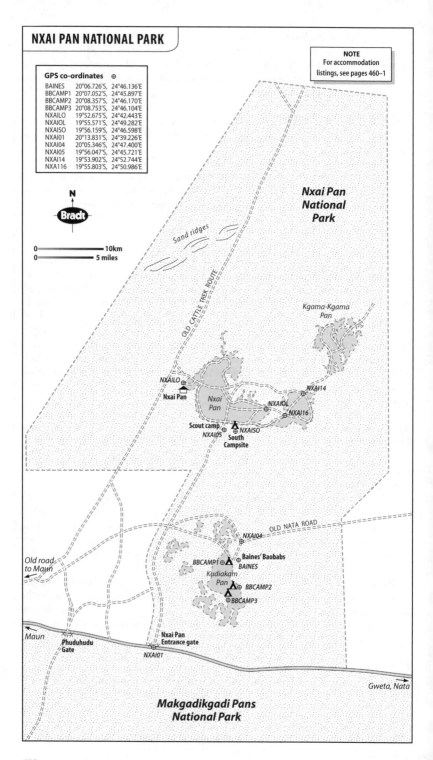

NXAI PAN NATIONAL PARK

NOTE
For accommodation
listings, see pages 460–1

GPS co-ordinates ⊕
BAINES   20°06.726'S, 24°46.136'E
BBCAMP1   20°07.052'S, 24°45.897'E
BBCAMP2   20°08.357'S, 24°46.170'E
BBCAMP3   20°08.753'S, 24°46.104'E
NXAILO   19°52.675'S, 24°42.443'E
NXAIOL   19°55.571'S, 24°49.282'E
NXAISO   19°56.159'S, 24°46.598'E
NXAI01   20°13.831'S, 24°39.226'E
NXAI04   20°05.346'S, 24°47.400'E
NXAI05   19°56.047'S, 24°45.721'E
NXAI14   19°53.902'S, 24°52.744'E
NXA116   19°55.803'S, 24°50.986'E

N
Bradt

0 ————— 10km
0 ————— 5 miles

Nxai Pan
National
Park

Sand ridges

OLD CATTLE TREK ROUTE

Kgama-Kgama
Pan

NXAILO ⊕
Nxai Pan

NXAH14

Nxai
Pan

NXAIOL

NXAI16

Scout camp   NXAISO
NXAI05   South
Campsite

OLD NATA ROAD

NXAI04

Old road
to Maun

Baines' Baobabs
BBCAMP1 ⊕   ⊕ BAINES
Kudiakam
Pan   ⊕ BBCAMP2
BBCAMP3

Maun   Nxai Pan
Phuduhudu   Entrance gate
Gate
NXAI01

Gweta, Nata

Makgadikgadi Pans
National Park

very common species here are the umbrella thorn (*Vachellia tortilis*) and bastard umbrella thorn (*Vachellia luederitzii*).

During the rains, the pans sprout a profusion of wild flowers, including the spectacular brunsvigia lily (*Brunsvigia radulosa*), which brings a splash of red to the summer landscape.

Around and between the pans the vegetation differs according to soil type. Acacias are the dominant trees on sandy soils, with stands of silver clusterleaf (*Terminalia sericea*), and – particularly in disturbed areas – dense thickets of sickle bush (*Dichrostachys cinerea*). Mopane (*Colophospermum mopane*) dominates the richer clayey soils to the north and east, carpeting the dusty ground with its golden butterfly leaves and bursting into a flush of green with the rains. Elsewhere, mixed sand and clay support various combretum species, with their wind-borne winged pods, while a richer selection of shrubs thrive on the lime-rich calcrete ridges, including the trumpet thorn (*Catophractes alexandrii*), Western rhigozum (*Rhigozum brevispinosum*) and purple-pod terminalia (*Terminalia prunoides*). Visit South Camp to see some fine examples of these.

Of all the area's trees, the best known must be the great baobabs (*Adansonia digitata*) – in particular the famous Baines' Baobabs that overlook Kudiakam Pan, which were painted by the renowned Victorian explorer and artist Thomas Baines on 22 May 1862, and have changed little in the 155 years since. They are not the only baobabs around, but they're certainly the most celebrated.

Fauna From December to April, Nxai Pan is a breeding ground for large herbivores. Game viewing can be spectacular at the start of this season, when thousands of animals are dropping their young and predators are drawn to the easy pickings. After good rains the lush green grasslands teem with huge concentrations of Burchell's zebra, blue wildebeest and springbok (here at the northeastern limit of their range), while healthy numbers of other grazers include gemsbok, eland and red hartebeest.

Large giraffe herds, sometimes over 40 strong, move across the pans between the acacia 'islands', which they prune into characteristic hourglass shapes. The mopane woodland, mainly to the north of Nxai Pan, shelters browsers such as impala and kudu, which often venture out on to the pans for the permanent waterholes and rich mineral salts. The impala is a versatile species, being able to adapt its diet to graze or browse, according to what is on offer, and Nxai Pan is one of the few areas where impala and springbok occur side by side – their habitats elsewhere generally being mutually exclusive.

In summer, small herds of breeding elephant can sometimes be seen around Kgama-Kgama Pan in the northeast of the park, while lone bulls disperse across the area at other times – generally on the fringes of the mopane. Other visitors from the north include the occasional tsessebe, at about the southern limit of their appearance in the Kalahari. In winter the great herds disperse from the pans, leaving few grazers except the hardy springbok, and a few timid steenbok that find shelter in the thickets.

Predators are well represented on Nxai Pan. Lion can be heard throughout the year: in summer they follow the zebra and wildebeest herds; during the dry season they remain to hunt springbok around the few permanent waterholes. The springbok herds also draw cheetah: Nxai Pan offers perfect open terrain for this coursing predator, and has a good reputation for sightings. Meanwhile wandering packs of wild dog occasionally turn up in pursuit of the same quarry.

Spotted hyena can sometimes be heard at night, especially when there are large concentrations of game around, while the more elusive brown hyena hunts and scavenges for smaller prey items around the pans. Black-backed jackal and honey badger are both versatile smaller predators that occur throughout the area, the latter sometimes foraging in association with the pale-chanting goshawk.

Aardwolf and bat-eared fox snap up harvester termites on the open grasslands. The former is strictly nocturnal and seldom seen; the latter is diurnal in winter and nocturnal in the hotter summer months, foraging in loose family groups with ears cocked to the ground for termite rustlings.

African wildcat and small-spotted genet hunt the acacia bush after dark for small rodents and roosting birds, while by day yellow mongoose comb open sandy areas for scorpions, slender mongoose hunt the acacia scrub, alone or in pairs, and banded mongoose rummage through the woodland in large, sociable colonies.

Other smaller mammals found here include lesser bushbaby, aardvark and porcupine, with spring hare on the grassland and scrub hare in the woodland. By day, tree squirrels are common and noisy inhabitants of the mopane.

Birdlife Nxai Pan's rich avifauna comprises a mixture of grassland, acacia scrub and mopane woodland birds, with a total of 217 species recorded in Hugh Chittenden's *Top Birding Spots of Southern Africa* (see *Appendix 3,* page 543). Each habitat has its own typical residents.

Grassland birds include ant-eating chat, white-browed sparrow weaver, capped wheatear and pale-chanting goshawk. White-browed robin, pied babbler and chinspot batis are found in the acacia scrub. Red-billed hornbill, red-billed spurfowl and barred owl prefer the mopane.

BROOD PARASITES

Cuckoos are not the only cheats of the bird world. Whydahs (Viduidae) are also brood parasites that lay their eggs in other birds' nests. Like cuckoos, each species of whydah exploits a specific host, and all of them choose waxbills (Estrildidae). However, unlike cuckoos, whydahs do not evict the eggs or nestlings of their host, so young whydahs grow up alongside their step-siblings, not instead of them.

To enhance the deception, a whydah's eggs – and there are usually two of them – perfectly mimic the colour of its host's clutch, and, once hatched, the whydah nestlings have exactly the right arrangements of gape spots inside their bills to dupe their step-parents into feeding them. A male whydah can even mimic the song of its host to distract it from the nest while the female goes about her devious business undisturbed. Breeding male whydahs are lively, conspicuous birds, who flaunt extravagant tail plumes in dancing display flights – though outside the breeding season they are indistinguishable from the drab females.

Three species of whydah occur in the pans region, of which the most typical is the shaft-tailed whydah (*Vidua regia*), easily recognised by the long thin tail-plumes of a breeding male, each tipped with a pennant. This species frequents sandy clearings in acacia thickets, often in association with its host, the violet-eared waxbill, and apparently without any animosity between them. The other two species are the pin-tailed whydah (*Vidua macroura*), which parasitises the common waxbill and prefers well-watered areas, and the paradise whydah (*Vidua paradisaea*), which parasitises the melba finch and is a common bird of acacia savannah.

The distinction between adjacent habitats is reflected in the parallel distributions of similar species. For example, double-banded coursers and northern black korhaans – both Kalahari specialists – occur only on the open grasslands, while bronze-winged coursers and red-crested korhaans, their close relatives, stick to the surrounding woodlands.

Resident raptors, such as bateleur (or short-tailed eagle), martial eagle, tawny eagle and brown snake eagle, are joined in summer by an influx of migrants, including steppe buzzard, western red-footed kestrel and yellow-billed kite. Raptor watching can be superb at this time, with more unusual species such as lesser-spotted eagle and hobby sometimes joining the throng at termite emergences.

Kori bustards, secretary birds and (in summer) white storks hunt the grasslands, and after good rains wattled cranes sometimes appear on the flashes. In spring the air resounds to the breeding displays of larks, including sabota, rufous-naped, red-capped, fawn-coloured, dusky and clapper. During summer the game herds are a focus of bird activity, with carmine and blue-cheeked bee-eaters hawking insects around the feet of springbok, zebra, red-billed and yellow-billed oxpeckers hitching rides on giraffes, and white-backed and lappet-faced vultures dropping from the sky on to carcasses.

Away from the pans, the campsites are a good place to search out the smaller passerines: violet-eared, black-cheeked and blue waxbills occur in the sandy acacia scrub together with melba and scaly-feathered finches, while shaft-tailed and paradise whydahs – brood parasites on waxbills (see box, opposite) – dash about in extravagant breeding finery. Baobabs are always worth checking, since they often provide roosting or nesting sites for rollers, hornbills and various owls.

WHEN TO VISIT The game at Nxai is fairly erratic – it can be excellent, though sometimes it will disappoint. If there have been good rains, then between December and April you have a very good chance of witnessing large herds of springbok, gemsbok, giraffe and migrating zebra, plus a scattering of other species. However, note that this is also the time when the pans are at their most treacherous, and driving at its most muddy.

I last visited in February, during a year of good rains, and we had good general game, with large numbers of zebra, although in two days we didn't see a single large carnivore. Conversely, a recent visitor in April was rewarded with sightings of both cheetah and lion during a one-night stay. Reliable reports suggest that game densities remain more or less constant until around August, when – as the dry season progresses and the waterholes dry up – the game becomes sparser and less dependable. Nxai can be a hot and unrewarding park at the height of October's heat.

GETTING THERE AND AWAY Unless you are staying at the new lodge, in which case you will normally arrive by air, you really need a vehicle to visit Nxai Pan National Park. Whether you have your own or are driven by one of the mobile-safari operators from Maun, you should come with all your fuel, water and food – there are no shops or fuel pumps here.

The route is very easy to find. The gate on the main road (⊕ NXAI01 20°13.831'S, 24°39.226'E), 0.5km to the east of the old cutline, heralded a new entrance in 2009. This is about 135km from Maun and 157km from Nata, and is very well signposted so you're unlikely to miss it. This is where you need to sign and present your entry permit.

There's one track north here, paralleling the old cutline (which until 2009 was the only access road to the park), and leading after some 36km to the scout post.

After driving on sand for around 18km, you'll reach a junction, where a right turn leads to Kudiakam Pan and Baines' Baobabs (see page 462 for directions). Continue straight, bearing north-northeast for a further 18km and you'll reach the scout camp (⊕ NXAI05 19°56.047'S, 24°45.721'E), which is at the south end of the main pan, near the waterhole. Nowadays this is fundamentally a base for the staff looking after the campsites but you can also get information here about the state of the roads and ask the guides about game movements within the park.

If you're driving yourself, follow the track round the pan from the scout camp to a junction. Here, turn west towards the Old Cattle Trek Route, pass the sign for the HATAB campsite, and continue for a further kilometre.

⌂ WHERE TO STAY

Along with the long-established campsites at Nxai Pan, there is a smart lodge to the west of the pan, opening up this park to visitors who would not consider camping.

Of the campsites around the pan itself, only the southern one with ten pitches remains open. However, three campsites can also be found close to the famous Baines' Baobabs, reversing a previous ban on camping in that area.

⌂ **Nxai Pan** [map 456] (9 chalets) Contact Kwando Safaris, page 224; ⊕ NXAILO 19°52.675'S, 24°42.443'E. Opened in Feb 2009, & the 1st lodge to be built inside the national park, Nxai Pan is located on an area of flat, open grassland, 47km from the new park gate, or 8.3km from the old one. The lodge forms a shallow crescent facing west over a distant waterhole that attracts a phenomenal number of elephant. A particularly welcoming local team affords a homely atmosphere that is quite a highlight.

At the heart of the lodge is a substantial if narrow thatched building, entirely open on one side, but with roll-down canvas blinds with plastic 'windows' to keep out the worst excesses of the weather. Inside, light wooden furniture lends a somewhat Scandinavian air to the bar, lounge & dining area, which flow almost seamlessly from one end to the other. These look over an extensive wooden deck with a small pool near the bar, & a firepit in front. A telescope situated on the main deck is the perfect opportunity to explore the night sky, with the help of a guide, while a curio shop at the back offers a range of gifts & merchandise.

Flanking the main building, & mirroring it in style, are individual chalets, linked by glossy raised wooden walkways that snake behind the complex. A door at the back of each leads into a long & open room, with twin beds – or a dbl – in the centre, & sliding doors with mesh panels opening on to a wooden deck. At one end, there are inside & outside showers, twin washbasins & a separate

toilet, while at the other are a desk, low table & chairs. A family room has a 2nd small twin room attached to the lounge.

Morning or afternoon game drives within the immediate area can be extended to full-day trips to Kudiakam Pan & Baines' Baobabs, with late-evening drives an option, & overnight trips on the pans planned too. Short informative nature walks are possible, too, since although the lodge is inside the national park, it sits within its own 5ha concession. These are conducted by a Bushman tracker, & are a great opportunity to share in their knowledge, sense of humour & passion for the land. *US$577 pp (sgl supp't US$220 Apr–Nov), inc FB, most drinks, activities & laundry.* ⊕ *All year.* ★★★

Å **South Campsite** [map 456] (10 pitches) Contact Xomae Group, pages 132–3; ⊕ NXAISO 19°56.159'S, 24°46.598'E. The closest campsite to the entrance, South Camp is probably the busier site – but it benefits from a lovely location. It's situated in a grove of purple-pod terminalia trees (*Terminalia prunioides*) which cast a good shade, making it relatively cool. There are separate ablution blocks for men & women, each with showers & flush toilets. *US$38 pp, exc park fees.* ⊕ *All year.*

Å **Baines' Baobabs** [map 456] (3 sites) Contact Xomae Group, pages 132–3. There are 3 separate campsites around Baines' Baobabs. The closest one to the famous baobabs themselves, at ⊕ BBCAMP1 20°07.052'S, 24°45.897'E, is on an island, separated from the baobabs by a salt pan. The other 2 sites (⊕ BBCAMP2 20°08.357'S, 24°46.170'E & ⊕ BBCAMP3 20°08.753'S, 24°46.104'E) lie further south along the eastern edge of the pan. Each of the sites is equipped with a long-drop loo & bucket shower, but there is no water, so make sure you bring everything you need for the duration of your stay. *US$50 pp, exc park fees.* ☺ *All year.*

WHAT TO SEE AND DO Nxai's a great park for watching the herds of plains game, and is certainly somewhere that you need to be patient. Don't rush around in search of predators; instead take your time and you'll see much more. The waterholes are very open and exposed here, so park a good distance away and you won't disturb the animals drinking.

Finally, note that the night sky here is often phenomenally clear – as it is across the centre of the Kalahari. So if you can bring a star chart as well as your route maps, you'll enjoy it all the more. First on your list should be to identify the Southern Cross, and use it to find due south. When gazing up, try using your binoculars and you'll be amazed how many more stars you can see.

Nxai and Kgama-Kgama pans These are the main pans of the complex. They're covered with grasses and dotted with clumps of acacias – and have always provided me with the best game viewing in this park.

Getting around In the dry season you'll find most of the roads in the area of the pan are good and hard, a pleasant contrast to the thick sand that you ploughed through to reach here.

When the rains come you'll have to be much more careful as many roads on the pan itself turn very muddy. Then the sand road in will be the easiest section, and the park itself will provide the problems. Make sure your self-sufficient vehicle includes a spade, and always carry some wood with you, both for campfires and for sticking under the wheels when you get stuck.

From Nxai Pan to Kgama-Kgama Pan The road which leads off east towards Kgama-Kgama Pan runs through dense bush, affording little visibility either side. To reach the pan, head east from the scout post for about 10km, passing South Camp on your right. This should bring you to a junction of the tracks (⊕ NXAI16 19°55.803'S, 24°50.986'E). From here one track (clearly marked on most maps) leads off to loop around to the southeast and then turn north.

However, another track leads off heading north of east, before turning northeast, and after almost 5km reaches another junction (⊕ NXAI14 19°53.902'S, 24°52.744'E).

The alternative, which leads roughly west, across the north end of the small pan to the east of Nxai, heads through an interesting area of mostly mopane woodland, mixed with some denser groves of terminalias, and even in May, some of the pans here retained water. This eventually leads west to North Camp (⊕ NXAINO 19°52.707'S, 24°47.358'E).

Kudiakam Pan and Baines' Baobabs Sandwiched between Nxai Pan and the main road, Kudiakam is the largest of an interesting complex of pans lying in sparse bush east of the track to Nxai. The game here doesn't usually match Nxai's, but the main attraction is an extraordinarily beautiful group of trees known as Baines' Baobabs, which stand at a spectacular site on the eastern edge of the pan. They were immortalised in a painting by Thomas Baines who came here in May 1862 with James Chapman and wrote:

A lone circuit brought me, with empty pouch, to the clump of baobabs we had seen yesterday from the wagon; five full-sized trees, and two or three younger ones were standing, so that when in leaf their foliage must form one magnificent shade. One gigantic trunk had fallen and lay prostrate but still, losing none of its vitality, bent forth branches and young leaves like the rest … The general colour of the immense stems was grey and rough: but where the old bark had peeled and curled off, the new (of that peculiar metallic coppery-looking red and yellow which Dr Livingstone was wont so strenuously to object in my pictures) shone through over large portions, giving them, according to light or shade, a red or yellow, grey or a deep purple tone.

The baobabs themselves have changed very little since Baines painted them, and the one lying prostrate is still thriving, having lost none of its vitality.

Having thought of the baobabs with reference to a fairly recent Victorian painter, it's perhaps worth reminding ourselves that Baines was far from the first person here. Lawrence Robbins (see *Appendix 3*, page 541) and others have conducted archaeological surveys of this area and discovered extensive remains dating from the Middle Stone Age period, 'especially on the eastern side within a 4km radius of the Baines baobab grove', according to Robbins. Many stone tools were found, plus ostrich eggshell remains, a zebra's tooth and the fossilised bone of a hippopotamus.

This site has been dated to about 105,000–128,000 years old, around which time this was probably a beach location on the edge of the great superlake. This Middle Stone Age period has a special resonance, as this is the period during which we think the first *Homo sapiens* appeared.

Getting there and away The easiest way is to follow the directions to Nxai Pan by turning off the main Maun–Nata road at the new gate (✪ NXAI01 20°13.831'S, 24°39.226'E) into the national park, which is well signposted. After heading north for 18km, you'll find a track off to the east. This track splits very soon, after about 0.9km, and both roads lead to the baobabs.

Dry-season route The right fork heads almost directly for Baines' Baobabs (✪ BAINES 20°06.726'S, 24°46.136'E). It is the more direct route, but it crosses the surface of the pans, so do not try this unless you know what you're doing and are sure they will be dry. (It should be fine after about August, though don't take this as a guarantee!) Even the guides at the main gate mentioned that they always try to take the more northerly wet-season route where possible.

Wet-season route Taking the left fork is more reliable if you're travelling earlier in the year, as it bends around slightly to the north, taking about 14.4km to reach a crossroads at ✪ NXAI04 20°05.346'S, 24°47.400'E. Here you meet the old road between Maun and Nata; this is about 3.6km from the trees themselves. There's a network of small tracks around here, so head straight and then look for tracks off to the right, or turn right and find a track to your left – you can't miss them (✪ BAINES 20°06.726'S, 24°46.136'E).

MAKGADIKGADI PANS

The Sua and Ntwetwe pans that comprise Makgadikgadi cover 12,000km² to the south of the Nata–Maun road. The western side is protected within a national park, while the east is either wilderness or cattle-ranching land. These are among the largest salt pans in the world and have few landmarks. So you're left to use the flat, distant horizon as your only line of reference – and even that dissolves into a haze of shimmering mirages in the heat of the afternoon sun. During the rains this desolate area comes to life, with huge migrating herds of zebra, wildebeest, and occasionally (if the pans fill with water) pelicans and many thousands of flamingos. A couple of odd outcrops of isolated rock in and around the pans add to their sense of mystery, as well as providing excellent vantage points from which to view the endless expanse of silver, grey and blue.

Makgadikgadi Pans National Park lies on the west of the pans, incorporating the western end of Ntwetwe Pan and a larger adjacent area of grassland and acacia woodland. The flora and fauna there are sufficiently different, especially around the Boteti River, to warrant a separate section, towards the end of this chapter, entitled *Makgadikgadi Pans National Park* (pages 476–84).

BACKGROUND INFORMATION This section concentrates on the main salt pans, Sua and Ntwetwe, and the areas of grassland immediately around them which encompass many scattered smaller pans.

Geography and geology As discussed on page 450, Sua and Ntwetwe lie at the centre of the great prehistoric lake basin that circumscribes the whole region. On top of this is an ancient mantle of wind-blown Kalahari sands – deposited during the Tertiary period, as the subcontinent was levelled by erosion. Exposed rock is a rarity on the surface of this scrubbed and scoured landscape. However, beneath the sand lie ancient Karoo deposits 300 million years old, comprising basalt larva, sandstone and shales and containing such valuable minerals as gold, silver, copper and nickel.

During the Cretaceous period, 80 million years ago, rifts and buckles in the earth's crust allowed 'pipes' of molten material – known as kimberlite – to punch their way up from below. Diamonds formed under conditions of massive heat and pressure in these kimberlite pipes. Today they are mined at Orapa, just south of Ntwetwe Pan.

A few isolated outcrops of igneous rock extrude from the surface of the pans, notably Kubu Island and Kukome Island on Sua Pan. Apart from these, and some fossilised barchan (crescent-shaped) dunes to the west, the pans themselves are flat and featureless expanses of dry, sterile salt. However, after good summer rains they are transformed into shimmering lakes, giving a glimpse of what the great superlake must once have been like. The rainwater that pours down on them is augmented in really wet years by seasonal flows from the east: the Nata, Tutume, Semowane and Mosetse rivers. Also, again only in exceptional years, an overspill from the Okavango makes its way to the west side of Ntwetwe, via the Boteti River.

Flora and fauna highlights The saline conditions of the pans themselves have a strong local influence on their surrounding vegetation. Broadly speaking this becomes richer and more diverse the further you travel from the pan edges, creating a loose concentric series of 'succession' zones, each of which supports a distinctive fauna. These zones effectively chart the gradual demise of the ancient superlake.

Flora There is no plant life on the surface of the pans, since nothing can tolerate the excessively high concentration of mineral salts, and wind erosion scours the exposed dusty surface, quickly denuding it of any vegetation that tries to take hold. The immediate fringes are carpeted with more or less uninterrupted grassland, consisting primarily of *Digitarias* species, which can survive despite the irregular herd movements. Between the pans can also be found patches of prickly salt grass (*Odyssea paucinervis*), a yellowish, spiky species that tolerates high salinity (salt crystals can sometimes be seen on the leaves).

Summer rains bring lush growth to the grasses, which flower in a wind-rippled sea of green. Then you'll also see a scattering of short-lived wild flowers bloom among the grasses, including crimson lilies, acanthus and wild hibiscus (*Hibiscus calyphyllus*). In areas of thicker sand ridges, the runners of the tsama melon (*Citrullus lanatus*) sprawl across the sand, its swollen fruit providing life-sustaining moisture for a myriad animals, from gerbils to gemsbok. In winter, cropped and shrivelled, the grasses are reduced to a sparse golden mantle over the dusty plains, scattering their seeds to the wind.

Here and there, small hollows in the rolling grassland trap wind-blown detritus, creating pockets of richer soil that support scattered trees and shrubs. The most common trees are various acacia species, such as the umbrella thorn (*Vachellia tortilis*), which, with their fine leaves for minimising water loss and wicked thorns to deter browsers, are ideally suited to survive this arid environment. The hardy camelthorn (*Vachellia erioloba*) thrives in areas of deeper sand, often in an almost lifeless state of disintegration, by tapping deep reserves of groundwater with its long roots.

The shepherd's tree (*Boscia albitrunca*) with its distinct white trunk and dense, invaluable shade, is another versatile pioneer of sandy Kalahari soils. The grasslands are studded with stands of fan palms (*Hyphaenea petersiana*), with their hard, cricket-ball-sized fruit known as vegetable ivory. Thick groves of this elegant tree occur beyond the northwest shores of Ntwetwe Pan and along the Maun–Nata road.

KALAHARI MELONS

There are at least eight species of the pumpkin family in Botswana, of which the tsama melon (*Citrullus lanatus*) is the most distinctive and frequently seen. It is found throughout the region, and is particularly common after a good rainy season. Then, even after most of the rest of the vegetation is brown and shrivelled, you'll find tempting round melons beside the sandiest of roads – often apparently on their own.

During the dry season these become important sources of moisture for many animals, especially the gemsbok, and are also used by the local people. To get drinking water from one of these, you first cut off the top, like a boiled egg. The centre can then be cut out and eaten. Then take a stick and mash the rest of the pulp while it's in the melon, and this can be eaten. Take care not to eat the pips. These are best roasted and pounded, when they make an edible meal that can be cooked with water. Sometimes you'll come across a bitter fruit, which you should not eat as it may cause poisoning.

Another fairly common species is the gemsbok melon (*Citrullus naudianus*), which has similar sprawling tendrils and an oval fruit, covered in blunt fleshy spines. Unlike the tsama melon, this is a perennial plant with a long underground tuber. Inside the fruit is a jelly-like, translucent green which can be eaten raw (again, discarding the pips usually), though it doesn't taste very good. It's slightly more palatable when roasted beside the fire overnight – but I wouldn't recommend that you throw away your muesli or yoghurt before tasting it!

In the far northeast of Sua Pan, the seasonal Nata River spreads out into a small delta formation which is quite different from the rest of the region. Here there's a band of tall dry riverine forest along the banks of the Nata, and a thickening of the ground cover lining the braided channels. Phragmites reeds thrive in the brackish conditions here, and when this delta is in flood the area can seem quite lush.

Further from the pans, the grassland gives way to a denser bush. To the east, a mixed sand and clay soil supports a greater variety of woodland trees, including tamboti (*Spirostachys africana*), marula (*Scleoroclarya birrea*) and monkey thorn (*Senegalia galpinii*), while a belt of mopane woodland (*Colophospermum mopane*) also grows in the more heavily clayey soil around Nata and along the eastern boundary of Sua Pan.

The mighty baobabs (*Adansonia digitata*) are perhaps the region's best-known and most easily identified trees. These iconic, drought-resistant giants occur scattered around the pans and on isolated rock outcrops such as Kubu Island, where they have stood as landmarks for millennia. The swollen trunks of many are engraved with the signatures of generations of thirsty travellers. Among the baobabs on Kubu some other more unusual species take advantage of this rocky, island niche, including the African star-chestnut (*Sterculia africana*) and common corkwood (*Commiphora pyracanthoides*).

Fauna Large mammals are scarce around the pans. This is partly because of the hostile nature of the terrain, partly because this is cattle-ranching country, where wild animals have been marginalised by the activities of people, and partly because of the destructive effect that veterinary control fences have had on animal migration patterns.

There is no doubt that cattle fences to the south (page 494) have had a significant impact on the populations of herbivores, and especially the blue wildebeest. Now blue wildebeest are seldom seen around Sua Pan and certainly not in the vast herds that built up during the 1950s, when populations are estimated to have peaked at about 250,000. Further west, though, in the area where Ntwetwe Pan borders the national park, great numbers of zebra and wildebeest arrive with the rains between November and December, feeding on the nutritious new grasses. Many move on in February and March, but others stay, attracted by regularly pumped waterholes in the area.

A permanent scattering of springbok inhabits the grasslands around the pans, too. These hardy and versatile antelope manage without water for long periods, and withstand the harshest daytime temperatures by orientating their white rumps towards the sun to deflect the worst of its ultraviolet rays.

Other large mammals are thin on the ground, being more abundant towards the west of Ntwetwe and the adjacent grazing grounds of Makgadikgadi Pans National Park (pages 478–81). However, a scrutiny of the pan surface can reveal the tracks of a surprising range of visitors, including rare wandering elephants or giraffe. Zebra and gemsbok are sometimes seen trekking wearily through the heat haze as they cross the pans between grazing areas, while red hartebeest are frequent visitors to the grasslands, where they can subsist on poorer grasses than many species.

The encrusted tracks of lion or cheetah sometimes appear on the pan surface, particularly towards the west, but the comparative lack of large herbivores means that larger predators are scarce, and a wandering lion is apt to be shot by cattle ranchers. More common are the smaller nocturnal carnivores that can survive the harsh conditions and thrive on smaller pickings.

Brown hyena inhabit the area, and occasionally these elusive predators may be observed at close quarters from Jack's Camp, on the western shores of Ntwetwe, where they have been studied by zoologists. Their catholic diet includes tsama melons and ostrich eggs, as well as spring hares, young springbok, smaller mammals and carrion.

Black-backed jackal, bat-eared fox and African wildcat are widespread, while yellow mongoose is common in sandy areas, where it is an accomplished killer of scorpions. At night, a legion of smaller mammals moves out across the grasslands. Spring hares thrive on damaged grassland and are common around villages, where up to 60 may occur per hectare. Their eyes shine brightly in torchlight, and casting a beam around your campsite will usually reveal at least one foraging nearby.

Aardvarks are found (though seldom seen) in open areas with plenty of termites, scrub hares hide up in acacia thickets, and porcupines occur anywhere. Acacias provide shelter for lesser bushbabies, which feed on their gum during winter when insects are less abundant. This diminutive, nocturnal primate performs astonishing leaps from tree to tree and seldom comes to the ground, progressing on its hind legs in huge hops when it does. Common rodents include typical Kalahari species such as ground squirrel, Damara mole rat, hairy-footed gerbil and black-tailed tree rat.

Birdlife The Makgadikgadi Pans are perhaps best known for their birdlife, specifically the great concentration of waterbirds in the Nata River delta after good rains (December–April). In good years, tens of thousands of flamingos, both lesser and greater, arrive to breed, visible from the air as a pink shimmer across the surface of the lake. They are sustained by a rich soup of algae – and brine shrimps, whose eggs lie dormant in the baked clay of the pan surface throughout the dry season.

This gathering represents the largest breeding flamingo population in southern Africa, and can peak at over 100,000 birds. However, it is a very unpredictable phenomenon. Even after good rains the flamingos have a life-and-death race against time to breed before the waters dry up, and they may not return again for years. In 1976, over 5,000 young flamingos, still unable to fly, were observed from the air trekking *en masse* across the barren pans in search of new water when their breeding shallows evaporated. What became of them is not recorded.

The flamingos can best be seen in the Nata Sanctuary (page 471). Here, when the flood is full, you will also find pelicans (both white and pink-backed), herons and egrets, cormorants and darters, waders (including avocet, black-winged stilt, blacksmith lapwing, wood sandpiper and ruff), black-necked grebe, red-knobbed coot, and ducks (including red-billed teal and white-faced duck). Other species more typical of the Okavango floodplains also occur at this time, including fish eagles,

SPRING HARES

The spring hare is actually a true rodent, and not a hare at all. Weighing about 3kg, this bizarre animal looks like a cross between a rabbit and a kangaroo, with its long ears and thick black-tipped tail. It progresses in ambling hops on long hind legs, with forelegs clasped in front and tail balanced behind.

Spring hares live in burrows by day, in which they doze off upright, having plugged the hole with dirt. By night they graze on grass and crops, and dig for roots, corms and tubers. This animal is a prized delicacy for many nocturnal predators, including owls, honey badgers and caracals. It also figures prominently on the local human menu. It has been estimated that over 2.5 million spring hares are hunted annually in Botswana – hooked out of their holes during the day – providing the protein equivalent of 20,000 cows.

saddle-billed storks and, occasionally, wattled cranes. The reedbeds themselves provide a breeding habitat for weavers, bishops and reed warblers.

The open grasslands surrounding the pans are home to many typical Kalahari ground-nesting birds, including ostriches, which are sometimes seen far out on the pans themselves, kori bustards and secretary birds. Some smaller species, including capped wheatear and ant-eating chat, take this a stage further by nesting, like rodents, in underground burrows. All four of southern Africa's sandgrouse (Namaqua, Burchell's, double-banded and yellow-throated) occur around the pans. These delicately plumaged birds are most often seen in the evening, flying rapidly towards a waterhole with rippling calls. Males will waddle in to immerse their absorbent belly feathers and carry water back many kilometres to their young on the nest.

More conspicuous by day is the boldly marked male northern black korhaan (formerly called the white-quilled korhaan), who calls with a noisy 'karak karak karak' as he takes off and circles slowly in territorial display, before fluttering to the ground with yellow legs dangling. Like all korhaans, the brooding female relies on her cryptic camouflage to remain hidden. Another common species, the double-banded courser, is superbly adapted to withstand the harsh conditions of the pans. It does not need any drinking water, and can survive extreme overheating while protecting its single egg from the fierce Makgadikgadi sun.

In this largely featureless habitat, any point of elevation can prove a good spot for birds. The baobabs on Kubu Island provide roosting and nesting sites for barn owls and rollers (both lilac-breasted and purple). Many tall stands of date palms harbour breeding palm swifts, and the occasional pair of red-necked falcons. Isolated thorn trees support the massive untidy nests of secretary birds or vultures (both white-backed and lappet-faced).

The acacia woodland holds a wide selection of birds typical of this habitat across the region (pages 458–9). Red-billed spurfowl, white-browed robin and violet-eared waxbill forage low down in the thickets, while lilac-breasted roller and long-tailed shrike perch more conspicuously in the taller acacias. Bateleurs (or short-tailed eagles) and martial eagles patrol the skies, and a host of bulbuls, babblers, hornbills, barbets, sunbirds, flycatchers and others occupy the niches in between.

The area around Nata Lodge is particularly rich in woodland species. In summer, migrant raptors such as steppe buzzard, western red-footed kestrel and yellow-billed kite join resident predators such as greater kestrel, pale chanting goshawk and marsh owl, and after good rains, Montagu's and pallid harriers may be seen quartering the grasslands in drifting, elegant flight.

Other common summer migrants include white stork, red-backed and lesser grey shrikes and European and carmine bee-eaters, while seed-eaters such as red-billed quelea and black-eared finchlark arrive to breed in large numbers, taking advantage of the seasonally abundant grass seeds.

GETTING AROUND With a large number of tracks in the area, I have not even tried to describe them all in detail here. However, if you're driving around by yourself, rather than with a local guide who knows the area well, then navigation issues should preoccupy you. Outside the national park, visiting the pans is all about exploring for yourself. If you want set routes to follow, perhaps it's not for you.

If you're ready for a small expedition, then take note of the highlights and landmarks mentioned here, with GPS co-ordinates, and use the Shell map (mentioned on page 146) to keep some realistic idea of where you are. That said, because of the size of the pans and their very remote situation, you must follow some basic safety rules:

15

- Take at least one reliable GPS with you – and many more batteries than you think you'll need.
- Carry much more fuel than you expect to use.
- Carry enough water and food for your whole time in the pans area, plus a few days' safety margin.
- Travel with a minimum of two fully equipped 4x4s, and preferably also a satellite phone.
- Arrange a rendezvous for when you leave the pans, and someone to raise the alarm if you don't arrive. Leave a rough route plan with them.

It's difficult for me to emphasise enough just how dangerous the pans can be. There are periodic deaths of people who visit the area without the proper back-up and preparation, and then get into difficulties. It's different from many areas in Botswana because:

- The sun is merciless on the pans' surface; there's absolutely no shade.
- If you break through the crust of the pans to the wet silt beneath, then getting out is very difficult, even with a second vehicle. Remember: there will be no wood around; no branches to put under the wheels.
- There are so many different tracks on the pans (each diverging vehicle makes a new one), that often there simply isn't a 'right' track which most vehicles take. Thus, it may be weeks or months before someone takes the same route that you do, and passes you.

SUA PAN Sua Pan is the eastern of the twin pans, and extends roughly southwards from the town of Nata (pages 484–6) in its northeast corner. On its southern shore is the village of Mosu; to its north lies the Maun–Nata road; to its west it is divided from Ntwetwe Pan by a thin strip of grassland.

Sua (sometimes spelled 'Sowa') is the Setswana word for 'salt', and it is this mineral residue from the vanished superlake that dominates the geology and ecology of the pan. Once, salt was laboriously collected from the pan surface by the San and carried away on donkeys. Today it is mined by Botswana Ash (Botash), a joint enterprise in which the Botswana government is the major shareholder, and taken out by rail. The company supplies sodium carbonate on an industrial scale for use in the manufacture of paper, glass and steel. Their mine is situated along the Sua Spit, a tongue of grassland that extends halfway across the pan from its eastern shore.

The Nata River feeds Sua Pan from the northeast (bringing the rains from Zimbabwe) and, in good years, it floods from December to April with shallow, warm water. Where the fresh water of the river meets the saline pan, a brackish delta of silted reedbeds has formed. In summer, this corner of the pan attracts great concentrations of breeding waterbirds, notably flamingos (see box, page 470).

GPS REFERENCES FOR SUA PAN MAP (opposite)

KUBU-I	20°53.737'S, 25°49.421'E	TSHWAG	20°48.094'S, 25°45.608'E
KUKOME	20°55.001'S, 26°12.203'E	TSIVET	20°58.620'S, 25°37.178'E
KWADIB	20°54.907'S, 26°16.571'E	TURNM1	21°19.468'S, 25°33.742'E
MMATSH	21°08.590'S, 25°39.214'E	TURNM2	20°55.990'S, 25°40.015'E
THABAT	20°42.606'S, 25°47.476'E		

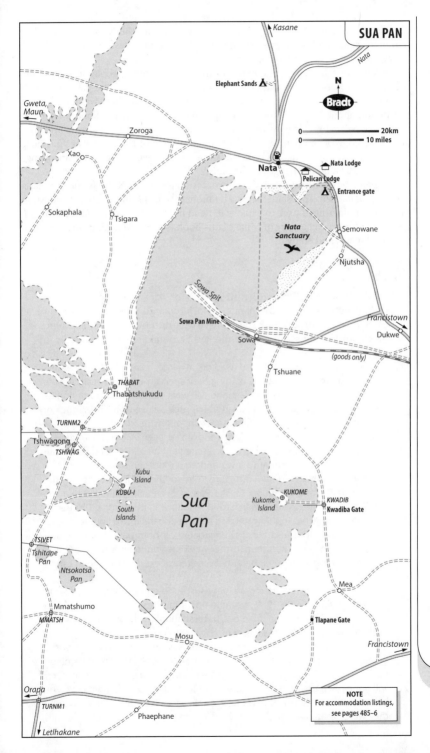

Kasane

Nata

Elephant Sands

N

Bradt

0   20km
0   10 miles

*Gweta,
Maun*

Zoroga

Xao

Nata

Nata Lodge

Pelican Lodge

Entrance gate

Sokaphala

Tsigara

Semowane

*Nata
Sanctuary*

Njutsha

Sowa Spit

Sowa Pan Mine

Francistown

Sowa

Dukwe

(goods only)

Tshuane

THABAT
Thabatshukudu

TURNM2

Tshwagong

TSHWAG

*Kubu
Island*

KUBU-I

*South
Islands*

*Sua
Pan*

KUKOME

Kukome
Island

KWADIB
Kwadiba Gate

TSIVET
*Tshitane
Pan*

*Ntsokotsa
Pan*

Mea

Mmatshumo

MMATSH

Tlapane Gate

Mosu

Francistown

Orapa

TURNM1

Phaephane

Letlhakane

NOTE
For accommodation listings,
see pages 485–6

The Kalahari's Great Salt Pans   MAKGADIKGADI PANS

15

This delta – an area of 230km² – is now protected within the Nata Sanctuary. The flamingos can usually be viewed from the bird hide on the eastern shore, but after heavy rain, access may not be possible.

Evidence of the former lake exists in the form of fossil pebble beaches along the shores of Kubu Island and other granite outcrops around the pan, and fossil diatoms and molluscs on the pan surfaces. These reveal that there was a prolonged wet period about 14,000–17,000 years ago and, more recently, a flood only 1,500 years ago. Near the village of Mosu in the south, an escarpment rises some 40m above the edge of the pan, showing the erosive force of the great lake that once washed against these cliffs. Here there is also one of several subterranean springs that emerge around the fringes of the pans.

The pan is a remarkable area, with the occasional spot like Kubu Island that has a magic all of its own. That said, there's a lot more than just Nata Sanctuary and Kubu here – but it does need time to explore it. Read my warning under *Getting around*, pages 467–8; then get a copy of Mike Main's book (see *Appendix 3*, page 543) and a few good maps, and enjoy it!

FLAMINGOS

Of the world's half-dozen or so species of flamingo, two are found within southern Africa: the greater (*Phoenicopterus ruber*) and the lesser (*Phoenicopterus minor*). Both species have wide distributions, from southern Africa north into East Africa and the Red Sea, and are highly nomadic in their habits.

Flamingos are usually found wading in large areas of shallow saline water where they filter feed by holding their specially adapted beaks upside down in the water. The lesser flamingo will walk or swim while swinging its head from side to side, mainly taking blue-green algae from the surface of the water. The larger greater flamingo will hold its head submerged while filtering out small organisms (detritus and algae), even stirring the mud with its feet to help the process. Both species are very gregarious and flocks can have millions of birds, though a few hundred is more common.

Only occasionally do flamingos breed in southern Africa, choosing the Makgadikgadi Pans, Namibia's Etosha Pan or even Lake Ngami. When the conditions are right (usually March to June, following the rains), both species build low mud cones in the water and lay one or (rarely) two eggs in a small hollow on the top. These are then incubated by both parents for about a month, until they hatch. After a further week the young birds flock together and start to forage with their parents. Some ten weeks later the young can fly and fend for themselves.

During this time the young are very susceptible to the shallow water in the pans drying out. In 1969, a rescue operation was mounted in Namibia when the main Etosha Pan dried out, necessitating the moving of thousands of chicks to nearby Fischer's Pan, which was still covered in water.

The best way to tell the two species apart is by their beaks: that of the greater flamingo is almost white with a black tip, while the lesser flamingo has a uniformly dark beak. If you are further away then the body of the greater will appear white, while that of the lesser looks smaller and more pink. The best place to see them in Botswana is certainly Sua Pan – although even there they will only appear if the rains have filled some of the pan.

Where to stay Most visitors to this area spend the night at one of the variety of options in Nata (pages 484–6). An alternative would be to camp at Nata Sanctuary (see below). There has been sporadic talk of a new lodge to be built at Sowa for some time now, but this has yet to be substantiated.

Nata Sanctuary (⊕ *all year 07.00–19.00 daily; P55 pp, plus P45/vehicle, camping P35 pp*) A conservation area was originally established in the northeast corner of Sua Pan with the help of the Kalahari Conservation Society in the 1980s, to protect the important seasonal wetland areas around the Nata Delta. However, although the villagers at Nata were consulted about the plans, the wider community in the area didn't benefit from it.

This area encompassed cattle-grazing land owned by four communities: Nata, Sepako, Maposa and Mmaxotae. In the early 1990s, it was realised that without the support of these communities, conservation in the area couldn't be effective. Eventually, as part of a ground-breaking community project, the communities moved about 3,000 head of cattle out of the area, and fencing began. In 1993, Nata Sanctuary was opened to the public, and in the same year it won the prestigious Tourism for Tomorrow award for the southern hemisphere.

Now Nata Sanctuary conserves an ecologically sensitive and important natural environment, and also effectively returns money to the communities for doing so. That said, the fences have become less effective over the years, so you'll probably see the odd cow as you drive around. Consider this an illustration of the increasing difficulties facing wildlife conservation areas in marginal regions of Africa but don't be put off; this is still an excellent area for birding and well worth exploring.

Nata Sanctuary generally makes a very easy place to visit for a day or two, either based in Nata or camping at the sanctuary itself. That said, while the birding is at its best during the rainy season, this is also the time when the roads are likely to be impassable, so if you're intent on spending some time in the sanctuary, then it's wise to check the situation before you set off. Arguably the best time to visit is around April, at the end of the rainy season.

Flora and fauna See pages 463–7 for notes on the general flora and fauna of the pan, but note that a number of mammals have been enclosed (or reintroduced) within the fenced boundaries of this reserve, including gemsbok, springbok, hartebeest, kudu, eland, zebra, reedbuck, jackal, fox, monkey, steenbok, squirrel and spring hare.

Getting there and away The colourfully decorated entrance to Nata Sanctuary is about 17km southeast of Nata, next to the main road to Francistown. It's very well signposted in both directions.

Where to stay Many visitors to the sanctuary stay at one of the lodges in nearby Nata (pages 484–6), but the sanctuary does have its own campsite.

⋀ **Campsite** [map 449] A fire in 2008 destroyed much of the older structure here, but the campsite was rapidly rebuilt, & for a time was really smart. Since then it hasn't been looked after very well & is in need of investment in both facilities & staff. That said, just 300m from the sanctuary entrance – so quite close to the road – are a few relatively shady pitches, each with braai stand & picnic table. Ablution blocks, 1 each for men & women, have flush toilets & showers. *Camping P35 pp.*

Kubu Island In the southwest of Sua Pan lies an isolated granite outcrop some 10m high and 1km long, known as Kubu Island. It forms the shape of a crescent, and its slopes are terraced with fossil beaches of wave-rounded pebbles, providing startling evidence of the prehistoric lake's former water levels. Crowned with an array of ancient, gnarled baobabs and surrounded on three sides by a vast grey emptiness, Kubu has a unique atmospheric beauty.

At night, with the wind moaning through the baobabs, it is easy to imagine the waves of a great inland sea lapping at its pebble beaches. Many of the island's rocks are white, covered in ancient, fossilised guano from the waterbirds that used to perch here when it was surrounded by the lake. The moonlight reflecting off the pan's white surface gives the place an almost supernatural atmosphere, which is heightened by the mystery of Kubu's former inhabitants. The shoreline is littered with Stone Age tools and arrowheads, while concentric drystone walls on the islands survive from a much more recent village, perhaps around AD1400–1600, and outside this are a number of stone cairns.

Archaeologists have linked these walls and cairns with the dynasty of Great Zimbabwe, and think that they were probably at the southwesternmost tip of that state. In *The Riddle of the Stone Walls* (see *Appendix 3*, page 540), Alec Campbell suggests that they could have been remote 'circumcision camps', to which the boys of the tribe were taken for circumcision and ceremonies leading to adulthood. It is suggested that perhaps ceremonies took place within the walls, and every class that 'graduated' then built a separate cairn.

Campbell also noted that the people of the nearest village, Tshwagong, hold Kubu and the nearby Thithaba Islands as sacred, and men over 16 years of age visit the islands to make contact with God, singing a particular song for rain and leaving offerings on the ground.

Kubu is a national monument, and there is now a warden stationed here to ensure that visitors don't damage anything.

Getting there and away One of the few operators to run trips to this area is Uncharted Africa (page 224), which offers quadbike excursions here from all their camps. In addition, their Kubu Island safari includes a couple of days at Kubu Island, travelling by quad bike and sleeping under the stars. Alternatively, you can drive yourself.

From the north there are endless possible routes to Kubu Island (⊕ KUBU-I 20°53.737'S, 25°49.421'E), and you can expect it to take about 3 to 4 hours from the main Maun–Nata road. Easiest is probably to take one of the many tracks that leave the main road between about 30km and 15km west of Nata. Follow your nose (or, more practically, your GPS) towards Thabatshukudu Village (⊕ THABAT 20°42.606'S, 25°47.476'E), which is about 70–75km south, depending on the track that you take.

From there it's about 10km southwest to the Tshwagong Veterinary Gate, through which any north–south traffic between Sua and Ntwetwe pans passes – so tracks will lead you there. This is about 3km north of the small village of Tshwagong (⊕ TSHWAG 20°48.094'S, 25°45.608'E), from where it's about 14km in a straight line southeast to Kubu Island. (There are several tracks here, so just head southeast and follow your GPS.)

Note that the track that leaves Gweta in a south then southeasterly direction, ending at the Tshwagong Veterinary Gate, passes over several long stretches of Ntwetwe Pan, and so is dangerously muddy during the wetter months of the year.

From the south it's best to start by heading for the village of Mmatshumo (⊕ MMATSH 21°08.590'S, 25°39.214'E). You'll find a number of tracks from the Orapa–Francistown road which will lead you here; the shortest leaves the main road around ⊕ TURNM1 21°19.468'S, 25°33.742'E. From there it's about 23km to Mmatshumo. Heading north from there, there's a good view of the pan to your right after about 5km, before the track bends west and back north to cross the small Tsitane Pan, crossing the veterinary fence at ⊕ TSIVET 20°58.620'S, 25°37.178'E. Then a straight track heading north-northeast brings you to Tshwagong (⊕ TSHWAG 20°48.094'S, 25°45.608'E) after about 20km.

Note that during the dry season you can take a short cut about 7km north of the vet fence, at around ⊕ TURNM2 20°55.990'S, 25°40.015'E, which heads east-northeast across the pan to Kubu; but don't try this when the pans are wet!

Other landmarks around Sua Pan
Places detailed here run south from Nata and Nata Sanctuary, then west and north to Kubu Island and beyond. Note that you should never attempt to drive across the pan from the east side to the west, or vice versa, even during the dry season.

Sowa Pan Mine (soda-ash factory) This modern industrial complex seems strangely out of place here, especially as it is easily reached, 40km along a tarred road. The turn-off is about 48km south of Nata on the road to Francistown.

Kukome Island On the eastern shore of Sua Pan, roughly opposite Kubu, Kukome (also spelled 'Kukonje') Island (⊕ KUKOME 20°55.001'S, 26°12.203'E) has similar fossil beaches and ancient remains. To reach here, first head for the Kwadiba Veterinary Gate (⊕ KWADIB 20°54.907'S, 26°16.571'E) on the east side of Sua Pan, from where a track leads west for about 7km to Kukome Island. (Beware: the GPS point given for the Kwadiba Gate on older editions of the Shell map doesn't seem correct to me.)

Mmatshumo Mmatshumo (⊕ MMATSH 21°08.590'S, 25°39.214'E) is a small village on the south side of the pans, between Sua and Ntwetwe pans, as well as an important waypoint when you're navigating yourself around.

South Islands About 7km south of Kubu, far out on the pan, are two other small islands. They too have baobab trees and the larger one, on the east, has a series of rock cairns along its spine.

Thabatshukudu Thabatshukudu (⊕ THABAT 20°42.606'S, 25°47.476'E) is another village – notable for the landmark of its colourfully painted general dealer's store – and another useful waypoint when navigating yourself around.

NTWETWE PAN Ntwetwe Pan is the western twin of Sua, and is of a similar size and general topography, though aligned more east–west. It lies due south of the Nata–Maun road, between Gweta in the north and Orapa and Mopipi in the south. One finger extends to the north of the road, while to the southwest the pan breaks up into several smaller pans, including Lake Xau, just south of Mopipi. The old north–south trading route between Gweta and Mopipi crosses the centre of the pan, and the two famous isolated baobabs (Green's Baobab and Chapman's Baobab) that marked this route for early European explorers – including Livingstone, who left his initials here – still serve as landmarks for today's travellers.

Ntwetwe lacks the famous granite outcrops of Sua; its main points of elevation are fossilised barchan dunes that once crept across the surface of the lake during a dry period and were left stranded when waters rose again. Gabasadi Island is the

15

largest of these. The profiles of the dune islands show steps and lines of vegetation which, like Sua Pan's pebble beaches, are evidence of former higher lake levels.

Stone Age sites are scattered among the smaller pans that form the western shore of Ntwetwe. At Gutsha Pan, near Chapman's Baobab, there is a perennial spring. Here the San once dug pit traps lined with poisoned stakes to trap the plentiful game that came to drink. The remains of these traps, and the calcrete blinds behind which the hunters hid, are still visible today.

Where to stay
There are three camps on the northwest side of the pan: Jack's Camp, San Camp and Camp Kalahari, in that order of luxury. Though these are the only camps on the pans themselves, you could also visit this area on a day or overnight excursion with Planet Baobab or Gweta Lodge (page 487). Both offer a cheaper option, aimed at backpackers and people driving along the Nata–Maun road.

Jack's Camp, San Camp and Camp Kalahari can be contacted through Natural Selection (page 224). All three camps are usually reached by light aircraft from Maun; a private airstrip (⊕ SANAIR 20°29.504'S, 25°11.054'E) is 20 minutes' drive from camp. That said, they do accept self-drive vehicles in the dry season, but even then all such vehicles must be escorted to the camps from Planet Baobab (page 487).

Jack's Camp [map 448] (10 tents) Jack's
Camp was the original camp on the pans. When all the other safari operators in Botswana focused on game & the Delta, Jack's dared to offer something totally different – & succeeded in style.

A bushcamp was originally started in this area in the 1960s, by the late Jack Bousfield. After his tragic death in an aircraft accident, his son, Ralph, built a camp for visitors here which first opened in 1993. It's set in sparse forest of real fan palms, in grasslands on the edge of Ntwetwe Pan, overlooking Makgadikgadi Pans National Park.

Jack's is furnished in a 'traditional East African '40s safari style'. This means it's very comfortable, with 1st-class attention to detail, but it's not super-luxurious by any means. Jack's green tents are classic Meru-style, built on decks & set in a palm grove. Inside, 7 of the tents have twin beds with individual canopies, while the others have four-poster dbl beds, all with down pillows & duvets, high-quality linens & even Persian rugs. Each tent has an en-suite bathroom with indoor & outdoor shower, flush toilet & hot water. At night, lighting is by paraffin lamp – much more magical than electricity!

Jack's central 'mess tent' is really a series of grand canvas pavilions. The interior is lined with amber printed cotton, while the green of the outside blends with the surrounding bush. This is something of a canvas field museum, sheltering an eclectic selection of items (mostly local) including

stone tools, fossils of extinct mega-fauna (like giant zebra), prints, maps, historical etchings, & a fair-sized collection of Bushman beadwork. There's also a drinks tent, a library tent, a centralised dining tent & a separate tea tent, its floor scattered with a mass of Persian rugs & cushions, where tea & delicious cakes are usually served before the afternoon activities. Towards the front of camp, with great views, there's an open-sided pool pavilion, where guests can relax & cool off on summer afternoons. *From US$1,290 pp 10 Jan–Mar to US$1,750/2,260 pp sharing/sgl Aug, inc FB, drinks, activities, laundry, park fees. Flights to/from Maun US$344 pp each way, inc for stays of 4 nights or more; road transfers/escorted self-drive from Planet Baobab US$325/100 per vehicle (☼ dry season only). ☼ All year.* ★★★★★

☀ San Camp [map 448] (6 tents) The
smaller but no less exclusive satellite of Jack's Camp lies 20 mins' drive away, right on Ntwetwe Pan, & is open only during the dry season. Run by the same team as Jack's, it works in the same way, with similar activities & approach. Like Jack's, it's rustic but stylish & comfortable, its tents – of white rather than green, to reflect the stark landscape – lending something of an *Arabian Nights* feel. 3 linked pavilions, incorporating a central dining area flanked by a library to one side, & a tea tent & 'relaxation area' to the other, are lined in a subtle pinstripe, with dark colonial-

style furniture with brass fittings offset by Persian rugs. In addition, a yoga & meditation pavilion is situated right on the edge of the pan. In the individual tents, a veranda with a day bed leads through to a sitting area, then on to the bedroom (2 with four-poster dbl beds; the rest with twins), dressing room, & bathroom with flush toilet & hot water at the back. During 2017, work was in hand to reinforce the structure of the camp, with a view to opening it all year round.

Both Jack's & San Camp are 1st-rate camps offering something totally different from virtually all of the rest of Botswana's camps. San is slightly cheaper than Jack's (though both are expensive), but I prefer the atmosphere & environment here. Either makes a great 3-night stop, best at the very end of a fly-in trip to Botswana. *From US$1,250 pp sharing 16 Apr–14 Jun to US$1,485/1,965 pp sharing/sgl Aug, inc FB, drinks, activities, laundry & park fees. Transfers as Jack's Camp, see opposite. No credit cards.* ⊕ *16 Apr–15 Oct.* ★★★★★

🏠 **Camp Kalahari** [map 448] (11 tents) Standing among real fan palms & acacias, the former Makgadikgadi Camp is just 5mins from the edge of Ntwetwe Pan, south of Gweta. Central to the camp is a small, open-sided V-shaped structure under a thatched roof, with a pool (being enlarged in 2018) & a firepit in front. One 'wing' houses a long teak dining table; the other a cosy lounge area. The style has a distinctly tribal feel, with furniture from Ethiopia & Sudan, whereas the tented rooms hark back to the 1940s, complete with twin or dbl metal-framed beds & campaign safari furniture, offset by rich Indian & Moroccan textiles. 21st-century creature comforts come in the form of an en-suite bathroom & separate toilet, an alfresco shower, solar-powered lights & a solar geyser for hot water. One family tent has 2 rooms linked through the bathroom. In the front, safari furniture sits on a wooden veranda. Batteries can be charged in the main building. As an aside, there is a discreet electric fence around the camp, largely to protect the trees, but it doesn't entirely deter elephant or lion.

In addition to the activities detailed below, Camp Kalahari also offers horseriding safaris, with 3-, 4- & 5-night options, led by the very experienced David Foot. A 5-night itinerary includes 3 nights at Camp Kalahari & 2 nights fly-camping. The open pans & sparse vegetation combined with relatively low levels of dangerous game in the area make this ideal riding country. The style might be different from the more upmarket Jack's, but the activities (& effectively, the location) are the same, making this a winning combination. *From US$560 pp 10 Jan–Mar to US$830/1,160 pp sharing/sgl Aug, inc FB, drinks, activities, laundry, park fees; riding from US$760 pp sharing per night, depending on numbers, plus US$510 tour leader fee for whole group. Transfers as Jack's Camp, see opposite.* ⊕ *All year.* ★★★– ★★★★

Activities from camp

Activities from these camps vary with the season. When it's dry, around May–October, there's likely to be very little game around. That's fine, as it's not the focus of a trip here. Instead you'll explore the pans in 4x4s, on individual quad bikes and on foot, often with a Bushman tracker. These trips concentrate on the area's smaller wildlife, and also touch on its history and archaeology. At a nearby pan, old Stone Age flint axe-heads and arrowheads can be found on the surface, though (quite rightly) the guides insist that they should be left there.

During the wet season, around November–April, the pans can become quagmires. It's often impossible to use the quad bikes, and the 4x4 drives tend to stick to the grasslands on the edges of the pans. However, then there is a much greater density of wildlife around, with many migrant birds – including flamingo – and if you're lucky, large herds of plains game, including zebra and wildebeest. Throughout the year you may see brown hyena, and you can have the fascinating experience of interacting with a gang of habituated meerkats. As the camps are outside the national park, night drives are possible – when there's often more wildlife around than during the day.

Exploring Ntwetwe Pan

Like Sua Pan, Ntwetwe is an area for experienced Africa hands to explore in their own vehicles – though bear in mind my comments on safety under *Getting around* on pages 467–8. Alternatively, and much safer (albeit very expensive), fly in from Maun to one of the camps for three or four days and explore the pans and surrounding area with expert guides: on foot, by 4x4 or on quad bikes.

Ntwetwe Pan doesn't have anything quite so spectacular as Kubu Island, though it does have a few marvellous old baobabs and an island of its own.

Chapman's Baobab This famous landmark (⊕ CHAPMA 20°29.372'S, 25°14.898'E) was noted by Chapman when he passed with Thomas Baines in 1861. One of the largest trees in Africa, and designated a national monument, it used to be visible from some distance away. Sadly, though, it split into three and fell prostrate in January 2016. Despite this, shoots were appearing along some of the limbs 18 months later; it remains to be seen if some of these might serve to continue the tree's long line.

Note that there are endless tracks to the west of here, many made by nearby private safari camps, and so navigation can be especially difficult, rendering a GPS essential.

Green's Baobab Less well known than Chapman's, this tree (⊕ GREENS 20°25.497'S, 25°13.869'E) is close to the only permanent spring in the area, Gutsha Pan, and still bears the inscription 'Green's Expedition 1858–1859' carved into its bark.

Gabasadi Island In the middle of Ntwetwe, to the west of the usual north–south route across the pans, Gabasadi Island is a low mound protruding from the surface of the pan. It's actually a fossilised, crescent-shaped barchan dune, which you'll realise if you climb it.

MAKGADIKGADI PANS NATIONAL PARK

Makgadikgadi Pans National Park covers about 3,900km² in a roughly square-shaped block to the west of the pans. It extends from the western edge of Ntwetwe Pan – one corner of which is incorporated within the park, fragmented into a myriad smaller pans – westwards to the Boteti River, which marks the park's western boundary. To the north it meets the southern boundary of Nxai Pan National Park, from which it is separated only by the main Maun–Nata road. While for administrative purposes the two parks are often lumped together as Makgadikgadi and Nxai Pan National Park, here they are treated individually, as a reflection of their very different attractions.

BACKGROUND INFORMATION
Geography and geology About one-fifth of the national park consists of salt pan. The rest is rolling grasslands on Kalahari sands, rising here and there into fossilised dunes and low hills of thicker sand which mark prehistoric limits of the great Makgadikgadi superlake. The great breadth of the sandy Boteti watercourse and the riverine woodland that lines its steep banks are evidence of a major river that once carved a channel across central Botswana, carrying the waters of the Okavango into the Makgadikgadi basin.

Until 2008, the Boteti hadn't flooded properly for 16 years, but in early 2009 the water returned and began to advance south again. Today it flows right through to Lake Xau and stays throughout the dry season. That said, in 2013, many locals were predicting that after a couple of years of lower rainfall and floods, the river may

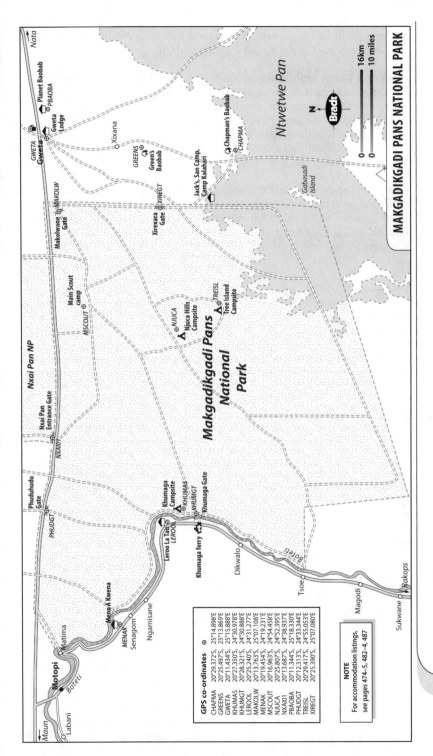

MAKGADIKGADI PANS NATIONAL PARK

Nata

Planet Baobab
☐ PBAOBA

Gweta
Lodge

☐P
GWETA Gweta

Xixana

GREENS
Green's
Baobab

Chapman's Baobab
CHAPMA

Ntwetwe Pan

Jack's, San Camp,
Camp Kalahari

Makolwane MAKOLW
Gate

Xirexara XIREGT
Gate

Gabasadi
Island

Main Scout
camp

MSCOUT

△ NJUCA
Njuca Hills
Campsite

TREISL
△ Tree Island
Campsite

Makgadikgadi Pans
National
Park

Nxai Pan NP

Nxai Pan
Entrance Gate

NXAI01

Phuduhudu
Gate

PHUDGT

Khumaga
Campsite

KHUMAS
△
KHUMGT
Khumaga Gate

Leroo La Tau
LEROOL

Khumaga ferry

Dikwalo

Boteti

Tsoe

Magodi

Rakops

Sukwane

Matima

Mena A Kwena

MENAK

Motopi

Maun

Boteti

Labani

Senagom

Ngamisane

GPS co-ordinates ⊕

CHAPMA	20°29.372'S,	25°14.898'E
GREENS	20°25.497'S,	25°13.869'E
GWETA	20°11.434'S,	25°15.888'E
KHUMAS	20°27.350'S,	24°30.978'E
KHUMGT	20°28.321'S,	24°30.888'E
LEROOL	20°25.240'S,	24°31.277'E
MAKOLW	20°13.763'S,	25°07.108'E
MENAK	20°19.454'S,	24°19.231'E
MSCOUT	20°16.963'S,	24°54.458'E
NJUCA	20°25.807'S,	24°52.395'E
NXAI01	20°13.687'S,	24°38.937'E
PBAOBA	20°11.344'S,	25°18.330'E
PHUDGT	20°12.313'S,	24°33.344'E
TREISL	20°29.417'S,	24°55.053'E
XIREGT	20°25.390'S,	25°07.080'E

NOTE
For accommodation listings,
see pages 474–5, 482–4, 487

⊕ N

Brandt

0 ───── 16km
0 ───── 10 miles

15

477

gradually revert back to its previous dry-season state in the coming years. Time will tell but for now the transformation is quite something.

Flora and fauna highlights
Makgadikgadi Pans National Park really contains a spectrum of environments, flora and fauna. Its east side, especially the southeast, is dominated by salt pans and grasslands – very much the same as the rest of Sua and Ntwetwe further east. Its western border, the Boteti River, is lined by thick riverine forest; here the wildlife has more in common with that found beside the Chobe or the Linyanti, or in the Okavango Delta. Between these two very different environments lies the body of the park.

Flora The vegetation on the east side of the park is very similar in pattern to that of the Makgadikgadi Pans (pages 463–7). Its diversity increases westwards as the saline influence of the pan is left behind; from the bare surface of the pan itself, through rolling grassland and the vegetated dunes of Njuca Hills, into thicker acacia scrub, and eventually to the dense riverine woodland along the banks of the Boteti River. Along the eastern border there are areas of palm-tree woodland, where groves of vegetable ivory palms (*Hyphaene petersiana*) grow among the tracts of tall grassland.

On raised ground between the salt pans, yellowish patches of prickly salt grass (*Odyssea paucinervis*) flourish, contrasting with clumps of the dark succulent *Chenopodiacea* species. Along the pan edges you may also find a cactus-like succulent, *Hoodia lugardii*, which periodically produces striking maroon flowers. The open grasslands are studded with islands of trees and denser vegetation, with such species as the trumpet thorn (*Catophractas alexandri*) and western rhigozum (*Rhigozum brevispinosum*) flowering among the acacia scrub.

Beside the deep sand that normally characterises the Boteti River, camelthorns (*Vachellia erioloba*), blackthorns (*Senegalia mellifera*) and silver clusterleaf (*Terminalia sericea*) dominate the riverine forest, interspersed with a few other riverine giants such as sycamore figs (*Ficus sycomorus*) and sausage trees (*Kigelia africana*). From the early 1990s until 2009, most of the 'riverbed' itself consisted of a sandy channel carpeted in grasses and punctuated by occasional muddy pools of water. Now though, with the river flowing as far as Lake Xau again, this has all disappeared. Typically, the river flows for a period of 20–40 years, followed by a similar period of seasonal flow only. Thus, if history repeats itself, the Boteti is now likely to flow at least until the 2020s – although reality could see the river revert back to a dry cycle relatively quickly.

Fauna In the wet season, Makgadikgadi Pans National Park boasts good concentrations of grazers that rival those of Nxai Pan to the north, and an aerial view shows the area to be latticed with a dense network of game trails. From about June onwards, herds of Burchell's zebra and blue wildebeest start a westward movement towards the lush grazing around the Boteti River, accompanied by smaller numbers of gemsbok, eland and red hartebeest. (The latter tend to come slightly later, in years when the rains have been exceptionally good.) These herds gradually congregate along the waterfront until, by November, this area becomes jam-packed with game. In attendance are leopard and lion, attracted by the high concentration of prey. You might also be lucky enough to glimpse the elusive white rhino.

In the ecozone between grassland and woodland, browsers such as kudu, bushbuck and grey duiker find a permanent home, while troops of baboons and vervet monkeys forage beneath the trees, and small numbers of giraffe and elephant often occur. The area also supports a small waterbuck population, resident pairs of bushbuck (locals say the same subspecies/race as the Chobe bushbuck) and – now that the Boteti is flowing once more – plenty of hippo. There are also some huge crocodiles, many of which survived for years in the caves along the banks of the riverbed and are now reaping the rewards of their patience.

In peak season, from September to November, the area around the Boteti can offer truly outstanding wildlife watching, and the air is filled with the hiccoughing calls of the milling zebra herds. However, with the arrival of the rains in December–January, the herds disperse. Some head north towards Nxai Pan; others gather in the grazing grounds of the southeast, where their migration route beyond the park to the Central Kalahari is blocked by a veterinary cordon fence. At this time, zebra and gemsbok may often be seen out on the pans in search of the mineral salts that are lacking on the Kalahari grasslands.

A healthy population of large predators, protected in the park from persecution by ranchers, includes lion, cheetah, leopard, spotted and brown hyena. Lion can be common during peak migration, with prides knocking down more zebra than they can consume and (be warned) sometimes wandering inquisitively through the campsites. Cheetah are less common, but may turn up anywhere where there are springbok, while leopard are permanent residents of the denser bush along the Boteti. Spotted hyena, like lion, follow the dry-season herds, while brown hyenas find life more productive (and less competitive) along the park's eastern side.

In the east of the park the campsite at Njuca Hills offers a panoramic base from which to explore the wildlife of the pans and grasslands. Herds of springbok, well adapted to survive the arid and exposed conditions, are common around the pans, while steenbok – usually found in pairs – are also widespread. Nocturnal predators

THE LIONS OF MAKGADIKGADI

Makgadikgadi is an erratic and uncertain place for lions. With the first rains, huge herds of zebra and wildebeest move out on to the plains to graze on the succulent grasses and drop their young. In the dry months this pulse of life ebbs back to the Boteti River, 50km to the west, leaving the plains largely deserted by large ungulates. The lions have had to adapt to these huge fluctuations and the unpredictability.

For some the solution is simply tracking the herds back to the Boteti for the dry months, where they must dodge the human residents on the west side of the river. Others stay behind amid the parched grasses, swirling dust devils and spring hares. This is not the place for huge ungainly prides; rather lionesses pair up and wander over large areas, often in excess of 1,000km², in order to find sufficient food. Males typically spread their time between two or more of these small, efficient prides. They can maintain territories of almost double that, walking up to 50km a night to patrol their vast swathes of baked wasteland.

Water is unavailable for up to seven months a year for these lions, so they must gain all their moisture from their prey. Immediately after killing large prey such as gemsbok they snick open the belly and stomach, slurping up the juices before they soak away into the sand. However, large prey is hard to find during the dry season, so they will hunt aardvarks and porcupines, and they increasingly look outside the eastern and western boundaries of the park for sustenance from herds of dopey, slow-moving livestock.

15

of the pan fringes include brown hyena, aardwolf, bat-eared fox and striped polecat, while black-backed jackal, African wildcat, honey badger and small spotted genet can occur anywhere in the park. Other small mammals include porcupine, aardvark, spring hare and scrub hare as well as a host of smaller rodents and insectivores (see the general section on pans fauna, pages 465–6).

In sandy areas, ground squirrels (here at the northern limit of their Kalahari range) forage by day in small colonies, holding up their tails as parasols against

THE CLANS OF THE MAKGADIKGADI

The brown hyena (*Hyaena brunnea*) is one of the three hyena species in southern Africa, the other two being a successful scavenger and hunter, the spotted hyena, and the insectivorous aardwolf. Brown hyena are classed as 'near threatened', with a total population of under 10,000 – of which the Makgadikgadi Pans National Park has about 150 adults.

The brown hyena has evolved to live in desert systems throughout southern Africa, where it occurs at low densities. This shy, nocturnal animal is a solitary forager that can survive independently of permanent surface water. Brown hyenas will eat virtually anything, apart from grass or herbage – and here their diet ranges from old carcasses or ostrich eggs to melons and scorpions.

The Makgadikgadi Brown Hyena Project was established near Jack's Camp in 2003 to improve the management and conservation of this elusive carnivore. This included investigating foraging strategies, scent-marking behaviour, space and resources requirements, and establishing the impact of the Makgadikgadi game fence on the populations of brown hyenas living on both sides of the fence, through changes in food availability and loss of access to the cattle areas. The project followed research in the same area by Glyn Maude as part of his PhD from the University of Bristol.

During the project, Glyn observed that individuals will often cover over 65km in a night when foraging in the Makgadikgadi. Here lion kills are an important source of food. Over the wet season, these are often zebra and wildebeest, while over the dry season, when food is more scarce, they can frequently be cattle and other livestock carcasses.

Brown hyenas are not truly solitary animals; they live in clans of between two and ten members. While clans' territories cover 200–1,000km², clan members are rarely seen together since they forage alone, only interacting with other clan members either by a chance meeting while foraging, or at a communal den site. Some brown hyenas, the males in particular, are not part of a clan but are nomadic. Clan members will often be tolerant of an intruder of the opposite sex, but will chase away same-sex intruders.

Brown hyenas are usually almost silent: their vocalisations are minimal. Long-distance communication is by a unique double scent mark deposited on grass stalks. These marks can be made as often as every 150m of foraging, and as well as communicating with other clan members, the scent mark is also a marker for the clan's territory. Defecations are also used as territorial markers and can be found in concentrations in 'latrine sites' which are often located along territorial boundaries. The presence of brown hyenas is more often indicated by their spoor or scent marks, as sightings of the animal in the wild are very uncommon.

the fierce sun and dashing for their burrows at any hint of danger. These sociable rodents associate amicably with yellow mongooses, who share their burrow systems and help keep a look-out for predators.

Reptiles Perhaps the most bizarre report from this park is of some of the Boteti's larger crocodiles which, when the river drops drastically during the dry season, or dries up completely, retreat into holes in the riverbank that they have dug for themselves. One such lair that I saw was a good 4–5m above the level of the water even in May, and would have been completely high and dry by October.

Birdlife The birdlife of Makgadikgadi Pans National Park is largely the same as that elsewhere in the greater Makgadikgadi region (pages 466–7), with a grading of species according to habitat, and a large summer influx of migrants.

The denser woodland along the Boteti also harbours more cover-loving species such as Meyer's parrot, woodland kingfisher, Burchell's coucal and Heuglin's robin, while the return of permanent water has attracted waterbirds such as black-winged stilts, pelicans, cranes and African fish eagles. Many raptors cruise the skies over the park, with Gabar goshawks hunting the thickets, secretary birds stalking the savannah, and vultures following the game herds in search of carcasses. In summer, storks, bee-eaters, kites, shrikes and other migrants move in and fan out across the grasslands.

GETTING AROUND If you're driving yourself here then ideally come armed with a copy of the Shell map of Botswana (see pages 145–6 for details), with its wealth of GPS co-ordinates. Then take to heart my caveats on pages 467–8, and you're ready to explore.

In most cases you can sign in and pay park fees at one of the main gates, including Makolwane (⊕ MAKOLW 20°13.763'S, 25°07.108'E) and Khumaga (⊕ KHUMGT 20°28.321'S, 24°30.888'E) gates. The Khumaga Gate is reached, when the Boteti is full, by a small but adequate ferry (m *7563 1663; P150/vehicle*). When the river is lower the crossing becomes a ford or even completely dry and driveable. Please note that the ferry operating times are the same as the park opening hours.

There are two further gates: the Phuduhudu Gate (⊕ PHUDGT 20°12.313'S, 24°33.344'E), on the Maun–Nata road and the Xirexara Gate (⊕ XIREGT 20°25.39'S, 25°07.08'E), on the eastern side of the park, but it is unclear if these gates allow visitors to pay park fees; we suspect not.

Note that if you enter the park at any other point – and there are several – then you should go straight to one of the gates to sign in. Meandering through the park without having signed in first is against the rules. If you have not paid park fees

---

OSTRICH BREEDING

Ostriches are particularly common in the eastern grasslands, and can often be seen from the main Nata–Maun road. These huge birds breed before the rains, with several females laying in a single scrape that may hold over 30 eggs. Incubation tends to rotate between the male at night (when his dark plumage is no longer vulnerable to overheating), and the female by day (when her drab plumage provides more effective camouflage). Youngsters from several broods gather together in large crèches, presided over by one adult pair, and can sometimes be seen gathering in the shadow of an adult for shade.

15

on entry then you will need to ensure you leave the park through one of the gates where you can.

Driving around, you'll find a basic network of sandy tracks that are clearly defined even in the rainy season, when the grass is very high. Moving away from these, though, the tracks are increasingly overgrown and difficult to follow. The more southerly roads, crossing the pans, are particularly hard to locate; arguably they are simply non-existent, washed away with each year's rains. Equally, those around the centre of the eastern side of the park are so numerous that they're totally confusing, complicated by a whole network of tracks used by the camps in the area.

Many visitors enter the park on one side and leave from another – which can make perfect sense. However, with the Boteti River now flowing all the way to Lake Xau, it's well worth checking that you can cross the river by ferry or ford before committing yourself to entering or leaving the park through the Khumaga Gate.

WHERE TO STAY Both the lodges to the north of Khumaga have spectacular settings on the western bank of the Boteti River, opposite the park. Although the campsite that was once adjacent to Leroo La Tau has now closed, campers have the choice of three campsites within the national park: Khumaga, Njuca Hills and Tree Island. As with all national parks' sites, these must be booked in advance (pages 131–3). In Khumaga Village itself, near to the ferry and the park entrance, Tiaan's Camp is a small, budget option for campers and non-campers alike.

Meno A Kwena Tented Camp [map 477] (8 tents) 686 0981; e reservations@menoakwena. com; www.menoakwena.com; ⊕ MENAK 20°19.454'S, 24°19.231'E (turn off from road ⊕ MENATN 20°16.310'S, 24°15.577'E or, slightly further south, MENATS 20°20.538'S, 24°17.848'E). Set on top of a 40m-high bank overlooking a bend in the Boteti River, which in recent years has been flowing all year, Meno A Kwena has a highly unusual location for a camp in Botswana, with superb river views. Now owned by Hennie Rawlinson in partnership with Natural Selection, it provides an authentic, low-impact safari experience.

Each Meru-style tent is built inside its own kraal – an enclosure of narrow tree trunks – with views over the river to the national park. The tents themselves are large & en suite, but they also have a secondary bucket-style shower (also with hot water) & a toilet in an adjacent rondavel. The rooms have proper twin beds (or a dbl) with down duvets, & are stylishly adorned, with brass dishes & colourful throws. Outside you'll find 2 safari chairs, a wooden day bed & a couple of safari chests – 1 containing tea & coffee. Across the site, more of those safari chests have been pressed into service as shelves, cupboards, tables & trunks, lending a slightly nomadic feel.

Sand paths through the bush link the rooms to a central tent of traditional green canvas, complete with guy ropes. The space is split between a fairly large bar, a dining area whose huge dining table is inset with glazed panels displaying local artefacts, & a comfortable lounge area. To the front is a sandy courtyard area, while overlooking the river is a rock pool that does service as a plunge pool, flanked by 2 small canvas shelters, & out of sight below is a wildlife hide. The relaxed atmosphere is accentuated by hand-crafted wrought-iron furniture & an eclectic selection of books; it's the sort of place where someone might pick up a guitar & start strumming.

While the normal 2 activities per day with a rest in between is on offer, there's considerable choice. From camp, activities focus on boat trips, & game drives to the Hippo Pools area of the park; normally this involves a boat into the park, then a game drive south, returning via the Khumaga ferry & a drive back to camp opposite the park. Seasonal day trips to Nxai Pan & Makgadikgadi Pans can be organised on request, as can mobile safaris to the salt pans & a meerkat colony or visits to the CKGR (both min 3 nights).

Perhaps more than most camps, Meno A Kwena attracts a wide range of visitors, including independent travellers, safari-goers & a number of NGO workers. *From US$445 pp Jan–Mar to US$840/1,170 Aug pp sharing/sgl, inc FB, drinks, all* activity, park fees, road transfers, laundry. ⊕ *All year.* ★★★–★★★★★

🏠 **Leroo La Tau** [map 477] (12 chalets) Contact Desert & Delta Safaris, pages 223–4; ✥ LEROOL 20°25.240'S, 24°31.277'E (turn off from road ✥ LEROTO 20°26.231'S, 24°27.935'E). This long-established lodge, perched 15m above the Boteti River, lies in an area that can provide remarkable game spectacles. In 2008, under the Desert & Delta umbrella, the lodge was fully refurbished, its chalets completely rebuilt to a high specification. Most guests arrive by air from Maun, although self-driving is also an option.

Until 2009, the star draw of the lodge was its extensive hide overlooking a large waterhole in the riverbed, with elephants & other wildlife in regular attendance. However, when water returns to the seasonal river, the waterhole is flooded & becomes part of the stream, shifting the game dynamic of the area. The hide, & another above by the firepit, still looks out on to some fantastic scenery with game often coming down to drink on the opposite bank of the river, but the immediacy of the animals is gone. In the dry season (Aug–Oct depending on the rains), water levels drop & the waterhole is once again pumped.

Up a few steps from the firepit is a small pool, surrounded by a lawn set with wooden loungers. The main lodge is set back again, one long wall fronted by a shady veranda. Inside, it's light & modern, but not austere, the teak flooring & tables offset by leather directors' chairs & a neutral décor. Most visitors dine as a group, but individual tables are always an option. Upstairs, above the bar, upholstered chairs & sofas are an enticing place to relax with a book, or to keep an eye on the river from the look-out window. Back at ground level, there's a shop, selling books & reasonably priced curios.

Guests stay in smart thatched chalets, built into the treeline, overlooking the Boteti. Each has a large veranda with 2 day beds & a table, from which glazed sliding doors, backed by screens, lead into the bedroom. Furnished with a dbl & a sgl bed, bedside lamps, a dressing table & a comfortable chair, these are modern & unfussy. In the bathroom, with twin basins & a huge shower, the loo shares the river view. Power is supplied by generator, & the hot water is efficient, though the water smells slightly of sulphur due to natural chemicals.

Visitors explore beyond camp on morning & afternoon game drives in 6-seater vehicles, either in a stretch of land enclosed by a loop of the Boteti or into the park. Either way, this represents lots of riverfront – which is where the game is usually concentrated. And despite being on a bend in the river within the park's perimeter fence, & surrounded by it on 3 sides, the lodge remains technically outside the park – so game drives can continue after dark. Guests staying 3 nights or more can opt for a full-day trip to Nxai Pan, but this must be pre-booked. *From US$560 pp Jan–Mar & Dec to US$995/1,293 pp sharing/sgl Jul–Oct, fully inc.* ⊕ *All year.* ★★★–★★★★★

🏠 **Tiaan's Camp** (6 chalets, camping) m 7715 2753, 7223 4998; e info@tiaanscamp.com; www.tiaanscamp.com; ✥ TIAAN 20°28.165'S, 24°30.875'E. This friendly owner-run camp on the edge of Khumaga Village provides cost-effective camping with easy access to the national park – though the sound of music & dogs can sometimes be heard. The chalets have electricity & en-suite bathrooms, & 8 campsites have ablution blocks with hot-water showers & flush toilets. There's also a small pool & a restaurant, which overlooks the Boteti River. *Camping P115 pp; all exc park fees, ferry crossings.* **$$**

⋀ **Khumaga Campsite** [map 477] (9 pitches) Contact SKL, page 132; ✥ KHUMAS 20°27.350'S, 24°30.978'E. Khumaga, sometimes written 'Xhumaga' or plain 'Kumaga', stands near the east bank of the (normally dry) Boteti River, close to one of the scout camps, & about 4km south of Leroo La Tau. It's a large, flat site, with extensive tree shade & a firepit for each pitch. There are 2 modern thatched ablution blocks, each divided for male & female campers, with flush toilets, washbasins & solar-heated showers. *US$50 pp, exc park fees, bed levy.* ⊕ *All year.*

⋀ **Njuca Hills Campsite** [map 477] (2 sites) Contact DWNP, page 132; ✥ NJUCA 20°25.807'S, 24°52.395'E. This basic site in the heart of the park, about 38km east of Khumaga, is slightly elevated (no more than about 20m), on one of a series of low, fossilised dunes, with an outcrop of trees for shade. Here you'll find no water or firewood, but there are pluses (aside from the seclusion): each site has a firepit, bucket shower & a long-drop toilet. Expect the main wildlife to be barking geckos & perhaps the odd curious yellow mongoose.

Just to emphasise the safety issues raised about travelling in any of the pans, visitors Richard & Vikki Threlfall wrote to me: 'We broke down at Njuca Hills Campsite, & were not found until the 3rd morning after discovering the problem! And then it was only pure chance.' Note that this happened at one of only 3 official campsites in the park, & realise that it would have taken a full-scale air search to find them if they'd been off the main routes. Do take heed of the safety issues detailed on pages 467–8, before

you travel anywhere in the pans area. *P30 pp, exc park fees.* ☺ *All year.*

☀ **⚑ Tree Island Campsite** [map 477] (3 sites) Contact DWNP, page 132; ✪ TREISL 20°29.417'S, 24°55.053'E. Situated on the edge of a deep pan, about 8km southeast of Njuca Hills, this is one of the most remote & isolated campsites in northern Botswana. Opened in 2012, it's the newest camp in the area & again there is no water: just long-drop toilets & bucket showers. *P30 pp; exc park fees.* ☺ *All year.*

WHAT TO SEE AND DO Like the bulk of Sua Pan or the rest of Ntwetwe Pan, the Makgadikgadi Pans National Park is really an area for experienced Africa hands to explore in their own vehicles – though bear in mind my comments on safety on pages 467–8. That said, in the late dry season you won't be quite so isolated if you stick to the road in the park which runs beside the Boteti River and stay at Khumaga Campsite, which will then have quite a few visitors. Alternatively, and much safer, stay at one of the lodges outside the park, exploring each area with their expert local guides: the pans on the eastern side with Jacks, San or Camp Kalahari, or the contrasting Boteti riverfront with Leroo La Tau or Meno A Kwena.

TOWNS AROUND THE PANS

The small towns around the pans, from Nata west to Motopi then south to Rakops, are rarely seen by those flying into the area's camps and tend to be used by visitors driving themselves simply to refuel and replenish basic supplies. That said, in May 2017, only Nata had a reliable supply of fuel. All the towns along this route have mobile-phone coverage, but don't expect any signal in the areas between them.

NATA Nata itself is a small place at the junction of the tar road to Maun, Kasane and Francistown. For many years it was little more than a filling stop for most people, where the vital garage relied on hand-cranked petrol pumps, and the well-stocked Sua Pan Bottle Store was always busy. Fuel is still the main reason for people to stop, though now the town boasts three modern fuel stations at the junction (NATA ✪ 20°12.693'S, 26°10.859'E), each with either a shop or a fast-food outlet. With these, plus a branch of Barclays Bank with an ATM, a post office, a new Choppies superstore with a Liquorama bottle store next door (over the river on the Francistown road), and a handful of local shops, Nata is a reasonable place to get organised. And if you're in need of repairs to your vehicle, try contacting Nata Garage on the Kasane road (✆ 621 1450).

With some decent places to stay, Nata is also a good choice for an overnight stop. Those planning to linger might seek out the nearby Nata Sanctuary (page 471), on the northern edge of Sua Pan, or use it as a base for exploring the pan as a whole. As an aside, staff at both Northgate Lodge and Pelican Lodge talk with enthusiasm about the wildlife at Dzibanana Pan, about 5km north of town close to the Zimbabwean border, which is reported when filled with water (roughly between April and August) to attract buffalo and sable.

🏠 **Where to stay and eat** When a fire destroyed the established Nata Lodge in 2008, other accommodation options opened up to fill the gap. Now, with the lodge rebuilt and the opening of the new Pelican Lodge, there is plenty of choice. It is also possible to camp at Nata Sanctuary (page 471). For campsites and lodges north of Nata, see *Kasane to Nata* (pages 252–4).

Most visitors to Nata are either self-catering or eat at their lodge. For those just passing through, the restaurants at Nata, Pelican and Northgate lodges are all open to non-residents. Alternatively, there's fast food in the form of Barcelos Flame-Grilled Chicken at the Engen garage, or a Wimpy at Caltex.

In and around Nata

🏠 **Nata Lodge** [map 449] (22 chalets, 10 Meru tents, camping) ✆620 0070; e reservations@natalodge.com; www.underonebotswanasky.com; ⊕ 20°13.448'S, 26°16.052'E. Nata Lodge lies about 10km east of Nata towards Francistown, & is well signposted just off the main road. It stands in a patch of sparse woodland with real fan palms & marula trees. It was completely rebuilt in 2009, following a fire that destroyed the original building.

The new-look lodge builds on the success of the old. Thatched wooden chalets raised on stilts have AC & twin beds, & their en-suite facilities incorporate a bath & outdoor shower. Two of the rooms have extra bunk beds, for families, & a 3rd is designed for improved access for those with limited mobility. The en-suite safari tents, also with twin beds & an outdoor shower, are tucked into the bush.

One room (23) has decking leading straight into the main area, where there are disabled toilets, making it suitable for those with limited mobility. Nearby is a very large campsite with space for 150 campers & separate male & female ablution blocks. The restaurant has seating indoors & out. At lunchtime there's a 'terrace menu', with evening meals either à la carte or, when it's busy, a braai dinner (*P205*). The pool is right in front of the bar area, & there's also a shop selling curios as well as books, maps & clothes. On an ad hoc basis, there are trips into Nata Sanctuary & on to the pans (*P265 pp/3hrs, min 2 people*). **$$$** *exc b/fast; camping P85 pp.* ⊕ *All year.*

🏠 **Pelican Lodge** [map 469] (51 chalets, 1 suite, camping) ✆247 0117; e reservations@pelicanlodge.co.bw; www.pelicanlodgebotswana.co.bw. About 7km south of Nata, on the Francistown road, Pelican Lodge is more a stark hotel than a lodge. With a series of large concrete, thatched buildings linked by thatched walkways on concrete slabs, it dominates a vast site. An indiscreet 3m fence surrounds the whole property, which at least helps to keep out livestock.

The reception area & à la carte restaurant are in different sections of one building, there's a bar in another room, & a totally separate building houses the 'Boma Bar' – a more informal restaurant where b/fast is served. And there's another well-stocked bar & big-screen TV. At the front of all this is an inviting swimming pool which, in keeping with everything else, is large & spread out. Most of the rooms are twin or dbl, but 3 are for families. All come with AC, satellite TV, tea & coffee station, writing desk, safe, fridge & phone, plus a couple of wicker chairs & a table. En-suite bathrooms have both a bath with a shower & an outside shower – though if privacy is your thing, go for the indoor option. Furthest away from the road, a well-designed campsite has a central braai & washing-up area, as well as a large ablution block for both sexes & a communal firepit. 3 sites sport their own private ablution blocks & braai stands. Activities include a tour of a local village, trips to Nata Sanctuary, game drives to Dzibanana Pan & bush walks.

Pelican Lodge is adequate for a 1-night stopover; the staff are helpful & friendly, & the food is varied & tasty. That said, it does feel as though it's trying to be all things to all people. With a campsite, a conference centre & guest rooms up to the 'presidential' suite, it's tempting to wish that they would concentrate on just one market. **$$–$$$** *exc b/fast; camping P90 pp.* ⊕ *All year.*

🏠 **Northgate Lodge** (22 rooms) ✆621 1156; e northgatelodge@reddysgroup.co.bw. Right in the centre of Nata, adjacent to the Caltex garage, this deceptively large lodge opened in 2008. It's urban in concept, with good-sized twin, dbl & family rooms built in blocks. Painted a deep red & with tiled floors, they're pleasant & modern with walk-in mosquito nets, kettle & TV, plus AC & a fridge in the more expensive rooms. Best are those overlooking the free-form pool or small garden rather than the garage. The bar & restaurant are open to non-residents, as are the internet facilities

(*P30/½hr*), & there's Wi-Fi throughout. There's also a limited amount of safe parking. Activities include trips to Dzibanana Pan & Nata Sanctuary. **$–$$$** *exc b/fast.* ⊕ *All year.*

 Nata Guest Inn (8 rooms) ☏621 1156; **m** 7145 0066; **e** nata.guest.inn@gmail.com. For a clean, inexpensive 1-night stopover, Nata Guest Inn is a good option. Built in 2004, its twin or dbl rooms are en suite with a bath or shower, & for a larger group there's a family room. Most rooms have AC, with plans to roll this out across the remainder soon. A small bar & restaurant is strictly for guests only, but activities will need to be organised elsewhere. **$$** *exc b/fast.* ⊕ *All year.*

 Maya Guest Inn (8 chalets) **m** 7477 1118, 7506 0791; **e** reservations@mayaguestinn. net; www.mayaguestinn.net. On the left of the main road towards Francistown, just before the river, this simple inn is a small complex of square, thatched chalets, with AC, kettle with tea & coffee, & TV. For meals you'll have to go elsewhere, but at least security should be thorough, as it's opposite the police station & there's a security guard on duty throughout the night. **$$** *exc b/fast.* ⊕ *All year.*

Further afield

⚔ Elephant Sands [map 469] (14 chalets, camping) **e** bookings@elephantsandsbotswana.com; www.elephantsands.com; ⊕ ELESAN 19°44.935'S, 26°04.265'E. Some 53km north of Nata, just 7km south of the vet fence, this once-simple campsite is about 500m west of the road & is clearly signposted. These days it has blossomed into a reasonably sized camp, although the original campsite persists, its spacious grounds popular with both independent campers & overlanders, who pitch in together & share rustic but clean open-air ablutions.

More comfortable are en-suite rondavels, their unusual semi-circular bathrooms with open-air showers, although these – like other options – run on solar power so have no AC or fans. There are also a couple of block-built family chalets under thatch, each sleeping 4 people. The newest additions are simply adorned en-suite Meru tents, which are built on stilts & overlook the waterhole. Elephant sightings are common, with cats & wild dogs also possible. As a result, visitors must stay within the confines of the camp – though that's no hardship with a large restaurant area, a separate bar, & a sunken boma surrounded by bush. **$$** *exc b/fast; camping P90 pp.* ⊕ *All year.*

GWETA Gweta (⊕ GWETA 20°11.434'S, 25°15.888'E) is a small, old village about 2km south of the road between Nata and Maun, about 205km from Maun and 100km from Nata. The **fuel station** just east of the junction (⊕ GWFUEL 20°11.438'S, 25°15.896'E) is no longer operational and despite plans to reinstate it, don't count on it. In the village, the rather grandly named Maano **supermarket** sells the basics, plus some freshish fruit and vegetables, but offered little in the way of service when last visited.

Getting there and away Gweta is very clearly signposted from the main road, in an area of mostly stunted mopane woodlands with the odd small clay pan. Turning off the main Maun–Nata road you'll come to a fork after about 2km, with a couple of shops on your right, and a post office on your left, before reaching the lodge, the entrance to which is visible from the fork on the left.

There are very regular **bus** services between Maun and Francistown, with up to five a day to and from Nata. They usually turn into town and stop in the centre, near the Maano supermarket. If not, ask the driver to stop on the road beside the turn-off to Planet Baobab. From here, the trip to Maun is about 3 hours and costs around P50; Francistown is some 4 hours away, at about P70.

 Where to stay The choices here are starkly different: the traditional Gweta Lodge in the village itself, or the funky, rustic-trendy Planet Baobab about 4km to the east. Both can be used as a base to explore Ntwetwe Pan or the Makgadikgadi Pans National Park, although most self-drive visitors will probably opt to camp nearer the pans instead. That said, both also offer day and overnight trips on to the pans, including quadbike excursions, so can be ideal for those without a vehicle. For accommodation right on the pans, see pages 474–5. There are also campsites in the national park (pages 482–4).

🏠 **Gweta Lodge** [map 449] (15 rooms, camping) ☎621 2220; **e** gwetalodge@botsnet. bw; www.gwetalodge.com. This old restcamp has undergone something of a transformation over the years. At the centre is a thatched bar & lounge area, with a small but sparkling pool in front. Twin, dbl & family en-suite rooms have fans, mosi nets & tiled floors. The smaller rondavels are much nicer than they look, with fans & modern en-suite facilities. Across the entrance track is a level, grassy campsite, with toilets & showers, some pre-erected tents, & 3 further twin rooms. It used to be quite compact, so could get noisy as the site is popular with groups, but a recent redesign has spread things out somewhat. Campers can use the bar, pool & lounge at the lodge. Meals are served in the homely if old-fashioned restaurant, which is entirely separate.

Activities include village tours (*P150 pp*), quadbiking on to the pans (*P1,600 pp*), & overnight fly-camping in Nxai Pan, the Makgadikgadi, Ntwetwe Pan & the Central Kalahari (*around P1,350 pp/day, min 2 people*). **$$** *exc b/fast; camping P80 pp.* ⊕ *All year.*

🏠 **Planet Baobab** [map 449] (18 huts, camping) **m** 7233 8344; reservations: ☎+27 11 447 4407; **e** res2@unchartedafrica.com; www. unchartedafrica.com. From the giant aardvark at the entrance (⊕ PBAOBA 20°11.344'S, 25°18.330'E) to the subterranean feel of the reception 'tunnel', Planet Baobab does indeed seem to be on another planet. Set in a grove of giant baobabs, it is just south of the main Nata–Maun road, & combines a Makgadikgadi Pans experience for a clientele who can't afford the prices of the trio of camps on the pans with somewhere interesting to stop for those driving past.

A sense of fun is evident in the well-furnished lodge, with bold local designs used to exuberant effect on the extensive surfaces of polished concrete. The focus is a funky bar area, dominated by a large, curved bar & lit by chandeliers made from local beer bottles. Seating is on hide-covered chairs at small concrete-plinth tables & there's a fine collection of interesting artefacts on the walls. Service is friendly, though food – served here or in the similarly styled restaurant – is nothing special. That said, those booked on a fully inclusive itinerary can choose dishes from a pan-African

menu. Outside is a superb 18m-diameter circular pool, with a shallow area for children & thatched gazebos at the side.

Traditional thatched 'mud' huts – actually brick clad in cement – offer intriguing accommodation, with everything inside rounded as if it were made of mud. Although similar in design, the Baobab chalets are slightly more spacious than the Bakalanga. A sgl bed is built into each side of the room, under a mosquito net, & there's an en-suite washbasin, toilet & shower. 3 family huts have a dbl bed too, & a designated parking spot outside. All are well designed, with glazed windows & trendy wall mirrors, but lighting is really poor, so take a torch.

The campsite has 4 showers & toilets (separated for men & women) built into a large & stylish thatched rondavel – complete with lights set into the walls & clothes-hooks made from branches. Each site has a thatched shelter with power & washing-up facilities to hand.

A variety of trips can be organised out of Planet Baobab. These include a guided 2hr village & cattlepost tour (*P495 pp*), which takes in a visit to the local primary school, Gweta's kgotla (traditional court), & a stop at the traditional healer, as well as a meal with a local family (typically of sorghum, mealie meal, seswaa, wild spinach, mopane worms in season, wild beans & perhaps creamy baobab fruit milkshake). There's always a chance to sample some of the local sorghum beer, too (it's an acquired taste!). With advance notice, a similar meal can be prepared in the restaurant, at P125 pp. A 2nd option is a 2hr baobab bushwalk & sundowner (*P190 pp*), concentrating on the environment, the traditional uses of plants & animals, the history of the area & perhaps some local stories. Further afield are ½-day, full-day & overnight trips to Ntwetwe Pan (*P960–1,660 pp, inc quadbikes*), & a full-day Nxai Pan excursion (*P2,045 pp*) – or, between Nov & Mar, a full-day game drive to follow the zebra & wildebeest migration inside the national park. All excursions are for a min of 2 people, & on Nxai Xini Pan can involve sleeping out on a bedroll under the stars. With minimal dangerous game around, this is all you need & is a great way to sleep. *Camping P78 adult. Visa & Mastercard accepted.* ⊕ *All year.* **$$$**

LIONS VS LIVESTOCK

When Graham Hemson worked as a guide at Jack's Camp, he was studying for a PhD on lion ecology and conservation in the Makgadikgadi area as part of Oxford University's Wildlife Conservation Research Unit. In 1999, he estimated that there were about 39 lions in the Makgadikgadi area, where he investigated their impact on people, and vice versa.

Every year lions kill hundreds of domestic animals in and around the Makgadikgadi Pans National Park, which brings them into conflict with the herders and owners. In retaliation people have, in the past, laid out traps and poison, and hunted lions outside the park with ruthless efficiency. As a result, between November 1999 and May 2000, at least 12 lions were killed.

However, contrary to common belief, Graham's research indicated that livestock predation does not happen mainly inside the kraal, but rather out in the grazing areas and sometimes inside the park. Although lions will tackle livestock in the villages, often they can simply pick off the many untended stragglers. An interesting ecological response to the predictability of livestock as prey is that lions that eat livestock have substantially smaller home ranges than those that are dependent on migratory prey, or scarce desert species.

Typically, this livestock predation is only a problem when wild prey is scarce. When zebra and wildebeest migrate out of their territories, lions are forced to change their preferences abruptly.

After surveying the local inhabitants, Graham found that many of the people in charge of the livestock were elderly women; often their husbands were living in town, running more lucrative family businesses. These women were physically unable to keep track of their cattle – resulting in a large number of stray animals which made a veritable manmade buffet for lions.

Following Graham's conclusions, Botswana's Department of Wildlife has lobbied its Veterinary Department to consider rerouting a proposed disease control fence around the Makgadikgadi, to help prevent the wildlife from straying into cattle country. Meanwhile strategies have been developed to help the local people minimise their losses, and to discourage them from killing more lions before the fence is built.

MOTOPI A few kilometres west of the Makgadikgadi Pans National Park, this large village is now linked to the main Maun–Nata road by a bridge (⊕ MOTOBR 20°12.723'S, 24°07.600'E) over the Boteti River. The timing couldn't be more apt, since in 2009 the river flowed at this point for the first time in 16 years, making the original crossing point impassable. Apart from two general dealers, there's nothing to delay visitors. (Though as an aside, the original gravel road, signposted to Moreomaoto, leads to the river, affording some lovely views and a nice picnic spot.)

From Motopi, a good tarred road runs parallel to the western bank of the river as far as Rakops (126km) and Mopipi, then around to Orapa. From here the road splits, with one fork heading east for Francistown, and the other southeast for Letlhakane, Serowe and Palapye; both are now tarred and of good quality. Most of this area is flat, cattle-farming territory, much of it lush and green during the rains, though with the vegetation thinning out as you head south towards Rakops. If you don't fancy pulling off into the bush, several picnic spots along the side of the road offer the chance to stop.

KHUMAGA The village of Khumaga just east of the main road marks another gate (KHUMGT 20°28.321'S, 24°30.888'E) into the Makgadikgadi Pans National Park, leading directly to the scout post and Khumaga Campsite via a ferry across the Boteti River. Tiaan's Camp (page 483) is on the left as you approach the ferry crossing from the main road.

RAKOPS Reachable entirely on tarmac from Maun, Rakops (✪ RAKOPS 21°02.136'S, 24°24.432'E) is notable as the last outpost passed on many trips into the Central Kalahari Game Reserve.

The village itself sprawls to the east of the road. A ragged remnant of tar runs down the centre of the road, flanked by widely spaced huts and bungalows, and a few general stores. A small fuel station is about 500m from the main road (bear right after the first crossroads and it's on the right), but supplies are erratic; many people opt to travel the extra 60km to Mopipi.

Where to stay While there is nowhere to stay in Rakops itself, there's a useful little lodge and campsite just 7km north of the turning off the main road, and a similar-size motel just south of the town.

Xere Motel [map 448] (11 rooms) ☏ 297 5068; m 7267 5568; ✪ XERMOT 21°02.834'S, 24°24.008'E. Continuing south along the main road, pass the 1st turning to Rakops on your left, & after a further 3km you'll arrive at the Xere Motel. Established in 2004, its identical dbl rooms are small but clean & comfortable, with AC, satellite TV, fridge & en-suite shower, bath & toilet. There's an à la carte restaurant on site & laundry can be done at extra cost. **$** *exc b/fast.* ⊕ *All year.*

Rakops River Lodge [map 448] (10 chalets, camping) ☏ 393 2711; m 7143 4129; e enquires@rakopsriverlodge.com; www.

rakopsriverlodge.com; ✪ RKRLO 20°59.189'S, 24°21.748'E. Close to the eastern side of the road, this simple but clean & very friendly motel – formerly the Sekgwa Sa Metsi Motel – opened under this name in 2012. Its small chalets each have a dbl or twin beds & tiled, en-suite facilities with bath & shower attachment, & 6 have AC. A couple of family rooms were being constructed in late 2013. Visitors can cook up their own braai, or eat in the large if rather empty dining area. The 9 pitches at the campsite have running water & a unisex ablution block, with power available on request. **$** *exc b/fast; camping P130 pp.* ⊕ *All year.*

ORAPA AND LETLHAKANE **Orapa** is at the heart of Botswana's diamond-mining operations, producing around 12% of the world's gem-quality diamonds. This makes it by far the most important town in the country to Botswana's economy, and hence security there is very tight. You're not allowed in, or out, without permission from the diamond company Debswana, which isn't given easily. Hence it's effectively off-limits to visitors and there's a road that detours around the south side of the mine.

There's also a major diamond mine at **Letlhakane**, about 30km southeast of Orapa, on the Serowe road, and there's active prospecting continuing throughout the region for more diamond pipes. More usefully for visitors, Letlhakane is also one of the few places where you can buy entry permits for the national parks.

For the safari visitor, the road south from Orapa is notable in that it leads, after some 220km, to the **Khama Rhino Sanctuary** (*www.khamarhinosanctuary.org.bw*). Described by one mobile safari operator as 'a really well laid-out and cared-for park with good wildlife and excellent facilities', it's a refuge for both white and black rhino. While its location falls outside the scope of this guide, it's a good stopover on the road between Maun and the south for self-drive tourists and thus is worthy of mention.

15

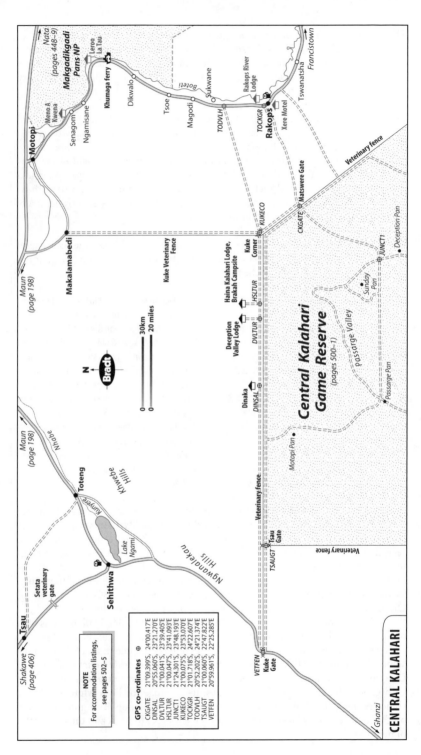

CENTRAL KALAHARI

NOTE
For accommodation listings, see pages 502–5

GPS co-ordinates ⊕

CKGATE	21°09.399'S, 24°00.417'E
DINSAL	20°55.060'S, 23°21.270'E
DVLTUR	21°00.041'S, 23°39.405'E
HSLTUR	21°00.047'S, 23°41.093'E
JUNCT1	21°24.301'S, 23°48.193'E
KUKECO	21°00.075'S, 23°53.070'E
TOCKGR	21°01.718'S, 24°22.607'E
TODVLH	20°52.202'S, 24°21.374'E
TSAUGT	21°00.060'S, 22°47.822'E
VETFEN	20°59.961'S, 22°25.285'E

16

The Central Kalahari

Covering about 52,800km², the Central Kalahari Game Reserve (or the CKGR, as it's usually known) is one of the world's largest game reserves. It dominates the centre of Botswana, the wider region that I refer to in this chapter as simply the 'Central Kalahari'. This is Africa at its most remote and esoteric: a vast sandsheet punctuated by a few huge open plains, occasional salt pans and the fossil remains of ancient riverbeds.

The CKGR isn't for everybody. The game is often sparse and can seem limited, with only occasional elephant and no buffalo; the distances are huge, along bush tracks of variable quality; and until 2009, the facilities were limited to a handful of campsites. So without a fully equipped vehicle (preferably two) and lots of bush experience, it was probably not the place for you. The converse is that if you've already experienced enough of Africa to love the feeling of space and the sheer freedom of real wilderness areas, then this reserve is completely magical; it's the ultimate wilderness destination.

In a change of policy, however, the authorities have permitted the establishment of two small lodges within the reserve, thus opening it up to those who don't have the experience, the time or the equipment to come here alone. As a middle ground, there are also a number of mobile safaris operating in the area.

Owing to limitations of space, this is only a short introduction to the area. It's intended to give you a feel for the Central Kalahari and the CKGR (the area of it which most visitors will see) and tell you how to get there and what it's like. I've assumed that most visitors will only be visiting the northern section of the park – Piper Pans and north – as that's generally regarded as the most interesting area. It's also the obvious part of the reserve to link into a trip with the more popular northern regions of Chobe and the Okavango.

BACKGROUND INFORMATION

HISTORY The Central Kalahari Game Reserve was declared a game park in 1961, on the very eve of independence. At that time, there was increasing international publicity about the San. With the prevalent view of their 'idyllic' hunter-gatherer lifestyle came a growing concern that this was threatened, and that they might become 'extinct'. The British Protectorate of Bechuanaland was the focus for this, so the authorities decided to protect the heart of the Kalahari for the San.

At the time, there was no way to set aside one particular area for an ethnic group. Neither the British authorities nor the Tswana, who were being groomed for government, wanted any discrimination among its citizens based on race. This would have set a dangerous precedent, with echoes of the tribal 'bantustans' created by the apartheid regime in South Africa.

Back in the 1960s, legislation to proclaim a separate area for a separate ethnic group didn't exist. Nor was any wanted by a new country anxious to avoid ethnic divisions. Hence the heart of the Central Kalahari was protected from further development or agricultural encroachment as a 'game park' – even though it was intended as a place of sanctuary for the San. Thus the Central Kalahari Game Reserve was proclaimed. (Still to this day the Botswana government has a strict policy of not discriminating – positively or negatively – between any of the ethnic groups in the country. 'We're all Tswana' is their wise approach, designed to minimise any ethnic tensions. However, there lies the nub of a problem. If a group like the San are allowed to live and hunt in a 'game reserve', why shouldn't any other Tswana citizen? Many who are concerned for the San argue that they need positive discrimination, while others maintain that such moves would be racist.)

In keeping with its origins, the CKGR remained largely closed for around 30 years; visitors needed special approval and permits, which were not lightly granted. During this time its most famous visitors were probably Mark and Delia Owens, a couple of young and idealistic animal researchers from America who lived on a tree-island in Deception Valley for about seven years (1974–80), and subsequently wrote a best-selling book, *Cry of the Kalahari* (see *Appendix 3,* page 541), based on their experiences.

Then, in the late 1980s and early 1990s, the park started to open up more, first allowing in organised groups with tour operators and, only in recent years, individual travellers in their own vehicles. However, despite the opening of two small lodges in 2009, numbers remain largely limited by the number of campsites available, so it still feels very much a wilderness destination.

PEOPLE When the CKGR was declared a reserve, a population of around 5,000 San people lived within its boundaries. In the 1990s, a borehole had been installed at the small village of Xade, where some of the park's game scouts were based. Research in 1996 estimated that the population in the reserve had fallen below 1,500, a significant proportion of whom had moved to live in the vicinity of Xade, near this fairly reliable source of water.

In the 1980s, the government's stated policy was to encourage relocation of the people to New Xade, a village which was created outside the reserve. The resulting removals of the people, and the highly controversial court case that resulted, are discussed in detail on pages 97–8. Note that this remains a very contentious and political topic.

GEOGRAPHY AND LANDSCAPE Despite its huge area, the Central Kalahari has relatively little scenic variation. Most of it is covered by an enormous, undulating sandsheet. Within the CKGR itself, the north of the park contains the most varied scenery; here you'll find a network of vegetated salt pans and a few fossilised riverbeds. There are a number of places within the reserve, including Motopi Pan, Passage Pan, Letiahau Pan and Piper Pans, where water is pumped by the park's authorities, creating permanent waterholes.

FLORA AND FAUNA If you're expecting to find stark differences between contrasting environments within this Kalahari reserve, you'll be disappointed. There are subtle changes between its different landscapes, but there isn't the variation here that you'll find around Chobe or the Okavango. Because of this, the animal species found here vary little from area to area – and this is one reason why the Central Kalahari is an area for old Africa hands, and not first-time safari-goers.

Flora People on their first trip through the Kalahari are often struck by just how green and vegetated it is, in contrast to their mental image of a desert. In fact most of the Kalahari is covered in a thin, mixed bush with a fairly low canopy height, dotted with occasional larger trees. Beneath this is a rather sparse ground-covering of smaller bushes, grasses and herbs.

To be a little more precise, the Central Kalahari's vegetation is dominated by *Terminalia sericea* sandveld (page 15), standing on deep sand. The most common species within this are the silver terminalia itself (*Terminalia sericea*), the Kalahari appleleaf (*Philenoptera nelsii*) and Kalahari sand acacias (*Vachellia luederitzii*), which occasionally form thickets. These vary from bushes to substantial trees, growing to a maximum height of around 10m. (Their flattened canopies are easily confused with the umbrella thorn (*Vachellia tortilis*), earning them the alternative name of bastard, or false, umbrella thorn.)

Other common trees include the distinctive purple-pod terminalia (*Terminalia prunioides*), which seem to grow best in areas where there is more clay in the soil; shepherd's trees (*Boscia albitrunca*), with their characteristic whitish bark; and feverberry trees (*Croton megalobotrys*). Bladethorns (*Senegalia fleckii*) and their close cousins the bluethorns (*Senegalia erubescens*), are common bushes with fine, feathery foliage but keen, curved barbs. Inevitably you'll spot plenty of old, gnarled camelthorn trees (*Vachellia erioloba*).

Beneath these you'll commonly find a variety of low bushes and shrubs including wild seringa bushes (*Burkea africana*) and bushwillows (*Combretum collinum*). Meanwhile on the ground one of the more common grasses is the lovely silky Bushman grass (*Stipagrostis uniplumis*).

Look carefully, perhaps helped by a good guide, and you'll find plenty to interest you here including, during the wetter months of the year, many flowers and herbs. The beautifully curving flowers of the cat's tail (*Hermbstaedtia odorata*) form spectacular pink patches in damper areas. More entertaining are the bright-red fruits of the balsam pear (*Momordica balsamina*) which, when ripe, fall to the ground and pop themselves open automatically if disturbed. In *Common Wild Flowers of the Okavango Delta* (see *Appendix 3*, page 542), Veronica Roodt reports that the young leaves of this plant are used as a vegetable, and while a few will use the fruits in cooking, many communities treat them as poisonous or use them in medicines.

Fauna Game viewing anywhere in the Central Kalahari area can be a stark contrast to the amazing densities of game that can often be seen in the Okavango–Linyanti–Chobe region. To get the best out of the CKGR, you'll require lots of time and patience, often just watching and waiting. The big game is here, but on average it occurs in very low densities – as you'd expect in such a harsh, arid environment. The only way to get around this is, as mentioned on page 494, to visit when it congregates on the open pans in the north.

Springbok are probably the most numerous of the **large herbivores** in the park today. That said, the game populations in the Central Kalahari seem to have been fluctuating fairly wildly, at least for the last century, and perhaps longer. In his book, *A Comment on Kalahari Wildlife and the Khukhe Fence* (see *Appendix 3*, page 540), Alec Campbell suggests that over this period human activities and interference have altered the balance of the wildlife populations in the Kalahari substantially, and led indirectly to population explosions and crashes.

Currently springbok disperse in small herds across the park during the dry season, but congregate in very large numbers on the short grass plains found on pans and fossil riverbeds during and shortly after the rains. (Note that this is exactly the opposite of the usual situation for many mammals, including elephants and buffalo, which gather in larger herds as the dry season progresses, only to disperse during the rains.)

These successful antelope are both browsers and grazers, which can derive all the moisture that they need from their food, provided that the plants they eat contain at least 10% water. They'll often rest by day and eat at night, thus maximising the moisture content of their fodder by including dew on it.

Springbok populations are very elastic: they are able to reproduce very speedily when conditions are favourable, allowing them to repopulate rapidly after a bad drought. With good conditions females can produce two calves in 13 months, while even six-month-old ewes will conceive, giving birth to their first lamb when they are barely a year old. To maximise the survival of their offspring, the females gather together in maternal herds and synchronise their births, thus presenting predators with a short-term surplus of easily caught young lambs.

The Central Kalahari's population of blue wildebeest has, at times within the last century, swelled to enormous proportions. In his work *A Comment on Kalahari Wildlife and the Khukhe Fence* (see *Appendix 3*, page 540), Campbell describes them as peaking in the 1960s when 'herds of 50 and 100 had so accumulated in the Matsheng and Okwa area that they stretched unbroken for many kilometres and numbered hundreds of thousands'. Thane Riney, an ecologist there at the time, was familiar with the vast herds of the Serengeti yet still referred to these as 'the largest herds of plains game left in Africa today'. Wildebeest populations were then estimated at up to 250,000 animals, but within a few years lack of water, grazing and the existence of veterinary cordon fences had conspired to wipe them out from much of the Central Kalahari. Today you'll find small groups of wildebeest in the CKGR, but I've never seen them in large numbers.

Probably the area's most common large antelope are gemsbok (also known as oryx), which can be seen in congregations of hundreds on the short grass plains during the rains, but usually occur in smaller groupings during the rest of the year. These magnificent antelope are supremely adapted for desert living. They can survive fluctuations of their body temperature up to 45°C (when 42°C would kill most mammals) because of a series of blood vessels, known as the carotid rete, located immediately below their brain. These effectively cool the blood before it reaches the animal's brain – the organ most adversely affected by temperature variations.

Red hartebeest can also be found here in good numbers, as can eland and – an amazing sight – giraffe. Kudu occur, but generally in quite small numbers: either small bachelor groups or family groups consisting of an old male, several females and a number of youngsters. Common duiker are occasionally seen, too, but if you catch a glimpse of a small antelope bounding away from you, it's much more likely to be a steenbok.

The main **predators** here are lion, cheetah, leopard and spotted hyena, which generally occur in a low density, matching their prey species. The lion prides range over large territories and are bonded by loose associations; members spend most of their time apart from each other, living alone or in pairs, and meeting relatively infrequently. Individual lions will often hunt a variety of smaller prey, like bat-eared foxes and porcupines, as well as the larger antelope more commonly thought of as lion fodder.

Similarly, the Central Kalahari's leopard have a very catholic diet, ranging from mice and spring hares to ground squirrels and wildcats, plus steenbok, springbok and calves of the larger antelope.

The park's cheetah seem to be more nomadic than the lion or leopard. In other parks, where game densities are higher, cheetah often lose their kills to these larger cats. Thus the CKGR's relatively low density of predators makes it a good place for cheetah. Hence this is one of sub-Saharan Africa's better parks for spotting them – at least at times when the springbok concentrate on the pans and riverbeds.

Among the **scavengers and insectivores** found here are the brown hyena (the original object of study for Mark and Delia Owens; see *Appendix 3*, page 541), black-backed jackal, caracal, Cape fox, bat-eared fox, aardwolf, genet and wildcat. However, as there is no facility for night drives in the reserve, only black-backed jackal and bat-eared fox are commonly seen as they aren't strictly nocturnal.

TUNNEL VISION

Just below the surface of the Kalahari lies a labyrinth of tunnels excavated by the Damara mole-rat (*Cryptomis damarensis*), the only member of this endemic African family to occur in the Kalahari. Mole-rats are rodents, and unlike true moles, which are insectivores, they feed entirely on plant matter – specifically underground storage organs such as bulbs, corms, tubers and desert cucumbers.

They have plump, cylindrical bodies, short, sturdy limbs and formidable projecting incisors for chiselling out the tunnels in which they live their entire lives. Earth excavated by the teeth is shuffled backwards by the forefeet, and when enough has accumulated the mole-rat reverses up a side tunnel, pushing it to the surface to form a 'molehill'. Digging is easiest when the soil is wet, so the rains prompt a flurry of activity: in one month, one colony of 16 Damara mole-rats was recorded digging 1km of tunnels and shifting 2.5 tonnes of soil to the surface. Not bad for an animal that weighs no more than 300g.

This Herculean effort uncovers enough food to last the colony through the dry season until the next rains. Meanwhile soil is shifted around and burrows modified to create a complex of chambers, passageways and latrines.

Damara mole-rats are the most sociable of their family. This is a necessary adaptation to the harsh Kalahari environment, where numbers bring more success to a team of blind foragers in search of an erratic, scattered food supply. Their complex societies are more like those of a social insect than a mammal. A colony averages around 15–25 members, occasionally up to 40, but only one pair – the dominant male and female – are reproductive. All others help forage, dig and rear the young, but suppress their fertility, being effectively like sterile worker-termites.

The dominant female breeds all year, producing a litter of between one and five pups after an 80-day gestation in a nest chamber 2m below ground. Hierarchies are reinforced aggressively, and each year about 10% of a colony's members leave to breed and found new colonies. Mole-rats communicate underground with snorts and squeals, and drum with their hind feet on tunnel walls to relay seismic messages to mates or rivals.

Though the casual visitor is unlikely ever to see a mole-rat, a range of canny predators, notably the mole snake (*Pseudaspis cana*), have learned to watch as a pile of fresh soil accumulates and will snatch the digger just as it approaches the surface.

Meanwhile the diurnal yellow mongoose is sometimes seen scampering around in search of insects, and families of meerkats (or suricats) are among the most entertaining and endearing of all the park's residents.

Birdlife The birdlife here is very varied, with Africa's largest bird, the ostrich, doing particularly well. I've never seen more free-roaming ostriches during May, when Deception Valley seemed to be dotted by large flocks of them.

Weighing 14–19kg, kori bustards are the world's heaviest flying birds and are also common, stepping around the plains in search of insects, small reptiles and mammals.

Closely related to the kori are the smaller korhaans; the northern black korhaan (or white-quilled korhaan, or white-winged) is one of the area's most obvious birds. The conspicuous black-and-white males have a harsh, raucous call and can be seen flying up and then falling back to the ground in endless display flights. Related red-crested korhaans are a little less obvious, and less common, though equally spectacular when displaying.

Doves are well represented with Cape turtle doves, laughing doves and, especially, Namaqua doves all being very common. All the species of sandgrouse found in southern Africa – double-banded, Burchell's, yellow-throated and Namaqua – live here. Watch in the mornings as flocks of Namaqua sandgrouse fly to waterholes. They drink and also wade into the water, where each male has specially adapted feathers on his breast, which act like a sponge to soak up water. He then flies up to 80km back to his nest, where the chicks drink from the feathers.

Large flocks of red-billed queleas resemble leaves blowing on a stiff autumn breeze as they swarm down from the trees in search of grass seeds or to drink from a muddy puddle. Even more colourful in the summer months are the male whydahs – pin-tailed, shaft-tailed and paradise – whose exuberant breeding plumage includes a disproportionately long tail. These are brood parasites – laying their eggs in the nest of other birds (see box, page 458).

The Central Kalahari's most common raptor is the pale-chanting goshawk: a light-grey bird, with pink legs and black ends to its wings and tail. It's usually seen hunting from a conspicuous perch, perhaps a fence post beside a track or the top of a small thorn bush, or occasionally hopping about the ground foraging. If disturbed it'll usually fly off low, swooping to land on a similar perch – even if that's another fence post from which it'll shortly be disturbed again. Equally visible during the summer months is the yellow-billed kite.

Black-shouldered kites and rock kestrels, both of which often hunt by hovering in flight, are common here. Bateleurs (or short-tailed eagles), black-breasted and brown snake eagles, martial and tawny eagles, and lanner falcons are also around, with the last making something of a speciality of hunting birds as they come to drink at waterholes.

PRACTICAL INFORMATION

WHEN TO VISIT The Kalahari is really unlike any other game area in sub-Saharan Africa in that its game is probably at its most spectacular during and shortly after the rains – from around January to April. Then the animals gather where the best rain has been and the sweetest grazing is, which usually means on the pans. These can be a magnificent sight, with very large herds of springbok and gemsbok, accompanied by good numbers of giraffe and ostrich plus groups of blue wildebeest, hartebeest and eland. Inevitably these attract increased predator activity from lion, cheetah and the odd leopard.

Having said that, this is also the time when the weather, and in particular the driving conditions, can be at their least hospitable. If there has been much rain then the road from Rakops to the Matswere Gate and beyond becomes a series of mud-holes lined by black-cotton soil, which is rock-hard when dry, but feels like treacle when wet. Meanwhile areas of pans in the park become large, shallow lakes where both navigation and traction present a challenge to any vehicle. Any group coming at this time must be fully prepared for heavy rain, and should expect to have to dig out their vehicle from the mud a number of times.

As a compromise for those who are not fond of endless mud, a favourite time to visit is just after the rains, around March–May, depending on when the rains stop. Then most of the surface water has disappeared, and the black-cotton soil isn't nearly as treacherous as it would have been a few months earlier. The game concentrations will still be good, albeit perhaps not *quite* so spectacular, but your overall experience will probably be much more enjoyable. That is, unless you really enjoy digging your vehicle out of knee-deep mud …

GETTING THERE AND AWAY There are four entrances into the CKGR. Of these, the most widely used is the Matswere Gate, which is on the eastern side of the reserve. From here it's just 38km to the north end of Deception Valley and the nearest campsites.

The new Tsau Gate (✪ TSAUGT 21°00.060'S, 22°47.822'E), in the northwest corner of the reserve, lies 39km east of the main Maun–Ghanzi road, along the southern side of the veterinary fence that defines the reserve's northern border. The closest campsites to the gate are at Motopi Pan.

The other entrances, Khutse Gate in the far south and Xade Gate to the west, some 80km from Piper Pans, are best suited to those exploring the more southerly areas of the reserve.

Driving yourself Driving yourself into the Central Kalahari is only a viable option for experienced and bush-wise adventurers with their own fully equipped 4x4s. Even they might consider travelling with two 4x4 vehicles and should have fail-safe plans for back-up assistance in the event of an emergency.

There are now four usual routes to the reserve, three to the Matswere Gate on the eastern side, and one to the new Tsau Gate at the northwest corner.

From the Maun–Ghanzi road to the Matswere Gate About 119km from Ghanzi and 167km from Maun, on the tarred Maun–Ghanzi road, you'll have to stop and pass through the Kuke Veterinary Fence (✪ VETFEN 20°59.961'S, 22°25.285'E). Immediately north of this, you'll find a good, wide gravel road that heads off on a bearing fractionally south of east. After a few kilometres, this thoroughfare bends round to the left, and there's a small turning into the bush on the right. Take this, and you'll find a simple sand track with two clear ruts for your wheels (welcome to the Kalahari!). The veterinary fence will be literally inches from your right side.

Expect only the occasional 4x4 to pass you; this isn't a busy track. Beneath your wheels you'll sometimes find patches of hard ground with bands of calcrete rocks. Then there are mud-holes, where thick clay is a sticky hazard during the rains (when this route is perfectly possible, but time-consuming). However, most of the track is good, fairly hard sand on which a reasonably experienced bush driver should be able to average 50km/h.

At times now you'll find yourself travelling parallel to several fences, and sometimes with one on each side of you. Beware of startling antelope here; they'll run in front of the vehicle with no escape, and become exhausted easily if you drive too fast.

Around 128km after the tar you'll reach a left turning (⊕ DVLTUR 21°00.041'S, 23°39.405'E) which is clearly signposted to Deception Valley Lodge (pages 504–5). The lodge is about 9km north from here along a winding track that crosses the lodge's own airstrip (⊕ DVLAIR 20°58.897'S, 23°39.515'E). Back on the main track, a further 3km brings you to the entrance to Haina Kalahari Lodge (⊕ HSLTUR 21°00.047'S, 23°41.093'E).

Almost 23km after passing this, you'll reach Phefodiaka veterinary checkpoint, widely known as Kuke Corner (⊕ KUKECO 21°00.075'S, 23°53.070'E; ⊕ 06.00–22.00). Here a gate marks the junction of four veterinary fences. As at other vet-fence checkpoints, you will probably be asked if you're carrying any red meat, which cannot be taken east across the fence. To the left a straight cutline heads due north to Makalamabedi. Continuing straight on brings you after 52km to the main Maun–Rakops road, coming out north of Rakops (⊕ TODVLH 20°52.202'S, 24°21.374'E). To the right, a well-used track follows the line of the fence, roughly south-southeast (bearing about 143°). This can be quite rutted and tedious driving, but after about 21.5km leads to the Matswere Gate into the CKGR (⊕ CKGATE 21°09.399'S, 24°00.417'E).

From the Maun–Ghanzi road to the Tsau Gate The road east to the Tsau Gate is a turning off the Maun–Ghanzi road just south of the Kuke Veterinary Fence (⊕ VETFEN 20°59.961'S, 22°25.285'E). From here, it follows straight along the southern side of the fence for about 39km, to reach the Tsau Gate (⊕ TSAUGT 21°00.060'S, 22°47.822'E) into the reserve. After the gate, continue along the fence for a further 32km, before turning south (⊕ MOTCUT 21°00.194'S, 23°06.400'E) towards Motopi Pan. It's important to be aware that you cannot cross the vet fence into or out of the reserve at any point along its northern boundary.

From Rakops to the Matswere Gate Between Rakops (⊕ RAKOPS 21°02.136'S, 24°24.432'E; page 489) and the CKGR's Matswere Gate there is one main track, fringed by a few detours and side-tracks. The turning from the tar road (⊕ TOCKGR 21°01.718'S, 24°22.607'E) is clearly signposted to the west, just 200m north of the turning to Rakops.

The track is pretty clear on the ground, following a bearing of about 250° until after around 41km you reach the veterinary fence that doubles as the park's boundary. This is the location of the smart new Matswere Gate (⊕ CKGATE 21°09.399'S, 24°00.417'E). When it's wet during the early months of the year, this is one of the muddiest, and hence trickiest, sections of track in the region, with patches of black-cotton soil that can trap even the most careful driver. I've heard tales of this section alone taking several days to pass, with frequent stops to dig out – so don't tackle it lightly. Later in the year, the track hardens to a roller-coaster ride where you bounce in and out of a succession of dry mud-holes; even then it's fairly slow going.

South along the cutline from Makalamabedi to the Matswere Gate I haven't driven the full length of this route, but I believe it's probably the most scenic route between Maun and the CKGR, though with the advent of the tar road between Maun and Rakops it's probably no longer the quickest. You'll find the north end of this at the small village of Makalamabedi, southeast of Maun, and southwest of Motopi. If you're coming from Maun, turn south off the main Maun–Nata road just before the Makalamabedi control post (⊕ MAKACP 20°11.219'S, 23°51.739'E), and take the tar road to Makalamabedi. From here, simply follow the cutline due south (driving on the eastern side of the veterinary fence) to Kuke Corner (⊕ KUKECO 21°00.075'S, 23°53.070'E), then continue south for a further 21.5km to the main Matswere Gate (⊕ CKGATE 21°09.399'S, 24°00.417'E).

Without your own vehicle If, like most visitors to Botswana, you don't have the knowledge, experience or equipment for this kind of a trip, there are now several options to visit the CKGR.

Fly-in trips Now that there are two exclusive lodges in the reserve (pages 502–4), the option of incorporating a fly-in trip to the CKGR into a broader itinerary has become a reality.

Group trips A few of Botswana's larger safari companies have scheduled group trips, leaving on specific pre-planned dates, which include time camping within the CKGR; see the main listings in *Chapter 5, Planning and Preparation* (pages 123–4), *Chapter 8, Maun, Tour operators and safari companies* (pages 223–7) and *Chapter 9, Kasane and the Northeast, Tour operators, safari companies and travel agents* (pages 247–8). Check out what they have running and read between the lines to make sure you understand exactly how much of their time is within the CKGR: occasionally, quite long trips will spend far too short a time in the park.

Private mobile trips If you have a fairly generous budget, then the same operators (and many of the smaller ones) will be delighted to organise a private trip for two or more people, for which you'll be able to specify the departure date and the timings. Expect the costs to be high though – in the region of US$400–450 per person per night. (Larger groups and longer expeditions are generally less expensive than smaller groups and shorter trips.)

Book a short trip from a lodge If you just want a few days in the park, then it's worth checking with Meno A Kwena or Haina Kalahari Lodge (pages 482–3 and 505). They will sometimes organise short, simple, guided camping expeditions into the park. Typically these come with a few nights either side at their lodge.

GETTING ORGANISED A visit to the CKGR requires a lot of organisation before you even start to drive there. You must book a place to stay and make arrangements to bring all your water, food, equipment and supplies. Brackish water is sometimes available at the Matswere Gate, but it isn't safe to drink and cannot be relied upon. Note that all the land outside the park falls into private farms and concessions, and so camping 'outside the gate' is not a practical option. Here, the nearest place to camp is the Brakah Campsite at Haina Kalahari Lodge.

GETTING AROUND The main entrance into the CKGR, and one of the few places where there's a break in the veterinary fence, is at the smart new Matswere Gate (⊕ CKGATE 21°09.399'S, 24°00.417'E). Here you can sign in, check on the state of the roads inside the park and use the toilet facilities. If you ask the scouts politely, it's sometimes possible to fill up with brackish water – which is fine for showers, but not suitable for drinking. (You should have arrived with all your own water, but if you didn't, then make the most of this. There are no waterpoints inside the reserve.) Remember that you must have prepaid your park entry fees at one of the designated points; see page 131.

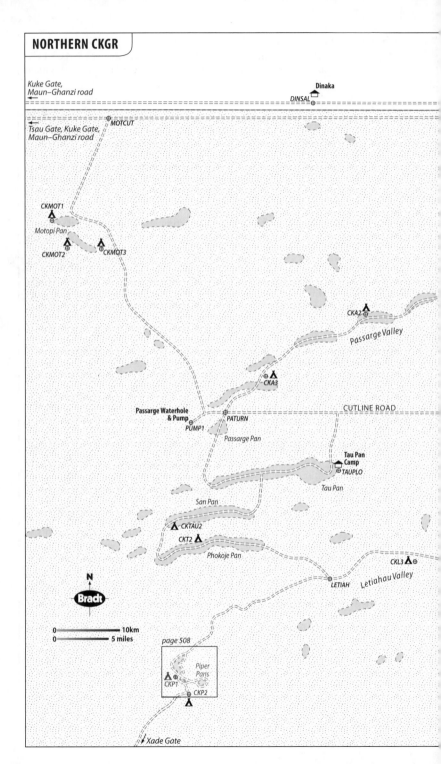

NORTHERN CKGR

Kuke Gate,
Maun–Ghanzi road

Dinaka

DINSAL

MOTCUT

Tsau Gate, Kuke Gate,
Maun–Ghanzi road

CKMOT1

Motopi Pan

CKMOT2   CKMOT3

CKA2

Passarge Valley

CKA3

Passarge Waterhole
& Pump   PATURN   CUTLINE ROAD

PUMP1

Passarge Pan

Tau Pan
Camp

TAUPLO

Tau Pan

San Pan

CKTAU2

CKT2

Phokoje Pan   CKL3

N   LETIAH   Letiahau Valley

Bradt

0 _____ 10km
0 _____ 5 miles   page 508

Piper
Pans

CKP1

CKP2

Xade Gate

500

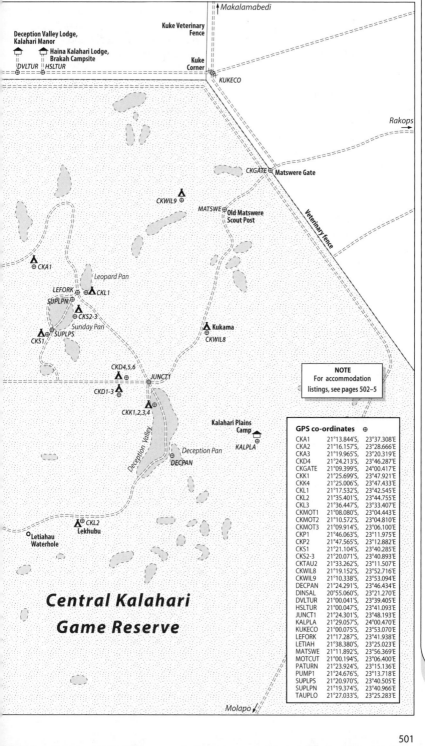

Central Kalahari Game Reserve

Location	Coordinates	
GPS co-ordinates ⊕		
CKA1	21°13.844'S,	23°37.308'E
CKA2	21°16.157'S,	23°28.666'E
CKA3	21°19.965'S,	23°20.319'E
CKD4	21°24.213'S,	23°46.287'E
CKGATE	21°09.399'S,	24°00.417'E
CKK1	21°25.699'S,	23°47.921'E
CKK4	21°25.006'S,	23°47.433'E
CKL1	21°17.532'S,	23°42.545'E
CKL2	21°35.401'S,	23°44.755'E
CKL3	21°36.447'S,	23°33.407'E
CKMOT1	21°08.080'S,	23°04.443'E
CKMOT2	21°10.572'S,	23°04.810'E
CKMOT3	21°09.914'S,	23°06.100'E
CKP1	21°46.063'S,	23°11.975'E
CKP2	21°47.565'S,	23°12.882'E
CKS1	21°21.104'S,	23°40.285'E
CKS2-3	21°20.071'S,	23°40.893'E
CKTAU2	21°33.262'S,	23°11.507'E
CKWIL8	21°19.152'S,	23°52.716'E
CKWIL9	21°10.338'S,	23°53.094'E
DECPAN	21°24.291'S,	23°46.434'E
DINSAL	20°55.060'S,	23°21.270'E
DVLTUR	21°00.041'S,	23°39.405'E
HSLTUR	21°00.047'S,	23°41.093'E
JUNCT1	21°24.301'S,	23°48.193'E
KALPLA	21°29.057'S,	24°00.470'E
KUKECO	21°00.075'S,	23°53.070'E
LEFORK	21°17.287'S,	23°41.938'E
LETIAH	21°38.380'S,	23°25.023'E
MATSWE	21°11.892'S,	23°56.369'E
MOTCUT	21°00.194'S,	23°06.400'E
PATURN	21°23.924'S,	23°15.136'E
PUMP1	21°24.676'S,	23°13.718'E
SUPLPS	21°20.970'S,	23°40.505'E
SUPLPN	21°19.374'S,	23°40.966'E
TAUPLO	21°27.033'S,	23°25.283'E

NOTE
For accommodation
listings, see pages 502–5

Deception Valley Lodge,
Kalahari Manor
Haina Kalahari Lodge,
Brakah Campsite
DVLTUR HSLTUR

↑ Makalamabedi

Kuke Veterinary
Fence

Kuke
Corner

KUKECO

Rakops →

CKGATE ⊕ Matswere Gate

CKWIL9 ⊕

MATSWE ⊕ Old Matswere
Scout Post

Veterinary fence

⊕ CKA1

Leopard Pan

LEFORK ⊕
SUPLPN ⊕   ⊕ CKL1

⊕ CKS2-3

Sunday Pan

⊕ SUPLPS

⊕ CKS1

⊕ Kukama
CKWIL8

CKD4,5,6
⊕   JUNCT1

CKD1-3 ⊕

CKK1,2,3,4

Kalahari Plains
Camp
KALPLA

Deception Pan

Deception Valley

DECPAN ⊕

⊕ CKL2
Lekhubu

Letiahau
Waterhole

↓ Molapo

The presence of a few signposts and distance markers within the reserve makes navigation a little easier than in the past, at least at first glance – but don't be fooled. Stray just a few metres from the main track and you could rapidly find yourself completely lost without a compass, a GPS, and a hefty degree of common sense.

Driving conditions In the dry season, the general quality of the tracks in the park is surprising. Many of them, particularly those which follow the valleys, are really very good. You might have expected to be constantly ploughing through deep sand, but it's not like that. Of course there are patches of deep and tricky sand, and also stretches of black-cotton soil (rock-hard when dry; virtually impassable if very wet), but many of the road surfaces are easy and hard when it's dry. During the rainy months it's important to seek advice from the wardens at the entrance gate, and from other visitors to the park. Some sections can be particularly treacherous, and you could save yourself hours – or even days – of digging.

 WHERE TO STAY Until 2009, visitors to the CKGR had two accommodation options: stay either within the park, using the park's demarcated campsites, or at one of the lodges outside the park boundary, which are not close enough for day trips (though they remain useful either as destinations in their own right, or as comfortable stops at the start and end of trips into the park). Now, however, two new lodges are situated inside the park boundary, which opens up the reserve to those who would not consider camping.

Inside the park While the lodges open up the CKGR to a wider range of visitors, there are plenty of challenges, including a relatively limited road network. These companies have a reputation for excellent guiding, though, so you should expect a real insight into the Kalahari's unique ecosystems, including the ways in which animals, birds & plants adapt to life in a region where lack of water is a serious problem.

Lodges

✳ 🏠 **Kalahari Plains Camp** [map 501] (10 tents) Contact Wilderness Safaris, page 225; ✛ KALPLA 21°29.057'S, 24°00.470E. At the end of 2009, Wilderness moved their tented camp from its temporary home north of Deception Valley to an open, but entirely secluded pan further south, some 20km from the valley. Here, where permanent water has been found, accommodation is in good-sized chalets constructed of wood & canvas , built on wooden platforms & specially designed to mediate the Kalahari's extremes of temperature. Each is tastefully furnished, the open front & roll-up windows are netted against mosquitoes, while inside the rooms are furnished with comfortable twin or dbl beds, electric lights & a fan (using solar power), & a small desk with chair. A couple

of canvas chairs invite relaxation on the shaded veranda, while at the back are an en-suite shower, flush toilet & twin washbasins. On the roof of each chalet is a flat wooden deck which doubles as a sleep-out area, with mattresses made up on request for alfresco nights under the stars.

Similar in style is the thatched main area, reached along sand paths through the bush. This is long & narrow, open on all sides, but with roll-down panels to protect against the elements. To one side of the central bar is the dining area & a large fridge full of cold drinks; to the other, comfortable chairs with low tables & a small but relevant library. Outside, a swimming pool is surrounded by its own deck.

Access to the camp is either by air into an airstrip 9km from camp, or – for those with their own vehicles – by road. If you're driving yourself, follow the directions on pages 498–9 for the Matswere Gate. From here, follow the signs towards Deception Valley for about 38km. Continue south through the valley, until the road forks at the end. Here you take the left fork towards Deception Pan for some 1km, then turn left on to a track known as the Northern Access Road. After a further 25km, you will reach Kalahari Plains Camp.

The location of the camp within the national park means that activities are limited to game drives during daylight hours, but they also organise walks from camp to learn about Bushman culture & history. *From US$670/875 Jun–Oct to US$965/1,255 Nov–Dec, inc FB, local drinks, park fees, activities.* ☺ *All year.* ★★★★

🏠 **Tau Pan Camp** [map 500] (9 chalets) Contact Kwando Safaris, page 224; ✪ TAUPLO 21°27.033'S, 23°25.283'E. Built on top of a low ridge, dominating the surrounding bush & with commanding views west across Tau Pan itself, this self-styled 'camp' has very much the feel of a lodge. If you're driving yourself, follow the main westerly track from the Matswere Gate for 78km, then turn south to Tau Pan (✪ TAUPTO 21°24.073'S, 23°25.656'E) for a further 6km to the lodge. The lodge is visible from miles around &, although its thatch is rapidly blending

into the environment, the same can't be said for the metal-roofed kitchen, even with its coat of green paint. Most visitors, however, arrive by air at the new airstrip, just 3km away, so see none of this.

The light design hand behind the camp at Nxai Pan has clearly been at work here, too: witness the long, narrow central building built in a slight curve, the pool to one side of the deck, & the curio shop at the back. Similar, too, is the open view across the plains, with roll-down blinds to keep the elements at bay. Here, though, the wood is darker than at its sister camp, & simple sand paths link the hub to each chalet. Sliding doors with mesh panels lead from a shaded deck into each spacious room, with roll-down blinds installed against the cold winter nights. Rooms are quite spacious, the centre is taken up by twin or dbl beds. To one side are a desk & leather armchairs; to the other, a

CAMPSITES

There are several designated campsites across the northern CKGR [map 500–501], with quite a good concentration around Deception Valley. Each of the sites is designed for just one group camping at any one time – with a maximum of two vehicles and six people – so once you have pre-booked a site, you should not be sharing it with anyone else. Historically, all these sites were totally undeveloped: just cleared patches of ground with no water, toilets or showers. Now, however, most of the sites have a long-drop toilet and a separate bucket shower, enclosed by simple rush screens, and a firepit. That said, you must still bring all the water you need, as well as all your food. And note that the vegetation around these facilities can get very overgrown, so digging your own toilet may be a more attractive option than fighting through the bush. (Don't forget a spade, and matches to burn any tissue paper before burying it.)

As with the rest of Botswana's parks, it's essential that you book and pay for these campsites in advance. Payment of park fees, however, is more flexible, with the option to pay in advance or at certain gates on entry. No matter how you pay, all fees must be settled before you will be allowed into the park. See pages 130–3 for how to do this, and details of the costs.

Within the CKGR, six sites – Lekhubu, Letiahau, Piper, Sunday, Passarge and Motopi – are operated by Bigfoot Tours (page 132), with rates for international visitors currently set at US$50 per person, excluding park fees. Other campsites within the reserve still fall within the remit of the DWNP, whose camping fees remain at P30 per person. It's worth noting, however, that there is a high expectation of park fees – and thus presumably attendant campsite and vehicle fees – being increased within the life of this book.

Each of the CKGR's campsites has a unique code. These are signposted on the ground as CKK1, CKK2, CKD1, etc, but for computer-booking purposes have been redesignated as CKKOR-01, CKKOR-02, CKDEC-01, etc. I've made notes on some of these on pages 506–10, identifying most of them with comments and GPS locations.

bathroom – with inside & outside showers, twin basins & separate toilet. Lighting for ceiling & bedside lamps is powered by solar panels. There's also a family chalet, sleeping up to 4 people.

Game drives explore the remote area around the camp, with day trips to Deception Valley a further option. There are also nature walks, conducted by the lodge's Bushman trackers. And with the huge Kalahari skies, stargazing is a must! *US$577 pp all year (sgl supp't US$220 Apr–Nov), inc FB, most drinks, activities, laundry.* ⊕ *All year.* ★★★

Campsites See box, page 503.

Outside the park There are 3 lodges close to the park's northern boundary: Dinaka, Deception Valley Lodge & the adjacent Haina Kalahari Lodge, which also has a campsite. Ideally these should be booked in advance, as if they're full it's a long way to the nearest alternative options. Note that they are at least 2hrs' drive from the Matswere Gate, & over 3hrs from the area within the CKGR known as Deception Valley. A possible alternative could be Meno A Kwena Tented Camp (pages 482–3), which stands beside the western border of Makgadikgadi Pans National Park, at least 3hrs' drive from the park's entrance gate. While this is not an option for day trips, the lodge does offer overnight trips into the CKGR.

For those coming from the west, there are other accommodation options around Ghanzi, including Grasslands Bushman Lodge (m *7210 4270; www. grasslandlodge.com*) & the tented Edo's Camp (m *7212 0399;* e *edosbooking@gmail.com*), but these fall outside the scope of this book.

🏠 **Dinaka** [map 500] (8 tents) Contact Ker & Downey, page 224; ⊕ DINSAL 20°55.060′S, 23°21.270′E. Set in its own 20,000ha private reserve, Dinaka is accessible by road, & also has its own airstrip. Following a change of ownership in 2017, the camp is being upgraded; completion is scheduled for Mar 2018, & with that will come a change in the rates.

The new safari tents will be well spaced & raised up on wooden decks with walkways connecting to the central area, looking out over a permanent waterhole. Each will have twin beds, or a dbl, with fully plumbed indoor & outdoor showers & flush

toilet. For families, there'll be a 2-bedroom tent, sharing a spacious en-suite bathroom.

Fronting the waterhole, Dinaka's main area encloses a few comfortable couches, a bar & the dining table – although private dining can be organised too. A small plunge pool is a boon during the hotter months. All areas of camp are accessible by wheelchair.

Game drives with no more than 4 guests per vehicle (except on request) form the mainstay of the activities, with afternoon game drives often continuing into the evening. Guided bush walks offer the chance to get closer to nature, while on a San Bushman walk you can learn about the traditional lifestyle of the San. Birding is a plus, too, with more than 200 different bird species recorded on the reserve. Dinaka also has a number of strategically positioned hides & we're reliably informed that these offer productive game viewing in the dry season. Eland numbers are particularly good here, & lion & leopard have also been seen regularly. *From US$530 pp Mar & Dec to US$1,010/1,295 Jul–Oct pp sharing/sgl, inc FB, local drinks, laundry, activities.* ⊕ *All year.* ★★★–★★★★★

🏠 **Deception Valley Lodge** [map 501] (8 chalets) \+27 0823 556910; e res1@ footsteps-in-africa.com; www.dvl.co.za; ⊕ DVLOD 20°57.182′S, 23°38.988′E. Old-fashioned style & comfort are the watchwords at Deception Valley Lodge, which is set in one of the country's more remote locations. As with the wider Central Kalahari area, it has a relative lack of big game, which tends to suit old Africa hands more than 1st-time visitors. The lodge has its own airstrip, but if you're driving yourself, see the directions on pages 497–9.

From a narrow veranda with simple chairs & a table, sliding doors lead into each thatched chalet. Heavy teak furniture dominates the bedroom (or 2 bedrooms in the family chalet), which has copious wardrobe space & twin beds (or a king-size dbl) under four-poster mosquito nets. Comfortable mattresses are covered with high-quality cotton sheets & down quilts – which you'll need as the Kalahari's temperatures plummet at night. A blanket box doubles as a lockable safe. The separate lounge has a sofa & a large glass coffee table on a colourful rug, while the bathroom – set between the 2 rooms – has a free-standing, claw-foot iron bath, & a door leading to an excellent outside shower. Hot water is derived from a gas geyser, & electricity powers a ceiling fan in each room, a well-stocked fridge/minibar in the lounge & any number of lamps & lights – yet in the daytime, the whole remains rather dark.

The chalets are widely separated from each other, & linked by low wooden walkways to a good pool with sunloungers & the lodge's main reception. Here, the lounge & dining areas are furnished with careful attention to detail, including ostrich-eggshell lampshades, framed Bushman artefacts on the walls, & hand-crafted wrought-iron chairs. A curio shop sells a limited range of T-shirts, quilted jackets & souvenirs.

The veranda incorporates a large 'apron' deck, where leather couches & low tables create an appealing outdoor seating area, while beyond is an outdoor dining area, a prime spot for watching the porcupine that roam through camp in the evening. About 75m in front is a productive waterhole, where on one visit, giraffe, oryx, zebra & wildebeest all turned up regularly.

Activities focus on day & night drives & walks on the lodge's 150km² concession, which shares its southern boundary with the CKGR. (Note that drives don't normally visit the game reserve, which – because of the location of the park gate – is too far for a comfortable day trip.) The landscape, flora & fauna are similar to that found on the fringes of the main reserve, although being much smaller & fenced, the concession doesn't get the large wet-season congregations that are a major attraction of the CKGR between Dec & May. In fact, the best season to visit Deception Valley Lodge is the more traditional game-viewing period of Jun–Sep. The reserve encompasses a number of waterholes & natural pans surrounded by larger trees, with a hide beside one that can be productive as game such as lion is not deterred by the fences. There's plenty to look at, & with good guiding – helped by San trackers – visitors should also spot many of the smaller attractions. 'Bushman' walks, accompanied by the lodge's San guides, incorporate genuine & enjoyable demonstrations of their traditional skills. Children are welcome, but families must take a private game vehicle. *From US$508 pp Jan–Mar to US$635/826 pp sharing/sgl Jul–Oct, inc FB, drinks, laundry & activities.* ⊕ *All year.* ★★★

🏠 **Haina Kalahari Lodge** [map 501] (9 rooms) `\`683 0238/9; e res@ hainakalaharilodge.com; www. hainakalaharilodge.com; ⊕ HAISAL 20°56.964'S, 23°40.689'E. On a 120km² concession to the east of Deception Valley Lodge, Haina benefits from the same environment & wildlife, but with a more modern feel. It is accessed from the same track (⊕ HSLTUR 21°00.047'S, 23°41.093'E).

Central to the lodge is an open-sided wooden structure under thatch, housing the bar, dining area & comfortable chairs, with roll-down canvas sides against inclement weather. To one side is a firepit surrounded by chairs, & to the front is a small pool. Accommodation is in dbl or twin Meru tents. All are en suite, but 3 larger 'superior' tents are finished to a higher specification than the others. All tents have good beds under mosquito nets, a stove to make hot drinks, a lockable box, & a deck at the front with chairs. In the family unit, for up to 4 people, 2 tents share the 1 deck. As distances from the main area to some of the tents are quite long, a golf cart is available to ferry you to the rooms on request. Hot water & power comes from solar panels, with a generator as back-up, while water is desalinated to make it drinkable. Batteries can be charged at any time.

In addition to day & night game drives, guided walks & an opportunity to find out about Bushman culture, the lodge organises quadbike excursions (*US$48/hr pp*), & day trips (*US$50 pp*) into the CKGR, each for a min of 4 people. Campers may drive around the concession, or pay to take part in walks or night drives. *US$436 pp sharing Jan–Jun & Nov–Dec, US$530 Jul–Oct; 'superior' tent US$542 Jan–Jun & Nov–Dec, US$694 Jul–Oct; all inc FB, local drinks, local activities; exc quad bikes, CKGR trips.* ⊕ *All year.* ★★★–★★★★★

⛺ **Brakah Campsite** [map 501] Contact Haina Kalahari Lodge, above; ⊕ 20°59.299'S, 23°41.910'E. A drive of some 6km from Haina Kalahari Lodge brings you to its secluded campsite, with space for up to 24 campers on 5 tree-shaded pitches. There's a simple, reed-fenced ablution block with showers & flush toilets, a washing-up area with saline water, & firewood at P45 per bundle. Meals can be pre-booked at the lodge; otherwise, you'll need to bring all your own fuel, food & fresh water. *Camping US$27 pp, plus US$11/vehicle.* ⊕ *All year.*

For most visitors, being in a pristine area that is as remote as the CKGR is an end in itself. Just being able to camp, move around and watch the wildlife at leisure in such a beautiful wilderness, with the certainty that you'll see very few other vehicles, is the real attraction here. So don't rush around looking for 'sights', as there really aren't any. Just take time to enjoy where you are!

That said, detailed here are some of the areas that you may visit, including a few notes on some of the various campsites, with their names, and both old on-the-ground codes and booking codes. Your permit for camping in the CKGR will specify the precise campsites booked for you on each night – and these can't be changed when you're here.

If you're entering and leaving via the Matswere Gate then a lovely week's circuit can be made by starting around Sunday and Leopard pans, then heading north and west along Passarge Valley, south via the western link to Piper Pans, and then returning northeast through Letiahau and Deception valleys. This is the order in which I've described these areas.

Should you want to stop closer to the Matswere Gate, there are two campsites along that route, the first, CKWIL-09, close to the old Matswere Scout Post (✪ CKWIL9 21°10.338'S, 23°53.094'E), and the second, CKWIL-08, about 12km further into the reserve (✪ CKWIL8 21°19.152'S, 23°52.716'E).

SUNDAY AND LEOPARD PANS Just north of Deception Valley are two fairly large pans: Sunday and Leopard. A waymarked 9km 'loop' – really more of a 5km semi-circular detour off the main track to Leopard Pan – allows you to drive around the edge of Sunday Pan rather than stick to the central track. It starts in the south at ✪ SUPLPS 21°20.970'S, 23°40.505'E, continuing round to rejoin the original track at ✪ SUPLPN 21°19.374'S, 23°40.966'E.

Any of the **campsites** around these pans make a good first stop if you enter the reserve via the Matswere Gate and plan on heading to the area around Passarge Valley. The more southerly Sunday Pan has three campsites. The first, CKS1, or CKSUN-02, is slightly left of the track when you're driving north, at ✪ CKS1 21°21.104'S, 23°40.285'E. Further on, the turn-off to the second and third sites (CKS2 and CKS3, or CKSUN-04 and 03) is to the right, at ✪ CKS2-3 21°20.071'S, 23°40.893'E. All are pleasant, in the edge of the bush close to the main open area of the pan.

Towards Leopard Pan about 5km further north, is a fourth campsite, CKL1, or CKSUN-01 (✪ CKL1 21°17.532'S, 23°42.545'E).

PASSARGE VALLEY This is a long valley with many pans and several campsites. Approaching from the east, it's easily reached from Leopard Pan by finding the junction of tracks to the north of the pan (✪ LEFORK 21°17.287'S, 23°41.938'E), and heading north from there.

Initially the landscape is quite a thick mixture of small trees and bushes: typical Kalahari sandveld. Then after about 13km you'll find an old green sign saying: 'Passarge Valley. Help keep this valley pristine by staying on the track.' Gradually – now heading southwest – you descend into a valley with a more open landscape and more grassland. About 9.5km further there's a turning south to Manong **Campsite**, coded CKA1/CKPAS-01 (✪ CKA1 21°13.844'S, 23°37.308'E), a lovely campsite set very much on its own.

Continuing in the valley for another 18km you'll then find a track to the north signposted to Kgokong Campsite, CKA2/CKPAS-02 (✪ CKA2 21°16.157'S,

23°28.666'E). Here the valley is really stunning: open grassland dotted with a few small tree-islands. The campsite is in the thickets just off to the side, slightly above the floor of the valley.

Further southwest, the third of Passarge's campsites is Kukama Campsite, CKA3/ CKPAS-03 (◈ CKA3 21°19.965'S, 23°20.319'E), in a small group of trees beside a fairly scrubby pan. This is about 12km northeast of the junction with the park's main east–west cutline track, at ◈ PATURN 21°23.924'S, 23°15.136'E.

PASSARGE PAN AND MOTOPI PAN A little beyond the southwest end of the Passarge Valley track, Passarge Pan is on the south side of the track which leads to a water pump (◈ PUMP1 21°24.676'S, 23°13.718'E). North of here a track leads through some lovely country dotted with small pans to Motopi Pan, where three new **campsites** have been established: CKMOT-01 (◈ CKMOT1 21°08.080'S, 23°04.443'E), CKMOT-02 (◈ CKMOT2 21°10.572'S, 23°04.810'E) and CKMOT-03 (◈ CKMOT3 21°09.914'S, 23°06.100'E). This track leads ultimately to the double fence which is the northern boundary of the reserve (◈ MOTCUT 21°00.194'S, 23°06.400'E). Note that there is no open gate here, and no direct way in or out of the reserve at this point. However, when you reach the fence you'll find a decent track that lies parallel to the fence. To the right, this runs east beside the fence, and then southeast from Kuke Corner (still confined within the park's boundary fence) to the main Matswere Gate. To the left a similar track runs west to the new Tsau Gate (◈ TSAUGT 21°00.060'S, 22°47.822'E), and from there to the Kuke Gate on the main Maun–Ghanzi road.

THE WESTERN LINK On the northeast side of Passarge Pan, the track south towards Phukwi, Tau, San and Phokoje pans starts at ◈ PATURN 21°23.924'S, 23°15.136'E. This track is the start of the 'western link', which eventually heads south towards Piper Pans.

You'll see from the map that this track seems to zigzag, always heading either north–south or east–west; this is because the inter-dune valleys (with their string of pans) run east–west. These valleys usually make the best game-viewing areas. They are linked by tracks running north–south, across the top of the dunes.

Note that on this track, the first few kilometres south of the main cutline track (◈ PATURN) is very boggy; I'd expect this to be exceedingly challenging during the rains.

For an alternative route south, you can enter the western link via Tau Pan. To do this, first turn east along the cutline towards the north end of Deception Valley. About 18km from ◈ PATURN, there's a track which heads almost due south to Phukwi Pan. For many years there was a campsite on this route, at Tau Pan, but this was closed when Tau Pan Camp was completed in 2009. In its place comes a new site, CKTAU-02, at San Pan (◈ CKTAU2 21°33.262'S, 23°11.507'E). In addition, there is CKT2/CKTAU-03 (◈ CKT2 21°35.278'S, 23°16.332'E), which is roughly halfway along the track that follows Phokoje Pan. Heading east along this, the track splits off southeast from Phokoje Pan about 18km before its junction (◈ LETIAH 21°38.380'S, 23°25.023'E) with the main track from the Letiahau Valley to Piper Pans.

PIPER PANS Piper Pans are as far south as most people visit in the northern section of the park, and as far as I'll describe in this chapter. If you are wondering if it's worth the effort to get here, the answer is a resounding 'yes'. And that's despite a badly corrugated section of road just north of this area.

The complex of pans is only a few kilometres across, but it's a stunning stretch of perfectly flat grass. In the rains it's green, and often covered with springbok and

16

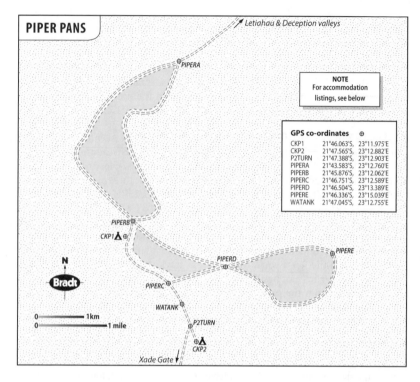

PIPER PANS

Letiahau & Deception valleys

PIPERA

NOTE
For accommodation
listings, see below

GPS co-ordinates	⊕
CKP1	21°46.063'S, 23°11.975'E
CKP2	21°47.565'S, 23°12.882'E
P2TURN	21°47.388'S, 23°12.903'E
PIPERA	21°43.583'S, 23°12.760'E
PIPERB	21°45.876'S, 23°12.062'E
PIPERC	21°46.751'S, 23°12.589'E
PIPERD	21°46.504'S, 23°13.389'E
PIPERE	21°46.336'S, 23°15.039'E
WATANK	21°47.045'S, 23°12.755'E

PIPERB
CKP1
N
Bradt
PIPERD
PIPERE
PIPERC
WATANK
0   1km
0   1 mile
P2TURN
CKP2
Xade Gate

gemsbok. By as early as May, it has usually turned a beautiful gold, like a field of ripe barley.

There are two **campsites** here. CKP1/CKPIP-01 (⊕ CKP1 21°46.063'S, 23°11.975'E), slightly further north, is in a grove of rather lovely trees on the west side of the track, but close to the edge of the pan.

The second site, CKP2/CKPIP-02 (⊕ CKP2 21°47.565'S, 23°12.882'E) is further south, up higher on a low fossilised dune. This is just beyond a prominent green water tank (⊕ WATANK 21°47.045'S, 23°12.755'E) which stands at the top of a fossilised dune, beside the track which leads, around 72km later, to Xade.

Around the outside edge of the pan itself there's a 7km circular track that is well worth exploring, although impassable during the rains. The eastern side of this (around ⊕ PIPERE 21°46.336'S, 23°15.039'E) is particularly treacherous black-cotton soil, while it often seems to disappear on the southern side. It's a lovely circuit, but very slow driving even when dry, as the hardened earth is very uneven.

LETIAHAU VALLEY Approaching from the south and Piper Pans, the road to Matswere leads first through Letiahau and then Deception Valley. About 12km northeast of the junction (⊕ LETIAH 21°38.380'S, 23°25.023'E), which is the turning north for the western link, the track enters the picturesque Letiahau Valley. A further 4km on there's a small turning south from the road which, after about 100m, leads to a group of trees in a bushy plain where the Letiahau **Campsite**, coded CKWIL-06 (⊕ CKL3 21°36.447'S, 23°33.407'E) is situated. Around 6km further east, a tiny loop takes a closer look at the permanent Letiahau waterhole.

About 20km east of the first campsite is a second one called Lekhubu, CKWIL-07 (⊕ CKL2 21°35.401'S, 23°44.755'E), off on the south side of the road. Continuing

On one morning's game viewing, driving slowly north into the end of Deception Valley, we spotted something unfamiliar moving in the distance. Training our binoculars, we could see a woman waving. We signalled that we'd seen her and continued, eventually taking a right track to head in her direction.

Approaching with some trepidation, we found a distressed Tswana woman on her own. She'd been standing on the roof of the 4x4 all morning, trying to attract attention. In fact she was one of the park's staff who, together with a few colleagues, had been driving from the Matswere Scout Post to Xade (I never learned why they were on a side-track off the main route!).

It seems that late the previous day the fuel filter in their old Land Rover had sprung a bad leak, marooning them there. They'd slept overnight but, with little water or food, her colleagues had set off to walk the 50km or so back to Matswere, and perhaps find visitors on the way who could help.

I spent a petrol-soaked hour under the vehicle, attempting a bush repair with no success, before offering her a lift back to the park's office. However, it transpired that this was the scout camp's only vehicle, so they wouldn't be able to do much. Hours later a better-equipped, modern Land Rover approached; it carried a bush-wise South African couple who travelled with what seemed like a garage full of spares and tools. The park workers had managed to flag this vehicle down and enlist the couple's help.

They were lucky. The park's remaining staff would have been virtually powerless to help, even if they'd known about the breakdown. Fortunately these visitors had the right tools and spare parts, so a repair was soon made. All set off again to Xade in their clapped-out Land Rover with few supplies. I hope they got there.

The morals of this story are simple:

- Don't expect any help from the park's staff: they probably won't have the vehicles or resources.
- Don't come to the CKGR without some basic spares, a simple tool kit and another vehicle to help you out.
- A satellite phone isn't totally necessary, but is a wise back-up, so bring one if possible.
- Ample food and water are absolutely essential: bring more than you expect to need.

east from this, the track backs around to take a more northerly line as it approaches Deception Valley.

DECEPTION PAN This open pan (⊕ DECPAN 21°24.291'S, 23°46.434'E) at the southern end of the valley is found by taking a short detour, about 1.5km from the main track. It fills with water during the rains, but for the rest of the year it's flat, cracked mud, tinged a vivid red colour by a small red water plant which flourishes when it's full.

DECEPTION VALLEY This is a broad inter-dune valley running roughly north–south; it's thought to be the bed of a fossil river. During and after good rains this is carpeted in luscious green grass that attracts dense concentrations of game. It's the park's most famous location, and where Mark and Delia Owens (see *Appendix 3*, page 541) lived. If you are visiting the northern section of the park for five to six days, then my advice is for you to save this as a highlight for your last couple of days.

Because it is the park's most famous area, and relatively close (35km) to the Matswere Scout Post entrance, this is the place where you're most likely to see other visitors. It's also the area with the most campsites.

Towards the northern end of Deception Valley, on the west side, a track splits off to pass beside the four kori campsites (CKK1–CKK4, or CKKOR-01 to CKKOR-04), which are spread across a distance of almost 1km. The most southerly one is located at ✪ CKK1 21°25.699'S, 23°47.921'E, and the most northerly at ✪ CKK4 21°25.006'S, 23°47.433'E. They're in fairly sparse bush on the edge of the main pan, and generally very close to any animal action there – though with the exception of CKK4, views of the pan are usually obscured by vegetation. There's also limited privacy, as a track runs almost through some of the sites.

Deception Valley's other campsites are all set north of the pan, higher up in fairly thick woodlands with some of the best shade in the park. There are six of these (CKD1–CKD6, or CKDEC-01 to CKDEC-06), three on either side of the cutline road. CKD4 (✪ CKD4 21°24.213'S, 23°46.287'E) consists of a roughly circular area that has been cleared of trees and bushes. Each campsite is separated from its neighbours by a few hundred metres, making them very secluded and private.

When you leave the park, simply drive towards the north of Deception Valley. There you'll find several small junctions with signposts, as the tracks along the valley are intersected by the straight cutline road. Head east to ✪ JUNCT1 21°24.301'S, 23°48.193'E, and continue on to sign out at the Matswere Gate (✪ CKGATE 21°09.399'S, 24°00.417'E).

17

Livingstone and the Victoria Falls

I've included here a brief chapter on Livingstone and the Victoria Falls as many visitors to northern Botswana will either start or end their trips here. The Victoria Falls are a magnificent sight, and few can resist a couple of nights here in addition to time on safari.

Until the 1990s, Livingstone often remained unseen, and some even viewed it with suspicion, being bigger and less well known than the small Zimbabwean town that shares the name of the waterfall. Today, though, Livingstone has become popular in its own right; its riverside lodges are close to the Falls, and yet a perfect complement to Botswana's small camps, and it offers all the thrills and spills that have come to characterise the area. While Zimbabwe's small town of Victoria Falls is re-emerging from the country's recent troubled politics, most visitors now choose to stay on the northern (Livingstone) side. Yet the two sides of the Falls offer different views, and it is worth seeing both to appreciate the whole waterfall. Thus many visitors still venture across the border for an afternoon to see the waterfall from the Zimbabwean side.

This chapter aims to give you an overview of Livingstone: what to do, where to stay and how to get organised. For comprehensive details on Livingstone and the Falls, and on Zambia as a whole, see the latest edition of my *Zambia: The Bradt Travel Guide*.

LIVINGSTONE

GETTING THERE AND AWAY
By air Livingstone's international airport (m *0977 770961*), just 5km northwest of the town centre, underwent an extensive programme of upgrading and redevelopment in 2013.

The spacious entrance hall of the new terminal has pleasant waiting rooms, airline offices, banks (⏲ *08.15–16.00 Mon–Fri, 08.15–noon/15.00 Sat*) with ATMs, a post office, bureau de change, car-hire kiosks and a desk for Bushtracks Africa. You can also buy curios and sundries such as sweets and postcards. A coffee shop (⏲ *07.00–18.00 daily*) serves local dishes and a range of snacks, then once you've passed through passport control you'll find a small bar, 'private' lounge (*US$25 pp, inc unlimited drinks*) and a café with breakfast options, snacks and light meals on offer. There's a bag-wrapping service here, you'll also find a duty-free shop and a few more curio outlets, including Kubu Crafts. Complimentary Wi-Fi is available throughout.

Airlines Both Comair and South African Airways have daily flights between Johannesburg and Livingstone, taking around 1½ hours. Kenya Airways flies three times a week between Nairobi and Livingstone, while Airlink flies daily to Nelspruit in South Africa. Internal and charter airlines include:

LIVINGSTONE & VICTORIA FALLS

↑ *Lusaka*

Livingstone
Airport

AIRPORT ROAD

pages 514–15

HILLCREST

LIVINGSTONE

NORTH
END

MARAMBA

MALOTA

DAMBWA
NORTH

*Riverside lodges,
Elephant Café,
Kazungula,
(Botswana)*

NAKATINDI ROAD

FALLS VIEW

LIBUYU

Park gate

KASHITU

in special use only

Channa's
Motors

Railway
station

LINDA

DAMBWA

Bushtracks
Africa

Waya Waya

Falls Park
shopping centre

Maramba

Mosi-oa-Tunya
National Park

*Old Drift
Cemetery*

Game Park gate

Zambezi

ZAMBIA

(ROYAL MILE)

SICHANGO RD

Livingstone
Reptile Park

N

Bradt

The Boat Club
African Queen

Vuma

*Siloka
Island*

0 ————— 2km
0 ————— 1 mile

ZIMBABWE

Picnic
site

*Mukuni
Village*

VICTORIA FALLS

Entrance
gate

Victoria Falls
(waterfall)

Baobab tree

Airstrip

Entrance to Falls/
curio market

VICTORIA FALLS ROAD

page 523

Gorge
swing

Mosi-oa-Tunya
National Park

Songwe

Zambezi

↓ *Hwange, Bulawayo*

512

✈ **Proflight** ✆0213 324745; e reservations@
proflight-zambia.com, livingstonesales@proflight-
zambia.com; www.flyzambia.com
✈ **Wilderness Air** ✆0213 321578/80; m 0966
770485 (24hr); e reservations@wilderness-air.
co.zm; www.wilderness-air.com

By bus Construction has been underway
for several years now on a major new bus
station [515 B6] between Nakatindi and
Kafubu Road, just west of the town centre.
Originally scheduled for completion in
2013 for the UNWTO General Assembly,
it's still very much a work in progress.
Once it opens, all bus companies will
relocate their booking offices there,
including one of the town's most reliable
companies, Shalom, and Mazhandu
Family Bus Services, making the service
much easier for passengers. Until then,
buses are leaving from the main terminus
off Chimemwe Road.

Most are headed to Lusaka, but for
visitors to or from Botswana, your best
bet is to board the Mazhandu Family Bus
to Mongu, which stops in Kazungula and
Sesheke. It's wise to buy tickets the day
before, and to be at the bus station at least half an hour before departure, since
buses often leave early if they're full.

LIVINGSTONE & VICTORIA FALLS
For listings, see pages 518–21

🛏 **Where to stay**
1   Avani Victoria Falls Resort..........C6
2   Chrismar Hotel.............................B4
3   David Livingstone Safari
      Lodge & Spa................................B4
4   Maramba River Lodge.................C4
5   Protea Hotel Livingstone...........C3
6   Royal Livingstone.........................C5
7   Royal Sichango Village................B4
8   Stanley Safari Lodge...................D5
9   Victoria Falls Waterfront............B4

Off map
      Riverside lodges: A3
         Islands of Siankaba
         The River Club
         Royal Chundu Zambezi
            River & Island Lodge
         Sindabezi Island
         Sussi & Chuma
         Thorntree River Lodge
         Toka Leya
         Tongabezi
         Waterberry Zambezi
            Lodge

✖ **Where to eat and drink**
      Avani.....................................(see 1)
      Royal Livingstone..................(see 6)
      Victoria Falls Waterfront.....(see 9)
10   Zigzag... B3
Off map
      Elephant Café............................A3

Driving west Those heading west, into Botswana, Namibia's Caprivi Strip
or western Zambia, should take the Nakatindi Road – signposted as the M10 –
that runs west, past the lodges along the river. After about 70km this comes to
Kazungula – where you can take the ferry across the Zambezi into Botswana, near
Kasane, or continue northwest within Zambia to Sesheke.

GETTING AROUND Livingstone town is small enough to walk around, as is the Falls
area. To travel between the two, or to the airport, use one of the plentiful light-blue
taxis that congregate at the main taxi stand [514 B2] or on Mosi-oa-Tunya Road
opposite the craft market [514 E3]. A taxi between town and either the Falls or
the airport will cost around Kw70–100/US$7–10 for up to four passengers. To the
riverside lodges, you'll be charged from around Kw150–200/US$15–20, depending
on the location. Negotiate – and be sure to agree on the price in advance.

By bus Minibuses run to the Falls [512 C6] from the Town Centre Market in the
centre of Livingstone throughout the day, departing when they are full.

Driving yourself Driving yourself in Livingstone is pretty straightforward, and
most lodges, and hotels and the larger restaurants have secure parking. Cars can
be hired with or without a driver (the former is often a cheaper option). For a self-
drive safari, you can rent a 4x4 with full kit.

For listings, see pages 516–21

Where to stay

1 Green Tree Lodge............A3
2 Jollyboys Backpackers......C5
3 Jollyboys Camp.............E6
4 Likute Guesthouse..........E3
5 Ngolide Lodge..............D8
6 Olga's Guesthouse..........D6

Where to eat and drink

7   Café Zambezi..............D7
8   Da Fusion.................B2
9   Fez Bar...................D6
10 The Golden Leaf...........D8
11 Hungry Lion...........(see 6)
    Olga's................(see 6)
12 Wonderbake................B1

LINDA

KUNWA   ROAD
KASOLO   ROAD
MULELE   ROAD
SEKUTE   ROAD
KWAME   NKRUMAH   ROAD
NYASA   ROAD
NGOMA   ROAD
CHIPEMBI ROAD
SIAMBELELE ROAD
JOHANE   ROAD

Livingstone Royal Golf & Country Club
Golf course

Central police station

see inset

SENANGA ROAD
TANZANIA ROAD
MAKAMBO ROAD
Southern Medical Centre
Total
Puma
KABOMPO RD
Kobil
Pharmacy
Church
NAKATINDI ROAD
MOSI-OA-TUNYA ROAD
Mosi-oa-Tunya Square
Kubu Crafts
Wild Side Tours & Safaris
Railway station

LIMULUNGA   ROAD
CHITIMUKULU   ROAD
NKUMBI   ROAD
KAFUBU ROAD

Protea Hotel Livingstone, Waya Waya, SES, Zigzag, Victoria Falls, Zimbabwe

Riverside lodges, Elephant Café, Kazungula (Botswana)
M10
New bus station
NAKATINDI ROAD
KAFUBU ROAD
LITUNGA ROAD
CHISHIMBA FALLS ROAD
Protea Hotel Livingstone, Waya Waya

DAMBWA CENTRAL
KALANGA ROAD
UNDI STREET
NJOVO ST
MONGU STREET
Railway Museum

400m
400yds

N
Bradt

515

In town, you're likely to come across any number of volunteers to look after your car. If you're prepared to trust someone then – in spite of considerable protestations to the contrary – a tip of about Kw3–5/US$0.30–0.50 should be about right, depending on the length of time you're away.

There are several 24-hour fuel stations on the main Mosi-oa-Tunya Road.

WHERE TO STAY Numerous bush lodges occupy charming locations along the Zambezi River, some near enough to enjoy the attractions and activities of the Falls easily, others further upstream and more remote. Closer to town, and to the Falls, an increasing number of upmarket hotels, some on the river, and others in a more urban setting, offer Western creature comforts. At the cheaper end of the market, staying in a guesthouse or in-town lodge, where you may meet African travellers or volunteers from overseas, can add a multi-cultural dimension to your visit, while backpacker accommodation tends to cater strictly to the international budget traveller.

Accommodation options listed here are among the best in an increasingly crowded market. For the purposes of this guide, we have concentrated on those that are either relatively close to the Falls or within easy reach of the Botswana border at Kazungula. For full details of these and other options, see my companion guide, *Zambia: The Bradt Travel Guide*.

Game park and close to the Falls

 Stanley Safari Lodge [512 D5] (10 cottages) Robin Pope Safaris; reservations ☎+265 993 504600; m 0967 848615; e info@

robinpopesafaris.net; www.robinpopesafaris. net. With the spray of the Falls in the distance & sweeping vistas towards the Zambezi, the lodge is best suited as a place to chill out, relax & unwind.

Inside the high electric fence, vast, fairly formal gardens with a central infinity pool are backed by a beautifully designed thatched building with an open-aspect lounge, bar & dining area, free Wi-Fi, & a wine cellar for candlelit tastings. Stylish 'cottages' with king-size or twin beds are all slightly different, some with a 'loo with a view' & an outside shower & bath, others more enclosed. The honeymoon suite has its own plunge pool & fireplace, & the family room, with a paddling pool, & bucket shower around a tree, works well for children. *Cottage US$415–520; open suite US$460–610; closed suite US$520–680; all pp sharing, FBA; inc local drinks, laundry & airport transfers.* ★ ★ ★

⌂ **David Livingstone Safari Lodge & Spa** [512 B4] (77 rooms) ✆0213 324601; e lodge@ dlslandspa.com; www.aha.co.za/davidlivingstone. This efficient, 5-star hotel under steep thatch has a prime spot on the river. The main reception, rooms, restaurants & infinity pool command excellent views of the river & the lodge's own riverboat, the *Lady Livingstone*. Basketwork lampshades, terracotta pots & wooden sculptures dominate the décor in the communal areas, & concrete walkways with rustic railings lead to tastefully appointed rooms with small balconies. There's Wi-Fi throughout, plus an award-winning spa, a gym, gift shop & activity centre. The lodge offers complimentary shuttles to Livingstone town & the Falls. $$$$$

⌂ **Royal Livingstone** [512 C5] (173 rooms) Mosi-oa-Tunya Rd; m 0978 777044/7; reservations ✆+27 10 003 8977; e royallivingstone@ anantaracom; www.royal-livingstone.anantara. com. If the broad, low, white frontage is rather unassuming at first glance, inside all is spacious & elegant, with an old-world attention to detail & service that befits its 5 stars. Sweeping lawns lead down to an unparalleled frontage along the Zambezi, just a 15min walk along the river from the Falls, though hotel staff are also on hand with golf carts. Views from the pool & riverfront massage tents are also stunning, especially with zebra, impala & giraffe grazing in the grounds. $$$$$

⌂ **Avani Victoria Falls Resort** [512 C6] (212 rooms) 393 Mosi-oa-Tunya Rd; m 0978 777044; reservations ✆+27 10 003 8977; e victoriafalls@minorhotels.com; www. minorhotels.com/en/avani/victoria-falls. Known as the Zambezi Sun until Minor Hotels took over in 2014, this lively 3-star offering is rather North African in style, with earthy red buildings overlooking extensive lawns. Vervet monkeys romp through the grounds & a large pool snakes through the centre. The location is unbeatable: though you can't see them from the hotel, you're just a few hundred metres' walk from the lip of the Falls & the curio market, & with unrestricted access. $$$$$

⌂ **Chrismar Hotel** [512 B4] (99 rooms) Sichango Rd; ✆0213 323141, 0213 324578; e book@chrismarhotels.co.zm; www. chrismarhotels.com. This mid-market hotel near the entrance to the national park is well thought out & offers good value for money. While it is not on the river, its bush setting is enhanced by numerous fountains & water features, including the largest swimming pool in town (a popular expat party hang-out), complete with a sunken bar in the middle. Rooms with AC, TV & Wi-Fi, in a range of styles up to executive suites, are set around spacious grounds, & wouldn't disgrace a hotel of far better quality. $$$$

⌂ **Victoria Falls Waterfront** [512 B4] (23 rooms, 12 tents, camping) Off Sichango Rd; ✆0213 320606–8; m 0968 320606; e waterfront@ safpar.com; www.thevictoriafallswaterfront.com. This large, secure & affordable complex sits on the riverfront within Mosi-oa-Tunya National Park, just 4km upstream of the Falls – with some of the best sunset views over the Zambezi. It's broadly split into 2 sites: 1 has a spacious restaurant with a pizza oven, a large bar (with satellite TV), a sunken pool, & the best of the accommodation; the other houses the Adventure Village with a natural-style rock pool, a 2nd bar & an auditorium, plus a decidedly noisy, though sociable, camping area, popular with overland trucks. Renovations in 2018 will include the addition of further chalets. *Camping US$13 pp.* $$$$

⌂ **Royal Sichango Village** [512 B4] (14 chalets, camping) Sichango Rd; ✆0213 322446; e info@ bushfront.com. Previously known as The Bushfront Lodge, Royal Sichango borders the national park a few kilometres upriver from the Falls, with thatched chalets set among indigenous vegetation. Chalets have en-suite bathrooms with potted plants; deluxe chalets have AC & satellite TV. There's also space for 80+ campers in 3 individual tent pitches, with modern ablutions & a braai area, plus a large bar/ lounge with free Wi-Fi, DSTV, a restaurant & a small pool. *Camping US$10 pp.* $$$–$$$$

⌂ **Maramba River Lodge** [512 C4] (9 chalets, 23 tents, camping) ✆0213 324189; m 0976

587511; e reservations@marambariverlodge. com; www.maramba-zambia.com. This well-established lodge & campsite is a real oasis in the bush, with green lawns & mature trees beloved of hippos & elephants – so it's important to be on the alert at all times. Particularly good for families, the lodge has a dedicated activity booking office, pool, children's play area, craft shop & fully licensed riverside bar & restaurant, with Wi-Fi. En-suite accommodation ranges from tented chalets to simple twin-bedded safari tents, while campers share an ablution block. *Camping US$10 pp.* **$$$**

Beside the Zambezi: upriver [off 512 A3] Lodges & camps are listed here in order of their proximity to the Falls.

Toka Leya [512 A3] (12 tented chalets) Contact Wilderness Safaris, page 225. 5km or so from Livingstone, & set within the national park, Toka Leya's canvas & natural wood chalets face the river from wide wooden verandas. Glass sliding doors lead to a bedroom & dressing area, with four-poster beds enveloped by mosi nets, desk, chairs, plus AC/ heating & a fan. It's all airy & spacious, with Persian-style rugs & bright lamps to liven up the understated décor. Wooden walkways link the chalets to the main lounge & restaurant area, down to the bar, tree-shaded deck & carved metal firepit – as well as a small infinity pool, & simple riverside spa. Explore with boat trips, game drives & birding/nature walks, or book trips further afield. *US$625–795 pp sharing, FBA, inc local drinks, laundry, 2 activities/day; exc spa treatments.* ★★★–★★★★★

Sussi & Chuma [512 A3] (12 chalets, 2 houses) Named after David Livingstone's loyal friends, who carried his body from Zambia back to Dar es Salaam, the lodge is set in the national park just 15mins' drive from Livingstone. Raised on stilts & tucked into an area of riverine forest, the chalets are reminiscent of treehouses. With remodelling due in 2018 you can expect spacious, wide-open rooms with high thatched ceilings & exposed rafters, complemented by cream walls & natural fabrics, & with more private en-suite facilities. 2 Chuma houses, each with 2 en-suite bedrooms, private plunge pool, chef & butler, are great for families or small groups. *Chalet US$585–720 pp sharing, house US$800–990 pp sharing, FBA, inc local drinks, park fees, laundry; exc spa treatments. Children under 6 in houses only.* ★★★–★★★★★

Thorntree River Lodge (10 suites) +27 21 701 0270; e info@africanbushcamps.com; www.africanbushcamps.com. 15km from the Falls, within the national park, Thorntree was completely redeveloped & reopened in 2017. Spacious, light chalets with private plunge pools blend into the surrounding landscape, with the stylish main area encompassing a comfortable bar, wine cellar, lounge & dining area with riverside deck & firepit. Adjacent huts house a spa, gym & curio shop, plus library with DSTV & Wi-Fi. *US$600/780 low/ high season, pp sharing, FBA, inc drinks, transfers, laundry & park fees.* ★★★–★★★★★

The River Club [512 A3] (11 chalets) 0213 327457; m 0962 650138; e reservations@ theriverclubzambia.com; www.theriverclubzambia. com. Nestled among indigenous trees within spacious grounds, The River Club has stunning views over the Zambezi. The atmosphere is distinctly colonial, with décor & service to match. Large, thatched, stilted chalets boast teak furniture & beautifully polished floors, while 3 suites offer larger decks, a family unit & private plunge pools. It's elegant – yet with a stunning infinity pool, a gym, tennis court, sauna & jacuzzi, AC, & Wi-Fi throughout, there's more than a nod to the modern era. *River suite US$426–523, luxury suite US$476– 695, all pp sharing, FBA, inc drinks & laundry; exc transfers.* ★★★–★★★★★

✳ **Tongabezi** (5 cottages, 6 houses) 0213 327450; m 0979 312766; e reservations@ tongabezi.com; www.tongabezi.com. Set on a sweeping bend of the Zambezi, 15km west of town, Tongabezi's setting is matched by excellent service. Individual & tastefully decorated cottages & houses are all different – & carefully secluded – with the services of a dedicated private valet. Sumptuous meals are served on the riverside deck, near to the swimming pool & firepit, or in the dining room – a spacious, stylish building perched on the hillside, with captivating views. You can even arrange to dine on a floating 'sampan' – perhaps after a relaxing massage. A new, large swimming pool & gym are due to be completed in 2018. *Cottage US$655/775, house US$755/875, Nut & Dog House US$875/995, low/high season (Nov– May/Jun–Oct), pp sharing, FBA, inc local drinks & laundry; exc transfers, park fees. 40% sgl supp't high season; no children under 7.* ★★★★

Sindabezi Island [512 A3] (5 chalets) Contact via Tongabezi, above. A short boat trip downstream from Tongabezi, Sindabezi offers barefoot luxury on an island retreat that looks across into the national park. Its en-suite chalets are private, comfortable & deceptively spacious. During the day, mealtimes are taken in the shade of the ebony trees; in the evening, enjoy a drink by the campfire, or take in the surroundings from the high viewing deck. *Chalet US$520/595, honeymoon chalet US$560/676, low/high season (Nov–May/ Jun–Oct), pp sharing, FBA, inc drinks, laundry & transfers to/from island.* ★★★–★★★★★

☀ 🏠 **Waterberry Zambezi Lodge** [512 A3] (7 chalets) 📞0213 327455; enquiries +44 (0)1379 873474; e reservations@waterberrylodge.com; www.waterberrylodge.com. Set in a secluded position on the banks of the Zambezi, 35mins' drive from Livingstone, Waterberry offers style, comfort & service worthy of its modest price tag. Comfortable & clean rooms, named after local birds, are all en suite with fans & mosi nets, plus small lounge areas. Grouped around the 2-storey main building & pool, & set in beautifully manicured gardens, with a lagoon, play area & nature trails, the site is open & welcoming – though as it's frequented by hippos, a degree of caution is needed with children. Waterberry's River Farmhouse, with 4 bedrooms, spacious lounge & dining room, its own chef & a private swimming pool, is well suited to families. *US$445 pp sharing, farmhouse US$510 pp up to 4 guests (additional guest US$445), FBA, inc local drinks, laundry & transfers.* ★★★

🏠 **Islands of Siankaba** [512 A3] (6 chalets, 1 honeymoon/VIP chalet) 📞0213 327490; reservations 📞0211 260279; m 0977 720530; e info@siankaba.net; www.siankaba.net. This exclusive lodge, offering superb cuisine & considerable attention to detail, is 55km from Livingstone, so stay here & enjoy it for its own sake. Reached by a short boat ride, Siankaba lies on 2 separate islands. One houses the large chalets, nestled among the trees & regally furnished with four-poster beds, teak furniture & claw-footed bathtubs. On the other is the restaurant & bar/ lounge area, with natural décor & tables on the terrace for alfresco dining. A secluded pool & spa are hidden among the trees, a nature trail runs round the island & bikes & mekoro allow you to explore. *Chalet US$456/617; honeymoon chalet US$609/630 low/high season, pp sharing, FBA, inc drinks, laundry & transfers. No children under 10.* ★★★

🏠 **Royal Chundu Zambezi River & Island Lodge** [514 A3] (10 river suites, 4 island villas) Lodge 📞0213 327060; reservations: 📞+27 13 751 1038; e reservations@royalchundu.com; www. royalchundu.com. 1½hrs' drive from the Falls, the upmarket Royal Chundu is on a wooded private stretch of the river, visited by just the occasional canoeist, & a haven for birds. At its heart, linked by walkways to solid & very smart chalets that boast all the accoutrements of a 5-star hotel, a sparkling infinity pool overlooks the river. A TV lounge, small library & computer room are tucked well away, but more typical are the floating riverside spa & formal dining room – complete with fireplace, polished silver, fine wines & cigars. On a separate island, exclusive villas offer luxury & utmost privacy, with four-poster beds, outside bathtubs & private dining & spa experiences. Do take part in their canoeing b/fast: it's a highlight. *River Lodge US$910; Island Lodge US$1,127, all pp sharing FB, inc drinks, laundry & airport transfers; exc spa treatments.* ★★★★★

In town
🏠 **Protea Hotel Livingstone** [512 C3] (80 rooms, 13 apts) Mosi-oa-Tunya Rd; 📞0213 324630; e reservations@phlivingstone.co.zm; www.proteahotels.com. Just south of the railway, this surprisingly elegant hotel has dbl, twin & family rooms, classically styled & comfortable, surrounding an attractive courtyard. You'll also find a large swimming pool, a restaurant & bar, & plenty of loungers. As well as a formal restaurant, the hotel has its own activity centre & curio shop, free Wi-Fi, secure parking & a business centre. **$$$$**

🏠 **Green Tree Lodge** [514 A3] (6 chalets) 2015 Kombe Dr; 📞0213 322631; m 0977 630159; e greentreelodge@livingstonezambia.com; www. greentreelodgezambia.com. Individual en-suite chalets boast dbl or twin beds, AC, fridge, TV, Wi-Fi & kettle, & its own veranda, & a new family chalet was added in 2017. The lodge has a welcoming pool & bar, a small restaurant & secure parking. **$$$**

🏠 **Likute Guesthouse** [514 E3] (13 rooms) 62 Likute Way; 📞0213 323661/264; m 0977 603971; e likute_guest_house@yahoo.com. Within a small walled complex, the clean & welcoming Likute has large en-suite rooms with AC, mosi nets, satellite TV, kettle & fridge. The staff are friendly, meals are available on request & there's secure parking. **$$**

17

Ngolide Lodge [515 D8] (16 rooms) 110 Mosi-oa-Tunya Rd; 0213 321091/2; e ngolidelodge@gmail.com; www.ngolidelodge. com. More of a mini-hotel than a lodge, this thatched building is well built & compact, if a bit dark. Small but comfortable & well-equipped rooms under high thatch lead off a central quadrangle that is surrounded by a shallow 'moat' & open gardens. There's Wi-Fi access & a licensed bar. The lodge also runs the nearby Golden Leaf restaurant, serving among the best Indian cuisine in Livingstone. **$$**

Olga's Guesthouse [515 D6] (8 rooms) Nakatindi Rd; 0213 324160; e info@olgasproject. com; www.olgasproject.com. Clean & comfortable thatched en-suite rooms with mosi nets & fans were added here in 2012, though the associated (& popular) pizza place (see opposite) is well established. All proceeds go to the Local Youth Community Training Centre, which provides training to local orphans & disadvantaged youths. Discounts are available for NGO workers & clergy. **$$**

Jollyboys Backpackers [515 C5] (14 en-suite rooms, 11 with shared ablutions, 32 dorm beds, camping) 34 Kanyanta Rd; 0213

324229, 0213 322086; e res@backpackzambia. com; www.backpackzambia.com. The ever-popular Jollyboys occupies a central, tree-shaded site just a few mins' walk from the town centre. Owner-run & friendly, it deserves its reputation as the quintessential backpackers' lodge. En-suite, shared ablution & dorm (with AC!) rooms are set around a thatched courtyard, & at its heart is a wonderful sunken lounge with plenty of cushions. As well as a pool table, table tennis & enticing rock swimming pool, there's an open-plan bar with DSTV, a restaurant, & self-catering kitchen. Free Wi-Fi, activity centre, bike hire, laundry service, secure parking & a book exchange complete the picture. *8-bed dorm US$15–18 pp; en-suite room US$65; shared ablutions room US$45; camping US$9 pp.* **$–$$** *exc b/fast.*

Jollyboys Camp [515 E6] (32 dorm beds, 8 en-suite rooms, 6 twin chalets, camping) 80 Chipembi Rd; 0213 324756; e res@ backpackzambia.com; www.backpackzambia.com. This offshoot of Jollyboys has a greater focus on family & group accommodation – there's even a jungle gym for the kids. *Dorm bed US$14; camping US$7 pp.* **$–$$** *exc b/fast.*

✕ WHERE TO EAT AND DRINK

Restaurants Livingstone's independent and hotel restaurants offer a wide variety of cuisine at fairly decent prices. It's worth remembering that hotel establishments, while usually more expensive, often cater to foreign tastes.

Elephant Café [512 A3] 0213 320606/8; www.elephant.cafe; ⏰ b/fast 06.10–10.00, lunch 10.00–14.30, high tea 14.15–18.15, dinner 15.15–21.15. Opened in 2016, 10km upriver from the Falls, this elephant interaction combined with sumptuous dining is an experience not to miss. Previously used for elephant rides, the elephants here are relaxed & well fed, & you can meet these gentle giants

before tucking into a 4-course meal (*US$230*), sourced with local ingredients. Advance booking is essential – opt for the speedboat transfer to make the most of the riverside location. **$$$$$** *inc drinks, transfers.*

Avani [512 C6] Mosi-oa-Tunya Rd; 0213 321122. There's an alfresco grill by the pool, ideal for light lunches & snacks. In the evening, try the buffet dinner (*US$35–45*): a selection of grilled

RESTAURANT PRICE CODES	
Based on average cost of a main course	
$$$$$	US$20+; £15+; Kw200+
$$$$	US$14–20; £20–15; Kw140–200
$$$	US$9–14; £6.50–10; Kw90–140
$$	US$6–9; £4.50–6.50; Kw60–90
$	under US$6; under £4.50; under Kw60

kebabs, burgers & pizzas to order, plus salads & desserts. $$$$$

✕ **Royal Livingstone** [512 C5] Mosi-oa-Tunya Rd; ☎0213 321122. This elegant hotel has a fabulous restaurant with surprisingly reasonable prices. The setting is lovely, the service excellent, & the food some of the best in town. Go early for sundowners overlooking the Falls. Booking essential. $$$$$

✕ **Victoria Falls Waterfront** [512 B4] Sichango Rd; ☎0213 320606–8. Enjoy b/fast, lunch or dinner with magnificent views of the Zambezi at affordable prices. The food is good & plentiful with the usual variety of chicken dishes, burgers, soups, sandwiches & daily specials served by friendly staff. The pizza oven is a popular addition & there is also a full bar. $$$–$$$$

✕ **Zigzag** [512 B3] Industrial Rd; ☎0213 322814; ⏰ 07.00–21.00 daily. A welcome respite from the hustle & bustle of town, shaded by fruit trees. Zigzag has varied choices for b/fast, coffee & cakes, lunch & dinner. There's also a children's menu & play area, & a fully licensed bar. $$$–$$$$

✕ **The Golden Leaf** [515 D8] 110 Mosi-oa-Tunya Rd; ☎0213 321266; ⏰ noon–22.00 daily. Originally part of Ngolide Lodge, this small Indian restaurant has a varied menu, with fish, mutton & chicken dishes, & plenty of veggie options. It's popular, so do book in advance. $$–$$$

✕ **Olga's** [515 D6] Nakatindi Rd; ☎0213 324160; www.olgasproject.com; ⏰ 07.30–22.00 daily. This is the place for pizzas, cooked in a traditional wood-fired oven, as well as pastas & salads. The thatched eating area incorporates crafts & furniture made by members of the local Community Training Centre, with profits fed back to the centre. There's Wi-Fi, too, & a take-away service is available. $$–$$$

✳ ✕ **Café Zambezi** [515 D7] Mosi-oa-Tunya Rd; ☎0213 323189; ⏰ 07.00–midnight daily. A great mix of African & Caribbean food (try the crocodile poppers) & an extensive drinks list is often accompanied by live, local music. Popular with locals & expats alike. $–$$

Take-aways and fast food There are several take-aways in town, including Wonderbake [514 B1], one of the best & most popular, & the Hungry Lion on the corner with Mutelo St [514 B2], serving the usual fare of chips, burgers, samosas, sandwiches & soft drinks. Falls Park shopping centre [512 C3] is also a useful source of fast food.

ENTERTAINMENT AND NIGHTLIFE Livingstone's nightlife centres largely around dancing and drinking, although the various restaurant bars offer a pleasant atmosphere if you simply want to relax and chat. For sundowners, join the crowd at the Victoria Falls Waterfront [512 B4], overlooking the river. The Fez Bar [515 D6] is a lively venue most nights – a favourite hang-out for expats. Other popular options are Da Fusion [512 B2] and Café Zambezi [515 D7]. For live music, there's a band at Avani [512 C6] most evenings and at weekends.

SHOPPING With both the Falls Park shopping centre [512 C3] and Mosi-oa-Tunya Square [515 D6] (commonly referred to as the 'Shoprite Centre'), options for shopping in Livingstone have improved considerably in recent years. There are also a couple of markets, and several shops along the main Mosi-oa-Tunya Road. Opening hours are usually around 09.00–17.00 Monday to Friday, and Saturday mornings, unless otherwise stated.

There's no specific **bookshop** in town any more, but several of the hotel gift shops stock a selection of novels and magazines, as well as wildlife reference books and regional travel guides. If you like bargaining, head for one of the craft markets (page 528) for **curios and gifts**. If not, then one of the tourist-orientated shops might suit you much better. Many of these can be found along Mosi-oa-Tunya Road, or try Kubu Crafts [515 D6] (*airport & Mosi-oa-Tunya Sq; www.kubucrafts. com*), offering crafts from all over Africa, or Waya Waya [512 C3] (*opposite Protea Hotel; www.wayawaya.no*), a social enterprise set up to teach local women to handcraft bags and accessories.

COMMUNICATIONS

Internet The majority of accommodation and many of the restaurants and cafés in Livingstone offer Wi-Fi (usually free for guests), though you'll still find a few internet cafés dotted around town. While rates are low and comparable, the standard of computers, speed and service varies.

Post Livingstone's post office [514 B1] (↘ *0213 245689, 0213 324797;* ⊕ *08.00–18.00 Mon–Fri, 08.00–14.00 Sat*) lies in the centre of town in a sprawling complex of banks and shops, adjacent to the main road.

Telephone SIM cards for both Airtel and the state-owned Zamtel are obtainable from numerous outlets across town; look out for their signs at shopping malls and on Mosi-oa-Tunya Road.

OTHER PRACTICALITIES

Banks and changing money Livingstone has several major banks near the main post office [514 B1], and various bureaux de change dotted throughout town. Most of the banks have ATMs, for which you'll generally need a Visa card rather than Mastercard. More convenient, but with the least favourable exchange rate, is to change money at a hotel or lodge. Avoid the freelance 'money-changers' who tend to congregate around the town centre and at the border.

Car repairs and spares The two biggest workshops in town are Foley's Africa (*Industrial Rd;* ↘ *0213 320888;* e *info@foleysafrica.com; www.foleysafrica.com*), which caters for Land Rovers; and Bennett Engineering, also known as Harry's workshop [512 C3] (↘ *0213 321611, 0213 322380;* m *0978 308936;* e *hbennett@iconnect.zm*), opposite Falls Park.

For more basic repairs, contact Kobil [515 D6] (m *0977 884345*) at the corner of Nakatindi Road, or Channa's Motors [512 C3] (*Mosi-oa-Tunya Rd;* ↘ *0213 320468*), just across the railway line. Punctures and tyre repairs can be handled by the Total fuel station on Mosi-oa-Tunya Road [515 D5], while for parts or vehicle accessories, head for Autoworld [514 A2] (*Mosi-oa-Tunya Rd;* ↘ *0213 320264;* e *autoworld@zamtel.zm*).

Medical facilities The local hospitals are not up to the standard of those in the West, and medical facilities are limited, but in the event of an emergency, contact:

✚ **SES** [515 D8] Speciality Emergency Services, Activity Centre, Avani Victoria Falls Resort; m 0977 740307/8; e livingstoneparamedic@ses-zambia. com; www.ses-zambia.com. The local base is staffed with South African-trained paramedics.

Pharmacies For cosmetics, toiletries or medicines there are several good pharmacies on and around Mosi-oa-Tunya Road, stocking a selection of items including insect repellents, beauty products, suncreams, medical supplies, baby supplies, batteries and more. Each has a trained pharmacist, who can offer advice on medications and fill prescriptions. Otherwise, both the Spar Super Store in Falls Park shopping centre [512 C3] and Shoprite in Mosi-oa-Tunya Square [515 D6] sell a variety of health and beauty products.

Tourist information The Zambia Tourism Board [514 A2] (*Mosi-oa-Tunya Rd;* ↘ *0213 321404/5;* e *livingstone@zambia.travel; www.zambiatourism.com;* ⊕ *08.00–*

17.00 Mon-Fri, 09.00–noon Sat) has an office at the tourist centre next to the Livingstone Museum.

WHAT TO SEE AND DO

The area around Victoria Falls has been a major crossroads for travellers for over a hundred years, from the early missionaries and traders, to the backpackers, overland trucks and package tourists of the last few decades. Apart from simply marvelling at one of the world's greatest waterfalls, there are now lots of ways to occupy yourself for a few days. Details of the options listed here are available at most places to stay, but should you be at a loss, try one of the following:

Bushtracks Africa [512 C3] Mosi-oa-Tunya Rd; ☏0213 323232; e victoriafalls@bushtracksafrica. com; www.bushtracksafrica.com
SafPar [512 B4] Victoria Falls Waterfront; ☏0213 320606/8; m 0973 403270; e zaminfo@safpar. com; www.safpar.net

Wild Side Tours & Safaris [515 D7] 131 Mosi-oa-Tunya Rd; ☏0213 323726; m 0978 323726; e wild@iconnect.zm

VICTORIA FALLS We can be sure that the Falls were well known to the native peoples of southern Africa well before any European 'discovered' them. After the San/Bushmen hunter-gatherers, the Toka Leya people inhabited the area, and it was probably they who christened the Falls Shongwe. Later, the Ndebele knew the Falls as the aManza Thunqayo, and after that the Makololo referred to them as Mosi-oa-Tunya. However, their first written description comes to us from Dr David Livingstone in November 1855:

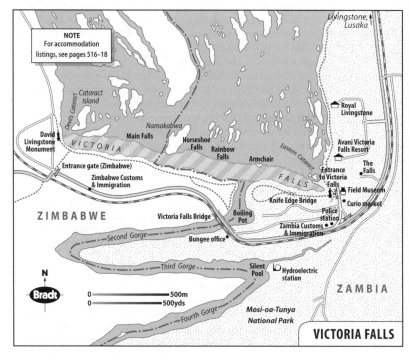

VICTORIA FALLS

It had never been seen before by European eyes; but scenes so lovely must have been gazed upon by angels in their flight.

The Falls are 1,688m wide and average just over 100m in height. Around 550 million litres (750 million during peak months) cascade over the lip every minute, making this one of the world's greatest waterfalls. Closer inspection shows that this immense curtain of water is interrupted by gaps, where small islands stand on the lip of the Falls. These effectively split the Falls into smaller waterfalls, known as (from west to east) the Devil's Cataract, the Main Falls, the Horseshoe Falls, the Rainbow Falls and the Eastern Cataract.

Around the Falls is a genuinely important and interesting rainforest, with plant species (especially ferns) rarely found elsewhere in Zimbabwe or Zambia, sustained by the clouds of spray, which blanket the immediate vicinity of the Falls. You'll also find various monkeys and baboons here, while the lush canopy shelters Livingstone's lourie among other birds.

The flow, and hence the spray, is greatest just after the end of the rainy season – around March or April, depending upon the rains – then decreases gradually until about December. During low water, a light raincoat (available for rent on site) is useful for wandering between the viewpoints on the Zimbabwean side, though it's not necessary in Zambia, but at high water a raincoat is largely ineffective as the spray soaks you in seconds. Anything that you want to keep dry must be wrapped in several layers of plastic or, better, ziplock or dry bags.

The Falls never seem the same twice, so try to visit several times, under different light conditions. At sunrise, both Danger Point and Knife-edge Point are fascinating – position yourself carefully to see your shadow in the mists, with three concentric rainbows appearing as halos. (Photographers will find polarising filters invaluable in capturing the rainbows on film, as the light from the rainbows at any time of day is polarised.) Moonlight is another fascinating time, when the Falls take on an ethereal glow and the waters blend into one smooth mass which seems frozen over the rocks.

On the Zambian side (⏰ 06.00–19.00 daily; US$20 pp), viewing the Falls could not be easier. For photographers, the area is best in the early morning, when the sun is behind you and illuminates the Falls, or in the late afternoon when you may catch a stunning sunset. When the river is at its lowest, towards the end of the dry season, the channels on this side may have dried up, yet while the Falls will be less spectacular then, their fascinating geology, normally obscured by spray, is revealed.

You can easily explore on your own, or organise a professional guide for a detailed explanation of the formation of the Falls and gorges, the river, local history and flora and fauna.

From the Zimbabwean side (⏰ summer 06.00–18.00 daily, winter from 06.30; US$30 pp), viewing the Falls is more regulated, and may be easiest organised through a tour operator, who will also handle visas and transport. If you're planning to visit independently, allow at least half a day, and expect a fair delay at the border. Tickets are valid for the whole day, so you can return for no extra cost during the same day – though be prepared for the generally pleasant but very persistent vendors and 'guides' along the way.

LIVINGSTONE ISLAND Accessed exclusively through Tongabezi (page 518), Livingstone (or Namakabwa) Island is where Dr Livingstone first viewed the Falls. Trips are run between July and March, subject to water levels. Gaze over the edge, perhaps chancing a thrilling dip in the Devil's Pool right on the Falls' edge, or having a gourmet meal – breakfast, lunch or high tea – in an exclusive setting.

When the water's at its lowest, around October and November, you can sometimes even walk across the top of the Falls.

RIVER CRUISES Floating on the Upper Zambezi with a glass in one hand, and a pair of binoculars in the other, is one of the region's highlights. Nowadays booze-cruise boats operate round the clock – and sometimes all congregate close together – but this is still a great way to take a gentle look around the Zambezi's islands, with national parks on both sides of the river.

Most elegant of the river boats are the ***African Queen*** [512 B4] and the ***Lady Livingstone***, whose most popular excursions are the sunset cruises. Smaller, less formal craft ply the same route at rather lower cost.

FISHING EXCURSIONS If you dream of hooking a tigerfish then a day on the Zambezi with a knowledgeable guide can help make it come true. Half- and full-day fishing trips can be organised for both novice and experienced anglers as well as fly-fishermen, to include fishing tackle, boat hire, fuel, transfers, a qualified guide and refreshments.

THRILLS AND SPILLS The Falls area is indisputably *the* adventure capital of southern Africa. There is an amazing and seemingly endless variety of ways to get your shot of adrenalin, though none comes cheaply. If you wish to do multiple activities, check out the many combination packages on offer as these can be slightly cheaper than booking individually. Whatever you plan, expect to sign an indemnity form before your activity starts.

On the Zambian side there is a single cable car at Rapid 25 to bring clients out of the gorge after river trips, with the cost often included in the activity price.

Flight of Angels Named after Livingstone's famous comment, 'Flight of Angels' describes any sightseeing trip over the Falls by microlight or helicopter. This is a good way to get a feel for the geography of the area, and is surprisingly worthwhile. If you're arriving from Kasane, or leaving for there, consider combining a sightseeing flight and an air transfer.

Microlight Essentially sightseeing from a propeller-powered armchair 500m above the ground, this is the closest you'll get to soaring like a bird over the Falls. Microlights are affected by the slightest turbulence, so if you book in advance, it's best to specify early morning or late afternoon, when conditions are ideal.

Helicopter The most expensive way to see the Falls is tremendous fun. A 15-minute trip takes in the Falls and the national park, or for 30 minutes you will fly over the gorges below the Falls as well; at extra cost, you can stop in the gorge for a picnic, or – if you plan to raft or riverboard – you save yourself the walk up and take an exhilarating helicopter lift instead, gaining an aerial view of the Falls and Zambezi gorges.

Bungee jumping Organised by an offshoot of the original New Zealand bungee pioneers, you jump – solo or tandem – from the middle of the main bridge between Zambia and Zimbabwe. With the Zambezi 111m below you, it is among the highest commercial bungee jumps in the world, and not for the nervous.

Bridge walks There's no-one better positioned to show you the ins and outs (or the ups and downs!) of the Victoria Falls Bridge than the bungee folks, whose intimate

17

bridge knowledge will not only fascinate you but have you clambering around and underneath the bridge like a monkey. With safety harness on and accompanied by a guide, you have the opportunity to explore the bridge's superstructure while hearing all about its construction and riveting history. While not as adrenalin-charged as bungee jumping, it's still bound to get your heart beating faster as you navigate your way high above the Zambezi.

Abseiling, high-wiring, gorge swing and slide A popular option on the adventure menu is the Zambezi swing, a cable swing set across the gorge which, together with a 90m-high cable slide (flying fox), abseiling (rappelling) and 'rap' jumps (rappelling forwards) down the side of the gorge, offers daring fun for all ages.

Swing participants are harnessed to ropes attached to the cable's sliding pulley and, after stepping off the cliff face, experience a heart-stopping 53m, three-second free-fall, followed by an exhilarating pendulum-like swing across the gorge, accelerating up to 140km/h (with a pull of roughly 2.5-times gravity) for some 2 minutes before being lowered to the ground. It's definitely not for the faint-hearted, though participants as young as eight and as old as 76 have braved it. It's even possible to try it out in tandem.

Slightly tamer is the high wire or flying fox, set on another static cable stretched across the gorge. With harness and pulley, you leap off a platform and 'fly' (slide) across the gorge some 90m above the ground. It can be done in either a sitting or a flying position, and is suitable for children.

Canoeing on the Upper Zambezi Canoeing down the Upper Zambezi is a cool occupation on hot days, and the best way to explore the upper river, its islands and channels. Zimbabwe's Zambezi National Park stretches all along the western shore providing ample opportunity for game viewing, while lodges, farms, villages and bush dot the Zambian side as you head downstream. The silence of canoes makes them ideal for floating up to antelope, elephants or crocodiles. Birdlife is prolific – you may hear the cry of the African fish eagle or see pied kingfishers hover and dive. Hippos provide the excitement, and are treated with respect and given lots of space. All canoe trips are accompanied by a licensed river guide, and sometimes also a motorboat for additional safety. Canoes range from two-seater open-decked kayaks to inflatable 'crocodiles'.

No prior canoeing experience is necessary, and once you are used to the water, the better guides will encourage you to concentrate on the wildlife.

White-water rafting The Zambezi below the Falls is one of the world's most renowned stretches of white water. The rapids below the Falls are mostly graded IV and V – somewhere between 'very difficult' and 'for experts only' – but the majority of them don't need skill to manoeuvre the boat once it is within the rapids, so absolute beginners are usually allowed to take part. Nevertheless, although a trained river guide pilots every raft, you should think very carefully about committing yourself if you have no experience. Boats do flip over, and the consequences can be severe. It's also important to ensure that your chosen operator will give a thorough safety briefing before departure, explaining what to do in the event of a capsize.

Rafting is offered from both Zambia and Zimbabwe, but the entry points and length of trips vary according to the water levels. From July to January, when the water is low, and the river's waves and troughs (or 'drops') are more pronounced, there are full- or half-day trips, while in high-water months (February to July), only half-day trips are offered. If the water is too high, rafting is suspended until it recedes to a safer level.

Riverboarding Thrilling for the fit who swim strongly, riverboarding is not for the faint of heart. After donning fins, lifejacket and helmet, you and your foam board (the size of a small surfboard) will be taught the basic skills before getting an opportunity to 'surf' the big waves of the Zambezi – accompanied by a safety raft.

White-water kayaking Even those without experience can try tandem kayaking with a qualified guide, who manoeuvres the kayak through rapids while you assist with paddle power. All participants must be confident swimmers.

ROYAL LIVINGSTONE EXPRESS The whistle of a steam loco rarely fails to stir a frisson of excitement, and Livingstone's foray into steam is no exception. Restored with meticulous attention to detail, the locos and wooden carriages are polished until they gleam, attracting plenty of attention from trackside villages. Large windows, as well as an observation car, ensure good visibility for all, and – if elephant, buffalo or other game are spotted – the train will sometimes stop for a better view. As the journey progresses, drinks are served before an unhurried dinner, enhanced by soft lighting and classical music. You may stop for sunset views on the Victoria Falls Bridge, and tours can also be taken through Mosi-oa-Tunya National Park.

CULTURAL ATTRACTIONS AND TOURS
Museums
Livingstone Museum [514 A2] Livingstone's main museum more than justifies a visit. To start with, there's an excellent three-dimensional map showing how the Zambezi River flows over Victoria Falls and downstream into the gorges, which puts everything into good perspective. Then there are exhibits on the Stone Age, and features on Zambian culture, politics, history, animals and traditional village life. Watch out, too, for the 'History' exhibition – it's easily missed but, with a unique collection of David Livingstone's personal possessions, including many of his letters, it's a must. Staff are friendly and knowledgeable and guided tours are included.

Railway Museum [515 A8] This collection of beautifully preserved old steam locomotives and memorabilia celebrating the iron horse's history in Livingstone was badly damaged by fire and is now more for extreme railway buffs. Fortunately, though, the 1922 10th Class 156 out of Glasgow that used to take pride of place has now been put to work hauling the *Royal Livingstone Express*.

Field Museum [map 523] Directly across from the entrance gate to Victoria Falls, this is signed as an information centre, but is more of a small interpretation centre. It's well worth a visit for an understanding of the geology, archaeology and history of the Falls.

Markets
Livingstone has many colourful local markets offering everything from fresh produce to secondhand clothes (*salaula*), from hand-fashioned metal pots to live chickens, from *chitenjes* (the traditional African cloth) to hand-crafted wood furniture and more. In addition to the large and fascinating Maramba Market [off 514 G4], there is also Porters' Market, further north [off 514 G2]. For something

17

smaller and closer to town, try Zimbabwe, Central or Town Centre Market (take your pick of the names!), down the road from Shoprite and next to the minibus station [514 B2].

Craft markets Livingstone is one of the best places in Zambia to buy crafts – either from the outstanding curio market near the Falls [map 523], where the goods come from as far as the Democratic Republic of Congo and Malawi, or at the equally good Mukuni Park Curio Market [514 E3] in town, where local artisans, craftsmen and traders sell their wares. The best buys are *makenge* baskets from Zambia's Western Province, malachite and heavy woodcarvings: hippos, elephants, rhinos, giraffes and smaller statues, though do consider the ethics of encouraging any further exploitation of hardwoods. Note, too, that some wooden items, especially wooden salad bowls and tall giraffes, are prone to cracking once you get them home due to changes in climate, and that very rarely are 'antiques' sold at craft markets anything other than fakes.

The curio markets are places to bargain hard, but are more sophisticated than they appear; traders will accept most currencies and sometimes credit cards.

Village visits While some of the lodges organise independent visits to local villages for their guests, there are organised trips to different villages. Most popular among these, although quite commercial, is **Mukuni Village** [off 512 D5], where you can visit local huts, view villagers at work, watch curio-making and sample traditional beer and food.

Historical tour of Livingstone A guided historical tour traces Livingstone's fascinating history, taking in many historical buildings and accented by colourful characters, intriguing tales and a once-vibrant social life.

SPORTS AND SPAS Many of Livingstone's hotels and lodges have small gyms or even tennis courts for their guests to use, or trained massage therapists on hand, but some facilities are open to all. Of note are the **spas** at the Royal Livingstone (page 517) and David Livingstone Safari Lodge and Spa (page 517).

Golfers can play at the Livingstone Royal Golf and Country Club [515 G6] (\0213 320440), which has an 18-hole course and a renovated colonial-style club building.

WILDLIFE ENCOUNTERS
Mosi-oa-Tunya National Park Much of the Zambian area around the Falls is protected within the tiny Mosi-oa-Tunya National Park. You can drive yourself around easily, or go by 4x4 with a tour operator. There are even walking safaris, led by licensed safari guides.

A few hours' driving could yield sightings of most of the common antelope and some fine giraffe, as well as buffalo, elephant and zebra. There is also the chance of spotting white rhino. Even wild dog are present, but there are no lion, leopard or other big cats.

Birdwatching Even the casual visitor with little interest will often see fish eagles, Egyptian geese, lots of kingfishers, numerous different bee-eaters, Hadeda and sacred ibis, and various other storks, egrets and herons. Meanwhile, avid birdwatchers will be seeking the more elusive birds like the rare Taita falcon, rock pratincoles and African skimmers.

Elephant interaction In 2017, Zambezi Elephant Trails made the decision to phase out elephant riding. However, the elephants, all originally orphaned or born to animals already involved with the elephant encounters, cannot safely be released back into the wild. Thus, a new project was born. In conjunction with SafariParExcellence, Zambezi Elephant Trails has introduced the Elephant Café (page 520), which aims to encourage guests to interact with the elephants rather than ride on them. The new venture is already popular, creating both a safe and relaxed environment for the animals, and a means to support them.

Livingstone Reptile Park [512 C4] This attraction offers the opportunity to see some huge crocs at close quarters. Picnic tables are set in the landscaped grounds and there's a café serving the park's signature 'Croc Bite'.

Walking with lions For visitors, the appeal of this encounter is the opportunity to walk with lion cubs, which are bred specially for the programme. Clearly this is very appealing to some people – but it's also very controversial; do consider the ethics before deciding whether or not to take part.

SEND US YOUR SNAPS!

We'd love to follow your adventures using our *Botswana* guide – why not send us your photos and stories via Twitter (*@BradtGuides*) and Instagram (*@bradtguides*) using the hashtag #botswana? Alternatively, you can upload your photos directly to the gallery on the Botswana destination page via our website (w *bradtguides.com/botswana*).

17

Tracks and signs

An extract from Southern African Wildlife: A Visitor's Guide *by Mike Unwin*

Animals seldom parade across the bush the way they do across a TV screen. In fact, the untamed wilderness, far from teeming with wall-to-wall wildlife, can sometimes seem a disappointingly empty place. But there is much more to see than simply the animals themselves, and the trained eye will find the land littered with evidence of their presence or passing: tracks and trails, pellets and droppings, diggings and rubbings, torn branches, flattened grass, feathers, nests and bones. These clues, often known by the Afrikaans word spoor, tell the story of what happened when nobody was looking.

Some awareness of tracks and signs will greatly enrich your own understanding of wildlife. Trackers, like forensic detectives, combine acute eyesight and vigilance with great patience, a photographic memory and the imagination to reconstruct a complete picture from a few scattered fragments. It is a humbling experience to watch an expert in action: a mere scratch in the soil can not only identify the animal responsible, but also reveal its age, sex, size, where it was heading, how it was moving, when it passed by and why.

MAKING TRACKS

Every animal that touches the ground leaves tracks. Some are easily recognised; others are more puzzling. Most small creatures, such as lizards, can only be identified to a broad generic level, but many larger mammal species have unique signatures. No two individuals of any species are identical, and the tracks of many show marked differences of size and shape between forefeet and hindfeet or between male and female. Conditions underfoot are critical to tracking. The clearest tracks are laid on surfaces that hold an impression, such as firm mud or damp sand. Hard, baked soil is too resistant, while soft sand allows slippage that distorts the shape.

Weather is also important: wind and rain can help to date tracks, but may erode or completely obliterate them. Neither overcast weather nor a midday sun are very helpful to trackers. Early morning is the best time to look – partly because tracks are still fresh, but also because the low light and slanting shadows throw any imprint into sharper relief.

THE HEAVY BRIGADE The bigger the animal, the harder its footfall. Elephants leave huge, round tracks, up to half a metre across, with the hindfeet smaller and more oval than the forefeet. In soft mud they create knee-deep craters that become sunbaked into a treacherous pitted moonscape. On hard ground, the latticework of cracks on their soles leaves a distinct, mosaic-like impression, even though the circular track outline may be invisible. A small heap of soil in front of each print indicates the elephant's direction (the rear of each track shows a clean edge). Rhino tracks have a cloverleaf shape, with each foot showing three distinct toes. On hard ground only the curved outer rim of each toenail may be visible. White rhinos have larger tracks (up to 30cm long) than black rhinos (about 24cm), with relatively broader toe marks. Hippos leave tracks of a similar size, but spaced more closely together and showing four clear toes on each foot. Their regular trails to and from water leave two, deep, parallel ruts either side of a central ridge.

ON THE HOOF Most ungulates leave symmetrical cloven-hoofed tracks. Those of antelope differ in little other than size, though some, like an impala's, are pointed, while others, like a kudu's, are more rounded. Identification often depends upon other clues: for example, an impala's tracks are likely to be in a herd and unlikely to be on a hillside. A few antelope show more unusual tracks: a sitatunga's are very long (over 15cm in the male) and widely splayed for bounding over marshy terrain, while klipspringers drill neat round holes with their cylindrical tip-toed hooves. A giraffe's enormous hooves (up to 20cm long) leave imprints like a steam iron, spaced far apart by its great stride. A buffalo has tracks like a cow's – larger and rounder than any antelope's except an eland. A warthog's are also quite rounded, with the two halves clearly separated. Zebra, with only a single big hoof on each foot, leave horseshoe tracks, the size of a donkey's.

PADS, PAWS AND CLAWS Most predator tracks show the typical pad and toes arrangement of domestic cats and dogs. The crucial things to look for are size, shape, number of toes and whether or not claws are visible. The male lion's are the biggest (up to 15cm long) and, like all cats, each shows four well-spaced, rounded toes and two small indentations in the back of the pad. Except for the cheetah, whose claws are permanently extended, cats do not leave claw marks. Conversely, all dog tracks show claws, and most have a longer, narrower shape than a cat's, with all four toes set in front of the pad. A hyena's tracks also show claws, but the curved toes are tucked closer together and the back of the pad slopes at a distinct diagonal. Spotted hyena tracks are about 10cm long, similar in size to a leopard's, and are commonly found around campsites. Mustelid tracks have five toes: an otter's show the hand-like spread of its dextrous fingers; a honey badger's show the furrows of its long claws, set well ahead of the toes. A genet's neat tracks resemble a tiny cat's – four-toed, clawless and rounded – but spaced close together by its short-legged gait. Most mongooses leave small, clawed tracks, some showing a fifth hind toe set back behind the four in front.

MAMMAL VARIATIONS An aardvark's tracks show only three toes on each foot, each one capped with a heavy claw mark, and its meandering trail is scattered with freshly excavated soil. Monkeys leave five-toed hand prints, with the opposable thumb or big toe clearly visible on each. A baboon's look particularly human, and are often confusingly overlaid where a whole troop has been active. A lesser bushbaby hops upright between trees, so leaves only the prints of its hindfeet. Squirrel tracks show longer hind feet than forefeet, and usually lead to and from a burrow or tree. A hare leaves tracks in sets of four, each of which shows the two front feet placed in line, one ahead of the other, and the overlapping back feet placed side-by-side in front. Rat and mice tracks are tiny and show four front toes, five hind toes and sometimes the drag mark of the tail.

BIRDS Bird tracks can be roughly classified by the shape and arrangement of the toes. Most have three toes pointing forward and one back. In some, such as starlings or hornbills, the hind toe points straight back, while in others, such as doves, it is set at a slight angle. Korhaans and dikkops show no hind toe at all, while an ostrich show only two toes in each of its enormous (20cm long) tracks and at least a metre's stride between them. The pattern of a bird's tracks reflects the way in which it moves: robins place both feet together in a series of well-spaced hops; doves follow a winding trail in which the feet move alternately in quick, short steps.

SCALE TRAILS The undulating motion of a typical snake leaves a series of S-shaped ripples, where each curve has pushed against surface irregularities to propel the body forward. A few heavy-bodied snakes, such as pythons and puff adders, can also grip the ground with their belly to push themselves along caterpillar-fashion, leaving a broad, straight furrow,

ANIMAL TRACKS (DRAWN TO SCALE)

Ground squirrel

Hippopotamus

Elephant

Baboon

Plains zebra

30cm

Aardvark

Giraffe

White rhino

Warthog

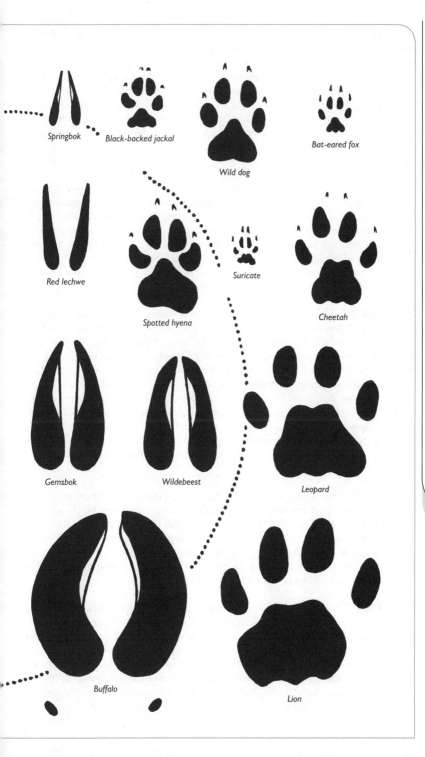

Springbok

Black-backed jackal

Wild dog

Bat-eared fox

Red lechwe

Spotted hyena

Suricate

Cheetah

Gemsbok

Wildebeest

Leopard

Buffalo

Lion

stamped with the impression of belly scales and bisected by the thin drag-line of the tail tip. The sidewinding Peringuey's adder leaves a strange sequence of disconnected bracket marks where each violent undulation has flung its body off the hot sand.

Other distinctive reptile tracks include the riverbank mud-chute of a crocodile – whose tracks show five splayed toes on the forefeet, four toes on the longer back feet, and a heavy furrow gouged by the tail – and the large, long-clawed prints of a monitor lizard, spaced either side of its wavy tail drag line. Smaller lizards inscribe neat, winding tramlines of closely spaced prints which, in soft surfaces such as sand, can be hard to distinguish from those of beetles and other larger invertebrates.

DROPPINGS

Unsavoury as they may seem, droppings can speak volumes about the whereabouts and behaviour of animals. Many male mammals delineate their territory using the strategically placed whiff of dung. Some, such as rhino and civet, build up big middens with regular deposits; others, such as hyena and many antelope, roll in theirs to soak up the scent and spread it around. Some droppings are visible from a great distance: a splash of white often reveals the nest or roost of birds such as vultures or cormorants, while dassie colonies stain the rocks yellow and brown with their viscous urine.

DEPOSITING A LOAD An elephant scatters its fibrous, football-sized droppings anywhere, and elephant country remains littered with dung long after the herds have moved on. When fresh, these droppings are full of goodies, and a host of foragers, from baboons to francolins, pick through the steaming contents in search of seeds, fruits and pods. White rhino dung is fine in texture, consisting entirely of grass, whereas black rhino dung is full of twigs and other woody matter. Over time, a bull rhino builds up a waist-deep midden, spread over several square metres, into which he scrapes deep grooves with his hind feet to pick up the scent. In areas where both rhino species occur, one may deposit its dung on the midden of the other. Hippo scatter their dung with their tail, plastering it messily over vegetation beside their trails. Buffalo droppings are black and loose, falling in folded 'pats' like domestic cattle's, and are often left trampled and smeared by the traffic of the herd.

PILES OF PELLETS Antelope leave neat piles of dark pellets, each pointed at one end and indented at the other. Many, such as impala, use communal dung heaps. Antelope are so efficient at deriving moisture and sustenance from their food that even the largest species have remarkably small, dry droppings – though a wildebeest's may congeal in sticky clumps. A giraffe's droppings, also amazingly small, are widely scattered by their great drop. Zebras deposit their dark, kidney-shaped droppings in neat mounds, which grow paler with age and break down into heaps of fine, dry grass.

SMELLY SCATS Carnivore droppings – or scats – are cylindrical sausages, often pointed or twisted at one end – as any dog-owner will confirm. Because of their meat content, they tend to be smellier than those of herbivores. Hyena droppings are green when fresh, but turn to a conspicuous chalky white because of their high bone content. A lion's may also whiten with age, but can be black with blood, and are usually full of fur. Civet droppings are surprisingly large, and often contain the hard undigested exoskeletons of millipedes, as well as berries and insect husks. Otter droppings, or spraints, consist mostly of crushed crab shell and are deposited at the water's edge.

WHO'S AT HOME?

Many animals can be detected by the homes they build. Bird nests are the best known, and some, such as the enormous thatches of sociable weavers or hammerkops often provide shelter for a whole community of other animals. Tree holes offer a desirable residence to anything from hornbills and hoopoes to bushbabies and squirrels, and a promising-looking cavity is always worth watching during the breeding season. Burrows should be checked for signs of life: a complex of small holes may indicate a mongoose or ground squirrel colony, while a big burrow may house either the aardvark that dug it, or more recent tenants such as warthogs, wildcats or porcupines – so look out for signs of occupation, such as a snake skin or porcupine quill.

The state of an area's vegetation can also betray local residents with no permanent home. A flattened depression in long grass might be where a waterbuck bedded down for the night, while tattered bushes could be the work of a territorial bull sable, who thrashes them with his horns. Deep parallel gashes gouged into a tree trunk are the calling card of the local leopard, and a shiny tree stump beside a mud wallow is a 'rubbing post', polished to a smooth finish by generations of itchy rhinos.

FEEDING SIGNS

A good look at the landscape soon reveals who had what for dinner. Elephant are the messiest of eaters: freshly broken branches, peeled strips of bark and tussocks of grass tossed across the track are all sure signs of their presence, as are deep holes dug in sandy riverbeds for fresh water. Big grazers such as hippo or rhino trim clearly defined and well-managed lawns. Giraffe prune thorn trees up to a height of six metres, creating a visible browse line, and leave glistening strings of saliva in overhead branches. Kudu leave bushes frayed and nibbled at head height, while black rhino will even munch thorny, poisonous euphorbias, sometimes demolishing them entirely. Many smaller animals also refashion the landscape in their search for food: bark stripped from the foot of a tree trunk is probably the work of porcupines; excavations at the base of an anthill show where an aardvark dug for termites; a hillside littered with overturned stones shows the methodical foraging of baboons for lizards and scorpions.

Predators usually leave evidence of their kills, though even a large carcass quickly disappears beneath an army of scavengers, as hyenas scatter the bones, vultures strip the skin, blowfly maggots consume the final shreds of flesh and ants clean the last drops of blood from the soil. Even the keratin of an antelope horn is food for the larvae of the horn-boring moth, which leaves strange tubular casts along its length. Leopards often cheat scavengers, at least for a while, by hoisting their kill into a tree, so look out for hooves overhead. A scattering of feathers may reveal the regular plucking post of a raptor – which tears out tough flight feathers individually, leaving small, V-shaped punctures on the shafts, whereas a mammalian predator rips them out in clumps, shearing right through the quills with its teeth. Owls and other birds of prey regurgitate pellets of undigested bones and fur, often found beneath their roosts, while some shrikes impale prey such as lizards and grasshoppers on acacia thorns and barbed-wire fences.

A1

Appendix 2

based on an original compiled by Phil Deutschle

Setswana is the national language of Botswana, while English is the official language. In practice, though many people speak other languages at home, most will be able to converse in Setswana. English will be spoken by those who have been to school, or who have been outside the country. In a country with a high level of education, this means most people, with the exception of the older generation in rural areas.

Learning to speak a little Setswana is easy and, even in educated circles, trying to speak a few words of the language will mark you out as showing respect for the country's culture. It will open many doors, and will really make a difference to how you are received. Carry the most important phrases on a slip of paper, and practise whenever you can.

PRONUNCIATION The only difficult sound in Setswana is the g, usually pronounced like ch in the Scottish 'loch' or German 'ich'. If you have trouble with that, just say the g like an ordinary h. The r is often rolled, especially if it's written 'rr'. Vowels and other consonants are pronounced as follows:

a	like a in China
e	like ay in day
i	like ee in see
o	like o in go
ph	like p in put
th	like t in table
u	like oo in too
x	like k in kite (also used to represent a click, as in Nxai)

Note, however, that Setswana is not entirely phonetic, and some letters may not be pronounced at all.

GREETINGS Greetings are relatively easy to master, as you can practise them with everyone you meet. They'll also get you instant results; using them is almost guaranteed to bring a smile to the face of those you greet – while sending out the message that you're not an arrogant foreigner who can't be bothered to learn a word of Setswana. So even if you never master anything else in Setswana, do learn the basic greetings and it'll make your trip so much easier and more pleasant.

English	Setswana
Words in underlined italics are optional	

Hello (literally 'Greetings Sir/Madam')	*Dumela Rra/Mma*
How did you rise?	*O tsogile jang?*
I have risen *well*	*Ke tsogile sentle*
How did you spend the day?	*O tlhotse jang?*
I spent the day *well*	*Ke tlhotse sentle*
How are you? (informal)	*O kae?*
I'm fine (lit, 'I'm here')	*Ke teng*
It's OK	*Go siame*
I am going	*Ke a tsamaya*
Stay well (said to someone staying)	*Sala sentle*
Go well (said to someone going)	*Tsamaya sentle*
Sleep well	*Robala sentle*

ESSENTIAL WORDS

Yes	*Ee*
No	*Nnyaa*
Thank you	*Ke aleboga, Ke itumetse* (lit, 'I am happy')
Excuse me!	*Sorry!*

BASIC QUESTIONS AND ANSWERS

What's your name? (formal)	*Leina la gago ke mang?*
My name is …	*Leina la me ke …*
Who are you? (informal)	*O mang?*
I'm …	*Ke …*
How goes it?	*Wa reng?*
It goes OK	*Ga ke bue*
Where are you from? or	
Where are you coming from?	*O tswa kae?*
I'm (coming) from …	*Ke tswa kwa …*
Where are you going?	*O ya kae?*
I'm going to …	*Ke ya …*
What's the time?	*Nako ke mang?*
Where's the shop?	*Shopo e kae?*
What do you want?	*O batla eng?*
I want …	*Ke batla/kopa …*
There is none	*Ga go na*
How much?	*Ke bokae?*
It's expensive/cheap	*Go a tura/tshipi*
What is this *in Setswana*?	*Se ke eng ka Setswana?*
What do you do? (your job)	*O dira eng?*

NUMBERS Unusually, numbers are said in English.

FOOD AND DRINK

water	*metse*	sugar	*sukiri*
tea	*tee*	mealie meal	*dupr*
coffee	*kofee*	meat	*fnama*
milk	*mashi*		

OTHER USEFUL WORDS AND PHRASES

I don't know *Setswana*	*Ga ke itse <u>Setswana</u>*
It tastes good	*Go monate*
I'm satisfied (regarding food)	*Ke kgotshe*
Men/Women (written on toilets)	*Banna/Basadi*
Far/near	*Kgakala/gaufi*
I'm asking for money/tobacco	*Ke kopa madi/motsoko*
I have no money/tobacco	*Ga ke na madi/motsoko*

PHOTOGRAPHER DETAILS

Appendix 3

FURTHER INFORMATION

BOOKS AND JOURNALS
Historical interest

Andersson, Charles John *Lake Ngami and the River Okavango* Originally published late 1850s; republished as a facsimile reprint by Struik, Cape Town, 1967. Records Namibia and Botswana in the 1850s through the eyes of one of the first traders and hunters in the area.

Baines, Thomas *Explorations in South-west Africa* London, 1864. Although linked more with the countries further east, the travels of Baines, as he accompanied Livingstone and others, makes good reading and is well illustrated by the author.

Bolaane, Dr Maitseo M M *Chiefs, Hunters and San in the Creation of the Moremi Game Reserve, Okavango Delta: Multiracial Interactions and Initiatives, 1956–1979* Botswana, 2013. A scholarly investigation into the social and political climate that underpinned the creation of Moremi Game Reserve in 1962.

Fawcus, Peter and Tilbury, Alan *Botswana: The Road to Independence* Co-publisher Botswana Society, Gaborone, 2000. The authors of this were two of Britain's most senior administrators during the final decade that led to Botswana's independence. Their book paints a rare picture (quite densely packed with detail) of a country's smooth transition from a colonial protectorate to an independent state – and has a particularly interesting foreword by Sir Ketumile Masire, one of Botswana's former presidents.

Gordon, Robert J *The Bushman Myth: The Making of a Namibian Underclass* Westview Press, Colorado and Oxford, 1992. If you, like me, had accepted the received wisdom that Bushmen are the last descendants of Stone Age man, pushed to living in splendid isolation in the Kalahari, then you must read this. It places the Bushmen in an accurate historical context and deconstructs many of the myths we have created about them. Despite being mainly based on facts about the San in Namibia, it's still well worth reading for an understanding of their position in contemporary Botswana.

Grant, Sandy *Botswana and its National Heritage* Melrose Books, Ely, 2012. This is as much a history of Botswana pre-independence than a dry record of its culture. Accessible text adds colour to many historical events and anecdotes, but it's the monochrome photographs from the archives that bring it to life. By the same author is *Botswana: An Historical Anthology*.

Head, Bessie *Serowe: Village of the Rain Wind* Heinemann, UK, 2008. This fascinating collection of oral-history transcripts records villagers' memories of their past, and especially the deeds of their enlightened leaders, Khama the Great, who ruled from 1875 to 1923, Tshekedi Khama (1926–59), his son from a second marriage, and Sir Seretse Khama, Khama's grandson by his first-born son Segkoma II (1923–25), who became first president of the independent Botswana.

Henk, Dan 'The Botswana Defence Force: Evolution of a Professional African Military', *African Security Review*, Volume 13, No 4, 2004.

Lane, Paul, Reid, Andrew and Segobya, Alinah (eds) *The Archaeology of Botswana* Co-publisher Botswana Society, Gaborone, 1998. This is a detailed and academic overview of the archaeology of Botswana, as well as how archaeology has progressed in the country to date. It's an excellent reference, but not a light read.

Livingstone, David *Missionary Travels and Researches in South Africa* John Murray, London, 1857. This classic is fascinating reading, over a century after it was written.

Reader, John *Africa: A Biography of the Continent* Penguin Books, London, 1997. Over 700 pages of highly readable history, interwoven with facts and statistics, to make a remarkable overview of Africa's past. Given that Botswana's boundaries were imposed from Europe, its history must be looked at from a pan-African context to be understood. This book can show you that wider view; it is compelling and essential reading. (Chapters 41 and 42 deal with the early settlers in the Cape, and are largely devoted to the Lozi people.)

Shortridge, G C *The Mammals of South West Africa* Heinemann, London, 1934. This is more of historical interest than a practical field guide.

Tlou, Thomas and Campbell, Alec *History of Botswana* Macmillan Botswana, Gaborone, 1997.

Williams, Susan *Colour Bar: The Triumph of Seretse Khama and His Nation* Penguin, UK, 2007. This recent book documents the impact of the marriage of Sir Seretse Khama and Lady Ruth Williams Khama.

Botswana Notes and Records The Botswana Society has published an annual journal, *Botswana Notes and Records*, since 1969. It contains 'scientific, and semi-scientific articles and notes, written by amateur as well as professional experts on subjects of permanent interest relating to Botswana'. This is an amazing archive of reliable information, which I've only scratched the surface of here – it's a real treasure trove for anyone interested in Botswana. During my researches I've read many articles and made reference to some of them, including the main ones, which are mentioned here:

Andringa, J 'The Climate of Botswana in Histograms', Volume 16 (1984), pages 117–26.

Campbell, Alec 'A Comment on Kalahari Wildlife and the Khukhe Fence', Volume 13 (1981), pages 111–18.

Campbell, Alec 'The Riddle of the Stone Walls', Volume 23 (1991), pages 243–50.

Cooke, H J and Baillieul, T 'The Caves of Ngamiland: An Interim Report on Explorations and Fieldwork 1972–74', Volume 6 (1974), pages 147–56.

Cooper, Dr S M 'Clan Size of Spotted Hyenas in the Savuti Region of Chobe National Park, Botswana', Volume 21 (1989), pages 121–33.

Garner, R A and Ritter, R C 'Resurvey of Gcwihaba Cave and Exploration of the Aha Sinkhole Caves', Volume 26 (1994), pages 183–8.

Gieske, A 'Modelling of Surface Outflow from the Okavango Delta', Volume 28 (1996), pages 165–92.

Hitchcock, Robert 'A Chronology of Major Events Relating to the Central Kalahari Game Reserve', Volume 31 (1999), pages 105–17.

Mann, P M and Ritter, R C 'Further Exploration and Resurvey of !WaDoum Cave', Volume 27 (1995), pages 13–20.

Parsons, Q N 'Franz or Klikko, the Wild Dancing Bushman: A Case Study in Khoisan Stereotyping', Volume 20 (1989), pages 71–6.

Ramsay, Jeff 'Some Notes on the Colonial Era History of the Central Kalahari Game Reserve Region', Volume 20 (1989), pages 91–4.

Renew, Audrey 'Some Edible Wild Cucumbers of Botswana', Volume 1 (1968), pages 5–8.

Ritter, R C and Garner, R A 'Discovery and Preliminary Exploration of a New Cave in the Gcwihaba Valley', Volume 26 (1994), pages 55–65.

Ritter, Ron and Mann, Paul 'Discovery and Exploration of Two New Caves in the Northwest District', Volume 27 (1995), pages 1–12.

Robbins, Lawrence H 'The Middle Stone Age of Kudiakam Pan', Volume 20 (1989), pages 41–50.

Robbins, L H and Campbell, A C 'The Depression Rock Shelter Site, Tsodilo Hills', Volume 20 (1989), pages 1–3.

Robbins, L H, Murphy, M L, Campbell, A C and Brook, G A 'Excavations at the Tsodilo Hills Rhino Cave', Volume 28 (1996), pages 23–45.

Sommerlatte, M W L 'A Preliminary Report on the Number, Distribution and Movement of Elephants in the Chobe National Park with Notes on Browse Utilisation', Volume 7 (1975), pages 121–9.

Van der Post, Cornelius 'Putting the Bushmen on the Map of Botswana', Volume 32 (2000), pages 107–15.

Viljoen, P C 'New Locality Record for the Klipspinger', Volume 12 (1980), page 169.

Williamson, D T and J E 'An Assessment of the Impact of Fences on Large Herbivore Biomass in the Kalahari', Volume 13 (1981), pages 107–10.

Yellen, J E, Brooks, A S, Stuckenrath, R and Welbourne, R 'A Terminal Pleistocene Assemblage from Drotsky's Cave, Western Ngamiland', Volume 19 (1987), pages 1–6.

Language and culture

Davis, Ronald and researchers at Stanford University 'Y chromosome sequence variation and the history of human populations' *Nature Genetics,* November 2000.

Dunbar, R 'Why gossip is good for you' *New Scientist,* 21 November 1992, pages 28–31.

Rantao, Paul Mmolotsi *Setswana Culture and Tradition* Pentagon Publishers, Gaborone, 2006. A straightforward introduction to the traditional Setswana lifestyle, covering everything from social structure and daily rituals to religious beliefs and practices.

Biography

Allison, Peter *Don't Run Whatever You Do: My Adventures as a Safari Guide* Nicholas Brealey Publishing, London, 2007. Light-hearted and easy reading, this behind-the-scenes series of anecdotes might just make you look at your safari guide in a new light.

Carruthers, Jane and Arnold, Marion *Life and Work of Thomas Baines* Fernwood Press, South Africa, 1995, reprinted 1996.

Davies, Caitlin *Place of Reeds: A True African Love Story* Simon & Schuster, London, 2006. Set in Maun in the early 1990s, this intensely personal and sometimes disturbing memoir is enriched by a very strong sense of place and a fascinating insight into the culture of northern Botswana.

Horton, Bernard *My Forever Heartache: Four Years of Discovery with the Kalahari Bushmen* Black Crake Books, Maun, 2013.

Owens, Mark and Delia *Cry of the Kalahari* HarperCollins, UK, 1986. A highly personal account of the authors' seven years in the Central Kalahari Game Reserve in the 1970s, during which time they conducted studies focusing largely on lions and brown hyena, and set up a conservation project.

Paton, Alan *Lost City of the Kalahari* University of KwaZulu Natal Press, South Africa, 2005. In 1886, the ruins of a 'lost city' in the Kalahari were described by G A Farin in *Through the Kalahari Desert*. Seventy years later, in 1956, seven adventurers set out in search of this mythical city, among them Alan Paton, author of *Cry, the Beloved Country*. This is the story of their expedition.

Randall, Will *Botswana Time* Abacus, UK, 2005. The author's stint as a teacher in Kasane makes light-hearted if hardly memorable reading.

Slaughter, Carolyn *Before the Knife: Memories of an African Childhood* Doubleday, UK, 2002. For a young white girl, growing up in the British Protectorate of Bechuanaland was in itself unusual, but even in this context the author's childhood was outside the norm. Beyond her personal horror is pre-independence Botswana, described with both affection and, at times, a stark realism.

van der Post, Laurens *The Lost World of the Kalahari* Hogarth Press, London, 1958; many subsequent reprints by Penguin. Laurens van der Post's classic account of how he journeyed into the heart of the Kalahari Desert in search of a 'pure' Bushman group – eventually found at the Tsodilo Hills. His almost mystical description of the Bushmen is fascinating, so long as you can cope with the rather dated, turgid prose. You then need to read Robert J Gordon's very different book, *The Bushman Myth* (page 539), to put it in perspective.

Field guides Although the choice of field guides continues to increase, those listed here are among the best. Top of your list should be Veronica Roodt's *Trees and Shrubs of the Okavango Delta*, even if you're not that interested in trees and shrubs. Serious birders should seek out *Birds of Botswana* while Richard Estes' *The Safari Companion* is a great general book on mammalian behaviour.

Butchart, Duncan *Wildlife of the Okavango: Common Animals and Plants* Struik Nature, Cape Town, 2000. Slim enough to take on a game drive, this handy guide with generally good photographs is an ideal first reference – albeit no substitute for a dedicated bird book.

Coates Palgrave, Keith and Coates Palgrave, Meg (eds) *Trees of Southern Africa* Struik, Cape Town, 3rd edn 2003. The definitive guide to the region's trees is a must-have for natural-history buffs.

Estes, Richard *The Safari Companion* Russell Friedman Books, South Africa, 1993 (co-published Tutorial Press, Zimbabwe and Chelsea Green Publishing, Vermont). While slightly too thick to be an ideal travelling companion, this is a real treasure chest of information on animal behaviour. It covers all the main animal species found in mainland Africa, from duikers and dwarf antelope to cats, dogs and the great apes. For each it includes a brief description of its social systems and forms of communication, along with helpful outlines of body postures and diagrams to explain typical forms of behaviour. If you've longed to decipher the language of animals, and have the time to stop and watch rather than simply tick game off a list, then you must bring this book.

Hancock, Peter and Randall, Richard *The Okavango Companion* Sandor Books, Maun, 2016. Covers most of the common animals and plants that you'll find in the Delta.

Hancock, Peter and Weiersbye, Ingrid *Birds of Botswana* Princeton University Press, New Jersey, 2016. A scholarly but very accessible field guide to Botswana's birds, with excellent illustrations. This is definitely the one for serious birders.

Newman, Kenneth *Newman's Birds of Southern Africa* Struik Publishers, South Africa, 2010. Republished numerous times since its first edition in 1988, Newman's has become one of the standard field guides to birds in southern Africa, south of the Kunene and Zambezi rivers. It also covers most species found in Zambia.

Roodt, Veronica *Common Wild Flowers of the Okavango Delta* Shell Oil Botswana, Gaborone, 1998. The second book in Shell's 'Field Guide' series is a little more specialist than the first book on trees, but still manages to comment on diverse topics from the formula for gunpowder to the treatment of scorpion stings. It's well worth getting, even for flower identification beyond the Delta.

Roodt, Veronica *Trees and Shrubs of the Okavango Delta* Shell Oil Botswana, Gaborone, 1998. This first book in Shell's 'Field Guide' series isn't just about trees or shrubs, and doesn't restrict its comments rigidly to the Okavango – but it is a masterpiece. Veronica Roodt has lived and worked in Moremi for many years, researching the plants of the area. This book is ostensibly just a field guide to slightly over 60 of the more common trees and shrubs in the area, but in reality it's a fascinating treatise on the insects and animals associated with all of them, plus the medicinal uses and local superstitions attached to each. It's well worth buying a copy as soon as you get to Botswana, even if you're not that interested in trees; it reads very well!

Roodt, Veronica *Wild Flowers, Waterplants and Grasses of the Okavango Delta and Kalahari* Veronica Roodt Publications, South Africa, 2011. Bringing together coverage of Chobe and the Makgadikgadi Pans as well as the Delta and the Kalahari, this field guide with excellent photographs is a must. There's also a companion volume, *Mammals of Botswana and Surrounding Areas*.

Sinclair, Ian, Hockey, Phil and Tarboton, Warwick *Sasol Birds of Southern Africa* Struik, South Africa, 4th edn 2011. First published in 1993, so a more recent addition to the market than Newman's, this is particularly useful for the illustrations of birds at different stages of their development, and in flight.

Unwin, Mike *Southern African Wildlife: A Visitor's Guide* Bradt Travel Guides, UK, 2nd edn 2011. A compact, single-volume guide to the habitats, identification and behavioural characteristics of the region's wildlife. A well-written text, which includes sections on tracks and signs, is matched by exceptionally good photographs.

Other useful guides

Bulpin, T V *Discovering Southern Africa* Discovering Southern Africa Productions, South Africa (distributed by Book Sales). Part guidebook and part history book, this covers mainly South Africa but also extends into Namibia and Zimbabwe. A weighty tome with useful background views and information, written from a South African perspective.

Campbell, Alec *The Guide to Botswana* Winchester Press, Johannesburg, first published 1968. Alec Campbell is perhaps the leading authority on Botswana's natural areas and history, having not only lived in Botswana for most of his life, but also held posts as the Director of National Parks and later as the Director of the National Museum of Botswana. There were several very substantial editions to this early guide which give insights into what Botswana was like decades ago. It's also fascinating to contrast and compare his guides with more contemporary guidebooks.

Campbell, Alec and Coulson, David *African Rock Art*: *Painting and Engraving on Stone* Abrams, New York, 2001. Campbell's informative text underpins some stunning photography, making this so much more than a coffee-table book.

Chittenden, Hugh (compiler) *Top Birding Spots of Southern Africa* Southern Book Publishers, South Africa, 1992. This useful, practical book details about 400 sites for keen birdwatchers, listing local specialities and endemic species with a checklist of key species for each site. Some of its simple maps are now out of date, though I'm not aware of it being reprinted in the last decade.

Dodwell, Christina *An Explorer's Handbook: Travel, Survival and Bush Cookery* Hodder and Stoughton, London, 1984. Over 170 pages of practical and amusing anecdotes, including chapters on 'unusual eatables', 'building an open fire' and 'tested exits from tight corners'. Practical advice for both possible and most unlikely eventualities – and it's a great read.

Gifford, James and Stockhall, Steven *Wildlife Photography in Botswana: A practical guide* Enlivened, Botswana, 2010. From technical know-how and equipment to where and how to photograph wildlife in Botswana, this is a helpful manual both for first-time photographers and those seeking more advanced skills – with some superb images.

Main, Mike *African Adventurer's Guide to Botswana* New Holland, UK, 2001. Mike Main is a leading authority on all things to do with Botswana, and especially its wilder areas. This book builds on the earlier *Visitor's Guide to Botswana*. It features route descriptions for some very offbeat 4x4 trips, including a few GPS points and schematic maps of the routes.

Main, Mike *Kalahari: Life's Variety in Dune and Delta* Macmillan, UK, 1988.

Rattray, Gordon *Access Africa* Bradt Travel Guides, UK, 2009. An invaluable guide to Africa's major safari areas for travellers with limited mobility.

Coffee-table picture books

Bailey, Adrian *Okavango: Africa's Wetland Wilderness* Struik Publishers, Cape Town, 1998. Bright colour plates and an informative text make this a good coffee-table overview of the Delta.

Balfour, Daryl and Sharna *Chobe: Africa's Untamed Wilderness* Southern Books, Johannesburg, 1997. An almost day-by-day account of a year that this renowned couple spent in Chobe and Selinda. Good pictures and a readable diary-format style give a fair picture of the changing seasons and the wildlife.

Forester, Bob, Murray-Hudson, Mike and Cherry, Lance *The Swamp Book: A View of the Okavango* Southern Books, Johannesburg, 1989. This interesting and quirky coffee-table book includes highly readable sections on the Okavango Delta and some of its more common flora and fauna, as well as comments on a few interesting historical accounts of travel there. Photographs include several taken underwater.

Gifford, James *Savute: Botswana's Wildlife Kingdom* HPH Publishing, South Africa, 2017. James Gifford's photographs capture both the drama and the wild beauty of the Savute region.

Lanting, Frans *Okavango: Africa's Last Eden* Chronicle Books, San Francisco, 1993. Probably the ultimate in coffee-table books includes minimal text but many impressive and beautiful images that were originally commissioned for *National Geographic* magazine.

McNutt, John and Boggs Ross, Lesley (text), Heldring, Hélène and Hamman, Dave (photography) *Running Wild: Dispelling the Myths of the African Wild Dog* Southern Books, Johannesburg, 1996. Some beautiful pictures of dogs in the Delta (the 'Mombo Pack' in the early 1990s) plus informative text about their behaviour and group dynamics – put into the context of observations made throughout northern Botswana.

Pickford, Peter and Beverly *The Miracle Rivers: The Okavango and Chobe of Botswana* Southern Books, Johannesburg, 1999. A coffee-table book with some colour plates and grainy black-and-white shots. The text is a mixture of quotes and travelogue with attention (and almost homage) paid to various hunting operations.

Ross, Karen *Okavango: Jewel of the Kalahari* BBC Enterprises Ltd, London, 1987. Written by Karen Ross in parallel with her research for a short series of films, produced by Partridge Films for the BBC. The film series is stunning, and certainly raised the UK's awareness of the Okavango Delta considerably when it was first shown. The book's also first class. Its photography is good, though not exceptional, but the depth of its text raises it well above the normal standard of coffee-table books. Though perhaps slightly dated now, it is still well worth getting hold of.

Walker, Clive *Savuti: The Vanishing River* Southern Books, Johannesburg, 1991. Using many simple line drawings, and just a sprinkling of generally impressive photographs, this is less pictorial than most coffee-table books. It concentrates mainly on Walker's personal experiences in Savuti, where he spent time with Lloyd Wilmot, among others, and witnessed the final drying out of the Savuti Channel. It's a good read, though too large to travel with easily.

Health

Wilson-Howarth, Dr Jane *The Essential Guide to Travel Health: Don't Let Bugs Bites and Bowels Spoil Your Trip* Cadogan Books, London, 2009. Formerly simply *Bugs, Bites and Bowels,* this amusing and erudite overview of the hazards of tropical travel is small enough to take with you.

Wilson-Howarth, Dr Jane and Ellis, Dr Matthew *Your Child Abroad: A Travel Health Guide* Bradt Travel Guides, UK, 3rd edn ebook 2014. Full of practical first-hand advice from two leading medical experts. An indispensable guide if you plan to travel abroad with young children.

Novels

Dow, Unity *Far and Beyon'* Spinifex Press, Australia, 2000. Tackling the complex issues of the role of women in society, and the conflict of the traditional and modern world, this is the first of Unity Dow's novels. Botswana's first female high-court judge, she brings her experience of the legal profession to her deceptively simple stories. Later books, also published by Spinifex, are *The Screaming of the Innocent* (2002), *Juggling Truths* (2003), and *The Heavens May Fall* (2007).

Head, Bessie *Maru* Heinemann, UK, 1972. The uplifting story of a Masarwa orphan's experiences of racial prejudice at a time when the Bushmen were treated as slaves by the dominant peoples of Botswana. South African by birth, Bessie Head came to Botswana as a refugee and was granted citizenship after 15 years. Her other novels include *When Rain Clouds Gather* (1968) and *A Question of Power* (1974), both published by Heinemann.

McCall-Smith, Alexander *The No 1 Ladies' Detective Agency* Abacus, UK, 2003. Mma Precious Ramotswe and her detective agency have been taken to the hearts of readers worldwide, but her roots are firmly in Gaborone. McCall-Smith's gently humorous tales, of which this is the first, are set in the context of modern-day Botswana, and will enrich even the shortest visit to the country.

Children's field guides

SASOL *'My first' guides* Penguin Random House, South Africa. I highly recommend this series of A4 paperback books for young children (age 3–7) on safari. They are accurate, clearly organised, well illustrated and concisely written. The layout is good and the use of a graphic key means that even children who cannot read are able to decipher the pertinent points for each creature. Accompanying colouring books are available for many of the guides.

My First Book of Southern African Mammals 2008. 58 of the most common and popular African mammals with large colour illustrations, simple text and a key to the animals' size, tracks and diet.

My First Book of Southern African Animal Tracks 2014. A good tracking book with clear illustrations of the animal and its tracks, plus a child-friendly scale to show the size of the tracks.

My First Book of Southern African Birds: Volume 1 2006. An excellent first reference book featuring the 56 most striking and commonly seen southern African bird species. Each page features a large illustration of each bird, with a small paragraph of information and a clear key to the food eaten, nesting style and the bird's track.

My First Book of Southern African Birds: Volume 2 2009. A further 58 birds introduced in identical style to volume 1.

My First Book of Southern African Insects 2009. Features 58 of the most common, colourful and unusual insects, from ants and dragonflies to beetles and bees.

My First Book of Southern African Creepy-Crawlies 2010. A companion to *Southern African Insects*, this showcases 58 spiders, snails, millipedes and other creepy crawlies. The key shows the creatures' size, diet and when it is active.

My First Book of Southern African Snakes and Other Reptiles 2007. As well as 56 snakes, this covers other reptiles, from lizards to tortoises. It illustrates the reptile itself, with information about its home, diet, size, reproduction – and danger rating.

Newman, Kenneth *What's That Bird? A Starter's Guide to Birds of Southern Africa* Struik, South Africa, 3rd edition 2004. Written by the famous birder, Kenneth Newman, this is an excellent bird book for older children and adults new to African birdwatching. It's comprehensive and full of useful spotting tips: a great starter guide.

Children's novels

Botumile, Bontekanye *The Elephant Story* (2006), *Patterns in the Sky* (2007), *The Seed Children* (2008), Thari-e-Ntsho Storytellers, Maun (*www.botswanastories.com*). This series of illustrated books for primary-school children combines Botswana legends with notes on topics such as traditional remedies.

McNeice, Angus, Maisie and Travers *The Lion Children* Orion Books Ltd, London, 2001. This entertaining scrapbook about life in the bush was written by three British children whose lives were transformed when their parents moved to the Okavango (around NG34) to research lions. While basically a children's book, it's a lot of fun to read and occasionally quite insightful.

Travel narratives from Bradt

Jackman, Brian *Savannah Diaries* Bradt, 2014. A celebration of Africa's wild places and creatures, seen through the eyes of one of Africa's most distinguished observers.

Jackman, Brian and Scott, Jonathan and Angela *The Marsh Lions: The Story of an African Pride* Bradt, 2012. A wildlife classic, this is a compelling and fascinating account of the daily drama of life and death in Kenya's finest big-game country.

Kent, Princess Michael of *A Cheetah's Tale* Bradt, 2017. A wonderful story of a vanished Africa, of a girl growing up and of the incredible bond that can exist between humans and animals.

Scott, Jonathan and Angela *The Leopard's Tale* Bradt, 2013. A unique and moving portrait of Africa, and the most intimate record ever written about the secretive lives of leopards.

Other Bradt Africa guides
For a full list of Bradt's Africa guides, see www.bradtguides.com/shop.

Briggs, Philip *South Africa Highlights* Bradt, 2011.
McIntyre, Chris *Namibia* Bradt, 2015.
McIntyre, Chris *Zambia* Bradt, 2016.
Murray, Paul *Zimbabwe* Bradt, 2016.

Useful websites
For the websites of Botswana's most widely read newspapers, see pages 157–8. A selection of the web's most interesting resources on Botswana might include, in alphabetical order:

http://anthro.fullerton.edu/Okavango A site by the Okavango researcher John Bock, which focuses on the peoples of the Okavango area – though it also includes numerous links to other sites of interest concerning Botswana.

www.bidpa.bw Home for the Botswana Institute for Development Policy Analysis (BIDPA). It's a fairly dry NGO site but includes some quite detailed papers on Botswana's economic development.

www.botswanatourism.co.bw The official website of the Botswana Tourism Board, complete with useful contacts, is both colourful and accessible.

https://clio.columbia.edu/?q=botswana&datasource=quicksearch&search_field=all_fields&search=true Columbia University's Department of African Studies is a good starting place for information on Botswana, with basic summaries and lots of good links.

www.expert.africa The home page for Expert Africa, run by this guide's author, incorporates Google maps featuring many locations within Botswana and more lodge reviews than any other site apart from Trip Advisor.

www.gov.bw The home page of Botswana's government, though many of its links are no longer functioning. That said, if you want to email a minister, download the customs regulations or read the latest budget speech – this is the place.

http://library.stanford.edu/areas/african-collections With a long page of links to sites relating to Botswana – some useful, others not – this is a helpful starting point if you're surfing around seeking information.

PUBLISHER'S NOTE   *Adrian Phillips, Managing Director*

Botswana is one of those 'trip-of-a-lifetime' destinations, and Bradt has long led the way with its guide to a country that promises some of Africa's very best safari experiences. Chris McIntyre has deep, first-hand experience of Botswana's tourist infrastructure, and he and his team have worked hard to ensure that the book remains accurate and thoroughly up to date. The result is a flagship title that embodies everything that Bradt does well, providing insightful background information, superb wildlife coverage (including a brand-new, full-colour section giving a guide to what you'll see) and detailed, personal reviews.

Fifth edition published July 2018
First published 2003

Bradt Travel Guides Ltd
IDC House, The Vale, Chalfont St Peter, Bucks SL9 9RZ, England
www.bradtguides.com
Print edition published in the USA by The Globe Pequot Press Inc,
PO Box 480, Guilford, Connecticut 06437-0480

Text copyright © 2018 Chris McIntyre
Maps copyright © 2018 Bradt Travel Guides Ltd Includes map data © OpenStreetMap
contributors
Photographs copyright © 2018 Individual photographers (page 538)
Project Managers: Anna Moores and Carys Homer
Cover research: Pepi Bluck, Perfect Picture

ISBN: 978 1 78477 093 8 (print)
e-ISBN: 978 1 78477 548 3 (e-pub)
e-ISBN: 978 1 78477 449 3 (mobi)

British Library Cataloguing in Publication Data
A catalogue record for this book is available from the British Library

Photographs For photographer details, see page 538
Front cover Zebras in the Okavango Delta (RDT/G)
Back cover Mokoro trip (SS); wild dog (SS)
Title page Elephants in the Okavango Delta (JG); San woman (SS); little bee-eater (OP/S)

Illustrations Annabel Milne and Carole Vincer
Maps David McCutcheon FBCart.S
Typeset by Ian Spick, Bradt Travel Guides Ltd
Production managed by Jellyfish Print Solutions; printed in India
Digital conversion by www.dataworks.co.in

Acknowledgements

This fifth edition, like its predecessors, couldn't have been written without the help of many people who have not yet been mentioned – some with previous editions, and some with this one.

In the past, Duncan, Purbs, Occy, Fritz and Simon all helped with different aspects of previous editions; all are remembered here with thanks. I am grateful to Wilderness Safaris for kind permission to borrow from their diagrams for the illustrations in *Chapter 1*. And on a personal note, my wife, Susie and children, James and Charlotte, have made great travelling companions over the years!

In Botswana, many have helped with the various editions of this guidebook, and its predecessor the *Guide to Namibia & Botswana* – and to them all I owe my thanks. I hope that those who aren't mentioned here will forgive the omissions, but those who have helped most recently include Mark and Nicola at Bush Ways, Adam Chapman from &Beyond; Colin Bell and Dave van Smeerdijk from Natural Selection; Hilton, Alex, Shelley and Dereck Joubert from Great Plains; Fran Hird and the team at Ker & Downey Botswana; Beks Ndlovu and Weena at African Bush Camps; Sue Smart and Ying Yi Ho from the Kwando team; Ralph from Uncharted Africa; numerous people at Wilderness Safaris – but especially Kim Nixon and Grant Woodrow; Emily and Gabi at the Garden Lodge; Alistair Rankin, Chris Kruger, Elcke and Shaun at Machaba; and all at Nogatsaa Pans Lodge. Many thanks, too, to Karen Riekert and Trish Williams in Kasane for their help with last-minute queries; to traveller Russell Fowler for many insightful comments on the text; and in Livingstone to Kim at Jollyboys Backpackers and the team at Waterberry Zambezi Lodge.

Thanks also to hundreds of Expert Africa's travellers who have helped with feedback after their trips and allowed us to publish their unedited feedback on www.expert.africa; these online reports now form an invaluable first-hand record of the country's better lodges and camps, from which I learn a lot.

In writing this, I'm aware that there are many above who know much more about Botswana than I. Among them, three experts really stand out: Alec Campbell, Mike Main and Veronica Roodt. All have written amazing, scholarly works on Botswana which have been a real inspiration, and all kindly offered their help to me. Beside their erudite works (recommended in *Appendix 3, Further Information*), this book pales – but I hope that it may introduce Botswana, and their works, to a wider audience.

Finally, Bradt's team who've worked with me on this book – including Anna Moores, Carys Homer and David McCutcheon – have been supremely patient and encouraging. That which is good and correct owes much to their care and attention; errors and omissions are all my own.

Index

Page numbers in **bold** indicate main entries; those in *italics* indicate maps.

INDEX OF ADVERTISERS